GLIMPSES OF UNFAMILIAR JAPAN

知られぬ日本の面影

The author in native Japanese attire.

GLIMPSES
OF UNFAMILIAR
JAPAN

LAFCADIO HEARN

With a new foreword by **Donald Richie**

TWO VOLUMES IN ONE

TUTTLE PUBLISHING
Tokyo • Rutland, Vermont • Singapore

"Books to Span the East and West"

Tuttle Publishing was founded in 1832 in the small New England town of Rutland, Vermont [USA]. Our core values remain as strong today as they were then—to publish best-in-class books which bring people together one page at a time. In 1948, we established a publishing office in Japan—and Tuttle is now a leader in publishing English-language books about the arts, languages and cultures of Asia. The world has become a much smaller place today and Asia's economic and cultural influence has grown. Yet the need for meaningful dialogue and information about this diverse region has never been greater. Over the past seven decades, Tuttle has published thousands of books on subjects ranging from martial arts and paper crafts to language learning and literature—and our talented authors, illustrators, designers and photographers have won many prestigious awards. We welcome you to explore the wealth of information available on Asia at **www.tuttlepublishing.com**.

Tuttle Publishing, an imprint of Periplus Editions (HK) Ltd.

www.tuttlepublishing.com

Copyright © 2009 Periplus Editions (HK) Ltd.
Cover Image: Japanese Gallery, London

Library of Congress Cataloging-in-Publication Data

Hearn, Lafcadio, 1850-1904.
  Glimpses of unfamiliar Japan: two volumes in one / by Lafcadio Hearn.
    xx, 580 p. : ill. ; 21 cm.
  Originally published : 1976.
  Includes bibliographical references and index.
    ISBN 978-4-8053-1025-0 (pbk. : alk. Paper)
  1. Japan – Description and travel. 2. Japan – Social life and customs. I. Title.
  DS809.H43 2009
  952.03'1--dc2
                2008037798

This Edition 978-0-8048-4755-1/
978-4-8053-1025-0 (for sale in Japan only)

Distributed by

North America, Latin America & Europe
Tuttle Publishing
364 Innovation Drive
North Clarendon, VT 05759-9436 U.S.A.
Tel: 1 (802) 773-8930; Fax: 1 (802) 773-6993
info@tuttlepublishing.com
www.tuttlepublishing.com

Asia Pacific
Berkeley Books Pte. Ltd.
3 Kallang Sector #04-01
Singapore 349278
Tel: (65) 6741-2178; Fax: (65) 6741-2179
inquiries@periplus.com.sg
www.tuttlepublishing.com

Japan
Tuttle Publishing
Yaekari Building 3rd Floor
5-4-12 Osaki Shinagawa-ku
Tokyo 141 0032
Tel: (81) 3 5437-0171; Fax: (81) 3 5437-0755
sales@tuttle.co.jp
www.tuttle.co.jp

25 24 23 22 21
10 9 8 7 6 5 4   2108TP

Printed in Singapore

TO THE FRIENDS

WHOSE KINDNESS ALONE RENDERED POSSIBLE

MY SOUJOURN IN THE ORIENT—

TO

PAYMASTER MITCHELL McDONALD, U. S. N.

AND

BASIL HALL CHAMBERLAIN, ESQ.

Emeritus Professor of Philology and Japanese in the Imperial Univenity of Tōkyō

I DEDICATE THIS VOLUME

IN TOKEN OF

AFFECTION AND GRATITUDE.

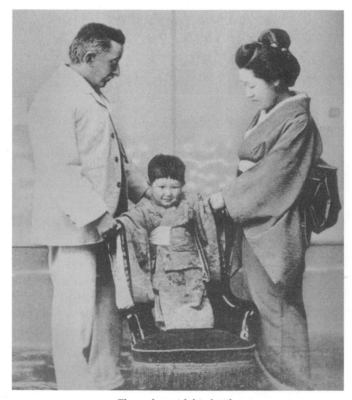
The author with his family.

TABLE OF CONTENTS

INTRODUCTION

Though Lafcadio Hearn went on to write a dozen more books on Japan, this collection of first impressions remains his most popular. Among the reasons is that here, more than elsewhere, the author most vividly captured a place that so affected him that he stayed for the rest of his life. The modern reader can still, through these pages, experience that "first charm of Japan, intangible and volatile as a perfume."

Hearn (1850-1894) was forty years old when he arrived in 1890. Japan had been "opened" for more than three decades and could no longer be called the "hermit empire" as it had been earlier. Foreign ships were being admitted into ports, roads were being built, tourists were appearing in large numbers. Japan was so well known when Hearn first came, that he wondered if there was enough unfamiliar to write about.

He had been contributing to Harper's magazine and had already published pieces on the West Indies and other exotic places where he had lived. When it was determined that he would next go to the Japan, he agreed to his publisher's terms but added that in a country already so well trodden he wondered whether they could expect him to come up with anything new.

This was why, when he collected the twenty-seven "sketches" which comprise this book, he insisted upon the title of *Glimpses of an Unfamiliar Japan*. In this way he could contrast his work to the impressions of others and claim the authenticity which he thought his account deserved. And, though the publisher removed that significant article, "an," perhaps hoping for a less seemingly qualified title, Hearn's pieces still maintain a definite difference from the country that travelers perhaps thought they already knew.

In the preface to this first collection of impressions Hearn states that "the rare charm of Japanese life" is not to be found in its Europeanized cities. Rather, it is to be discovered in "the great common people," those who live far from foreign influence, "who still cling to their delightful old customs, their picturesque dress...This is the life of which a foreign observer can never weary, if fortunate and sympathetic enough to enter into it."

Hearn was certainly sympathetic in that he had happily lived among the great common people in places as far from European influence as New Orleans and Martinique. And he was fortunate in that enough remained of old Japan (outside the major cities) that he could write about it.

Since he had posited an "unfamiliar" Japan, he had to discover it. And, since he was creating a kind of utopia for himself and his readers he had to find a dystopia to set it off. Consequently, he much disliked Tokyo, Yokohama, Osaka, the big modern cities of the new Japan, places where we are forced "sometimes to doubt whether the course of our boasted Western progress is really in the direction of moral development," and which, incidentally, were all the Japan that most foreigners saw.

Utopia was, according to the first chapter of Hearn's first book, found on the very first day, when he left the European quarter of Yokohama to enter the "Japanese town" that surrounded it. "It is with the delicious surprise of the first journey through Japanese streets...that one first received the real sensation of being in the Orient." Here was an unfamiliar Japan waiting for him to describe it.

Hearn's euphoria is palpable in "My First Day in the Orient," this earliest account of his chosen land. The excitement and exhilaration is there on the page, turning into the ecstatic as you read. In one of his last essays, "Strangeness and Charm," (from *Japan: An Attempt at Interpretation*, 1904) he returns to that enchanted first day. "I remember especially the wonder and delight of the vision. This wonder and delight have never passed away; they are often revived for me even now by some chance happening, after fourteen years of sojourn."

The extraordinary charm of Japan rested in its perceived strangeness, and in Hearn's own romantic temperament. "Really you are happy because you have entered bodily into Fairyland— into a world that is not, and never could be your own." The West Indies had been pleasingly different but nothing as wonderfully strange as Japan could seem.

And it was just this strangeness that Hearn treasured. In this first essay he writes "elfish everything seems; for everything as well as everybody is small and queer, and mysterious; the little houses under their blue roofs, the little shop-fronts hung with blue, and the smiling little people in their blue costumes. The illusion is only broken by the occasional passing of a tall foreigner..."

Like many early foreign writers on Japan ("land of the topsy-turvy") Hearn was infantilizing the place but while most writers were castigating the Japanese as for being (from the Western point of view) childlike, Hearn was praising them for it. Here were folk living in an innocent naturalness which he felt that Europe and America had long lost.

This difference was to be celebrated and the traveler was invited to revel in. Hence, perhaps, the style of these early writings, the continual use of such terms as "small," "tiny," "curious," "delicate;" the comparison with elves and with fairyland—none of this intended as in any way condescending.

Later Hearn found the style of these early essays so "florid" that he was tempted to rewrite to "sober them down," but what he was really writing about in these first essays was himself and his own ecstatic discovery of a place that was truly different. And it was not just the little people and their curious ways.

As he would write in his 1904 essay, looking back at these first impressions, "the underlying strangeness of this world—the psychological strangeness—is much more startling than the visible and superficial." (This is still true. The contemporary traveler, now more than a hundred years later, finds that Tokyo-Osaka looks like Dallas-Fort Worth but certainly does not act like it.)

Hearn communicated his excited enthusiasm not only through a heightened vocabulary, but also by using the present tense throughout, as though he wanted what was happening to him to happen to his reader as well. He wants us to live what he calls "the dream of the Romantics," to feel that the past "though senescent, is alive around you"; he wants you "to have the sensation of returning through twenty centuries into the life of a happier world."

This is what Hearn himself did. He found the unfamiliar but real Japan in the distant and beloved city of Matsue; found time to write this first book in the much disliked new city of Kumamoto. Along the way he married, began raising a family, took Japanese citizenship and a Japanese name (Koizumi Yakumo), began wearing kimono, and found it "somewhat irksome to use a chair."

It was on the tatami floor that Hearn wrote his *Glimpses of an Unfamiliar Japan*. Its format is very like that of his earlier *Two Years in the French West Indies*, a collection of essays that mixed story-telling, scholarship, and autobiography. But it was much longer. There were eventually over 1500 pages of manuscript. The original edition of the published work took two volumes and this new paperback edition is over 500 pages. Even so, Hearn could in 1893, while finishing the book, write his friend and benefactor Basil Hall Chamberlain that "for every page written as many was ten were repressed." The reason for this was apparently the ease of its creation. You just "move the pen and the ghosts do the writing."

Chamberlain, already an important and influential figure in Japanese studies, had befriended Hearn when the author first arrived. It was he who arranged the teaching posts in both Matsue and Kumamoto, and who was influential in giving Hearn his later professorship at Tokyo Imperial University.

Though they were later to have their differences, in 1893, the year that some six of the pieces in *Glimpses of an Unfamiliar Japan* were published in an American periodical, Chamberlain was appreciative of the book and wrote the author that "your accuracy of detail seems to almost as wonderful as your beautiful style."

Later Chamberlain wrote more about this accuracy of detail. He recalled that Hearn "saw details very distinctly while being incapable of understanding them as a whole." This was because "blind of one eye, he was extremely short-sighted of the other. On entering a room his habit was to grope all around, closely examining the wallpaper, the backs of books, pictures, curios. Of these he could have drawn an exact catalogue, but he had never properly seen either the horizon or the stars."

Perhaps then some of the strangeness and much of that quaint beauty that Hearn attributes to the rural Japan of 1890 is the result of an impaired vision. Of that first enchanted day he writes: "There is some charm unutterable in the morning air, cool with the coolness of Japanese spring and wind-waves from the snowy cone of Fuji; a charm perhaps due rather to softest lucidity than to any positive tone—an atmospheric limpidity extraordinary, with only a suggestion of blue in it, through which the most distant objects appear focused with amazing sharpness." Since it was extreme shortsightedness from which he suffered in his single eye, it would follow that the sharpness of objects far away was amazing but that anything nearer was of an extraordinary atmospheric limpidity.

Likewise, because Hearn did not learn to read and write Japanese and his command of the spoken tongue was mostly inefficient, he depended upon what he heard, what he was told. In the first of the essays he meets the first of these necessary informants—the student priest Akira (scholars have discovered that the boy's family name was Manabe) whom we see literally teaching the enchanted author. Later the main informant was Setsuko, Hearn's wife (and whose family name, Koizumi, became his) and though she is never directly acknowledged it is she who told him (in the pidgin Anglo-Japanese that they had evolved) the various facts and stories that make up this and all the rest of his books.

Triply challenged in that he could not properly see, read, or write, Hearn still remains our earliest authority, our first vision of Japan. This is because he found in Japan a surpassing beauty, a lovable picturesqueness, and a place for himself. Since he was an aesthete he could find that the Japanese were too. If he worshiped beauty, then so did they. In the process of searching out beauty imperiled by change, in chronicling traditional life soon to disappear, he became a witness.

We read Hearn because of his partial but loving description of what once existed everywhere a century ago but now is rarely glimpsed. At the same time, through this vanished Japan, we recognize something still. Kimono are not common, the countryside is no longer picturesque, the architecture is no longer quaint and wee but as vaunting as anything found in New York, Paris, or Shanghai, yet much exclusively Japanese remains.

And this we still can (and so) posit as "opposite" to our Western ways—ways of thinking, of taking for granted, of assuming, and of presuming as well. This original Japan that is here early glimpsed is, to this extant, still with us and if Hearn were still with us he might recognize it and rejoice.

Donald Richie
Tokyo, 2009

PUBLISHER'S FOREWORD

THIS book was first published in 1894, after Lafcadio Hearn had lived in Japan for some four years. Even though his residence there had been comparatively brief, he had already succeeded in making himself a splendid interpreter of that country to the West—an interpreter without parallel in his own time and a man who could explain Japan as though he himself were a Japanese. He depended largely upon events to impress his readers, and he searched for words that would describe them with the utmost vividness. He steeped himself in the old legends of Japan and put them into the best of English with the artistry and the freedom of a born storyteller. Both his own soul and the soul of Japan are in his writing, and it is small wonder that the writing continues to live, for it invariably has the ring of truth. Even though much has changed in Japan since he came under the spell of that country, what he had to say about it still has a remarkable validity, for the Japanese spirit has changed considerably less than the material conditions of Japanese life. In a word, the Japanese character and the Japanese tradition are still fundamentally the same as Hearn found them to be, and for this reason his books are still extremely revealing to readers in the West.

The present book combines the two volumes of the original edition into one. Its title is apt, for the book takes the reader into a world that few Westerners saw in the late nineteenth and the early twentieth centuries. Here are the customs, the superstitions, the charming scenery, the revelations of Japanese character, and all the other elements that Hearn found so bewitching. Here, for example, are essays on such subjects as the Japanese garden, the household shrine, the festivals, and the bewildering

Japanese smile—all aspects of Japanese life that have endured in spite of the changes that have taken place during the modernization of Japan. Here, too, is "My First Day in the Orient," still as exciting to read as it was one hundred years ago because it conveys so expertly the feelings of the foreigner who is making his first acquaintance with Japan. Indeed, the reader is astonished over and over again at how much of Hearn remains true for our own time.

It is truly surprising that *Glimpses of Unfamiliar Japan* should have had to wait until now to be reissued, for it is as fresh and revealing today as it was when it first appeared in 1894, and the publisher is most gratified to offer it here in a new form for a new generation of readers who are making their own discovery of Japan, just as Hearn did some one hundred-plus years ago.

PREFACE

In the Introduction to his charming "Tales of Old Japan," Mr. Mitford wrote in 1871: "The books which have been written of late years about Japan have either been compiled from official records, or have contained the sketchy impressions of passing travelers. Of the inner life of the Japanese the world at large knows but little: their religion, their superstitions, their ways of thought, the hidden springs by which they move—all these are as yet mysteries."

This invisible life referred to by Mr. Mitford is the Unfamiliar Japan of which I have been able to obtain a few glimpses. The reader may, perhaps, be disappointed by their rarity; for a residence of little more than four years among the people—even by one who tries to adopt their habits and customs—scarcely suffices to enable the foreigner to begin to feel at home in this world of strangeness. None can feel more than the author himself how little has been accomplished in these volumes, and how much remains to do.

The popular religious ideas—especially the ideas derived from Buddhism—and the curious superstitions touched upon in these sketches are little shared by the educated classes of New Japan. Except as regards his characteristic indifference toward abstract ideas in general and metaphysical speculation in particular, the Occidentalized Japanese of today stands almost on the intellectual plane of the cultivated Parisian or Bostonian. But he is inclined to treat with undue contempt all conceptions of the supernatural; and toward the great religious questions of the hour his attitude is one of perfect apathy. Rarely does his university training in modern philosophy impel him to attempt any independent study of relations, either sociological or psychological. For him, superstitions are simply superstitions; their relation to the emotional nature of the people interests him not at all.* And this not only because he thoroughly understands that people, but because the class to which he belongs is still unreasoningly, though quite naturally, ashamed of its older beliefs. Most of us who now call ourselves agnostics can recollect the feelings with which, in the period of our fresh emancipation from a faith far more irrational than Buddhism, we looked back upon the gloomy theology of our fathers. Intellectual Japan has become agnostic within only a few decades; and the suddenness of this mental revolution sufficiently explains the principal, though not perhaps all the causes of the present attitude of the superior class toward Buddhism. For the time being it certainly borders upon intolerance; and while such is the feeling even to religion as distinguished from superstition, the feeling toward superstition as distinguished from religion must be something stronger still.

But the rare charm of Japanese life, so different from that of all other lands, is not to be found in its Europeanized circles. It is to be found among the great common people, who represent in Japan, as in all countries, the national virtues, and who still cling to their delightful old customs, their picturesque dresses, their Buddhist images, their household shrines, their beautiful and touching worship of ancestors. This is the life of which a foreign observer can never weary, if fortunate and sympathetic enough to enter into it—the life that forces him sometimes to doubt whether the course of our boasted Western progress is really in the direction of moral development. Each day, while the years pass, there will be revealed to him some strange and unsuspected beauty in it. Like other life, it has its darker side; yet even this is brightness compared with the darker side of Western existence. It has its foibles, its follies, its vices, its cruelties; yet the

---

* In striking contrast to this indifference is the strong, rational, farseeing conservatism of Viscount Tōrio—a noble exception.

more one sees of it, the more one marvels at its extraordinary goodness, its miraculous patience, its never-failing courtesy, its simplicity of heart, its intuitive charity. And to our own larger Occidental comprehension, its commonest superstitions, however contemned at Tōkyō, have rarest value as fragments of the unwritten literature of its hopes, its fears, its experience with right and wrong—its primitive efforts to find solutions for the riddle of the Unseen. How much the lighter and kindlier superstitions of the people add to the charm of Japanese life can, indeed, be understood only by one who has long resided in the interior. A few of their beliefs are sinister—such as that in demon-foxes, which public education is rapidly dissipating; but a large number are comparable for beauty of fancy even to those Greek myths in which our noblest poets of today still find inspiration; while many others, which encourage kindness to the unfortunate, and kindness to animals, can never have produced any but the happiest moral results. The amusing presumption of domestic animals, and the comparative fearlessness of many wild creatures in the presence of man; the white clouds of gulls that hover about each incoming steamer in expectation of an alms of crumbs; the whirring of doves from temple-eaves to pick up the rice scattered for them by pilgrims; the familiar storks of ancient public gardens; the deer of holy shrines, awaiting cakes and caresses; the fish which raise their heads from sacred lotus-ponds when the stranger's shadow falls upon the water—these and a hundred other pretty sights are due to fancies which, though called superstitious, inculcate in simplest form the sublime truth of the Unity of Life. And even when considering beliefs less attractive than these—superstitions of which the grotesqueness may provoke a smile—the impartial observer would do well to bear in mind the words of Lecky:

"Many superstitions do undoubtedly answer to the Greek conception of slavish 'fear of the Gods,' and have been productive of unspeakable misery to mankind; but there are very many others of a different tendency. Superstitions appeal to our hopes as well as our fears. They often meet and gratify the inmost longings of the heart. They offer certainties where reason can only afford possibilities or probabilities. They supply conceptions on which the imagination loves to dwell. They sometimes impart even a new sanction to moral truths. Creating wants which they alone can satisfy, and fears which they alone can quell, they often become essential elements of happiness; and their consoling efficacy is most felt in the languid or troubled hours when it is most needed. We owe more to our illusions than to our knowledge. The imagination, which is altogether constructive, probably contributes more to our happiness than the reason, which in the sphere of speculation is mainly critical and destructive. The rude charm which, in the hour of danger or distress, the savage clasps so confidently to his breast, the sacred picture which is believed to shed a hallowing and protecting influence over the poor man's cottage, can bestow a more real consolation in the darkest hour of human suffering than can be afforded by the grandest theories of philosophy....No error can be more grave than to imagine that when a critical spirit is abroad the pleasant beliefs will all remain, and the painful ones alone will perish."

That the critical spirit of modernized Japan is now indirectly aiding rather than opposing the efforts of foreign bigotry to destroy the simple, happy beliefs of the people, and substitute those cruel superstitions which the West has long intellectually outgrown—the fancies of an unforgiving God and an everlasting hell—is surely to be regretted. More than a hundred and sixty years ago Kaempfer wrote of the Japanese: "In the practice of virtue, in purity of life and outward devotion, they far outdo the Christians." And except where native morals have suffered by foreign contamination, as in the open ports, these words are true of the Japanese today. My own conviction, and that of many impartial and more experienced observers of Japanese life, is that Japan has nothing whatever to gain by conversion to Christianity, either morally or otherwise, but very much to lose.

Of the twenty-seven sketches composing these volumes, four were originally purchased by various newspaper syndicates, and reappear in a considerably altered form, and six were published in the "Atlantic Monthly" (1891-93). The remainder, forming the bulk of the work, are new.

L.H.

Kumamoto, Kyūshū, Japan, *May*, 1894.

1

MY FIRST DAY IN THE ORIENT

"Do not fail to write down your first impressions as soon as possible," said a kind English professor whom I had the pleasure of meeting soon after my arrival in Japan: "they are evanescent, you know; they will never come to you again, once they have faded out; and yet of all the strange sensations you may receive in this country you will feel none so charming as these." I am trying now to reproduce them from the hasty notes of the time, and find that they were even more fugitive than charming; something has evaporated from all my recollections of them—something impossible to recall. I neglected the friendly advice, in spite of all resolves to obey it: I could not, in those first weeks, resign myself to remain indoors and write, while there was yet so much to see and hear and feel in the sun-steeped ways of the wonderful Japanese city. Still, even could I revive all the lost sensations of those first experiences, I doubt if I could express and fix them in words. The first charm of Japan is intangible and volatile as a perfume.

It began for me with my first kuruma-ride out of the European quarter of Yokohama into the Japanese town; and so much as I can recall of it is hereafter set down.

I.

It is with the delicious surprise of the first journey through Japanese streets—unable to make one's kuruma-runner understand anything but gestures, frantic gestures to roll on anywhere, everywhere, since all is unspeakably pleasurable and new—that one first receives the real sensation of being in the Orient, in this Far East so much read of, so long dreamed of, yet, as the eyes bear witness, heretofore all unknown. There is a romance even in the first full consciousness of this rather commonplace fact; but for me this consciousness is transfigured inexpressibly by the divine beauty of the day. There is some charm unutterable in the morning air, cool with the coolness of Japanese spring and wind-waves from the snowy cone of Fuji; a charm perhaps due rather to softest lucidity than to any positive tone—an atmospheric limpidity extraordinary, with only a suggestion of blue in it, through which the most distant objects appear focused with amazing sharpness. The sun is only pleasantly warm; the jinriki-sha, or kuruma, is the most cosy little vehicle imaginable; and the street-vistas, as seen above the dancing white mushroom-shaped hat of my sandaled runner, have an allurement of which I fancy that I could never weary.

Elfish everything seems; for everything as well as everybody is small, and queer, and mysterious: the little houses under their blue roofs, the little shop-fronts hung with blue, and the smiling little people in their blue costumes. The illusion is only broken by the occasional passing of a tall foreigner, and by diverse shop-signs bearing announcements in absurd attempts at English. Nevertheless such discords only serve to emphasize reality; they never materially lessen the fascination of the funny little streets.

'Tis at first a delightfully odd confusion only, as you look down one of them, through an interminable flutter of flags and swaying of dark blue drapery, all made beautiful and mysterious with Japanese or Chinese lettering. For there are no immediately discernible laws of construction or decoration: each building seems to have a fantastic prettiness of its own; nothing is exactly like anything else, and all is bewilderingly novel. But gradually, after an hour passed in the quarter, the eye begins to recognize in a vague way some general plan in the construction of these low, light, queerly-gabled wooden houses, mostly unpainted, with their first stories all open to the street, and thin strips of roofing sloping above each shop-front, like awnings, back to the miniature balconies of paper-screened second stories. You begin to understand the common plan of the tiny shops, with their matted floors well raised above the street level, and the general perpendicular arrangement of sign-lettering, whether undulating on drapery or glimmering on gilded and lacquered signboards. You observe that the same rich dark blue which dominates in popular costume rules also in shop draperies, though there is a sprinkling of other tints—bright blue and white and red (no greens or yellows). And then you note also that the dresses of the laborers are lettered with the same wonderful lettering as the shop draperies. No arabesques could produce such an effect. As modified for decorative purposes, these ideographs have a speaking symmetry which no design without a meaning could possess. As they appear on the back of a workman's frock—pure white on dark blue—and large enough to be easily read at a great distance (indicating some guild or company of which the wearer is a member or employee), they give to the poor cheap garment a factitious appearance of splendor.

And finally, while you are still puzzling over the mystery of things, there will come to you like a revelation the knowledge that most of the amazing picturesqueness of these streets is simply due to the profusion of Chinese and Japanese characters in white, black, blue, or gold, decorating everything—even surfaces of doorposts and paper screens. Perhaps, then, for one moment, you will imagine the effect of English lettering substituted for those magical characters; and the mere idea will give to whatever aesthetic sentiment you may possess a brutal shock, and you will become, as I have become, an enemy of the Romaji-Kwai—that society founded for the ugly utilitarian purpose of introducing the use of English letters in writing Japanese.

II.

An ideograph does not make upon the Japanese brain any impression similar to that created in the Occidental brain by a letter or combination of letters—dull, inanimate symbols of vocal sounds. To the Japanese brain an ideograph is a vivid picture: it lives; it speaks; it gesticulates. And the whole space of a Japanese street is full of such living characters—figures that cry out to the eyes, words that smile or grimace like faces.

What such lettering is, compared with our own lifeless types, can be understood only by those who have lived in the farther East. For even the printed characters of Japanese or Chinese imported texts give no suggestion of the possible beauty of the same characters as modified for decorative inscriptions, for sculptural use, or for the commonest advertising purposes. No rigid convention fetters the fancy of the calligrapher or designer: each strives to make his characters more beautiful than any others; and generations upon generations of artists have been toiling from time immemorial with like emulation, so that through centuries and centuries of tireless effort and study, the primitive hieroglyph or ideograph has been evolved into a thing of beauty indescribable. It consists only of a certain number of brushstrokes; but in each stroke there is an undiscoverable secret art of grace, proportion, imperceptible curve, which actually makes it seem alive, and bears witness that even during the lightning-moment of its creation the artist felt with his brush for the ideal shape of the stroke *equally along its entire length,* from head to tail. But the art of the strokes is not all; the art of their combination is that which produces the enchantment, often so as to astonish the Japanese themselves. It is not surprising, indeed, considering the strangely personal, animate, esoteric aspect of Japanese lettering, that there should be wonderful legends of calligraphy, relating how words written by holy experts became incarnate, and descended from their tablets to hold converse with mankind.

III.

My kurumaya calls himself "Cha." He has a white hat, which looks like the top of an enormous mushroom; a short blue wide-sleeved jacket; blue drawers, closefitting as "tights," and reaching to his ankles; and light straw sandals bound upon his bare feet with cords of palmetto-fiber. Doubtless he typifies all the patience, endurance, and insidious coaxing powers of his class. He has already manifested his power to make me give him more than the law allows; and I have been warned against him in vain. For the first sensation of having a human being for a horse, trotting between shafts, unwearyingly bobbing up and down before you for hours, is alone enough to evoke a feeling of compassion. And when this human being, thus trotting between shafts, with all his hopes, memories, sentiments, and comprehensions, happens to have the gentlest smile, and the power to return the least favor by an apparent display of infinite gratitude, this compassion becomes sympathy, and provokes unreasoning impulses to self-sacrifice. I think the sight of the profuse perspiration has also something to do with the feeling, for it makes one think of the cost of heart-beats and muscle contractions, likewise of chills, congestions, and pleurisy. Cha's clothing is drenched; and he mops his face with a small sky-blue towel, with figures of bamboo sprays and sparrows in white upon it, which towel he carries wrapped about his wrist as he runs.

That, however, which attracts me in Cha—Cha considered not as a motive power at all, but as a personality—I am rapidly learning to discern in the multitudes of faces turned toward us as we roll through these miniature streets. And perhaps the supremely pleasurable impression of this morning is that produced by the singular gentleness of popular scrutiny. Everybody looks at you curiously; but there is never anything disagreeable, much less hostile in the gaze: most commonly it is accompanied by a smile or half smile. And the ultimate consequence of all these kindly curious looks and smiles is that the stranger finds himself thinking of fairy-land. Hackneyed to the degree of provocation this statement no doubt is: everybody describing the sensations of his first Japanese day talks of the land as fairy-land, and of its people as fairy-folk. Yet there is a natural reason for this unanimity in choice of terms to describe what is almost impossible to describe more accurately at the first essay. To find one's self suddenly in a world where everything is upon a smaller and daintier scale than with us—a world of lesser and seemingly kindlier beings, all smiling at you as if to wish you well—a world where all movement is slow and soft, and voices are hushed—a world where land, life, and sky are unlike all that one has known elsewhere—this is surely the realization, for imaginations nourished with English folklore, of the old dream of a World of Elves.

IV.

The traveler who enters suddenly into a period of social change—especially change from a feudal past to a democratic present—is likely to regret the decay of things beautiful and the ugliness of things new. What of both I may yet discover in Japan I know not; but today, in these exotic streets, the old and the new mingle so well that one seems to set off the other. The line of tiny white telegraph poles carrying the world's news to papers printed in a mixture of Chinese and Japanese characters; an electric bell in some tea-house with an Oriental riddle of text pasted beside the ivory button; a shop of American sewing-machines next to the shop of a maker of Buddhist images; the establishment of a photographer beside the establishment of a manufacturer of straw sandals: all these present no striking incongruities, for each sample of Occidental innovation is set into an Oriental frame that seems adaptable to any picture. But on the first day, at least, the Old alone is new for the stranger, and suffices to absorb his attention. It then appears to him that everything Japanese is delicate, exquisite, admirable—even a pair of common wooden chopsticks in a paper bag with a little drawing upon it; even a package of toothpicks of cherry-wood, bound with a paper wrapper wonderfully lettered in three different colors; even the little sky-blue towel, with designs of flying sparrows upon it, which the jinrikisha man uses to wipe his face. The bank bills, the commonest copper coins, are things of beauty. Even the piece of plaited colored string used by the shopkeeper in tying up your last purchase is a pretty curiosity. Curiosities and dainty objects bewilder you by their very multitude: on either side of you, wherever you turn your eyes, are countless wonderful things as yet incomprehensible.

But it is perilous to look at them. Every time you dare to look, something obliges you to buy it—unless, as may often happen, the smiling vender invites your inspection of so many varieties of one article, each specially and all unspeakably desirable, that you flee away out of mere terror at your own impulses. The shopkeeper never asks you to buy; but his wares are enchanted, and if you once begin buying you are lost. Cheapness means only a temptation to commit bankruptcy; for the resources of irresistible artistic cheapness are inexhaustible. The largest steamer that crosses the Pacific could not contain what you wish to purchase. For, although you may not, perhaps, confess the fact to yourself, what you really want to buy is not the contents of a shop; you want the shop and the shopkeeper, and streets of shops with their draperies and their habitants, the whole city and the bay and the mountains begirdling it, and Fujiyama's white witchery overhanging it in the speckless sky, all Japan, in very truth, with its magical trees and luminous atmosphere, with all its cities and towns and temples, and forty millions of the most lovable people in the universe.

Now there comes to my mind something I once heard said by a practical American on hearing of a great fire in Japan: "Oh! those people can afford fires; their houses are so cheaply built." It is true that the frail wooden houses of the common people can be cheaply and quickly replaced; but that which was within them to make them beautiful cannot—and every fire is an art tragedy. For this is the land of infinite hand-made variety; machinery has not yet been able to introduce sameness and utilitarian ugliness in cheap production (except in response to foreign demand for bad taste to suit vulgar markets), and each object made by the artist or artisan differs still from all others, even of his own making. And each time something beautiful perishes by fire, it is a something representing an individual idea.

Happily the art impulse itself, in this country of conflagrations, has a vitality which survives each generation of artists, and defies the flame that changes their labor to ashes or melts it to shapelessness. The idea whose symbol has perished will reappear again in other creations—perhaps after the passing of a century—modified, indeed, yet recognizably of kin to the thought of the past. And every artist is a ghostly worker. Not by years of groping and sacrifice does he find his highest expression; the sacrificial past is within him; his art is an inheritance; his fingers are guided by the dead in the delineation of a flying bird, of the vapors of mountains, of the colors of the morning and the evening, of the shape of branches and the spring burst of flowers: generations of skilled workmen have given him their cunning, and revive in the wonder of his drawing. What was conscious effort in the beginning became unconscious in later centuries—becomes almost automatic in the living man—becomes the art instinctive. Wherefore, one colored print by a Hokusai or Hiroshige, originally sold for less than a cent, may have more real art in it than many a Western painting valued at more than the worth of a whole Japanese street.

V.

Here are Hokusai's own figures walking about in straw raincoats, and immense mushroom-shaped hats of straw, and straw sandals—bare-limbed peasants, deeply tanned by wind and sun; and patient-faced mothers with smiling bald babies on their backs, toddling by upon their geta (high, noisy, wooden clogs), and robed merchants squatting and smoking their little brass pipes among the countless riddles of their shops.

Then I notice how small and shapely the feet of the people are—whether bare brown feet of peasants, or beautiful feet of children wearing tiny, tiny geta, or feet of young girls in snowy tabi. The tabi, the white digitated stocking, gives to a small light foot a mythological aspect—the white cleft grace of the foot of a fauness. Clad or bare, the Japanese foot has the antique symmetry: it has not yet been distorted by the infamous footgear which has deformed the feet of Occidentals.

Of every pair of Japanese wooden clogs, one makes in walking a slightly different sound from the other, as *kring* to *krang;* so that the echo of the walker's steps has an alternate rhythm of tones. On a pavement, such as that of a railway station, the sound obtains immense sonority; and a crowd will sometimes intentionally fall into step, with the drollest conceivable result of drawling wooden noise.

VI.

"Tera e yuke!"

I have been obliged to return to the European hotel—not because of the noon-meal, as I really begrudge myself the time necessary to eat it, but because I cannot make Cha understand that I want to visit a Buddhist temple. Now Cha understands; my landlord has uttered the mystical words:

"Tera e yuke!"

A few minutes of running along broad thoroughfares lined with gardens and costly ugly European buildings; then passing the bridge of a canal stocked with unpainted sharp-prowed craft of extraordinary construction, we again plunge into narrow low bright pretty streets—into another part of the Japanese city. And Cha runs at the top of his speed between more rows of little ark-shaped houses, narrower above than below; between other unfamiliar lines of little open shops. And always over the shops little strips of blue-tiled roof slope back to the paperscreened chamber of upper floors; and from all the facades hang draperies dark blue, or white, or crimson—foot-breadths of texture covered with beautiful Japanese lettering, white on blue, red on black, black on white. But all this flies by swiftly as a dream. Once more we cross a canal; we rush up a narrow street rising to meet a hill; and Cha, halting suddenly before an immense flight of broad stone steps, sets the shafts of his vehicle on the ground that I may dismount, and, pointing to the steps, exclaims:

"*Tera!*"

I dismount, and ascend them, and, reaching a broad terrace, find myself face to face with a wonderful gate, topped by a tilted, peaked, many-cornered Chinese roof. It is all strangely carven, this gate. Dragons are intertwined in a frieze above its open doors; and the panels of the doors themselves are similarly sculptured; and there are gargoyles—grotesque lion heads—protruding from the eaves. And the whole is gray, stone-colored; to me, nevertheless, the carvings do not seem to have the fixity of sculpture; all the snakeries and dragonries appear to undulate with a swarming motion, elusively, in eddyings as of water.

I turn a moment to look back through the glorious light. Sea and sky mingle in the same beautiful pale clear blue. Below me the billowing of bluish roofs reaches to the verge of the unruffled bay on the right, and to the feet of the green wooded hills flanking the city on two sides. Beyond that semicircle of green hills rises a lofty range of serrated mountains, indigo silhouettes. And enormously high above the line of them towers an apparition indescribably lovely—one solitary snowy cone, so filmily exquisite, so spiritually white, that but for its immemorially familiar outline, one would surely deem it a shape of cloud. Invisible its base remains, being the same delicious tint as the sky: only above the eternal snow-line its dreamy cone appears, seeming to hang, the ghost of a peak, between the luminous land and the luminous heaven—the sacred and matchless mountain, Fujiyama.

And suddenly, a singular sensation comes upon me as I stand before this weirdly sculptured portal—a sensation of dream and doubt. It seems to me that the steps, and the dragon-swarming gate, and the blue sky arching over the roofs of the town, and the ghostly beauty of Fuji, and the shadow of myself there stretching upon the gray masonry, must all vanish presently. Why such a feeling? Doubtless because the forms before me—the curved roofs, the coiling dragons, the Chinese grotesqueries of carving— do not really appear to me as things new, but as things dreamed: the sight of them must have stirred to life forgotten memories of picture-books. A moment, and the delusion vanishes; the romance of reality returns, with freshened consciousness of all that which is truly and deliciously new; the magical transparencies of distance, the wondrous delicacy of the tones of the living picture, the enormous height of the summer blue, and the white soft witchery of the Japanese sun.

VII.

I pass on and climb more steps to a second gate with similar gargoyles and swarming of dragons, and enter a court where graceful votive lanterns of stone stand like monuments. On my right and left two great grotesque stone lions are sitting—the lions of Buddha, male and female. Beyond is a long low light building, with curved and gabled roof of blue tiles, and three wooden steps before its entrance. Its sides are simple wooden screens covered with thin white paper. This is the temple.

On the steps I take off my shoes; a young man slides aside the screens closing the entrance, and bows me a gracious welcome. And I go in, feeling under my feet a softness of matting thick as bedding. An immense square apartment is before me, full of an unfamiliar sweet smell—the scent of Japanese incense; but after the full blaze of the sun, the paper-filtered light here is dim as moonshine; for a minute or two I can see nothing but gleams of gilding in a soft gloom. Then, my eyes becoming accustomed to the obscurity, I perceive against the paper-paned screens surrounding the sanctuary on three sides shapes of enormous flowers cutting like silhouettes against the vague white light. I approach and find them to be paper flowers—symbolic lotus-blossoms beautifully colored, with curling leaves gilded on the upper surface and bright green beneath. At the dark end of the apartment, facing the entrance, is the altar of Buddha, a rich and lofty altar, covered with bronzes and gilded utensils clustered to right and left of a shrine like a tiny gold temple. But I see no statue; only a mystery of unfamiliar shapes of burnished metal, relieved against darkness, a darkness behind the shrine and altar—whether recess or inner sanctuary I cannot distinguish.

The young attendant who ushered me into the temple now approaches, and, to my great surprise, exclaims in excellent English, pointing to a richly decorated gilded object between groups of candelabra on the altar:

"That is the shrine of Buddha."

"And I would like to make an offering to Buddha," I respond.

"It is not necessary," he says, with a polite smile.

But I insist; and he places the little offering for me upon the altar. Then he invites me to his own room, in a wing of the building—a large luminous room, without furniture, beautifully matted. And we sit down upon the floor and chat. He tells me he is a student in the temple. He learned English in Tōkyō, and speaks it with a curious accent, but with fine choice of words. Finally he asks me—

"Are you a Christian?"

And I answer truthfully: "No."

"Are you a Buddhist?"

"Not exactly."

"Why do you make offerings if you do not believe in Buddha?"

"I revere the beauty of his teaching, and the faith of those who follow it."

"Are there Buddhists in England and America?"

"There are, at least, a great many interested in Buddhist philosophy."

And he takes from an alcove a little book, and gives it to me to examine. It is an English copy of Olcott's "Buddhist Catechism."

"Why is there no image of Buddha in your temple?" I ask.

"There is a small one in the shrine upon the altar," the student answers; "but the shrine is closed. And we have several large ones. But the image of Buddha is not exposed here every day— only upon festal days. And some images are exposed only once or twice a year."

From my place, I can see, between the open paper screens, men and women ascending the steps, to kneel and pray before the entrance of the temple. They kneel with such naive reverence, so gracefully and so naturally, that the kneeling of our Occidental devotees seems a clumsy stumbling by comparison. Some only join their hands; others clap them three times loudly and slowly; then they bow their heads, pray silently for a moment, and rise and depart. The shortness of the prayers impresses me as something novel and interesting. From time to time I hear the clink and rattle of brazen coin cast into the great wooden money-box at the entrance.

I turn to the young student, and ask him:

"Why do they clap their hands three tames before they pray?"

He answers:

"Three times for the Sansai, the Three Powers; Heaven, Earth, Man."

"But do they clap their hands to call the Gods, as Japanese clap their hands to summon their attendants?"

"Oh, no!" he replies. "The clapping of hands represents only the awakening from the Dream of the Long Night."*

"What night? What dream?" He hesitates some moments before making answer:

"The Buddha said: All beings are only dreaming in this fleeting world of unhappiness."

---

* I do not think this explanation is correct; but it is interesting, as the first which I obtained upon the subject. Properly speaking, Buddhist worshipers should not clap the hands, but only rub them softly together. Shintō worshipers always clap their hands four times.

"Then the clapping of hands signifies that in prayer the soul awakens from such dreaming?"

"Yes."

"You understand what I mean by the word 'soul?'"

"Oh, yes! Buddhists believe the soul always was—always will be."

"Even in Nirvana?"

"Yes."

While we are thus chatting the Chief Priest of the temple enters—very aged man—accompanied by two young priests, and I am presented to them; and the three bow very low, showing me the glossy crowns of their smoothly-shaven heads, before seating themselves in the fashion of gods upon the floor. I observe they do not smile; these are the first Japanese I have seen who do not smile: their faces are impassive as the faces of images. But their long eyes observe me very closely, while the student interprets their questions, and while I attempt to tell them something about the translations of the Sutras in our "Sacred Books of the East," and about the labors of Beal and Burnouf and Feer and Davids and Kern, and others. They listen without change of countenance, and utter no word in response to the young student's translation of my remarks. Tea, however, is brought in and set before me in a tiny cup, placed in a little brazen saucer, shaped like a lotus-leaf; and I am invited to partake of some little sugar-cakes (*kwashi*), stamped with a figure which I recognize as the Swastika, the ancient Indian symbol of the Wheel of the Law.

As I rise to go, all rise with me; and at the steps the student asks for my name and address.

"For," he adds, "you will not see me here again, as I am going to leave the temple. But I will visit you."

"And your name?" I ask.

"Call me Akira," he answers.

At the threshold I bow my good-by; and they all bow very, very low—one blue-black head, three glossy heads like balls of ivory. And as I go, only Akira smiles.

VIII.

"Tera?" queries Cha, with his immense white hat in his hand, as I resume my seat in the jinrikisha at the foot of the steps. Which no doubt means, do I want to see any more temples? Most certainly I do: I have not yet seen Buddha.

"Yes, tera, Cha."

And again begins the long panorama of mysterious shops and tilted eaves, and fantastic riddles written over everything. I have no idea in what direction Cha is running. I only know that the streets seem to become always narrower as we go, and that some of the houses look like great wickerwork pigeon-cages only, and that we pass over several bridges before we halt again at the foot of another hill. There is a lofty flight of steps here also, and before them a structure which I know is both a gate and a symbol, imposing, yet in no manner resembling the great Buddhist gateway seen before. Astonishingly simple all the lines of it are: it has no carving, no coloring, no lettering upon it; yet it has a weird solemnity, an enigmatic beauty. It is a torii.

"Miya," observes Cha. Not a tera this time, but a shrine of the gods of the more ancient faith of the land—a miya.

I am standing before a Shintō symbol; I see for the first time, out of a picture at least, a torii. How describe a torii to those who have never looked at one even in a photograph or engraving? Two lofty columns, like gate-pillars, supporting horizontally two cross-beams, the lower and lighter beam, having its ends fitted into the columns a little distance below their summits; the uppermost and larger beam supported upon the tops of the columns, and projecting well beyond them to right and left. That is a torii: the construction varying little in design, whether made of stone, wood, or metal. But this description can give no correct idea of the appearance of a torii, of its majestic aspect, of its mystical suggestiveness as a gateway. The first time you see a noble one, you will imagine, perhaps, that you see the colossal model of some beautiful Chinese letter towering against the sky; for all the lines of the thing have the grace of an animated ideograph—have the bold angles and curves of characters made with four sweeps of a master-brush.*

Passing the torii I ascend a flight of perhaps one hundred stone steps, and find at their summit a second torii, from whose lower cross-beam hangs festooned the mystic shimenawa. It is in this case a hempen rope of perhaps two inches in diameter through its greater length, but tapering off at either end like a snake. Sometimes the shimenawa is made of bronze, when the torii itself is of bronze; but according to tradition it should be made of straw, and most commonly is. For it represents the straw rope which the deity Futo-tama-no-mikoto stretched behind the Sun-goddess, Ama-terasu-oho-mi-Kami, after Ameno-ta-jikara-wo-no-Kami, the Heavenly-handstrength-god, had pulled her out, as is told in that ancient myth of Shintō which Professor Chamberlain has translated.† And the shimenawa, in its commoner and simpler form, has pendent tufts of straw along its entire length, at regular intervals, because originally made, tradition declares, of grass pulled up by the roots which protruded from the twist of it.

Advancing beyond this torii, I find myself in a sort of park or pleasure ground on the summit of the hill. There is a small temple on the right; it is all closed up; and I have read so much about the disappointing vacuity of Shintō temples that I do not regret the absence of its guardian. And I see before me what is infinitely more interesting—a grove of cherry-trees covered with something unutterably beautiful—a dazzling mist of snowy blossoms clinging like summer cloud-fleece about every branch

---

* The Various writers, following the opinion of the Japanologue Satow, have sated that the torii was originally a bird-perch for fowls offered up to the gods at Shintō shrines—"not as food, but to give warning of daybreak." The etymology of the word is said to be "bird-rest" by some authorities; but Aston, not less of an authority, derives it from words which would give simply the meaning of a gateway. See Chamberlain's *Things Japanese*, pp. 429,480.

† Professor Basil Hall Chamberlain has held the extraordinary position of Professor of *Japanese* in the Imperial University of Japan—no small honor to English philology!

and twig; and the ground beneath them, and the path before me, is white with the soft, thick, odorous snow of fallen petals.

Beyond this loveliness are flower-plots surrounding tiny shrines; and marvelous grotto-work, full of monsters—dragons and mythologic beings chiseled in the rock; and miniature landscape work with tiny groves of dwarf trees, and Lilliputian lakes, and microscopic brooks and bridges and cascades. Here, also, are swings for children. And here are belvederes, perched on the verge of the hill, wherefrom the whole fair city, and the whole smooth bay speckled with fishing-sails no bigger than pin-heads, and the far, faint, high promontories reaching into the sea, are all visible in one delicious view—blue-penciled in a beauty of ghostly haze indescribable.

Why should the trees be so lovely in Japan? With us, a plum or cherry tree in flower is not an astonishing sight; but here it is a miracle of beauty so bewildering that, however much you may have previously read about it, the real spectacle strikes you dumb. You see no leaves—only one great filmy mist of petals. Is it that the trees have been so long domesticated and caressed by man in this land of the gods, that they have acquired souls, and strive to show their gratitude, like women loved, by making themselves more beautiful for man's sake? Assuredly they have mastered men's hearts by their loveliness, like beautiful slaves. That is to say, Japanese hearts. Apparently there have been some foreign tourists of the brutal class in this place, since it has been deemed necessary to set up inscriptions in English announcing that "IT IS FORBIDDEN TO INJURE THE TREES."

IX.

"Tera?"

"Yes, Cha, tera."

But only for a brief while do I traverse Japanese streets. The houses separate, become scattered along the feet of the hills: the city thins away through little valleys, and vanishes at last behind. And we follow a curving road overlooking the sea. Green hills slope steeply down to the edge of the way on the right; on the left, far below, spreads a vast stretch of dun sand and salty pools to a line of surf so distant that it is discernible only as a moving white thread. The tide is out; and thousands of cockle-gatherers are scattered over the sands, at such distances that their stooping figures, dotting the glimmering seabed, appear no larger than gnats. And some are coming along the road before us, returning from their search with well-filled baskets—girls with faces almost as rosy as the faces of English girls.

As the jinrikisha rattles on, the hills dominating the road grow higher. All at once Cha halts again before the steepest and loftiest flight of temple steps I have yet seen.

I climb and climb and climb, halting perforce betimes, to ease the violent aching of my quadriceps muscles; reach the top completely out of breath; and find myself between two lions of stone; one showing his fangs, the other with jaws closed. Before me stands the temple, at the farther end of a small bare plateau surrounded on three sides by low cliffs—a small temple, looking very old and gray. From a rocky height to the left of the building, a little cataract rumbles down into a pool, ringed in by a palisade. The voice of the water drowns all other sounds. A sharp wind is blowing from the ocean: the place is chill even in the sun, and bleak, and desolate, as if no prayer had been uttered in it for a hundred years.

Cha taps and calls, while I take off my shoes upon the worn wooden steps of the temple; and after a minute of waiting, we hear a muffled step approaching and a hollow cough behind the paper screens. They slide open; and an old white-robed priest appears, and motions me, with a low bow, to enter. He has a kindly face; and his smile of welcome seems to me one of the most exquisite I have ever been greeted with. Then he coughs again, so badly that I think if I ever come here another time, I shall ask for him in vain.

I go in, feeling that soft, spotless, cushioned matting beneath my feet with which the floors of all Japanese buildings are covered. I pass the indispensable bell and lacquered reading-desk; and before me I see other screens only, stretching from floor to ceiling. The old man, still coughing, slides back one of these upon the right, and waves me into the dimness of an inner sanctuary, haunted by faint odors of incense. A colossal bronze lamp, with snarling gilded dragons coiled about its columnar stem, is the first object I discern; and, in passing it, my shoulder sets ringing a festoon of little bells suspended from the lotus-shaped summit of it. Then I reach the altar, gropingly, unable yet to distinguish forms clearly. But the priest, sliding back screen after screen, pours in light upon the gilded brasses and the inscriptions; and I look for the image of the Deity or presiding Spirit between the altar-groups of convoluted candelabra. And I see—only a mirror, a round, pale disk of polished metal, and my own face therein, and behind this mockery of me a phantom of the far sea.

Only a mirror! Symbolizing what? Illusion? or that the Universe exists for us solely as the reflection of our own souls? or the old Chinese teaching that we must seek the Buddha only in our own hearts? Perhaps some day I shall be able to find out all these things.

As I sit on the temple steps, putting on my shoes preparatory to going, the kind old priest approaches me again, and, bowing, presents a bowl. I hastily drop some coins in it, imagining it to be a Buddhist almsbowl, before discovering it to be full of hot water. But the old man's beautiful courtesy saves me from feeling all the grossness of my mistake. Without a word, and still preserving his kindly smile, he takes the bowl away, and, returning presently with another bowl, empty, fills it with hot water from a little kettle, and makes a sign to me to drink.

Tea is most usually offered to visitors at temples; but this little shrine is very, very poor; and I have a suspicion that the old priest suffers betimes for want of what no fellow-creature should be permitted to need. As I descend the windy steps to the roadway I see him still looking after me, and I hear once more his hollow cough.

Then the mockery of the mirror recurs to me. I am beginning to
wonder whether I shall ever be able to discover that which I seek—
outside of myself! That is, outside of my own imagination.

X.

"Tera?" once more queries Cha.

"Tera, no—it is getting late. Hotel, Cha."

But Cha, turning the corner of a narrow street, on our homeward route, halts the jinrikisha before a shrine or tiny temple
scarcely larger than the smallest of Japanese shops, yet more of a
surprise to me than any of the larger sacred edifices already visited. For, on either side of the entrance, stand two monster-figures,
nude, blood-red, demoniac, fearfully muscled, with feet like lions,
and hands brandishing gilded thunderbolts, and eyes of delirious
fury; the guardians of holy things, the Ni-Ō, or "Two Kings."*
And right between these crimson monsters a young girl stands
looking at us; her slight figure, in robe of silver gray and girdle
of iris-violet, relieved deliciously against the twilight darkness
of the interior. Her face, impassive and curiously delicate, would
charm wherever seen; but here, by strange contrast with the
frightful grotesqueries on either side of her, it produces an effect
unimaginable. Then I find myself wondering whether my feeling
of repulsion toward those twin monstrosities be altogether just,
seeing that so charming a maiden deems them worthy of venera-
tion. And they even cease to seem ugly as I watch her standing
there between them, dainty and slender as some splendid moth,
and always naively gazing at the foreigner, utterly unconscious

---

* These Ni-Ō, however, the first I saw in Japan, were very clumsy figures. There are
magnificent Ni-Ō to be seen in some of the great temple gateways in Tōkyō, Kyōto,
and elsewhere. The grandest of all are those in the Ni-Ō Mon, or "Two Kings' Gate,"
of the huge Tōdaiji temple at Nara. They are eight hundred years old. It is impossible
not to admire the conception of stormy dignity and hurricane-force embodied in those
colossal figures.

Prayers are addressed to the Ni-Ō, especially by pilgrims. Most of their statues are
disfigured by little pellets of white paper, which people chew into a pulp and then spit at
them. There is a curious superstition that if the pellet sticks to the statue the prayer is
heard: if, on the other hand, it falls to the ground, the prayer will not be answered.

that they might have seemed to him both unholy and uncomely.
What are they? Artistically they are Buddhist transformations of
Brahma and of Indra. Enveloped by the absoring, all-transform-
ing magical atmosphere of Buddhism, Indra can now wield his
thunderbolts only in defense of the faith which has dethroned
him: he has become a keeper of the temple gates; nay, has even
become a servant of Bosatsu *(Bodhisattvas)*, for this is only a
shrine of Kwannon, Goddess of Mercy, not yet a Buddha.

"Hotel, Cha, hotel!" I cry out again, for the way is long, and the
sun sinking—sinking in the softest imaginable glow of topazine
light. I have not seen Shaka (so the Japanese have transformed
the name Sakya-Muni); I have not looked upon the face of the
Buddha. Perhaps I may be able to find his image tomorrow,
somewhere in this wilderness of wooden streets, or upon the
summit of some yet unvisited hill.

The sun is gone; the topaz-light is gone; and Cha stops to light
his lantern of paper; and we hurry on again, between two long
lines of painted paper lanterns suspended before the shops: so
closely set, so level those lines are, that they seem two interminable strings of pearls of fire. And suddenly a sound—solemn,
profound, mighty—peals to my ears over the roofs of the town,
the voice of the tsurigane, the great temple-bell of Nogiyama.

All too short the day seemed. Yet my eyes have been so long
dazzled by the great white light, and so confused by the sorcery
of that interminable maze of mysterious signs which made each
street vista seem a glimpse into some enormous *grimoire*, that
they are now weary even of the soft glowing of all these paper
lanterns, likewise covered with characters that look like texts
from a Book of Magic. And I feel at last the coming of that
drowsiness which always follows enchantment.

XI.

"*Amma-kamishimo-go-hyakmon!*"
A woman's voice ringing through the night, chanting in a tone

of singular sweetness words of which each syllable comes through my open window like a wavelet of flute-sound. My Japanese servant, who speaks a little English, has told me what they mean, those words;

"*Amma-kamishimo-go-hyakmon!*"

And always between these long, sweet calls I hear a plaintive whistle, one long note first, then two short ones in another key. It is the whistle of the amma, the poor blind woman who earns her living by shampooing the sick or the weary, and whose whistle warns pedestrians and drivers of vehicles to take heed for her sake, as she cannot see. And she sings also that the weary and the sick may call her in.

"*Amma-kamishimo-go-hyakmon!*"

The saddest melody, but the sweetest voice. Her cry signifies that for the sum of "five hundred mon" she will come and rub your weary body "above and below," and make the weariness or the pain go away. Five hundred mon are the equivalent of five sen (Japanese cents); there are ten rin to a sen, and ten mon to one rin. The strange sweetness of the voice is haunting—makes me even wish to have some pains, that I might pay five hundred mon to have them driven away.

I lie down to sleep, and I dream. I see Chinese texts—multitudinous, weird, mysterious—fleeing by me, all in one direction; ideographs white and dark, upon sign-boards, upon paper screens, upon backs of sandaled men. They seem to live, these ideographs, with conscious life; they are moving their parts, moving with a movement as of insects, monstrously, like *phasmidœ*. I am rolling always through low, narrow, luminous streets in a phantom jinrikisha, whose wheels make no sound. And always, always, I see the huge white mushroom-shaped hat of Cha dancing up and down before me as he runs.

2

THE WRITING OF KŌBŌDAISHI

I.

KŌBŌDAISHI, most holy of Buddhist priests, and founder of the Shingon-shū—which is the sect of Akira—first taught the men of Japan to write the writing called Hiragana and the syllabary I-ro-ha; and Kōbōdaishi was himself the most wonderful of all writers, and the most skillful wizard among scribes.

And in the Book, Kōbōdaishi-ichi-dai-ki, it is related that when he was in China, the name of a certain room in the palace of the Emperor having become effaced by time, the Emperor sent for him and bade him write the name anew. Thereupon Kōbōdaishi took a brush in his right hand, and a brush in his left, and one brush between the toes of his left foot, and another between the toes of his right, and one in his mouth also; and with those five brushes, so holding them, he limned the characters upon the wall. And the characters were beautiful beyond any that had ever been seen in China—smooth-flowing as the ripples in the current of a river. And Kobodaishi then took a brush, and with it from a distance spattered drops of ink upon the wall; and the drops as they fell became transformed and turned into beautiful characters. And the Emperor gave to Kobodaishi the name Gohitsu-Oshō, signifying The Priest who writes with Five Brushes.

At another time, while the saint was dwelling in Taka-wasan, near to Kyōto, the Emperor, being desirous that Kōbōdaishi should write the tablet for the great temple called Kongō-jo-ji, gave the tablet to a messenger and bade him carry it to Kōbōdaishi, that Kōbōdaishi might letter it. But when the Emperor's messenger, bearing the tablet, came near to the place where Kōbōdaishi dwelt, he found a river before him so much swollen by rain that no man might cross it. In a little while, however, Kōbōdaishi appeared upon the farther bank, and, hearing from the messenger what the Emperor desired, called to him to hold up the tablet. And the messenger did so; and Kōbōdaishi, from his place upon the farther bank, made the movements of the letters with his brush; and as fast as he made them they appeared upon the tablet which the messenger was holding up.

II.

Now in that time Kōbōdaishi was wont to meditate alone by the river-side; and one day, while so meditating, he was aware of a boy standing before him, gazing at him curiously. The garments of the boy were as the garments worn by the needy; but his face was beautiful. And while Kōbōdaishi wondered, the boy asked him: "Are you Kōbōdaishi, whom men call 'Gohitsu-Oshō'—the priest who writes with five brushes at once?" And Kōbōdaishi answered: "I am he." Then said the boy: "If you be he, write, I pray you, upon the sky." And Kōbōdaishi, rising, took his brush, and made with it movements toward the sky, as if writing; and presently upon the face of the sky the letters appeared, most beautifully wrought. Then the boy said: "Now I shall try;" and he wrote also upon the sky as Kōbōdaishi had done. And he said again to Kōbōdaishi: "I pray you, write for me—write upon the surface of the river." Then Kōbōdaishi wrote upon the water a poem in praise of the water; and for a moment the characters remained, all beautiful, upon the face of the stream, as if they had fallen upon it like leaves; but presently they moved with the current and floated away. "Now I will try," said the boy; and he wrote upon the water the Dragon-character—the character *Ryū*, in the writing which is called Sōsho, the "Grass-character;" and the character remained upon the flowing surface, and moved not. But Kōbōdaishi saw that the boy had not placed the *ten*, the little dot belonging to the character, beside it. And he asked the boy: "Why did you not put the *ten?*" "Oh, I forgot!" answered the boy; "please put it there for me," and Kōbōdaishi then made the dot. And, lo! the Dragon-character became a Dragon; and the Dragon moved terribly in the waters; and the sky darkened with thunder-clouds, and blazed with lightnings; and the Dragon ascended in a whirl of tempest to heaven.

Then Kōbōdaishi asked the boy: "Who are you?" And the boy made answer: "I am he whom men worship on the mountain Gotai; I am the Lord of Wisdom—Monju Bosatsu!" And even as he spoke the boy became changed; and his beauty became luminous like the beauty of gods; and his limbs became radiant, shedding soft light about. And, smiling, he rose to heaven and vanished beyond the clouds.

III.

But Kōbōdaishi himself once forgot to put the *ten* beside the character *Ō* on the tablet which he painted with the name of the Gate Ō-Te-mon of the Emperor's palace. And the Emperor at Kyōto having asked him why he had not put the *ten* beside the character, Kōbōdaishi answered: "I forgot; but I will put it on now." Then the Emperor bade ladders be brought; for the tablet was already in place, high above the gate. But Kōbōdaishi, standing on the pavement before the gate, simply threw his brush at the tablet; and the brush, so thrown, made the *ten* there most admirably, and fell back into his hand.

Kobodaishi also painted the tablet of the gate called Ko-ka-mon of the Emperor's palace at Kyōto. Now there was a man, dwelling near that gate, whose name was Kino Momoye; and he ridiculed the characters which Kōbōdaishi had made, and pointed to one of them, saying: "Why, it looks like a swaggering wrestler!" But the same night Momoye dreamed that a wrestler had come to his bedside and leaped upon him, and was beating him with his fists. And, crying out with the pain of the blows, he awoke, and saw the wrestler rise in air, and change into the written character he had laughed at, and go back to the tablet over the gate.

And there was another writer, famed greatly for his skill, named Onomo Toku, who laughed at some characters on the tablet of the Gate Shukaku-mon, written by Kōbōdaishi; and he said, pointing to the character *Shu:* "Verily *shu* looks like the character 'rice.'" And that night he dreamed that the character he had mocked at became a man; and that the man fell upon him and beat him, and jumped up and down upon his face many times—even as a kometsuki, a rice-cleaner, leaps up and down to move the hammers that beat the rice—saying the while:

"Lo! I am the messenger of Kōbōdaishi!" And, waking, he found himself bruised and bleeding as one that had been grievously trampled.

And long after Kobodaishi's death it was found that the names written by him on the two gates of the Emperor's palace—Bi-fuku-mon, the Gate of Beautiful Fortune; and Ko-ka-mon, the Gate of Excellent Greatness—were well-nigh effaced by time. And the Emperor ordered a Dainagon,* whose name was Yukinari, to restore the tablets. But Yukinari was afraid to perform the command of the Emperor, by reason of what had befallen other men; and, fearing the divine anger of Kōbōdaishi, he made offerings, and prayed for some token of permission. And the same night, in a dream, Kobodaishi appeared to him, smiling gently, and said: "Do the work even as the Emperor desires, and have no fear." So he restored the tablets in the first month of the fourth year of Kwanko, as is recorded in the book, Hon-cho-bun-sui.

And all these things have been related to me by my friend Akira.

---

* *Dainagon*, the title of a high officer in the ancient Imperial Court

3

JIZŌ

I.

I HAVE passed another day in wandering among the temples, both Shintō and Buddhist. I have seen many curious things; but I have not yet seen the face of the Buddha.

Repeatedly, after long wearisome climbing of stone steps, and passing under gates full of gargoyles—heads of elephants and heads of lions—and entering shoeless into scented twilight, into enchanted gardens of golden lotus-flowers of paper, and there waiting for my eyes to become habituated to the dimness, I have looked in vain for images. Only an opulent glimmering confusion of things half-seen—vague altar-splendors created by gilded bronzes twisted into riddles, by vessels of indescribable shape, by enigmatic texts of gold, by mysterious glittering pendent things—all framing in only a shrine with doors fast closed.

What has most impressed me is the seeming joyousness of popular faith. I have seen nothing grim, austere, or self-repressive. I have not even noted anything approaching the solemn. The bright temple courts and even the temple steps are thronged with laughing children, playing curious games; and mothers, entering the sanctuary to pray, suffer their little ones to creep about the matting and crow. The people take their religion lightly and cheerfully: they drop their cash in the great alms-box, clap their hands, murmur a very brief prayer, then turn to laugh and talk and smoke their little pipes before the temple entrance. Into some shrines, I have noticed the worshipers do not enter at all; they merely stand before the doors and pray for a few seconds, and make their small offerings. Blessed are they who do not too much fear the gods which they have made.

II.

Akira is bowing and smiling at the door. He slips off his sandals, enters in his white digitated stockings, and, with another smile and bow, sinks gently into the proffered chair. Akira is an interesting boy. With his smooth beardless face, and clear bronze skin, and blue-black hair trimmed into a shock that shadows his forehead to the eyes, he has almost the appearance, in his long wide-sleeved robe and snowy stockings, of a young Japanese girl.

I clap my hands for tea, hotel tea, which he calls "Chinese tea." I offer him a cigar, which he declines; but with my permission, he will smoke his pipe. Thereupon he draws from his girdle a Japanese pipe-case and tobacco-pouch combined; pulls out of the pipe-case a little brass pipe with a bowl scarcely large enough to hold a pea; pulls out of the pouch some tobacco so finely cut that it looks like hair, stuffs a tiny pellet of this preparation in the pipe, and begins to smoke. He draws the smoke into his lungs, and blows it out again through his nostrils. Three little whiffs, at intervals of about half a minute, and the pipe, emptied, is replaced in its case.

Meanwhile I have related to Akira the story of my disappointments.

"Oh, you can see him today," responds Akira, "if you will take a walk with me to the Temple of Zotokuin. For this is the Busshōe, the festival of the Birthday of Buddha. But he is very small, only a few inches high. If you want to see a great Buddha, you must go to Kamakura. There is a Buddha in that place, sitting upon a lotus; and he is fifty feet high."

So I go forth under the guidance of Akira. He says he may be able to show me "some curious things."

III.

There is a sound of happy voices from the temple, and the steps are crowded with smiling mothers and laughing children. Entering, I find women and babies pressing about a lacquered table in front of the doorway. Upon it is a little tub-shaped vessel of sweet tea—amacha; and standing in the tea is a tiny figure of Buddha, one hand pointing upward and one downward. The women, having made the customary offering, take up some of the tea with a wooden ladle of curious shape, and pour it over the statue, and then, filling the ladle a second time, drink a little, and give a sip to their babies. This is the ceremony of washing the statue of Buddha.

Near the lacquered stand on which the vessel of sweet tea rests is another and lower stand supporting a temple bell shaped like a great bowl. A priest approaches with a padded mallet in his hand and strikes the bell. But the bell does not sound properly: he starts, looks into it, and stoops to lift out of it a smiling Japanese baby. The mother, laughing, runs to relieve him of his burden; and priest, mother, and baby all look at us with a frankness of mirth in which we join.

Akira leaves me a moment to speak with one of the temple attendants, and presently returns with a curious lacquered box, about a foot in length, and four inches wide on each of its four sides. There is only a small hole in one end of it; no appearance of a lid of any sort.

"Now," says Akira, "if you wish to pay two sen, we shall learn our future lot according to the will of the gods."

I pay the two sen, and Akira shakes the box. Out comes a narrow slip of bamboo, with Chinese characters written thereon.

"Kitsu!" cries Akira. "Good-fortune. The number is fifty-and-one."

Again he shakes the box; a second bamboo slip issues from the slit.

"Dai kitsu! great good-fortune. The number is ninety-and-nine."

Once more the box is shaken; once more the oracular bamboo protrudes.

"Kyō!" laughs Akira. "Evil will befall us. The number is sixty-and-four."

He returns the box to a priest, and receives three mysterious papers, numbered with numbers corresponding to the numbers of the bamboo slips. These little bamboo slips, or divining-sticks, are called *mikuji*.

This, as translated by Akira, is the substance of the text of the paper numbered fifty-and-one:

"He who draweth forth this mikuji, let him live according to the heavenly law and worship Kwannon. If his trouble be a sickness, it shall pass from him. If he have lost aught, it shall be found. If he have a suit at law, he shall gain. If he love a woman, he shall surely win her—though he should have to wait. And many happinesses will come to him."

The dai-kitsu paper reads almost similarly, with the sole differences that, instead of Kwannon, the deities of wealth and prosperity—Daikoku, Bishamon, and Benten—are to be worshiped, and that the fortunate man will not have to wait at all for the woman loved. But the *kyo* paper reads thus:

"He who draweth forth this mikuji, it will be well for him to obey the heavenly law and to worship Kwannon the Merciful. If he have any sickness, even much more sick he shall become. If he have lost aught, it shall never be found. If he have a suit at law, he shall never gain it. If he love a woman, let him have no more expectation of winning her. Only by the most diligent piety can he hope to escape the most frightful calamities. And there shall be no felicity in his portion."

"All the same, we are fortunate," declares Akira. "Twice out of three times we have found luck. Now we will go to see another statue of Buddha."

And he guides me, through many curious streets, to the southern verge of the city.

IV.

Before us rises a hill, with a broad flight of stone steps sloping to its summit, between foliage of cedars and maples. We climb; and I see above me the Lions of Buddha waiting—the male yawning menace, the female with mouth closed. Passing between them, we enter a large temple court, at whose farther end rises another wooded eminence.

And here is the temple, with roof of blue-painted copper tiles, and tilted eaves and gargoyles and dragons, all weather-stained to one neutral tone. The paper screens are open, but a melancholy rhythmic chant from within tells us that the noonday service is being held: the priests are chanting the syllables of Sanscrit texts transliterated into Chinese—intoning the Sutra called the Sutra of the Lotus of the Good Law. One of those who chant keeps time by tapping with a mallet, cotton-wrapped, some grotesque object shaped like a dolphin's head, all lacquered in scarlet and gold, which gives forth a dull, booming tone—a mokugyo.

To the right of the temple is a little shrine, filling the air with fragrance of incense burning. I peer in through the blue smoke that curls up from half a dozen tiny rods planted in a small brazier full of ashes; and far back in the shadow I see a swarthy Buddha, tiara-coiffed, with head bowed and hands joined, just as I see the Japanese praying, erect in the sun, before the thresholds of temples. The figure is of wood, rudely wrought and rudely colored: still the placid face has beauty of suggestion.

Crossing the court to the left of the building, I find another flight of steps before me, leading up a slope to something mysterious still higher, among enormous trees. I ascend these steps also, reach the top, guarded by two small symbolic lions, and suddenly find myself in cool shadow, and startled by a spectacle totally unfamiliar.

Dark—almost black—soil, and the shadowing of trees immemorially old, through whose vaulted foliage the sunlight leaks thinly down in rare flecks: a crepuscular light, tender and solemn, revealing the weirdest host of unfamiliar shapes—a vast congregation of gray, columnar, mossy things, stony, monumental, sculptured with Chinese ideographs. And about them, behind them, rising high above them, thickly set as rushes in a marsh-verge, tall slender wooden tablets, like laths, covered with similar fantastic lettering, pierce the green gloom by thousands, by tens of thousands.

And before I can note other details, I know that I am in a hakaba, a cemetery—a very ancient Buddhist cemetery.

These laths are called in the Japanese tongue sotoba.* All have notches cut upon their edges on both sides near the top— five notches; and all are painted with Chinese characters on both faces. One inscription is always the phrase *"To promote Buddhahood"* painted immediately below the dead man's name; the inscription upon the other surface is always a sentence in Sanscrit whose meaning has been forgotten even by those priests who perform the funeral rites. One such lath is planted behind the tomb as soon as the monument *(haka)* is set up; then another every seven days for forty-nine days; then one after the lapse of a hundred days; then one at the end of a year; then one after the passing of three years; and at successively longer periods others are erected during one hundred years.

And in almost every group I notice some quite new, of freshly planed unpainted white wood, standing beside others gray or even black with age; and there are many, still older, from whose surface all the characters have disappeared. Others are lying on the somber clay. Hundreds stand so loose in the soil that the least breeze jostles and clatters them together.

Not less unfamiliar in their forms, but far more interesting, are the monuments of stone. One shape I know represents five of the Buddhist elements: a cube supporting a sphere which upholds a pyramid on which rests a shallow square cup with four crescent edges and tilted corners, and in the cup a pyriform body

---

* Derived from the Sanscrit *stupa*.

poised with the point upwards. These successively typify Earth, Water, Fire, Wind, Ether, the five substances wherefrom the body is shaped, and into which it is resolved by death; the absence of any emblem for the Sixth element, *Knowledge,* touches more than any imagery conceivable could do. And, nevertheless, in the purpose of the symbolism, this omission was never planned with the same idea that it suggests to the Occidental mind.

Very numerous also among the monuments are low, square, flat-topped shafts, with a Japanese inscription in black or gold, or merely cut into the stone itself. Then there are upright slabs of various shapes and heights, mostly rounded at the top, usually bearing sculptures in relief. Finally, there are many curiously angled stones, or natural rocks, dressed on one side only, with designs etched upon the smoothed surface. There would appear to be some meaning even in the irregularity of the shape of these slabs; the rock always seems to have been broken out of its bed at five angles, and the manner in which it remains balanced perpendicularly upon its pedestal is a secret that the first hasty examination fails to reveal.

The pedestals themselves vary in construction; most have three orifices in the projecting surface in front of the monument supported by them, usually one large oval cavity, with two small round holes flanking it. These smaller holes serve for the burning of incense-rods; the larger cavity is filled with water. I do not know exactly why. Only my Japanese companion tells me "it is an ancient custom in Japan thus to pour out water for the dead." There are also bamboo cups on either side of the monument in which to place flowers.

Many of the sculptures represent Buddha in meditation, or in the attitude of exhorting; a few represent him asleep, with the placid, dreaming face of a child, a Japanese child; this means Nirvana. A common design upon many tombs also seems to be two lotus-blossoms with stalks intertwined.

In one place I see a stone with an English name upon it, and above that name a rudely chiseled cross. Verily the priests of Buddha have blessed tolerance; for this is a Christian's tomb!

And all is chipped and moldered and mossed; and the gray stones stand closely in hosts of ranks, only one or two inches apart, ranks of thousands upon thousands, always in the shadow of the great trees. Overhead innumerable birds sweeten the air with their trilling; and far below, down the steps behind us, I still hear the melancholy chant of the priests, faintly, like a humming of bees.

Akira leads the way in silence to where other steps descend into a darker and older part of the cemetery; and at the head of the steps, to the right, I see a group of colossal monuments, very tall, massive, mossed by time, with characters cut more than two inches deep into the gray rock of them. And behind them, in lieu of laths, are planted large sotoba, twelve to fourteen feet high, and thick as the beams of a temple roof. These are graves of priests.

V.

Descending the shadowed steps, I find myself face to face with six little statues about three feet high, standing in a row upon one long pedestal. The first holds a Buddhist incense-box; the second, a lotus; the third, a pilgrim's staff *(tsue):* the fourth is telling the beads of a Buddhist rosary; the fifth stands in the attitude of prayer, with hands joined; the sixth bears in one hand the shakujō, or mendicant priest's staff, having six rings attached to the top of it, and in the other hand the mystic jewel, Nio-i hō-jiu, by virtue whereof all desires may be accomplished. But the faces of the Six are the same: each figure differs from the other by the attitude only and emblematic attribute; and all are smiling the like faint smile. About the neck of each figure a white cotton bag is suspended; and all the bags are filled with pebbles; and pebbles have been piled high also about the feet of the statues, and upon their knees, and upon their shoulders; and even upon their aureoles of stone, little pebbles are balanced. Archaic, mysterious, but inexplicably touching, all these soft childish faces are.

Roku Jizō—"The Six Jizō"—these images are called in the speech of the people; and such groups may be seen in many a Japanese cemetery. They are representations of the most beautiful and tender figure in Japanese popular faith, that charming divinity who cares for the souls of little children, and consoles them in the place of unrest, and saves them from the demons. "But why are those little stones piled about the statues?" I ask.

Well, it is because some say the child-ghosts must build little towers of stones for penance in the Sai-no-Kawara, which is the place to which all children after death must go. And the Oni, who are demons, come to throw down the little stone-piles as fast as the children build; and these demons frighten the children, and torment them. But the little souls run to Jizō, who hides them in his great sleeves, and comforts them, and makes the demons go away. And every stone one lays upon the knees or at the feet of Jizō, with a prayer from the heart, helps some child-soul in the Sai-no-Kawara to perform its long penance.*

"All little children," says the young Buddhist student who tells all this, with a smile as gentle as Jizō's own, "must go to the Sai-no-Kawara when they die. And there they play with Jizō. The Saino-Kawara is beneath us, below the ground.†

---

* "The real origin of the custom of piling stones before the images of Jizō and other divinities is not now known to the people. The custom is founded upon a passage in the famous Sutra, 'The Lotus of the Good Law.'

"Even the little boys who, in playing, erected here and there heaps of sand, with the intention of dedicating them as Stupas to the Ginas—they have all of them reached enlightenment."—*Saddharma Pundarika*, c. II. v. 81 (Kern's translation), "Sacred Books of the East," vol. xxi.

† The original Jizō has been identified by Orientalists with the Sanscrit *Kshitegarbha;* as Professor Chamberlain observes, the resemblance in sound between the names Jizō and Jesus "is quite fortuitous." But in Japan Jizō has become totally transformed: he may justly be called the most Japanese of all Japanese divinities. According to the curious old Buddhist book, *Sai no Kawara Kuchi zu sami no den,* the whole Sai-no-Kawara legend originated in Japan, and was first written by the priest Kuya Shōnin, in the sixth year of the period called Ten-Kei, in the reign of the 'Emperor Shuyaku, who died in the year 946. To Kuya was revealed, in the village of Sai-in, near Kyōto, during a night

"And Jizō has long sleeves to his robe; and they pull him by the sleeves in their play; and they pile up little stones before him to amuse themselves. And those stones you see heaped about the statues are put there by people for the sake of the little ones, most often by mothers of dead children who pray to Jizō. But grown people do not go to the Sai-no-Kawara when they die."*

And the young student, leaving the Roku-Jizō, leads the way to other strange surprises, guiding me among the tombs, showing me the sculptured divinities.

Some of them are quaintly touching; all are interesting; a few are positively beautiful.

The greater number have nimbi. Many are represented kneeling, with hands joined exactly like the figures of saints in old Christian art. Others, holding lotus-flowers, appear to dream the dreams that are meditations. One figure reposes on the coils of a great serpent. Another, coiffed with something resembling a tiara, has six: hands, one pair joined in prayer, the rest, extended, holding out various objects; and this figure stands upon a prostrate demon, crouching face downwards. Yet another image, cut in low relief, has arms innumerable.

The first pair of hands are joined, with the palms together; while from behind the line of the shoulders, arms reach out in all directions, vapory, spiritual, holding forth all kinds of objects as in answer to supplication, and symbolizing, perhaps, the omnipotence of love. This is but one of the many forms of Kwannon, the goddess of mercy, the gentle divinity who refused the rest of Nirvana to save the souls of men, and who is most frequently

---

passed by the dry bed of the neighboring river, Sai-no-Kawa (said to be the modern Serikawa), the condition of child-souls in the Meido. [Such is the legend in the book; but Professor Chamberlain has shown that the name *Sai-on Kawara,* as now written, signifies "The Dry Bed of the River of Souls," and modern Japanese faith places that river in the Meido.] Whatever be the true history of the myth, it is certainly Japanese; and the conception of Jizō as the lover and playfellow of dead children belongs to Japan.

There are many other popular forms of Jizō, one of the most common being that Koyasu-Jizō to whom pregnant women pray. There are but few roads in Japan upon which statues of Jizō may not be seen; for he is also the patron of pilgrims.

* Except those who have never married.

pictured as a beautiful Japanese girl. But here she appears as Senjiu-Kwannon (Kwannon-of-the-Thousand-Hands). Close by stands a great slab bearing upon the upper portion of its chiseled surface an image in relief of Buddha, meditating upon a lotus; and below are carven three weird little figures, one with hands upon its eyes, one with hands upon its ears, one with hands upon its mouth; these are Apes. "What do they signify?" I inquire. My friend answers vaguely, mimicing each gesture of the three sculptured shapes:

"*I see no bad thing; I hear no bad thing; I speak no bad thing.*"

Gradually, by dint of reiterated explanations, I myself learn to recognize some of the gods at sight. The figure seated upon a lotus, holding a sword in its hand, and surrounded by flickering fire, is Fudo-Sama—Buddha as the Unmoved, the Immutable: the Sword signifies Intellect; the Fire, Power. Here is a meditating divinity, holding in one hand a coil of ropes: the divinity is Buddha; those are the ropes which bind the passions and desires. Here also is Buddha slumbering, with the gentlest, softest Japanese face—a child face—and eyes closed, and hand pillowing the cheek, in Nirvana. Here is a beautiful virgin-figure, standing upon a lily: Kwannon-Sama, the Japanese Madonna. Here is a solemn seated figure, holding in one hand a vase, and lifting the other with the gesture of a teacher: Yakushi-Sama, Buddha the All-Healer, Physician of Souls.

Also, I see figures of animals. The Deer of Buddhist birth-stories stands, all grace, in snowy stone, upon the summit of tōrō, or votive lamps. On one tomb I see, superbly chiseled, the image of a fish, or rather the Idea of a fish, made beautifully grotesque for sculptural purposes, like the dolphin of Greek art. It crowns the top of a memorial column; the broad open jaws, showing serrated teeth, rest on the summit of the block bearing the dead man's name; the dorsal fin and elevated tail are elaborated into decorative impossibilities. "Mokugyo," says Akira. It is the same Buddhist emblem as that hollow wooden object,

lacquered scarlet-and-gold, on which the priests beat with a padded mallet while chanting the Sutra. And, finally, in one place I
perceive a pair of sitting animals, of some mythological species,
supple of figure as greyhounds. "Kitsune," says Akira—"foxes."
So they are, now that I look upon them with knowledge of their
purpose; idealized foxes, foxes spiritualized, impossibly graceful
foxes. They are chiseled in some gray stone. They have long, narrow, sinister, glittering eyes; they seem to snarl; they are weird,
very weird creatures, the servants of the Rice-God, retainers of
Inari-Sama, and properly belong, not to Buddhist iconography,
but the imagery of Shintō.

No inscriptions upon these tombs corresponding to our epi-
taphs. Only family names—the names of the dead and their
relatives, and a sculptured crest, usually a flower. On the sotoba,
only Sanscrit words.

Farther on, I find other figures of Jizō, single reliefs, sculptured upon tombs. But one of these is a work of art so charming
that I feel a pain at being obliged to pass it by. More sweet, assuredly, than any imaged Christ, this dream in white stone of the
playfellow of dead children, like a beautiful young boy, with gracious eyelids half closed, and face made heavenly by such a smile
as only Buddhist art could have imagined, the smile of infinite
lovingness and supremest gentleness. Indeed, so charming the
ideal of Jizō is that in the speech of the people, a beautiful face
is always likened to his—"Jizō-kao," as the face of Jizō.

VI.

And we come to the end of the cemetery, to the verge of the
great grove.

Beyond the trees, what caressing sun, what spiritual loveliness in the tender day! A tropic sky always seemed to me to hang
so low that one could almost bathe one's fingers in its lukewarm
liquid blue by reaching upward from any dwelling-roof. But this
sky, softer, fainter, arches so vastly as to suggest the heaven
of a larger planet. And the very clouds are not clouds, but only

dreams of clouds, so filmy they are; ghosts of clouds, diaphanous spectres, illusions!

All at once I become aware of a child standing before me, a very young girl who looks up wonderingly at my face; so light her approach that the joy of the birds and whispering of the leaves quite drowned the soft sound of her feet. Her ragged garb is Japanese; but her gaze, her loose fair hair, are not of Nippon only; the ghost of another race—perhaps my own—watches me through her flower-blue eyes. A strange playground surely is this for thee, my child; I wonder if all these shapes about thee do not seem very weird, very strange, to that little soul of thine. But no; 'Tis only I who seem strange to thee; thou hast forgotten the Other Birth, and thy father's world.

Half-caste, and poor, and pretty, in this foreign port! Better thou wert with the dead about thee, child! better than the splendor of this soft blue light the unknown darkness for thee. There the gentle Jizō would care for thee, and hide thee in his great sleeves, and keep all evil from thee, and play shadowy play with thee; and this thy forsaken mother, who now comes to ask an alms for thy sake, dumbly pointing to thy strange beauty with her patient Japanese smile, would put little stones upon the knees of the dear god that thou mightest find rest.

VII.

"Oh, Akira! you must tell me something more about Jizō, and the ghosts of the children in the Sai-no-Kawara."

"I cannot tell you much more," answers Akira, smiling at my interest in this charming divinity; "but if you will come with me now to Kuboyama, I will show you, in one of the temples there, pictures of the Sai-no-Kawara and of Jizō, and the Judgment of Souls."

So we take our way in two jinrikisha to the Temple Rin-ko-ji, on Kuboyama. We roll swiftly through a mile of many-colored narrow Japanese streets; then through a half mile of pretty suburban ways, lined with gardens, behind whose clipped hedges are homes light and dainty as cages of wicker-work; and then, leaving our vehicles, we ascend green hills on foot by winding paths, and traverse a region of fields and farms. After a long walk in the hot sun we reach a village almost wholly composed of shrines and temples.

The outlying sacred place—three buildings in one enclosure of bamboo fences—belongs to the Shingon sect. A small open shrine, to the left of the entrance, first attracts us. It is a dead house: a Japanese bier is there. But almost opposite the doorway is an altar covered with startling images.

What immediately rivets the attention is a terrible figure, all vermilion red, towering above many smaller images—a goblin shape with immense cavernous eyes. His mouth is widely opened as if speaking in wrath, and his brows frown terribly. A long red beard descends upon his red breast. And on his head is a strangely shaped crown, a crown of black and gold, having three singular lobes: the left lobe bearing an image of the moon; the right, an image of the sun; the central lobe is all black. But below it, upon the deep gold-rimmed black band, flames the mystic character signifying KING. Also, from the same crown-band protrude at descending angles, to left and right, two gilded sceptre-shaped objects. In one hand the King holds an object similar of form, but larger, his shaku or regal wand. And Akira explains.

This is Emma-Ō, Lord of Shadows, Judge of Souls, King of the Dead.* Of any man having a terrible countenance the Japanese are wont to say, "*His face is the face of Emma.*"

At his right hand white Jizō-Sama stands upon a many-petaled rosy lotus.

At his left is the image of an aged woman—weird Sodzu-Baba, she who takes the garments of the dead away by the banks of the River of the Three Roads, which flows through the phantom-world. Pale blue her robe is; her hair and skin are white; her face

---

* In Sanscrit, "Yama-Raja." But the Indian conception has been totally transformed by Japanese Buddhism.

is strangely wrinkled; her small, keen eyes are hard. The statue is very old; and the paint is scaling from it in places, so as to lend it a ghastly leprous aspect.

There are also images of the Sea-goddess Benten and of Kwannon-Sama, seated on summits of mountains forming the upper part of miniature landscapes made of some unfamiliar composition, and beautifully colored; the whole being protected from careless fingering by strong wire nettings stretched across the front of the little shrines containing the panorama. Benten has eight arms: two of her hands are joined in prayer; the others, extended above her, hold different objects—a sword, a wheel, a bow, an arrow, a key, and a magical gem. Below her, standing on the slopes of her mountain throne, are her ten robed attendants, all in the attitude of prayer; still farther down appears the body of a great white serpent, with its tail hanging from one orifice in the rocks, and its head emerging from another. At the very bottom of the hill lies a patient cow. Kwannon appears as Senjiu-Kwannon, offering gifts to men with all the multitude of her arms of mercy.

But this is not what we came to see. The pictures of heaven and hell await us in the Zen-Shū temple close by, whither we turn our steps.

On the way my guide tells me this:

"When one dies the body is washed and shaven, and attired in white, in the garments of a pilgrim. And a wallet (sanyabukkero), like the wallet of a Buddhist pilgrim, is hung about the neck of the dead; and in this wallet are placed three rin.* And these coin are buried with the dead.

---

* Funeral customs, as well as the beliefs connected with them, vary considerably in different parts of Japan. Those of the eastern provinces differ from those of the western and southern. The old practice of placing articles of value in the coffin—such as the metal mirror formerly buried with a woman, or the sword buried with a man of the Samurai caste—has become almost obsolete. But the custom of putting money in the coffin still prevails: in Iiumo the amount is always six rin, and these are called Rokudō-kane, or "The Money for the Six Roads."

"For all who die must, except children, pay three rin at the Sanzu-no-Kawa, 'The River of the Three Roads.' When souls have reached that river, they find there the Old Woman of the Three Roads, Sodzu-Baba, waiting for them: she lives on the banks of that river, with her husband, Ten Datsu-Ba. And if the Old Woman is not paid the sum of three rin, she takes away the clothes of the dead, and hangs them upon the trees."

VIII.

The temple is small, neat, luminous with the sun pouring into its widely opened shōji; and Akira must know the priests well, so affable their greeting is. I make a little offering, and Akira explains the purpose of our visit. Thereupon we are invited into a large bright apartment in a wing of the building, overlooking a lovely garden. Little cushions are placed on the floor for us to sit upon; and a smoking-box is brought in, and a tiny lacquered table about eight inches high. And while one of the priests opens a cupboard, or alcove with doors, to find the kakemono, another brings us tea, and a plate of curious confectionery consisting of various pretty objects made of a paste of sugar and rice flour. One is a perfect model of a chrysanthemum blossom; another is a lotus; others are simply large, thin, crimson lozenges bearing admirable designs—flying birds, wading storks, fish, even miniature landscapes. Akira picks out the chrysanthemum, and insists that I shall eat it; and I begin to demolish the sugary blossom, petal by petal, feeling all the while an acute remorse for spoiling so beautiful a thing.

Meanwhile four kakemono have been brought forth, unrolled, and suspended from pegs upon the wall; and we rise to examine them.

They are very, very beautiful kakemono, miracles of drawing and of color—subdued color, the color of the best period of Japanese art; and they are very large, fully five feet long and more than three broad, mounted upon silk.

And these are the legends of them:

First kakemono:

In the upper part of the painting is a scene from the Shaba, the world of men which we are wont to call the Real—a cemetery with trees in blossom, and mourners kneeling before tombs. All under the soft blue light of Japanese day.

Underneath is the world of ghosts. Down through the earth-crust souls are descending. Here they are flitting all white through inky darknesses; here farther on, through weird twilight, they are wading the flood of the phantom River of the Three Roads, Sanzu-no-Kawa. And here on the right is waiting for them Sodzu-Baba, the Old Woman of the Three Roads, ghastly and gray, and tall as a nightmare. From some she is taking their garments; the trees about her are heavily hung with the garments of others gone before.

Farther down I see fleeing souls overtaken by demons— hideous blood-red demons, with feet like lions, with faces half human, half bovine, the physiognomy of minotaurs in fury. One is rending a soul asunder. Another demon is forcing souls to reincarnate themselves in bodies of horses, of dogs, of swine. And as they are thus reincarnated they flee away into shadow.

Second kakemono:

Such a gloom as the diver sees in deep-sea water, a lurid twilight. In the midst a throne, ebon-colored, and upon it an awful figure seated—Emma Dai-Ō, Lord of Death and Judge of Souls, unpitying, tremendous. Frightful guardian spirits hover about him—armed goblins. On the left, in the foreground below the throne, stands the wondrous Mirror, Tabari-no-Kagami, reflecting the state of souls and all the happenings of the world. A landscape now shadows its surface—a landscape of cliffs and sand and sea, with ships in the offing. Upon the sand a dead man is lying, slain by a sword slash; the murderer is running away. Before this mirror a terrified soul stands, in the grasp of a demon, who compels him to look, and to recognize in the murderer's features his own face. To the right of the throne, upon a tall-stemmed flat stand, such as offerings to the gods are placed upon in the temples, a monstrous shape appears, like a double-faced head freshly cut off, and set upright upon the stump of the neck. The two faces are the Witnesses: the face of the Woman (*Mirume*) sees all that goes on in the Shaba; the other face is the face of a bearded man, the face of Kaguhana, who smells all odors, and by them is aware of all that human beings do. Close to them, upon a reading-stand, a great book is open, the record-book of deeds. And between the Mirror and the Witnesses white shuddering souls await judgment.

Farther down I see the sufferings of souls already sentenced. One, in lifetime a liar, is having his tongue torn out by a demon armed with heated pincers. Other souls, flung by scores into fiery carts, are being dragged away to torment. The carts are of iron, but resemble in form certain hand-wagons which one sees every day being pulled and pushed through the streets by bare-limbed Japanese laborers, chanting always the same melancholy alternating chorus, *Haidah! hei! haidah! hei!* But these demon-wagoners—naked, blood-colored, having the feet of lions and the heads of bulls—move with their flaming wagons at a run, like jinrikisha-men.

All the souls so far represented are souls of adults.

Third kakemono:

A furnace, with souls for fuel, blazing up into darkness. Demons stir the fire with poles of iron. Down through the upper blackness other souls are falling head downward into the flames.

Below this scene opens a shadowy landscape—a faint-blue and faint-gray world of hills and vales, through which a river serpentines—the Sai-no-Kawara.

Thronging the banks of the pale river are ghosts of little children, trying to pile up stones. They are very, very pretty, the child-souls, pretty as real Japanese children are (it is astonishing how well is child-beauty felt and expressed by the artists of Japan). Each child has one little short white dress.

In the foreground a horrible devil with an iron club has just dashed down and scattered a pile of stones built by one of the children. The little ghost, seated by the ruin of its work is crying with both pretty hands to its eyes. The devil appears to sneer. Other children also are weeping near by. But, lo! Jizō comes, all light and sweetness, with a glory moving behind him like a great full moon; and he holds out his shakujo, his strong and holy staff, and the little ghosts catch it and cling to it, and are drawn into the circle of his protection. And other infants have caught his great sleeves, and one has been lifted to the bosom of the god.

Below this Sai-no-Kawara scene appears yet another shadow-world, a wilderness of bamboos! Only white-robed shapes of women appear in it. They are weeping; the fingers of all are bleeding. With finger-nails plucked out must they continue through centuries to pick the sharp-edged bamboo-grass.

Fourth kakemono:

Floating in glory, Dai-Nichi-Nyorai, Kwannon-Sama, Amida Buddha. Far below them as hell from heaven surges a lake of blood, in which souls float. The shores of this lake are precipices studded with sword-blades thickly set as teeth in the jaws of a shark; and demons are driving naked ghosts up the frightful slopes. But out of the crimson lake something crystalline rises, like a beautiful, clear waterspout; the stem of a flower—a miraculous lotus, bearing up a soul to the feet of a priest standing above the verge of the abyss. By virtue of his prayer was shaped the lotus which thus lifted up and saved a sufferer.

Alas! there are no other kakemonos. There were several others: they have been lost!

No: I am happily mistaken; the priest has found, in some mysterious recess, one more kakemono, a very large one, which he unrolls and suspends beside the others. A vision of beauty, indeed! but what has this to do with faith or ghosts? In the foreground a garden by the waters of the sea, of some vast blue lake—a garden like that at Kanagawa, full of exquisite miniature landscape-work: cascades, grottoes, lily-ponds, carved bridges, and trees snowy with blossom, and dainty pavilions out jutting over the placid azure water. Long, bright, soft bands of clouds swim athwart the background. Beyond and above them rises a fairy magnificence of palatial structures, roof above roof, through an aureate haze like summer vapor: creations aerial, blue, light as dreams. And there are guests in these gardens, lovely beings, Japanee maidens. But they wear aureoles, starshining: they are spirits!

For this is Paradise, the Gokuraku; and all those divine shapes are Bosatsu. And now, looking closer, I perceive beautiful weird things which at first escaped my notice.

They are gardening, these charming beings! They are caressing the lotus-buds, sprinkling their petals with something celestial, helping them to blossom. And what lotus-buds! with colors not of this world. Some have burst open; and in their luminous hearts, in a radiance like that of dawn, tiny naked infants are seated, each with a tiny halo. These are Souls, new Buddhas, hotoke born into bliss. Some are very, very small; others larger; all seem to be growing visibly, for their lovely nurses are feeding them with something ambrosial. I see one which has left its lotus-cradle, being conducted by a celestial Jizō toward the higher splendors far away.

Above, in the loftiest blue, are floating tennin, angels of the Buddhist heaven, maidens with phoenix wings. One is playing with an ivory plectrum upon some stringed instrument, just as a dancing-girl plays her samisen; and others are sounding those curious Chinese flutes, composed of seventeen tubes, which are used still in sacred concerts at the great temples.

Akira says this heaven is too much like earth. The gardens, he declares, are like the gardens of temples, in spite of the celestial lotus-flowers; and in the blue roofs of the celestial mansions he discovers memories of the tea-houses of the city of Saikyō.*

Well, what after all is the heaven of any faith but ideal reiteration and prolongation of happy experiences remembered—the

---

* Literally "Western Capital,"—modern name of Kyōto, ancient residence of the emperors. The name "Tōkyō," on the other hand, signifies "Eastern Capital."

dream of dead days resurrected for us, and made eternal? And
if you think this Japanese ideal too simple, too naive, if you say
there are experiences of the material life more worthy of por-
trayal in a picture of heaven than any memory of days passed
in Japanese gardens and temples and tea-houses, it is perhaps
because you do not know Japan, the soft, sweet blue of its sky,
the tender color of its waters, the gentle splendor of its sunny
days, the exquisite charm of its interiors, where the least object
appeals to one's sense of beauty with the air of something not
made, but caressed, into existence.

IX.

"Now there is a wasan of Jizō," says Akira, taking from a shelf
in the temple alcove some much-worn, blue-covered Japanese
book. "A wasan is what you would call a hymn or psalm. This
book is two hundred years old: it is called Sai-no-Kawara-kuchi-
zu-sami-no-den, which is, literally, 'The Legend of the *Humming*
of the Sai-no-Kawara.' And this is the wasan;" and he reads me
the hymn of Jizō—the legend of the murmur of the little ghosts,
the legend of the humming of the Sai-no-Kawara—rhythmically,
like a song:*

"Not of this world is the story of sorrow.
The story of the Sai-no-Kawara,
At the roots of the Mountain of Shide;
Not of this world is the tale; yet 'tis most pitiful to hear.

---

* These first ten lines of the original will illustrate the measure of the wasan:

> Kore wa konoyo no koto narazu,
> Shide no yamaji no suso no naru,
> Sai-no-Kawara no monogatari
> Kiku ni tsuketemo aware nari
> Futatsu-ya, mitsu-ya, yotsu, itsutsu,
>
> To nimo taranu midorigo ga
> Sai-no-Kawara ni atsumari te,
> Chichi koishi! haha koishi!
> Koishi! koishi! to naku koe wa
> Konoyo no koe towa ko to kawari.

For together in the Sai-no-Kawara are assembled
Children of tender age in multitude—
Infants but two or three years old,
Infants of four or five, infants of less than ten:
In the Sai-no-Kawara are they gathered together.
And the voice of their longing for their parents,
The voice of their crying for their mothers and their fathers—
'*Chichi koishi! haha koishi!*'—
Is never as the voice of the crying of children in this world,
But a crying so pitiful to hear
That the sound of it would pierce through flesh and bone.
And sorrowful indeed the task which they perform—
Gathering the stones of the bed of the river,
Therewith to heap the tower of prayers.

Saying prayers for the happiness of father, they heap the first tower;

Saying prayers for the happiness of mother, they heap the second tower;

Saying prayers for their brothers, their sisters, and all whom they loved at home, they heap the third tower.

Such, by day, are their pitiful diversions.

But ever as the sun begins to sink below the horizon,
Then do the Oni, the demons of the hells, appear,
And say to them—'What is this that you do here?
'Lo! your parents still living in the Shaba-world
'Take no thought of pious offering or holy work:
'They do naught but mourn for you from the morning unto the evening.

'Oh, how pitiful! alas! how unmerciful!
'Verily the cause of the pains that you suffer
'Is only the mourning, the lamentation of your parents.' And saying also,
'Blame never us!'
The demons cast down the heaped-up towers,
They dash the stones down with their clubs of iron.

But lo! the teacher Jizō appears.

All gently he comes, and says to the weeping infants:

'Be not afraid, dears! be never fearful!

'Poor little souls, your lives were brief indeed!

'Too soon you were forced to make the weary journey to the Meido,

'The long journey to the region of the dead!

'Trust to me! I am your father and mother in the Meido,

'Father of all children in the region of the dead.'

And he folds the skirt of his shining robe about them;

So graciously takes he pity on the infants.

To those who cannot walk he stretches forth his strong shakujō;

And he pets the little ones, caresses them, takes them to his loving bosom.

So graciously he takes pity on the infants.

Namu Amida Butsu!"

4

A PILGRIMAGE TO ENOSHIMA

I.

KAMAKURA.

A long, straggling country village, between low wooded hills, with a canal passing through it. Old Japanese cottages, dingy, neutral-tinted, with roofs of thatch, very steeply sloping, above their wooden walls and paper shōji. Green patches on all the roof-slopes, some sort of grass; and on the very summits, on the ridges, luxurious growths of yane-shōbu,* the roof-plant, bearing pretty purple flowers. In the lukewarm air a mingling of Japanese odors, smells of saké, smells of seaweed soup, smells of daikon, the strong native radish; and dominating all, a sweet, thick, heavy scent of incense—incense from the shrines of gods.

Akira has hired two jinrikisha for our pilgrimage; a speckless azure sky arches the world; and the land lies glorified in a joy of sunshine. And yet a sense of melancholy, of desolation unspeakable, weighs upon me as we roll along the bank of the tiny stream, between the moldering lines of wretched little homes with grass growing on their roofs. For this moldering hamlet represents all that remains of the million-peopled streets of Yoritomo's capital, the mighty city of the Shōgunate, the ancient seat of feudal power, whither came the envoys of Kublai Khan demanding tribute, to lose their heads for their temerity. And only some of the

---

* Yane, "roof;" shōbu, "sweet-flag" (Acorus calamus).

unnumbered temples of the once magnificent city now remain, saved from the conflagrations of the fifteenth and sixteenth centuries, doubtless because built in high places, or because isolated from the maze of burning streets by vast courts and groves. Here still dwell the ancient gods in the great silence of their decaying temples, without worshipers, without revenues, surrounded by desolations of rice-fields, where the chanting of frogs replaces the sea-like murmur of the city that was and is not.

II.

The first great temple—En-gaku-ji—invites us to cross the canal by a little bridge facing its outward gate—a roofed gate with fine Chinese lines, but without carving. Passing it, we ascend a long, imposing succession of broad steps, leading up through a magnificent grove to a terrace, where we reach the second gate. This gate is a surprise; a stupendous structure of two stories—with huge sweeping curves of roof and enormous gables—antique, Chinese, magnificent. It is more than four hundred years old, but seems scarcely affected by the wearing of the centuries. The whole of the ponderous and complicated upper structure is sustained upon an open-work of round, plain pillars and crossbeams; the vast eaves are full of bird-nests; and the storm of twittering from the roofs is like a rushing of water. Immense the work is, and imposing in its aspect of settled power; but, in its way, it has great severity: there are no carvings, no gargoyles, no dragons; and yet the maze of projecting timbers below the eaves will both excite and delude expectation, so strangely does it suggest the grotesqueries and fantasticalities of another art. You look everywhere for the heads of lions, elephants, dragons, and see only the four-angled ends of beams, and feel rather astonished than disappointed. The majesty of the edifice could not have been strengthened by any such carving.

After the gate another long series of wide steps, and more trees, millennial, thick-shadowing, and then the terrace of the temple itself, with two beautiful stone lanterns (*tōrō*) at its entrance. The architecture of the temple resembles that of the gate, although on a lesser scale. Over the doors is a tablet with Chinese characters, signifying, "Great, Pure, Clear, Shining Treasure." But a heavy framework of wooden bars closes the sanctuary, and there is no one to let us in. Peering between the bars I see, in a sort of twilight, first a pavement of squares of marble, then an aisle of massive wooden pillars upholding the dim lofty roof, and at the farther end, between the pillars, Shaka, colossal, black-visaged, gold-robed, enthroned upon a giant lotus fully forty feet in circumference. At his right hand some white mysterious figure stands, holding an incense-box; at his left, another white figure is praying with clasped hands. Both are of superhuman stature. But it is too dark within the edifice to discern who they may be—whether disciples of the Buddha, or divinities, or figures of saints.

Beyond this temple extends an immense grove of trees—ancient cedars and pines—with splendid bamboos thickly planted between them, rising perpendicularly as masts to mix their plumes with the foliage of the giants: the effect is tropical, magnificent. Through this shadowing, a flight of broad stone steps slant up gently to some yet older shrine. And ascending them we reach another portal, smaller than the imposing Chinese structure through which we already passed, but wonderful, weird, full of dragons, dragons of a form which sculptors no longer carve, which they have even forgotten how to make, winged dragons rising, from a storm-whirl of waters or there into descending. The dragon upon the panel, of the left gate has her mouth closed; the jaws of the dragon on the panel of the right gate are open and menacing. Female and male they are, like the lions of Buddha. And the whirls of the eddying water, and the crests of the billowing, stand out from the panel in astonishing boldness of relief, in loops and curlings of gray wood time-seasoned to the hardness of stone.

The little temple beyond contains no celebrated image, but a shari only, or relic of Buddha, brought from India. And I cannot see it, having no time to wait until the absent keeper of the shari can be found.

III.

"Now we shall go to look at the big bell," says Akira.

We turn to the left as we descend, along a path cut between hills faced for the height of seven or eight feet with protection-walls made green by moss; and reach a flight of extraordinarily dilapidated steps, with grass springing between their every joint and break—steps so worn down and displaced by countless feet that they have become ruins, painful and even dangerous to mount. We reach the summit, however, without mishap, and find ourselves before a little temple, on the steps of which an old priest awaits us, with smiling bow of welcome, We return his salutation; but ere entering the temple turn to look at the tsurig-ane on the right—the famous bell.

Under a lofty open shed, with a tilted Chinese roof, the great bell is hung. I should judge it to be fully nine feet high, and about five feet in diameter, with lips about eight inches thick. The shape of it is not like that of our bells, which broaden toward the lips; this has the same diameter through all its height, and it is covered with Buddhist texts cut into the smooth metal of it. It is rung by means of a heavy swinging beam, suspended from the roof by chains, and moved like a battering-ram. There are loops of palm-fiber rope attached to this beam to pull it by; and when you pull hard enough, so as to give it a good swing, it strikes a moulding like a lotus-flower on the side of the bell. This it must have done many hundred times; for the square, flat end of it, though showing the grain of a very dense wood, has been bat-tered into a convex disk with ragged protruding edges, like the surface of a long-used printer's mallet.

A priest makes a sign to me to ring the bell. I first touch the great lips with my hand very lightly; and a musical murmur comes from them. Then I set the beam swinging strongly; and a sound deep as thunder, rich as the bass of a mighty organ—a sound enormous, extraordinary, yet beautiful—rolls over the hills and away. Then swiftly follows another and lesser and sweeter billowing of tone; then another; then an eddying of waves of echoes. Only once was it struck, the astounding bell; yet it continues to sob and moan for at least ten minutes!

And the age of this bell is six hundred and fifty years.*

In the little temple near by, the priest shows us a series of curious paintings, representing the six hundredth anniversary of the casting of the bell. (For this is a sacred bell, and the spirit of a god is believed to dwell within it.) Otherwise the temple has little of interest. There are some kakemono representing Iyeyasu and his retainers; and on either side of the door, separating the inner from the outward sanctuary, there are life-size images of Japanese warriors in antique costume. On the altars of the inner shrine are small images, grouped upon a miniature landscape-work of painted wood—the Jiugo-Dōji, or Fifteen Youths—the Sons of the Goddess Benten. There are gohei before the shrine, and a mirror upon it; emblems of Shintō. The sanctuary has changed hands in the great transfer of Buddhist temples to the state religion.

In nearly every celebrated temple little Japanese prints are sold, containing the history of the shrine, and its miraculous legends. I find several such things on sale at the door of the temple, and in one of them, ornamented with a curious engraving of the bell, I discover, with Akira's aid, the following traditions:

---

* At the time this paper was written, nearly three years ago, I had not seen the mighty bells at Kyōto and at Nara.

The largest bell in Japan is suspended in the grounds of the grand Jōdo temple of Chion-in, at Kyōto. Visitors are not allowed to sound it. It was cast in 1633. It weighs seventy-four tons, and requires, they say, twenty-five men to ring it properly. Next in size ranks the bell of the Daibutsu temple in Kyōto, which visitors are allowed to ring on payment of a small sum. It was cast in 1615, and weighs sixty-three tons. The wonderful bell of Tōdaiji, at Nara, although ranking only third, is perhaps the most interesting of all. It is thirteen feet six inches high, and nine feet in diameter; and its inferiority to the Kyōto bells is not in visible dimensions so much as in weight and thickness. It weighs thirty-seven tons. It was cast in 733, and is therefore one thousand one hundred and sixty years old. Visitors pay one cent to sound it once.

IV.

In the twelfth year of Bummei, this bell rang itself. And one who laughed on being told of the miracle, met with misfortune; and another, who believed, thereafter prospered, and obtained all his desires.

Now, in that time there died in the village of Tamanawa a sick man whose name was Ono-no-Kimi; and Ono-no-Kimi descended to the region of the dead, and went before the Judgment-Seat of Emma-Ō. And Emma, Judge of Souls, said to him, "You come too soon! The measure of life allotted you in the Shaba-world has not yet been exhausted. Go back at once." But Ono-no-Kimi pleaded, saying, "How may I go back, not knowing my way through the darkness?" And Emma answered him, "You can find your way back by listening to the sound of the bell of En-gaku-ji, which is heard in the Nan-en-budi world, going south." And Ono-no-Kimi went south, and heard the bell, and found his way through the darknesses, and revived in the Shaba-world.

Also in those days there appeared in many provinces a Buddhist priest of giant stature, whom none remembered to have seen before, and whose name no man knew, traveling through the land, and everywhere exhorting the people to pray before the bell of En-gaku-ji. And it was at last discovered that the giant pilgrim was the holy bell itself, transformed by supernatural power into the form of a priest. And after these things had happened, many prayed before the bell, and obtained their wishes.

V.

"Oh! there is something still to see," my guide exclaims as we reach the great Chinese gate again; and he leads the way across the grounds by another path to a little hill, previously hidden from view by trees. The face of the hill, a mass of soft stone perhaps one hundred feet high, is hollowed out into chambers, full of images. These look like burial caves; and the images seem funereal monuments. There are two stories of chambers—three above, two below; and the former are connected with the latter by a narrow interior stairway cut through the living rock. And all around the dripping walls of these chambers on pedestals are gray slabs, shaped exactly like the haka in Buddhist cemeteries, and chiseled with figures of divinities in high relief. All have glory-disks: some are naïve and sincere like the work of our own mediaeval image-makers. Several are not unfamiliar. I have seen before, in the cemetery of Kuboyama, this kneeling woman with countless shadowy hands; and this figure tiara-coiffed, slumbering with one knee raised, and cheek pillowed upon the left hand— the placid and pathetic symbol of the perpetual rest. Others, like Madonnas, hold lotus-flowers, and their feet rest upon the coils of a serpent. I cannot see them all, for the rock roof of one chamber has fallen in; and a sunbeam entering the ruin reveals a host of inaccessible sculptures half buried in rubbish.

But no!—this grotto-work is not for the dead; and these are not haka, as I imagined, but only images of the Goddess of Mercy. These chambers are chapels; and these sculptures are the En-gaku-ji-no-hyaka-Kwannon, "the Hundred Kwannons of Engaku-ji." And I see in the upper chamber above the stairs a granite tablet in a rock-niche, chiseled with an inscription in Sanscrit transliterated into Chinese characters, "Adoration to the great merciful Kwan-ze-on, who looketh down above the sound of prayer."*

VI.

Entering the grounds of the next temple, the Temple of Kencho-ji, through the "Gate of the Forest of Contemplative Words," and the "Gate of the Great Mountain of Wealth," one might almost fancy one's self reentering, by some queer mistake, the

---

* In Sanscrit, Avalokitesvara. The Japanese Kwannon, or Kwan-ze-on, is identical in origin with the Chinese virgin-goddess Kwanyin, adopted by Buddhism as an incarnation of the Indian Avalokitesvara. (*See Eitel's Handbook of Chinese Buddhism.*) But the Japanese Kwannon has lost all Chinese characteristics—has become artistically an idealization of all that is sweet and beautiful in the woman of Japan.

grounds of En-gaku-ji. For the third gate before us, and the imposing temple beyond it, constructed upon the same models as those of the structures previously visited, were also the work of the same architect. Passing this third gate—colossal, severe, superb—we come to a fountain of bronze before the temple doors, an immense and beautiful lotus-leaf of metal, forming a broad shallow basin kept full to the brim by a jet in its midst.

This temple also is paved with black and white square slabs, and we can enter it with our shoes. Outside it is plain and solemn as that of En-gaku-ji; but the interior offers a more extraordinary spectacle of faded splendor. In lieu of the black Shaka throned against a background of flamelets, is a colossal Jizō-Sama, with a nimbus of fire—a single gilded circle large as a wagon-wheel, breaking into fire-tongues at three points. He is seated upon an enormous lotus of tarnished gold—over the lofty edge of which the skirt of his robe trails down. Behind him, standing on ascending tiers of golden steps, are glimmering hosts of minia-ture figures of him, reflections, multiplications of him, ranged there by ranks of hundreds—the Thousand Jizō. From the ceil-ing above him droop the dingy splendors of a sort of dais-work, a streaming circle of pendants like a fringe, shimmering faintly through the webbed dust of centuries. And the ceiling itself must once have been a marvel; all beamed in caissons, each caisson containing, upon a gold ground, the painted figure of a flying bird. Formerly the eight great pillars supporting the roof were also covered with gilding; but only a few traces of it linger still upon their worm-pierced surfaces, and about the bases of their capitals. And there are wonderful friezes above the doors, from which all color has long since faded away, marvelous gray old carvings in relief; floating figures of tennin, or heavenly spirits playing upon flutes and biwa.

There is a chamber separated by a heavy wooden screen from the aisle on the right; and the priest in charge of the building slides the screen aside, and bids us enter. In this chamber is a drum elevated upon a brazen stand—the hugest I ever saw, fully eighteen feet in circumference. Beside it hangs a big bell, covered with Buddhist texts. I am sorry to learn that it is prohibited to sound the great drum. There is nothing else to see except some dingy paper lanterns figured with the swastika—the sacred Buddhist symbol called by the Japanese manji.

VII.

Akira tells me that in the book called Jizō-kyo-Kosui, this legend is related of the great statue of Jizō in this same ancient temple of Ken-cho-ji.

Formerly there lived at Kamakura the wife of a Rōnin* named Soga Sadayoshi. She lived by feeding silkworms and gathering the silk. She used often to visit the temple of Ken-chō-ji; and one very cold day that she went there, she thought that the image of Jizō looked like one suffering from cold; and she resolved to make a cap to keep the god's head warm—such a cap as the people of the country wear in cold weather. And she went home and made the cap and covered the god's head with it, saying, "Would I were rich enough to give thee a warm covering for all thine august body; but, alas! I am poor, and even this which I offer thee is unworthy of thy divine acceptance."

Now this woman very suddenly died in the fiftieth year of her age, in the twelfth month of the fifth year of the period called Chisho. But her body remained warm for three days, so that her relatives would not suffer her to be taken to the burning ground. And on the evening of the third day she came to life again.

Then she related that on the day of her death she had gone before the judgment-seat of Emma, king and judge of the dead. And Emma, seeing her, became wroth, and said to her: "You have been a wicked woman, and have scorned the teaching of the Buddha. All your life you have passed in destroying the lives of silkworms by putting them into heated water. Now you shall go

---

* Let the reader consult Mitford's admirable *Tales of Old Japan* for the full meaning of the term "Rōnin."

to the Kwakkto-Jigoku, and there burn until your sins shall be expiated." Forthwith she was seized and dragged by demons to a great pot filled with molten metal, and thrown into the pot, and she cried out horribly. And suddenly Jizō-Sama descended into the molten metal beside her, and the metal became like a flowing of oil and ceased to burn; and Jizō put his arms about her and lifted her out. And he went with her before King Emma, and asked that she should be pardoned for his sake, forasmuch as she had become related to him by one act of goodness. So she found pardon, and returned to the Shaba-world.

"Akira," I ask, "it cannot then be lawful, according to Buddhism, for any one to wear silk?"

"Assuredly not," replies Akira; "and by the law of Buddha priests are expressly forbidden to wear silk. Nevertheless," he adds with that quiet smile of his, in which I am beginning to discern suggestions of sarcasm, "nearly all the priests wear silk."

VIII.

Akira also tells me this:

It is related in the seventh volume of the book Kamakurashi that there was formerly at Kamakura a temple called Emmei-ji, in which there was enshrined a famous statue of Jizō, called Hadaka-Jizō, or Naked Jizō. The statue was indeed naked, but clothes were put upon it; and it stood upright with its feet upon a chessboard. Now, when pilgrims came to the temple and paid a certain fee, the priest of the temple would remove the clothes of the statue; and then all could see that, though the face was the face of Jizō, the body was the body of a woman.

Now this was the origin of the famous image of Hadaka-Jizō standing upon the chessboard. On one occasion the great prince Taira-no-Tokyori was playing chess with his wife in the presence of many guests. And he made her agree, after they had played several games, that whosoever should lose the next game would have to stand naked on the chessboard. And in the next game they played his wife lost. And she prayed to Jizō to save her from the shame of appearing naked. And Jizō came in answer to her prayer and stood upon the chessboard, and disrobed himself, and changed his body suddenly into the body of a woman.

IX.

As we travel on, the road curves and narrows between higher elevations, and becomes more somber. "*Oi! mate!*" my Buddhist guide calls softly to the runners; and our two vehicles halt in a band of sunshine, descending, through an opening in the foliage of immense trees, over a flight of ancient mossy steps. "Here," says my friend, "is the temple of the King of Death; it is called Emma-Do; and it is a temple of the Zen sect—Zen-Oji. And it is more than seven hundred years old, and there is a famous statue in it."

We ascend to a small, narrow court in which the edifice stands. At the head of the steps, to the right, is a stone tablet, very old, with characters cut at least an inch deep into the granite of it, Chinese characters signifying, "This is the Temple of Emma, King."

The temple resembles outwardly and inwardly the others we have visited, and, like those of Shaka and of the colossal Jizō of Kamakura, has a paved floor, so that we are not obliged to remove our shoes on entering. Everything is worn, dim, vaguely gray; there is a pungent scent of mouldiness; the paint has long ago peeled away from the naked wood of the pillars. Throned to right and left against the high walls tower nine grim figures— five on one side, four on the other—wearing strange crowns with trumpet-shapen ornaments; figures hoary with centuries, and so like to the icon of Emma, which I saw at Kuboyama, that I ask, "Are all these Emma?" "Oh, no!" my guide answers; "these are his attendants only—the Jiu-Ō, the Ten Kings." "But there are only nine?" I query. "Nine, and Emma completes the number. You have not yet seen Emma."

Where is he? I see at the farther end of the chamber an altar elevated upon a platform approached by wooden steps; but there is no image, only the usual altar furniture of gilded bronze and lacquerware. Behind the altar I see only a curtain about six feet square—a curtain once dark red, now almost without any definite hue—probably veiling some alcove. A temple guardian approaches, and invites us to ascend the platform. I remove my shoes before mounting upon the matted surface, and follow the guardian behind the altar, in front of the curtain. He makes me a sign to look, and lifts the veil with a long rod. And suddenly, out of the blackness of some mysterious profundity masked by that somber curtain, there glowers upon me an apparition at the sight of which I involuntarily start back—a monstrosity exceeding all anticipation—a Face.*

A Face tremendous, menacing, frightful, dull red, as with the redness of heated iron cooling into gray. The first shock of the vision is no doubt partly due to the somewhat theatrical manner in which the work is suddenly revealed out of darkness by the lifting of the curtain. But as the surprise passes I begin to recognize the immense energy of the conception—to look for the secret of the grim artist. The wonder of the creation is not in the tiger frown, nor in the violence of the terrific month, nor in the fury and ghastly color of the head as a whole: it is in the eyes—eyes of nightmare.

X.

Now this weird old temple has its legend.

Seven hundred years ago, it is said, there died the great image-maker, the great busshi, Unke-Sosei. And Unke-Sosei signifies "Unke who returned from the dead." For when he came before

---

* There is a delicious Japanese proverb, the full humor of which is only to be appreciated by one familiar with the artistic representations of the divinities referred to:

> *Karutoki no Jizō-gao,*
> *Nasutoki no Emma-gao.*

> ["Borrowing-time, the face of Jizō;
> Repaying-time, the face of Emma."]

Emma, the Judge of Souls, Emma said to him: "Living, thou madest no image of me. Go back unto earth and make one, now that thou hast looked upon me." And Unke found himself suddenly restored to the world of men; and they that had known him before, astonished to see him alive again, called him Unke-Sosei. And Unke-Sosei, bearing with him always the memory of the countenance of Emma, wrought this image of him, which still inspires fear in all who behold it; and he made also the images of the grim Jiu-Ō, the Ten Kings obeying Emma, which sit throned about the temple.

I want to buy a picture of Emma, and make my wish known to the temple guardian. Oh, yes, I may buy a picture of Emma, but I must first see the Oni. I follow the guardian out of the temple, down the mossy steps, and across the village highway into a little Japanese cottage, where I take my seat upon the floor. The guardian disappears behind a screen, and presently returns dragging with him the Oni—the image of a demon, naked, bloodred, indescribably ugly. The Oni is about three feet high. He stands in an attitude of menace, brandishing a club. He has a head shaped something like the head of a bulldog, with brazen eyes; and his feet are like the feet of a lion. Very gravely the guardian turns the grotesquery round and round, that I may admire its every aspect; while a naïf crowd collects before the open door to look at the stranger and the demon.

Then the guardian finds me a rude woodcut of Emma, with a sacred inscription printed upon it; and as soon as I have paid for it, he proceeds to stamp the paper with the seal of the temple. The seal he keeps in a wonderful lacquered box, covered with many wrappings of soft leather. These having been removed, I inspect the seal—an oblong, vermilion-red polished stone, with the design cut in intaglio upon it. He moistens the surface with red ink, presses it upon the corner of the paper bearing the grim picture, and the authenticity of my strange purchase is established forever.

XI.

You do not see the Dai-Butsu as you enter the grounds of his long-vanished temple, and proceed along a paved path across stretches of lawn; great trees hide him. But very suddenly, at a turn, he comes into full view and you start! No matter how many photographs of the colossus you may have already seen, this first vision of the reality is an astonishment. Then you imagine that you are already too near, though the image is at least a hundred yards away. As for me, I retire at once thirty or forty yards back, to get a better view. And the jinrikisha man runs after me, laughing and gesticulating, thinking that I imagine the image alive and am afraid of it.

But, even were that shape alive, none could be afraid of it. The gentleness, the dreamy passionlessness of those features—the immense repose of the whole figure—are full of beauty and charm. And, contrary to all expectation, the nearer you approach the giant Buddha, the greater this charm becomes. You look up into the solemnly beautiful face—into the half closed eyes that seem to watch you through their eyelids of bronze as gently as those of a child; and you feel that the image typifies all that is tender and calm in the Soul of the East. Yet you feel also that only Japanese thought could have created it. Its beauty, its dignity, its perfect repose, reflect the higher life of the race that imagined it; and, though doubtless inspired by some Indian model, as the treatment of the hair and various symbolic marks reveal, the art is Japanese.

So mighty and beautiful the work is, that you will not for some time notice the magnificent lotus-plants of bronze, fully fifteen feet high, planted before the figure, on either side of the great tripod in which incense-rods are burning.

Through an orifice in the right side of the enormous lotus-blossom on which the Buddha is seated, you can enter into the statue. The interior contains a little shrine of Kwannon, and a statue of the priest Yuten, and a stone tablet bearing in Chinese characters the sacred formula, *Namu Amida Butsu.*

A ladder enables the pilgrim to ascend into the interior of the colossus as high as the shoulders, in which are two little windows commanding a wide prospect of the grounds; while a priest, who acts as guide, states the age of the statue to be six hundred and thirty years, and asks for some small contribution to aid in the erection of a new temple to shelter it from the weather.

For this Buddha once had a temple. A tidal wave following an earthquake swept walls and roof away, but left the mighty Amida unmoved, still meditating upon his lotus.

XII.

And we arrive before the far-famed Kamakura temple of Kwannon—Kwannon, who yielded up her right to the Eternal Peace that she might save the souls of men, and renounced Nirvana to suffer with humanity for other myriad million ages—Kwannon, the Goddess of Pity and of Mercy.

I climb three flights of steps leading to the temple, and a young girl, seated at the threshold, rises to greet us. Then she disappears within the temple to summon the guardian priest, a venerable man, white-robed, who makes me a sign to enter.

The temple is large as any that I have yet seen, and, like the others, gray with the wearing of six hundred years. From the roof there hang down votive offerings, inscriptions, and lanterns in multitude, painted with various pleasing colors. Almost opposite to the entrance is a singular statue, a seated figure, of human dimensions and most human aspect, looking upon us with small weird eyes set in a wondrously wrinkled face. This face was originally painted flesh-tint, and the robes of the image pale blue; but now the whole is uniformly gray with age and dust, and its colorlessness harmonizes so well with the senility of the figure that one is almost ready to believe one's self gazing at a living mendicant pilgrim. It is Benzuru, the same personage whose famous image at Asakusa has been made featureless by the wearing touch of countless pilgrim-fingers. To left and right of the entrance are the Ni-Ō, enormously muscled, furious of aspect; their crimson bodies are speckled with a white scum of paper pellets spat at them by worshipers. Above the altar is a small but very pleasing image of Kwannon, with her entire figure relieved against an oblong halo of gold, imitating the flickering of flame.

But this is not the image for which the temple is famed; there is another to be seen upon certain conditions. The old priest presents me with a petition, written in excellent and eloquent English, praying visitors to contribute something to the maintenance of the temple and its pontiff, and appealing to those of another faith to remember that "any belief which can make men kindly and good is worthy of respect." I contribute my mite, and I ask to see the great Kwannon.

Then the old priest lights a lantern, and leads the way, through a low doorway on the left of the altar, into the interior of the temple, into some very lofty darkness. I follow him cautiously awhile, discerning nothing whatever but the flicker of the lantern; then we halt before something which gleams. A moment, and my eyes, becoming more accustomed to the darkness, begin to distinguish outlines; the gleaming object defines itself gradually as a Foot, an immense golden Foot, and I perceive the hem of a golden robe undulating over the instep. Now the other foot appears; the figure is certainly standing. I can perceive that we are in a narrow but also very lofty chamber, and that out of some mysterious blackness overhead ropes are dangling down into the circle of lantern-light illuminating the golden feet. The priest lights two more lanterns, and suspends them upon hooks attached to a pair of pendent ropes about a yard apart; then he pulls up both together slowly. More of the golden robe is revealed as the lanterns ascend, swinging on their way; then the outlines of two mighty knees; then the curving of columnar thighs under chiseled drapery, and, as with the still waving ascent of the lanterns the golden Vision towers ever higher through the gloom, expectation intensifies. There is no sound but the sound of the invisible pulleys overhead, which squeak like bats. Now above the golden girdle, the suggestion of a bosom. Then the glowing of a golden hand uplifted in benediction. Then another golden hand holding a lotus. And at last a Face, golden, smiling with eternal youth and infinite tenderness, the face of Kwannon.

So revealed out of the consecrated darkness, this ideal of divine feminity—creation of a forgotten art and time—is more than impressive. I can scarcely call the emotion which it produces admiration; it is rather reverence.

But the lanterns, which paused awhile at the level of the beautiful face, now ascend still higher, with a fresh squeaking of pulleys. And lo! the tiara of the divinity appears, with strangest symbolism. It is a pyramid of heads, of faces—charming faces of maidens, miniature faces of Kwannon herself.

For this is the Kwannon of the Eleven Faces—Jiu-ichi-men-Kwannon.

XIII

Most sacred this statue is held; and this is its legend.

In the reign of Emperor Gensei, there lived in the province of Yamato a Buddhist priest, Tokudo Shōnin, who had been in a previous birth Hoki Bosatsu, but had been reborn among common men to save their souls. Now at that time, in a valley in Yamato, Tokudo Shōnin, walking by night, saw a wonderful radiance; and going toward it found that it came from the trunk of a great fallen tree, a kusunoki, or camphor-tree. A delicious perfume came from the tree, and the shining of it was like the shining of the moon. And by these signs Tokudo Shōnin knew that the wood was holy; and he bethought him that he should have the statue of Kwannon carved from it. And he recited a sutra, and repeated the Nenbutsu, praying for inspiration; and even while he prayed there came and stood before him an aged man and an aged woman; and these said to him, "We know that your desire is to have the image of Kwannon-Sama carved from this tree with the help of Heaven; continue therefore, to pray, and we shall carve the statue."

And Toudu Shōnin did as they bade him; and he saw them easily split the vast trunk into two equal parts, and begin to carve each of the parts into an image. And he saw them so labor for three days; and on the third day the work was done—and he saw the two marvelous statues of Kwannon made perfect before him. And he said to the strangers: "Tell me, I pray you, by what names you are known." Then the old man answered: "I am Kasuga Myōjin." And the woman answered: "I am called Ten-shō-kō-dai-jin; I am the Goddess of the Sun." And as they spoke both became transfigured and ascended to heaven and vanished from the sight of Tokudo Shōnin.*

And the Emperor, hearing of these happenings, sent his representative to Yamato to make offerings, and to have a temple built. Also the great priest, Gyōgi-Bosatsu, came and consecrated the images, and dedicated the temple which by order of the Emperor was built. And one of the statues he placed in the temple, enshrining it, and commanding it: "Stay thou here always to save all living creatures! "But the other statue he cast into the sea, saying to it: "Go thou whithersoever it is best, to save all the living."

Now the statue floated to Kamakura. And there arriving by night it shed a great radiance all about it as if there were sunshine upon the sea; and the fishermen of Kamakura were awakened by the great light; and they went out in boats, and found the statue floating and brought it to shore. And the Emperor ordered that a temple should be built for it, the temple called Shin-haseidera, on the mountain called Kaiko-San, at Kamakura.

---

* This old legend has peculiar interest as an example of the efforts made by Buddhism to absorb the Shintō divinities, as it had already absorbed those of India and of China. These efforts were, to a great extent, successful prior to the disestablishment of Buddhism and the revival of Shintō as the state religion. But in Izumo, and other parts of western Japan, Shintō has always remained dominant, and has even appropriated and amalgamated much belonging to Buddhism.

XIV.

As we leave the temple of Kwannon behind us, there are no more dwellings visible along the road; the green slopes to left and right become steeper, and the shadows of the great trees deepen over us. But still, at intervals, some flight of venerable mossy steps, a carven Buddhist gateway, or a lofty torii, signals the presence of sanctuaries we have no time to visit: countless crumbling shrines are all around us, dumb witnesses to the antique splendor and vastness of the dead capital; and everywhere, mingled with perfume of blossoms, hovers the sweet, resinous smell of Japanese incense. Betimes we pass a scattered multitude of sculptured stones, like segments of four-sided pillars—old haka, the forgotten tombs of a long-abandoned cemetery; or the solitary image of some Buddhist deity—a dreaming Amida or faintly smiling Kwannon. All are ancient, time-discolored, mutilated; a few have been weather-worn into unrecognizability. I halt a moment to contemplate something pathetic, a group of six images of the charming divinity who cares for the ghosts of little children—the Roku-Jizō. Oh, how chipped and scurfed and mossed they are! Five stand buried almost up to their shoulders in a heaping of little stones, testifying to the prayers of generations; and votive yodarekake, infant bibs of diverse colors, have been put about the necks of these for the love of children lost. But one of the gentle god's images lies shattered and overthrown in its own scattered pebble-pile—broken perhaps by some passing wagon.

XV.

The road slopes before us as we go, sinks down between cliffs steep as the walls of a cañon, and curves. Suddenly we emerge from the cliffs, and reach the sea. It is blue like the unclouded sky—a soft dreamy blue.

And our path turns sharply to the right, and winds along cliff-summits overlooking a broad beach of dun-colored sand; and the sea wind blows deliriously with a sweet saline scent, urging the lungs to fill themselves to the very utmost; and far away before me, I perceive a beautiful high green mass, an island foliage-covered, rising out of the water about a quarter of a mile from the main-land—Enoshima, the holy island, sacred to the goddess of the sea, the goddess of beauty. I can already distinguish a tiny town, gray-sprinkling its steep slope. Evidently it can be reached today on foot, for the tide is out, and has left bare a long broad reach of sand, extending to it, from the opposite village which we are approaching, like a causeway.

At Katase, the little settlement facing the island, we must leave our jinrikisha and walk; the dunes between the village and the beach are too deep to pull the vehicle over. Scores of other jinriki-sha are waiting here in the little narrow street for pilgrims who have preceded me. But today, I am told, I am the only European who visits the shrine of Benten.

Our two men lead the way over the dunes, and we soon descend upon damp firm sand.

As we near the island the architectural details of the little town define delightfully through the faint sea-haze—curved bluish sweeps of fantastic roofs, angles of airy balconies, high-peaked curious gables, all above a fluttering of queerly shaped banners covered with mysterious lettering. We pass the sand flats; and the ever-open Portal of the Sea-city, the City of the Dragon-goddess, is before us, a beautiful torii. All of bronze it is, with shimenawa of bronze above it, and a brazen tablet inscribed with characters declaring: "This is the Palace of the Goddess of Enoshima." About the bases of the ponderous pillars are strange designs in *relievo,* eddyings of waves with tortoises struggling in the flow. This is really the gate of the city, facing the shrine of Benten by the land approach; but it is only the third torii of the imposing series through Katase: we did not see the others, having come by way of the coast.

And lo! we are in Enoshima. High before us slopes the single street, a street of broad steps, a street shadowy, full of multi-colored flags and dark blue drapery dashed with white fantasticalities, which are words, fluttered by the sea wind. It is lined with taverns and miniature shops. At every one I must pause to look; and to dare to look at anything in Japan is to want to buy it. So I buy, and buy, and buy!

For verily it is the City of Mother-of-Pearl, this Enoshima. In every shop, behind the lettered draperies there are miracles of shell-work for sale at absurdly small prices. The glazed cases laid flat upon the matted platforms, the shelved cabinets set against the walls, are all opalescent with nacreous things—extraordinary surprises, incredible ingenuities; strings of mother-of-pearl fish, strings of mother of-pearl birds, all shimmering with rainbow colors. There are little kittens of mother-of-pearl, and little foxes of mother-of-pearl, and little puppies of mother-of-pearl, and girls' hair-combs, and cigarette holders, and pipes too beautiful to use. There are little tortoises, not larger than a shilling, made of shells, that, when you touch them, however lightly, begin to move head, legs, and tail, all at the same time, alternately, withdrawing or protruding their limbs so much like real tortoises as to give one a shock of surprise. There are storks and birds, and beetles and butterflies, and crabs and lobsters, made so cunningly of shells, that only touch convinces you they are not alive. There are bees of shell, poised on flowers of the same material—poised on wire in such a way that they seem to buzz if moved only with the tip of a feather. There is shell-work jewelry indescribable, things that Japanese girls love, enchantments in mother-of-pearl, hairpins carven in a hundred forms, brooches, necklaces. And there are photographs of Enoshima.

XVI.

This curious street ends at another torii, a wooden torii, with a steeper flight of stone steps ascending to it. At the foot of the steps are votive stone lamps and a little well, and a stone tank at which all pilgrims wash their hands and rinse their mouths before approaching the temples of the gods. And hanging beside the tank are bright blue towels, with large white Chinese characters upon them. I ask Akira what these characters signify:

"*Ho-Keng* is the sound of the characters in the Chinese; but in Japanese the same characters are pronounced *Kenjitatematsuru*, and signify that those towels are most humbly offered to Benten. They are what you call votive offerings. And there are many kinds of votive offerings made to famous shrines. Some people give towels, some give pictures, some give vases; some offer lanterns of paper, or bronze, or stone. It is common to promise such offerings when making petitions to the gods; and it is usual to promise a torii. The torii may be small or great according to the wealth of him who gives it; the very rich pilgrim may offer to the gods a torii of metal, such as that below, which is the Gate of Enoshima."

"Akira, do the Japanese always keep their vows to the gods?"

Akira smiles a sweet smile, and answers:

"There was a man who promised to build a torii of good metal if his prayers were granted. And he obtained all that he desired. And then he built a torii with three exceedingly small needles."

XVII.

Ascending the steps, we reach a terrace, overlooking all the city roofs. There are Buddhist lions of stone and stone lanterns, mossed and chipped, on either side the torii; and the background of the terrace is the sacred hill, covered with foliage. To the left is a balustrade of stone, old and green, surrounding a shallow pool covered with scum of water-weed. And on the farther bank above it, out of the bushes, protrudes a strangely shaped stone slab, poised on edge, and covered with Chinese characters. It is a sacred stone, and is believed to have the form of a great frog, gama; wherefore it is called Gama-ishi, the Frog-stone. Here and there along the edge of the terrace are other graven monuments, one of which is the offering of certain pilgrims who visited the shrine of the sea-goddess one hundred times. On the right other flights of steps lead to loftier terraces; and an old man, who sits at the foot of them, making bird-cages of bamboo, offers himself as guide.

We follow him to the next terrace, where there is a school for the children of Enoshima, and another sacred stone, huge and shapeless: Fuku-ishi, the Stone of Good Fortune. In old times pilgrims who rubbed their hands upon it believed they would thereby gain riches; and the stone is polished and worn by the touch of innumerable palms.

More steps and more green-mossed lions and lanterns, and another terrace with a little temple in its midst, the first shrine of Benten. Before it a few stunted palm-trees are growing. There is nothing in the shrine of interest, only Shintō emblems. But there is another well beside it with other votive towels, and there is another mysterious monument, a stone shrine brought from China six hundred years ago. Perhaps it contained some far-famed statue before this place of pilgrimage was given over to the priests of Shintō. There is nothing in it now; the monolith slab forming the back of it has been fractured by the falling of rocks from the cliff above; and the inscription cut therein has been almost effaced by some kind of scum. Akira reads "*Dai-Nippon-goku-Enoshima-no-reiseki-ken...*" the rest is undecipherable. He says there is a statue in the neighboring temple, but it is exhibited only once a year, on the fifteenth day of the seventh month.

Leaving the court by a rising path to the left, we proceed along the verge of a cliff overlooking the sea. Perched upon this verge are pretty tea-houses, all widely open to the sea wind, so that, looking through them, over their matted floors and lacquered balconies one sees the ocean as in a picture-frame, and the pale clear horizon specked with snowy sails, and a faint blue-peaked shape also, like a phantom island, the far vapory silhouette of Ōshima. Then we find another torii, and other steps leading to a terrace almost black with shade of enormous evergreen trees, and surrounded on the seaside by another stone balustrade, velveted with moss. On the right more steps, another torii, another terrace; and more mossed green lions and stone lamps; and a monument inscribed with the record of the change whereby Enoshima passed away from Buddhism to become Shintō. Beyond, in the center of another plateau, the second shrine of Benten.

But there is no Benten! Benten has been hidden away by Shintō hands. The second shrine is void as the first. Nevertheless, in a building to the left of the temple, strange relics are exhibited. Feudal armor; suits of plate and chain-mail; helmets with visors which are demoniac masks of iron; helmets crested with dragons of gold; two-handed swords worthy of giants; and enormous arrows, more than five feet long, with shafts nearly an inch in diameter. One has a crescent head about nine inches from horn to horn, the interior edge of the crescent being sharp as a knife. Such a missile would take off a man's head; and I can scarcely believe Akira's assurance that such ponderous arrows were shot from a bow by hand only. There is a specimen of the writing of Nichiren, the great Buddhist priest—gold characters on a blue ground; and there is, in a lacquered shrine, a gilded dragon said to have been made by that still greater priest and writer and master-wizard, Kōbōdaishi.

A path shaded by overarching trees leads from this plateau to the third shrine. We pass a torii and beyond it come to a stone monument covered with figures of monkeys chiseled in relief. What the signification of this monument is, even our guide cannot explain. Then another torii. It is of wood; but I am told it replaces one of metal, stolen in the night by thieves. Wonderful thieves! that torii must have weighed at least a ton! More stone lanterns; then an immense court, on the very summit of the mountain, and there, in its midst, the third and chief temple of Benten. And before the temple is a large vacant space surrounded by a fence in such manner as to render the shrine totally inaccessible. Vanity and vexation of spirit!

There is, however, a little haiden, or place of prayer, with nothing in it but a money-box and a bell, before the fence, and facing the temple steps. Here the pilgrims make their offerings and pray. Only a small raised platform covered with a Chinese roof supported upon four plain posts, the back of the structure being closed by a lattice about breast high. From this praying-station we can look into the temple of Benten, and see that Benten is not there.

But I perceive that the ceiling is arranged in caissons; and in a central caisson I discover a very curious painting—a foreshortened Tortoise, gazing down at me. And while I am looking at it I hear Akira and the guide laughing; and the latter exclaims, "*Benten-Sama!*"

A beautiful little damask snake is undulating up the latticework, poking its head through betimes to look at us. It does not seem in the least afraid, nor has it much reason to be, seeing that its kind are deemed the servants and confidants of Benten. Sometimes the great goddess herself assumes the serpent-form; perhaps she has come to see us.

Near by is a singular stone, set on a pedestal in the court. It has the form of the body of a tortoise, and markings like those of the creature's shell; and it is held a sacred thing, and is called the Tortoise-stone. But I fear exceedingly that in all this place we shall find nothing save stones and serpents!

XVIII.

Now we are going to visit the Dragon cavern, not so called, Akira says, because the Dragon of Benten ever dwelt therein, but because the shape of the cavern is the shape of a dragon. The path descends toward the opposite side of the island, and suddenly breaks into a flight of steps cut out of the pale hard rock—exceedingly steep, and worn, and slippery, and perilous—overlooking the sea. A vision of low pale rocks, and surf bursting among them, and a tōrō or votive stone lamp in the center of them—all seen as in a bird's eye-view, over the verge of an awful precipice. I see also deep, round holes in one of the rocks. There used to be a tea-house below; and the wooden pillars supporting it were fitted into those holes.

I descend with caution; the Japanese seldom slip in their straw sandals, but I can only proceed with the aid of the guide. At almost every step I slip. Surely these steps could never have been thus worn away by the straw sandals of pilgrims who came to see only stones and serpents!

At last we reach a plank gallery carried along the face of the cliff above the rocks and pools, and following it round a projection of the cliff enter the sacred cave. The light dims as we advance; and the sea-waves, running after us into the gloom, make a stupefying roar, multiplied by the extraordinary echo. Looking back, I see the mouth of the cavern like a prodigious sharply angled rent in blackness, showing a fragment of azure sky.

We reach a shrine with no deity in it, pay a fee; and lamps being lighted and given to each of us, we proceed to explore a series of underground passages. So black they are that even with the light of three lamps, I can at first see nothing. In a while, however, I can distinguish stone figures in relief—chiseled on slabs like those I saw in the Buddhist graveyard. These are placed at regular intervals along the rock walls. The guide approaches his light to the face of each one, and utters a name, "Daikoku-Sama," "Fudō-Sama," "Kwannon-Sama." Sometimes in lieu of a statue there is an empty shrine only, with a money-box before it; and these void shrines have names of Shintō gods, "Daijingu," "Hachiman," "Inari-Sama." All the statues are black, or seem black in the yellow lamplight, and sparkle as if frosted. I feel as if I were in some mortuary pit, some subterranean burial-place of dead gods. Interminable the corridor appears; yet there is at last an end—an end with a shrine in it—where the rocky ceiling descends so low that to reach the shrine one must go down on hands and knees. And there is nothing in the shrine. This is the Tail of the Dragon.

We do not return to the light at once, but enter into other lateral black corridors—the Wings of the Dragon. More sable effigies of dispossessed gods; more empty shrines; more stone faces covered with saltpetre; and more money-boxes, possible only to reach by stooping, where more offerings should be made. And there is no Benten, either of wood or stone.

I am glad to return to the light. Here our guide strips naked, and suddenly leaps head foremost into a black deep swirling current between rocks. Five minutes later he reappears, and clambering out lays at my feet a living, squirming sea-snail and an enormous shrimp. Then he resumes his robe, and we reascend the mountain.

XIX.

"And this," the reader may say—"this is all that you went forth to see: a torii, some shells, a small damask snake, some stones?"

It is true. And nevertheless I know that I am bewitched. There is a charm indefinable about the place—that sort of charm which comes with a little ghostly thrill never to be forgotten.

Not of strange sights alone is this charm made, but of numberless subtle sensations and ideas interwoven and interblended: the sweet sharp scents of grove and sea; the blood-brightening, vivifying touch of the free wind; the dumb appeal of ancient mystic mossy things; vague reverence evoked by knowledge of treading soil called holy for a thousand years; and a sense of sympathy, as a human duty, compelled by the vision of steps of rock worn down into shapelessness by the pilgrim feet of vanished generations.

And other memories ineffaceable: the first sight of the sea-girt City of Pearl through a fairy veil of haze; the windy approach to the lovely island over the velvety soundless brown stretch of sand; the weird majesty of the giant gate of bronze; the queer, high-sloping, fantastic, quaintly gabled street, flinging down sharp shadows of aerial balconies; the flutter of colored draperies in the sea wind, and of flags with their riddles of lettering; the pearly glimmering of the astonishing shops.

And impressions of the enormous day—the day of the Land of the Gods—a loftier day than ever our summers know; and the glory of the view from those green sacred silent heights between sea and sun; and the remembrance of the sky, a sky spiritual as holiness, a sky with clouds ghost-pure and white as the light itself—seeming, indeed, not clouds but dreams, or souls of Bodhisattvas about to melt forever into some blue Nirvana.

And the romance of Benten, too—the Deity of Beauty, the Divinity of Love, the Goddess of Eloquence. Rightly is she likewise named Goddess of the Sea. For is not the Sea most ancient and most excellent of Speakers—the eternal Poet, chanter of that mystic hymn whose rhythm shakes the world, whose mighty syllables no man may learn?

XX.

We return by another route.

For a while the way winds through a long narrow winding valley between wooded hills: the whole extent of bottom-land is occupied by rice-farms; the air has a humid coolness, and one hears only the chanting of frogs, like a clattering of countless castanets, as the jinrikisha jolts over the rugged elevated paths separating the flooded rice-fields.

As we skirt the foot of a wooded hill upon the right, my Japanese comrade signals to our runners to halt, and himself dismounting, points to the blue-peaked roof of a little temple high-perched on the green slope. "Is it really worth while to climb up there in the sun?" I ask. "Oh, yes!" he answers: "it is the temple of Kishibojin—Kishibojin, the Mother of Demons!"

We ascend a flight of broad stone steps, meet the Buddhist guardian lions at the summit, and enter the little court in which the temple stands. An elderly woman, with a child clinging to her robe, comes from the adjoining building to open the screens for us; and taking off our footgear we enter the temple. Without, the edifice looked old and dingy; but within all is neat and pretty. The June sun, pouring through, the open shōji, illuminates an artistic confusion of brasses gracefully shaped and multi-colored things—images, lanterns, paintings, gilded inscriptions, pendent scrolls. There are three altars.

Above the central altar Amida Buddha sits enthroned on his mystic golden lotus in the attitude of the Teacher. On the altar to the right gleams a shrine of five miniature golden steps, where little images stand in rows, tier above tier, some seated, some erect, male and female, attired like goddesses or like daimyō: the Sanjiubanjin, or Thirty Guardians. Below, on the facade of the altar, is the figure of a hero slaying a monster. On the altar to the left is the shrine of the Mother-of-Demons.

Her story is a legend of horror. For some sin committed in a previous birth, she was born a demon, devouring her own children. But being saved by the teaching of Buddha, she became a divine being, especially loving and protecting infants; and Japanese mothers pray to her for their little ones, and wives pray to her for beautiful boys.

The face of Kishibojin* is the face of a comely woman. But her eyes are weird. In her right hand she bears a lotus-blossom; with her left she supports in a fold of her robe, against her half-veiled breast, a naked baby. At the foot of her shrine stands Jizō-Sama, leaning upon his shakujo. But the altar and its images do not form the startling feature of the temple-interior. What impresses the visitor in a totally novel way are the votive offerings. High before the shrine, suspended from strings stretched taut between tall poles of bamboo, are scores, no, hundreds, of pretty tiny dresses—Japanese baby-dresses of many colors. Most are made of poor material, for these are the thank-offerings of very poor simple women, poor country mothers, whose prayers to Kishibojin for the blessing of children have been heard.

And the sight of all those little dresses, each telling so naïvely its story of joy and pain—those tiny kimono shaped and sewn by docile patient fingers of humble mothers—touches irresistibly, like some unexpected revelation of the universal mother-love. And the tenderness of all the simple hearts that have testified thus to faith and thankfulness seems to thrill all about me softly, like a caress of summer wind.

---

* In Sanscrit "*Harîtî*"—Karitei-Bo is the Japanese name for one form of Kishibojin.

Outside the world appears to have suddenly grown beautiful; the light is sweeter; it seems to me there is a new charm even in the azure of the eternal day.

XXL.

Then, having traversed the valley, we reach a main road so level and so magnificently shaded by huge old trees that I could believe myself in an English lane—a lane in Kent or Surrey, perhaps—but for some exotic detail breaking the illusion at intervals; a torii, towering before temple-steps descending to the highway, or a sign-board lettered with Chinese characters, or the wayside shrine of some unknown god.

All at once I observe by the roadside some unfamiliar sculptures in relief—a row of chiseled slabs protected by a little bamboo shed; and I dismount to look at them, supposing them to be funereal monuments. They are so old that the lines of their sculpturing are half obliterated; their feet are covered with moss, and their visages are half effaced. But I can discern that these are not haka, but six images of one divinity; and my guide knows him—Kōshin, the God of Roads. So chipped and covered with scurf he is, that the upper portion of his form has become indefinably vague; his attributes have been worn away. But below his feet, on several slabs, chiseled cunningly, I can still distinguish the figures of the Three Apes, his messengers. And some pious soul has left before one image an humble votive offering—the picture of a black cock and a white hen, painted upon a wooden shingle. It must have been left here very long ago; the wood has become almost black, and the painting has been damaged by weather and by the droppings of birds. There are no stones piled at the feet of these images, as before the images of Jizō; they seem like things forgotten, crusted over by the neglect of generations—archaic gods who have lost their worshipers.

But my guide tells me, "The Temple of Kōshin is near, in the village of Fujisawa." Assuredly I must visit it.

XXII.

The temple of Kōshin is situated in the middle of the village, in a court opening upon the main street. A very old wooden temple it is, unpainted, dilapidated, gray with the grayness of all forgotten and weather-beaten things. It is some time before the guardian of the temple can be found, to open the doors. For this temple has doors in lieu of shōji—old doors that moan sleepily at being turned upon their hinges. And it is not necessary to remove one's shoes; the floor is matless, covered with dust, and squeaks under the unaccustomed weight of entering feet. All within is crumbling, moldering, worn; the shrine has no image, only Shintō emblems, some poor paper lanterns whose once bright colors have vanished under a coating of dust, some vague inscriptions. I see the circular frame of a metal mirror; but the mirror itself is gone. Whither? The guardian says: "No priest lives now in this temple; and thieves might come in the night to steal the mirror; so we have hidden it away." I ask about the image of Kōshin. He answers it is exposed but once in every sixty-one years: so I cannot see it; but there are other statues of the god in the temple court.

I go to look at them: a row of images, much like those upon the public highway, but better preserved. One figure of Kōshin, however, is different from the others I have seen—apparently made after some Hindoo model, judging by the Indian coiffure, mitre-shaped and lofty. The god has three eyes; one in the center of his forehead, opening perpendicularly instead of horizontally. He has six arms. With one hand he supports a monkey; with another he grasps a serpent; and the other hands hold out symbolic things—a wheel, a sword, a rosary, a sceptre. And serpents are coiled about his wrists and about his ankles; and under his feet is a monstrous head, the head of a demon, Amanjako, sometimes called Utatesa ("Sadness"). Upon the pedestal below the Three Apes are carven; and the face of an ape appears also upon the front of the god's tiara.

I see also tablets of stone, graven only with the god's name—votive offerings. And near by, in a tiny wooden shrine, is the figure of the Earth-god, Ken-ro-ji-jin, gray, primeval, vaguely wrought, holding in one hand a spear, in the other a vessel containing something indistinguishable.

XXIII.

Perhaps to uninitiated eyes these many-headed, many-handed gods at first may seem—as they seem always in the sight of Christian bigotry—only monstrous. But when the knowledge of their meaning comes to one who feels the divine in all religions, then they will be found to make appeal to the higher aestheticism, to the sense of moral beauty, with a force never to be divined by minds knowing nothing of the Orient and its thought. To me the image of Kwannon of the Thousand Hands is not less admirable than any other representation of human loveliness idealized bearing her name—the Peerless, the Majestic, the Peace-Giving, or even White Sui-Getsu, who sails the moonlit waters in her rosy boat made of a single lotus-petal; and in the triple-headed Shaka I discern and revere the mighty power of that Truth, whereby, as by a conjunction of suns, the Three Worlds have been illuminated.

But vain to seek to memorize the names and attributes of all the gods; they seem, self-multiplying, to mock the seeker; Kwannon the Merciful, is revealed as the Hundred Kwannon; the Six Jizō become the Thousand. And as they multiply before research, they vary and change: less multiform, less complex, less elusive the moving of waters than the visions of this Oriental faith. Into it, as into a fathomless sea, mythology after mythology from India and China and the farther East has sunk and been absorbed; and the stranger, peering into its deeps, finds himself, as in the tale of Undine, contemplating a flood in whose every surge rises and vanishes a Face—weird or beautiful or terrible—a most ancient shoreless sea of forms incomprehensibly interchanging and intermingling, but symbolizing the protean magic of that infinite Unknown that shapes and re-shapes forever all cosmic being.

XXIV.

I wonder if I can buy a picture of Kōshin. In most Japanese temples little pictures of the tutelar deity are sold to pilgrims, cheap prints on thin paper. But the temple guardian here tells me, with a gesture of despair, that there are no pictures of Kōshin for sale; there is only an old kakemono on which the god is represented. If I would like to see it he will go home and get it for me. I beg him to do me the favor; and he hurries into the street.

While awaiting his return, I continue to examine the queer old statues, with a feeling of mingled melancholy and pleasure. To have studied and loved an ancient faith only through the labors of palaeographers and archaeologists, and as a something astronomically remote from one's own existence, and then suddenly in after years to find the same faith a part of one's human environment—to feel that its mythology, though senescent, is *alive* all around you—is almost to realize the dream of the Romantics, to have the sensation of returning through twenty centuries into the life of a happier world. For these quaint Gods of Roads and Gods of Earth are really living still, though so worn and mossed and feebly worshiped. In this brief moment, at least, I am really in the Elder World—perhaps just at that epoch of it when the primal faith is growing a little old-fashioned, crumbling slowly before the corrosive influence of a new philosophy; and I know myself a pagan still, loving these simple old gods, these gods of a people's childhood.

And they need some human love, these naïf, innocent, ugly gods. The beautiful divinities will live forever by that sweetness of womanhood idealized in the Buddhist art of them: eternal are Kwannon and Benten; they need no help of man; they will compel reverence when the great temples shall all have become voiceless and priestless as this shrine of Kōshin is. But these kind, queer, artless, moldering gods, who have given ease to so many troubled minds, who have gladdened so many simple hearts, who have heard so many innocent prayers—how gladly would I prolong their beneficent lives in spite of the so-called "laws of progress" and the irrefutable philosophy of evolution!

The guardian returns, bringing with him a kakemono, very small, very dusty, and so yellow-stained by time that it might be a thousand years old. But I am disappointed as I unroll it; there is only a very common print of the god within—all outline. And while I am looking at it, I become for the first time conscious that a crowd has gathered about me—tanned kindly-faced laborers from the fields, and mothers with their babies on their backs, and school children, and jinrikisha men—all wondering that a stranger should be thus interested in their gods. And although the pressure about me is very, very gentle, like a pressure of tepid water for gentleness, I feel a little embarrassed. I give back the old kakemono to the guardian, make my offering to the god, and take my leave of Kōshin and his good servant.

All the kind oblique eyes follow me as I go. And something like a feeling of remorse seizes me at thus abruptly abandoning the void, dusty, crumbling temple, with its mirrorless altar and its colorless lanterns, and the decaying sculptures of its neglected court, and its kindly guardian whom I see still watching my retreating steps, with the yellow kakemono in his hand. The whistle of a locomotive warns me that I shall just have time to catch the train. For Western civilization has invaded all this primitive peace, with its webs of steel, with its ways of iron. This is not of thy roads, O Kōshin!—the old gods are dying along its ash-strewn verge!

5

AT THE MARKET OF THE DEAD

I.

IT is just past five o'clock in the afternoon. Through the open door of my little study the rising breeze of evening is beginning to disturb the papers on my desk, and the white fire of the Japanese sun is taking that pale amber tone which tells that the heat of the day is over. There is not a cloud in the blue—not even one of those beautiful white filamentary things, like ghosts of silken floss, which usually swim in this most ethereal of earthly skies even in the driest weather.

A sudden shadow at the door. Akira, the young Buddhist student, stands at the threshold slipping his white feet out of his sandal-thongs preparatory to entering, and smiling like the god Jizō.

"Ah! komban, Akira."

"Tonight," says Akira, seating himself upon the floor in the posture of Buddha upon the Lotus, "the Bon-ichi will be held. Perhaps you would like to see it?"

"Oh, Akira, all things in this country I should like to see. But tell me, I pray you, unto what may the Bon-ichi be likened?"

"The Bon-ichi," answers Akira, "is a market at which will be sold all things required for the Festival of the Dead; and the Festival of the Dead will begin tomorrow, when all the altars of the temples and all the shrines in the homes of good Buddhists will be made beautiful."

"Then I want to see the Bon-ichi, Akira, and I should also like to see a Buddhist shrine—a household shrine."

"Yes, will you come to my room?" asks Akira. "It is not far—in the Street of the Aged Men, beyond the Street of the Stony River, and near to the Street Everlasting. There is a butsuma there—a household shrine—and on the way I will tell you about the Bonku."

So, for the first time, I learn those things—which I am now about to write.

II.

From the 13th to the 15th day of July is held the Festival of the Dead—the Bommatsuri or Bonku—by some Europeans called the Feast of Lanterns. But in many places there are two such festivals annually; for those who still follow the ancient reckoning of time by moons hold that the Bommatsuri should fall on the 13th, 14th, and 15th days of the seventh month of the antique calendar, which corresponds to a later period of the year.

Early on the morning of the 13th, new mats of purest rice straw, woven expressly for the festival, are spread upon all Buddhist altars and within each butsuma or butsudan—the little shrine before which the morning and evening prayers are offered up in every believing home. Shrines and altars are likewise decorated with beautiful embellishments of colored paper, and with flowers and sprigs of certain hallowed plants—always real lotus-flowers when obtainable, otherwise lotus-flowers of paper, and fresh branches of shikimi (anise) and of misohagi (lespedeza). Then a tiny lacquered table—a zen—such as Japanese meals are usually served upon, is placed upon the altar, and the food offerings are laid on it. But in the smaller shrines of Japanese homes the offerings are more often simply laid upon the rice matting, wrapped in fresh lotus-leaves.

These offerings consist of the foods called somen, resembling our vermicelli, gozen, which is boiled rice, dango, a sort of tiny dumpling, eggplant, and fruits according to season—frequently uri and saikwa, slices of melon and watermelon, and plums and peaches. Often sweet cakes and dainties are added. Sometimes the offering is only O-sho-jin-gu (honorable uncooked food); more usually it is O-rio-gu (honorable boiled food); but it never includes, of course, fish, meats, or wine. Clear water is given to the shadowy guest, and is sprinkled from time to time upon the altar or within the shrine with a branch of misohagi; tea is poured out every hour for the viewless visitors, and everything is daintily served up in little plates and cups and bowls, as for living guests, with hashi (chopsticks) laid beside the offering. So for three days the dead are feasted.

At sunset, pine torches, fixed in the ground before each home, are kindled to guide the spirit-visitors. Sometimes, also, on the first evening of the Bommatsuri, welcome-fires (*mukaebi*) are lighted along the shore of the sea or lake or river by which the village or city is situated—neither more nor less than one hundred and eight fires; this number having some mystic significa-tion in the philosophy of Buddhism. And charming lanterns are suspended each night at the entrances of homes—the Lan-terns of the Festival of the Dead—lanterns of special forms and colors, beautifully painted with suggestions of landscape and shapes of flowers, and always decorated with a peculiar fringe of paper streamers.

Also, on the same night, those who have dead friends go to the cemeteries and make offerings there, and pray, and burn incense, and pour out water for the ghosts. Flowers are placed there in the bamboo vases set beside each haka, and lanterns are lighted and hung up before the tombs, but these lanterns have no designs upon them.

At sunset on the evening of the 15th only the offerings called Segaki are made in the temples. Then are fed the ghosts of the Circle of Penance, called Gakidō, the place of hungry spirits; and then also are fed by the priests those ghosts having no other friends among the living to care for them. Very, very small these offerings are—like the offerings to the gods.

III.

Now this, Akira tells me, is the origin of the Segaki, as the same is related in the holy book Busetsuuran-bongyo:

Dai-Mokenren, the great disciple of Buddha, obtained by merit the Six Supernatural Powers. And by virtue of them it was given him to see the soul of his mother in the Gakidō—the world of spirits doomed to suffer hunger in expiation of faults committed in a previous life. Mokenren saw that his mother suffered much; he grieved exceedingly because of her pain, and he filled a bowl with choicest food and sent it to her. He saw her try to eat; but each time that she tried to lift the food to her lips it would change into fire and burning embers, so that she could not eat. Then Mokenren asked the Teacher what he could do to relieve his mother from pain. And the Teacher made answer: "On the fifteenth day of the seventh month, feed the ghosts of the great priests of all countries." And Mokenren, having done so, saw that his mother was freed from the state of gaki, and that she was dancing for joy.* This is the origin also of the dances called Bon-Odori, which are danced on the third night of the Festival of the Dead throughout Japan.

Upon the third and last night there is a weirdly beautiful ceremony, more touching than that of the Segaki, stranger than the Bon-odori—the ceremony of farewell. All that the living may do to please the dead has been done; the time allotted by the powers of the unseen worlds unto the ghostly visitants is well-nigh past, and their friends must send them all back again.

Everything has been prepared for them. In each home small boats made of barley straw closely woven have been freighted with supplies of choice food, with tiny lanterns, and written messages of faith and love. Seldom more than two feet in length are these boats; but the dead require little room. And the frail craft

---

* It is related in the same ·book that Ananda having asked the Buddha how came Mokenren's mother to suffer in the Gakidō, the Teacher replied that in a previous incarnation she had refused, through cupidity, to feed certain visiting priests.

are launched on canal, lake, sea, or river—each with a miniature lantern glowing at the prow, and incense burning at the stern. And if the night be fair, they voyage long. Down all the creeks and rivers and canals the phantom fleets go glimmering to the sea; and all the sea sparkles to the horizon with the lights of the dead, and the sea wind is fragrant with incense.

But alas! it is now forbidden in the great seaports to launch the shōryōbune, "the boats of the blessed ghosts."

IV.

It is so narrow, the Street of the Aged Men, that by stretching out one's arms one can touch the figured sign-draperies before its tiny shops on both sides at once. And these little ark-shaped houses really seem toy-houses; that in which Akira lives is even smaller than the rest, having no shop in it, and no miniature second story. It is all closed up. Akira slides back the wooden amado which forms the door, and then the paper-paned screens behind it; and the tiny structure, thus opened, with its light unpainted woodwork and painted paper partitions, looks something like a great bird-cage. But the rush matting of the elevated floor is fresh, sweet-smelling, spotless; and as we take off our footgear to mount upon it, I see that all within is neat, curious, and pretty.

"The woman has gone out," says Akira, setting the smoking-box *(hibachi)* in the middle of the floor, and spreading beside it a little mat for me to squat upon.

"But what is this, Akira?" I ask, pointing to a thin board suspended by a ribbon on the wall—a board so cut from the middle of a branch as to leave the bark along its edges. There are two columns of mysterious signs exquisitely painted upon it.

"Oh, that is a calendar," answers Akira. "On the right side are the names of the months having thirty-one days; on the left, the names of those having less. Now here is a household shrine."

Occupying the alcove, which is an indispensable part of the structure of Japanese guest-rooms, is a native cabinet painted with figures of flying birds; and on this cabinet stands the butsuma. It is a small lacquered and gilded shrine, with little doors modeled after those of a temple gate—a shrine very quaint, very much dilapidated (one door has lost its hinges), but still a dainty thing despite its crackled lacquer and faded gilding. Akira opens it with a sort of compassionate smile; and I look inside for the image. There is none; only a wooden tablet with a band of white paper attached to it, bearing Japanese characters—the name of a dead baby girl—and a vase of expiring flowers, a tiny print of Kwannon, the Goddess of Mercy, and a cup filled with ashes of incense.

" Tomorrow," Akira says, "she will decorate this, and make the offerings of food to the little one."

Hanging from the ceiling, on the opposite side of the room, and in front of the shrine, is a wonderful, charming, funny, white-and-rosy mask—the face of a laughing, chubby girl with two mysterious spots upon her forehead, the face of Otafuku.* It twirls round and round in the soft air-current coming through the open shōji; and every time those funny black eyes, half shut with laughter, look at me, I cannot help smiling. And hanging still higher, I see little Shintō emblems of paper (*gohei*), a min-iature mitre-shaped cap in likeness of those worn in the sacred dances, a pasteboard emblem of the magic gem (*Niō-i hōjiu*) which the gods bear in their hands, a small Japanese doll, and a little wind-wheel which will spin around with the least puff of air, and other indescribable toys, mostly symbolic, such as are sold on festal days in the courts of the temples—the playthings of the dead child.

"Komban!" exclaims a very gentle voice behind us. The mother is standing there, smiling as if pleased at the stranger's interest in her butsuma—a middle-aged woman of the poorest class, not comely, but with a most kindly face. We return her evening

---

* A deity of good fortune.

greeting; and while I sit down upon the little mat laid before the hibachi, Akira whispers something to her, with the result that a small kettle is at once set to boil over a very small charcoal furnace. We are probably going to have some tea.

As Akira takes his seat before me, on the other side of the hibachi, I ask him:

"What was the name I saw on the tablet?"

"The name which you saw," he answers, "was not the real name. The real name is written upon the other side. After death another name is given by the priest. A dead boy is called Ryochi Dōji; a dead girl, Mioyo Dōnyo."

While we are speaking, the woman approaches the little shrine, opens it, arranges the objects in it, lights the tiny lamp, and with joined hands and bowed head begins to pray. Totally unembarrassed by our presence and our chatter she seems, as one accustomed to do what is right and beautiful heedless of human opinion; praying with that brave, true frankness which belongs to the poor only of this world—those simple souls who never have any secret to hide, either from each other or from heaven, and of whom Ruskin nobly said, "These are our holiest."

I do not know what words her heart is murmuring: I hear only at moments that soft sibilant sound, made by gently drawing the breath through the lips, which among this kind people is a token of humblest desire to please.

As I watch the tender little rite, I become aware of something dimly astir in the mystery of my own life—vaguely, indefinably familiar, like a memory ancestral, like the revival of a sensation forgotten two thousand years. Blended in some strange way it seems to be with my faint knowledge of an elder world, whose household gods were also the beloved dead; and there is a weird sweetness in this place, like a shadowing of Lares.

Then, her brief prayer over, she turns to her miniature furnace again. She talks and laughs with Akira; she prepares the tea, pours it out in tiny cups and serves it to us, kneeling in that graceful attitude—picturesque, traditional—which for six hundred years has been the attitude of the Japanese woman serving tea. Verily, no small part of the life of the woman of Japan is spent thus in serving little cups of tea. Even as a ghost, she appears in popular prints offering to somebody spectral tea-cups of spectral tea. Of all Japanese ghost-pictures, I know of none more pathetic than that in which the phantom of a woman kneeling humbly offers to her haunted and remorseful murderer a little cup of tea!

"Now let us go to the Bon-ichi," says Akira, rising; "she must go there herself soon, and it is already getting dark. *Sayōnara!*"

It is indeed almost dark as we leave the little house: stars are pointing in the strip of sky above the street; but it is a beautiful night for a walk, with a tepid breeze blowing at intervals, and sending long flutterings through the miles of shop draperies. The market is in the narrow street at the verge of the city, just below the hill where the great Buddhist temple of Zoto-Kuin stands—in the Motomachi, only ten squares away.

V.

The curious narrow street is one long blaze of lights—lights of lantern signs, lights of torches and lamps illuminating unfamiliar rows of little stands and booths set out in the thoroughfare before all the shop-fronts on each side; making two far-converging lines of multi-colored fire. Between these moves a dense throng, filling the night with a clatter of geta that drowns even the tide-like murmuring of voices and the cries of the merchant. But how gentle the movement!—there is no jostling, no rudeness; everybody, even the weakest and smallest, has a chance to see everything; and there are many things to see.

"*Hasu-no-hana!—hasu-no-ha!*" Here are the venders of lotus-flowers for the tombs and the altars, of lotus leaves in which to wrap the food of the beloved ghosts. The leaves, folded into bundles, are heaped upon tiny tables; the lotus-flowers, buds and blossoms intermingled, are fixed upright in immense bunches, supported by light frames of bamboo.

Ogara!—ogara-ya! White sheaves of long peeled rods. These are hemp-sticks. The thinner ends can be broken up into hashi for the use of the ghosts; the rest must be consumed in the mukaebi. Rightly all these sticks should be made of pine; but pine is too scarce and dear for the poor folk of this district, so the ogara are substituted.

"*Kawarake!—kawarake-ya!*" The dishes of the ghosts: small red shallow platters of unglazed earthenware; primeval pottery wrought after a fashion which now exists only for the dead—pottery shaped after a tradition older than the religion of Buddha.

"*Ya-bondoro-wa-irimasenka?*" The lanterns—the "bon"-lanterns—which will light the returning feet of the ghosts. All are beautiful. Some are hexagonal, like the lanterns of the great shrines; and some have the form of stars; and some are like great luminous eggs. They are decorated with exquisite paintings of lotus-flowers, and with, fringes of paper streamers choicely colored, or perhaps broad white paper ribbons in which charming suggestions of lotus-blossoms have been scissored out. And here are dead-white lanterns, round like moons; these are for the cemeteries.

"*O-kazari! O-kazari-ya!*" The venders of all articles of decoration for the Festival of the Dead. "*Komo-demo!—nandemo!*" Here are the fresh, white mats of rice straw for the butsumas and the altars; and here are the warauma, little horses made out of wisps of straw, for the dead to ride; and the waraushi, little oxen of straw which will do shadowy labor for them. All honorably cheap—*O-yasui!* Here also are the branches of shikimi for the altars, and sprays of misohagi wherewith to sprinkle water upon the Segaki.

"*O-kazari-mono-wa-irimasenka!*" Exquisite scarlet and white tassels of strings of rice grains, like finest bead-work; and wonderful paper decorations for the butsuma; and incense-sticks *(senko)* of all varieties, from the commonest, at a couple of cents a bundle, to the extremely dear, at one yen—long, light, chocolate-colored, brittle rods, slender as a pencil-lead, each bundle secured by straps of gilded and colored paper. You take one, light an end, and set the other end upright in a vessel containing soft ashes; it will continue to smolder, filling the air with fragrance, until wholly consumed.

"*Hotaru-ni-kirigirisu!—o-kodomo-shu-no-onagusami!—oyasuku-makemasu!*" Eh! what is all this? A little booth shaped like a sentry-box, all made of laths, covered with a red-and-white chess pattern of paper; and out of this frail structure issues a shrilling keen as the sound of leaking steam. "Oh, that is only insects," says Akira, laughing; "nothing to do with the Bonku." Insects, yes!—in cages! The shrilling is made by scores of huge green crickets, each prisoned in a tiny bamboo cage by itself. "They are fed with eggplant and melon rind," continues Akira, "and sold to children to play with." And there are also beautiful little cages full of fireflies—cages covered with brown mosquito-netting, upon each of which some simple but very pretty design in bright colors has been dashed by a Japanese brush. One cricket and cage, two cents. Fifteen fireflies and cage, five cents.

Here on a street corner squats a blue-robed boy behind a low wooden table, selling wooden boxes about as big as matchboxes, with red paper hinges. Beside the piles of these little boxes on the table are shallow dishes filled with clear water, in which extraordinary thin flat shapes are floating—shapes of flowers, trees, birds, boats, men, and women. Open a box; it costs only two cents. Inside, wrapped in tissue paper, are bundles of little pale sticks, like round matchsticks, with pink ends. Drop one into the water, it instantly unrolls and expands into the likeness of a lotus-flower. Another transforms itself into a fish. A third becomes a boat. A fourth changes to an owl. A fifth becomes a tea-plant, covered with leaves and blossoms.... So delicate are these things that, once immersed, you cannot handle them without breaking them. They are made of seaweed.

"*Tsukuri hana!—tsukuri-hana-wa-irimasenka?*" The sellers of artificial flowers, marvelous chrysanthemums and lotus-plants of paper, imitations of bud and leaf and flower so cunningly wrought that the eye alone cannot detect the beautiful trickery. It is only right that these should cost much more than their living counterparts.

VI.

High above the thronging and the clamor and the myriad fires of the merchants, the great Shingon temple at the end of the radiant street towers upon its hill against the starry night, weirdly, like a dream—strangely illuminated by rows of paper lanterns hung all along its curving eaves; and the flowing of the crowd bears me thither. Out of the broad entrance, over a dark gliding mass which I know to be heads and shoulders of crowding worshipers, beams a broad band of yellow light; and before reaching the lion-guarded steps I hear the continuous clanging of the temple gong, each clang the signal of an offering and a prayer. Doubtless a cataract of cash is pouring into the great alms-chest; for tonight is the Festival of Yakushi-Nyorai, the Physician of Souls. Borne to the steps at last, I find myself able to halt a moment, despite the pressure of the throng, before the stand of a lantern-seller selling the most beautiful lanterns that I have ever seen. Each is a gigantic lotus-flower of paper, so perfectly made in every detail as to seem a great living blossom freshly plucked; the petals are crimson at their bases, paling to white at their tips; the calyx is a faultless mimicry of nature, and beneath it hangs a beautiful fringe of paper cuttings, colored with the colors of the flower, green below the calyx, white in the middle, crimson at the ends. In the heart of the blossom is set a microscopic oil-lamp of baked clay; and this being lighted, all the flower becomes luminous, diaphanous—a lotus of white and crimson fire. There is a slender gilded wooden hoop by which to hang it up, and the price is four cents! How can people afford to make such things for four cents, even in this country of astounding cheapness?

Akira is trying to tell me something about the hyaku-hachi-no-mukaebi, the Hundred and Eight Fires, to be lighted tomorrow evening, which bear some figurative relation unto the Hundred and Eight Foolish Desires; but I cannot hear him for the clatter of the geta and the komageta, the wooden clogs and wooden sandals of the worshipers ascending to the shrine of Yakushi-Nyorai. The light straw sandals of the poorer men, the zōri and the waraji, are silent; the great clatter is really made by the delicate feet of women and girls, balancing themselves carefully upon their noisy geta. And most of these little feet are clad with spotless tabi, white as a white lotus. White feet of little blue-robed mothers they mostly are—mothers climbing patiently and smilingly, with pretty placid babies at their backs, up the hill to Buddha.

And while through the tinted lantern light I wander on with the gentle noisy people, up the great steps of stone, between other displays of lotus-blossoms, between other high hedgerows of paper flowers, my thought suddenly goes back to the little broken shrine in the poor woman's room, with the humble playthings hanging before it, and the laughing, twirling mask of Otafuku. I see the happy, funny little eyes, oblique and silky-shadowed like Otafuku's own, which used to look at those toys—toys in which the fresh child-senses found a charm that I can but faintly divine, a delight hereditary, ancestral. I see the tender little creature being borne, as it was doubtless borne many times, through just such a peaceful throng as this, in just such a lukewarm, luminous night, peeping over the mother's shoulder, softly clinging at her neck with tiny hands.

Somewhere among this multitude she is—the mother. She will feel again tonight the faint touch of little hands, yet will not turn her head to look and laugh, as in other days.

6

BON-ODORI

I.

OVER the mountains to Izumo, the land of the Kamiyo,[*] the land of the Ancient Gods. A journey of four days by kuruma, with strong runners, from the Pacific to the Sea of Japan; for we have taken the longest and least frequented route.

Through valleys most of this long route lies, valleys always open to higher valleys, while the road ascends, valleys between mountains with rice-fields ascending their slopes by successions of diked terraces which look like enormous green flights of steps. Above them are shadowing somber forests of cedar and pine; and above these wooded summits loom indigo shapes of farther hills overtopped by peaked silhouettes of vapory gray. The air is lukewarm and windless; and distances are gauzed by delicate mists; and in this tenderest of blue skies, this Japanese sky which always seems to me loftier than any other sky which I ever saw, there are only, day after day, some few filmy, spectral, diaphanous white wandering things: like ghosts of clouds, riding on the wind.

But sometimes, as the road ascends, the rice-fields disappear a while: fields of barley and of indigo, and of rye and of cotton, fringe the route for a little space; and then it plunges into forest shadows. Above all else, the forests of cedar sometimes border-

---

[*] The period in which only deities existed.

ing the way are astonishments; never outside of the tropics did I see any growths comparable for density and perpendicularity with these. Every trunk is straight and bare as a pillar: the whole front presents the spectacle of an immeasurable massing of pallid columns towering up into a cloud of somber foliage so dense that one can distinguish nothing overhead but branchings lost in shadow. And the profundities beyond the rare gaps in the palisade of blanched trunks are night-black, as in Doré's pictures of fir woods.

No more great towns; only thatched villages nestling in the folds of the hills, each with its Buddhist temple, lifting a tilted roof of blue-gray tiles above the congregation of thatched homesteads, and its miya, or Shintō shrine, with a torii before it like a great ideograph shaped in stone or wood. But Buddhism still dominates; every hilltop has its tera; and the statues of Buddhas or of Bodhisattvas appear by the roadside, as we travel on, with the regularity of milestones. Often a village tera is so large that the cottages of the rustic folk about it seem like little out-houses; and the traveler wonders how so costly an edifice of prayer can be supported by a community so humble. And everywhere the signs of the gentle faith appear: its ideographs and symbols are chiseled upon the faces of the rocks; its icons smile upon you from every shadowy recess by the way; even the very landscape betimes would seem to to have been moulded by the soul of it, where hills rise softly as a prayer. And the summits of some are domed like the head of Shaka, and the dark bossy frondage that clothes them might seem the clustering of his curls.

But gradually, with the passing of the days, as we journey into the loftier west, I see fewer and fewer tera. Such Buddhist temples as we pass appear small and poor; and the wayside images become rarer and rarer. But the symbols of Shintō are more numerous, and the structure of its miya larger and loftier. And the torii are visible everywhere, and tower higher, before the approaches to villages, before the entrances of courts guarded by strangely grotesque lions and foxes of stone, and before stairways of old mossed rock, upsloping, between dense growths of ancient cedar and pine, to shrines that molder in the twilight of holy groves.

At one little village I see, just beyond the torii leading to a great Shintō temple, a particularly odd small shrine, and feel impelled by curiosity to examine it. Leaning against its closed doors are many short gnarled sticks in a row, miniature clubs. Irreverently removing these, and opening the little doors, Akira bids me look within. I see only a mask—the mask of a goblin, a Tengu, grotesque beyond description, with an enormous nose—so grotesque that I feel remorse for having looked at it.

The sticks are votive offerings. By dedicating one to the shrine, it is believed that the Tengu may be induced to drive one's enemies away. Goblin-shaped though they appear in all Japanese paintings and carvings of them, the Tengu-Sama are divinities, lesser divinities, lords of the art of fencing and the use of all weapons.

And other changes gradually become manifest. Akira complains that he can no longer understand the language of the people. We are traversing regions of dialects. The houses are also architecturally different from those of the country-folk of the northeast; their high thatched roofs are curiously decorated with bundles of straw fastened to a pole of bamboo parallel with the roof-ridge, and elevated about a foot above it. The complexion of the peasantry is darker than in the northeast; and I see no more of those charming rosy faces one observes among the women of the Tōkyō districts. And the peasants wear different hats, hats pointed like the straw roofs of those little wayside temples curiously enough called *an* (which means a straw hat).

The weather is more than warm, rendering clothing oppressive; and as we pass through the little villages along the road, I see much healthy cleanly nudity: pretty naked children; brown men and boys with only a soft narrow white cloth about their loins, asleep on the matted floors, all the paper screens of the houses having been removed to admit the breeze. The men seem to be lightly and supply built; but I see no saliency of muscles;

the lines of the figure are always smooth. Before almost every dwelling, indigo, spread out upon little mats of rice straw, may be seen drying in the sun.

The country-folk gaze wonderingly at the foreigner. At various places where we halt, old men approach to touch my clothes, apologizing with humble bows and winning smiles for their very natural curiosity, and asking my interpreter all sorts of odd questions. Gentler and kindlier faces I never beheld; and they reflect the souls behind them; never yet have I heard a voice raised in anger, nor observed an unkindly act.

And each day, as we travel, the country becomes more beautiful—beautiful with that fantasticality of landscape only to be found in volcanic lands. But for the dark forests of cedar and pine, and this far faint dreamy sky, and the soft whiteness of the light, there are moments of our journey when I could fancy myself again in the West Indies, ascending some winding way over the mornes of Dominica or of Martinique. And, indeed, I find myself sometimes looking against the horizon glow for shapes of palms and ceibas. But the brighter green of the valleys and of the mountain-slopes beneath the woods is not the green of young cane, but of rice-fields—thousands upon thousands of tiny rice-fields no larger than cottage gardens, separated from each other by narrow serpentine dikes.

II.

In the very heart of a mountain range, while rolling along the verge of a precipice above rice-fields, I catch sight of a little shrine in a cavity of the cliff overhanging the way, and halt to examine it. The sides and sloping roof of the shrine are formed by slabs of unhewn rock. Within smiles a rudely chiseled image of Batō-Kwannon—Kwannon-with-the Horse's-Head—and before it bunches of wild flowers have been placed, and an earthen incense-cup, and scattered offerings of dry rice. Contrary to the idea suggested by the strange name, this form of Kwannon is not horse-headed; but the head of a horse is sculptured upon the tiara worn by the divinity. And the symbolism is fully explained by a large wooden sotoba planted beside the shrine, and bearing, among other inscriptions, the words, "*Batō Kwan-ze-on Bosatsu, giu ba bodai han ye.*" For Batō-Kwannon protects the horses and the cattle of the peasant; and he prays her not only that his dumb servants may be preserved from sickness, but also that their spirits may enter, after death, into a happier state of existence. Near the sotoba there has been erected a wooden framework about four feet square, filled with little tablets of pine set edge to edge so as to form one smooth surface; and on these are written, in rows of hundreds, the names of all who subscribed for the statue and its shrine. The number announced is ten thousand. But the whole cost could not have exceeded ten Japanese dollars (yen); wherefore I surmise that each subscriber gave not more than one rin—one tenth of one sen, or cent. For the hyakushō are unspeakably poor.*

In the midst of these mountain solitudes, the discovery of that little shrine creates a delightful sense of security. Surely nothing save goodness can be expected from a people gentle-hearted enough to pray for the souls of their horses and cows.†

As we proceed rapidly down a slope, my kurumaya swerves to one side with a suddenness that gives me a violent start, for

---

* *Hyakushō*, a peasant, husbandman. The two Chinese characters forming the word signify respectively, "a hundred" (*hyaku*), and "family name" (*sei*). One might be tempted to infer that the appellation is almost equivalent to our phrase, "their name is legion." And a Japanese friend assures me that the inference would not be far wrong. Anciently the peasants had no family name; each was known by his personal appellation, coupled with the name of his lord as possessor or ruler. Thus a hundred peasants on one estate would all be known by the name of their master.

† This custom of praying for the souls of animals is by no means general. But I have seen in the western provinces several burials of domestic animals at which such prayers were said. After the earth was filled in, some incense-rods were lighted above the grave in each instance, and the prayers were repeated in a whisper. A friend in the capital sends me the following curious information:

"At the Eko-in temple in Tokyo prayers are offered up every morning for the souls of certain animals whose ihai [mortuary tablets] are preserved in the building. A fee of thirty yen will procure burial in the temple-ground and a short service for any small domestic pet."

Doubtless similar temples exist elsewhere. Certainly no one capable of affection for our dumb friends and servants can mock these gentle customs.

the road overlooks a sheer depth of several hundred feet. It is merely to avoid hurting a harmless snake making its way across the path. The snake is so little afraid that on reaching the edge of the road it turns its head to look after us.

III.

And now strange signs begin to appear in all these rice-fields: I see everywhere, sticking up above the ripening grain, objects like white-feathered arrows. Arrows of prayer! I take one up to examine it. The shaft is a thin bamboo, split down for about one third of its length; into the slit a strip of strong white paper with ideographs upon it—an ofuda, a Shintō charm—is inserted; and the separated ends of the cane are then rejoined and tied together just above it. The whole, at a little distance, has exactly the appearance of a long, light, well-feathered arrow. That which I first examine bears the words, *"Yu-Asaki-jinja-kozen-son-chu-an-zen"* (From the God whose shrine is before the Village of Peace). Another reads, *"Miho-jinja-sho-gwan-jo-ju-go-kito-shu-go"* signifying that the Deity of the temple Mihojinja granteth fully every supplication made unto him. Everywhere, as we proceed, I see the white arrows of prayer glimmering above the green level of the grain; and always they become more numerous. Far as the eye can reach the fields are sprinkled with them, so that they make upon the verdant surface a white speckling as of flowers.

Sometimes, also, around a little rice-field, I see a sort of magical fence, formed by little bamboo rods supporting a long cord from which long straws hang down, like a fringe, and paper cuttings, which are symbols *(gohei),* are suspended at regular intervals. This is the shimenawa, sacred emblem of Shintō. Within the consecrated space enclosed by it no blight may enter—no scorching sun wither the young shoots. And where the white arrows glimmer the locust shall not prevail, nor shall hungry birds do evil.

But now I look in vain for the Buddhas. No more great tera, no Shaka, no Amida, no Dai-Nichi-Nyorai; even the Bosutsu have been left behind. Kwannon and her holy kin have disappeared; Kōshin, Lord of Roads, is indeed yet with us; but he has changed his name and become a Shintō deity: he is now Sarudahiko-no-mikoto; and his presence is revealed only by the statues of the Three Mystic Apes which are his, servants—

Mizaru, who sees no evil, covering his eyes with his hands,

Kikazaru, who hears no evil, covering his ears with his hands,

Iwazaru, who speaks no evil, covering his mouth with his hands.

Yet no! one Bosatsu survives in this atmosphere of magical Shintō: still by the roadside I see at long intervals the image of Jizō-Sama, the charming playfellow of dead children. But Jizō also is a little changed; even in his sextuple representation,* the Roku-Jizō, he appears not standing, but seated upon his lotas-flower; and I see no stones piled up before him, as in the eastern provinces.

IV.

At last, from the verge of an enormous ridge, the roadway suddenly slopes down into a vista of high peaked roofs of thatch and green-mossed eaves—into a village like a colored print out of old Hiroshige's picture-books, a village with all its tints and colors precisely like the tints and colors of the landscape in which it lies. This is Kami-Ichi, in the land of Hōki.

We halt before a quiet, dingy little inn, whose host, a very aged man, comes forth to salute me; while a silent, gentle crowd

---

* Why *six* Jizō instead of five or three or any other number, the reader may ask. I myself asked the question many times before receiving any satisfactory reply. Perhaps the following legend affords the most satisfactory explanation:

According to the Book *Taijo-Hoshi-mingyo-nenbutsu-den*, Jizō-Bosatsu was a woman ten thousand ko *(kalpas)* before this era, and became filled with desire to convert all living beings of the Six Worlds and the Four Births. And by virtue of the Supernatural Powers she multiplied herself and simultaneously appeared in all the Rokusshō or Six States of Sentient Existence at once, namely in the Jigoku, Gaki, Chikushō, Shura, Ningen, Tenjō, and converted the dwellers thereof. (A friend insists that in order to have done this Jizō must first have become a man.)

Among the many names of Jizō, such as "The Never Slumbering," "The Dragon-Praiser," "The Shining King," "Diamond-of-Pity," I find the significant appellation of "The Countless Bodied."

of villagers, mostly children and women, gather about the kuruma to see the stranger, to wonder at him, even to touch his clothes with timid smiling curiosity. One glance at the face of the old innkeeper decides me to accept his invitation. I must remain here until tomorrow: my runners are too wearied to go farther tonight.

Weather-worn as the little inn seemed without, it is delightful within. Its polished stairway and balconies are speckless, reflecting like mirror-surfaces the bare feet of the maidservants; its luminous rooms are fresh and sweet-smelling as when their soft mattings were first laid down. The carven pillars of the alcove (*toko*) in my chamber, leaves and flowers chiseled in some black rich wood, are wonders; and the kakemono or scroll-picture hanging there is an idyl, Hotei, God of Happiness, drifting in a bark down some shadowy stream into evening mysteries of vapory purple. Far as this hamlet is from all art centers, there is no object visible in the house which does not reveal the Japanese sense of beauty in form. The old gold-flowered lacquer-ware, the astonishing box in which sweetmeats (*Kwashi*) are kept, the diaphanous porcelain wine-cups dashed with a single tiny gold figure of a leaping shrimp, the tea-cup holders which are curled lotus-leaves of bronze, even the iron kettle with its figurings of dragons and clouds, and the brazen hibachi whose handles are heads of Buddhist lions, delight the eye and surprise the fancy. Indeed, wherever today in Japan one sees something totally uninteresting in porcelain or metal, something commonplace and ugly, one may be almost sure that detestable something has been shaped under foreign influence. But here I am in ancient Japan; probably no European eyes ever looked upon these things before.

A window shaped like a heart peeps out upon the garden, a wonderful little garden with a tiny pond and miniature bridges and dwarf trees, like the landscape of a teacup; also some shapely stones of course, and some graceful stone-lanterns, or tōrō, such as are placed in the courts of temples. And beyond these, through the warm dust, I see lights, colored lights, the lanterns of the Bonku, suspended before each home to welcome the coming of beloved ghosts; for by the antique calendar, according to which in this antique place the reckoning of time is still made, this is the first night of the Festival of the Dead.

As in all the other little country villages where I have been stopping, I find the people here kind to me with a kindness and a courtesy unimaginable, indescribable, unknown in any other country, and even in Japan itself only in the interior. Their simple politeness is not an art; their goodness is absolutely unconscious goodness; both come straight from the heart. And before I have been two hours among these people, their treatment of me, coupled with the sense of my utter inability to repay such kindness, causes a wicked wish to come into my mind. I wish these charming folk would do me some unexpected wrong, something surprisingly evil, something atrociously unkind, so that I should not be obliged to regret them, which I feel sure I must begin to do as soon as I go away.

While the aged landlord conducts me to the bath, where he insists upon washing me himself as if I were a child, the wife prepares for us a charming little repast of rice, eggs, vegetables, and sweetmeats. She is painfully in doubt about her ability to please me, even after I have eaten enough for two men, and apologizes too much for not being able to offer me more.

"There is no fish," she says, "for today is the first day of the Bonku, the Festival of the Dead; being the thirteenth day of the month. On the thirteenth, fourteenth, and fifteenth of the month nobody may eat fish. But on the morning of the sixteenth day, the fishermen go out to catch fish; and everybody who has both parents living may eat of it. But if one has lost one's father or mother then one must not eat fish, even upon the sixteenth day."

While the good soul is thus explaining I become aware of a strange remote sound from without, a sound I recognize through memory of tropical dances, a measured clapping of hands. But this clapping is very soft and at long intervals. And at still longer intervals there comes to us a heavy muffled booming, the tap of a great drum, a temple drum.

"Oh! we must go to see it," cries Akira; "it is the Bon-odori, the Dance of the Festival of the Dead. And you will see the Bon-odori danced here as it is never danced in cities—the Bon-odori of ancient days. For customs have not changed here; but in the cities all is changed."

So I hasten out, wearing only, like the people about me, one of those light wide-sleeved summer robes—yukata—which are furnished to male guests at all Japanese hotels; but the air is so warm that even thus lightly clad, I find myself slightly perspiring. And the night is divine—still, clear, vaster than nights of Europe, with a big white moon flinging down queer shadows of tilted eaves and horned gables and delightful silhouettes of robed Japanese. A little boy, the grandson of our host, leads the way with a crimson paper lantern; and the sonorous echoing of geta, the *koro-koro* of wooden sandals, fills all the street, for many are going whither we are going, to see the dance.

A little while we proceed along the main street; then, traversing a narrow passage between two houses, we find ourselves in a great open space flooded by moonlight. This is the dancing-place; but the dance has ceased for a time. Looking about me, I perceive, that we are in the court of an ancient Buddhist temple. The temple building itself remains intact, a low long peaked silhouette against the starlight; but it is void and dark and unhallowed now; it has been turned, they tell me, into a schoolhouse, The priests are gone; the great bell is gone; the Buddhas and the Bodhisattvas have vanished, all save one—a broken-handed Jizō of stone, smiling with eyelids closed, under the moon.

In the center of the court is a framework of bamboo supporting a great drum; and about it benches have been arranged, benches from the schoolhouse, on which villagers are resting. There is a hum of voices, voices of people speaking very low, as if expecting something solemn; and cries of children betimes, and soft laughter of girls. And far behind the court, beyond a low hedge of somber evergreen shrubs, I see soft white lights and a host of tall gray shapes throwing long shadows; and I know that the lights are the white lanterns of the dead (those hung in cemeteries only), and that the gray shapes are shapes of tombs.

Suddenly a girl rises from her seat, and taps the huge drum once. It is the signal for the Dance of Souls.

V.

Out of the shadow of the temple a processional line of dancers files into the moonlight and as suddenly halts—all young women or girls, clad in their choicest attire; the tallest leads; her comrades follow in order of stature; little maids of ten or twelve years compose the end of the procession. Figures lightly poised as birds—figures that somehow recall the dreams of shapes circling about certain antique vases; those charming Japanese robes, close-clinging about the knees, might seem, but for the great fantastic drooping sleeves, and the curious broad girdles confining them, designed after the drawing of some Greek or Etruscan artist. And, at another tap of the drum, there begins a performance impossible to picture in words, something unimaginable, phantasmal—a dance, an astonishment.

All together glide the right foot forward one pace, without lifting the sandal from the ground, and extend both hands to the right, with a strange floating motion and a smiling, mysterious obeisance. Then the right foot is drawn back, with a repetition of the waving of hands and the mysterious bow. Then all advance the left foot and repeat the previous movements, half-turning to the left. Then all take two gliding paces forward, with a single simultaneous soft clap of the hands, and the first performance is reiterated, alternately to right and left; all the sandaled feet gliding together, all the supple hands waving together, all the pliant bodies bowing and swaying together. And so slowly, weirdly, the processional movement changes into a great round, circling about the moonlit court and around the voiceless crowd of spectators.*

And always the white hands sinuously wave together, as if weaving spells, alternately without and within the round, now with palms upward, now with palms downward; and all the elfish sleeves hover duskily together, with a shadowing as of wings; and all the feet poise together with such a rhythm of complex motion, that, in watching it, one feels a sensation of hypnotism—as while striving to watch a flowing and shimmering of water.

And this soporous allurement is intensified by a dead hush. No one speaks, not even a spectator. And, in the long intervals between the soft clapping of hands, one hears only the shrilling of the crickets in the trees, and the shu-shu of sandals, lightly stirring the dust. Unto what, I ask myself, may this be likened? Unto nothing; yet it suggests some fancy of somnambulism—dreamers, who dream themselves flying, dreaming upon their feet.

And there comes to me the thought that I am looking at something immemorially old, something belonging to the unrecorded beginnings of this Oriental life, perhaps to the crepuscular Kamiyo itself, to the magical Age of the Gods; a symbolism of motion whereof the meaning has been forgotten for innumerable years. Yet more and move unreal the spectacle appears, with its silent smilings, with its silent bowings, as if obeisance to watchers invisible; and I find myself wondering whether, were I to utter but a whisper, all would not vanish forever, save the gray

---

* Since this sketch was written, I have seen the Bon-odori in many different parts of Japan; but I have never witnessed exactly the same kind of dance. Indeed, I would judge from my experiences in Izumo, in Oki, in Tottori, in Hoki, in Bingo, and elsewhere, that the Bon-odori is not danced in the same way in any two provinces. Not only do the motions and gestures vary according to locality, but also the airs of the songs sung—and this even when the words are the same. In some places the measure is slow and solemn; in others it is rapid and merry, and characterized by a queer jerky swing, impossible to describe. But everywhere both the motion and the melody are curious and pleasing enough to fascinate the spectator for hours. Certainly these primitive dances are of far greater interest than the performances of geisha. Although Buddhism may have utilized them and influenced them, they are beyond doubt incomparably older than Buddhism.

moldering court and the desolate temple, and the broken statue of Jizō, smiling always the same mysterious smile I see upon the faces of the dancers.

Under the wheeling moon, in the midst of the round, I feel as one within the circle of a charm. And verily this is enchantment; I am bewitched, bewitched by the ghostly weaving of hands, by the rhythmic gliding of feet, above all by the flitting of the marvelous sleeves—apparitional, soundless, velvety as a flitting of great tropical bats. No; nothing I ever dreamed of could be likened to this. And with the consciousness of the ancient hakaba behind me, and the weird invitation of its lanterns, and the ghostly beliefs of the hour and the place, there creeps upon me a nameless, tingling sense of being haunted. But no! these gracious, silent, waving, weaving shapes are not of the Shadowy Folk, for whose coming the white fires were kindled: a strain of song, full of sweet, clear quavering, like the call of a bird, gushes from some girlish mouth, and fifty soft voices join the chant:

> *Sorota swoimashita odorikoga sorota,*
> *Soroikite, kita hare yukata.*

"Uniform to view [*as ears of young rice ripening in the field*] all clad alike in summer festal robes, the company of dancers have assembled."

Again only the shrilling of the crickets, the shushu of feet, the gentle clapping; and the wavering hovering measure proceeds in silence, with mesmeric lentor—with a strange grace, which, by its very naïveté, seems old as the encircling hills.

Those who sleep the sleep of centuries out there, under the gray stones where the white lanterns are, and their fathers, and the fathers of their fathers' fathers, and the unknown generations behind them, buried in cemeteries of which the place has been forgotten for a thousand years, doubtless looked upon a scene like this. Nay! the dust stirred by those young feet was human life, and so smiled and so sang under this self-same moon, "with woven paces, and with waving hands."

Suddenly a deep male chant breaks the hush. Two giants have joined the round, and now lead it, two superb young mountain peasants nearly nude, towering head and shoulders above the whole of the assembly. Their kimono are rolled about their waists like girdles, leaving their bronzed limbs and torsos naked to the warm air; they wear nothing else save their immense straw hats, and white tabi, donned expressly for the festival. Never before among these people saw I such men, such thews; but their smiling beardless faces are comely and kindly as those of Japanese boys. They seem brothers, so like in frame, in movement, in the timbre of their voices, as they intone the same song:

> *No demo yama demo ko wa umioheyo,*
> *Sen ryō kura yori ho ga takara.*

"Whether brought forth upon the mountain or in the field, it matters nothing: more than a treasure of one thousand ryō, a baby precious is."

And Jizō, the lover of children's ghosts, smiles across the silence.

Souls close to nature's Soul are these; artless and touching their thought, like the worship of that Kishibojin to whom wives pray. And after the silence, the sweet thin voices of the women answer:

> *Oomu otoko ni sowa sanu oya wa,*
> *Oyade gozaranu ko no kataki.*

"The parents who will not allow their girl to be united with her lover; they are not the parents, but the enemies of their child."

And song follows song; and the round ever becomes larger; and the hours pass unfelt, unheard, while the moon wheels slowly down the blue steeps of the night.

A deep low boom rolls suddenly across the court, the rich tone of some temple bell telling the twelfth hour. Instantly the witchcraft ends, like the wonder of some dream broken by a sound; the chanting ceases; the round dissolves in an outburst of happy laughter, and chatting, and softly-voweled callings of flower-names which are names of girls, and farewell cries of "*Sayōnara!*" as dancers and spectators alike betake themselves homeward, with a great *koro-koro* of getas.

And I, moving with the throng, in the bewildered manner of one suddenly roused from sleep, know myself ungrateful. These silvery laughing folk who now toddle along beside me upon their noisy little clogs, stepping very fast to get a peep at my foreign face, these but a moment ago were visions of archaic grace, illusions of necromancy, delightful phantoms; and I feel a vague resentment against them for thus materializing into simple country-girls.

VI.

Lying down to rest, I ask myself the reason of the singular emotion inspired by that simple peasant chorus. Utterly impossible to recall the air, with its fantastic intervals and fractional tones; as well attempt to fix in memory the purlings of a bird; but the indefinable charm of it lingers with me still.

Melodies of Europe awaken within us feelings we can utter, sensations familiar as mother-speech, inherited from all the generations behind us. But how explain the emotion evoked by a primitive chant totally unlike anything in Western melody— impossible even to write in those tones which are the ideographs of our music-tongue?

And the emotion itself—what is it? I know not; yet I feel it to be something infinitely more old than I—something not of only one place or time, but vibrant to all common joy or pain of being, under the universal sun. Then I wonder if the secret does not lie in some untaught spontaneous harmony of that chant with Nature's most ancient song, in some unconscious kinship to the music of solitudes—all trillings of summer life that blend to make the great sweet Cry of the Land.

7

THE CHIEF CITY OF THE PROVINCE OF THE GODS

I.

THE first of the noises of a Matsue day comes to the sleeper like the throbbing of a slow, enormous pulse exactly under his ear. It is a great, soft, dull buffet of sound—like a heartbeat in its regularity, in its muffled depth, in the way it quakes up through one's pillow so as to be felt rather than heard. It is simply the pounding of the ponderous pestle of the kometsuki, the cleaner of rice—a sort of colossal wooden mallet with a handle about fifteen feet long horizontally balanced on a pivot. By treading with all his force on the end of the handle, the naked kometsuki elevates the pestle, which is then allowed to fall back by its own weight into the rice-tub. The measured muffled echoing of its fall seems to me the most pathetic of all sounds of Japanese life ; it is the beating, indeed, of the Pulse of the Land.

Then the boom of the great bell of Tōkōji, the Zenshū temple, shakes over the town; then come melancholy echoes of drumming from the tiny little temple of Jizō in the street Zaimokuchō, near my house, signaling the Buddhist hour of morning prayer. And finally the cries of the earliest itinerant venders begin—"Daikoyai! kabuya-kabu!"—the sellers of daikon and other strange vegetables. "Moyaya-moya!"—the plaintive call of the women who sell little thin slips of kindling-wood for the lighting of charcoal fires.

II.

Roused thus by these earliest sounds of the city's wakening life, I slide open my little Japanese paper window to look out upon the morning over a soft green cloud of spring foliage rising from the river-bounded garden below. Before me, tremulously mirroring everything upon its farther side, glimmers the broad glassy mouth of the Ōhashigawa, opening into the grand Shinji Lake, which spreads out broadly to the right in a dim gray frame of peaks. Just opposite to me, across the stream, the blue-pointed Japanese dwellings have their *to** all closed; they are still shut up like boxes, for it is not yet sunrise, although it is day.

But oh, the charm of the vision—those first ghostly love-colors of a morning steeped in mist soft as sleep itself resolved into a visible exhalation! Long reaches of faintly-tinted vapor cloud the far lake verge—long nebulous bands, such as you may have seen in old Japanese picture-books, and must have deemed only artistic whimsicalities unless you had previously looked upon the real phenomena. All the bases of the mountains are veiled by them, and they stretch athwart the loftier peaks at different heights like immeasurable lengths of gauze (this singular appearance the Japanese term "shelving"),[†] so that the lake appears incomparably larger than it really is, and not an actual lake, but a beautiful spectral sea of the same tint as the dawn-sky and mixing with it, while peak-tips rise like islands from the brume, and visionary strips of hill-ranges figure as league-long causeways stretching out of sight—an exquisite chaos, ever changing aspect as the delicate fogs rise, slowly, very slowly. As the sun's yellow rim comes into sight, fine thin lines of warmer tone—spectral violets and opalines—shoot across the flood, treetops take tender fire, and

---

* Thick solid sliding shutters of unpainted wood, which in Japanese houses serve both as shutters and doors.

† *Tanabiku.*

the unpainted facades of high edifices across the water change their wood-color to vapory gold through the delicious haze.

Looking sunward, up the long Ōhashigawa, beyond the many-pillared wooden bridge, one high-pooped junk, just hoisting sail, seems to me the most fantastically beautiful craft I ever saw—a dream of Orient seas, so idealized by the vapor is it; the ghost of a junk, but a ghost that catches the light as clouds do; a shape of gold mist, seemingly semi-diaphanous, and suspended in pale blue light.

III.

And now from the river-front touching my garden there rises to me a sound of clapping of hands—one, two, three, four claps—but the owner of the hands is screened from view by the shrubbery. At the same time, however, I see men and women descending the stone steps of the wharves on the opposite side of the Ōhashigawa, all with little blue towels tucked into their girdles. They wash their faces and hands and rinse their mouths—the customary ablution preliminary to Shintō prayer. Then they turn their faces to the sunrise and clap their hands four times and pray. From the long high white bridge come other clappings, like echoes, and others again from far light graceful craft, curved like new moons—extraordinary boats in which I see bare-limbed fisher-men standing with foreheads bowed to the goldern East. Now the clappings multiply—multiply at last into an almost continuous volleying of sharp sounds. For all the population are saluting the rising sun—O-Hi-San, the lady of Fire—Ama-terasu-oho-mi-Kami, the Lady of Great Light* "*Konnichi-Sama*! Hail this day to thee, divinest Day-Maker! Thanks unutterable unto thee, for this thy sweet light, making beautiful the world!" So, doubtless, the thought, if not the utterance, of countless hearts. Some turn to the sun only, clapping their hands; yet many turn also to

---

* *Ama-terasu-oho-mi-Kami* literally signifies "the Heaven-Shining-Great-August-Divinity." (See Professor Chamberlain's translation of the *Kojiki*.)

the West, to holy Kitzuki, the immemorial shrine; and not a few turn their faces successively to all the points of heaven, murmuring the names of a hundred gods; and others, again, after having saluted the Lady of Fire, look toward high Ichibata, toward the place of the great temple of Yakushi-Nyorai, who giveth sight to the blind—not clapping their hands as in Shintō worship, but only rubbing the palms softly together after the Buddhist manner. But all—for in this most antique province of Japan all Buddhists are Shintōists likewise—utter the archaic words of Shintō prayer: *"Harai tamai kiyome tamai to Kami imi tami."*

Prayer to the most ancient gods who reigned before the coming of Buddha, and who still reign her in their own Izumo-land—in the Land of Reed Plains, in the Place of the issuing of Clouds; prayer to the deities of primal chaos and primeval sea and of the beginnings of the world—strange gods with long weird names, kindred of U-hiji-ni-no-Kami, the First Mud-Lord, kindred of Su-hiji-ni-no-Kami, the First Sand-Lady; prayer to those who came after them—the gods of strength and beauty, the world-fashioners, makers of the mountains and the isles, ancestors of those sovereigns whose lineage still is names "The Sun's Succession;" prayer to the Three Thousand Gods "residing within the provinces," and to the Eight Hundred Myriads who dwell in the azure Takama-no-hara—in the blue Plain of High Heaven. *"Nippon-koku-chu-yaoyorozu-no-Kami-gami-sama!"*

IV.

"Ho—ke-kyō!"

My uguisu is awake at last, and utters his morning prayer. You do not know what an uguisu is? An uguisu is a holy little bird that professes Buddhism. All uguisu have professed Buddhism from time immemorial; all uguisu preach alike to men the excellence of the divine Sutra.

"Ho—ke-kyō!"

In the Japanese tongue "Ho-ke-kyō; in Sanscrit, Saddharma-pundarika: "The Sutra of the Lotus of the Good Law," the di-

vine book of the Nichiren sect. Very brief, indeed, is my little
feathered Buddhist's confession of faith—only the sacred name
reiterated over and over again like a litany, with liquid bursts of
twittering between.

"*Ho—ke-kyō!*"

Only this one phrase, but how deliciously he utters it! With
what slow amorous ecstasy he dwells upon its golden syllables!

It hath been written: "He who shall keep, read, teach, or write
this Sutra shall obtain eight hundred good qualities of the Eye.
He shall see the whole Triple Universe down to the great hell
Aviki, and up to the extremity of existence. He shall obtain
twelve hundred good qualities of the Ear. He shall hear all sounds
in the Triple Universe—sounds of gods, goblins, demons, and
beings not human."

"*Ho—ke-kyō!*"

A single word only. But it is also written: "He who shall joyfully
accept but a single word from this Sutra, incalculably greater
shall be his merit than the merit of one who should supply all
beings in the four hundred thousand Asankhyeyas of worlds with
all the necessaries for happiness."

"*Ho—ke-kyō!*"

Always he makes a reverent little pause after uttering it and
before shrilling out his ecstatic warble, his bird-hymn of praise.
First the warble; then a pause of about five seconds; then a
slow, sweet, solemn utterance of the holy name in a tone as of
meditative wonder; then another pause; then another wild, rich,
passionate warble. Could you see him, you would marvel how so
powerful and penetrating a soprano could ripple from so minute
a throat; for he is one of the very tiniest of all feathered singers,
yet his chant can be heard far across the broad river, and children
going to school pause daily on the bridge, a whole cho away, to
listen to his song. And uncomely withal: a neutral-tinted mite,
almost lost in his immense box-cage of hinoki wood, darkened
with paper screens over its little wire-grated windows, for he
loves the gloom.

Delicate he is and exacting even to tyranny. All his diet must be laboriously triturated and weighed in scales, and measured out to him at precisely the same hour each day. It demands all possible care and attention merely to keep him alive. He is precious, nevertheless. "Far and from the uttermost coasts is the price of him," so rare he is. Indeed, I could not have afforded to buy him. He was sent to me by one of the sweetest ladies in Japan, daughter of the governor of Izumo, who, thinking the foreign teacher might feel lonesome during a brief illness, made him the exquisite gift of this dainty creature.

V.

The clapping of hands has ceased; the toil of the day begins; continually louder and louder the pattering of geta over the bridge. It is a sound never to be forgotten, this pattering of geta over the Ōhashi—rapid, merry, musical, like the sound of an enormous dance; and a dance it veritably is. The whole population is moving on tiptoe, and the multitudinous twinkling of feet over the verge of the sunlit roadway is an astonishment. All those feet are small, symmetrical—light as the feet of figures painted on Greek vases—and the step is always taken toes first; indeed, with geta it could be taken no other way, for the heel touches neither the geta nor the ground, and the foot is tilted forward by the wedge-shaped wooden sole. Merely to stand upon a pair of geta is difficult for one unaccustomed to their use, yet you see Japanese children running at full speed in geta with soles at least three inches high, held to the foot only by a forestrap fastened between the great toe and the other toes, and they never trip and the geta never falls off. Still more curious is the spectacle of men walking in bokkuri or takageta, a wooden sole with wooden supports at least five inches high lifted underneath it so as to make the whole structure seem the lacquered model of a wooden bench. But the wearers stride as freely as if they had nothing upon their feet.

Now children begin to appear, hurrying to school. The undulation of the wide sleeves of their pretty speckled robes, as they run, looks precisely like a fluttering of extraordinary butterflies. The junks spread their great white or yellow wings, and the funnels of the little steamers which have been slumbering all night by the wharves begin to smoke.

One of the tiny lake steamers lying at the opposite wharf has just opened its steam-throat to utter the most unimaginable, piercing, desperate, furious howl. When that cry is heard everybody laughs. The other little steamboats utter only plaintive mooings, but unto this particular vessel—newly built and launched by a rival company—there has been given a voice expressive to the most amazing degree of reckless hostility and savage defiance. The good people of Matsue, upon hearing its voice for the first time, gave it forthwith a new and just name—Ōkami-Maru. "Maru" signifies a steamship. "Ōkami" signifies a wolf.

VI.

A very curious little object now comes slowly floating down the river, and I do not think that you could possibly guess what it is.

The Hotoke, or Buddhas, and the beneficent Kami are not the only divinities worshiped by the Japanese of the poorer classes. The deities of evil, or at least some of them, are duly propitiated upon certain occasions, and requited by offerings whenever they graciously vouchsafe to inflict a temporary ill instead of an irremediable misfortune.* (After all, this is no more irrational than the thanksgiving prayer at the close of the hurricane season in the West Indies, after the destruction by storm of twenty-two thousand lives.) So men sometimes pray to Ekibiogami, the God of Pestilence, and to Kaze-no-Kami, the God of Wind and of Bad Colds, and to Hoso-no-Kami, the God of Smallpox, and to divers evil genii.

Now when a person is certainly going to get well of smallpox a feast is given to the Hoso-no-Kami, much as a feast is given to

---

* "The gods who do harm are to be appeased, so that they may not punish those who have offended them." Such are the words of the great Shintō teacher, Hirata, as translated by Mr. Satow in his article, *The Revival of Pure Shintau.*

the Fox-God when a possessing fox has promised to allow himself to be cast out. Upon a sando-wara, or small straw mat, such as is used to close the end of a rice-bale, one or more kawarake, or small earthenware vessels, are placed. These are filled with a preparation of rice and red beans, called adzukimeshi, whereof both Inari-Sama and Hoso-no-Kami are supposed to be very fond. Little bamboo wands with gobei (paper cuttings) fastened to them are then planted either in the mat or in the adzukimeshi, and the color of these gohei must be red. (Be it observed that the gohei of other Kami are always white.) This offering is then either suspended to a tree, or set afloat in some running stream at a considerable distance from the home of the convalescent. This is called "seeing the God off."

VII.

The long white bridge with its pillars of iron is recognizably modern. It was, in fact, opened to the public only last spring with great ceremony. According to some most ancient custom, when a new bridge has been built the first persons to pass over it must be the happiest of the community. So the authorities of Matsue sought for the happiest folk, and selected two aged men who had both been married for more than half a century, and who had had not less than twelve children, and had never lost any of them. These good patriarchs first crossed the bridge, accompanied by their venerable wives, and followed by their grown-up children, grandchildren, and great-grandchildren, amidst a great clamor of rejoicing, the showering of fireworks, and the firing of cannon.

But the ancient bridge so recently replaced by this structure was much more picturesque, curving across the flood and supported upon multitudinous feet, like a long-legged centipede of the innocuous kind. For three hundred years it had stood over the stream firmly and well, and it had its particular tradition.

When Horiō Yoshiharu, the great general who became daimyo of Izumo in the Keichō era, first undertook to put a bridge over the mouth of this river, the builders labored in vain; for there appeared to be no solid bottom for the pillars of the bridge to rest upon. Millions of great stones were cast into the river to no purpose, for the work constructed by day was swept away or swallowed up by night. Nevertheless, at last the bridge was built, but the pillars began to sink soon after it was finished; then a flood carried half of it away, and as often as it was repaired so often it was wrecked. Then a human sacrifice was made to appease the vexed spirits of the flood. A man was buried alive in the riverbed below the place of the middle pillar, where the current is most treacherous, and thereafter the bridge remained immovable for three hundred years.

This victim was one Gensuke, who had lived in the street Saikamachi; for it had been determined that the first man who should cross the bridge wearing hakama without a machi* should be put under the bridge; and Gensuke sought to pass over not having a machi in his hakama, so they sacrificed him. Wherefore the midmost pillar of the bridge was for three hundred years called by his name—Gensuke-bashira. It is averred that upon moonless nights a ghostly fire flitted about that pillar—always in the dead watch hour between two and three; and the color of the light was red, though I am assured that in Japan, as in other lands, the fires of the dead are most often blue.

VIII.

Now some say that Gensuke was not the name of a man, but the name of an era, corrupted by local dialect into the semblance of a personal appellation. Yet so profoundly is the legend believed, that when the new bridge was being built thousands of country-folk were afraid to come to town; for a rumor arose that a new victim was needed, who was to be chosen from among them, and that it had been determined to make the choice from

---

* *Machi*, a stiff piece of pasteboard or other material sewn into the waist of the hakama at the back, so as to keep the folds of the garment perpendicular and neat-looking.

those who still wore their hair in queues after the ancient manner. Wherefore hundreds of aged men cut off their queues. Then another rumor was circulated to the effect that the police had been secretly instructed to seize the one-thousandth person of those who crossed the new bridge the first day, and to treat him after the manner of Gensuke. And at the time of the great festival of the Rice-God, when the city is usually thronged by farmers coming to worship at the many shrines of Inari, this year there came but few; and the loss to local commerce was estimated at several thousand yen.

IX.

The vapors have vanished, sharply revealing a beautiful little islet in the lake, lying scarcely half a mile away—a low, narrow strip of land with a Shintō shrine upon it, shadowed by giant pines; not pines like ours, but huge, gnarled, shaggy, tortuous shapes, vast-reaching like ancient oaks. Through a glass one can easily discern a torii, and before it two symbolic lions of stone (Kara-ahishi), one with its head broken off, doubtless by its having been overturned and dashed about by heavy waves during some great storm. This islet is sacred to Benten, the Goddess of Eloquence and Beauty, wherefore it is called Benten-no-shima. But it is more commonly called Yomega-shima, or "The Island of the Young Wife," by reason of a legend. It is said that it arose in one night, noiselessly as a dream, bearing up from the depths of the lake the body of a drowned woman who had been very lovely, very pious, and very unhappy. The people, deeming this a sign from heaven, consecrated the islet to Benten, and thereon built a shrine unto her, planted trees about it, set a torii before it, and made a rampart about it with great curiously-shaped stones; and there they buried the drowned woman.

Now the sky is blue down to the horizon, the air is a caress of spring. I go forth to wander through the queer old city.

X.

I perceive that upon the sliding doors, or immediately above the principal entrance of nearly every house, are pasted oblong white papers bearing ideographic inscriptions; and overhanging every threshold I see the sacred emblem of Shintō, the little rice-straw rope with its long fringe of pendent stalks. The white papers at once interest me; for they are ofuda, or holy texts and charms, of which I am a devout collector. Nearly all are from temples in Matsue or its vicinity; and the Buddhist ones indicate by the sacred words upon them to what particular shū, or sect, the family belongs—for nearly every soul in this community professes some form of Buddhism as well as the all-dominant and more ancient faith of Shintō. And even one quite ignorant of Japanese ideographs can nearly always distinguish at a glance the formula of the great Nichiren sect from the peculiar appearance of the column of characters composing it, all bristling with long sharp points and banneret zigzags, like an army; the famous text *Namu-myō-hō-ren-ge-kyō*, inscribed of old upon the flag of the great captain Kato Kiyomasa, the extirpator of Spanish Christianity, the glorious *vir ter execrandus* of the Jesuits. Any pilgrim belonging to this sect has the right to call at whatever door bears the above formula and ask for alms or food.

But by far the greater number of the ofuda are Shintō. Upon almost every door there is one ofuda especially likely to attract the attention of a stranger, because at the foot of the column of ideographs composing its text there are two small figures of foxes, a black and a white fox, facing each other in a sitting posture, each with a little bunch of rice-straw in its mouth, instead of the more usual emblematic key. These ofuda are from the great Inari temple of Oshiroyama,* within the castle grounds, and are charms against fire. They represent, indeed, the only form of assurance against fire yet known in Matsue—so far, at

---

* Kushi-no-ki-Matsuhira-Inari-Daimyōjin.

least, as wooden dwellings are concerned. And although a single spark and a high wind are sufficient in combination to obliterate a larger city in one day, great fires are unknown in Matsue, and small ones are of rare occurrence.

The charm is peculiar to the city; and of the Inari in question this tradition exists:

When Naomasu, the grandson of Iyeyasu, first came to Matsue to rule the province, there entered into his presence a beautiful boy, who said: "I came hither from the home of your august father in Echizen, to protect you from all harm. But I have no dwelling-place, and am staying therefore at the Buddhist temple of Fu-mon-in. Now if you will make for me a dwelling within the castle grounds, I will protect from fire the buildings there and the houses of the city, and your other residence likewise which is in the capital. For I am Inari Shinyemon." With these words he vanished from sight. Therefore Naomasu dedicated to him the great temple which still stands in the castle grounds, surrounded by one thousand foxes of stone.

XI.

I now turn into a narrow little street, which, although so ancient that its dwarfed two-story houses have the look of things grown up from the around, is called the Street of the New Timber. New the timber may have been one hundred and fifty years ago; but the tints of the structures would ravish an artist—the somber ashen tones of the wood-work, the furry browns of old thatch, ribbed and patched and edged with the warm soft green of those velvety herbs and mosses which flourish upon Japanese roofs.

However, the perspective of the street frames in a vision more surprising than any details of its moldering homes. Between very lofty bamboo poles, higher than any of the dwellings, and planted on both sides of the street in lines, extraordinary black nets are stretched, like prodigious cobwebs against the sky, evoking sudden memories of those monster spiders which figure in Japanese mythology and in the picture-books of the old artists.

But these are only fishing-nets of silken thread; and this is the street of the fishermen. I take my way to the great bridge.

XII.

A stupendous ghost!

Looking eastward from the great bridge over those sharply beautiful mountains, green and blue, which tooth the horizon, I see a glorious specter towering to the sky. Its base is effaced by far mists: out of the air the thing would seem to have shaped itself—a phantom cone, diaphanously gray below, vaporously white above, with a dream of perpetual snow—the mighty mountain of Daisen.

At the first approach of winter it will in one night become all blanched from foot to crest; and then its snowy pyramid so much resembles that Sacred Mountain, often compared by poets to a white inverted fan, half opened, hanging in the sky, that it is called Izumo-Fuji, "the Fuji of Izumo." But it is really in Hōki, not in Izumo, though it cannot be seen from any part of Hōki to such advantage as from here. It is the one sublime spectacle of this charming land; but it is visible only when the air is very pure. Many are the marvelous legends related concerning it, and somewhere upon its mysterious summit the Tengu are believed to dwell.

XIII.

At the farther end of the bridge, close to the wharf where the little steamboats are, is a very small Jizō temple (*Jizō-dō*). Here are kept many bronze drags; and whenever any one has been drowned and the body not recovered, these are borrowed from the little temple and the river is dragged. If the body be thus found, a new drag must be presented to the temple.

From here, half a mile southward to the great Shintō temple of Tenjin, deity of scholarship and calligraphy, broadly stretches Tenjinmachi, the Street of the Rich Merchants, all draped on either side with dark blue hangings, over which undulate with

every windy palpitation from the lake white wondrous ideographs, which are names and signs, while down the wide way, in
white perspective, diminishes a long line of telegraph poles.

Beyond the temple of Tenjin the city is again divided by a river,
the Shindotegawa, over which arches the bridge Tenjin-bashi.
Again beyond this other large quarters extend to the hills and
curve along the lake shore. But in the space between the two
rivers is the richest and busiest life of the city, and also the vast
and curious quarter of the temples. In this islanded district are
likewise the theatres, and the place where wrestling-matches are
held, and most of the resorts of pleasure.

Parallel with Tenjinmachi runs the great street of the Buddhist
temples, or Teramachi, of which the eastern side is one unbroken
succession of temples—a solid front of court walls tile-capped,
with imposing gateways at regular intervals. Above this long
stretch of tile-capped wall rise the beautiful tilted massive lines
of gray-blue temple roofs against the sky. Here all the sects dwell
side by side in harmony—Nichiren-shū, Shingon-shū, Zen-shū,
Tendai-shū, even that Shin-shū, unpopular in Izumo because
those who follow its teaching strictly must not worship the
Kami. Behind each temple court there is a cemetery, or *hakaba*;
and eastward beyond these are other temples, and beyond them
yet others—masses of Buddhist architecture mixed with shreds
of gardens and miniature homesteads, a huge labyrinth of moldering courts and fragments of streets.

Today, as usual, I find I can pass a few hours very profitably
in visiting the temples; in looking at the ancient images seated
within the cups of golden lotus-flowers under their aureoles of
gold; in buying curious mamori; in examining the sculptures of
the cemeteries, where I can nearly always find some dreaming
Kwannon or smiling Jizō well worth the visit.

The great courts of Buddhist temples are places of rare interest for one who loves to watch the life of the people; for these
have been for unremembered centuries the playing-places of
the children. Generations of happy infants have been amused

in them. All the nurses, and little girls who carry tiny brothers or sisters upon their backs, go thither every morning that the sun shines; hundreds of children join them; and they play at strange, funny games—"Oni-gokko," or the game of Devil, "Kage-Oni," which signifies the Shadow and the Demon, and "Mekusangokko," which is a sort of "blindman's buff."

Also, during the long summer evenings, these temples are wrestling-grounds, free to all who love wrestling; and in many of them there is a dohyō-ba, or wrestling-ring. Robust young laborers and sinewy artisans come to these courts to test their strength after the day's tasks are done, and here the fame of more than one now noted wrestler was first made. When a youth has shown himself able to overmatch at wrestling all others in his own district, he is challenged by champions of other districts; and if he can overcome these also, he may hope eventually to become a skilled and popular professional wrestler.

It is also in the temple courts that the sacred dances are performed and that public speeches are made. It is in the temple courts, too, that the most curious toys are sold, on the occasion of the great holidays—toys most of which have a religious signification.

There are grand old trees, and ponds full of tame fish, which put up their heads to beg for food when your shadow falls upon the water. The holy lotus is cultivated therein.

"Though growing in the foulest slime, the flower remains pure and undefiled.

"And the soul of him who remains ever pure in the midst of temptation is likened unto the lotus.

"Therefore is the lotus carven or painted upon the furniture of temples; therefore also does it appear in all the representations of our Lord Buddha.

"In Paradise the blessed shall sit at ease enthroned upon the-cups of golden lotus-flowers."*

---

* From an English composition by one of my Japanese pupils.

A bugle-call rings through the quaint street; and round the corner of the last temple come marching a troop of handsome young riflemen, uniformed somewhat like French light infantry, marching by fours so perfectly that all the gaitered legs move as if belonging to a single body, and every sword-bayonet catches the sun at exactly the same angle, as the column wheels into view. These are the students of the Shihan-Gakkō, the College of Teachers, performing their daily military exercises. Their professors give them lectures upon the microscopic study of cellular tissues, upon the segregation of developing nerve structure, upon spectrum analysis, upon the evolution of the color sense, and upon the cultivation of bacteria in glycerine infusions. And they are none the less modest and knightly in manner for all their modern knowledge, nor the less reverentially devoted to their dear old fathers and mothers whose ideas were shaped in the era of feudalism.

XIV.

Here come a band of pilgrims, with yellow straw overcoats, "rain-coats" *(mino)*, and enormous yellow straw hats, mushroom-shaped, of which the down-curving rim partly hides the face. All carry staffs, and wear their robes well girded up so as to leave free the lower limbs, which are enclosed in white cotton leggings of a peculiar and indescribable kind. Precisely the same sort of costume was worn by the same class of travelers many centuries ago; and just as you now see them trooping by—whole families wandering together, the pilgrim child clinging to the father's hand—so may you see them pass in quaint procession across the faded pages of Japanese picture books a hundred years old.

At intervals they halt before some shop-front to look at the many curious things which they greatly enjoy seeing, but which they have no money to buy.

I myself have become so accustomed to surprises, to interesting or extraordinary sights, that when a day happens to pass during which nothing remarkable has been heard or seen I feel vaguely discontented. But such blank days are rare: they occur in my own case only when the weather is too detestable to permit of going out-of-doors. For with ever so little money one can always obtain the pleasure of looking at curious things. And this has been one of the chief pleasures of the people in Japan for centuries and centuries, for the nation has passed its generations of lives in making or seeking such things. To divert one's self seems, indeed, the main purpose of Japanese existence, beginning with the opening of the baby's wondering eyes. The faces of the people have an indescribable look of patient expectancy— the air of waiting for something interesting to make its appearance. If it fail to appear, they will travel to find it: they are astonishing pedestrians and tireless pilgrims, and I think they make pilgrimages not more for the sake of pleasing the gods than of pleasing themselves by the sight of rare and pretty things. For every temple is a museum, and every hill and valley throughout the land has its temple and its wonders.

Even the poorest farmer, one so poor that he cannot afford to eat a grain of his own rice, can afford to make a pilgrimage of a month's duration; and during that season when the growing rice needs least attention hundreds of thousands of the poorest go on pilgrimages. This is possible, because from ancient times it has been the custom for everybody to help pilgrims a little; and they can always find rest and shelter at particular inns (*Kichinyado*) which receive pilgrims only, and where they are charged merely the cost of the wood used to cook their food.

But multitudes of the poor undertake pilgrimages requiring much more than a month to perform, such as the pilgrimage to the thirty-three great temples of Kwannon, or that to the eighty-eight temples of Kōbodaishi; and these, though years be needed to accomplish them, are as nothing compared to the enormous Sengaji, the pilgrimage to the thousand temples of the Nichiren sect. The time of a generation may pass ere this can be made. One may begin it in early youth, and complete it only when youth is long past. Yet there are several in Matsue, men and women, who have made this tremendous pilgrimage, seeing all Japan, and supporting themselves not merely by begging, but by some kinds of itinerant peddling.

The pilgrim who desires to perform this pilgrimage carries on his shoulders a small box, shaped like a Buddhist shrine, in which he keeps his spare clothes and food. He also carries a little brazen gong, which he constantly sounds while passing through a city or village, at the same time chanting the *Namihmyō-hō-ren-ge-kyō;* and he always bears with him a little blank book, in which the priest of every temple visited stamps the temple seal in red ink. The pilgrimage over, this book with its one thousand seal impressions becomes an heirloom in the family of the pilgrim.

XV.

I too must make divers pilgrimages, for all about the city, beyond the waters or beyond the hills, lie holy places immemorially old.

Kitzuki, founded by the ancient gods, who "made stout the pillars upon the nethermost rock bottom, and made high the cross-beams to the Plain of High Heaven,"—Kitzuki, the Holy of Holies, whose high-priest claims descent from the Goddess of the Sun; and Ichibata, famed shrine of Yakushi-Nyorai, who giveth sight to the blind—Ichibata-no-Yakushi, whose lofty temple is approached by six hundred and forty steps of stone; and Kiomidzu, shrine of Kwannon of the Eleven Faces, before whose altar the sacred lire has burned without ceasing for a thousand years; and Sada, where the Sacred Snake lies coiled forever on the sambo of the gods; and Oba, with its temples of Izanami and Izanagi, parents of gods and men, the makers of the world; and Yaegaki, whither lovers go to pray for unions with the beloved; and Kaka, Kaka-ura, Kaka-no-Kukedo San—all these I hope to see.

But of all places, Kaka-ura! Assuredly I must go to Kaka.

Few pilgrims go thither by sea, and boatmen are forbidden to go there if there be even wind enough "to move three hairs." So that whosoever wishes to visit Kaka must either wait for a period of dead calm—very rare upon the coast of the Japanese Sea—or journey thereunto by land; and by land the way is difficult and wearisome. But I must see Kaka. For at Kaka, in a great cavern by the sea, there is a famous Jizō of stone; and each night, it is said, the ghosts of little children climb to the high cavern and pile up before the statue small heaps of pebbles; and every morning, in the soft sand, there may be seen the fresh prints of tiny naked feet, the feet of the infant ghosts. It is also said that in the cavern there is a rock out of which comes a stream of milk, as from a woman's breast; and the white stream flows forever, and the phantom children drink of it. Pilgrims bring with them gifts of small straw sandals—the zori that children wear—and leave them before the cavern, that the feet of the little ghosts may not be wounded by the sharp rocks. And the pilgrim treads with caution, lest he should overturn any of the many heaps of stones; for if this be done the children cry.

XVI.

The city proper is as level as a table, but is bounded on two sides by low demilunes of charming hills shadowed with evergreen foliage and crowned with temples or shrines. There are thirty-five thousand souls dwelling in ten thousand houses forming thirty-three principal and many smaller streets; and from each end of almost every street, beyond the hills, the lake, or the eastern rice-fields, a mountain summit is always visible—green, blue, or gray according to distance. One may ride, walk, or go by boat to any quarter of the town; for it is not only divided by two rivers, but is also intersected by numbers of canals crossed by queer little bridges curved like a well-bent bow. Architecturally (despite such constructions in European style as the College of Teachers, the great public school, the Kenchō, the new post-office), it is much like other quaint Japanese towns; the structure of its temples, taverns, shops, and private dwellings is the same as in other cities of the western coast. But doubtless owing to the fact that Matsue remained a feudal stronghold until a time within the memory of thousands still living, those feudal distinctions of caste so sharply drawn in ancient times are yet indicated with singular exactness by the varying architecture of different districts. The city can be definitely divided into three architectural quarters: the district of the merchants and shop-keepers, forming the heart of the settlement, where all the houses are two stories high; the district of the temples, including nearly the whole southeastern part of the town; and the district or districts of the shizoku (formerly called samurai), comprising a vast number of large, roomy, garden-girt, one-story dwellings. From these elegant homes, in feudal days, could be summoned at a moment's notice five thousand "two-sworded men" with their armed retainers, making a fighting total for the city alone of probably not less than thirteen thousand warriors. More than one-third of all the city buildings were then samurai homes; for Matsue was the military center of the most ancient province of Japan. At both ends of the town, which curves in a crescent along the lakeshore, were the two main settlements of samurai; but just as some of the most important temples are situated outside of the temple district, so were many of the finest homesteads of this knightly caste situated in other quarters. They mustered most thickly, however, about the castle, which stands today on the summit of its citadel hill—the Oshiroyama—solid as when first built long centuries ago, a vast and sinister shape, all iron-gray, rising against the sky from a cyclopean foundation of stone. Fantastically grim the thing is, and grotesquely complex in detail; looking somewhat like a huge pagoda, of which the second, third, and fourth stories have been squeezed down and telescoped into one another by their own weight. Crested at its summit, like a feudal helmet, with two colossal fishes of bronze lifting their curved bodies sky ward from either angle of the roof, and bristling with horned gables and gargoyled eaves and tilted puzzles of tiled roofing at every story, the creation is a veritable architectural dragon, made up of magnificent monstrosities—

a dragon, moreover, full of eyes set at all conceivable angles, above, below, and on every side. From under the black scowl of the loftiest eaves, looking east and south, the whole city can be seen at a single glance, as in the vision of a soaring hawk; and from the northern angle the view plunges down three hundred feet to the castle road, where walking figures of men appear no larger than flies.

XVII.

The grim castle has its legend.

It is related that, in accordance with some primitive and barbarous custom, precisely like that of which so terrible a souvenir has been preserved for us in the most pathetic of Servian ballads, "The Foundation of Skadra," a maiden of Matsue was interred alive under the walls of the castle at the time of its erection, as a sacrifice to some forgotten gods. Her name has never been recorded; nothing concerning her is remembered except that she was beautiful and very fond of dancing.

Now after the castle had been built, it is said that a law had to be passed forbidding that any girl should dance in the streets of Matsue. For whenever any maiden danced the hill Oshiroyama would shudder, and the great castle quiver from basement to summit.

XVIII.

One may still sometimes hear in the streets a very humorous song, which every one in town formerly knew by heart, celebrating the Seven Wonders of Matsue. For Matsue was formerly divided into seven quarters, in each of which some extraordinary object or person was to be seen. It is now divided into five religious districts, each containing a temple of the state religion. People living within those districts are called ujiko, and the temple the ujigami, or dwelling-place of the tutelary god. The ujiko must support the ujigami. (Every village and town has at least one ujigami.)

There is probably not one of the multitudinous temples of Matsue which has not some marvelous tradition attached to it; each of the districts has many legends; and I think that each of the thirty-three streets has its own special ghost story. Of these ghost stories I cite two specimens: they are quite representative of one variety of Japanese folklore.

Near to the Fu-mon-in temple, which is in the northeastern quarter, there is a bridge called Adzukitogi-bashi, or The Bridge of the Washing of Peas. For it was said in other years that nightly a phantom woman sat beneath that bridge washing phantom peas. There is an exquisite Japanese iris-flower, of rainbow-violet color, which flower is named kaki-tsubata; and there is a song about that flower called kaki-tsubata-no-uta. Now this song must never be sung near the Adzuki-togi-bashi, because, for some strange reason which seems to have been forgotten, the ghosts haunting that place become so angry upon hearing it that to sing it there is to expose one's self to the most frightful calamities. There was once a samurai who feared nothing, who one night went to that bridge and loudly sang the song. No ghost appearing, he laughed and went home. At the gate of his house he met a beautiful tall woman whom he bad never seen before, and who, bowing, presented him with a lacquered box— *fumi-bako*—such as women keep their letters in. He bowed to her in his knightly way; but she said, "I am only the servant—this is my mistress's gift," and vanished out of his sight. Opening the box, be saw the bleeding head of a young child. Entering his house, he found upon the floor of the guest-room the dead body of his own infant son with the head torn off.

Of the cemetery Dai-Oji, which is in the street called Naka-baramachi, this story is told:

In Nakabaramachi there is an ameya, or little shop in which midzu-ame is sold—the amber-tinted syrup, made of malt, which is given to children when milk cannot be obtained for them. Every night at a late hour there came to that shop a very pale woman, all in white, to buy one rin* worth of midzu-ame. The ame-seller wondered that she was so thin and pale, and often questioned her kindly; but she answered nothing. At last one night he followed her, out of curiosity. She went to the cemetery; and he became afraid and returned.

The next night the woman came again, but bought no midzu-ame, and only beckoned to the man to go with her. He followed her, with friends, into the cemetery. She walked to a certain tomb, and there disappeared; and they heard, under the ground, the crying of a child. Opening the tomb, they saw within it the corpse of the woman who nightly visited the ameya, with a living infant, laughing to see the lantern light, and beside the infant a little cup of midzu-ame. For the mother had been prematurely buried; the child was born in the tomb, and the ghost of the mother had thus provided for it—love being stronger than death.

XIX.

Over the Tenjin-bashi, or Bridge of Tenjin, and through small streets and narrow of densely populated districts, and past many a tenantless and moldering feudal homestead, I make my way to the extreme southwestern end of the city, to watch the sunset from a little sobaya† facing the lake. For to see the sun sink from this sobaya is one of the delights of Matsue.

There are no such sunsets in Japan as in the tropics: the light is gentle as a light of dreams; there are no furies of color; there are no chromatic violences in nature in this Orient. All in sea or sky is tint rather than color, and tint vapor-toned. I think that the exquisite taste of the race in the matter of colors and of tints, as exemplified in the dyes of their wonderful textures, is largely attributable to the sober and delicate beauty of nature's tones in this all-temperate world where nothing is garish.

---

* *Rin*, one-tenth of one cent. A small round copper coin with a square hole in the middle.

† An inn where soba is sold.

Before me the fair vast lake sleeps, softly luminous, far-ringed with chains of blue volcanic hills shaped like a sierra. On my right, at its eastern end, the most ancient quarter of the city spreads its roofs of blue-gray tile; the houses crowd thickly down to the shore, to dip their wooden feet into the flood. With a glass I can see my own windows and the far-spreading of the roofs beyond, and above all else the green citadel with its grim castle, grotesquely peaked. The sun begins to set, and exquisite astonishments of tinting appear in water and sky.

Dead rich purples cloud broadly behind and above the indigo blackness of the serrated hills—mist purples, fading upward smokily into faint vermilions and dim gold, which again melt up through ghostliest greens into the blue. The deeper waters of the lake, far away, take a tender violet indescribable, and the silhouette of the pine-shadowed island seems to float in that sea of soft sweet color. But the shallower and nearer is cut from the deeper water by the current as sharply as by a line drawn, and all the surface on this side of that line is a shimmering bronze—old rich ruddy gold-bronze.

All the fainter colors change every five minutes—wondrously change and shift like tones and shades of fine shot-silks.

XX.

Often in the streets at night, especially on the nights of sacred festivals *(matsuri)*, one's attention will be attracted to some small booth by the spectacle of an admiring and perfectly silent crowd pressing before it. As soon as one can get a chance to look one finds there is nothing to look at but a few vases containing sprays of flowers, or perhaps some light gracious branches freshly cut from a blossoming tree. It is simply a little flower-show, or, more correctly, a free exhibition of master skill in the arrangement of flowers. For the Japanese do not brutally chop off flower-heads to work them up into meaningless masses of color, as we barbarians do: they love nature too well for that; they know how much the natural charm of the flower depends upon its setting and mounting, its relation to leaf and stem, and they select a single graceful branch or spray just as nature made it. At first you will not, as a Western stranger, comprehend such an exhibition at all: you are yet a savage in such matters compared with the commonest coolies about you. But even while you are still wondering at popular interest in this simple little show, the charm of it will begin to grow upon you, will become a revelation to you; and, despite your Occidental idea of self-superiority, you will feel humbled by the discovery that all flower displays you have ever seen abroad were only monstrosities in comparison with the natural beauty of those few simple sprays. You will also observe how much the white or pale blue screen behind the flowers enhances the effect by lamp or lantern light. For the screen has been arranged with the special purpose of showing the exquisiteness of plant shadows; and the sharp silhouettes of sprays and blossoms cast thereon are beautiful beyond the imagining of any Western decorative artist.

XXI.

It is still the season of mists in this land whose most ancient name signifies the Place of the Issuing of Clouds. With the passing of twilight a faint ghostly brume rises over lake and landscape, spectrally veiling surfaces, slowly obliterating distances. As I lean over the parapet of the Tenjin-bashi, on my homeward way, to take one last look eastward, I find that the mountains have already been effaced. Before me there is only a shadowy flood far vanishing into vagueness without a horizon—the phantom of a sea. And I become suddenly aware that little white things are fluttering slowly down into it from the fingers of a woman standing upon the bridge beside me, and murmuring something in a low sweet voice. She is praying for her dead child. Each of those little papers she is dropping into the current bears a tiny picture of Jizō, and perhaps a little inscription. For when a child dies the mother buys a small woodcut (*hanko*) of Jizō, and with it prints the image of the divinity upon one hundred little papers. And she sometimes also writes upon the papers words signifying "For the sake of..."—inscribing never the living, but the kaimyo or soul-name only, which the Buddhist priest has given to the dead, and which is written also upon the little commemorative tablet kept within the Buddhist household shrine, or *butsuma*. Then, upon a fixed day (most commonly the forty-ninth day after the burial), she goes to some place of running water and drops the little papers therein one by one; repeating, as each slips through her fingers, the holy invocation, "*Namu Jizō, Dai Bosatsu!*"

Doubtless this pious little woman, praying beside me in the dusk, is very poor. Were she not, she would hire a boat and scatter her tiny papers far away upon the bosom of the lake. (It is now only after dark that this may be done; for the police—I know not why—have been instructed to prevent the pretty rite, just as in the open ports they have been instructed to prohibit the launching of the little straw boats of the dead, the shōryōbune).

But why should the papers be cast into running water? A good old Tendai priest tells me that originally the rite was only for the souls of the drowned, but now these gentle hearts believe that all waters flow downward to the Shadow-world and through the Sai-no-Kawara, where Jizō is.

XXII.

At home again, I slide open once more my little paper window, and look out upon the night. I see the paper lanterns flitting over the bridge, like a long shimmering of fireflies. I see the spectres of a hundred lights trembling upon the black flood. I see the broad shōji of dwellings beyond the river suffused with the soft yellow radiance of invisible lamps; and upon those lighted spaces I can discern slender moving shadows, silhouettes of graceful women. Devoutly do I pray that glass may never become universally adopted in Japan—there would be no more delicious shadows.

I listen to the voices of the city awhile. I hear the great bell of Tōkōji rolling its soft Buddhist thunder across the dark, and the songs of the night-walkers whose hearts have been made merry with wine, and the long sonorous chanting of the night-peddlers.

"*U-mu-don-yai-soba-yai!*" It is the seller of hot soba, Japanese buckwheat, making his last round.

"*Umai handan, machibito endan, usemono ninsō kasō kichikyō no urainai!*" The cry of the itinerant fortune-teller.

"*Ame-yu!*" The musical cry of the seller of midzuame, the sweet amber syrup which children love.

"*Amai!*" The shrilling call of the seller of ama zaké, sweet rice wine.

"*Kawachi-no-kuni-hiotan-yama-koi-no-tsuji-ura!*" The peddler of love-papers, of divining-papers, pretty tinted things with little shadowy pictures upon them. When held near a fire or a lamp, words written upon them with invisible ink begin to appear. These are always about sweethearts, and sometimes tell one what he does not wish to know. The fortunate ones who read them believe themselves still more fortunate; the unlucky abandon all hope; the jealous become even more jealous than they were before.

From all over the city there rises into the night a sound like the bubbling and booming of great frogs in a marsh—the echoing of the tiny drums of the dancing-girls, of the charming geisha. Like the rolling of a waterfall continually reverberates the multitudinous pattering of geta upon the bridge. A new light rises in the east; the moon is wheeling up from behind the peaks, very large and weird and wan through the white vapors. Again I hear the sounds of the clapping of many hands. For the wayfarers are paying obeisance to O-Tsuki-San: from the long bridge they are saluting the coming of the White Moon-Lady.*

---

* According to the mythology of the *Kojiki* the Moon-Deity is a male divinity. But the common people know nothing of the *Kojiki*, written in an archaic Japanese which only the learned can read; and they address the moon as O-Tsuki-Saa, or "Lady Moon," just as the old Greek idylists did.

I sleep, to dream of little children, in some moldering mossy temple court, playing at the game of Shadows and of Demons.

8

KITZUKI: THE MOST ANCIENT SHRINE OF JAPAN

SHINKOKU is the sacred name of Japan—Shinkoku, "The Country of the Gods;" and of all Shinkoku the most holy ground is the land of Izumo. Hither from the blue Plain of High Heaven first came to dwell awhile the Earth-makers, Izanagi and Izanami, the parents of gods and of men; somewhere upon the border of this land was Izanami buried; and out of this land into the black realm of the dead did Izanagi follow after her, and seek in vain to bring her back again. And the tale of his descent into that strange nether world, and of what there befell him, is it not written in the Kojiki?* And of all legends primeval concerning the Underworld this story is one of the weirdest—more weird than even the Assyrian legend of the Descent of Ishtar.

Even as Izumo is especially the province of the gods, and the place of the childhood of the race by whom Izanagi and Izanami are yet worshiped, so is Kitzuki of Izumo especially the city of the gods, and its immemorial temple the earliest home of the ancient faith, the great religion of Shintō.

Now to visit Kitzuki has been my most earnest ambition since I learned the legends of the Kojiki concerning it; and this ambition

---

* The most ancient book extant in the archaic tongue of Japan. It is the most sacred scripture of Shintō. It has been admirably translated, with copious notes and commentaries, by Professor Basil Hall Chamberlain, of Tōkyō.

has been stimulated by the discovery that very few Europeans have visited Kitzuki, and that none have been admitted into the great temple itself. Some, indeed, were not allowed even to approach the temple court. But I trust that I shall be somewhat more fortunate; for I have a letter of introduction from my dear friend Nishida Sentaro, who is also a personal friend of the high pontiff of Kitzuki. I am thus assured that even should I not be permitted to enter the temple—a privilege accorded to but few among the Japanese themselves—I shall at least have the honor of an interview with the Guji, or Spiritual Governor of Kitzuki, Senke Takanori, whose princely family trace back their descent to the Goddess of the Sun.*

I.

I leave Matsue for Kitzuki early in the afternoon of a beautiful September day; taking passage upon a tiny steamer in which everything, from engines to awnings, is Lilliputian. In the cabin one must kneel. Under the awnings one cannot possibly stand upright. But the miniature craft is neat and pretty as a toy model, and moves with surprising swiftness and steadiness. A handsome naked boy is busy serving the passengers with cups of tea and with cakes, and setting little charcoal furnaces before those who desire to smoke: for all of which a payment of about three quarters of a cent is expected.

I escape from the awnings to climb upon the cabin roof for a view; and the view is indescribably lovely. Over the lucent level of the lake we are steaming toward a far-away heaping of beautiful shapes, colored with that strangely delicate blue which tints all distances in the Japanese atmosphere—shapes of peaks and headlands looming up from the lake verge against a porcelain-

---

* The genealogy of the family is published in a curious little book with which I was presented at Kitzuki. Senke Takanori is the eighty-first Pontiff Governor (formerly called *Kokuzō*) of Kitzuki. His lineage is traced back through sixty-five generations of Kokuzō and sixteen generations of earthly deities to Ama-terasu and her brother Susanoō-no-mikoto.

white horizon. They show no details whatever. Silhouettes only they are—masses of absolutely pure color. To left and right, framing in the Shinjiko, are superb green surgings of wooded hills. Great Yakuno-San is the loftiest mountain before us, north-west. Southeast, behind us, the city has vanished; but proudly towering beyond looms Daisen—enormous, ghostly blue and ghostly white, lifting the cusps of its dead crater into the region of eternal snow. Over all arches a sky of color faint as a dream.

There seems to be a sense of divine magic in the very atmosphere, through all the luminous day, brooding over the vapory land, over the ghostly blue of the flood—a sense of Shintō. With my fancy full of the legends of the Kojiki, the rhythmic chant of the engines comes to my ears as the rhythm of a Shintō ritual mingled with the names of gods:

> *Koto-shiro-nushi-no-Kami,*
> *Oho-kuni-nushi-no-Kami.*

II.

The great range on the right grows loftier as we steam on; and its hills, always slowly advancing toward us, begin to reveal all the rich details of their foliage. And lo! on the tip of one grand wood-clad peak is visible against the pure sky the many-angled roof of a great Buddhist temple. That is the temple of Ichibata, upon the mountain Ichibata-yama, the temple of Yakushi-Nyorai, the Physician of Souls. But at Icbibata he reveals himself more specially as the healer of bodies, the Buddha who giveth sight unto the blind. It is believed that whosoever has an affection of the eyes will be made well by praying earnestly at that great shrine; and thither from many distant provinces do afflicted thousands make pilgrimage, ascending the long weary mountain path and the six hundred and forty steps of stone leading to the windy temple court upon the summit, whence may be seen one of the loveliest landscapes in Japan. There the pilgrims wash their eyes with the water of the sacred spring, and kneel before the shrine and murmur the holy formula of Ichibata: "*On-koro-koro-sendai-matōki-sowaka*,"—words of which the meaning has long been forgotten, like that of many a Buddhist invocation; Sanscrit words transliterated into Chinese, and thence into Japanese, which are understood by learned priests alone, yet are known by heart throughout the land, and uttered with the utmost fervor of devotion.

I descend from the cabin roof, and squat upon the deck, under the awnings, to have a smoke with Akira. And I ask:

"How many Buddhas are there, O Akira? Is the number of the Enlightened known?"

"Countless the Buddhas are," makes answer Akira; "yet there is truly but one Buddha; the many are forms only. Each of us contains a future Buddha. Alike we all are except in that we are more or less unconscious of the truth. But the vulgar may not understand these things, and so seek refuge in symbols and in forms."

"And the Kami—the deities of Shintō?"

"Of Shintō I know little. But there are eight hundred myriads of Kami in the Plain of High Heaven—so says the Ancient Book. Of these, three thousand one hundred and thirty and two dwell in the various provinces of the land; being enshrined in two thousand eight hundred and sixty-one temples. And the tenth month of our year is called the 'No-God-month,' because in that month all the deities leave their temples to assemble in the province of Izumo, at the great temple of Kitzuki; and for the same reason that month is called in Izumo, and only in Izumo, the 'God-is-month.' But educated persons sometimes call it the 'God-present-festival,' using Chinese words. Then it is believed the serpents come from the sea to the land, and coil upon the sambo, which is the table of the gods, for the serpents announce the coming; and the Dragon-King sends messengers to the temples of Izanagi and Izanami, the parents of gods and men."

"O Akira, many millions of Kami there must be of whom I shall always remain ignorant, for there is a limit to the power of memory; but tell me something of the gods whose names are most seldom uttered, the deities of strange places and of strange things, the most extraordinary gods."

"You cannot learn much about them from me," replies Akira. "You will have to ask others more learned than I. But there are gods with whom it is not desirable to become acquainted. Such are the God of Poverty, and the God of Hunger, and the God of Penuriousness, and the God of Hindrances and Obstacles. These are of dark color, like the clouds of gloomy days, and their faces are like the faces of gaki."[*]

"With the God of Hindrances and Obstacles, O Akira, I have had more than a passing acquaintance. Tell me of the others."

"I know little about any of them," answers Akira, "excepting Bimbogami. It is said there are two gods who always go together—Fuku-no-Kami, who is the God of Luck, and Bimbogami, who is the God of Poverty. The first is white, and the second is black."

"Because the last," I venture to interrupt, "is only the shadow of the first. Fuku-no-Kami is the Shadow-caster, and Bimbogami the Shadow; and I have observed, in wandering about this world, that wherever the one goeth, eternally followeth after him the other."

Akira refuses his assent to this interpretation, and resumes:

"When Bimbogami once begins to follow anyone it is extremely difficult to be free from him again. In the village of Umitsu, which is in the province of Omi, and not far from Kyōto, there once lived a Buddhist priest who during many years was grievously tormented by Bimbogami. He tried oftentimes without avail to drive him away; then he strove to deceive him by proclaiming aloud to all the people that he was going to Kyōto. But instead of going to Kyōto he went to Tsuruga, in the province of Echizen; and when he reached the inn at Tsuruga there came forth to meet him a boy lean and wan like a gaki. The boy said to him, 'I have been waiting for you'—and the boy was Bimbogami.

---

[*] In Sanscrit *pretas*. The gaki are the famished ghosts of that Circle of Torment in hell whereof the penance is hunger; and the months of some are "smaller than the points of needles."

"There was another priest who for sixty years had tried in vain to get rid of Bimbogami, and who resolved at last to go to a distant province. On the night after he had formed this resolve he had a strange dream, in which he saw a very much emaciated boy, naked and dirty, weaving sandals of straw *(waraji),* such as pilgrims and runners wear; and he made so many that the priest wondered, and asked him, 'For what purpose are you making so many sandals?' And the boy answered, 'I am going to travel with you. I am Bimbogami.'"

"Then is there no way, Akira, by which Bimbogami may be driven away?"

"It is written," replies Akira, "in the book called Jizō-Kyō-Kosui that the aged Enjobo, a priest dwelling in the province of Owari, was able to get rid of Bimbogami by means of a charm. On the last day of the last month of the year he and his disciples and other priests of the Shingon sect took branches of peach-trees and recited a formula, and then, with the branches, imitated the action of driving a person out of the temple, after which they shut all the gates and recited other formulas. The same night Enjobo dreamed of a skeleton priest in a broken temple weeping alone, and the skeleton priest said to him, 'After I had been with you for so many years, how could you drive me away?' But always thereafter until the day of his death, Enjobo lived in prosperity."

III.

For an hour and a half the ranges to left and right alternately recede and approach. Beautiful blue shapes glide toward us, change to green, and then, slowly drifting behind us, are all blue again. But the far mountains immediately before us—immovable, unchanging—always remain ghosts. Suddenly the little steamer turns straight into the land—a land so low that it came into sight quite unexpectedly—and we puff up a narrow stream between rice-fields to a queer, quaint, pretty village on the canal bank—Shōbara. Here I must hire jinrikisha to take us to Kitzuki.

There is not time to see much of Shōbara if I hope to reach
Kitzuki before bedtime, and I have only a flying vision of one
long wide street (so picturesque that I wish I could pass a day
in it), as our kuruma rush through the little town into the open
country, into a vast plain covered with rice-fields. The road
itself is only a broad dike, barely wide enough for two jinrikisha to pass each other upon it. On each side the superb plain is
bounded by a mountain range shutting off the white horizon.
There is a vast silence, an immense sense of dreamy peace, and
a glorious soft vapory light over everything, as we roll into the
country of Hyasugi to Kaminawoë. The jagged range on the left
is Shusai-yama, all sharply green, with the giant Daikoku-yama
overtopping all; and its peaks bear the names of gods. Much
more remote, upon our right, enormous, pansy-purple, tower
the shapes of the Kita-yama, or northern range; filing away in
tremendous procession toward the sunset, fading more and more
as they stretch west, to vanish suddenly at last, after the ghostliest conceivable manner, into the uttermost day.

All this is beautiful; yet there is no change while hours pass.
Always the way winds on through miles of rice-fields, white-
speckled with paper-winged shafts which are arrows of prayer.
Always the voice of frogs—a sound as of infinite bubbling.
Always the green range on the left, the purple on the right, fading westward into a tall file of tinted spectres which always melt
into nothing at last, as if they were made of air. The monotony
of the scene is broken only by our occasional passing through
some pretty Japanese village, or by the appearance of a curious
statue or monument at an angle of the path, a roadside Jizō,
or the grave of a wrestler, such as may be seen on the bank of
the Hiagawa, a huge slab of granite sculptured with the words,
"*Ikumo Matsu kikusuki.*"

But after reaching Kandogori, and passing over a broad but
shallow river, a fresh detail appears in the landscape. Above the
mountain chain on our left looms a colossal blue silhouette, almost saddle-shaped, recognizable by its outline as a once mighty

volcano. It is now known by various names, but it was called in ancient times Sa-hime-yama; and it has its Shintō legend.

It is said that in the beginning the God of Izumo, gazing over the land, said, "This new land of Izumo is a land of but small extent, so I will make it a larger land by adding unto it." Having so said, he looked about him over to Korea, and there he saw land which was good for the purpose. With a great rope he dragged therefrom four islands, and added the land of them to Izumo. The first island was called Ya-o-yo-ne, and it formed the land where Kitzuki now is. The second island was called Sada-no-kuni, and is at this day the site of the holy temple where all the gods do yearly hold their second assembly, after having first gathered together at Kitzuki. The third island was called in its new place Kura-mi-no-kuni, which now forms Shimane-gori. The fourth island became that place where stands the temple of the great god at whose shrine are delivered unto the faithful the charms which protect the rice-fields.*

Now in drawing these islands across the sea into their several places the god looped his rope over the mighty mountain of Daisen and over the mountain Sa-hime-yama; and they both bear the marks of that wondrous rope even unto this day. As for the rope itself, part of it was changed into the long island of ancient times† called Yomi-ga-hama, and a part into the Long Beach of Sono.

After we pass the Hori-kawa the road narrows and becomes rougher and rougher, but always draws nearer to the Kita-yama range. Toward sundown we have come close enough to the great hills to discern the details of their foliage. The path begins to rise; we ascend slowly through the gathering dusk. At last there

---

* Mionoseki.

† Now solidly united with the mainland. Many extraordinary changes, of rare interest to the physiographer and geologist, have actually taken place along the coast of Izumo and in the neighborhood of the great lake. Even now, each year some change occurs. I have seen several very strange ones.

appears before us a great multitude of twinkling lights. We have reached Kitzuki, the holy city.

IV.

Over a long bridge and under a tall torii we roll into upward-sloping streets. Like Enoshima, Kitzuki has a torii for its city gate; but the torii is not of bronze. Then a flying vision of open lamp-lighted shop-fronts, and lines of luminous shōji under high-tilted eaves, and Buddhist gateways guarded by lions of stone, and long, low, tile-coped walls of temple courts over-topped by garden shrubbery, and Shintō shrines prefaced by other tall torii; but no sign of the great temple itself. It lies toward the rear of the city proper, at the foot of the wooded mountains; and we are too tired and hungry to visit it now. So we halt before a spacious and comfortable-seeming inn—the best, indeed, in Kitzuki—and rest ourselves and eat, and drink saké out of exquisite little porcelain cups, the gift of some pretty singing-girl to the hotel. Thereafter, as it has become much too late to visit the Guji, I send to his residence by a messenger my letter of introduction, with an humble request in Akira's hand-writing, that I may be allowed to present myself at the house before noon the next day.

Then the landlord of the hotel, who seems to be a very kindly person, comes to us with lighted paper lanterns, and invites us to accompany him to the Oho-yashiro.

Most of the houses have already closed their wooden sliding doors for the night, so that the streets are dark, and the lanterns of our landlord indispensable; for there is no moon, and the night is starless. We walk along the main street for a distance of about six squares, and then, making a turn, find ourselves before a superb bronze torii, the gateway to the great temple avenue.

V.

Effacing colors and obliterating distances, night always magnifies by suggestion the aspect of large spaces and the effect of large objects. Viewed by the vague light of paper lanterns, the approach to the great shrine is an imposing surprise—such a surprise that I feel regret at the mere thought of having to see it tomorrow by disenchanting day: a superb avenue lined with colossal trees, and ranging away out of sight under a succession of giant torii, from which are suspended enormous shimenawa, well worthy the grasp of that Heavenly-Hand-Strength Deity whose symbols they are. But, more than by the torii and their festooned symbols, the dim majesty of the huge avenue is enhanced by the prodigious trees—many perhaps thousands of years old—gnarled pines whose shaggy summits are lost in darkness. Some of the mighty trunks are surrounded with a rope of straw: these trees are sacred. The vast roots, far-reaching in every direction, look in the lantern-light like a writhing and crawling of dragons.

The avenue is certainly not less than a quarter of a mile in length; it crosses two bridges and passes between two sacred groves. All the broad lands on either side of it belong to the temple. Formerly no foreigner was permitted to pass beyond the middle torii. The avenue terminates at a lofty wall pierced by a gateway resembling the gateways of Buddhist temple courts, but very massive. This is the entrance to the outer court; the ponderous doors are still open, and many shadowy figures are passing in or out.

Within the court all is darkness, against which pale yellow lights are gliding to and fro like a multitude of enormous fireflies—the lanterns of pilgrims. I can distinguish only the looming of immense buildings to left and right, constructed with colossal timbers. Our guide traverses a very large court, passes into a second, and halts before an imposing structure whose doors are still open. Above them, by the lantern glow, I can see a marvelous frieze of dragons and water, carved in some rich wood by the hand of a master. Within I can see the symbols of Shintō, in a side shrine on the left; and directly before us the lanterns reveal a surface of matted floor vaster than anything I had expected to find. Therefrom I can divine the scale of the edifice which I suppose to be the temple. But the landlord tells us this is not the temple, but only the *Haiden* or Hall of Prayer, before which the people make their orisons. By day, through the open doors, the temple can be seen. But we cannot see it tonight, and but few visitors are permitted to go in. " The people do not enter even the court of the great shrine, for the most part," interprets Akira; "they pray before it at a distance. Listen!"

All about me in the shadow I hear a sound like the splashing and dashing of water—the clapping of many hands in Shintō prayer.

"But this is nothing," says the landlord; "there are but few here now. Wait until tomorrow, which is a festival day."

As we wend our way back along the great avenue, under the torn and the giant trees, Akira interprets for me what our landlord tells him about the sacred serpent.

"The little serpent," he says, "is called by the people the august Dragon-Serpent; for it is sent by the Dragon-King to announce the coming of the gods. The sea darkens and rises and roars before the coming of Ryū-ja-Sama. Ryū-ja-Sama we call it because it is the messenger of Ryūgū-jō, the palace of the dragons; but it is also called Hakuja, or the White Serpent."*

---

* The Hakuja, or White Serpent, is also the servant of Benten, or Ben-zai-ten, Goddess of Love, of Beauty, of Eloquence, and of the Sea. "The Hakuja has the face of an ancient man, with white eyebrows, and wears upon its head a crown." Both goddess and serpent can be identified with ancient Indian mythological beings, and Buddhism first introduced both into Japan. Among the people, especially perhaps in Izumo, certain divinities of Buddhism are often identified, or rather confused, with certain Kami, in popular worship and parlance.

Since this sketch was written, I have had opportunity of seeing a Ryū-ja within a few hours after its capture. It was between two and three feet long, and about one inch in diameter at its thickest girth. The upper part of the body was a very dark brown, and the belly yellowish white; toward the tail there were some beautiful yellowish mottlings. The body was not cylindrical, but curiously four-sided—like those elaborately woven

"Does the little serpent come to the temple of its own accord?"

"Oh, no. It is caught by the fishermen. And only one can be caught in a year, because only one is sent; and whoever catches it and brings it either to the Kitzuki-no-oho-yashiro, or to the temple Sadajinja, where the gods hold their second assembly during the Kami-ari-zuki, receives one hyō* of rice in recompense. It costs much labor and time to catch a serpent; but whoever captures one is sure to become rich in after time."†

"There are many deities enshrined at Kitzuki, are there not?" I ask.

"Yes; but the great deity of Kitzuki is Oho-kuni-nushi-no-Kami,‡ whom the people more commonly call Daikoku. Here also is worshiped his son, whom many call Ebisu. These deities are usually pictured together: Daikoku seated upon bales of rice, holding the Red Sun against his breast with one hand, and in the other grasping the magical mallet of which a single stroke gives wealth; and Ebisu bearing a fishing-rod, and holding under his arm a great tai-fish. These gods are always represented with

---

whip-lashes which have four edges. The tail was flat and triangular, like that of certain fish. A Japanese teacher, Mr. Watanabe, of the Normal School of Matsue, identified the little creature as a hydrophid of the species called *Pelamis bicolor*. It is so seldom seen, however, that I think the foregoing superficial description of it may not be without interest to some readers.

* Ippyo, one *hyō*; 2½ hyō make one *koku* = 5.13 bushels. The word *hyō* means also the bag made to contain one hyō.

† Either at Kitzuki or at Sada it is possible sometimes to buy a serpent. On many a "household-god-shelf" in Matsue the little serpent may be seen. I saw one that had become brittle and black with age, but was excellently preserved by some process of which I did not learn the nature. It had been admirably posed in a tiny wire cage, made to fit exactly into a small shrine of white wood, and must have been, when alive, about two feet four inches in length. A little lamp was lighted daily before it, and some Shintō formula recited by the poor family to whom it belonged.

‡ Translated by Professor Chamberlain the "Deity Master-of-the-Great-Land"—one of the most ancient divinities of Japan, but in popular worship confounded with Daikoku, God of Wealth. His son, Koto-shiro-nushi-no-Kami, is similarly confounded with Ebisu, or Yebisu, the patron of honest labor. The origin of the Shintō custom of clapping the hands in prayer is said by some Japanese writers to have been a sign given by Koto-shiro-nushi-no-Kami.

Both deities are represented by Japanese art in a variety of ways. Some of the twin images of them sold at Kitzuki are extremely pretty as well as curious.

smiling faces; and both have great ears, which are the sign of wealth and fortune."

VI.

A little wearied by the day's journeying, I get to bed early, and sleep as dreamlessly as a plant until I am awakened about daylight by a heavy, regular, bumping sound, shaking the wooden pillow on which my ear rests—the sound of the katsu of the kometsuki beginning his eternal labor of rice-cleaning. Then the pretty musume of the inn opens the chamber to the fresh mountain air and the early sun, rolls back all the wooden shutters into their casings behind the gallery, takes down the brown mosquito net, brings a hibachi with freshly kindled charcoal for my morning smoke, and trips away to get our breakfast.

Early as it is when she returns, she brings word that a messenger has already arrived from the Guji, Senke Takanori, high descendant of the Goddess of the Sun. The messenger is a dignified young Shintō priest, clad in the ordinary Japanese full costume, but wearing also a superb pair of blue silken hakama, or Japanese ceremonial trousers, widening picturesquely towards the feet. He accepts my invitation to a cup of tea, and informs me that his august master is waiting for us at the temple.

This is delightful news, but we cannot go at once. Akira's attire is pronounced by the messenger to be defective. Akira must don fresh white tabi and put on hakama before going into the august presence: no one may enter thereinto without hakama. Happily Akira is able to borrow a pair of hakama from the landlord; and, after having arranged ourselves as neatly as we can, we take our way to the temple, guided by the messenger.

VII.

I am agreeably surprised to find, as we pass again under a magnificent bronze torii which I admired the night before, that the approaches to the temple lose very little of their imposing character when seen for the first time by sunlight. The majesty of the trees remains astonishing; the vista of the avenue is grand; and the vast spaces of groves and grounds to right and left are even more impressive than I had imagined. Multitudes of pilgrims are going and coming; but the whole population of a province might move along such an avenue without jostling. Before the gate of the first court a Shintō priest in full sacerdotal costume waits to receive us: an elderly man, with a pleasant kindly face. The messenger commits us to his charge, and vanishes through the gateway, while the elderly priest, whose name is Sasa, leads the way.

Already I can hear a heavy sound, as of surf, within the temple court; and as we advance the sound becomes sharper and recognizable—a volleying of handclaps. And passing the great gate, I see thousands of pilgrims before the Haiden, the same huge structure which I visited last night. None enter there: all stand before the dragon-swarming doorway, and cast their offerings into the money-chest placed before the threshold; many making contribution of small coin, the very poorest throwing only a handful of rice into the box.* Then they clap their hands and bow their heads before the threshold, and reverently gaze through the Hall of Prayer at the loftier edifice, the Holy of Holies, beyond it. Each pilgrim remains but a little while, and claps his hands but four times; yet so many are coming and going that the sound of the clapping is like the sound of a cataract.

Passing by the multitude of worshipers to the other side of the Haiden, we find ourselves at the foot of a broad flight of iron-bound steps leading to the great sanctuary—steps which I am told no European before me was ever permitted to approach. On the lower steps the priests of the temple, in full ceremonial costume, are waiting to receive us. Tall men they are, robed in violet and purple silks shot through with dragon-patterns in gold. Their lofty fantastic headdresses, their voluminous and beauti-

---

* Very large donations are made to this temple by wealthy men. The wooden tablets without the Haiden, on which are recorded the number of gifts and the names of the donors, mention several recent presents of 1,000 yen, or dollars; and donations of 500 yen are not uncommon. The gift of a high civil official ia rarely less than 50 yen.

ful costume, and the solemn immobility of their hierophantic attitudes make them at first sight seem marvelous statues only. Somehow or other there comes suddenly back to me the memory of a strange French print I used to wonder at when a child, representing a group of Assyrian astrologers. Only their eyes move as we approach. But as I reach the steps all simultaneously salute me with a most gracious bow, for I am the first foreign pilgrim to be honored by the privilege of an interview in the holy shrine itself with the princely hierophant, their master, descendant of the Goddess of the Sun—he who is still called by myriads of humble worshipers in the remoter districts of this ancient province Ikigami, "the living deity." Then all become absolutely statuesque again.

I remove my shoes, and am about to ascend the steps, when the tall priest who first received us before the outer gate indicates, by a single significant gesture, that religion and ancient custom require me, before ascending to the shrine of the god, to perform the ceremonial ablution. I hold out my hands; the priest pours the pure water over them thrice from a ladle-shaped vessel of bamboo with a long handle, and then gives me a little blue towel to wipe them upon, a votive towel with mysterious white characters upon it. Then we all ascend; I feeling very much like a clumsy barbarian in my ungraceful foreign garb.

Pausing at the head of the steps, the priest inquires my rank in society. For at Kitzuki hierarchy and hierarchical forms are maintained with a rigidity as precise as in the period of the gods; and there are special forms and regulations for the reception of visitors of every social grade. I do not know what flattering statements Akira may have made about me to the good priest; but the result is that I can rank only as a common person—which veracious fact doubtless saves me from some formalities which would have proved embarrassing, all ignorant as I still am of that finer and more complex etiquette in which the Japanese are the world's masters.

VIII.

The priest leads the way into a vast and lofty apartment opening for its entire length upon the broad gallery to which the stairway ascends. I have barely time to notice, while following him, that the chamber contains three immense shrines, forming alcoves on two sides of it. Of these, two are veiled by white curtains reaching from ceiling to matting—curtains decorated with perpendicular rows of black disks about four inches in diameter, each disk having in its center a golden blossom. But from before the third shrine, in the farther angle of the chamber, the curtains have been withdrawn; and these are of gold brocade, and the shrine before which they hang is the chief shrine, that of Oho-kuni-nushi-no-Kami. Within are visible only some of the ordinary emblems of Shintō, and the exterior of that Holy of Holies into which none may look. Before it a long low bench, covered with strange objects, has been placed, with one end toward the gallery and one toward the alcove. At the end of this bench, near the gallery, I see a majestic bearded figure, strangely coifed and robed all in white, seated upon the matted floor in hierophantic attitude. Our priestly guide motions us to take our places in front of him and to bow down before him. For this is Senke Takanori, the Guji of Kitzuki, to whom even in his own dwelling none may speak save on bended knee, descendant of the Goddess of the Sun, and still by multitudes revered in thought as a being superhuman. Prostrating myself before him, according to the customary code of Japanese politeness, I am sainted in return with that exquisite courtesy which puts a stranger immediately at ease. The priest who acted as our guide now sits down on the floor at the Guji's left hand; while the other priests, who followed us to the entrance of the sanctuary only, take their places upon the gallery without.

IX.

Senke Takanori is a youthful and powerful man. As he sits there before me in his immobile hieratic pose, with his strange lofty headdress, his heavy curling beard, and his ample snowy sacerdotal robe broadly spreading about him in statuesque undulations, he realizes for me all that I had imagined, from the suggestion of old Japanese pictures, about the personal majesty of the ancient princes and heroes. The dignity alone of the man would irresistibly compel respect; but with that feeling of respect there also flashes through me at once the thought of the profound reverence paid him by the population of the most ancient province of Japan, the idea of the immense spiritual power in his hands, the tradition of his divine descent, the sense of the immemorial nobility of his race; and my respect deepens into a feeling closely akin to awe. So motionless he is that he seems a sacred statue only—the temple image of one of his own deified ancestors. But the solemnity of the first few moments is agreeably broken by his first words, uttered in a low rich basso, while his dark, kindly eyes remain motionlessly fixed upon my face. Then my interpreter translates his greeting—large fine phrases of courtesy—to which I reply as I best know how, expressing my gratitude for the exceptional favor accorded me.

"You are, indeed," he responds through Akira, "the first European ever permitted to enter into the Oho-yashiro. Other Europeans have visited Kitzuki and a few have been allowed to enter the temple court; but you only have been admitted into the dwelling of the god. In past years, some strangers who desired to visit the temple out of common curiosity only were not allowed to approach even the court; but the letter of Mr. Nishida, explaining the object of your visit, has made it a pleasure for us to receive you thus."

Again I express my thanks; and after a second exchange of courtesies the conversation continues through the medium of Akira.

"Is not this great temple of Kitzuki," I inquire, "older than the temples of Ise?"

"Older by far," replies the Guji; "so old, indeed, that we do not well know the age of it. For it was first built by order of the Goddess of the Sun, in the time when deities alone existed. Then it was exceedingly magnificent—it was three hundred and twenty feet high. The beams and the pillars were larger than any existing timber could furnish; and the framework was bound together firmly with a rope made of taku* fiber, one thousand fathoms long.

"It was first rebuilt in the time of the Emperor Sui-nin.† The temple so rebuilt by order of the Emperor Sui-nin was called the Structure of the Iron Rings, because the pieces of the pillars, which were composed of the wood of many great trees, had been bound fast together with huge rings of iron. This temple was also splendid, but far less splendid than the first, which had been built by the gods, for its height was only one hundred and sixty feet.

"A third time the temple was rebuilt, in the reign of the Empress Sai-mei; but this third edifice was only eighty feet high. Since then the structure of the temple has never varied; and the plan then followed has been strictly preserved to the least detail in the construction of the present temple.

"The Oho-yashiro has been rebuilt twenty-eight times; and it has been the custom to rebuild it every sixty-one years. But in the long period of civil war it was not even repaired for more than a hundred years. In the fourth year of Tai-ei, one Amako Tsune Hisa, becoming Lord of Izumo, committed the great temple to the charge of a Buddhist priest, and even built pagodas about it, to the outrage of the holy traditions. But when the Amako family were succeeded by Moro Mototsugo, this latter purified the

---

* *Taku* is the Japanese name for the paper mulberry.
† See the curious legend in Professor Chamberlain's translation of the Kojiki.

temple, and restored the ancient festivals and ceremonies which before had been neglected."

"In the period when the temple was built upon a larger scale," I ask, "were the timbers for its construction obtained from the forests of Izurno?"

The priest Sasa, who guided us into the shrine, makes answer:

"It is recorded that on the fourth day of the seventh month of the third year of Ten-in one hundred large trees came floating to the seacoast of Ki-tzuki, and were stranded there by the tide. With these timbers the temple was rebuilt in the third year of Ei-kyu; and that structure was called the Building-of-the-Trees-which-came-floating. Also in the same third year of Ten-in, a great tree-trunk, one hundred and fifty feet long, was stranded on the seashore near a shrine called Ube-no-yashiro, at Miyanoshita-mura, which is in Inaba. Some people wanted to cut the tree; but they found a great serpent coiled around it, which looked so terrible that they became frightened, and prayed to the deity of Ube-no-yashiro to protect them; and the deity revealed himself, and said: 'Whensoever the great temple in Izumo is to be rebuilt, one of the gods of each province sends timber for the building of it, and this time it is my turn. Build quickly, therefore, with that great tree which is mine.' And therewith the god disappeared. From these and from other records we learn that the deities have always superintended or aided the building of the great temple of Kitzuki."

"In what part of the Oho-yashiro," I ask, "do the august deities assemble during the Kami-ari-zuki?"

"On the east and west sides of the inner court," replies the priest Sasa, "there are two long buildings called the Jiu-ku-sha. These contain nineteen shrines, no one of which is dedicated to any particular god; and we believe it is in the Jiu-ku-sha that the gods assemble."

"And how many pilgrims from other provinces visit the great shrine yearly?" I inquire.

"About two hundred and fifty thousand," the Guji answers. "But the number increases or diminishes according to the condition of the agricultural classes; the more prosperous the season, the larger the number of pilgrims. It rarely falls below two hundred thousand."

X.

Many other curious things the Guji and his chief priest then related to me; telling me the sacred name of each of the courts, and of the fences and holy groves and the multitudinous shrines and their divinities; even the names of the great pillars of the temple, which are nine in number, the central pillar being called the august Heart-Pillar of the Middle. All things within the temple grounds have sacred names, even the torii and the bridges.

The priest Sasa called my attention to the fact that the great shrine of Oho-kuni-nushi-no-Kami faces west, though the great temple faces east, like all Shintō temples. In the other two shrines of the same apartment, both facing east, are the first divine Ko-kuzō of Izumo, his seventeenth descendant, and the father of Nominosukune, wise prince and famous wrestler. For in the reign of the Emperor Sui-nin one Kehaya of Taima had boasted that no man alive was equal to himself in strength. Nominosukune, by the emperor's command, wrestled with Kehaya, and threw him down so mightily that Kehaya's ghost departed from him. This was the beginning of wrestling in Japan; and wrestlers still pray unto Nominosukune for power and skill.

There are so many other shrines that I could not enumerate the names of all their deities without wearying those readers unfamiliar with the traditions and legends of Shintō. But nearly all those divinities who appear in the legend of the Master of the Great Land are still believed to dwell here with him, and here their shrines are: the beautiful one, magically born from the jewel worn in the tresses of the Goddess of the Sun, and called by men the Torrent Mist Princess; and the daughter of the Lord of the World of Shadows, she who loved the Master of the Great

Land, and followed him out of the place of ghosts to become his wife; and the deity called "Wondrous-Eight-Spirits," grandson of the "Deity of Water-Gates," who first made a fire-drill and platters of red clay for the august banquet of the god at Kitzuki; and many of the heavenly kindred of these.

XI.

The priest Sasa also tells me this:

When Naomasu, grandson of the great Iyeyasu, and first daimyō of that mighty Matsudaira family who ruled Izumo for two hundred and fifty years, came to this province, he paid a visit to the Temple of Kitzuki, and demanded that the miya of the shrine within the shrine should be opened that he might look upon the sacred objects—upon the shintai, or body of the deity. And this being an impious desire, both of the Kokuzō* unitedly protested against it. But despite their remonstrances and their pleadings, he persisted angrily in his demand, so that the priests found themselves compelled to open the shrine. And the miya being opened, Naomasu saw within it a great awabi† of nine holes—so large that it concealed everything behind it. And when he drew still nearer to look, suddenly the awabi changed itself into a huge serpent more than fifty feet in length‡—and it massed its black coils before the opening of the shrine, and hissed like the sound of raging fire, and looked so terrible, that Naomasu and those

---

* From a remote period there have been two Kokuzō in theory, although but one incumbent. Two branches of the same family claim ancestral right to the office—the rival houses of Senke and Kitajima. The government has decided always in favor of the former; but the head of the Kitajima family has usually been appointed Vice-Kokuzō. A Kitajima today holds the lesser office.

The term Kokuzō is not, correctly speaking, a spiritual, but rather a temporal title. The Kokuzō has always been the emperor's deputy to Kitzuki—the person appointed to worship the deity in the emperor's stead; but the real spiritual title of such a deputy is that still borne by the present Guji—"Mitsuye-Shiro."

† *Haliotis tuberculata*, or "sea-ear." The curious shell is pierced with a row of holes, which vary in number with the age and size of the animal it shields.

‡ Literally, "ten hirō," or Japanese fathoms.

with him fled away—having been able to see naught else. And ever thereafter Naomasu feared and reverenced the god.

XII.

The Guji then calls my attention to the quaint relics lying upon the long low bench between us, which is covered with white silk: a metal mirror, found in preparing the foundation of the temple when rebuilt many hundred years ago; agatama jewels of onyx and jasper; a Chinese flute made of jade; a few superb swords, the gifts of shōguns and emperors; helmets of splendid antique workmanship; and a bundle of enormous arrows with double-pointed heads of brass, fork-shaped and keenly edged.

After I have looked at these relics and learned something of their history, the Guji rises and says to me, "Now we will show you the ancient fire-drill of Kitzuki, with which the sacred fire is kindled."

Descending the steps, we pass again before the Haiden, and enter a spacious edifice on one side of the court, of nearly equal size with the Hall of Prayer. Here I am agreeably surprised to find a long handsome mahogany table at one end of the main apartment into which we are ushered, and mahogany chairs placed all about it for the reception of guests. I am motioned to one chair, my interpreter to another; and the Guji and his priests take their seats, also at the table. Then an attendant sets before me a handsome bronze stand about three feet long, on which rests an oblong something carefully wrapped in snow-white cloths. The Guji removes the wrappings; and I behold the most primitive form of fire-drill known to exist in the Orient.* It is simply a very thick piece of solid white plank, about two and a half feet long, with a line of holes drilled along its upper edge, so that the upper part of each hole breaks through the sides of the plank. The sticks which produce the fire, when fixed in the holes and

---

* The fire-drill used at the Shintō temples of Ise is far more complicated in construction, and certainly represents a much more advanced stage of mechanical knowledge than the Kitzuki fire-drill indicates.

rapidly rubbed between the palms of the hands, are made of a lighter kind of white wood; they are about two feet long, and as thick as a common lead pencil.

While I am yet examining this curious simple utensil, the invention of which tradition ascribes to the gods, and modern science to the earliest childhood of the human race, a priest places upon the table a light, large wooden box, about three feet long, eighteen inches wide, and four inches high at the sides, but higher in the middle, as the top is arched like the shell of a tortoise. This object is made of the same hinoki wood as the drill; and two long slender sticks are laid beside it. I at first suppose it to be another fire-drill. But no human being could guess what it really is. It is called the koto-ita, and is one of the most primitive of musical instruments; the little sticks are used to strike it. At a sign from the Guji two priests place the box upon the floor, seat themselves on either side of it, and taking up the little sticks begin to strike the lid with them, alternately and slowly, at the same time uttering a most singular and monotonous chant. One intones only the sounds, "*Ang! ang!*" and the other responds, "*Ong! ong!*" The koto-ita gives out a sharp, dead, hollow sound as the sticks fall upon it in time to each utterance of "*Ang! ang!*" "*Ong! ong!*"*

XIII.

These things I learn:

Each year the temple receives a new fire-drill; but the fire-drill is never made in Kitzuki, but in Kumano, where the traditional regulations as to the manner of making it have been preserved from the time of the gods. For the first Kokuzō of Izumo, on becoming pontiff, received the fire-drill for the great temple from the hands of the deity who was the younger brother of the Sun-Goddess, and is now enshrined at Kumano. And from

---

* During a subsequent visit to Kitzuki I learned that the koto-ita is used only as a sort of primitive "tuning" instrument: it gives the right tone for the true chant which I did not hear during my first visit. The true chant, an ancient Shinto hymn, is always preceded by the performance above described.

his time the firedrills for the Oho-yashiro of Kitzuki have been made only at Kumano.

Until very recent times the ceremony of delivering the new fire-drill to the Guji of Kitzuki always took place at the great temple of Oba, on the occasion of the festival called Unohi-matsuri. This ancient festival, which used to be held in the eleventh month, became obsolete after the Revolution everywhere except at Oba in Izumo, where Izanami-no-Kami, the mother of gods and men, is enshrined.

Once a year, on this festival, the Kokuzō always went to Oba, taking with him a gift of double ricecakes. At Oba he was met by a personage called the Kame-da-yu, who brought the fire-drill from Kumano and delivered it to the priests at Oba. According to tradition, the Kame-da-yu had to act a somewhat ludicrous role, so that no Shintō priest ever cared to perform the part, and a man was hired for it. The duty of the Kame-da-yu was to find fault with the gift presented to the temple by the Kokuzō; and in this district of Japan there is still a proverbial saying about one who is prone to find fault without reason, "He is like the Kame-da-yu."

The Kame-da-yu would inspect the rice-cakes and begin to criticise them. "They are much smaller this year," he would observe, "than they were last year." The priests would reply: "Oh, you are honorably mistaken; they are in truth very much larger." "The color is not so white this year as it was last year; and the rice-flour is not finely ground." For all these imaginary faults of the mochi the priests would offer elaborate explanations or apologies.

At the conclusion of the ceremony the sakaki branches used in it were eagerly bid for, and sold at high prices, being believed to possess talismanic virtues.

XIV.

It nearly always happened that there was a great storm either on the day the Kokuzō went to Oba, or upon the day he returned therefrom. The journey had to be made during what is in Izumo the most stormy season (December by the new calendar). But in popular belief these storms were in some tremendous way connected with the divine personality of the Kokuzo, whose attributes would thus appear to present some curious analogy with those of the Dragon-God. Be that as it may, the great periodical storms of the season are still in this province called Kokuzō-aré* and it is still the custom in Izumo to say merrily to the guest who arrives or departs in a time of tempest, "Why, you are like the Kokuzō!"

XV.

The Guji waves his hand, and from the farther end of the huge apartment there comes a sudden burst of strange music—a sound of drums and bamboo flutes; and turning to look, I see the musicians, three men, seated upon the matting, and a young girl with them. At another sign from the Guji the girl rises. She is barefooted and robed in snowy white, a virgin priestess. But below the hem of the white robe I see the gleam of hakama of crimson silk. She advances to a little table in the middle of the apartment, upon which a queer instrument is lying, shaped somewhat like a branch with twigs bent downward, from each of which hangs a little bell. Taking this curious object in both hands, she begins a sacred dance, unlike anything I ever saw before. Her every movement is a poem, because she is very graceful; and yet her performance could scarcely be called a dance, as we understand the word; it is rather a light swift walk within a circle, during which she shakes the instrument at regular intervals, making all the little bells ring. Her face remains impassive as a beautiful mask, placid and sweet as the face of a dreaming Kwannon; and her white feet are pure of line as the feet of a marble nymph. Altogether, with her snowy raiment and white flesh and passionless face, she seems rather a beautiful living statue than

---

* The tempest of the Kokuzō.

a Japanese maiden. And all the while the weird flutes sob and shrill, and the muttering of the drums is like an incantation.

What I have seen is called the Dance of the Miko, the Divineress.

XVI.

Then we visit the other edifices belonging to the temple: the storehouse; the library; the hall of assembly, a massive structure two stories high, where may be seen the portraits of the Thirty-Six Great Poets, painted by Tosano Mitsu Oki more than a thousand years ago, and still in an excellent state of preservation. Here we are also shown a curious magazine, published monthly by the temple—a record of Shintō news, and a medium for the discussion of questions relating to the archaic texts.

After we have seen all the curiosities of the temple, the Guji invites us to his private residence near the temple to show us other treasures—letters of Yoritomo, of Hideyoshi, of Iyeyasu; documents in the handwriting of the ancient emperors and the great shōguns, hundreds of which precious manuscripts he keeps in a cedar chest. In case of fire the immediate removal of this chest to a place of safety would be the first duty of the servants of the household.

Within his own house, the Guji, attired in ordinary Japanese full dress only, appears no less dignified as a private gentleman than he first seemed as pontiff in his voluminous snowy robe. But no host could be more kindly or more courteous or more generous. I am also much impressed by the fine appearance of his suite of young priests, now dressed, like himself, in the national costume; by the handsome, aquiline, aristocratic faces, totally different from those of ordinary Japanese—faces suggesting the soldier rather than the priest. One young man has a superb pair of thick black moustaches, which is something rarely to be seen in Japan.

At parting our kind host presents me with the ofuda, or sacred charms given to pilgrims—two pretty images of the chief deities of Kitzuki—and a number of documents relating to the history of the temple and of its treasures.

XVII.

Having taken our leave of the kind Guji and his suite, we are guided to Inasa-no-hama, a little sea-bay at the rear of the town, by the priest Sasa, and another kannushi. This priest Sasa is a skilled poet and a man of deep learning in Shintō history and the archaic texts of the sacred books. He relates to us many curious legends as we stroll along the shore.

This shore, now a popular bathing resort—bordered with airy little inns and pretty tea-houses—is called Inasa because of a Shintō tradition that here the god Oho-kuni-nushi-no-Kami, the Master-of-the-Great-Land, was first asked to resign his dominion over the land of Izumo in favor of Masa-ka-a-katsukachi-hayabi-ame-no-oshi-ho-mimi-no-mikoto; the word Inasa signifying "Will you consent or not?"* In the thirty-second section of the first volume of the Kojiki the legend is written: I cite a part thereof:

"The two deities (Tori-bune-no-Kami and Takemika-dzu-chi-no-wo-no-Kami), descending to the little shore of Inasa in the land of Izumo, drew their swords ten handbreadths long, and stuck them upside down on the crest of a wave, and seated themselves cross-legged upon the points of the swords, and asked the Deity Master-of-the-Great-Land, saying: 'The Heaven-Shining-Great-August-Deity and the High-Integrating-Deity have charged us and sent us to ask, saying: "We have deigned to charge our august child with thy dominion, as the land which he should govern. So how is thy heart?"' He replied, saying: 'I am unable to say. My son Ya-he-koto-shironushi-no-Kami will be the one to tell you'...So they asked the Deity again, saying: 'Thy son Kotoshiro-nushi-no-Kami has now spoken thus. Hast thou

---

* That is, according to Motoöri, the commentator. Or more briefly "No or yes?" This is, according to Professor Chamberlain, a mere fanciful etymology; but it is accepted by Shintō faith, and for that reason only is here given.

other sons who should speak?' He spoke again, saying: 'There is my other son, Take-mi-na-gata-no Kami'...While he was thus speaking the Deity Take-mi-na-gata-no-Kami came up [from the sea], bearing on the tips of his fingers a rock which it would take a thousand men to lift, and said, 'I should like to have a trial of strength.'"

Here, close to the beach, stands a little miya called Inasa-no-kami-no-yashiro, or, the Temple of the God of Inasa; and therein Take-mika-dzu-chi-no-Kami, who conquered in the trial of strength, is enshrined. And near the shore the great rock which Take-mi-na-gatano-Kami lifted upon the tips of his fingers, may be seen rising from the water. And it is called Chihikinoiha.

We invite the priests to dine with us at one of the little inns facing the breezy sea; and there we talk about many things, but particularly about Kitzuki and the Kokuzo.

XVIII.

Only a generation ago the religious power of the Kokuzō extended over the whole of the province of the gods; he was in fact as well as in name the Spiritual Governor of Izumo. His jurisdiction does not now extend beyond the limits of Kitzuki, and his correct title is no longer Kokuzō, but Guji.* Yet to the simple-hearted people of remoter districts he is still a divine or semi-divine being, and is mentioned by his ancient title, the inheritance of his race from the epoch of the gods. How profound a reverence was paid to him in former ages can scarcely be imagined by any who have not long lived among the country folk of Izumo. Outside of Japan perhaps no human being, except the Dalai Lama of Tibet, was so humbly venerated and so religiously beloved. Within Japan itself only the Son of Heaven, the "Tenshi-Sama," standing as mediator "between his people

---

* The title of Kokuzō, indeed, still exists, but it is now merely honorary, having no official duties connected with it. It is actually borne by Baron Senke, the father of Senke Takanori, residing in the capital. The active religious duties of the Mitsuye-shiro now devolve upon the Guji.

and the Sun" received like homage; but the worshipful reverence paid to the Mikado was paid to a dream rather than to a
person, to a name rather than to a reality, for the Tenshi-Sama
was ever invisible as a deity "divinely retired," and in popular
belief no man could look upon his face and live.* Invisibility and
mystery vastly enhanced the divine legend of the Mikado. But
the Kokuzō, within his own province, though visible to the multitude and often journeying among the people, received almost
equal devotion; so that his material power, though rarely, if ever,
exercised, was scarcely less than that of the Daimyō of Izumo
himself. It was indeed large enough to render him a person
with whom the shōgunate would have deemed it wise policy to
remain upon good terms. An ancestor of the present Guji even
defied the great Taikō Hideyoshi, refusing to obey his command
to furnish troops with the haughty answer that he would receive
no order from a man of common birth.† This defiance cost the
family the loss of a large part of its estates by confiscation, but
the real power of the Kokuzō remained unchanged until the
period of the new civilization.

Out of many hundreds of stories of a similar nature, two little
traditions may be cited as illustrations of the reverence in which
the Kokuzō was formerly held.

It is related that there was a man who, believing himself to
have become rich by favor of the Daikoku of Kitzuki, desired
to express his gratitude by a gift of robes to the Kokuzō. The
Kokuzō courteously declined the proffer; but the pious worshiper persisted in his purpose, and ordered a tailor to make
the robes. The tailor, having made them, demanded a price that
almost took his patron's breath away. Being asked to give his reason for demanding such a price, he made answer: "Having made
robes for the Kokuzō, I cannot hereafter make garments for any

* As late as 1890 I was told by a foreign resident, who had traveled much in the interior of the country, that in certain districts many old people may be met with who still
believe that to see the face of the emperor is "to become a Buddha"—that is, to die.

† Hideyoshi, as is well known, was not of princely extraction.

other person. Therefore I must have money enough to support me for the rest of my life."

The second story dates back to about one hundred and seventy years ago.

Among the samurai of the Matsue clan in the time of Nobukori, fifth daimyō of the Matsudaira family, there was one Sugihara Kitoji, who was stationed in some military capacity at Kitzuki. He was a great favorite with the Kokuzō, and used often to play at chess with him. During a game, one evening, this officer suddenly became as one paralyzed, unable to move or speak. For a moment all was anxiety and confusion; but the Kokuzō said: "I know the cause. My friend was smoking, and although smoking disagrees with me, I did not wish to spoil his pleasure by telling him so. But the Kami, seeing that I felt ill, became angry with him. Now I shall make him well." Whereupon the Kokuzō uttered some magical word, and the officer was immediately as well as before.

XIX.

Once more we are journeying through the silence of this holy land of mists and of legends; wending our way between green leagues of ripening rice white sprinkled with arrows of prayer, between the far processions of blue and verdant peaks whose names are the names of gods. We have left Kitzuki far behind. But as in a dream I still see the mighty avenue, the long succession of torii with their colossal shimenawa, the majestic face of the Guji, the kindly smile of the priest Sasa, and the girl priestess in her snowy robes dancing her beautiful ghostly dance. It seems to me that I can still hear the sound of the clapping of hands, like the crashing of a torrent. I cannot suppress some slight exultation at the thought that I have been allowed to see what no other foreigner has been privileged to see—the interior of Japan's most ancient shrine, and those sacred utensils and quaint rites of primitive worship so well worthy the study of the anthropologist and the evolutionist.

But to have seen Kitzuki as I saw it is also to have seen something much more than a single wonderful temple. To see Kitzuki is to see the living center of Shintō, and to feel the life-pulse of the ancient faith, throbbing as mightily in this nineteenth century as ever in that unknown past whereof the Kojiki itself, though written in a tongue no longer spoken, is but a modern record.* Buddhism, changing form or slowly decaying through the centuries, might seem doomed to pass away at last from this Japan to which it came only as an alien faith; but Shintō, unchanging and vitally unchanged, still remains all dominant in the land of its birth, and only seems to gain in power and dignity with time.† Buddhism has a voluminous theology, a profound philosophy, a literature vast as the sea. Shintō has no philosophy, no code of ethics, no metaphysics; and yet, by its very immateriality, it can resist the invasion of Occidental religious thought as no other Orient faith can. Shintō extends a welcome to Western science, but remains the irresistible opponent of Western religion; and the foreign zealots who would strive against it are astounded to find the power that foils their uttermost efforts indefinable as magnetism and invulnerable as air. Indeed the best of our scholars have never been able to tell us what Shintō is. To some it appears to be merely ancestor-worship, to others ancestor-worship combined with nature-worship; to others, again, it seems to be no religion at all; to the missionary of the more ignorant class it is the worst form of heathenism. Doubtless the difficulty of explaining Shintō has been due simply to the fact that the sinologists have sought for the source of it in books: in the Kojiki and the Nihongi, which are its histories; in the Norito, which are its prayers; in the commentaries of Motowori and

---

* The Kojiki dates back, as a written work, only to A.D. 712. But its legends and records are known to have existed in the form of oral literature from a much more ancient time.

† In certain provinces of Japan Buddhism practically absorbed Shintō in other centuries, but in Izumo Shintō absorbed Buddhism; and now that Shintō is supported by the state there is a visible tendency to eliminate from its cult certain elements of Buddhist origin.

Hirata, who were its greatest scholars. But the reality of Shintō lives not in books, nor in rites, nor in commandments, but in the national heart, of which it is the highest emotional religious expression, immortal and ever young. Far underlying all the surface crop of quaint superstitions and artless myths and fantastic magic there thrills a mighty spiritual force, the whole soul of a race with all its impulses and powers and intuitions. He who would know what Shintō is must learn to know that mysterious soul in which the sense of beauty and the power of art and the fire of heroism and magnetism of loyalty and the emotion of faith have become inherent, immanent, unconscious, instinctive.

Trusting to know something of that Oriental soul in whose joyous love of nature and of life even the unlearned may discern a strange likeness to the soul of the old Greek race, I trust also that I may presume some day to speak of the great living power of that faith now called Shintō, but more anciently Kami-no-michi, or "The Way of the Gods."

9

IN THE CAVE OF THE CHILDREN'S GHOSTS

I.

It is forbidden to go to Kaka if there be wind enough "to move three hairs."

Now an absolutely windless day is rare on this wild western coast. Over the Japanese Sea, from Korea, or China, or boreal Siberia, some west or northwest breeze is nearly always blowing. So that I have had to wait many long months for a good chance to visit Kaka.

Taking the shortest route, one goes first to Mitsuara from Matsue, either by kuruma or on foot. By kuruma this little journey occupies nearly two hours and a half, though the distance is scarcely seven miles, the road being one of the worst in all Izumo. You leave Matsue to enter at once into a broad plain, level as a lake, all occupied by rice-fields and walled in by wooded hills. The path, barely wide enough for a single vehicle, traverses this green desolation, climbs the heights beyond it, and descends again into another and a larger level of rice-fields, surrounded also by hills. The path over the second line of hills is much steeper; then a third rice-plain must be crossed and a third chain of green altitudes, lofty enough to merit the name of mountains. Of course one must make the ascent on foot: it is no small labor for a kurumaya to pull even an empty kuruma up to the top; and how he manages to do so without breaking the little vehicle is a mystery, for the path is stony and rough as the bed of a torrent. A tiresome climb I find it; but the landscape view from the summit is more than compensation.

Then descending, there remains a fourth and last wide level of rice-fields to traverse. The absolute flatness of the great plains between the ranges, and the singular way in which these latter "fence off" the country into sections, are matters for surprise even in a land of surprises like Japan. Beyond the fourth rice-valley there is a fourth hillchain, lower and richly wooded, on reaching the base of which the traveler must finally abandon his kuruma, and proceed over the hills on foot. Behind them lies the sea. But the very worst bit of the journey now begins. The path makes an easy winding ascent between bamboo growths and young pine and other vegetation for a shaded quarter of a mile, passing before various little shrines and pretty homesteads surrounded by high-hedged gardens. Then it suddenly breaks into steps, or rather ruins of steps—partly hewn in the rock, partly built, everywhere breached and worn—which descend, all edgeless, in a manner amazingly precipitous, to the village of Mitsuura. With straw sandals, which never slip, the country folk can nimbly hurry up or down, such a path; but with foreign footgear one slips at nearly every step; and when you reach the bottom at last, the wonder of how you managed to get there, even with the assistance of your faithful kurumaya, keeps you for a moment quite unconscious of the fact that you are already in Mitsu-ura.

II.

Mitsu-ura stands with its back to the mountains, at the end of a small deep bay hemmed in by very high cliffs. There is only one narrow strip of beach at the foot of the heights; and the village owes its existence to that fact, for beaches are rare on this part of the coast. Crowded between the cliffs and the sea, the houses have a painfully compressed aspect; and somehow the greater number give one the impression of things created out of wrecks of junks. The little streets, or rather alleys, are full of boats and skeletons of boats and boat timbers; and everywhere, suspended from bamboo poles much taller than the houses, immense bright brown fishing-nets are drying in the sun. The whole curve of the beach is also lined with boats, lying side by side, so that I wonder how it will be possible to get to the water's edge without climbing over them. There is no hotel; but I find hospitality in a fisherman's dwelling, while my kurumaya goes somewhere to hire a boat for Kaka-ura.

In less than ten minutes there is a crowd of several hundred people about the house, half-clad adults and perfectly naked boys. They blockade the building; they obscure the light by filling up the doorways and climbing into the windows to look at the foreigner. The aged proprietor of the cottage protests in vain, says harsh things; the crowd only thickens. Then all the sliding screens are closed. But in the paper panes there are holes; and at all the lower holes the curious take regular turns at peeping. At a higher hole I do some peeping myself. The crowd is not prepossessing: it is squalid, dull-featured, remarkably ugly. But it is gentle and silent; and there are one or two pretty faces in it which seem extraordinary by reason of the general homeliness of the rest.

At last my kurumaya has succeeded in making arrangements for a boat; and I effect a sortie to the beach, followed by the kurumaya and by all my besiegers. Boats have been moved to make a passage for us, and we embark without trouble of any sort. Our crew consists of two scullers—an old man at the stern, wearing only a rokushaku about his loins, and an old woman at the bow, fully robed and wearing an immense straw hat shaped like a mushroom. Both of course stand to their work and it would be hard to say which is the stronger or more skillful sculler. We passengers squat Oriental fashion upon a mat in the center of the boat, where a hibachi, well stocked with glowing charcoal, invites us to smoke.

III.

The day is clear blue to the end of the world, with a faint wind from the east, barely enough to wrinkle the sea, certainly more than enough to "move three hairs." Nevertheless the boatwoman and the boatman do not seem anxious; and I begin to wonder whether the famous prohibition is not a myth. So delightful the transparent water looks, that before we have left the bay I have to yield to its temptation by plunging in and swimming after the boat. When I climb back on board we are rounding the promontory on the right; and the little vessel begins to rock. Even under this thin wind the sea is moving in long swells. And as we pass into the open, following the westward trend of the land, we find ourselves gliding over an ink-black depth, in front of one of the very grimmest coasts I ever saw.

A tremendous line of dark iron-colored cliffs, towering sheer from the sea without a beach, and with never a speck of green below their summits; and here and there along this terrible front, monstrous beetlings, breaches, fissures, earthquake rendings, and topplings-down. Enormous fractures show lines of strata pitched up skyward, or plunging down into the ocean with the long fall of cubic miles of cliff. Before fantastic gaps, prodigious masses of rock, of all nightmarish shapes, rise from profundities unfathomed. And though the wind today seems trying to hold its breath, white breakers are reaching far up the cliffs, and dashing their foam into the faces of the splintered crags. We are too far to hear the thunder of them; but their ominous sheetlightning fully explains to me the story of the three hairs. Along this goblin coast on a wild day there would be no possible chance for the strongest swimmer or the stoutest boat; there is no place for the foot, no hold for the hand, nothing but the sea raving against a precipice of iron. Even today, under the feeblest breath imaginable, great swells deluge us with spray as they splash past. And for two long hours this jagged frowning coast towers by; and, as we toil on, rocks rise around us like black teeth; and always, far away, the foam-bursts gleam at the feet of the implacable cliffs. But there are no sounds save the lapping and plashing of passing swells, and the monotonous creaking of the sculls upon their pegs of wood.

At last, at last, a bay—a beautiful large bay, with a demilune of soft green hills about it, overtopped by far blue mountains—and in the very farthest point of the bay a miniature village, in front of which many junks are riding at anchor: Kaka-ura.

But we do not go to Kaka-ura yet; the Kukedo are not there. We cross the broad opening of the bay, journey along another half mile of ghastly sea precipice, and finally make for a lofty promontory of naked Plutonic rock. We pass by its menacing foot, slip along its side, and lo! at an angle opens the arched mouth of a wonderful cavern, broad, lofty, and full of light, with no floor but the sea. Beneath us, as we slip into it, I can see rocks fully twenty feet down. The water is clear as air. This is the Shin-Kukedo, called the New Cavern, though assuredly older than human record by a hundred thousand years.

IV.

A more beautiful sea-cave could scarcely be imagined. The sea, tunneling the tall promontory through and through, has also, like a great architect, ribbed and groined and polished its mighty work. The arch of the entrance is certainly twenty feet above the deep water, and fifteen wide; and trillions of wave tongues have licked the vault and walls into wondrous smoothness. As we proceed, the rockroof steadily heightens and the way widens. Then we unexpectedly glide under a heavy shower of fresh water, dripping from overhead. This spring is called the ō-chōzubachi or mitarashi* of Shin-Ku-kedo-San. From the high vault at this

---

* Such are the names given to the water-vessels or cisterns at which Shintō worshipers must wash their hands and rinse their mouths ere praying to the Kami. A mitarashi or ō-chōzubachi is placed before every Shintō temple. The pilgrim to Shin-Kukedo-San should perform this ceremonial ablution at the little rock-spring above described, before entering the sacred cave. Here even the gods of the cave are said to wash after having passed through the seawater.

point it is believed that a great stone will detach itself and fall upon any evil-hearted person who should attempt to enter the cave. I safely pass through the ordeal!

Suddenly as we advance the boatwoman takes a stone from the bottom of the boat, and with it begins to rap heavily on the bow; and the hollow echoing is reiterated with thundering repercussions through all the cave. And in another instant we pass into a great burst of light, coming from the mouth of a magnificent and lofty archway on the left, opening into the cavern at right angles. This explains the singular illumination of the long vault, which at first seemed to come from beneath; for while the opening was still invisible all the water appeared to be suffused with light. Through this grand arch, between outlying rocks, a strip of beautiful green undulating coast appears, over miles of azure water. We glide on toward the third entrance to the Kukedo, opposite to that by which we came in; and enter the dwelling-place of the Kami and the Hotoke, for this grotto is sacred both to Shintō and to Buddhist faith. Here the Kukedo reaches its greatest altitude and breadth. Its vault is fully forty feet above the water, and its walls thirty feet apart. Far up on the right, near the roof, is a projecting white rock, and above the rock an orifice wherefrom a slow stream drips, seeming white as the rock itself.

This is the legendary Fountain of Jizō, the fountain of milk at which the souls of dead children drink. Sometimes it flows more swiftly, sometimes more slowly; but it never ceases by night or day. And mothers suffering from want of milk come hither to pray that milk may be given unto them; and their prayer is heard. And mothers having more milk than their infants need come hither also, and pray to Jizō that so much as they can give may be taken for the dead children; and their prayer is heard, and their milk diminishes.

At least thus the peasants of Izumo say.

And the echoing of the swells leaping against the rocks without, the rushing and rippling of the tide against the walls, the heavy rain of percolating water, sounds of lapping and gurgling and splashing, and sounds of mysterious origin coming from no visible where, make it difficult for us to hear each other speak. The cavern seems full of voices, as if a host of invisible beings were holding tumultuous converse.

Below us all the deeply lying rocks are naked to view as if seen through glass. It seems to me that nothing could be more delightful than to swim through this cave and let one's self drift with the sea-currents through all its cool shadows. But as I am on the point of jumping in, all the other occupants of the boat utter wild cries of protest. It is certain death! men who jumped in here only six months ago were never heard of again! this is sacred water, Kami-no-umi!

And as if to conjure away my temptation, the boatwoman again seizes her little stone and raps fearfully upon the bow. On finding, however, that I am not sufficiently deterred by these stories of sudden death and disappearance, she suddenly screams into my ear the magical word,

"SAMÉ!"

Sharks! I have no longer any desire whatever to swim through the many-sounding halls of Shin-Ku-kedo-San.

I have lived in the tropics!

And we start forthwith for Kyū-Kukedo-San, the Ancient Cavern.

V.

For the ghastly fancies about the Kami-no-umi, the word "samé" afforded a satisfactory explanation. But why that long, loud, weird rapping on the bow with a stone evidently kept on board for no other purpose? There was an exaggerated earnestness about the action which gave me an uncanny sensation— something like that which moves a man while walking at night upon a lonesome road, full of queer shadows, to sing at the top of his voice. The boatwoman at first declares that the rapping was made only for the sake of the singular echo. But after some cautious further questioning, I discover a much more sinister reason for the performance. Moreover, I learn that all the sea-men and seawomen of this coast do the same thing when passing through perilous places, or places believed to be haunted by the Ma. What are the Ma?

Goblins!

VI.

From the caves of the Kami we retrace our course for about a quarter of a mile; then make directly for an immense perpendicular wrinkle in the long line of black cliffs. Immediately before it a huge dark rock towers from the sea, whipped by the foam of breaking swells. Rounding it, we glide behind it into still water and shadow, the shadow of a monstrous cleft in the precipice of the coast. And suddenly, at an unsuspected angle, the mouth of another cavern yawns before us; and in another moment our boat touches its threshold of stone with a little shock that sends a long sonorous echo, like the sound of a temple drum, booming through all the abysmal place. A single glance tells me whither we have come. Far within the dusk I see the face of a Jizō, smiling in pale stone, and before him, and all about him, a weird congregation of gray shapes without shape—a host of fantasticalities that strangely suggest the wreck of a cemetery. From the sea the ribbed floor of the cavern slopes high through deepening shadows back to the black mouth of a farther grotto; and all that slope is covered with hundreds and thousands of forms like shattered haka. But as the eyes grow accustomed to the gloaming it becomes manifest that these were never haka; they are only little towers of stone and pebbles deftly piled up by long and patient labor.

"*Shinda kodomo no shigoto,*" my kurumaya murmurs with a compassionate smile; "all this is the work of the dead children."

And we disembark. By counsel, I take off my shoes and put on a pair of zori, or straw sandals provided for me, as the rock is extremely slippery. The others land barefoot. But how to proceed soon becomes a puzzle: the countless stone-piles stand so close together that no space for the foot seems to be left between them.

"*Mada michi ga arimasŭ!*" the boatwoman announces, leading the way. There is a path.

Following after her, we squeeze ourselves between the wall of the cavern on the right and some large rocks, and discover a very, very narrow passage left open between the stone-towers. But we are warned to be careful for the sake of the little ghosts: if any of their work be overturned, they will cry. So we move very cautiously and slowly across the cave to a space bare of stone-heaps, where the rocky floor is covered with a thin layer of sand, detritus of a crumbling ledge above it. And in that sand I see light prints of little feet, children's feet, tiny naked feet, only three or four inches long—*the footprints of the infant ghosts.*

Had we come earlier, the boatwoman says, we should have seen many more. For 'tis at night, when the soil of the cavern is moist with dews and drippings from the roof, that they leave their footprints upon it; but when the heat of the day comes, and the sand and the rocks dry up, the prints of the little feet vanish away.

There are only three footprints visible, but these are singularly distinct. One points toward the wall of the cavern; the others toward the sea. Here and there, upon ledges or projections of the rock, all about the cavern, tiny straw sandals—children's zori—are lying: offerings of pilgrims to the little ones, that their feet may not be wounded by the stones. But all the ghostly foot prints are prints of naked feet.

Then we advance, picking our way very, very carefully between the stone-towers, toward the mouth of the inner grotto, and reach the statue of Jizō before it. A seated Jizō, carven in granite, holding in one hand the mystic jewel by virtue of which all wishes may be fulfilled; in the other his shakujo, or pilgrim's staff. Before him (strange condescension of Shintō faith!) a little torii has been erected, and a pair of gohei! Evidently this gentle divinity has no enemies; at the feet of the lover of children's ghosts, both creeds unite in tender homage.

I said feet. But this subterranean Jizō has only one foot. The carven lotus on which he reposes has been fractured and broken: two great petals are missing; and the right foot, which must have rested upon one of them, has been knocked off at the ankle. This, I learn upon inquiry, has been done by the waves. In times of great storm the billows rush into the cavern like raging Oni, and sweep all the little stone towers into shingle as they come, and dash the statues against the rocks. But always during the first still night after the tempest the work is reconstructed as before!

"*Hotoke ga shimpai shite; naki-naki tsumi naoshimasŭ.*" They make mourning, the hotoke; weeping, they pile up the stones again, they rebuild their towers of prayer.

All about the black mouth of the inner grotto the bone-colored rock bears some resemblance to a vast pair of yawning jaws. Downward from this sinister portal the cavern-floor slopes into a deeper and darker aperture. And within it, as one's eyes become accustomed to the gloom, a still larger vision of stone towers is disclosed; and beyond them, in a nook of the grotto, three other statues of Jizō smile, each one with a torii before it. Here I have the misfortune to upset first one stone-pile and then another, while trying to proceed. My kurumaya, almost simultaneously, ruins a third. To atone therefor, we must build six new towers, or double the number of those which we have cast down. And while we are thus busied, the boatwoman tells of two fishermen who remained in the cavern through all one night, and heard the humming of the viewless gathering, and sounds of speech, like the speech of children murmuring in multitude.

VII.

Only at night do the shadowy children come to build their little stone-heaps at the feet of Jizō; and it is said that every night the stones are changed. When I ask why they do not work by day, when there is none to see them, I am answered: "O-Hi-San*

---

* "The August Fire-Lady;" or, "the August Sun-Lady," Ama-terasu-oho-mi-Kami.

might see them; *the dead exceedingly fear the Lady-Sun.*"

To the question, "Why do they come from the sea?" I can get no satisfactory answer. But doubtless in the quaint imagination of this people, as also in that of many another, there lingers still the primitive idea of some communication, mysterious and awful, between the world of waters and the world of the dead. It is always over the sea, after the Feast of Souls, that the spirits pass murmuring back to their dim realm, in those elfish little ships of straw which are launched for them upon the sixteenth day of the seventh moon. Even when these are launched upon rivers, or when floating lanterns are set adrift upon lakes or canals to light the ghosts upon their way, or when a mother bereaved drops into some running stream one hundred little prints of Jizō for the sake of her lost darling, the vague idea behind the pious act is that all waters flow to the sea and the sea itself unto the "Nether-distant Land."

Some time, somewhere, this day will come back to me at night, with its visions and sounds: the dusky cavern, and its gray hosts of stone climbing back into darkness, and the faint prints of little naked feet, and the weirdly smiling images, and the broken syllables of the waters, inward-borne, multiplied by husky echoings, blending into one vast ghostly whispering, like the humming of the Sai-no-Kawara.

And over the black-blue bay we glide to the rocky beach of Kaka-ura.

VIII.

As at Mitsu-ura, the water's edge is occupied by a serried line of fishing-boats, each with its nose to the sea; and behind these are ranks of others; and it is only just barely possible to squeeze one's way between them over the beach to the drowsy, pretty, quaint little streets behind them. Everybody seems to be asleep when we first land: the only living creature visible is a cat, sitting on the stern of a boat; and even that cat, according to Japanese beliefs, might not be a real cat, but an o-baké or a nekomata—in short, a goblin-cat, *for it has a long tail.* It is hard work to discover the solitary hotel: there are no signs; and every house seems a private house, either a fisherman's or a farmer's. But the little place is worth wandering about in. A kind of yellow stucco is here employed to cover the exterior of walls; and this light warm tint under the bright blue day gives to the miniature streets a more than cheerful aspect.

When we do finally discover the hotel, we have to wait quite a good while before going in; for nothing is ready; everybody is asleep or away, though all the screens and sliding-doors are open. Evidently there are no thieves in Kaka-ura. The hotel is on a little hillock, and is approached from the main street (the rest are only miniature alleys) by two little flights of stone steps. Immediately across the way I see a Zen temple and a Shintō temple, almost side by side.

At last a pretty young woman, naked to the waist, with a bosom like a Naiad, comes running down the street to the hotel at a surprising speed, bowing low with a smile as she hurries by us into the house. This little person is the waiting-maid of the inn, O-Kayo-San—a name signifying "Years of Bliss." Presently she reappears at the threshold, fully robed in a nice kimono, and gracefully invites us to enter, which we are only too glad to do. The room is neat and spacious; Shintō kakemono from Kitzuki are suspended in the toko and upon the walls; and in one corner I see a very handsome Zen-butsudan, or household shrine. (The form of the shrine, as well as the objects of worship therein, vary according to the sect of the worshipers.) Suddenly I become aware that it is growing strangely dark; and looking about me, perceive that all the doors and windows and other apertures of the inn are densely blocked up by a silent, smiling crowd which has gathered to look at me. I could not have believed there were so many people in Kaka-ura.

In a Japanese house, during the hot season, everything is

thrown open to the breeze. All the shōji or sliding paper-screens, which serve for windows; and all the opaque paper-screens (*fusuma*) used in other seasons to separate apartments, are removed. There is nothing left between floor and roof save the frame or skeleton of the building; the dwelling is literally *unwalled*, and may be seen through in any direction. The landlord, finding the crowd embarrassing, closes up the building in front. The silent, smiling crowd goes to the rear. The rear is also closed. Then the crowd masses to right and left of the house; and both sides have to be closed, which makes it insufferably hot. And the crowd make gentle protest.

Wherefore our host, being displeased, rebukes the multitude with argument and reason, yet without lifting his voice. (Never do these people lift up their voices in anger.) And what he says I strive to translate, with emphases, as follows:

"You-as-for! outrageousness doing—*what* marvelous is?

"*Theatre* is not!

"*Juggler* is not!

"*Wrestler* is not!

"*What* amusing is?

"Honorable-G*uest* this is!

"Now august-to-eat-time-is; to-look-at *evil* matter is. *Honorable-returning-time*-in-to-look-at-as-for-is-good."

But outside, soft laughing voices continue to plead; pleading, shrewdly enough, only with the feminine portion of the family: the landlord's heart is less easily touched. And these, too, have their arguments:

"Oba-San!

"O-Kayo-San!

"Shōji-to-open-condescend!—want to see!

"*Though-we-look-at, Thing-that-by-looking-at-is-worn-out-it-is-not!*

"So that not-to-hinder looking-at is good.

"Hasten therefore to open!"

As for myself, I would gladly protest against this sealing-up, for there is nothing offensive nor even embarrassing in the gaze of these innocent, gentle people; but as the landlord seems to be personally annoyed, I do not like to interfere. The crowd, however, does not go away: it continues to increase, waiting for my exit. And there is one high window in the rear, of which the paper-panes contain some holes; and I see shadows of little people climbing up to get to the holes. Presently there is an eye at every hole.

When I approach the window, the peepers drop noiselessly to the ground, with little timid bursts of laughter, and run away. But they soon come back again. A more charming crowd could hardly be imagined: nearly all boys and girls, half-naked because of the heat, but fresh and clean as flowerbuds. Many of the faces are surprisingly pretty; there are but very few which are not extremely pleasing. But where are the men, and the old women? Truly, this population seems not of Kaka-ura, but rather of the Sai-no-Kawara. The boys look like little Jizō.

During dinner, I amuse myself by poking pears and little pieces of radish through the holes in the shōji. At first there is much hesitation and silvery laughter; but in a little while the silhouette of a tiny hand reaches up cautiously, and a pear vanishes away. Then a second pear is taken, without snatching, as softly as if a ghost had appropriated it. Thereafter hesitation ceases, despite the effort of one elderly woman to create a panic by crying out the word *Mahōtsukai,* "wizard." By the time the dinner is over and the shōoji removed, we have all become good friends. Then the crowd resumes its silent observation from the four cardinal points.

I never saw a more striking difference in the appearance of two village populations than that between the youth of Mitsu-ura and of Kaka. Yet the villages are but two hours' sailing dis-tance apart. In remoter Japan, as in certain islands of the West Indies, particular physical types are developed apparently among communities but slightly isolated; on one side of a mountain a population may be remarkably attractive, while upon the other you may find a hamlet whose inhabitants are decidedly unpre-possessing. But nowhere in this country have I seen a prettier *jeunesse* than that of Kaka-ura.

"*Returning-time-in-to-look-at-as-for-is-good.*" As we descend to the bay, the whole of Kaka-ura, including even the long-invisible ancients of the village, accompanies us; making no sound except the pattering of geta. Thus we are escorted to our boat. Into all the other craft drawn up on the beach the younger folk clamber lightly, and seat themselves on the prows and the gunwales to gaze at the marvelous *Thing-that-by-looking-at-worn-out-is-not.* And all smile, but say nothing, even to each other: somehow the experience gives me the sensation of being asleep; it is so soft, so gentle, and so queer withal, just like things seen in dreams. And as we glide away over the blue lucent water I look back to see the people all waiting and gazing still from the great semicircle of boats; all the slender brown child-limbs dangling from the prows; all the velvety-black heads motionless in the sun; all the boy-faces smiling Jizō-smiles; all the black soft eyes still watching, tirelessly watching, the *thing-that-by-looking-at-worn-out-is-not.* And as the scene, too swiftly receding, diminishes to the width of a kake-mono, I vainly wish that I could buy this last vision of it, to place it in my toko, and delight my soul betimes with gazing thereon. Yet another moment, and we round a rocky point; and Kaka-ura vanishes from my sight forever. So all things pass away.

Assuredly those impressions which longest haunt recollection are the most transitory: we remember many more instants than minutes, more minutes than hoars; and who remembers an entire day? The sum of the remembered happiness of a lifetime is the creation of seconds. What is more fugitive than a smile? Yet when does the memory of a vanished smile expire? or the soft regret which that memory may evoke?

Regret for a single individual smile is something common to normal human nature; but regret for the smile of a population, for a smile considered as an abstract quality, is certainly a rare sensation, and one to be obtained, I fancy, only in this Orient land whose people smile forever like their own gods of stone. And this precious experience is already mine; I am regretting the smile of Kaka.

Simultaneously there comes the recollection of a strangely grim Buddhist legend. Once the Buddha smiled; and by the wondrous radiance of that smile were countless worlds illuminated. But there came a Voice, saying: *"It is not real! It cannot last!"* And the light passed.

10

AT MIONOSEKI

Seki wa yoi toko,
Asahi wo ukete;
O-Yama arashiga
Soyo-soyoto!

SONG OF MIONOSEKI.

[Seki is a goodly place, facing the morning sun. There, from the holy mountains, the winds blow softly, softly—*soyo-soyoto.*]

I.

THE God of Mionoseki hates eggs, hen's eggs. Likewise he hates hens and chickens, and abhors the Cock above all living creatures. And in Mionoseki there are no cocks or hens or chickens or eggs. You could not buy a hen's egg in that place even for twenty times its weight in gold.

And no boat or junk or steamer could be hired to convey to Mionoseki so much as the feather of a chicken, much less an egg. Indeed, it is even held that if you have eaten eggs in the morning you must not dare to visit Mionoseki until the following day. For the great deity of Mionoseki is the patron of mariners and the ruler of storms; and woe unto the vessel which bears unto his shrine even the odor of an egg.

Once the tiny steamer which runs daily from Matsue to Mionoseki encountered some unexpectedly terrible weather on her outward journey, just after reaching the open sea. The crew insisted that something displeasing to Koto-shiro-nushi-no-Kami must have been surreptitiously brought on board. All the passengers were questioned in vain. Suddenly the captain discerned upon the stem of a little brass pipe which one of the men was smoking, smoking in the face of death, like a true Japanese, *the figure of a crowing cock!* Needless to say, that pipe was thrown overboard. Then the angry sea began to grow calm; and the little vessel safely steamed into the holy port, and cast anchor before the great torii of the shrine of the god!

II.

Concerning the reason why the Cock is thus detested by the Great Deity of Mionoseki, and banished from his domain, divers legends are told; but the substance of all of them is about as follows: As we read in the Kojiki, Koto-shiro-nushi-no-Kami, Son of the Great Deity of Kitsuki, was wont to go to Cape Miho,* "to pursue birds and catch fish." And for other reasons also he used to absent himself from home at night, but had always to return before dawn. Now, in those days the Cock was his trusted servant, charged with the duty of crowing lustily when it was time for the god to return. But one morning the bird failed in its duty; and the god, hurrying back in his boat, lost his oars, and had to paddle with his hands; and his hands were bitten by the wicked fishes.

Now the people of Yasugi, a pretty little town on the lagoon of Naka-umi, through which we pass upon our way to Mionoseki, most devoutly worship the same Koto-shiro-nushi-no-Kami; and nevertheless in Yasugi there are multitudes of cocks and hens and chickens; and the eggs of Yasugi cannot be excelled for size and quality. And the people of Yasugi aver that one may better serve the deity by eating eggs than by doing as the people of Mionoseki do; for whenever one eats a chicken or devours an egg, one destroys an enemy of Koto-shiro-nushi-no-Kami.

---

* Mionoseki.

III.

From Matsue to Mionoseki by steamer is a charming journey in fair weather. After emerging from the beautiful lagoon of Naka-umi into the open sea, the little packet follows the long coast of Izumo to the left. Very lofty this coast is, all cliffs and hills rising from the sea, mostly green to their summits, and many cultivated in terraces, so as to look like green pyramids of steps. The bases of the cliffs are very rocky; and the curious wrinklings and corrugations of the coast suggest the work of ancient volcanic forces. Far away to the right, over blue still leagues of sea, appears the long low shore of Hōki, faint as a mirage, with its far beach like an endless white streak edging the blue level, and beyond it vapory lines of woods and cloudy hills, and over everything, looming into the high sky, the magnificent ghostly shape of Daisen, snow-streaked at its summit.

So for perhaps an hour we steam on, between Hōki and Izumo; the rugged and broken green coast on our left occasionally revealing some miniature hamlet sheltered in a wrinkle between two hills; the phantom coast on the right always unchanged. Then suddenly the little packet whistles, heads for a grim promontory to port, glides by its rocky foot, and enters one of the prettiest little bays imaginable, previously concealed from view. A shell-shaped gap in the coast—a semicircular basin of clear deep water, framed in by high corrugated green hills, all wood-clad. Around the edge of the bay the quaintest of little Japanese cities, Mionoseki.

There is no beach, only a semicircle of stone wharves, and above these the houses, and above these the beautiful green of the sacred hills—with a temple roof or two showing an angle through the foliage. From the rear of each house steps descend to deep water; and boats are moored at all the backdoors. We moor in front of the great temple, the Miojinja. Its great paved avenue slopes to the water's edge, where boats are also moored at steps of stone; and looking up the broad approach, one sees a grand stone torii, and colossal stone lanterns, and two magnificent sculptured lions, karashishi, seated upon lofty pedestals, and looking down upon the people from a height of fifteen feet or more. Beyond all this the walls and gate of the outer temple court appear, and beyond them, the roofs of the great haiden, and the pierced projecting cross-beams of the loftier Go-Miojin, the holy shrine itself, relieved against the green of the wooded hills. Picturesque junks are lying in ranks at anchor; there are two deep-sea vessels likewise, of modern build, ships from Ōsaka. And there is a most romantic little breakwater built of hewn stone, with a stone lantern perched at the end of it; and there is a pretty humped bridge connecting it with a tiny island on which I see a shrine of Benten, the Goddess of Waters.

I wonder if I shall be able to get any eggs!

IV.

Unto the pretty waiting maiden of the inn Shimaya I put this scandalous question, with an innocent face but a remorseful heart:

"*Ano ne! tamago wa arimasenka?*"

With the smile of a Kwannon she makes reply:

"*Hé! Ahiru-no tamago-ga sukoshi gozarimasŭ.*"

Delicious surprise!

There augustly exist eggs—*of ducks!*

But there exist no ducks. For ducks could not find life worth living in a city where there is only deep-sea water. And all the ducks' eggs come from Sakai.

V.

This pretty little hotel, whose upper chambers overlook the water, is situated at one end, or nearly at one end, of the crescent of Mionoseki, and the Miojinja almost, at the other, so that one must walk through the whole town to visit the temple, or else cross the harbor by boat. But the whole town is well worth seeing. It is so tightly pressed between the sea and the bases of the hills that there is only room for one real street; and this is so narrow that a man could anywhere jump from the second story of a house upon the water-side into the second story of the opposite house upon the land-side. And it is as picturesque as it is narrow, with its awnings and polished balconies and fluttering figured draperies. From this main street several little *ruelles* slope to the water's edge, where they terminate in steps; and in all these miniature alleys long boats are lying, with their prows projecting over the edge of the wharves, as if eager to plunge in. The temptation to take to the water I find to be irresistible: before visiting the Miojinja I jump from the rear of our hotel into twelve feet of limpid sea, and cool myself by a swim across the harbor.

On the way to Miojinja, I notice, in multitudes of little shops, fascinating displays of baskets and utensils made of woven bamboo. Fine bamboo-ware is indeed the meibutsu, the special product of Mionoseki; and almost every visitor buys some nice little specimen to carry home with him.

The Miojinja is not in its architecture more remarkable than ordinary Shintō temples in Izumo; nor are its interior decorations worth describing in detail. Only the approach to it over the broad sloping space of level pavement, under the granite torii, and between the great lions and lamps of stone, is noble. Within the courts proper there is not much to be seen except a magnificent tank of solid bronze, weighing tons, which must have cost many thousands of yen. It is a votive offering. Of more humble ex-votos, there is a queer collection in the shamusho or business building on the right of the haiden: a series of quaintly designed and quaintly colored pictures, representing ships in great storms, being guided or aided to port by the power of Koto-shiro-nushi-no-Kami. These are gifts from ships.

The ofuda are not so curious as those of other famous Izumo temples; but they are most eagerly sought for. Those strips of white paper, bearing the deity's name, and a few words of promise, which are sold for a few rin, are tied to rods of bamboo, and planted in all the fields of the country roundabout. The most curious things sold are tiny packages of rice-seeds. It is alleged that whatever you desire will grow from these rice-seeds, if you plant them uttering a prayer. If you desire bamboos, cotton-plants, peas, lotus-plants, or watermelons, it matters not; only plant the seed and believe, and the desired crop will arise.

VI.

Much more interesting to me than the ofuda of the Miojinja are the yōraku, the pendant ex-votos in the Hojinji, a temple of the Zen sect which stands on the summit of the beautiful hill above the great Shintō shrine. Before an altar on which are ranged the images of the Thirty-three Kwannons, the thirty-three forms of that Goddess of Mercy who represents the ideal of all that is sweet and pure in the Japanese maiden, a strange, brightly colored mass of curious things may be seen, suspended from the carven ceiling. There are hundreds of balls of worsted and balls of cotton thread of all colors; there are skeins of silk and patterns of silk weaving and of cotton weaving; there are broidered purses in the shape of sparrows and other living creatures; there are samples of bamboo plaiting and countless specimens of needlework. All these are the votive offerings of school children, little girls only, to the Maid-mother of all grace and sweetness and pity. So soon as a baby girl learns something in the way of woman's work—sewing, or weaving, or knitting, or broidering, she brings her first successful effort to the temple as an offering to the gentle divinity, "whose eyes are beautiful," she "who looketh down above the sound of prayer." Even the infants of the Japanese kindergarten bring their first work here—pretty papercuttings, scissored out and plaited into divers patterns by their own tiny flower-soft hands.

VII.

Very sleepy and quiet by day is Mionoseki: only at long intervals one hears laughter of children, or the chant of oarsmen rowing the most extraordinary boats I ever saw outside of the tropics;

boats heavy as barges, which require ten men to move them. These stand naked to the work, wielding oars with cross-handles (imagine a letter T with the lower end lengthened out into an oar-blade). And at every pull they push their feet against the gunwales to give more force to the stroke; intoning in every pause a strange refrain of which the soft melancholy calls back to me certain old Spanish Creole melodies heard in West Indian waters:

> A-ra-ho-no-san-no-sa,
> I-ya-ho-en-ya!
> Ghi!
> Ghi!

The chant begins with a long high note, and descends by fractional tones with almost every syllable, and faints away at last into an almost indistinguishable hum. Then comes the stroke, "Ghi!—ghi!"

But at night Mionoseki is one of the noisiest and merriest little havens of Western Japan. From one horn of its crescent to the other the fires of the shokudai, which are the tall lights of banquets, mirror themselves in the water; and the whole air palpitates with sounds of revelry. Everywhere one hears the booming of the tsudzumi, the little hand-drums of the geisha, and sweet plaintive chants of girls, and tinkling of samisen, and the measured clapping of hands in the dance, and the wild cries and laughter of the players at ken. And all these are but echoes of the diversions of sailors. Verily, the nature of sailors differs but little the world over. Every good ship which visits Mionoseki leaves there, so I am assured, from three hundred to five hundred yen for saké and for dancing-girls. Much do these mariners pray the Great Deity who hates eggs to make calm the waters and favorable the winds, so that Mionoseki may be reached in good time without harm. But having come hither over an unruffled sea with fair soft breezes all the way, small indeed is the gift which they give to the temple of the god, and marvelously large the sums which they pay unto geisha and keepers of taverns. But the god is patient and long-suffering—except in the matter of eggs.

However, these Japanese seamen are very gentle compared with our own Jack Tars, and not without a certain refinement and politeness of their own. I see them sitting naked to the waist at their banquets; for it is very hot, but they use their chopsticks as daintily and pledge each other in saké almost as graciously as men of a better class. Likewise they seem to treat their girls very kindly. It is quite pleasant to watch them feasting across the street. Perhaps their laughter is somewhat more boisterous and their gesticulation a little more vehement than those of the common citizens; but there is nothing resembling real roughness—much less rudeness. All become motionless and silent as statues—fifteen fine bronzes ranged along the wall of the zashiki,* when some pretty geisha begins one of those histrionic dances which, to the Western stranger, seem at first mysterious as a performance of witchcraft, but which really are charming translations of legend and story into the language of living grace and the poetry of woman's smile. And as the wine flows, the more urbane becomes the merriment—until there falls upon all that pleasant sleepiness which saké brings, and the guests, one by one, smilingly depart. Nothing could be happier or gentler than their evening's joviality; yet sailors are considered in Japan an especially rough class. What would be thought of our own roughs in such a country?

Well, I have been fourteen months in Izumo; and I have not yet heard voices raised in anger, or witnessed a quarrel: never have I seen one man strike another, or a woman bullied, or a child slapped. Indeed I have never seen any real roughness anywhere that I have been in Japan, except at the open ports, where the poorer classes seem, through contact with Europeans, to lose their natural politeness, their native morals—even their capacity for simple happiness.

---

* *Zashiki*, the best and largest room of a Japanese dwelling; the guest-room of a private house, or the banquet-room of a public inn.

VIII.

Last night I saw the seamen of Old Japan: today I shall see those of New Japan. An apparition in the offing has filled all this little port with excitement—an Imperial man-of-war. Everybody is going out to look at her; and all the long boats that were lying in the alleys are already hastening, full of curious folk, to the steel colossus. A cruiser of the first class, with a crew of five hundred.

I take passage in one of those astounding craft I mentioned before—a sort of barge propelled by ten exceedingly strong naked men, wielding enormous oars—or rather, sweeps—with cross-handles. But I do not go alone: indeed I can scarcely find room to stand, so crowded the boat is with passengers of all ages, especially women who are nervous about going to sea in an ordinary sampan. And a dancing-girl jumps into the crowd at the risk of her life, just as we push off—and burns her arm against my cigar in the jump. I am very sorry for her; but she laughs merrily at my solicitude. And the rowers begin their melancholy somnolent song,

> *A-ra-ho-no-san-no-sa*
> *Iya-ho-en-ya!*
> *Ghi!*
> *Ghi!*

It is a long pull to reach her—the beautiful monster, towering motionless there in the summer sea, with scarce a curling of thin smoke from the mighty lungs of her slumbering engines; and that somnolent song of our boatmen must surely have some ancient magic in it; for by the time we glide alongside I feel as if I were looking at a dream. Strange as a vision of sleep, indeed, this spectacle: the host of quaint craft hovering and trembling around that tremendous bulk; and all the long-robed, wide-sleeved multitude of the antique port-men, women, children—the gray and the young together—crawling up those mighty flanks in one ceaseless stream, like a swarming of ants. And all this with a great humming like the humming of a hive—a sound made up of low laughter, and chattering in undertones, and subdued murmurs of amazement. For the colossus overawes them—this ship of the Tenshi-Sama, the Son of Heaven; and they wonder like babies at the walls and the turrets of steel, and the giant guns, and the mighty chains, and the stern bearing of the white-uniformed hundreds looking down upon the scene without a smile, over the iron bulwarks. Japanese those also— yet changed by some mysterious process into the semblance of strangers. Only the experienced eye could readily decide the nationality of those stalwart marines: but for the sight of the Imperial arms in gold, and the glimmering ideographs upon the stern, one might well suppose one's self gazing at some Spanish or Italian ship-of-war manned by brown Latin men.

I cannot possibly get on board. The iron steps are occupied by an endless chain of clinging bodies—blue-robed boys from school, and old men with gray queues, and fearless young mothers holding fast to the ropes with over-confident babies strapped to their backs, and peasants, and fishers, and dancing-girls. They are now simply sticking there like flies: somebody has told them they must wait fifteen minutes. So they wait with smiling patience, and behind them in the fleet of high-prowed boats hundreds more wait and wonder. But they do not wait for fifteen minutes! All hopes are suddenly shattered by a stentorian announcement from the deck: "*Mo jikan ga naikara, miseru koto dekimasen!*" The monster is getting up steam—going away: nobody else will be allowed to come on board. And from the patient swarm of clingers to the handropes, and the patient waiters in the fleet of boats, there goes up one exceedingly plaintive and prolonged "*Aa!*" of disappointment, followed by artless reproaches in Izumo dialect: "*Gun-jin wa uso iwanuka to omoya!—usotsukidana!—aa! so dana!*" ["War-people-as-for-lies-never-say—that-we-thought!—*Aa-aa-aa!*"] Apparently the gun-jin are accustomed to such scenes; for they do not even smile.

But we linger near the cruiser to watch the hurried descent of the sightseers into their boats, and the slow ponderous motion of the chain-cables ascending, and the swarming of sailors down over the bows to fasten and unfasten mysterious things. One, bending head-downwards, drops his white cap; and there is a race of boats for the honor of picking it up. A marine leaning over the bulwarks audibly observes to a comrade: "*Aa! gwaikojin dana!—nani shi ni kite iru darō?*"—The other vainly suggests: "*Yasu-no-senkyōshi darō.*" My Japanese costume does not disguise the fact that I am an alien; but it saves me from the imputation of being a missionary. I remain an enigma. Then there are loud cries of "*Abunai!*"—if the cruiser were to move now there would be swamping and crushing and drowning unspeakable. All the little boats scatter and flee away.

Our ten naked oarsmen once more bend to their cross-handled oars, and recommence their ancient melancholy song. And as we glide back, there comes to me the idea of the prodigious cost of that which we went forth to see, the magnificent horror of steel and steam and all the multiple enginery of death, paid for by those humble millions who toil forever knee-deep in the slime of rice-fields, yet can never afford to eat their own rice! Far cheaper must be the food they live upon; and nevertheless, merely to protect the little that they own, such nightmares must be called into existence—monstrous creations of science mathematically applied to the ends of destruction.

How delightful Mionoseki now seems, drowsing far off there under its blue tiles at the feet of the holy hills!—immemorial Mionoseki, with its lamps and lions of stone, and its god who hates eggs!—pretty fantastic Mionoseki, where all things, save the schools, are mediaeval still: the high-pooped junks, and the long-nosed boats, and the plaintive chants of oarsmen!

> *A-ra-ho-no-san-no-sa,*
> *Iya-ho-en-ya!*
> *Ghi!*
> *Ghi!*

And we touch the mossed and ancient wharves of stone again: over one mile of lucent sea we have floated back a thousand years! I turn to look at the place of that sinister vision; and lo!— there is nothing there! Only the level blue of the flood under the hollow blue of the sky; and, just beyond the promontory, one far, small white speck: the sail of a junk. The horizon is naked. Gone!—but how soundlessly, how swiftly! She makes nineteen knots. And, oh! Koto-shiro-nushi-no-Kami, there probably existed eggs on board!

11

NOTES ON KITZUKI

I.

KITZUKI, July 20, 1891.

AKIRA is no longer with me. He has gone to Kyoto, the holy Buddhist city, to edit a Buddhist magazine; and I already feel without him like one who has lost his way—despite his reiterated assurances that he could never be of much service to me in Izumo, as he knew nothing about Shintō.

But for the time being I am to have plenty of company at Kitzuki, where I am spending the first part of the summer holidays; for the little city is full of students and teachers who know me. Kitzuki is not only the holiest place in the San-indō; it is also the most fashionable bathing resort. The beach at Inasa bay is one of the best in all Japan; the beach hotels are spacious, airy, and comfortable; and the bathing houses, with hot and cold fresh-water baths in which to wash off the brine after a swim, are simply faultless. And in fair weather, the scenery is delightful, as you look out over the summer space of sea. Closing the bay on the right, there reaches out from the hills overshadowing the town a mighty, rugged, pine-clad spur—the Kitzuki promontory. On the left a low long range of mountains serrate the horizon beyond the shore-sweep, with one huge vapory shape towering blue into the blue sky behind them—the truncated silhouette of Sanbeyama. Before you the Japanese Sea touches the sky. And there, upon still clear nights, there appears a horizon of fire—the torches of hosts of fishing-boats riding at anchor three and four miles away—so numerous that their lights seem to the naked eye a band of unbroken flame. The Guji has invited me and one of my friends to see a great harvest dance at his residence on the evening of the festival of Tenjin. This dance—Honen-odori—is peculiar to Izumo; and the oppotunity to witness it in this city is a rare one, as it is going to be performed only by order of the Guji.

II.

The robust pontiff himself loves the sea quite as much as any one in Kitzuki; yet he never enters a beach hotel, much less a public bathing house. For his use alone a special bathing house has been built upon a ledge of the cliff overhanging the little settlement of Inasa: it is approached by a narrow pathway shadowed by pine-trees; and there is a torii before it, and shimenawa. To this little house the Guji ascends daily during the bathing season, accompanied by a single attendant, who prepares his bathing dresses, and spreads the clean mats upon which he rests after returning from the sea. The Guji always bathes robed. No one but himself and his servant ever approaches the little house, which commands a charming view of the bay: public reverence for the pontiff's person has made even his restingplace holy ground. As for the country-folk, they still worship him with hearts and bodies. They have ceased to believe as they did in former times, that any one upon whom the Kokuzō fixes his eye at once becomes unable to speak or move; but when he passes among them through the temple court they still prostrate themselves along his way, as before the Ikigami.

III.

KITZUKI, July 23d.

Always, through the memory of my first day at Kitzuki, there will pass the beautiful white apparition of the Miko, with her perfect passionless face, and strange, gracious, soundless tread, as of a ghost.

Her name signifies "the Pet," or "the Darling of the Gods,"— Mi-ko.

The kind Guji, at my earnest request, procured me—or rather, had taken for me—a photograph of the Miko, in the attitude of her dance, upholding the mystic suzu, and wearing, over her crimson hakama, the snowy priestess-robe descending to her feet.

And the learned priest Sasa told me these things concerning the Pet of the Gods, and the Miko-kagura—which is the name of her sacred dance.

Contrary to the custom at the other great Shintō temples of Japan, such as Ise, the office of miko at Kitzuki has always been hereditary. Formerly there were in Kitzuki more than thirty families whose daughters served the Oho-yasbiro as miko: today there are but two, and the number of virgin priestesses does not exceed six—the one whose portrait I obtained being the chief. At Ise and elsewhere the daughter of any Shintō priest may become a miko; but she cannot serve in that capacity after becoming nubile; so that, except in Kitzuki, the miko of all the greater temples are children from ten to twelve years of age. But at the Kitzuki Oho-yashiro the maiden-priestesses are beautiful girls of between sixteen and nineteen years of age; and sometimes a favorite miko is allowed to continue to serve the gods even after having been married. The sacred dance is not difficult to learn: the mother or sister teaches it to the child destined to serve in the temple. The miko lives at home, and visits the temple only upon festival days to perform her duties. She is not placed under any severe discipline or restrictions; she takes no special vows; she risks no dreadful penalties for ceasing to remain a virgin. But her position being one of high honor, and a source of revenue to her family, the ties which bind her to duty are scarcely less cogent than those vows taken by the priestesses of the antique Occident.

Like the priestesses of Delphi, the miko was in ancient times also a divineress—a living oracle, uttering the secrets of the future when possessed by the god whom she served. At no temple does the miko now act as sibyl, oracular priestess, or divineress. But there still exists a class of divining-women, who claim to hold communication with the dead, and to foretell the future, and who call themselves miko—practicing their profession secretly; for it has been prohibited by law.

In the various great Shintō shrines of the Empire the Miko-kagura is differently danced. In Kitzuki, most ancient of all, the dance is the most simple and the most primitive. Its purpose being to give pleasure to the gods, religious conservatism has preserved its traditions and steps unchanged since the period of the beginning of the faith. The origin of this dance is to be found in the Kojiki legend of the dance of Ame-no-uzume-no-mikoto—she by whose mirth and song the Sun-goddess was lured from the cavern into which she had retired, and brought back to illuminate the world. And the suzu—the strange bronze instrument with its cluster of bells which the miko uses in her dance—still preserves the form of that bamboo-spray to which Ame-no-uzume-no-mikoto fastened small bells with grass, ere beginning her mirthful song.

IV.

Behind the library in the rear of the great shrine, there stands a more ancient structure which is still called the Miko-yashiki, or dwelling-place of the miko. Here in former times all the maiden-priestesses were obliged to live, under a somewhat stricter discipline than now. By day they could go out where they pleased; but they were under obligation to return at night to the yashiki before the gates of the court were closed. For it was feared that the Pets of the Gods might so far forget themselves as to condescend to become the darlings of adventurous mortals. Nor was the fear at all unreasonable; for it was the duty of a miko to be singularly innocent as well as beautiful. And one of the most beautiful miko who belonged to the service of the Oho-yashiro did actually so fall from grace—giving to the Japanese world a romance which you can buy in cheap printed form at any large bookstore in Japan.

Her name was O-Kuni, and she was the daughter of one Nakamura Mongoro of Kitzuki, where her descendants still live at the present day. While serving as dancer in the great temple she fell in love with a rōnin named Nagoya Sanza—a desperate, handsome vagabond, with no fortune in the world but his sword. And she left the temple secretly, and fled away with her lover toward Kyōto. All this must have happened not less than three hundred years ago.

On their way to Kyōto they met another rōnin, whose real name I have not been able to learn. For a moment only this "wave-man" figures in the story, and immediately vanishes into the eternal Night of death and all forgotten things. It is simply recorded that he desired permission to travel with them, that he became enamored of the beautiful miko, and excited the jealousy of her lover to such an extent that a desperate duel was the result, in which Sanza slew his rival.

Thereafter the fugitives pursued their way to Kyoto without other interruption. Whether the fair O-Kuni had by this time found ample reason to regret the step she had taken, we cannot know. But from the story of her after-life it would seem that the face of the handsome ronin who had perished through his passion for her became a haunting memory.

We next hear of her in a strange role at Kyōto. Her lover appears to have been utterly destitute; for, in order to support him, we find her giving exhibitions of the Miko-kagura in the Shijo-Kawara—which is the name given to a portion of the dry bed of the river Kamagawa—doubtless the same place in which the terrible executions by torture took place. She must have been looked upon by the public of that day as an outcast. But her extraordinary beauty seems to have attracted many spectators, and to have proved more than successful as an exhibition.

Sanza's purse became well filled. Yet the dance of O-Kuni in the Shijo-Kawara was nothing more than the same dance which the miko of Kitzuki dance today, in their crimson hakama and snowy robes—a graceful gliding walk.

The pair next appear in Tōkyō—or, as it was then called, Yedo—as actors. O-Kuni, indeed, is universally credited by tradition with having established the modern Japanese stage—the first profane drama. Before her time only religious plays, of Buddhist authorship, seem to have been known. Sanza himself became a popular and successful actor, under his sweetheart's tuition. He had many famous pupils, among them the great Saruwaka, who subsequently founded a theatre in Yedo; and the theatre called after him Saruwakaza, in the street Saruwakachō, remains even unto this day. But since the time of O-Kuni, women have been—at least until very recently—excluded from the Japanese stage; their parts, as among the old Greeks, being taken by men or boys so effeminate in appearance and so skillful in acting that the keenest observer could never detect their sex.

Nagoya Sanza died many years before his companion. O-Kuni then returned to her native place, to ancient Kitzuki, where she cut off her beautiful hair, and became a Buddhist nun. She was learned for her century, and especially skillful in that art of poetry called Renga; and this art she continued to teach until her death. With the small fortune she had earned as an actress she built in Kitzuki the little Buddhist temple called Rengaji, in the very heart of the quaint town—so called because there she taught the art of Renga. Now the reason she built the temple was that she might therein always pray for the soul of the man whom the sight of her beauty had ruined, and whose smile, perhaps, had stirred something within her heart whereof Sanza never knew. Her family enjoyed certain privileges for several centuries because she had founded the whole art of the Japanese stage; and until so recently as the Restoration the chief of the descendants of Nakamura Mongorō was always entitled to a share in the profits of the Kitzuki theatre, and enjoyed the title of Zamoto. The family is now, however, very poor.

I went to see the little temple of Rengaji, and found that it had disappeared. Until within a few years it used to stand at the foot of the great flight of stone steps leading to the second Kwannondera, the most imposing temple of Kwannon in Kitzuki. Nothing now remains of the Rengaji but a broken statue of Jizō, before which the people still pray. The former court of the little temple has been turned into a vegetable garden, and the material of the ancient building utilized, irreverently enough, for the construction of some petty cottages now occupying its site. A peasant told me that the kakemono and other sacred objects had been given to the neighboring temple, where they might be seen.

V.

Not far from the site of the Rengaji, in the grounds of the great hakaba of the Kwannondera, there stands a most curious pine. The trunk of the tree is supported, not on the ground, but upon four colossal roots which lift it up at such an angle that it looks like a thing walking upon four legs. Trees of singular shape are often considered to be the dwelling places of Kami; and the pine in question affords an example of this belief. A fence has been built around it, and a small shrine placed before it, prefaced by several small torii; and many poor people may be seen, at almost any hour of the day, praying to the Kami of the place. Before the little shrine I notice, besides the usual Kitzuki ex-voto of seaweed, several little effigies of horses made of straw. Why these offerings of horses of straw? It appears that the shrine is dedicated to Kōshin, the Lord of Roads; and those who are anxious about the health of their horses pray to the Road-God to preserve their animals from sickness and death, at the same time bringing these straw effigies in token of their desire. But this role of veterinarian is not commonly attributed to Kōshin; and it appears that something in the fantastic form of the tree suggested the idea.

VI.

Kitzuki, July 24th.

Within the first court of the Oho-yashiro, and to the left of the chief gate, stands a small timber structure, ashen-colored with age, shaped like a common miya or shrine. To the wooden gratings of its closed doors are knotted many of those white papers upon which are usually written vows or prayers to the gods. But on peering through the grating one sees no Shintō symbols in the dimness within. It is a stable! And there, in the central stall, is a superb horse—looking at you. Japanese horseshoes of straw are suspended to the wall behind him. He does not move. He is made of bronze!

Upon inquiring of the learned priest Sasa the story of this horse, I was told the following curious things:

On the eleventh day of the seventh month, by the ancient calendar,* falls the strange festival called Minige, or "The Body-escaping." Upon that day, 'tis said that the Great Deity of Kitzuki leaves his shrine to pass through all the streets of the city, and along the seashore, after which he enters into the house of the Kokuzō. Wherefore upon that day the kokuzō was always wont to leave his house; and at the present time, though he does not actually abandon his home, he and his family retire into certain apartments, so as to leave the larger part of the dwelling free for the use of the god. This retreat of the Kokuzō is still called the Minige.

Now while the great Deity Oho-kuni-nushi-no-Kami is passing through the streets, he is followed by the highest Shintō priest of the shrine—this kannushi having been formerly called

---

* Fourteenth of August.

Bekkwa. The word "Bekkwa" means "special" or "sacred fire" and the chief kannushi was so called because for a week before the festival he had been nourished only with special food cooked with the sacred fire, so that he might be pure in the presence of the God. And the office of Bekkwa was hereditary; and the appellation at last became a family name. But he who performs the rite today is no longer called Bekkwa.

Now while performing his function, if the Bekkwa met any one upon the street, he ordered him to stand aside with the words: "Dog, give way!" And the common people believed, and still believe, that anybody thus, spoken to by the officiating kannushi would be changed into a dog. So on that day of the Minige nobody used to go out into the streets after a certain hour, and even now very few of the people of the little city leave their homes during the festival.*

After having followed the deity through all the city, the Bekkwa used to perform, between two and three o'clock in the darkness of the morning, some secret rite by the seaside. (I am told this rite is still annually performed at the same hour.) But, except the Bekkwa himself, no man might be present; and it was believed, and is still believed by the common people, that were any man, by mischance, to see the rite he would instantly fall dead, or become transformed into an animal.

So sacred was the secret of that rite, that the Bekkwa could not even utter it *until after he was dead,* to his successor in office.

Therefore, when he died, the body was laid upon the matting of a certain inner chamber of the temple, and the son was left alone with the corpse, after all the doors had been carefully closed. Then, at a certain hour of the night, the soul returned into the body of the dead priest, and he lifted himself up, and whispered the awful secret into the ear of his son—and fell back dead again.

---

* In the pretty little seaside hotel Inaba-ya, where I lived during my stay in Kitzuki, the kind old hostess begged her guests with almost tearful earnestness not to leave the house during the Minige.

But what, you may ask, has all this to do with the Horse of Bronze?

Only this:

Upon the festival of the Minige, the Great Deity of Kitzuki rides through the streets of his city upon the Horse of Bronze.

VII.

The Horse of Bronze, however, is far from being the only statue in Izumo which is believed to run about occasionally at night: at least a score of other artistic things are, or have been, credited with similar ghastly inclinations. The great carven dragon which writhes above the entrance of the Kitzuki haiden used, I am told, to crawl about the roofs at night, until a carpenter was summoned to cut its wooden throat with a chisel, after which it ceased its perambulations. You can see for yourself the mark of the chisel on its throat! At the splendid Shintō temple of Kasuga, in Matsue, there are two pretty life-size bronze deer—stag and doe—the heads of which seemed to me to have been separately cast, and subsequently riveted very deftly to the bodies. Nevertheless I have been assured by some good country-folk that each figure was originally a single casting, but that it was afterwards found necessary to cut off the heads of the deer to make them keep quiet at night. But the most unpleasant customer of all this uncanny fraternity to have encountered after dark was certainly the monster tortoise of Gesshōji temple in Matsue, where the tombs of the Matsudairas are. This stone colossus is almost seventeen feet in length and lifts its head six feet from the ground. On its now broken back stands a prodigious cubic monolith about nine feet high, bearing a half-obliterated inscription. Fancy—as Izumo folks did— this mortuary incubus staggering abroad at midnight, and its hideous attempts to swim in the neighboring lotus-pond! Well, the legend runs that its neck *had* to be broken in consequence of this awful misbehavior. But really the thing looks as if it could only have been broken by an earthquake.

VIII.

At the Oho-yashiro it is the annual festival of the God of Scholarship, the God of Calligraphy—Tenjin. Here in Kitzuki, the festival of the Divine Scribe, the Tenjin-Matsuri, is still observed according to the beautiful old custom which is being forgotten elsewhere. Long ranges of temporary booths have been erected within the outer court of the temple; and in these are suspended hundreds of long white tablets, bearing specimens of calligraphy. Every schoolboy in Kitzuki has a sample of his best writing on exhibition. The texts are written only in Chinese characters—not in hirakana or katakana—and are mostly drawn from the works of Confucius or Mencius.

To me this display of ideographs seems a marvelous thing of beauty—almost a miracle, indeed, since it is all the work of very, very young boys. Rightly enough, the word "to write" *(kaku)* in Japanese signifies also to "paint" in the best artistic sense. I once had an opportunity of studying the result of an attempt to teach English children the art of writing Japanese. These children were instructed by a Japanese writing-master; they sat upon the same bench with Japanese pupils of their own age, beginners like-wise. But they could never learn like the Japanese children. The ancestral tendencies within them rendered vain the efforts of the instructor to teach them the secret of a shapely stroke with the brush. It is not the Japanese boy alone who writes; the fingers of the dead move his brush, guide his strokes.

Beautiful, however, as this writing seems to me, it is far from winning the commendation of my Japanese companion, himself a much experienced teacher. "The greater part of this work," he declares, "is very bad." While I am still bewildered by this sweeping criticism, he points out to me one tablet inscribed with rather small characters, adding: "Only that is tolerably good."

"Why," I venture to observe, "that one would seem to have cost much less trouble; the characters are so small."

"Oh, the size of the characters has nothing to do with the matter," interrupts the master, "it is a question of form."

"Then I cannot understand. What you call very bad seems to me exquisitely beautiful."

"Of course you cannot understand," the critic replies; "it would take you many years of study to understand. And even then"—

"And even then?"

"Well, even then you could only partly understand."

Thereafter I hold my peace on the topic of calligraphy.

IX.

Vast as the courts of the Oho-yashiro are, the crowd within them is now so dense that one must move very slowly, for the whole population of Kitzuki and its environs has been attracted here by the matsuri. All are making their way very gently toward a little shrine built upon an island in the middle of an artificial lake and approached by a narrow causeway. This little shrine, which I see now for the first time (Kitzuki temple being far too large a place to be all seen and known in a single visit), is the Shrine of Tenjin. As the sound of a waterfall is the sound of the clapping of hands before it, and myriads of rin, and bushels of handfuls of rice, are being dropped into the enormous wooden chest there placed to receive the offerings. Fortunately this crowd, like all Japanese crowds, is so sympathetically yielding that it is possible to traverse it slowly in any direction, and thus to see all there is to be seen. After contributing my mite to the coffer of Tenjin, I devote my attention to the wonderful display of toys in the outer courts.

At almost every temple festival in Japan there is a great sale of toys, usually within the court itself—a miniature street of small booths being temporarily erected for this charming commerce. Every matsuri is a children's holiday. No mother would think of attending a temple-festival without buying her child a toy: even the poorest mother can afford it; for the price of the toys sold in a temple court varies from one fifth of one sen,* or Japanese cent, to three or four sen; toys worth so much as five sen being rarely displayed at these little shops. But cheap as they are, these frail playthings are full of beauty and suggestiveness, and, to one who knows and loves Japan, infinitely more interesting than the costliest inventions of a Parisian toy-manufacturer. Many of them, however, would be utterly incomprehensible to an English child. Suppose we peep at a few of them.

Here is a little wooden mallet, with a loose tiny ball fitted into a socket at the end of the handle. This is for the baby to suck. On either end of the head of the mallet is painted the mystic *tomoye*—that Chinese symbol, resembling two huge commas so united as to make a perfect circle, which you may have seen on the title-page of Mr. Lowell's beautiful "Soul of the Far East." To you, however, this little wooden mallet would seem in all probability just a little wooden mallet and nothing more. But to the Japanese child it is full of suggestions. It is the mallet of the Great Deity of Kitzuki, Oho-kuninushi-no-Kami—vulgarly called Daikoku—the God of Wealth, who, by one stroke of his hammer gives fortune to his worshipers.

Perhaps this tiny drum, of a form never seen in the Occident *(tsudzumi)*, or this larger drum with a *mitsudomoye*, or triple-comma symbol, painted on each end, might seem to you without religious signification; but both are models of drums used in the Shintō and the Buddhist temples. This queer tiny table is a miniature sambo: it is upon such a table that offerings are presented to the gods. This curious cap is a model of the cap of a Shintō priest. Here is a toy miya, or Shintō shrine, four inches high. This bunch of tiny tin bells attached to a wooden handle might seem to you something corresponding to our Occidental tin rattles; but it is a model of the sacred suzu used by the virgin priestess in her dance before the gods. This face of a smiling chubby girl,

---

* There are ten rin to one sen, and ten mon to one rin, or one thousand to one sen. The majority of the cheap toys sold at the matsuri cost from two to nine rin. The rin is a circular copper coin with a square hole in the middle for stringing purposes.

with two spots upon her forehead—a mask of baked clay—is the traditional image of Ame-no-uzume-no-mikoto, commonly called Otafuka, whose merry laughter lured the Goddess of the Sun out of the cavern of darkness. And here is a little Shintō priest in full hieratic garb: when this little string between his feet is pulled, he claps his hands as if in prayer.

Hosts of other toys are here—mysterious to the uninitiated European, but to the Japanese child full of delightful religious meaning. In these faiths of the Far East there is little of sternness or grimness—the Kami are but the spirits of the fathers of the people; the Buddhas and the Bosatsu were men. Happily the missionaries have not succeeded as yet in teaching the Japanese to make religion a dismal thing. These gods smile forever: if you find one who frowns, like Fudo, the frown seems but half in earnest; it is only Emma, the Lord of Death, who somewhat appalls. Why religion should be considered too awful a subject for children to amuse themselves decently with never occurs to the common Japanese mind. So here we have images of the gods and saints for toys—Tenjin, the Deity of Beautiful Writing—and Uzume, the laughter-loving—and Fukusuke, like a happy school-boy—and the Seven Divinities of Good Luck, in a group—and Fukurojin, the God of Longevity, with head so elongated that only by the aid of a ladder can his barber shave the top of it—and Hotei, with a belly round and huge as a balloon—and Ebisu, the Deity of markets and of fishermen, with a tai-fish under his arm—and Daruma, ancient disciple of Buddha, whose legs were worn off by uninterrupted meditation.

Here likewise are many toys which a foreigner could scarcely guess the meaning of, although they have no religious significa-tion. Such is this little badger, represented as drumming upon its own belly with both forepaws. The badger is believed to be able to use its belly like a drum, and is credited by popular supersti-tion with various supernatural powers. This toy illustrates a pretty fairy-tale about some hunter who spared a badger's life and was rewarded by the creature with a wonderful dinner and a musical performance. Here is a hare sitting on the end of the handle of a wooden pestle which is set horizontally upon a pivot. By pulling a little string, the pestle is made to rise and fall as if moved by the hare. If you have been even a week in Japan you will recognize the pestle as the pestle of a kometsuki, or rice-cleaner, who works it by treading on the handle. But what is the hare? This hare is the Hare-in-the-Moon, called Usagi-no-kometsuki: if you look up at the moon on a clear night you can see him cleaning his rice.

Now let us see what we can discover in the way of cheap ingenuities.

Tombō, "the Dragon-Fly." Merely two bits of wood joined together in the form of a T. The lower part is a little round stick, about as thick as a match, but twice as long; the upper piece is flat, and streaked with paint. Unless you are accustomed to look for secrets, you would scarcely be able to notice that the flat piece is trimmed along two edges at a particular angle. Twirl the lower piece rapidly between the palms of both hands, and suddenly let it go. At once the strange toy rises revolving in the air, and then sails away slowly to quite a distance, performing extraordinary gyrations, and imitating exactly—to the eye at least—the hovering motion of a dragon-fly. Those little streaks of paint you noticed upon the top-piece now reveal their purpose; as the tombō darts hither and thither, even the tints appear to be those of a real dragon-fly; and even the sound of the flitting toy imitates the dragon-fly's hum. The principle of this pretty invention is much like that of the boomerang; and an expert can make his tombō, after flying across a large room, return into his hand. All the tombō sold, however, are not as good as this one; we have been lucky. Price, one tenth of one cent!

Here is a toy which looks like a bow of bamboo strung with wire. The wire, however, is twisted into a corkscrew spiral. On this spiral a pair of tiny birds are suspended by a metal loop. When the bow is held perpendicularly with the birds at the upper end of the string, they descend whirling by their own weight, as if circling round one another; and the twittering of two birds is imitated by the sharp grating of the metal loop upon the spiral wire. One bird flies head upward, and the other tail upward. As soon as they have reached the bottom, reverse the bow, and they will recommence their wheeling flight. Price, two cents— because the wire is dear.

O-Saru, the "Honorable Monkey."* A little cotton monkey, with a blue head and scarlet body, hugging a bamboo rod. Under him is a bamboo spring; and when you press it, he runs up to the top of the rod. Price, one eighth of one cent.

O-saru. Another Honorable Monkey. This one is somewhat more complex in his movements, and costs a cent. He runs up a string, hand over hand, when you pull his tail.

Tōri-Kago. A tiny gilded cage, with a bird in it, and plum flowers. Press the edges of the bottom of the cage, and a minuscule wind-instrument imitates the chirping of the bird. Price, one cent.

Karuwazashi, the Acrobat. A very loose-jointed wooden boy clinging with both hands to a string stretched between two bamboo sticks, which are curiously rigged together in the shape of an open pair of scissors. Press the ends of the sticks at the bottom; and the acrobat tosses his legs over the string, seats himself upon it, and finally turns a somersault. Price, one sixth of one cent.

Kobiki, the Sawyer. A figure of a Japanese workman, wearing only a fundoshi about his loins, and standing on a plank, with a long saw in his hands. If you pull a string below his feet, he will go to work in good earnest, sawing the plank. Notice that he pulls the saw towards him, like a true Japanese, instead of pushing it from him, as our own carpenters do. Price, one tenth of one cent.

Chie-no-ita, the "Intelligent Boards," or better, perhaps, "The Planks of Intelligence." A sort of chain composed of about a

---

* Why the monkey is so respectfully mentioned in polite speech, I do not exactly know; but I think that the symbolical relation of the monkey, both to Buddhism and to Shintō, may perhaps account for the use of the prefix "O" (honorable) before its name.

dozen flat square pieces of white wood, linked together by ribbons. Hold the thing perpendicularly by one end-piece; then turn the piece at right angles to the chain; and immediately all the other pieces tumble over each other in the most marvelous way without unlinking. Even an adult can amuse himself for half an hour with this: it is a perfect *trompe-l'oeil* in mechanical adjustment. Price, one cent.

Kitsune-Tanuki. A funny flat paper mask with closed eyes. If you pull a pasteboard slip behind it, it will open its eyes and put out a tongue of surprising length. Price, one sixth of one cent.

Chin. A little white dog, with a collar round its neck. It is in the attitude of barking. From a Buddhist point of view, I should think this toy somewhat immoral. For when you slap the dog's head; it utters a sharp yelp, as of pain. Price, one sen and five rin. Rather dear.

Fuki-agari-koboshi, the Wrestler Invincible. This is still dearer; for it is made of porcelain, and very nicely colored. The wrestler squats upon his hams. Push him down in any direction, he always returns of his own accord to an erect position. Price, two sen.

Oroga-Heika-Kodomo, the Child Reverencing His Majesty the Emperor. A Japanese schoolboy with an accordion in his hands, singing and playing the national anthem, or Kimiga. There is a little windbellows at the bottom of the toy; and when you operate it, the boy's arms move as if playing the instrument, and a shrill small voice is heard. Price, one cent and a half.

Jishaku. This, like the preceding, is quite a modern toy. A small wooden box containing a magnet and a tiny top made of a red wooden button with a steel nail driven through it. Set the top spinning with a twirl of the fingers; then hold the magnet over the nail, and the top will leap up to the magnet and there continue to spin, suspended in air. Price, one cent.

It would require at least a week to examine them all. Here is a model spinning-wheel, absolutely perfect, for one fifth of one cent. Here are little day tortoises which swim about when you put them into water—one rin for two. Here is a box of toysoldiers—

samurai in full armor—nine rin only. Here is a Kaze-Kuruma, or wind-wheel—a wooden whistle with a paper wheel mounted before the orifice by which the breath is expelled, so that the wheel turns furiously when the whistle is blown—three rin. Here is an Ogi, a sort of tiny quadruple fan sliding in a sheath. When expanded it takes the shape of a beautiful flower—one rin.

The most charming of all these things to me, however, is a tiny doll—O-Hina-San (Honorable Miss Hina)—or *beppin* ("beautiful woman"). The body is a phantom only—a flat stick covered with a paper kimono—but the head is really a work of art. A pretty oval face with softly shadowed oblique eyes—looking shyly downward—and a wonderful maiden coiffure, in which the hair is arranged in bands and volutes and ellipses and convolutions and foliole curlings most beautiful and extraordinary. In some respects this toy is a costume model, for it imitates exactly the real coiffure of Japanese maidens and brides. But the expression of the face of the beppin is, I think, the great attraction of the toy; there is a shy, plaintive sweetness about it impossible to describe, but deliciously suggestive of a real Japanese type of girl-beauty. Yet the whole thing is made out of a little crumpled paper, colored with a few dashes of the brush by an expert hand. There are no two O-Hina-San exactly alike out of millions; and when you have become familiar by long residence with Japanese types, any such doll will recall to you some pretty face that you have seen. These are for little girls. Price, five rin.

X.

Here let me tell you something you certainly never heard of before in relation to Japanese dolls—not the tiny O-Hina-San I was just speaking about, but the beautiful life-sized dolls representing children of two or three years old; real toy-babes which, although far more cheaply and simply constructed than our finer kinds of Western dolls, become, under the handling of a Japanese girl, infinitely more interesting. Such dolls are well dressed, and look so lifelike—little slanting eyes, shaven pates, smiles, and all!—that as seen from a short distance the best eyes might be deceived by them. Therefore in those stock photographs of Japanese life, of which so many thousands are sold in the open ports, the conventional baby on the mother's back is most successfully represented by a doll. Even the camera does not betray the substitution. And if you see such a doll, though held quite close to you, being made by a Japanese mother to reach out its hands, to move its little bare feet, and to turn its head, you would be almost afraid to venture a heavy wager that it was only a doll. Even after having closely examined the thing, you would still, I fancy, feel a little nervous at being left alone with it, so perfect the delusion of that expert handling.

Now there is a belief that some dolls do actually become alive.

Formerly the belief was less rare than it is now. Certain dolls were spoken of with a reverence worthy of the Kami, and their owners were envied folk. Such a doll was treated like a real son or daughter; it was regularly served with food; it had a bed, and plenty of nice clothes, and a name. If in the semblance of a girl, it was O-Toku-San; if in that of a boy, Tokutarō-San. It was thought that the doll would become angry and cry if neglected, and that any ill-treatment of it would bring ill-fortune to the house. And, moreover, it was believed to possess supernatural powers of a very high order.

In the family of one Sengoku, a samurai of Matsue, there was a Tokutarō-San which had a local reputation scarcely inferior to that of Kishibōjin—she to whom Japanese wives pray for offspring. And childless couples used to borrow that doll, and keep it for a time—ministering unto it—and furnish it with new clothes before gratefully returning it to its owners. And all who did so, I am assured, became parents, according to their heart's desire. "Sengoku's doll had a soul." There is even a legend that once, when the house caught fire, the Tokutarō-San ran out safely into the garden of its own accord!

The idea about such a doll seems to be this: The new doll is only a doll. But a doll which is preserved for a great many years in one family,* and is loved and played with by generations of children, gradually acquires a soul. I asked a charming Japanese girl: "How can a doll live?"

"Why," she answered, " *if you love it enough,* it will live!"

What is this but Renan's thought of a deity in process of evolution, uttered by the heart of a child?

XI.

But even the most beloved dolls are worn out at last, or get broken in the course of centuries. And when a doll must be considered quite dead, its remains are still entitled to respect. Never is the corpse of a doll irreverently thrown away. Neither is it burned or cast into pure running water, as all sacred objects of the miya must be when they have ceased to be serviceable. And it is not buried. You could not possibly imagine what is done with it.

It is dedicated to the God Kojin,†—a somewhat mysterious divinity, half-Buddhist, half-Shintō. The ancient Buddhist images of Kōjin represented a deity with many arms; the Shintō Kōjin of Izumo has, I believe, no artistic representation whatever. But in almost every Shintō, and also in many Buddhist, temple grounds, is planted the tree called enoki,‡ which is sacred to him, and in which he is supposed by the peasantry to dwell; for they pray before the enoki always to Kōjin. And there is usually a small shrine placed before the tree, and a little torii also. Now you may often see laid upon such a shrine of Kōjin, or at the foot of his sacred tree, or in a hollow thereof—if there be any hollow—pathetic remains of dolls. But a doll is seldom given to

---

* As many fine dolls really are. The superior class of O-Hina-San, such as figure in the beautiful displays of the O-Hina-no-Matsuri at rich homes, are heirlooms. Dolls are not given to children to break; and Japanese children seldom break them. I saw at a Doll's Festival in the house of the Governor of Izumo, dolls one hundred years old—charming figurines in ancient court costume.

† Not to be confounded with Eoshin, the God of Roads.

‡ *Celtis Willldenowiana.* Sometimes, but rarely, a pine or other tree is substituted for the enoki.

Kōjin during the lifetime of its possessor. When you see one thus exposed, you may be almost certain that it was found among the effects of some poor dead woman—the innocent memento of her girlhood, perhaps even also of the girlhood of her mother and of her mother's mother.

XII.

And now we are to see the Hōnen-odori—which begins at eight o'clock. There is no moon; and the night is pitch-black overhead: but there is plenty of light in the broad court of the Guji's residence, for a hundred lanterns have been kindled and hung out. I and my friend have been provided with comfortable places in the great pavilion which opens upon the court, and the pontiff has had prepared for us a delicious little supper.

Already thousands have assembled before the pavilion—young men of Kitzuki and young peasants from the environs, and women and children in multitude, and hundreds of young girls. The court is so thronged that it is difficult to assume the possibility of any dance. Illuminated by the lantern-light, the scene is more than picturesque: it is a carnivalesque display of gala-costume. Of course the peasants come in their ancient attire: some in rain-coats *(mino),* or overcoats of yellow straw; others with blue towels tied round their heads; many with enormous mushroom hats—all with their blue robes well tucked up. But the young townsmen come in all guises and disguises. Many have dressed themselves in female attire; some are all in white duck, like police; some have mantles on; others wear shawls exactly as a Mexican wears his zarape; numbers of young artisans appear almost as lightly clad as in working-hours, barelegged to the hips, and barearmed to the shoulders. Among the girls some wonderful dressing is to be seen—ruby-colored robes, and rich grays and browns and purples, confined with exquisite obi, or girdles of figured satin; but the best taste is shown in the simple and very graceful black and white costumes worn by some maidens of the better classes—dresses especially made for dancing, and not to be worn at any other time. A few shy damsels have completely masked themselves by tying down over their cheeks the flexible brims of very broad straw hats. I cannot attempt to talk about the delicious costumes of the children: as well try to describe without paint the variegated loveliness of moths and butterflies.

In the center of this multitude I see a huge rice-mortar turned upside down; and presently a sandaled peasant leaps upon it lightly, and stands there—with an open paper umbrella above his head. Nevertheless it is not raining. That is the Ondotori, the leader of the dance, who is celebrated through all Izumo as a singer. According to ancient custom, the leader of the Hōnen-odori* always holds an open umbrella above his head while he sings.

Suddenly, at a signal from the Guji, who has just taken his place in the pavilion, the voice of the Ondo-tori, intoning the song of thanksgiving, rings out over all the murmuring of the multitude like a silver cornet. A wondrous voice, and a wondrous song, full of trills and quaverings indescribable, but full also of sweetness and true musical swing. And as he sings, he turns slowly round upon his high pedestal, with the umbrella always above his head; never halting in his rotation from right to left, but pausing for a regular interval in his singing, at the close of each two verses, when the people respond with a joyous outcry: "*Yo-ha-to-nai!— ya-ha-to-nai!*" Simultaneously an astonishingly rapid movement of segregation takes place in the crowd; two enormous rings of dancers form, one within the other, the rest of the people pressing back to make room for the odori. And then this great double-round, formed by fully five hundred dancers, begins also to revolve from right to left—lightly, fantastically—all the tossing of arms and white twinkling of feet keeping faultless time to the measured syllabification of the chant. An immense wheel the dance is, with the Ondo-tori for its axis—always turning slowly upon his rice-mortar, under his open umbrella, as he sings the song of harvest thanksgiving:

---

* Literally, "The Dance of the Fruitful Year."

> *Ichi-wa—*
>   *Izumo-no-Taisha-Sama-ye;*
> *Ni-ni-wa—*
>   *Niigata-no-Irokami-Sama-ye;*
> *San-wa—*
>   *Sanuki-no-Kompira-Sama-ye;*
> *Shi-ni-wa—*
>   *Shinano-no-Zenkoji-Sama-ye;*
> *Itsutsu—*
>   *Ichibata-O-Yakushi-Sama-ye;*
> *Roku-niwa—*
>   *Rakkakudo-no-O-Jizo-Sama-ye;*
> *Nanatsu—*
>   *Nana-ura-no-O-Ebisu-Sama-ye;*
> *Yattsu—*
>   *Yawata-no-Hachiman-Sama-ye*
> *Kokonotsu—*
>   *Koya-no-Oteradera-ye;*
> *To-niwa—*
>   *Tokoro-no-Ujigami-Sama-ye.**

And the voices of all the dancers in unison roll out the chorus:

>   *Ya-ha-to-nai!*
>   *Ya-ha-to-nai!*

Utterly different this whirling joyous Hōnen-odori from the
Bon-odori which I witnessed last year at Shimo-Ichi, and which

---

* "First—unto the Taisha-Sama of Izumo;
   Second—to Irokami-Sama of Niigata;
   Third—unto Kompira-Sama of Sanuki;
   Fourth—unto Zenkoji-Sama of Shinano;
   Fifth—to O-Yakushi-San of Ichibata;
   Sixth—to O-Jizo-Sama of Rokkakudo;
   Seventh—to O-Ebisu-Sama of Nana-ura;
   Eighth—unto Hachiman-Sama of Yawata;
   Ninth—unto every holy shrine of Koya;
   Tenth—to the Ujigami-Sama of our village."
Japanese readers will appreciate the ingenious manner in which the numeral at the
beginning of each phrase is repeated in the name of the sacred place sung of.

seemed to me a very dance of ghosts. But it is also much more difficult to describe. Each dancer makes a half-wheel alternately to left and right, with a peculiar bending of the knees and tossing up of the hands at the same time—as in the act of lifting a weight above the head; but there are other curious movements—jerky with the men, undulatory with the women—as impossible to describe as water in motion. These are decidedly complex, yet so regular that five hundred pairs of feet and hands mark the measure of the song as truly as if they were under the control of a single nervous system.

It is strangely difficult to memorize the melody of a Japanese popular song, or the movements of a Japanese dance; for the song and the dance have been evolved through an aesthetic sense of rhythm in sound and in motion as different from the corresponding Occidental sense as English is different from Chinese. We have no ancestral sympathies with these exotic rhythms, no inherited aptitudes for their instant comprehension, no racial impulses whatever in harmony with them. But when they have become familiar through study, after a long residence in the Orient, how nervously fascinant the oscillation of the dance, and the singular swing of the song!

This dance, I know, began at eight o'clock; and the Ondo-tori, after having sung without a falter in his voice for an extraordinary time, has been relieved by a second. But the great round never breaks, never slackens its whirl; it only enlarges as the night wears on. And the second Ondo-tori is relieved by a third; yet I would like to watch that dance forever.

"What time do you think it is? "my friend asks, looking at his watch.

"Nearly eleven o'clock," I make answer.

"Eleven o'clock! It is exactly eight minutes to three o'clock. And our host will have little time for sleep before the rising of the sun."

12

AT HINOMISAKI

KITZUKI, August 10, 1891.

MY Japanese friends urge me to visit Hinomisaki, where no European has ever been, and where there is a far-famed double temple dedicated to Amaterasu-oho-mi-Kami, the Lady of Light, and to her divine brother Take-haya-susa-no-wo-no-mikoto. Hinomisaki is a little village on the Izumo coast about five miles from Kitzuki. It may be reached by a mountain path, but the way is extremely steep, rough, and fatiguing. By boat, when the weather is fair, the trip is very agreeable. So, with a friend, I start for Hinomisaki in a very cozy ryosen, skillfully sculled by two young fishermen.

Leaving the pretty bay of Inasa, we follow the coast to the right—a very lofty and grim coast without a beach. Below us the clear water gradually darkens to inky blackness, as the depth increases; but at intervals pale jagged rocks rise up from this nether darkness to catch the light fifty feet under the surface. We keep tolerably close to the cliffs, which vary in height from three hundred to six hundred feet—their bases rising from the water all dull iron-gray, their sides and summits green with young pines and dark grasses that toughen in seawind. All the coast is abrupt, ravined, irregular—curiously breached and fissured. Vast masses of it have toppled into the sea; and the black ruins project from the deep in a hundred shapes of menace. Sometimes our boat glides between a double line of these, or takes a zigzag course through labyrinths of reef-channels. So swiftly and deftly is the little craft impelled to right and left, that one could almost believe it sees its own way and moves by its own intelligence. And again we pass by extraordinary islets of prismatic rock, whose sides, just below the water-line, are heavily mossed with seaweed. The polygonal masses composing these shapes are called by the fishermen "tortoise-shell stones." There is a legend that once Oho-kuni-nushi-no-Kami, to try his strength, came here, and, lifting up one of these masses of basalt, flung it across the sea to the mountain of Sanbeyama. At the foot of Sanbe the mighty rock thus thrown by the Great Deity of Kitzuki may still be seen, it is alleged, even unto this day.

More and more bare and rugged and ghastly the coast becomes as we journey on, and the sunken ledges more numerous, and the protruding rocks more dangerous, splinters of strata piercing the sea surface from a depth of thirty fathoms. Then suddenly our boat makes a dash for the black cliff, and shoots into a tremendous cleft of it—an earthquake fissure with sides lofty and perpendicular as the walls of a cañon—and lo! there is daylight ahead. This is a miniature strait, a short cut to the bay. We glide through it in ten minutes, reach open water again, and Hinomisaki is before us—a semicircle of houses clustering about a bay curve, with an opening in their center, prefaced by a torii.

Of all bays I have ever seen, this is the most extraordinary. Imagine an enormous sea-cliff torn out and broken down level with the sea, so as to leave a great scoop-shaped hollow in the land, with one original fragment of the ancient cliff still standing in the middle of the gap—a monstrous square tower of rock, bearing trees upon its summit. And a thousand yards out from the shore rises another colossal rock; fully one hundred feet high. This is known by the name of Fumishima or Okyōgashima; and the temple of the Sun-goddess, which we are now about to see, formerly stood upon that islet. The same appalling forces which formed the bay of Hinomisaki doubtless also detached the gigantic mass of Fumishima from this iron coast.

We land at the right end of the bay. Here also there is no beach; the water is black-deep close to the shore, which slopes up rapidly. As we mount the slope, an extraordinary spectacle is before us. Upon thousands and thousands of bamboo frames—shaped somewhat like our clothes-horses—are dangling countless pale yellowish things, the nature of which I cannot discern at first glance. But a closer inspection reveals the mystery. Millions of cuttlefish drying in the sun! I could never have believed that so many cuttlefish existed in these waters. And there is scarcely any variation in the dimensions of them: out of ten thousand there is not the difference of half an inch in length.

II.

The great torii which forms the sea-gate of Hinomisaki is of white granite, and severely beautiful. Through it we pass up the main street of the village—surprisingly wide for about a thousand yards, after which it narrows into a common highway which slopes up a wooded hill and disappears under the shadow of trees. On the right, as you enter the street, is a long vision of gray wooden houses with awnings and balconies—little shops, little two-story dwellings of fishermen—and ranging away in front of these other hosts of bamboo frames from which other millions of freshly caught cuttlefish are hanging. On the other side of the street rises a Cyclopean retaining wall, massive as the wall of a daimyō's castle, and topped by a lofty wooden parapet pierced with gates; and above it tower the roofs of majestic buildings, whose architecture strongly resembles that of the structures of Kitzuki; and behind all appears a beautiful green background of hills. This is the Hinomisaki-jinja. But one must walk some considerable distance up the road to reach the main entrance of the court, which is at the farther end of the inclosure, and is approached by an imposing broad flight of granite steps.

The great court is a surprise. It is almost as deep as the outer court of the Kitzuki-no-oho-yashiro, though not nearly so wide; and a paved cloister forms two sides of it. From the court gate a

broad paved walk leads to the haiden and shamusho at the opposite end of the court—spacious and dignified structures above
whose roofs appears the quaint and massive gable of the main
temple, with its fantastic cross-beams. This temple, standing
with its back to the sea, is the shrine of the Goddess of the Sun.
On the right side of the main court, as you enter, another broad
flight of steps leads up to a loftier court, where another fine
group of Shintō buildings stands—a haiden and a miya; but these
are much smaller, like miniatures of those below. Their woodwork also appears to be quite new. The upper miya is the shrine
of the god Susano-ō,*—brother of Ama-terasu-oho-mi-Kami.

III.

To me the great marvel of the Hinomisaki-jinja is that structures so vast, and so costly to maintain, can exist in a mere
fishing hamlet, in an obscure nook of the most desolate coast
of Japan. Assuredly the contributions of peasant pilgrims alone
could not suffice to pay the salary of a single kannushi; for
Hinomisaki, unlike Kitzuki, is not a place possible to visit in all
weathers. My friend confirms me in this opinion; but I learn
from him that the temples have three large sources of revenue.
They are partly supported by the Government; they receive
yearly large gifts of money from pious merchants; and the revenues from lands attached to them also represent a considerable
sum. Certainly a great amount of money must have been very
recently expended here; for the smaller of the two miya seems
to have just been wholly rebuilt; the beautiful joinery is all white
with freshness, and even the carpenters' odorous chips have not
yet been all removed.

At the shamusho we make the acquaintance of the Guji of
Hinomisaki, a noble-looking man in the prime of life, with one

---

* This deity is seldom called by his full name, which has been shortened by common
usage into Susano-ō-no-mikoto.

of those fine aquiline faces rarely to be met with except among
the high aristocracy of Japan. He wears a heavy black moustache,
which gives him, in spite of his priestly robes, the look of a
retired army officer. We are kindly permitted by him to visit the
sacred shrines; and a kannushi is detailed to conduct us through
the buildings.

Something resembling the severe simplicity of the Kitzuki-
no-oho-yashiro was what I expected to see. But this shrine of
the Goddess of the Sun is a spectacle of such splendor that for
the first moment I almost doubt whether I am really in a Shintō
temple. In very truth there is nothing of pure Shintō here. These
shrines belong to the famous period of Ryōbu-Shintō, when the
ancient faith, interpenetrated and allied with Buddhism, adopted the ceremonial magnificence and the marvelous decorative art
of the alien creed. Since visiting the great Buddhist shrines of
the capital, I have seen no temple interior to be compared with
this. Daintily beautiful as a casket is the chamber of the shrine.
All its elaborated woodwork is lacquered in scarlet and gold; the
altarpiece is a delight of carving and color; the ceiling swarms
with dreams of clouds and dragons. And yet the exquisite taste
of the decorators—buried, doubtless, five hundred years ago—
has so justly proportioned the decoration to the needs of surface,
so admirably blended the colors, that there is no gaudiness, no
glare, only an opulent repose.

This shrine is surrounded by a light outer gallery which is not
visible from the lower court; and from this gallery one can study
some remarkable friezes occupying the spaces above the doorways and below the eaves—friezes surrounding the walls of the
miya. These, although exposed for many centuries to the terrific
weather of the western coast, still remain masterpieces of quaint
carving. There are apes and hares peeping through wonderfully
chiseled leaves, and doves and demons, and dragons writhing
in storms. And while looking up at these, my eye is attracted
by a peculiar velvety appearance of the woodwork forming the

immense projecting eaves of the roof. Under the tiling it is more than a foot thick. By standing on tiptoe I can touch it; and I discover that it is even more velvety to the touch than to the sight. Further examination reveals the fact that this colossal roofing is not solid timber, only the beams are solid. The enormous pieces they support are formed of countless broad slices thin as the thinnest shingles, superimposed and cemented together into one solid-seeming mass. I am told that this composite woodwork is more enduring than any hewn timber could be. The edges, where exposed to wind and sun, feel to the touch just like the edges of the leaves of some huge thumb-worn volume; and their stained velvety yellowish aspect so perfectly mocks the appearance of a book, that while trying to separate them a little with my fingeirs, I find myself involuntarily peering for a running-title and the number of a folio!

We then visit the smaller temple. The interior of the sacred chamber is equally rich in lacquered decoration and gilding; and below the miya itself there are strange paintings of weird foxes—foxes wandering in the foreground of a mountain landscape. But here the colors have been damaged somewhat by time; the paintings have a faded look. Without the shrine are other wonderful carvings, doubtless executed by the same chisel which created the friezes of the larger temple.

I learn that only the shrine-chambers of both temples are very old; all the rest has been more than once rebuilt. The entire structure of the smaller temple and its haiden, with the exception of the shrine-room, has just been rebuilt—in fact, the work is not yet quite done—so that the emblem of the deity is not at present in the sanctuary. The shrines proper are never repaired, but simply reinclosed in the new buildings when reconstruction becomes a necessity. To repair them or restore them today would be impossible: the art that created them is dead. But so excellent their material and its lacquer envelope that they have suffered little in the lapse of many centuries from the attacks of time.

One more surprise awaits me—the homestead of the high pontiff, who most kindly invites us to dine with him; which hospitality is all the more acceptable from the fact that there is no hotel in Hinomisaki, but only a kichinyado* for pilgrims.

The ancestral residence of the high pontiffs of Hinomisaki occupies, with the beautiful gardens about it, a space fully equal to that of the great temple courts themselves. Like most of the oldfashioned homes of the nobility and of the samurai, it is but one story high—an immense elevated cottage, one might call it. But the apartments are lofty, spacious, and very handsome—and there is a room of one hundred mats.† A very nice little repast, with abundance of good wine, is served up to us—and I shall always remember one curious dish, which I at first mistake for spinach. It is seaweed, deliciously prepared—not the common edible seaweed, but a rare sort, fine like moss.

After bidding farewell to our generous host, we take an uphill stroll to the farther end of the village. We leave the cuttlefish behind; but before us the greater part of the road is covered with matting, upon which indigo is drying in the sun. The village terminates abruptly at the top of the hill, where there is another grand granite torii—a structure so ponderous that it is almost as difficult to imagine how it was ever brought up the hill as to understand the methods of the builders of Stonehenge. From this torii the road descends to the pretty little seaport of U-Ryō, on the other side of the cape; for Hinomisaki is situated on one side of a great promontory, as its name implies—a mountain range projecting into the Japanese Sea.

---

* A *kichinyado* is an inn at which the traveler is charged only the price of the wood used for fuel in cookng his rice.

† The thick fine straw mats, fitted upon the floor of every Japanese room, are always six feet long by three feet broad. The largest room in the ordinary middle class house is a room of eight mats. A room of one hundred mats is something worth seeing.

IV.

The family of the Guji of Hinomisaki is one of the oldest of the Kwazoku or noble families of Izumo; and the daughters are still addressed by the antique title of Princess—O-Hime-San. The ancient official designation of the pontiff himself was Kengyō, as that of the Kitzuki pontiff was Kokuzō; and the families of the Hinomisaki and of the Kitzuki Guji are closely related.

There is one touching and terrible tradition in the long history of the Kengyōs of Hinomisaki, which throws a strange light upon the social condition of this province in feudal days. Seven generations ago, a Matsudaira, Daimyō of Izumo, made with great pomp his first official visit to the temples of Hinomisaki, and was nobly entertained by the Kengyō—doubtless in the same chamber of a hundred mats which we today were privileged to see. According to custom, the young wife of the host waited upon the regal visitor, and served him with dainties and with wine. She was singularly beautiful; and her beauty, unfortunately, bewitched the Daimyō. With kingly insolence he demanded that she should leave her husband and become his concubine. Although astounded and terrified, she answered bravely, like the true daughter of a samurai, that she was a loving wife and mother, and that, sooner than desert her husband and her child, she would put an end to her life with her own hand. The great Lord of Izumo sullenly departed without further speech, leaving the little household plunged in uttermost grief and anxiety; for it was too well known that the prince would suffer no obstacle to remain in the way of his lust or his hate.

The anxiety, indeed, proved to be well founded. Scarcely had the Daimyō returned to his domains when he began to devise means for the ruin of the Kengyō. Soon afterward, the latter was suddenly and forcibly separated from his family, hastily tried for some imaginary offense, and banished to the islands of Oki. Some say the ship on which he sailed went down at sea with all on board. Others say that he was conveyed to Oki, but only to die there of misery and cold. At all events, the old Izumo records state that, in the year corresponding to 1661 A.D., "the Kengyō Takatoshi died in the land of Oki."

On receiving news of the Kengyō's death, Matsudaira scarcely concealed his exultation. The object of his passion was the daughter of his own Karō, or ministers, one of the noblest samurai of Matsue, by name Kamiya. Kamiya was at once summoned before the Daimyō, who said to him: "Thy daughter's husband being dead, there exists no longer any reason that she should not enter into my household. Do thou bring her hither." The Karō touched the floor with his forehead, and departed on his errand.

Upon the following day he reentered the prince's apartment, and, performing the customary prostration, announced that his lord's commands had been obeyed—that the victim had arrived.

Smiling for pleasure, the Matsudaira ordered that she should be brought at once into his presence. The Karō prostrated himself, retired, and presently returning, placed before his master a kubi-oke* upon which lay the freshly-severed head of a beautiful woman—the head of the young wife of the dead Kengyō—with the simple utterance:

"This is my daughter."

Dead by her own brave will—but never dishonored.

Seven generations have been buried since the Matsudaira strove to appease his remorse by the building of temples and the erection of monuments to the memory of his victim. His own race died with him: those who now bear the illustrious name of that long line of daimyōs are not of the same blood; and the grim ruin of his castle, devoured by vegetation, is tenanted only by lizards and bats. But the Kamiya family endures; no longer wealthy, as in feudal times, but still highly honored in their native city.

---

* The kubi-oke was a lacquered tray with a high rim and a high cover. The name signifies "head-box." It was the ancient custom to place the head of a decapitated person upon a kubi-oke before conveying the ghastly trophy into the palace of the prince desirous of seeing it.

And each high pontiff of Hinomisaki chooses always his bride from among the daughters of that valiant race.

NOTE: The Kengyō of the above tradition was enshrined by Matsudaira in the temple of Shiyeki-jinja, at Ōyama, near Matsue. This miya was built for an atonement; and the people still pray to the spirit of the Kengyō. Near this temple formerly stood a very popular theatre, also erected by the Daimyō in his earnest desire to appease the soul of his victim; for he had heard that the Kengyō was very fond of theatrical performances. The temple is still in excellent preservation; but the theatre has long since disappeared; and its site is occupied by a farmer's vegetable garden.

13

SHINJŪ

I.

SOMETIMES they simply put their arms round each other, and lie down together on the iron rails, just in front of an express train. (They cannot do it in Izumo, however, because there are no railroads there yet.) Sometimes they make a little banquet for themselves, write very strange letters to parents and friends, mix something bitter with their rice-wine, and go to sleep forever. Sometimes they select a more ancient and more honored method: the lover first slays his beloved with a single sword stroke, and then pierces his own throat. Sometimes with the girl's long crape-silk under-girdle (*koshi-obi*) they bind themselves fast together, face to face, and so embracing leap into some deep lake or stream. Many are the modes by which they make their way to the Meido, when tortured by that world-old sorrow about which Schopenhauer wrote so marvelous a theory.

Their own theory is much simpler.

None love life more than the Japanese; none fear death less. Of a future world they have no dread; they regret to leave this one only because it seems to them a world of beauty and of happiness; but the mystery of the future, so long oppressive to Western minds, causes them little concern. As for the young lovers of whom I speak, they have a strange faith which effaces mysteries for them. They turn to the darkness with infinite trust. If they are too unhappy to endure existence, the fault is not another's, nor yet the world's; it is their own.; it is *innen*, the result of errors in a previous life. If they can never hope to be united in this world, it is only because in some former birth they broke their promise to wed, or were otherwise cruel to each other. All this is not heterodox. But they believe likewise that by dying together they will find themselves at once united in another world, though Buddhism proclaims that self-destruction is a deadly sin. Now this idea of winning union through death is incalculably older than the faith of Shaka; but it has somehow borrowed in modern time from Buddhism a particular ecstatic coloring, a mystical glow. *Hasu no hana no ue ni oite matan.* On the lotus-blossoms of paradise they shall rest together. Buddhism teaches of transmigrations countless, prolonged through millions of millions of years, before the soul can acquire the Infinite Vision, the Infinite Memory, and melt into the bliss of Nehan, as a white cloud melts into the summer's blue. But these suffering ones think never of Nehan; love's union, their supremest wish, may be reached, they fancy, through the pang of a single death. The fancies of all, indeed—as their poor letters show—are not the same. Some think themselves about to enter Amida's paradise of light; some see in their visional hope the saki-no-yo only, the future rebirth, when, beloved shall meet beloved again, in the all-joyous freshness of another youth; while the idea of many, indeed of the majority, is vaguer far—only a shadowy drifting together through vapory silences, as in the faint bliss of dreams.

They always pray to be buried together. Often this prayer is refused by the parents or the guardians, and the people deem this refusal a cruel thing, for 'tis believed that those who die for love of each other will find no rest, if denied the same tomb. But when the prayer is granted the ceremony of burial is beautiful and touching. From the two homes the two funeral processions issue to meet in the temple court, by light of lanterns. There, after the recitation of the kyō, and the accustomed impressive ceremonies, the chief priest utters an address to the souls of the dead. Compassionately he speaks of the error and the sin;

of the youth of the victims, brief and comely as the flowers that blossom and fall in the first burst of spring. He speaks of the Illusion—Mayoi—which so wrought upon them; he recites the warning of the Teacher. But sometimes he will even predict the future reunion of the lovers in some happier and higher life, reechoing the popular heart-thought with a simple eloquence that makes his hearers weep. Then the two processions form into one, which takes its way to the cemetery where the grave has already been prepared. The two coffins are lowered together, so that their sides touch as they rest at the bottom of the excavation. Then the yama-no-mono* folk remove the planks which separate the pair—making the two coffins into one; above the reunited dead the earth is heaped; and a haka, bearing in chiseled letters the story of their fate, and perhaps a little poem, is placed above the mingling of their dust.

II.

These suicides of lovers are termed "jōshi" or "shinjū"—(both words being written with the same Chinese characters)—signifying "heart-death," "passion-death," or "love-death." They most commonly occur, in the case of women, among the jorō† class; but occasionally also among young girls of a more respectable class. There is a fatalistic belief that if one shinjū occurs among the inmates of a jorōya, two more are sure to follow. Doubtless the belief itself is the cause that cases of shinjū do commonly occur in series of three.

The poor girls who voluntarily sell themselves to a life of shame for the sake of their families in time of uttermost distress do not, in Japan (except, perhaps, in those open ports where European vice and brutality have become demoralizing influences), ever reach that depth of degradation to which their Western sisters

---

* *Yama-no-mono* ("mountain-folk,"—so called from their settlement on the hills above Tokōji)—a pariah-class whose special calling is the washing of the dead and the making of graves.

† *Jorō*: a courtesan.

descend. Many indeed retain, through all the period of their terrible servitude, a refinement of manner, a delicacy of sentiment, and a natural modesty that seem, under such conditions, as extraordinary as they are touching.

Only yesterday a case of shinjū startled this quiet city. The servant of a physician in the street called Nadamachi, entering the chamber of his master's son a little after sunrise, found the young man lying dead with a dead girl in his arms. The son had been disinherited. The girl was a jorō. Last night they were buried, but not together; for the father was not less angered than grieved that such a thing should have been.

Her name was Kane. She was remarkably pretty and very gentle; and from all accounts it would seem that her master had treated her with a kindness unusual in men of his infamous class. She had sold herself for the sake of her mother and a child-sister. The father was dead, and they had lost everything. She was then seventeen. She had been in the house scarcely a year when she met the youth. They fell seriously in love with each other at once. Nothing more terrible could have befallen them; for they could never hope to become man and wife. The young man, though still allowed the privileges of a son, had been disinherited in favor of an adopted brother of steadier habits. The unhappy pair spent all they had for the privilege of seeing each other: she sold even her dresses to pay for it. Then for the last time they met by stealth, late at night, in the physician's house, drank death, and laid down to sleep forever.

I saw the funeral procession of the girl winding its way by the light of paper lanterns—the wan dead glow that is like a shimmer of phosphorescence—to the Street of the Temples, followed by a long train of women white-hooded, white-robed, white-girdled, passing all soundlessly—a troop of ghosts.

So through blackness to the Meido the white Shapes flit—the eternal procession of Souls—in painted Buddhist dreams of the Under-world

III.

My friend who writes for the "San-in Shimbun," which tomorrow will print the whole sad story, tells me that compassionate folk have already decked the new-made graves with flowers and with sprays of shikimi.* Then drawing from a long native envelope a long, light, thin roll of paper covered with beautiful Japanese writing, and unfolding it before me, he adds:

"She left this letter to the keeper of the house in which she lived: it has been given to us for publication. It is very prettily written. But I cannot translate it well; for it is written in woman's language. The language of letters written by women is not the same as that of letters written by men. Women use particular words and expressions. For instance, in men's language 'I' is watakushi, or ware, or yo, or boku, according to rank or circumstance, but in the language of woman, it is warawa. And women's language is very soft and gentle; and I do not think it is possible to translate such softness and amiability of words into any other language. So I can only give you an imperfect idea of the letter."

And he interprets, slowly, thus:

"I leave this letter:

"As you know, from last spring I began to love Tashirō-San; and he also fell in love with me. And now, alas!—the influence of our relation in some previous birth having come upon us—and the promise we made each other in that former life to become wife and husband having been broken—even today I must travel to the Meido.

"You not only treated me very kindly, though you found me so stupid and without influence,† but you likewise aided in many

---

* *Illicium religiosum.*

† Literally: "without shadow" or "shadowless."

ways for my worthless sake my mother and sister. And now, since I have not been able to repay you even the one-myriadth part of that kindness and pity in which you enveloped, me—pity great as the mountains and the sea,* —it would not be without just reason that you should hate me as a great criminal.

"But though I doubt not this which I am about to do will seem a wicked folly, I am forced to it by conditions and by my own heart. Wherefore I still may pray you to pardon my past faults. And though I go to the Meido, never shall I forget your mercy to me—great as the mountains and the sea. From under the shadow of the grasses† I shall still try to recompense you—to send back my gratitude to you and to your house. Again, with all my heart I pray you: do not be angry with me.

"Many more things I would like to write. But now my heart is not a heart; and I must quickly go. And so I shall lay down my writing-brush.

"It is written so clumsily, this.

"Kane thrice prostrates herself before you.

"From KANE.

"To——SAMA."

"Well, it is a characteristic shinjū letter," my friend comments, after a moment's silence, replacing the frail white paper in its envelope. "So I thought it would interest you. And now, although it is growing dark, I am going to the cemetery to see what has been done at the grave. Would you like to come with me?"

We take our way over the long white bridge, up the shadowy Street of the Temples, toward the ancient hakaba of Miokoji— and the darkness grows as we walk. A thin moon hangs just above the roofs of the great temples.

Suddenly a far voice, sonorous and sweet—a man's voice— breaks into song under the starred night: a song full of strange

---

* *Umi-yama-no-on.*
† *Kusaba-no-kagé.*

charm and tones like warblings—those Japanese tones of popular emotion which seem to have been learned from the songs of birds. Some happy workman returning home. So clear the thin frosty air that each syllable quivers to us; but I cannot understand the words:

> *Saité yuké toya, ano ya wo saité;*
> *Yuké ba chikayoru nushi no soba.*

"What is that?" I ask my friend,

He answers:

"A love-song. '*Go forward, straight forward that way, to the house that thou seest before thee; the nearer thou goest thereto, the nearer to her* shalt thou be.'"

---

* Or "him." This is a free rendering. The word "nushi" simply refers to the owner of the house.

14

YAEGAKI-JINJA

UNTO Yaegaki-jinja, which is in the village of Sakusa in Iu, in the Land of Izumo, all youths and maidens go who are in love, and who can make the pilgrimage. For in the temple of Yaegaki at Sakusa, Take-haya-susa-no-wo-no-mikoto and his wife Inadahime and their son Sa-ku-sa-no-mikoto are enshrined. And these are the Deities of Wedlock and of Love; and they set the solitary in families; and by their doing are destinies coupled even from the hour of birth. Wherefore one should suppose that to make pilgrimage to their temple to pray about things long since irrevocably settled were simple waste of time. But in what land did ever religious practice and theology agree? Scholiasts and priests create or promulgate doctrine and dogma; but the good people always insist upon making the gods according to their own heart—and these are by far the better class of gods. Moreover, the history of Susano-ō, the Impetuous Male Deity, does not indicate that destiny had anything to do with his particular case: he fell in love with the Wondrous Inada Princess at first sight— as it is written in the Kojiki:

"Then Take-haya-susa-no-wo-no-mikoto descended to a place called Tori-kami at the headwaters of the River Hi in the land of Idzumo. At this time a chopstick came floating down the stream. So Take-haya-susa-no-wo-no-mikoto, thinking that there must be people at the headwaters of the river, went up it in quest of them. And he came upon an old man and an old woman who had a young girl between them, and were weeping. Then he deigned to ask: 'Who are ye?' So the old man replied, saying: 'I am an Earthly Deity, son of the Deity Oho-yama-tsu-mi-no-Kami. I am called by the name of Ashi-nadzu-chi; my wife is called by the name of Te-nadzu-chi; and my daughter is called by the name of Kushi-Inada-hime.' Again he asked: 'What is the cause of your crying?' The old man answered, saying: 'I had originally eight young daughters. But the eight-forked serpent of Koshi has come every year, and devoured one; and it is now its time to come, wherefore we weep.' Then he asked him: 'What is its form like?' The old man answered, saying: 'Its eyes are like akakagachi; it has one body with eight heads and eight tails. Moreover, upon its body grow moss and sugi and hinoki trees. Its length extends over eight valleys and eight hills; and if one look at its belly, it is all constantly bloody and inflamed.' Then Take-haya-susa-no-wo-no-mikoto said to the old man: 'If this be thy daughter, wilt thou offer her to me?' He replied: 'With reverence; but I know not thine august name.' Then he replied saying: 'I am elder brother to Ama-terasu-oho-mi-Kami. So now I have descended from heaven.' Then the Deities Ashi-nadzu-chi and Te-nadzu-chi said: 'If that be so, with reverence will we offer her to thee.' So Take-haya-susa-no-wo-no-mikoto, at once taking and changing the young girl into a close-toothed comb, which he stuck into his august hair-bunch, said to the Deities Ashi-nadzu-chi and Te-nadzu-chi: 'Do you distill some eightfold refined liquor. Also make a fence round about; in that fence make eight gates; at each gate tie a platform; on each platform put a liquor-vat; and into each vat pour the eightfold refined liquor, and wait.' So as they waited after having prepared everything in accordance with his bidding, the eight-forked serpent came and put a head into each vat and drank the liquor. Thereupon it was intoxicated, and all the heads lay down and slept. Then Take-haya-susa-no-wo-no-mikoto drew the ten-grasp sabre that was augustly girded upon him, and cut the serpent in pieces, so that the River Hi flowed on changed into a river of blood.

"Then Take-haya-susa-no-wo-no-mikoto sought in the Land of Idzumo where he might build a palace.

"When this great Deity built the palace, clouds rose up thence. Then he made an august song:

> "*Ya-kumo tatsu:*
> Idzumo ya-he-gaki;
> *Tsuma-gaki ni*
>   *Ya-he-gaki tsukuru:*
>   *Sono ya-he-gaki wo!*"*

Now the temple of Yaegaki takes its name from the words of the august song Ya-he-gaki, and therefore signifies the Temple of the Eightfold Fence. And ancient commentators upon the sacred books have said that the name of Idzumo (which is now Izumo), as signifying the Land of the Issuing of Clouds, was also taken from that song of the god.†

II.

Sakusa, the hamlet where the Yaegaki-jinja stands, is scarcely more than one ri south from Matsue. But to go there one must follow tortuous paths too rough and steep for a kuruma; and of three ways, the longest and roughest happens to be the most interesting. It slopes up and down through bamboo groves and primitive woods, and again serpentines through fields of rice and barley, and plantations of indigo and of ginseng, where the scenery is always beautiful or odd. And there are many famed Shintō temples to be visited on the road, such as Take-uchi-jinja, dedicated to the venerable minister of the Empress Jingō, Take-uchi, to whom men now pray for health and for length of

---

* "Eight clouds arise. The eightfold [or, *manifold*] fence of Idzumo makes an eightfold [or, *manifold*] fence for the spouses to retire within. Oh! that eightfold fence!" This is said to be the oldest song in the Japanese language. It has been differently translated by the great scholars and commentators. The above version and text are from Professor B. H. Chamberlain's translation of the *Kojiki* (pp. 60-64).

† Professor Chamberlain disputes this etymology for excellent reasons. But in Izumo itself the etymology is still accepted, and will be accepted, doubtless, until the results of foreign scholarship in the study of the archaic texts is more generally known.

years; and Okusa-no-miya, or Rokusho-jinja, of the five greatest shrines in Izumo; and Manai-jinja, sacred to Izanagi, the Mother of Gods, where strange pictures may be obtained of the Parents of the World; and Oba-no-miya, where Izanami is enshrined, also called Kamoshi-jinja, which means, "The Soul of the God."

At the Temple of the Soul of the God, where the sacred fire-drill used to be delivered each year with solemn rites to the great Kokuzō of Kitzuki, there are curious things to be seen—a colossal grain of rice, more than an inch long, preserved from that period of the Kainiyō when the rice grew tall as the tallest tree and bore grains worthy of the gods; and a caldron of iron in which the peasants say that the first Kokuzō came down from heaven; and a cyclopean tōrō, formed of rocks so huge that one cannot imagine how they were ever balanced upon each other; and the Musical Stones of Oba, which chime like bells when smitten. There is a tradition that these cannot be carried away beyond a certain distance; for 'tis recorded that when a daimyō named Matsudaira ordered one of them to be conveyed to his castle at Matsue, the stone made itself so heavy that a thousand men could not move it farther than the Ōhashi bridge. So it was abandoned before the bridge; and it lies there imbedded in the soil even unto this day.

All about Oba you may see many sekirei or wagtails—birds sacred to Izanami and Izanagi—for a legend says that from the sekirei the gods first learned the art of love. And none, not even the most avaricious farmer, ever hurts or terrifies these birds. So that they do not fear the people of Oba, nor the scarecrows in the fields.

The God of Scarecrows is Sukuna-biko-na-no-Kami.

III.

The path to Sakusa, for the last mile of the journey, at least, is extremely narrow, and has been paved by piety with large flat rocks laid upon the soil at intervals of about a foot, like an inter-minable line of stepping-stones. You cannot walk between them nor beside them, and you soon tire of walking upon them; but they have the merit of indicating the way, a matter of no small importance where fifty rice-field paths branch off from your own at all bewildering angles. After having been safely guided by these stepping-stones through all kinds of labyrinths in rice valleys and bamboo groves, one feels grateful to the peasantry for that clue-line of rocks. There are some quaint little shrines in the groves along this path—shrines with curious carvings of dragons and of lion-heads and flowing water—all wrought ages ago in good keyaki-wood,* which has become the color of stone. But the eyes of the dragons and the lions have been stolen because they were made of fine crystal-quartz, and there was none to guard them, and because neither the laws nor the gods are quite so much feared now as they were before the period of Meiji.

Sakusa is a very small cluster of farmers' cottages before a temple at the verge of a wood—the temple of Yaegaki. The stepping-stones of the path vanish into the pavement of the court, just before its lofty unpainted wooden torii. Between the torii and the inner court, entered by a Chinese gate, some grand old trees are growing, and there are queer monuments to see.

On either side of the great gateway is a shrine compartment, inclosed by heavy wooden gratings on two sides; and in these compartments are two grim figures in complete armor, with bows in their hands and quivers of arrows upon their backs—the Zuijin, or ghostly retainers of the gods, and guardians of the gate. Before nearly all the Shintō temples of Izumo, except Kitzuki, these Zuijin keep grim watch. They are probably of Buddhist origin; but they have acquired a Shintō history and Shintō names.† Originally, I am told, there was but one Zuijin-

---

* *Planeca Japonica.*

† So absolutely has Shintō in Izumo monopolized the Karashishi, or stone lions, of Buddhist origin, that it is rare in the province to find a pair before any Buddhist temple. There is even a Shintō myth, about their introduction into Japan from India, by the Fox-God!

Kami, whose name was Toyo-kushi-iwa-ma-to-no-mikoto. But at a certain period both the god and his name were cut in two—perhaps for decorative purposes. And now he who sits upon the left is called Toyoiwa-ma-to-no-mikoto; and his companion on the right, Kushi-iwa-ma-to-no-mikoto.

Before the gate, on the left side, there is a stone monument upon which is graven, in Chinese characters, a poem in Hokku, or verse of seventeen syllables, composed by Chō-un:

> *Ko-ka-ra-shi-ya*
> *Ka-mi-no-mi-yu-ki-no*
> *Ya-ma-no-a-to.*

My companion translates the characters thus: "Where high heap the dead leaves, there is the holy place upon the hills, where dwell the gods." Near by are stone lanterns and stone lions, and another monument—a great five-cornered slab set up and chiseled—bearing the names in Chinese characters of the Ji-jin, or Earth-Gods—the Deities who protect the soil: Uga-no-mitama-no-mikoto (whose name signifies the August Spirit-of-Food), Amaterasu-oho-mi-Kami, Ona-muji-no-Kami, Kaki-yasu-hime-no-Kami, Sukuna-hiko-na-no-Kami (who is the Scarecrow God). And the figure of a fox in stone sits before the Name of the August Spirit-of-Food.

The miya or Shintō temple itself is quite small—smaller than most of the temples in the neighborhood, and dingy, and be-grimed with age. Yet, next to Kitzuki, this is the most famous of Izumo shrines. The main shrine, dedicated to Susano-ō and Inadahime and their son, whose name is the name of the hamlet of Sakusa, is flanked by various lesser shrines to left and right. In one of these smaller miya the spirit of Ashi-nadzu-chi, father of Inada-hime, is supposed to dwell; and in another that of Te-nadzu-chi, the mother of Inada-hime. There is also a small shrine of the Goddess of the Sun. But these shrines have no curious fea-tures. The main temple offers, on the other hand, some displays of rarest interest.

To the gray weather-worn gratings of the doors of the shrine hundreds and hundreds of strips of soft white paper have been tied in knots: there is nothing written upon them, although each represents a heart's wish and a fervent prayer. No prayers, indeed, are so fervent as those of love. Also there are suspended many little sections of bamboo, cut just below joints so as to form water receptacles: these are tied together in pairs with a small straw cord which also serves to hang them up. They contain offerings of sea-water carried here from no small distance. And mingling with the white confusion of knotted papers there dangle from the gratings many tresses of girls' hair—love-sacrifices*—and numerous offerings of seaweed, so filamentary and so sunblackened that at some little distance it would not be easy to distinguish them from long shorn tresses. And all the woodwork of the doors and the gratings, both beneath and between the offerings, is covered with a speckling of characters graven or written, which are names of pilgrims. And my companion reads aloud the well-remembered name of—AKIRA!

If one dare judge the efficacy of prayer to these kind gods of Shintō from the testimony of their worshipers, I should certainly say that Akira has good reason to hope. Planted in the soil, all round the edge of the foundations of the shrine, are multitudes of tiny paper flags of curious shape *(nobori)* pasted upon splinters of bamboo. Each of these little white things is a banner of victory, and a lover's witness of gratitude.† You will find such little flags stuck into the ground about nearly all the great Shintō temples of Izumo. At Kitzuki they cannot even be counted—any more than the flakes of a snow-storm.

---

* Such offerings are called Gwan-hodoki. *Gwan wo hodoki*, "to make a vow."

† A pilgrim whose prayer has been heard usually plants a single nobori as a token. Sometimes you may see nobori of five colors *(goshiki)*—black, yellow, red, blue, and white—of which one hundred or one thousand have been planted by one person. But this is done only in pursuance of some very special row.

And here is something else that you will find at most of the famous miya in Izumo—a box of little bamboo sticks, fastened to a post before the doors. If you were to count the sticks, you would find their number to be exactly one thousand. They are counters for pilgrims who make a vow to the gods to perform a sendo-mairi. To perform a sendo-mairi means to visit the temple one thousand times. This, however, is so hard to do that busy pious men make a sort of compromise with the gods, thus: they walk from the shrine one foot beyond the gate, and back again to the shrine, one thousand times—all in one day, keeping count with the little splints of bamboo.

There is one more famous thing to be seen before visiting the holy grove behind the temple, and that is the Sacred Tama-tsubaki, or Precious-Camellia of Yaegaki. It stands upon a little knoll, fortified by a projection-wall, in a rice-field near the house of the priest; a fence has been built around it, and votive lamps of stone placed before it. It is of vast age, and has two heads and two feet; but the twin trunks grow together at the middle. Its unique shape, and the good quality of longevity it is believed to possess in common with all of its species, cause it to be revered as a symbol of undying wedded love, and as tenanted by the Kami who hearken to lovers' prayers—en-musubi-no-kami.

There is, however, a strange superstition about tsubaki-trees; and this sacred tree of Yaegaki, in the opinion of some folk, is a rare exception to the general ghastliness of its species. For tsubaki-trees are goblin trees, they say, and walk about at night; and there was one in the garden of a Matsue samurai which did this so much that it had to be cut down. Then it writhed its arms and groaned, and blood spurted at every stroke of the axe.

IV.

At the spacious residence of the kannushi some very curious ofuda and o-mamori—the holy talismans and charms of Yaegaki—are sold, together with pictures representing Take-haya-susa-no-wo-nomikoto and his bride Inada-hime surrounded by the "manifold fence" of clouds. On the pictures is also printed the august song whence the temple derives its name of Yaegaki-jinja—"*Ya kumo tatsu Idzumo ya-he-gaki.*" Of the o-mamori there is quite a variety; but by far the most interesting is that labeled: "*Izumo-Yaegaki-jinja-en-musubi-on-hina*" (August wedlock-producing "hina" of the temple of Yaegaki of Izumo). This oblong, folded paper, with Chinese characters and the temple seal upon it, is purchased only by those in love, and is believed to assure nothing more than the desired union. Within the paper are two of the smallest conceivable doll-figures *(hina)*, representing a married couple in antique costume—the tiny wife folded to the breast of the tiny husband by one long-sleeved arm. It is the duty of whoever purchases this mamori to return it to the temple if he or she succeed in marrying the person beloved. As already stated, the charm is not supposed to assure anything more than the union: it cannot be accounted responsible for any consequences thereof. He who desires perpetual love must purchase another mamori labeled: "*Renri-tama-tsubaki-aikyō-goki-to-on-mamori*" (August amulet of august prayer-for-kindling-love of the jewel-precious tsubaki—tree-of-Union). This charm should maintain at constant temperature the warmth of affection—it contains only a leaf of the singular double-bodied camellia-tree before mentioned. There are also small amulets for exciting love, and amulets for the expelling of diseases, but these have no special characteristics worth dwelling upon.

Then we take our way to the sacred grove—the Okuno-in, or Mystic Shades of Yaegaki.

V.

This ancient grove—so dense that when you first pass into its shadows out of the sun all seems black—is composed of colossal cedars and pines, mingled with bamboo, tsubaki (*Camellia Japonica*), and sakaki, the sacred and mystic tree of Shintō. The dimness is chiefly made by the huge bamboos. In nearly all sacred groves bamboos are thickly set between the trees, and their feathery foliage, filling every lofty opening between the heavier crests, entirely cuts off the sun. Even in a bamboo grove where no other trees are, there is always a deep twilight.

As the eyes become accustomed to this green gloaming, a pathway outlines itself between the trees—a pathway wholly covered with moss, velvety, soft, and beautifully verdant. In former years, when all pilgrims were required to remove their footgear before entering the sacred grove, this natural carpet was a boon to the weary. The next detail one observes is that the trunks of many of the great trees have been covered with thick rush matting to a height of seven or eight feet, and that holes have been torn through some of the mats. All the giants of the grove are sacred; and the matting was bound about them to prevent pilgrims from stripping off their bark, which is believed to possess miraculous virtues. But many, more zealous than honest, do not hesitate to teat away the matting in order to get at the bark. And the third curious fact which you notice is that the trunks of the great bamboos are covered with ideographs—with the wishes of lovers and the names of girls. There is nothing in the world of vegetation so nice to write a sweetheart's name upon as the polished bark of a bamboo: each, letter, however lightly traced at first, enlarges and blackens with the growth of the bark, and never fades away.

The deeply mossed path slopes down to a little pond in the very heart of the grove—a pond famous in the land of Izumo. Here there are many imori, or water-newts, about five inches long, which have red bellies. Here the shade is deepest, and the stems of the bamboos most thickly tattooed with the names of girls. It is believed that the flesh of the newts in the sacred pond of Yaegaki possesses aphrodisiac qualities; and the body of the creature, reduced to ashes by burning, was formerly converted into love-powders. And there is a little Japanese song referring to the practice:

"*Hore-gusuri hoka niwa naika to imori ni toeba, yubi-wo marumete kore bakari*"*

The water is very clear; and there are many of these newts to be seen. And it is the custom for lovers to make a little boat of paper, and put into it one rin, and set it afloat, and watch it. So soon as the paper becomes wet through, and allows the water to enter it, the weight of the copper coin soon sends it to the bottom, where, owing to the purity of the water, it can be still seen distinctly as before. If the newts then approach and touch it, the lovers believe their happiness assured by the will of the gods; but if the newts do not come near it, the omen is evil. One poor little paper boat, I observe, could not sink at all; it simply floated to the inaccessible side of the pond, where the trees rise like a solid wall of trunks from the water's edge, and there became caught in some drooping branches. The lover who launched it must have departed sorrowing at heart.

Close to the pond, near the pathway, there are many camellia-bushes, of which the tips of the branches have been tied together, by pairs, with strips of white paper. These are shrubs of presage. The true lover must be able to bend two branches together, and to keep them united by tying a paper tightly about them—all with the fingers of one hand. To do this well is good luck. Nothing is written upon the strips of paper.

But there is enough writing upon the bamboos to occupy curiosity for many an hour, in spite of the mosquitoes. Most of the names are yobi-na—that is to say, pretty names of women; but there are likewise names of men—jitsumyō;† and, oddly enough, a girl's name and a man's are in no instance written together. To judge by all this ideographic testimony, lovers in Japan—or at

---

* "On being asked if there were any other love charm, the Newt replied, making a ring with two of his toes—'Only this.' The sign signifies, 'Money.'"

† There are no less than eleven principal kinds of Japanese names. The jitsumyō, or "true name," corresponds to our Christian name. On this intricate and interesting topic the reader should consult Professor B. H. Chamberlain's excellent little book, *Things Japanese*, pp. 250-255.

least in Izumo—are even more secretive than in our Occident. The enamored youth never writes his own jitsumyō and his sweetheart's yobi-na together; and the family name, or myōji, he seldom ventures to inscribe. If he writes his jitsumyō, then he contents himself with whispering the yobi-na of his sweetheart to the gods and to the bamboos. If he cuts her yobi-na into the bark, then he substitutes for his own name a mention of his existence and his age only, as in this touching instance:

> *Takata-Toki-to-en-musubi-negaimas.*
> *Jiu-hassai-no-otoko.**

This lover presumes to write his girl's whole name; but the example, so far as I am able to discover, is unique. Other enamored ones write only the yobi-na of their bewitchers; and the honorable prefix, "O," and the honorable suffix, "San," find no place in the familiarity of love. There is no "O-Haru-San," "O-Kin-San," "O-Take-San," "O-Kiku-San," but there are hosts of Haru, and Kin, and Take, and Kiku. Girls, of course, never dream of writing their lovers' names. But there are many geimyō here, "artistic names,"—names of mischievous geisha who worship the Golden Kitten, written by their saucy selves: Rakue and Asae and Wakai, Aikichi and Kotobuki and Kohachi, Kohana and Tamakichi and Katsuko, and Asakichi and Hanakichi and Katsukichi, and Chiyoe and Chiyotsuru. "Fortunate Pleasure," "Happy-Dawn," and "Youth" (such are their appellations), "Blest-Love" and "Length-of-Days," and "Blossom-Child" and "Jewel-of-Fortune" and "Child-of-Luck," and "Joyous-Sunrise" and "Flower-of-Bliss" and "Glorious Victory," and "Life-as-the-Stork's-for-a-thousand-years." Often shall he curse the day he was born who falls in love with Happy-Dawn; thrice unlucky the wight bewitched by the Child-of-Luck; woe unto him who hopes to cherish the Flower-of-Bliss; and more than once shall he wish himself dead whose heart is snared by Life-as-the-Stork's-for-a-thousand-years. And I see

---

* "That I may be wedded to Takata-Toki, I humbly pray. – A youth of eighteen."

that somebody who inscribes his age as twenty and three has become enamored of young Wakagusa, whose name signifies the tender Grass of Spring. Now there is but one possible misfortune for you, dear boy, worse than falling in love with Wakagusa—and that is that she should happen to fall in love with you. Because then you would, both of you, write some beautiful letters to your friends, and drink death, and pass away in each other's arms, murmuring your trust to rest together upon the same lotus-flower in Paradise: "*Hasu no ha no ue ni oite matsu.*" Nay! pray the Deities rather to dissipate the bewitchment that is upon you:

> *Te ni toru na,*
> *Yahari no ni oke*
> *Gengebana.**

And here is a lover's inscription—in English! Who presumes to suppose that the gods know English? Some student, no doubt, who for pure shyness engraved his soul's secret in this foreign tongue of mine—never dreaming that a foreign eye would look upon it. "*I wish You, Haru!*" Not once, but four—no, five times!— each time omitting the preposition. Praying—in this ancient grove—in this ancient Land of Izumo—unto the most ancient gods in English! Verily, the shyest love presumes much upon the forbearance of the gods. And great indeed must be either the patience of Take-hayasusa-no-wo-no-mikoto, or the rustiness of the ten-grasp sabre that was augustly girded upon him.

---

* The gengebana (also called renge-so, and in Izumo miakobana) is an herb planted only for fertilizing purposes. Its flowers are extremely small, but so numerous that in their blossoming season miles of fields are colored by them a beautiful lilaceous blue. A gentleman who wished to marry a jorō despite the advice of his friends, was gently chided by them with the above little verse, which, freely translated, signifies: "Take it not into thy hand: the flowers of the gengebana are fair to view only when left all together in the field."

15

KITSUNE

I.

By every shady wayside and in every ancient grove, on almost every hilltop and in the outskirts of every village, you may see, while traveling through the Hondo country, some little Shintō shrine, before which, or at either side of which, are images of seated foxes in stone. Usually there is a pair of these, facing each other. But there may be a dozen, or a score, or several hundred, in which case most of the images are very small. And in more than one of the larger towns you may see in the court of some great miya a countless host of stone foxes, of all dimensions, from toy-figures but a few inches high to the colossi whose pedestals tower above your head, all squatting around the temple in tiered ranks of thousands. Such shrines and temples, everybody knows, are dedicated to Inari, the God of Rice. After having traveled much in Japan, you will find that whenever you try to recall any country-place you have visited, there will appear in some nook or corner of that remembrance a pair of green-and-gray foxes of stone, with broken noses. In my own memories of Japanese travel, these shapes have become *de rigueur*, as picturesque detail.

In the neighborhood of the capital and in Tōkyō itself—sometimes in the cemeteries—very beautiful idealized figures of foxes may be seen, elegant as greyhounds. They have long green or gray eyes of crystal quartz or some other diaphanous substance; and they create a strong impression as mythological conceptions.

But throughout the interior, fox-images are much less artistically fashioned. In Izumo, particularly, such stone-carving has a decidedly primitive appearance. There is an astonishing multiplicity and variety of fox-images in the Province of the Gods—images comical, quaint, grotesque, or monstrous, but, for the most part, very rudely chiseled. I cannot, however, declare them less interesting on that account. The work of the Tokkaido sculptor copies the conventional artistic notion of light grace and ghostliness. The rustic foxes of Izumo have no grace: they are uncouth; but they betray in countless queer ways the personal fancies of their makers. They are of many moods—whimsical, apathetic, inquisitive, saturnine, jocose, ironical; they watch and snooze and squint and wink and sneer; they wait with lurking smiles; they listen with cocked ears most stealthily, keeping their mouths open or closed. There is an amusing individuality about them all, and an air of knowing mockery about most of them, even those whose noses have been broken off. Moreover, these ancient country foxes have certain natural beauties which their modern Tōkyō kindred cannot show. Time has bestowed upon them divers speckled coats of beautiful soft colors while they have been sitting on their pedestals, listening to the ebbing and flowing of the centuries and snickering weirdly at mankind. Their backs are clad with finest green velvet of old mosses; their limbs are spotted and their tails are tipped with the dead gold or the dead silver of delicate fungi. And the places they most haunt are the loveliest— high shadowy groves where the uguisu sings in green twilight, above some voiceless shrine with its lamps and its lions of stone so mossed as to seem things born of the soil—like mushrooms.

I found it difficult to understand why, out of every thousand foxes, nine hundred should have broken noses. The main street of the city of Matsue might be paved from end to end with the tips of the noses of mutilated Izumo foxes. A friend answered my expression of wonder in this regard by the simple but suggestive word, "*Kodomo*" which means, "The children."

II.

Inari, the name by which the Fox-God is generally known, signifies "Load-of-Rice." But the antique name of the Deity is the August-Spirit-of-Food: he is the Uka-no-mi-tama-no-mikoto of the Kojiki.* In much more recent times only has he borne the name that indicates his connection with the fox-cult, Miketsu-no-Kami, or the Three-Fox-God. Indeed, the conception of the fox as a supernatural being does not seem to have been introduced into Japan before the tenth or eleventh century; and although a shrine of the deity, "with statues of foxes, may be found in the court of most of the large Shintō temples, it is worthy of note that in all the vast domains of the oldest Shintō shrine in Japan—Kitzuki—you cannot find the image of a fox. And it is only in modern art—the art of Toyokuni and others—that Inari is represented as a bearded man riding a white fox.†

Inari is not worshiped as the God of Rice only; indeed, there are many Inari, just as in antique Greece there were many deities called Hermes, Zeus, Athena, Poseidon—one in the knowledge of the learned, but essentially different in the imagination of the common people. Inari has been multiplied by reason of his different attributes. For instance, Matsue has a Kamiya-San-no-

---

* Toyo-uke-bime-no-Kami, or Uka-no-mi-tama (who has also eight other names), is a female divinity, according to the *Kojiki* and its commentators. Moreover, the greatest of all Shintō scholars, Hirata, as cited by Satow, says there is really no such god as Inari-San at all—that the very name is an error. But the common people have created the *God* Inari: therefore he must be presumed to exist—if only for folk-lorists; and I speak of him as a male deity because I see him so represented in pictures and carvings. As to his mythological existence, his great and wealthy temple at Kyōto is impressive testimony.

† The white fox is a favorite subject with Japanese artists. Some very beautiful kake-mono representing white foxes were on display at the Tōkyō exhibition of 1890. Phosphorescent foxes often appear in the old colored prints, now so rare and precious, made by artists whose names have become world-famous. Occasionally foxes are represented wandering about at night, with lambent tongues of dim fire—*kitsune-bi*—above their heads. The end of the fox's tail, both in sculpture and drawing, is ordinarily decorated with the symbolic jewel (*tama*) of old Buddhist art. I have in my possession one kake-mono representing a white fox with a luminous jewel in its tail. I purchased it at the Matsue temple of Inari—"O-Shiroyama-no-Inari-Sama." The art of the kakemono is clumsy; but the conception possesses curious interest.

Inari-San, who is the God of Coughs and Bad Colds—afflictions extremely common and remarkably severe in the Land of Izumo. He has a temple in the Kamachi at which he is worshiped under the vulgar appellation of Kaze-no-Kami and the politer one of Kamiya-San-no-Inari. And those who are cured of their coughs and colds after having prayed to him, bring to his temple offerings of tofu.

At Oba, likewise, there is a particular Inari, of great fame. Fastened to the wall of his shrine is a large box full of small clay foxes. The pilgrim who has a prayer to make puts one of these little foxes in his sleeve and carries it home. He must keep it, and pay it all due honor, until such time as his petition has been granted. Then he must take it back to the temple, and restore it to the box, and, if he be able, make some small gift to the shrine.

Inari is often worshiped as a healer; and still more frequently as a deity having power to give wealth. (Perhaps because all the wealth of Old Japan was reckoned in koku of rice.) Therefore his foxes are sometimes represented holding keys in their mouths. And from being the deity who gives wealth, Inari has also become in some localities the special divinity of the jorō class. There is, for example, an Inari temple worth visiting in the neighborhood of the Yoshiwara at Yokohama. It stands in the same court with a temple of Benten, and is more than usually large for a shrine of Inari. You approach it through a succession of torii, one behind the other: they are of different heights, diminishing in size as they are placed nearer to the temple, and planted more and more closely in proportion to their smallness. Before each torii sit a pair of weird foxes—one to the right and one to the left. The first pair are large as greyhounds; the second two are much smaller; and the sizes of the rest lessen as the dimensions of the torii lessen. At the foot of the wooden steps of the temple there is a pair of very graceful foxes of dark gray stone, wearing pieces of red cloth about their necks. Upon the steps themselves are white wooden foxes—one at each end of each step—each successive pair being smaller than the pair below; and at the threshold of the doorway are two very little foxes, not more than three inches high, sitting on sky-blue pedestals. These have the tips of their tails gilded. Then, if you look into the temple you will see on the left something like a long low table on which are placed thousands of tiny fox-images, even smaller than those in the doorway, having only plain white tails. There is no image of Inari; indeed, I have never seen an image of Inari as yet in any Inari temple. On the altar appear the usual emblems of Shintō; and before it, just opposite the doorway, stands a sort of lantern, having glass sides and a wooden bottom studded with nailpoints on which to fix votive candles.*

And here, from time to time, if you will watch, you will probably see more than one handsome girl, with brightly painted lips and the beautiful antique attire that no maiden or wife may wear, come to the foot of the steps, toss a coin into the money-box at the door, and call out: "*O-rōsoku!*" which means "an honorable candle." Immediately, from an inner chamber, some old man will enter the shrine-room with a lighted candle, stick it upon a nail-point in the lantern, and then retire. Such candle-offerings are always accompanied by secret prayers for good-fortune. But this Inari is worshiped by many besides members of the jorō class.

The pieces of colored cloth about the necks of the foxes are also votive offerings.

III.

Fox-images in Izumo seem to be more numerous than in other provinces, and they are symbols there, so far as the mass of the peasantry is concerned, of something else besides the worship of the Rice-Deity. Indeed, the old conception of the Deity of Rice-fields has been overshadowed and almost effaced among the lowest classes by a weird cult totally foreign to the spirit

---

* The Japanese candle has a large hollow paper wick. It is usually placed upon an iron point which enters into the orifice of the wick at the flat end.

of pure Shintō—the Fox-cult. The worship of the retainer has almost replaced the worship of the god. Originally the Fox was sacred to Inari only as the Tortoise is still sacred to Kompira; the Deer to the Great Deity of Kasuga; the Rat to Daikoku; the Tai-fish to Ebisu; the White Serpent to Benten; or the Centipede to Bishamon, God of Battles. But in the course of centuries the Fox usurped divinity. And the stone images of him are not the only outward evidences of his cult. At the rear of almost every Inari temple you will generally find in the wall of the shrine building, one or two feet above the ground, an aperture about eight inches in diameter and perfectly circular. It is often made so as to be closed at will by a sliding plank. This circular orifice is a Fox-hole, and if you find one open, and look within, you will probably see offerings of tofu or other food which foxes are supposed to be fond of. You will also, most likely, find grains of rice scattered on some little projection of woodwork below or near the hole, or placed on the edge of the hole itself; and you may see some peasant clap his hands before the hole, utter some little prayer, and swallow a grain or two of that rice in the belief that it will either cure or prevent sickness. Now the fox for whom such a hole is made is an invisible fox, a phantom fox—the fox respectfully referred to by the peasant as O-Kitsune-San. If he ever suffers himself to become visible, his color is said to be snowy white.

According to some, there are various kinds of ghostly foxes. According to others, there are two sorts of foxes only, the Inari-fox (O-Kitsune-San) and the wild fox (kitsune). Some people again class foxes into Superior and Inferior Foxes, and allege the existence of four Superior Sorts—Byakko; Kokko, Jenko, and Reiko—all of which possess supernatural powers. Others again count only three kinds of foxes—the Field-fox, the Man-fox, and the Inari-fox. But many confound the Field-fox or wild fox with the Man-fox, and others identify the Inari-fox with the Man-fox. One cannot possibly unravel the confusion of these beliefs, especially among the peasantry. The beliefs vary, moreover, in different districts. I have only been able, after a residence of fourteen months in Izumo, where the superstition is especially strong, and marked by certain unique features, to make the following very loose summary of them:

All foxes have supernatural power. There are good and bad foxes. The Inari-fox is good, and the bad foxes are afraid of the Inari-fox. The worst fox is the Ninko or Hito-kitsune (Man-fox): this is especially the fox of demoniacal possession. It is no larger than a weasel, and somewhat similar in shape, except for its tail, which is like the tail of any other fox. It is rarely seen, keeping itself invisible, except to those to whom it attaches itself. It likes to live in the houses of men, and to be nourished by them, and to the homes where it is well cared for it will bring prosperity. It will take care that the ricefields shall never want for water, nor the cooking-pot for rice. But if offended, it will bring misfortune to the household, and ruin to the crops. The wild fox (Nogitsune) is also bad. It also sometimes takes possession of people; but it is especially a wizard, and prefers to deceive by enchantment. It has the power of assuming any shape and of making itself invisible; but the dog can always see it, so that it is extremely afraid of the dog. Moreover, while assuming another shape, if its shadow fall upon water, the water will only reflect the shadow of a fox. The peasantry kill it; but he who kills a fox incurs the risk of being bewitched by that fox's kindred, or even by the *ki,* or ghost of the fox. Still if one eat the flesh of a fox, he cannot be enchanted afterwards. The Nogitsune also enters houses. Most families having foxes in their houses have only the small kind, or Ninko; but occasionally both kinds will live together under the same roof. Some people say that if the Nogitsune lives a hundred years it becomes all white, and then takes rank as an Inari-fox.

There are curious contradictions involved in these beliefs, and other contradictions will be found in the following pages of this sketch. To define the fox-superstition at all is difficult, not only on account of the confusion of ideas on the subject among the believers themselves, but also on account of the variety of elements out of which it has been shapen. Its origin is Chinese;* but in Japan it became oddly blended with the worship of a Shintō deity, and again modified and expanded by the Buddhist concepts of thaumaturgy and magic. So far as the common people are concerned, it is perhaps safe to say that they pay devotion to foxes chiefly because they fear them. The peasant still worships what he fears.

IV.

It is more than doubtful whether the popular notions about different classes of foxes, and about the distinction between the fox of Inari and the fox of possession, were ever much more clearly established than they are now, except in the books of old *literati*. Indeed, there exists a letter from Hideyoshi to the Fox-God which would seem to show that in the time of the great Taikō the Inari-fox and the demon fox were considered identical. This letter is still preserved at Nara, in the Buddhist temple called Todaiji:

> KYŌTO, the seventeenth day
> of the Third Month.

To INARI DAIMYOJIN:

My Lord—I have the honor to inform you that one of the foxes under your jurisdiction has bewitched one of my servants, causing her and others a great deal of trouble. I have to request that you will make minute inquiries into the matter, and endeavor to find out the reason of your subject misbehaving in this way, and let me know the result.

If it turns out that the fox has no adequate reason to give for his behavior, you are to arrest and punish him at once. If you hesitate to take action in this matter, I shall issue orders for the destruction of every fox in the land.

---

* See Professor Chamberlain's *Things Japanese*, under the title, "Demoniacal Possession."

Any other particulars that you may wish to be informed of in reference to what has occurred, you can learn from the high-priest YOSHIDA.

Apologizing for the imperfections of this letter, I have the honor to be

Your obedient servant,

HIDEYOSHI TAIKŌ.*

But there certainly were some distinctions established in localities, owing to the worship of Inari by the military caste. With the samurai of Izumo, the Rice-God, for obvious reasons, was a highly popular deity; and you can still find in the garden of almost every old shizoku residence in Matsue, a small shrine of Inari Daimyōjin, with little stone foxes seated before it. And in the imagination of the lower classes, all samurai families possessed foxes. But the samurai foxes inspired no fear. They were believed to be "good foxes;" and the superstition of the Ninko or Hito-kitsune does not seem to have unpleasantly affected any samurai families of Matsue during the feudal era. It is only since the military caste has been abolished, and its name, simply as a body of gentry, changed to *shizoku,*† that some families have become victims of the superstition through intermarriage with the *chōnin,* or mercantile classes, among whom the belief has always been strong.

By the peasantry the Matsudaira daimyō of Izumo were supposed to be the greatest fox-possessors. One of them was believed to use foxes as messengers to Tōkyō (be it observed that a fox can travel, according to popular credence, from Yokohama to London in a few hours); and there is some Matsue story about a fox having been caught in a trap‡ near Tōkyō, attached to

---

* Translated by Walter Dening.

† The word *shizoku* is simply the Chinese for *samurai*. But the term now means little more than "gentleman" in England.

‡ The fox-messenger travels unseen. But if caught in a trap, or injured, his magic fails him, and he becomes visible.

whose neck was a letter written by the prince of Izumo only the same morning. The great Inari temple of Inari in the castle grounds—O-Shiroyama-no-Inari-Sama—with its thousands upon thousands of foxes of stone, is considered by the country people a striking proof of the devotion of the Matsudaira, not to Inari, but to foxes.

At present, however, it is no longer possible to establish distinctions of genera in this ghostly zoology, where each species grows into every other. It is not even possible to disengage the *ki* or Soul of the Fox and the August-Spirit-of-Food from the confusion in which both have become hopelessly blended under the name Inari, by the vague conception of their peasant-worshipers. The old Shintō mythology is indeed quite explicit about the August-Spirit-of-Food, and quite silent upon the subject of foxes. But the peasantry in Izumo, like the peasantry of Catholic Europe, make mythology for themselves. If asked whether they pray to Inari as to an evil or a good deity, they will tell you that Inari is good, and that Inari-foxes are good. They will tell you of white foxes and dark foxes—of foxes to be reverenced and foxes to be killed—of the good fox which cries "kon-kon," and the evil fox which cries "kwaikwai." But the peasant possessed by the fox cries out: "I *am Inari—Tamabushi-no-Inari!*"—or some other Inari.

V.

Goblin foxes are peculiarly dreaded in Izumo for three evil habits attributed to them. The first is that of deceiving people by enchantment, either for revenge or pure mischief. The second is that of quartering themselves as retainers upon some family, and thereby making that family a terror to its neighbors. The third and worst is that of entering into people and taking diabolical possession of them and tormenting them into madness. This affliction is called "kitsune-tsuki."

The favorite shape assumed by the goblin fox for the purpose of deluding mankind is that of a beautiful woman; much less frequently the form of a young man is taken in order to deceive some one of the other sex. Innumerable are the stories told or written about the wiles of fox-women. And a dangerous woman of that class whose art is to enslave men, and strip them of all they possess, is popularly named by a word of deadly insult—*kitsune.*

Many declare that the fox never really assumes human shape; but that he only deceives people into the belief that he does so by a sort of magnetic power, or by spreading about them a certain magical effluvium.

The fox does not always appear in the guise of a woman for evil purposes. There are several stories, and one really pretty play, about a fox who took the shape of a beautiful woman, and married a man, and bore him children—all out of gratitude for some favor received—the happiness of the family being only disturbed by some odd carnivorous propensities on the part of the offspring. Merely to achieve a diabolical purpose, the form of a woman is not always the best disguise. There are men quite insusceptible to feminine witchcraft. But the fox is never at a loss for a disguise; he can assume more forms than Proteus. Furthermore, he can make you see or hear or imagine whatever he wishes you to see, hear, or imagine. He can make you see out of Time and Space; he can recall the past and reveal the future. His power has not been destroyed by the introduction of Western ideas; for did he not, only a few years ago, cause phantom trains to run upon the Tokkaido railway, thereby greatly confounding and terrifying the engineers of the company? But, like all goblins, he prefers to haunt solitary places. At night he is fond of making queer ghostly lights,* in semblance of lantern-fires, flit about dangerous places; and to protect yourself from this trick of his, it is necessary to learn that by joining your hands in a particular way, so as to leave a diamond-shaped aperture between the crossed fingers, you can extinguish the witch-fire at any distance simply

* The *Will-o' the-wisp* is called *Kitsune-bi*, or "fox-fire."

by blowing through the aperture in the direction of the light and uttering a certain Buddhist formula.

But it is not only at night that the fox manifests his power for mischief: at high noon he may tempt you to go where you are sure to get killed, or frighten you into going by creating some apparition or making you imagine that you feel an earthquake. Consequently the old-fashioned peasant, on seeing anything extremely queer, is slow to credit the testimony of his own eyes. The most interesting and valuable witness of the stupendous eruption of Bandai-San in 1888—which blew the huge volcano to pieces and devastated an area of twenty-seven square miles, leveling forests, turning rivers from their courses, and burying numbers of villages with all their inhabitants—was an old peasant who had watched the whole cataclysm from a neighboring peak as unconcernedly as if he had been looking at a drama. He saw a black column of ashes and steam rise to the height of twenty thousand feet and spread out at its summit in the shape of an umbrella, blotting out the sun. Then he felt a strange rain pouring upon him, hotter than the water of a bath. Then all became black; and he felt the mountain beneath him shaking to its roots, and heard a crash of thunders that seemed like the sound of the breaking of a world. But he remained quite still until everything was over. He had made up his mind not to be afraid—deeming that all he saw and heard was delusion wrought by the witchcraft of a fox.

VI.

Strange is the madness of those into whom demon foxes enter. Sometimes they run naked shouting through the streets. Sometimes they lie down and froth at the mouth, and yelp as a fox yelps. And on some part of the body of the possessed a moving lump appears under the skin, which seems to have a life of its own. Prick it with a needle, and it glides instantly to another place. By no grasp can it be so tightly compressed by a strong hand that it will not slip from under the fingers. Possessed folk are also said to speak and write languages of which they were totally ignorant prior to possession. They eat only what foxes are believed to like—tofu, aburagé,* azukimeshi, etc.—and they eat a great deal, alleging that not they, but the possessing foxes, are hungry.

It not unfrequently happens that the victims of fox-possession are cruelly treated by their relatives, being severely burned and beaten in the hope that the fox may be thus driven away. Then the Hōin† or Yamabushi is sent for—the exorciser. The exorciser argues with the fox, who speaks through the mouth of the possessed. When the fox is reduced to silence by religious argument upon the wickedness of possessing people, he usually agrees to go away on condition of being supplied with, plenty of tofu or other food; and the food promised must be brought immediately to that particular Inari temple of which the fox declares himself a retainer. For the possessing fox, by whomsoever sent, usually confesses himself the servant of a certain Inari, though sometimes even calling himself the god.

As soon as the possessed has been freed from the possessor, he falls down senseless, and remains for a long time prostrate. And it is said, also, that he who has once been possessed by a fox will never again be able to eat tofu, aburagé, azukimeshi, or any of those things which foxes like.

VII.

It is believed that the Man-fox (Hito-kitsune) cannot be seen. But if he goes close to still water, his SHADOW can be seen in the

---

* *Aburagé* is a name given to fried bean-curds or tofu. *Azukimeshi* is a preparation of red beans boiled with rice.

† The Hōin or Yamabushi was a Buddhist exorciser, usually a priest. Strictly speaking, the Hōin was a Yamabushi of higher tank. The Yamabushi used to practice divination as well as exorcism. They were forbidden to exercise these professions by the present government; and most of the little temples formerly occupied by them have disappeared or fallen into ruin. But among the peasantry Buddhist exorcisers are still called to attend cases of fox-possession, and while acting as exorcisers are still spoken of as Yamabushi.

water. Those "having foxes" are therefore supposed to avoid the vicinity of rivers and ponds.

The invisible fox, as already stated, attaches himself to persons. Like a Japanese servant, he belongs to the household. But if a daughter of that household marry, the fox not only goes to that new family, following the bride, but also _colonizes_ his kind in all those families related by marriage or kinship with the husband's family. Now every fox is supposed to have a family of seventy-five—neither more nor less than seventy-five—and all these must be fed. So that although such foxes, like ghosts, eat very little individually, it is expensive to have foxes. The fox-possessors _(kitsune-mochi)_ must feed their foxes at regular hours; and the foxes always eat first—all the seventy-five. As soon as the family rice is cooked in the kama (a great iron cooking-pot), the kitsune-mochi taps loudly on the side of the vessel, and uncovers it. Then the foxes rise up through the floor. And although their eating is soundless to human ear and invisible to human eye, the rice slowly diminishes. Wherefore it is fearful for a poor man to have foxes.

But the cost of nourishing foxes is the least evil connected with the keeping of them. Foxes have no fixed code of ethics, and have proved themselves untrustworthy servants. They may initiate and long maintain the prosperity of some family; but should some grave misfortune fall upon that family in spite of the efforts of its seventy-five invisible retainers, then these will suddenly flee away, taking all the valuables of the household along with them. And all the fine gifts that foxes bring to their masters are things which have been stolen from somebody else. It is therefore extremely immoral to keep foxes. It is also dangerous for the public peace, inasmuch as a fox, being a goblin, and devoid of human susceptibilities, will not take certain precautions. He may steal the next-door neighbor's purse by night and lay it at his own master's threshold, so that if the next-door neighbor happens to get up first and see it there is sure to be a row.

Another evil habit of foxes is that of making public what they hear said in private, and taking it upon themselves to create undesirable scandal. For example, a fox attached to the family of Kobayashi-San hears his master complain about his neighbor Nakayama-San, whom he secretly dislikes. Therewith the zealous retainer runs to the house of Nakayama-San, and enters into his body, and torments him grievously, saying: "I am the retainer of Kobayashi-San to whom you did such-and-such a wrong; and until such time as he command me to depart, I shall continue to torment you."

And last, but worst of all the risks of possessing foxes, is the danger that they may become wroth with some member of the family. Certainly a fox may be a good friend, and make rich the home in which he is domiciled. But as he is not human, and as his motives and feelings are not those of men, but of goblins, it is difficult to avoid incurring his displeasure. At the most unexpected moment he may take offense without any cause knowingly having been given, and there is no saying what the consequences may be. For the fox possesses Instinctive Infinite Vision—and the Ten-Ni-Tsun, or All-Hearing-Ear—and the Ta-Shin-Tsun, which is the Knowledge of the Most Secret Thoughts of Others—and Shiyuku, Mei-Tsun, which is the Knowledge of the Past—and Zhin-Kiyan-Tsun, which means the Knowledge of the Universal Present—and also the Powers of Transformation and of Transmutation.* So that even without including his special powers of bewitchment, he is by nature a being almost omnipotent for evil.

VIII.

For all these reasons, and doubtless many more, people believed to have foxes are shunned. Intermarriage with a fox-possessing family is out of the question; and many a beautiful and

---

* A most curious paper on the subject of *Ten-gan*, or Infinite Vision—being the translation of a Buddhist sermon by the priest Sata Kaiseki—appeared in vol. vii. of the *Transactions* of the Asiatic Society of Japan, from the pen of Mr. J. M. James. It contains an interesting consideration of the supernatural powers of the Fox.

accomplished girl in Izumo cannot secure a husband because of
the popular belief that her family harbors foxes. As a rule, Izumo
girls do not like to marry out of their own province; but the
daughters of a kitsune-mochi must either marry into the family of another kitsune-mochi, or find a husband far away from
the Province of the Gods. Rich fox-possessing families have not
overmuch difficulty in disposing of their daughters by one of the
means above indicated; but many a fine sweet girl of the poorer
kitsune-mochi is condemned by superstition to remain unwed-
ded. It is not because there are none to love her and desirous
of marrying her—young men who have passed through public
schools and who do not believe in foxes. It is because popular
superstition cannot be yet safely defied in country districts
except by the wealthy. The consequences of such defiance would
have to be borne, not merely by the husband, but by his whole
family, and by all other families related thereunto. Which are
consequences to be thought about!

Among men believed to have foxes there are some who know
how to turn the superstition to good account. The country-folk,
as a general rule, are afraid of giving offense to a kitsune-mochi,
lest he should send some of his invisible servants to take possession of them. Accordingly, certain kitsune-mochi have obtained
great ascendency over the communities in which they live. In
the town of Yonago, for example, there is a certain prosperous
chōnin whose will is almost law, and whose opinions are never
opposed. He is practically the ruler of the place, and in a fair
way of becoming a very wealthy man. All because he is thought
to have foxes.

Wrestlers, as a class, boast of their immunity from fox-possession, and care neither for kitsune-mochi nor for their spectral friends. Very strong men are believed to be proof against all
such goblinry. Foxes are said to be afraid of them, and instances
are cited of a possessing fox declaring: "I wished to enter into
your brother, but he was too strong for me; so I have entered

into you, as I am resolved to be revenged upon some one of your family."

IX.

Now the belief in foxes does not affect persons only: it affects property. It affects the value of real estate in Izumo to the amount of hundreds of thousands.

The land of a family supposed to have foxes cannot be sold at a fair price. People are afraid to buy it; for it is believed the foxes may ruin the new proprietor. The difficulty of obtaining a purchaser is most great in the case of land terraced for rice-fields, in the mountain districts. The prime necessity of such agriculture is irrigation—irrigation by a hundred ingenious devices, always in the face of difficulties. There are seasons when water becomes terribly scarce, and when the peasants will even fight for water. It is feared that on lands haunted by foxes, the foxes may turn the water away from one field into another, or, for spite, make holes in the dikes and so destroy the crop.

There are not wanting shrewd men to take advantage of this queer belief. One gentleman of Matsue, a good agriculturalist of the modern school, speculated in the fox-terror fifteen years ago, and purchased a vast tract of land in eastern Izumo which no one else would bid for. That land has sextupled in value, besides yielding generously under his system of cultivation; and by selling it now he could realize an immense fortune. His success, and the fact of his having been an official of the government, broke the spell: it is no longer believed that his farms are fox-haunted. But success alone could not have freed the soil from the curse of the superstition. The power of the farmer to banish the foxes was due to his official character. With the peasantry, the word "Government" is talismanic.

Indeed, the richest and the most successful farmer of Izumo, worth more than a hundred thousand yen, Wakuri-San of Chinomiya in Kandegori—is almost universally believed by the peasantry to be a kitsune-mochi. They tell curious stories about him. Some say that when a very poor man he found in the woods one day a little white fox-cub, and took it home, and petted it, and gave it plenty of tofu, adzukimeshi, and aburagé—three sorts of food which foxes love—and that from that day prosperity came to him. Others say that in his house there is a special zashiki, or guest-room for foxes; and that there, once in each month, a great banquet is given to hundreds of Hito-kitsune. But Chinomiya-no-Wakuri, as they call him, can afford to laugh at all these tales. He is a refined man, highly respected in cultivated circles where superstition never enters.

X.

When a Ninko comes to your house at night and knocks, there is a peculiar muffled sound about the knocking by which you can tell that the visitor is a fox—if you have experienced ears. For a fox knocks at doors with its tail. If you open, then you will see a man, or perhaps a beautiful girl, who will talk to you only in fragments of words, but nevertheless in such a way that you can perfectly well understand. A fox cannot pronounce a whole word, but a part only—as "Nish...*Sa*..." for "Nishida-*San,*" "*degoz*" for "*degozarimasu,*" or "*uch*...*de*...? "for" *uchi desūka?*" Then, if you are a friend of foxes, the visitor will present you with a little gift of some sort, and at once vanish away into the darkness. Whatever the gift may be, it will seem much larger that night than in the morning. Only a part of a fox-gift is real.

A Matsue shizoku, going home one night by way of the street called Horomachi, saw a fox running for its life pursued by dogs. He beat the dogs off with his umbrella, thus giving the fox a chance to escape. On the following evening he heard someone knock at his door, and on opening the *to* saw a very pretty girl standing there, who said to him: "Last night I should have died but for your august kindness. I know not how to thank you enough: this is only a pitiable little present." And she laid a small bundle at his feet and went away. He opened the bundle and found two beautiful ducks and two pieces of silver money—

those long, heavy, leaf-shaped pieces of money—each worth ten or twelve dollars—such as are now eagerly sought for by collectors of antique things. After a little while, one of the coins changed before his eyes into a piece of grass; the other was always good.

Sugitean-San, a physician of Matsue, was called one evening to attend a case of confinement at a house some distance from the city, on the hill called Shiragayama. He was guided by a servant carrying a paper lantern painted with an aristocratic crest.* He entered into a magnificent house, where he was received with superb samurai courtesy. The mother was safely delivered of a fine boy. The family treated the physician to an excellent dinner, entertained him elegantly, and sent him home, loaded with presents and money. Next day he went, according to Japanese etiquette, to return thanks to his hosts. He could not find the house: there was, in fact, nothing on Shiragayama except forest. Returning home, he examined again the gold which had been paid to him. All was good except one piece, which had changed into grass.

XI.

Curious advantages have been taken of the superstitions relating to the Fox-God.

In Matsue, several years ago, there was a tofuya which enjoyed an unusually large patronage. A tofuya is a shop where tofu is sold—a curd prepared from beans, and much resembling good custard in appearance. Of all eatable things, foxes are most fond of tofu and of soba, which is a preparation of buckwheat. There is even a legend that a fox, in the semblance of an elegantly attired man, once visited Nogi-no-Kuriharaya, a popular sobaya on the lake shore, and ate much soba. But after the guest was gone, the money he had paid changed into wooden shavings.

---

* All the portable lanterns used to light the way upon dark nights bear a *mon* or crest of the owner.

The proprietor of the tofuya had a different experience. A man in wretched attire used to come to his shop every evening to buy a chō of tofu, which he devoured on the spot with the haste of one long famished. Every evening for weeks he came, and never spoke; but the landlord saw one evening the tip of a bushy white tail protruding from beneath the stranger's rags. The sight aroused strange surmises and weird hopes. From that night he began to treat the mysterious visitor with obsequious kindness. But another month passed before the latter spoke. Then what he said was about as follows:

"Though I seem to you a man, I am not a man; and I took upon myself human form only for the purpose of visiting you. I come from Taka-machi, where my temple is, at which you often visit. And being desirous to reward your piety and goodness of heart, I have come tonight to save you from a great danger. For by the power which I possess I know that tomorrow this street will burn, and all the houses in it shall be utterly destroyed except yours. To save it I am going to make a charm. But in order that I may do this, you must open your go-down *(kura)* that I may enter, and allow no one to watch me; for should living eye look upon me there, the charm will not avail."

The shopkeeper, with fervent words of gratitude, opened his storehouse, and reverently admitted the seeming Inari, and gave orders that none of his household or servants should keep watch. And these orders were so well obeyed that all the stores within the storehouse, and all the valuables of the family, were removed without hindrance during the night. Next day the kura was found to be empty. And there was no fire.

There is also a well authenticated story about another wealthy shopkeeper of Matsue who easily became the prey of another pretended Inari. This Inari told him that whatever sum of money he should leave at a certain miya by night, he would find it doubled in the morning—as the reward of his lifelong piety. The shopkeeper carried several small sums to the miya, and found them doubled within twelve hours. Then he deposited larger sums, which were similarly multiplied; he even risked some hundreds of dollars, which were duplicated. Finally he took all his money out of the bank and placed it one evening within the shrine of the god—and never saw it again.

XII.

Vast is the literature of the subject of foxes—ghostly foxes. Some of it is old as the eleventh century. In the ancient romances and the modern cheap novel, in historical traditions and in popular fairytales, foxes perform wonderful parts. There are very beautiful and very sad and very terrible stories about foxes. There are legends of foxes discussed by great scholars, and legends of foxes known to every child in Japan—such as the history of Tamamonomae, the beautiful favorite of the Emperor Toba— Tamamonomae, whose name has passed into a proverb, and who proved at last to be only a demon fox with Nine Tails and Fur of Gold. But the most interesting part of fox-literature belongs to the Japanese stage, where the popular beliefs are often most humorously reflected—as in the following excerpts from the comedy of Hiza-Kuruge, written by one Jippensha Ikku:

> [Kidahachi and Iyaji are traveling from Yedo to Ōsaka. When within a short distance of Akasaka, Kidahachi hastens on in advance to secure good accommodations at the best inn. Iyaji, traveling along leisurely, stops a little while at a small wayside refreshment-house kept by an old woman.]

OLD WOMAN: Please take some tea, sir.

IYAJI: Thank you! How far is it from here to the next town?— Akasaka?

OLD WOMAN: About one ri. But if you have no companion, you had better remain here tonight, because there is a bad fox on the way, who bewitches travelers.

IYAJI: I am afraid of that sort of thing. But I must go on; for my companion has gone on ahead of me, and will be waiting for me.

[After having paid for his refreshments, Iyaji proceeds on his way. The night is very dark, and he feels quite nervous on account of what the old woman has told him. After having walked a considerable distance, he suddenly hears a fox yelping—*kon-kon.* Feeling still more afraid, he shouts at the top of his voice:]

IYAJI: Come near me, and I will kill you!

[Meanwhile Kidahachi, who has also been frightened by the old woman's stories, and has therefore determined to wait for Iyaji, is saying to himself in the dark: "If I do not wait for him, we shall certainly be deluded." Suddenly he hears Iyaji's voice, and cries out to him:]

KIDAHACHI: O Iyaji-San!

IYAJI: What are you doing there?

KIDAHACHI: I did intend to go on ahead; but I became afraid, and so I concluded to stop here and wait for you.

IYAJI (*who imagines that the fox has taken the shape of Kidahachi to deceive him*): Do not think that you are going to dupe me!

KIDAHACHI: That is a queer way to talk! I have some nice mochi* here which I bought for you.

IYAJI: Horse-dung cannot be eaten!†

KIDAHACHI: Don't be suspicious!—I am really Kidahachi.

IYAJI (*springing upon him furiously*): Yes! you took the form of Kidahachi just to deceive me!

KIDAHACHI: What do you mean?—What are you going to do to me?

IYAJI: I am going to kill you! (*Throws him down.*)

KIDAHACHI: Oh! you have hurt me very much—please leave me alone!

IYAJI: If you are really hurt, then let me see you in your real shape! (*They struggle together.*)

---

* Cakes made of rice flour and often sweetened with sugar.

† It is believed that foxes amuse themselves by causing people to eat horse-dung in the belief that they are eating mochi, or to enter a cesspool in the belief they are taking a bath.

KIDAHACHI: What are you doing?—putting your hand there?

IYAJI: I am feeling for your tail. If you don't put out your tail at once, I shall make you! (*Takes his towel, and with it ties Kidahachi's hands behind his back, and then drives him before him.*)

KIDAHACHI: Please untie me—please untie me first!

[By this time they have *almost* reached Akasaka, and Iyaji, seeing a dog, calls the animal, and drags Kidahachi close to it; for a dog is believed to be able to detect a fox through any disguise. But the dog takes no notice of Kidahachi. Iyaji therefore unties him, and apologizes; and they both laugh at their previous fears.]

XIII.

But there are some very pleasing forms of the Fox-God.

For example, there stands in a very obscure street of Matsue—one of those streets no stranger is likely to enter unless he loses his way—a temple called Jigyōba-no-Inari,* and also Kodomo-no-Inari, or "the Children's Inari." It is very small, but very famous; and it has been recently presented with a pair of new stone foxes, very large, which have gilded teeth and a peculiarly playful expression of countenance. These sit one on each side of the gate: the Male grinning with open jaws, the Female demure, with mouth closed.†

In the court you will find many ancient little foxes with noses, heads, or tails broken, two great Karashishi before which straw

---

* In Jigyōbamachi, a name signifying "earthwork-street." It stands upon land reclaimed from swamp.

† This seems to be the immemorial artistic law for the demeanor of all symbolic guardians of holy places, such as the Karashishi, and the Ascending and Descending Dragons carved upon panels, or pillars. At Kumano temple even the Suijin, or warrior-guardians, who frown behind the gratings of the chambers of the great gateway, are thus represented—one with mouth open, the other with closed lips.

On inquiring about the origin of this distinction between the two symbolic figures, I was told by a young Buddhist scholar that the male figure in such representations is supposed to be pronouncing the sound "Ă," and the figure with closed lips the sound of nasal "N"—corresponding to the Alpha and Omega of the Greek alphabet, and also emblematic of the Beginning and the End. In the Lotus of the Good Law, Buddha so reveals himself, as the cosmic Alpha and Omega, and the Father of the World—like Krishna in the *Bhagavad-Gita*.

sandals *(waraji)* have been suspended as votive offerings by somebody with sore feet who has prayed to the Karashishi-Sama that they will heal his affliction, and a shrine of Kōjin, occupied by the corpses of many children's dolls.*

The grated doors of the shrine of Jigyōba-no-Inari, like those of the shrine of Yaegaki, are white with the multitude of little papers tied to them, which papers signify prayers. But the prayers are special and curious. To right and to left of the doors, and also above them, odd little votive pictures are pasted upon the walls, mostly representing children in bathtubs, or children getting their heads shaved. There are also one or two representing children at play. Now the interpretation of these signs and wonders is as follows:

Doubtless you know that Japanese children, as well as Japanese adults, must take a hot bath every day; also that it is the custom to shave the heads of very small boys and girls. But in spite of hereditary patience and strong ancestral tendency to follow ancient custom, young children find both the razor and the hot bath difficult to endure, with their delicate skins. For the Japanese hot bath is very hot (not less than 110° F., as a general rule), and even the adult foreigner must learn slowly to bear it, and to appreciate its hygienic value. Also, the Japanese razor is a much less perfect instrument than ours, and is used without any lather, and is apt to hurt a little unless used by the most skillful hands. And finally, Japanese parents are not tyrannical with their children: they pet and coax, very rarely compel or terrify. So that it is quite a dilemma for them when the baby revolts against the bath or mutinies against the razor.

The parents of the child who refuses to be shaved or bathed have recourse to Jigyōba-no-Inari. The god is besought to send one of his retainers to amuse the child, and reconcile it to the

---

* There is one exception to the general custom of giving the dolls of dead children, or the wrecks of dolls, to Kōjin. Those images of the God of Calligraphy and Scholarship which are always presented as gifts to boys on the Boys' Festival are given, when broken, to Tenjin himself, not to Kōjin: at least such is the custom in Matsue.

new order of things, and render it both docile and happy. Also if a child is naughty, or falls sick, this Inari is appealed to. If the prayer be granted, some small present is made to the temple—sometimes a votive picture, such as those pasted by the door, representing the successful result of the petition. To judge by the number of such pictures, and by the prosperity of the temple, the Kodomo-no-Inari would seem to deserve his popularity. Even during the few minutes I passed in his court I saw three young mothers, with infants at their backs, come to the shrine and pray and make offerings. I noticed that one of the children remarkably pretty—had never been shaved at all. This was evidently a very obstinate case.

While returning from my visit to the Jigyōba Inari, my Japanese servant, who had guided me there, told me this story: The son of his next-door neighbor, a boy of seven, went out to play one morning, and disappeared for two days. The parents were not at first uneasy, supposing that the child had gone to the house of a relative, where he was accustomed to pass a day or two from time to time. But on the evening of the second day it was learned that the child had not been at the house in question. Search was at once made; but neither search nor inquiry availed. Late at night, however, a knock was heard at the door of the boy's dwelling, and the mother, hurrying out, found her truant fast asleep on the ground. She could not discover who had knocked. The boy, upon being awakened, laughed, and said that on the morning of his disappearance he had met a lad of about his own age, with very pretty eyes, who had coaxed him away to the woods, where they had played together all day and night and the next day at very curious funny games. But at last he got sleepy, and his comrade took him home. He was not hungry. The comrade promised "to come tomorrow."

But the mysterious comrade never came; and no boy of the description given lived in the neighborhood. The inference was that the comrade was a fox who wanted to have a little fun. The subject of the fun mourned long in vain for his merry companion.

XIV.

Some thirty years ago there lived in Matsue an ex-wrestler named Tobikawa, who was a relentless enemy of foxes and used to hunt and kill them. He was popularly believed to enjoy immunity from bewitchment because of his immense strength; but there were some old folks who predicted that he would not die a natural death. This prediction was fulfilled: Tobikawa died in a very curious manner. He was excessively fond of practical jokes. One day he disguised himself as a Tengu, or sacred goblin, with wings and claws and long nose, and ascended a lofty tree in a sacred grove near Rakusan, whither, after a little while, the innocent peasants thronged to worship him with offerings. While diverting himself with this spectacle, and trying to play his part by springing nimbly from one branch to another, he missed his footing and broke his neck in the fall.

XV.

But these strange beliefs are swiftly passing away. Year by year more shrines of Inari crumble down, never to be rebuilt. Year by year the statuaries make fewer images of foxes. Year by year fewer victims of fox-possession are taken to the hospitals to be treated according to the best scientific methods by Japanese physicians who speak German. The cause is not to be found in the decadence of the old faiths: a superstition outlives a religion. Much less is it to be sought for in the efforts of proselytizing missionaries from the West—most of whom profess an earnest belief in devils. It is purely educational. The omnipotent enemy of superstition is the public school, where the teaching of modern science is unclogged by sectarianism or prejudice; where the children of the poorest may learn the wisdom of the Occident; where there is not a boy or a girl of fourteen ignorant of the great names of Tyndall, of Darwin, of Huxley, of Herbert Spencer. The little hands that break the Fox-god's nose in mischievous play can also write essays upon the evolution of plants and about the geology of Izumo. There is no place for ghostly foxes in the beautiful nature-world revealed by new studies to the new generation. The omnipotent exorciser and reformer is the Kodomo.

16

IN A JAPANESE GARDEN

I.

My little two-story house by the Ōhashigawa, although dainty as a bird-cage, proved much too small for comfort at the approach of the hot season—the rooms being scarcely higher than steamship cabins, and so narrow that an ordinary mosquito-net could not be suspended in them. I was sorry to lose the beautiful lake view, but I found it necessary to remove to the northern quarter of the city, into a very quiet street behind the moldering castle. My new home is a katchiū-yashiki, the ancient residence of some samurai of high rank. It is shut off from the street, or rather roadway, skirting the castle moat by a long, high wall coped with tiles. One ascends to the gateway, which is almost as large as that of a temple court, by a low broad flight of stone steps; and projecting from the wall, to the right of the gate, is a lookout window, heavily barred, like a big wooden cage. Thence, in feudal days, armed retainers kept keen watch on all who passed by—invisible watch, for the bars are set so closely that a face behind them cannot be seen from the roadway. Inside the gate the approach to the dwelling is also walled in on both sides, so that the visitor, unless privileged, could see before him only the house entrance, always closed with white shōji. Like all samurai homes, the residence itself is but one story high, but there are fourteen rooms within, and these are lofty, spacious, and beautiful. There is, alas, no lake view nor any charming prospect. Part

of the O-Shiroyama, with the castle on its summit, half concealed by a park of pines, may be seen above the coping of the
front wall, but only a part; and scarcely a hundred yards behind
the house rise densely wooded heights, cutting off not only the
horizon, but a large slice of the sky as well. For this immure-
ment, however, there exists fair compensation in the shape of
a very pretty garden, or rather a series of garden spaces, which
surround the dwelling on three sides. Broad verandas overlook
these, and from a certain veranda angle I can enjoy the sight of
two gardens at once. Screens of bamboos and woven rushes, with
wide gateless openings in their midst, mark the boundaries of
the three divisions of the pleasure-grounds. But these structures
are not intended to serve as true fences; they are ornamental,
and only indicate where one style of landscape gardening ends
and another begins.

II.

Now a few words upon Japanese gardens in general.

After having learned—merely by seeing, for the practical
knowledge of the art requires years of study and experience,
besides a natural, instinctive sense of beauty—something about
the Japanese manner of arranging flowers, one can thereafter
consider European ideas of floral decoration only as vulgarities.
This observation is not the result of any hasty enthusiasm, but a
conviction settled by long residence in the interior. I have come
to understand the unspeakable loveliness of a solitary spray
of blossoms arranged as only a Japanese expert knows how to
arrange it—not by simply poking the spray into a vase, but by
perhaps one whole hour's labor of trimming and posing and
daintiest manipulation—and therefore I cannot think now of
what we Occidentals call a "bouquet" as anything but a vulgar
murdering of flowers, an outrage upon the color-sense, a brutality, an abomination. Somewhat in the same way, and for similar
reasons, after having learned what an old Japanese garden is, I
can remember our costliest gardens at home only as ignorant

displays of what wealth can accomplish in the creation of incongruities that violate nature.

Now a Japanese garden is not a flower garden; neither is it made for the purpose of cultivating plants. In nine cases out of ten there is nothing in it resembling a flower-bed. Some gardens may contain scarcely a sprig of green; some have nothing green at all, and consist entirely of rocks and pebbles and sand, although these are exceptional.* As a rule, a Japanese garden is a landscape garden, yet its existence does not depend upon any fixed allowance of space. It may cover one acre or many acres. It may also be only ten feet square. It may, in extreme cases, be much less; for a certain kind of Japanese garden can be contrived small enough to put in a tokonoma. Such a garden, in a vessel no larger than a fruit-dish, is called koniwa or tokoniwa, and may occasionally be seen in the tokonoma of humble little dwellings so closely squeezed between other structures as to possess no ground in which to cultivate an outdoor garden. (I say "an outdoor garden," because there are indoor gardens, both upstairs and downstairs, in some large Japanese houses.) The tokoniwa is usually made in some curious bowl, or shallow carved box, or quaintly shaped vessel impossible to describe by any English word. Therein are created minuscule hills with minuscule houses upon them, and microscopic ponds and rivulets spanned by tiny humped bridges; and queer wee plants do duty for trees, and curiously formed pebbles stand for rocks, and there are tiny tōrō, perhaps a tiny torii as well—in short, a charming and living model of a Japanese landscape.

Another fact of prime importance to remember is that, in order to comprehend the beauty of a Japanese garden, it is necessary

---

* Such as the garden attached to the abbot's palace at Tokuwamonji, cited by Mr. Conder, which was made to commemorate the legend of stones which bowed themselves in assent to the doctrine of Buddha. At Togo-ike, in Tottori-ken, I saw a very large garden consisting almost entirely of stones and sand. The impression which the designer had intended to convey was that of approaching the sea over a verge of dunes, and the illusion was beautiful.

to understand—or at least to learn to understand—the beauty of stones. Not of stones quarried by the hand of man, but of stones shaped by nature only. Until you can feel, and keenly feel, that stones have character, that stones have tones and values, the whole artistic meaning of a Japanese garden cannot be revealed to you. In the foreigner, however aesthetic he may be, this feeling needs to be cultivated by study. It is inborn in the Japanese; the soul of the race comprehends Nature infinitely better than we do, at least in her visible forms. But although, being an Occidental, the true sense of the beauty of stones can be reached by you only through long familiarity with the Japanese use and choice of them, the characters of the lessons to be acquired exist everywhere about you, if your life be in the interior. You cannot walk through a street without observing tasks and problems in the aesthetics of stones for you to master. At the approaches to temples, by the side of roads, before holy groves, and in all parks and pleasure-grounds, as well as in all cemeteries, you will notice large, irregular, flat slabs of natural rock—mostly from the river beds and water-worn—sculptured with ideographs, but unhewn. These have been set up as votive tablets, as commemorative monuments, as tombstones, and are much more costly than the ordinary cut-stone columns and haka chiseled with the figures of divinities in relief. Again, you will see before most of the shrines, nay, even in the grounds of nearly all large homesteads, great irregular blocks of granite or other hard rock, worn by the action of torrents, and converted into water-basins (*chodzubachi*) by cutting a circular hollow in the top. Such are but common examples of the utilization of stones even in the poorest villages; and if you have any natural artistic sentiment, you cannot fail to discover, sooner or later, how much more beautiful are these natural forms than any shapes from the hand of the stone-cutter. It is probable, too, that you will become so habituated at last to the sight of inscriptions cut upon rock surfaces, especially if you travel much through the country, that you will often find yourself involuntarily looking for texts or other chiselings where there are none, and could not possibly be, as if ideographs belonged by natural law to rock formation. And stones will begin, perhaps, to assume for you a certain individual or physiognomical aspect—to suggest moods and sensations, as they do to the Japanese. Indeed, Japan is particularly a land of suggestive shapes in stone, as high volcanic lands are apt to be; and such shapes doubtless addressed themselves to the imagination of the race at a time long prior to the date of that archaic text which tells of demons in Izumo "who made rocks, and the roots of trees, and leaves, and the foam of the green waters to speak."

As might be expected in a country where the suggestiveness of natural forms is thus recognized, there are in Japan many curious beliefs and superstitions concerning stones. In almost every province there are famous stones supposed to be sacred or haunted, or to possess miraculous powers, such as the Women's Stone at the temple of Hachiman at Kamakura, and the Sesshō-seki, or Death Stone of Nasu, and the Wealth-giving Stone at Enoshima, to which pilgrims pay reverence. There are even legends of stones having manifested sensibility, like the tradition of the Nodding Stones which bowed down before the monk Daita when he preached unto them the word of Buddha; or the ancient story from the Kojiki, that the Emperor O-Jin, being augustly intoxicated, "smote with his august staff a great stone in the middle of the Ohosaka road, *whereupon the stone ran away!*"*

Now stones are valued for their beauty; and large stones selected for their shape may have an aesthetic worth of hundreds of dollars. And large stones form the skeleton, or framework, in the design of old Japanese gardens. Not only is every stone chosen with a view to its particular expressiveness of form, but every stone in the garden or about the premises has its separate and individual name, indicating its purpose or its decorative duty. But I can tell you only a little, a very little, of the folk-lore of a Japanese garden; and if you want to know more about stones

---

* The *Kojiki*, translated by Professor B. H. Chamberlain, p. 254.

and their names, and about the philosophy of gardens, read the unique essay of Mr. Conder on the Art of Landscape Gardening in Japan,* and his beautiful book on the Japanese Art of Floral Decoration; and also the brief but charming chapter on Gardens, in Morse's Japanese Homes.†

III.

No effort to create an impossible or purely ideal landscape is made in the Japanese garden. Its artistic purpose is to copy faithfully the attractions of a veritable landscape, and to convey the real impression that a real landscape communicates. It is therefore at once a picture and a poem; perhaps even more a poem than a picture. For as nature's scenery, in its varying aspects, affects us with sensations of joy or of solemnity, of grimness or of sweetness, of force or of peace, so must the true reflection of it in the labor of the landscape gardener create not merely an impression of beauty, but a mood in the soul. The grand old landscape gardeners, those Buddhist monks who first introduced the art into Japan, and subsequently developed it into an almost occult science, carried their theory yet farther than this. They held it possible to express moral lessons in the design of a garden, and abstract ideas, such as Chastity, Faith, Piety, Content, Calm, and Connubial Bliss. Therefore were gardens contrived according to the character of the owner, whether poet, warrior, philosopher, or priest. In those ancient gardens (the art, alas, is passing away under the withering influence of the utterly commonplace Western taste) there were expressed

---

* Since this paper was written, Mr. Conder has published a beautiful illustrated volume—"Landscape Gardening in Japan. By Josiah Conder, F. R. I., B. A. Tōkyō: 1893." A photographic supplement to the work gives views of the most famous gardens in the capital and elsewhere.

† The observations of Dr. Rein on Japanese gardens are not to be recommended, in respect either to accuracy or to comprehension of the subject. Rein spent only two years in Japan, the larger part of which time he devoted to the study of the lacquer industry, the manufacture of silk and paper, and other practical matters. On these subjects his work is justly valued. But his chapters on Japanese manners and customs, art, religion, and literature show extremely little acquaintance with those topics.

both a mood of nature and some rare Oriental conception of a mood of man.

I do not know what human sentiment the principal division of my garden was intended to reflect; and there is none to tell me. Those by whom it was made passed away long generations ago, in the eternal transmigration of souls. But as a poem of nature it requires no interpreter. It occupies the front portion of the grounds, facing south; and it also extends west to the verge of the northern division of the garden, from which it is partly separated by a curious screen-fence structure. There are large rocks in it, heavily mossed; and divers fantastic basins of stone for holding water; and stone lamps green with years; and a shachihoko, such as one sees at the peaked angles of castle roofs—a great stone fish, an idealized porpoise, with its nose in the ground and its tail in the air.* There are miniature hills, with old trees upon them; and there are long slopes of green, shadowed by flowering shrubs, like river banks; and there are green knolls like islets. All these verdant elevations rise from spaces of pale yellow sand, smooth as a surface of silk and miming the curves and meanderings of a river course. These sanded spaces are not to be trodden upon; they are much too beautiful for that. The least speck of dirt would mar their effect; and it requires the trained skill of an experienced native gardener—a delightful old man he is—to keep them in perfect form. But they are traversed in various directions by lines of flat unhewn rock slabs, placed at slightly irregular distances from one another, exactly like stepping-stones across a brook. The whole effect is that of the shores of a still stream in some lovely, lonesome, drowsy place.

There is nothing to break the illusion, so secluded the garden is. High walls and fences shut out streets and contiguous things; and the shrubs and the trees, heightening and thickening

---

* This attitude of the shachihoko is somewhat *de rigueur*, whence the common expression *shachihoko dai*, signifying "to stand on one's head."

toward the boundaries, conceal from view even the roofs of the neighboring katchiū-yashiki. Softly beautiful are the tremulous shadows of leaves on the sunned sand; and the scent of flowers comes thinly sweet with every waft of tepid air; and there is a humming of bees.

IV.

By Buddhism all existences are divided into *Hijō,* things without desire, such as stones and trees; and *Ujō,* things having desire, such as men and animals. This division does not, so far as I know, find expression in the written philosophy of gardens; but it is a convenient one. The folklore of my little domain relates both to the inanimate and the animate. In natural order, the Hijō may be considered first, beginning with a singular shrub near the entrance of the yashiki, and close to the gate of the first garden.

Within the front gateway of almost every old samurai house, and usually near the entrance of the dwelling itself, there is to be seen a small tree with large and peculiar leaves. The name of this tree in Izumo is tegashiwa, and there is one beside my door. What the scientific name of it is I do not know; nor am I quite sure of the etymology of the Japanese name. However, there is a word tegashi, meaning a bond for the hands; and the shape of the leaves of the tegashiwa somewhat resembles the shape of a hand.

Now, in old days, when the samurai retainer was obliged to leave his home in order to accompany his daimyō to Yedo, it was customary, just before his departure, to set before him a baked tai* served up on a tegashiwa leaf. After this farewell repast, the leaf upon which the tai had been served was hung up above the door as a charm to bring the departed knight safely back again. This pretty superstition about the leaves of the tegashiwa had its

---

* The magnificent perch called tai (*Serranus marginalis*), which is very common along the Izumo coast, is not only justly prized as the most delicate of Japanese fish, but is also held to be an emblem of good fortune. It is a ceremonial gift at weddings and on congratulatory occasions. The Japanese call it also "the king of fishes."

origin not only in their shape but in their movement. Stirred by a wind they seemed to beckon—not indeed after our Occidental manner, but in the way that a Japanese signs to his friend to come, by gently waving his hand up and down with the palm towards the ground.

Another shrub to be found in most Japanese gardens is the nanten,* about which a very curious belief exists. If you have an evil dream, a dream which bodes ill luck, you should whisper it to the nanten early in the morning, and then it will never come true.† There are two varieties of this graceful plant: one which bears red berries, and one which bears white. The latter is rare. Both kinds grow in my garden. The common variety is placed close to the veranda (perhaps for the convenience of dreamers); the other occupies a little flowerbed in the middle of the garden, together with a small citron-tree. This most dainty citron-tree is called "Buddha's fingers,"‡ because of the wonderful shape of its fragrant fruits. Near it stands a kind of laurel, with lanciform leaves glossy as bronze; it is called by the Japanese yuzuri-ha,§ and is almost as common in the gardens of old samurai homes as the tegashiwa itself. It is held to be a tree of good omen, because no one of its old leaves ever falls off before a new one, growing

---

* *Nandina domeslica.*

† The most lucky of all dreams, they say in Izumo, is a dream of Fuji, the Sacred Mountain. Next in order of good omen is dreaming of a falcon (*taka*). The third best subject for a dream is the eggplant (*nasubi*). To dream of the sun or of the moon is very lucky; but it is still more so to dream of stars. For a young wife it is most fortunate to dream of *swallowing a star*: this signifies that she will become the mother of a beautiful child. To dream of a cow is a good omen; to dream of a horse is lucky, but it signifies traveling. To dream of rain or fire is good. Some dreams are held in Japan, as in the West, "to go by contraries." Therefore to dream of having one's house burned up, or of funerals, or of being dead, or of talking to the ghost of a dead person, is good. Some dreams which are good for women mean the reverse when dreamed by men; for example, it is good for a woman to dream that her nose bleeds, but for a man this is very bad. To dream of much money is a sign of loss to come. To dream of the *koi*, or of any fresh-water fish, is the most unlucky of all. This is curious, for in other parts of Japan the koi is a symbol of good fortune.

‡ *Tebushukan: Citrus sarkodactilis.*

§ Yuzuru signifies to resign in favor of another; ha signifies a leaf. The botanical name, as given in Hepburn's dictionary, is *Daphniphillum macropodum.*

behind it, has well developed. For thus the yuzuriha symbolizes hope that the father will not pass away before his son has become a vigorous man, well able to succeed him as the head of the family. Therefore, on every New Year's Day the leaves of the yuzuriha, mingled with fronds of fern, are attached to the shimenawa which is then suspended before every Izumo home.

V.

The trees, like the shrubs, have their curious poetry and legends. Like the stones, each tree has its special landscape name according to its position and purpose in the composition. Just as rocks and stones form the skeleton of the ground plan of a garden, so pines form the framework of its foliage design. They give body to the whole. In this garden there are five pines—not pines tormented into fantasticalities, but pines made wondrously picturesque by long and tireless care and judicious trimming. The object of the gardener has been to develop to the utmost possible degree their natural tendency to rugged line and massings of foliage—that spiny somber-green foliage which Japanese art is never weary of imitating in metal inlay or golden lacquer. The pine is a symbolic tree in this land of symbolism. Ever green, it is at once the emblem of unflinching purpose and of vigorous old age; and its needle-shaped leaves are credited with the power of driving demons away.

There are two sakuranoki,* Japanese cherry-trees—those trees whose blossoms, as Professor Chamberlain so justly observes, are "beyond comparison more lovely than anything Europe has to show." Many varieties are cultivated and loved; those in my garden bear blossoms of the most ethereal pink, a flushed white. When, in spring, the trees flower, it is as though fleeciest masses of cloud faintly tinged by sunset had floated down from the highest sky to fold themselves about the branches. This comparison is no poetical exaggeration; neither is it original: it is an

---

* *Cerasus pseudo-cerasus* (Lindley).

ancient Japanese description of the most marvelous floral exhibition which nature is capable of making. The reader who has never seen a cherry-tree blossoming in Japan cannot possibly imagine the delight of the spectacle. There are no green leaves; these come later: there is only one glorious burst of blossoms, veiling every twig and bough in their delicate mist; and the soil beneath each tree is covered deep out of sight by fallen petals as by a drift of pink snow.

But these are cultivated cherry-trees. There are others which put forth their leaves before their blossoms, such us the yama-zakura, or mountain cherry.* This too, however, has its poetry of beauty and of symbolism. Sang the great Shintō writer and poet, Motowori:

> Shikishima no
>   Yamato-gokoro wo
> Hito-towaba,
>   Asa-hi ni niou
> Yamazakura bana.†

Whether cultivated or uncultivated, the Japanese cherry-trees are emblems. Those planted in old samurai gardens were not cherished for their loveliness alone. Their spotless blossoms were regarded as symbolizing that delicacy of sentiment and blamelessness of life belonging to high courtesy and true knightliness. "As the cherry flower is first among flowers," says an old proverb, "so should the warrior be first among men."

Shadowing the western end of this garden, and projecting its smooth dark limbs above the awning of the veranda, is a superb

---

* About this mountain cherry there is a humorous saying which illustrates the Japanese love of puns. In order fully to appreciate it, the reader should know that Japanese nouns have no distinction of singular and plural. The word _ha_, as pronounced, may signify either "leaves" or "teeth;" and the word _hana_, either "flowers" or "nose." The yamazakura puts forth its ha (leaves) before its hana (flowers). Wherefore a man whose ha (teeth) project in advance of his hana (nose) is called a yamazakura. Prognathism is not uncommon in Japan, especially among the lower classes.

† "If one should ask you concerning the heart of a true Japanese, point to the wild cherry flower glowing in the sun."

umenoki, Japanese plum-tree, very old, and originally planted here, no doubt, as in other gardens, for the sake of the sight of its blossoming. The flowering of the umenoki,* in the earliest spring, is scarcely less astonishing than that of the cherry-tree, which does not bloom for a full month later; and the blossoming of both is celebrated by popular holidays. Nor are these, although the most famed, the only flowers thus loved. The wistaria, the convolvulus, the peony, each in its season, form displays of efflorescence lovely enough to draw whole populations out of the cities into the country to see them. In Izumo, the blossoming of the peony is especially marvelous. The most famous place for this spectacle is the little island of Daikonshima, in the grand Naka-umi lagoon, about an hour's sail from Matsue. In May the whole island flames crimson with peonies; and even the boys and girls of the public schools are given a holiday, in order that they may enjoy the sight.

Though the plum flower is certainly a rival in beauty of the sakura-no-hana, the Japanese compare woman's beauty—physical beauty—to the cherry flower, never to the plum flower. But womanly virtue and sweetness, on the other hand, are compared to the ume-no-hana, never to the cherry blossom. It is a great mistake to affirm, as some writers have done, that the Japanese never think of comparing a woman to trees and flowers. For grace, a maiden is likened to a slender willow;† for youthful charm, to the cherry-tree in flower; for sweetness of heart, to the blossoming plum-tree. Nay, the old Japanese poets have compared woman to all beautiful things. They have even sought similes from flowers for her various poses, for her movements, as in the verse—

---

* There are three noteworthy varieties: one bearing red, one pink and white, and one pure white flowers.

† The expression *yanagi-goshi*, "a willow-waist," is one of several in common use comparing slender beauty to the willow-tree.

Tateba shakuyaku;[*]
Suwareba botan;
Aruku sugatawa
Himeyuri[†] *no hana.*[‡]

Why, even the names of the humblest country girls are often those of beautiful trees or flowers prefixed by the honorific O:[§] O-Matsu (Pine), O-Také (Bamboo), O-Umé (Plum), O-Hana (Blossom), O-Iné (Ear-of-Young-Rice), not to speak of the professional flower-names of dancing-girls and of jorō. It has been argued with considerable force that the origin of certain tree-names borne by girls must be sought in the folk-conception of the tree as an emblem of longevity, or happiness, or good fortune, rather than in any popular idea of the beauty of the tree in itself. But however this may be, proverb, poem, song, and popular speech today yield ample proof that the Japanese comparisons of women to trees and flowers are in no wise inferior to our own in aesthetic sentiment.

VI.

That trees, at least Japanese trees, have souls, cannot seem an unnatural fancy to one who has seen the blossoming of the umenoki and the sakuranoki. This is a popular belief in Izumo and elsewhere. It is not in accord with Buddhist philosophy, and yet in a certain sense it strikes one as being much closer to cosmic truth than the old Western orthodox notion of trees as "things created for the use of man." Furthermore, there exist sev-

---

[*] *Peonia albifiora.* The name signifies the delicacy of beauty. The simile of the *botan* (the tree peony) can be fully appreciated only by one who is acquainted with the Japanese flower.

[†] Some say keshiyuri (poppy) instead of himeyuri. The latter is a graceful species of lily, *Lilium callosum.*

[‡] "Standing, she is a shakuyaku; seated, she is a botan; and the charm of her figure in walking is the charm of a himeyuri."

[§] In the higher classes of Japanese society today, the honorific O is not, as a rule, used before the names of girls, and showy appellations are not given to daughters. Even among the poor respectable classes, names resembling those of geisha, etc., are in disfavor. But those above cited are good, honest, everyday names.

eral odd superstitions about particular trees, not unlike certain West Indian beliefs which have had a good influence in checking the destruction of valuable timber. Japan, like the tropical world, has its goblin trees. Of these, the enoki *(Celtis Willldenowiana)* and the yanagi (drooping willow) are deemed especially ghostly, and are rarely now to be found in old Japanese gardens. Both are believed to have the power of haunting. *"Enoki ga bakeru,"* the Izumo saying is. You will find in a Japanese dictionary the word "bakeru" translated by such terms as "to be transformed," "to be metamorphosed," "to be changed," etc., but the belief about these trees is very singular, and cannot be explained by any such rendering of the verb "bakeru." The tree itself does not change form or place, but a spectre called Ki-no o-baké disengages itself from the tree and walks about in various guises.* Most often the shape assumed by the phantom is that of a beautiful woman. The tree spectre seldom speaks, and seldom ventures to go very far away from its tree. If approached, it immediately shrinks back into the trunk or the foliage. It is said that if either an old yanagi or a young enoki be cut blood will flow from the gash. When such trees are very young it is not believed that they have supernatural habits, but they become more dangerous the older they grow.

There is a rather pretty legend—recalling the old Greek dream of dryads—about a willow-tree which grew in the garden of a samurai of Kyōto. Owing to its weird reputation, the tenant of the homestead desired to cut it down; but another samurai dissuaded him, saying: "Rather sell it to me, that I may plant it in my garden. That tree has a soul; it were cruel to destroy its life."

---

* Mr. Satow has found in Hirata a belief to which this seems to some extent akin— the curious Shintō doctrine "according to which a divine being throws off portions of itself by a process of fissure, thus producing what are called waki-mi-tama—parted spirits, with separate functions." The great god of Izumo, Oho-kuni-nushi-no-Kami, is said by Hirata to have three such "parted spirits:" his rough spirit *(ara-mi-tama)* that punishes, his gentle spirit *(nigi-mi-tama)* that pardons, and his benedictory or beneficent spirit *(saki-mi-tama)* that blesses. There is a Shintō story that the rough spirit of this god once met the gentle spirit without recognizing it.

Thus purchased and transplanted, the yanagi flourished well in its new home, and its spirit, out of gratitude, took the form of a beautiful woman, and became the wife of the samurai who had befriended it. A charming boy was the result of this union. A few years later, the daimyo to whom the ground belonged gave orders that the tree should be cut down. Then the wife wept bitterly, and for the first time revealed to her husband the whole story. "And now," she added, "I know that I must die; but our child will live, and you will always love him. This thought is my only solace." Vainly the astonished and terrified husband sought to retain her. Bidding him farewell forever, she vanished into the tree. Needless to say that the samurai did everything in his power to persuade the daimyo to forego his purpose. The prince wanted the tree for the reparation of a great Buddhist temple, the San-jiu-san-gen-dō.* The tree was felled, but, having fallen, it suddenly became so heavy that three hundred men could not move it. Then the child, taking a branch in his little hand, said, "Come," and the tree followed him, gliding along the ground to the court of the temple.

Although said to be a bakemono-ki, the enoki sometimes receives highest religious honors; for the spirit of the god Kōjin, to whom old dolls are dedicated, is supposed to dwell within certain very ancient enoki trees, and before these are placed shrines whereat people make prayers.

VII.

The second garden, on the north side, is my favorite. It contains no large growths. It is paved with blue pebbles, and its center is occupied by a pondlet—a miniature lake fringed with rare plants, and containing a tiny island, with tiny mountains and dwarf peach-trees and pines and azaleas, some of which are perhaps more than a century old, though scarcely more than a

---

* Perhaps the most impressive of all the Buddhist temples in Kyōto. It is dedicated to Kwannon of the Thousand Hands, and is said to contain 33,333 of her images.

foot high. Nevertheless, this work, seen as it was intended to be seen, does not appear to the eye in miniature at all. From a certain angle of the guest-room looking out upon it, the appearance is that of a real lake shore with a real island beyond it, a stone's throw away. So cunning the art of the ancient gardener who contrived all this, and who has been sleeping for a hundred years under the cedars of Gesshōji, that the illusion can be detected only from the zashiki by the presence of an ishidōrō, or stone lamp, upon the island. The size of the ishidōrō betrays the false perspective, and I do not think it was placed there when the garden was made.

Here and there at the edge of the pond, and almost level with the water, are placed large flat stones, on which one may either stand or squat, to watch the lacustrine population or to tend the water-plants. There are beautiful water-lilies, whose bright green leaf-disks float oilily upon the surface (*Nuphar Japonica*), and many lotus plants of two kinds, those which bear pink and those which bear pure white flowers. There are iris plants growing along the bank, whose blossoms are prismatic violet, and there are various ornamental grasses and ferns and mosses. But the pond is essentially a lotus pond; the lotus plants make its greatest charm. It is a delight to watch every phase of their marvelous growth, from the first unrolling of the leaf to the fall of the last flower. On rainy days, especially, the lotus plants are worth observing. Their great cup-shaped leaves swaying high above the pond, catch the rain and hold it a while; but always after the water in the leaf reaches a certain level the stem bends, and empties the leaf with a loud splash, and then straightens again. Rainwater upon a lotus-leaf is a favorite subject with Japanese metal-workers, and metal-work only can reproduce the effect, for the motion and color of water moving upon the green oleaginous surface are exactly those of quicksilver.

VIII.

The third garden, which is very large, extends beyond the inclosure containing the lotus pond to the foot of the wooded hills which form the northern and northeastern boundary of this old samurai quarter. Formerly all this broad level space was occupied by a bamboo grove; but it is now little more than waste of grasses and wild flowers. In the northeast corner there is a magnificent well, from which ice-cold water is brought into the house through a most ingenious little aqueduct of bamboo pipes; and in the northwestern end, veiled by tall weeds, there stands a very small stone shrine of Inari, with two proportionately small stone foxes sitting before it. Shrine and images are chipped and broken, and thickly patched with dark green moss. But on the east side of the house one little square of soil belonging to this large division of the garden is still cultivated. It is devoted entirely to chrysanthemum plants, which are shielded from heavy rain and strong sun by slanting frames of light wood fashioned like shōji, with panes of white paper, and supported like awnings upon thin posts of bamboo. I can venture to add nothing to what has already been written about these marvelous products of Japanese floriculture considered in themselves; but there is a little story relating to chrysanthemums which I may presume to tell.

There is one place in Japan where it is thought unlucky to cultivate chrysanthemums, for reasons which shall presently appear; and that place is in the pretty little city of Himeji, in the province of Harima. Himeji contains the ruins of a great castle of thirty turrets; and a daimyō used to dwell therein whose revenue was one hundred and fifty-six thousand koku of rice. Now, in the house of one of that daimyō's chief retainers there was a maid-servant, of good family, whose name was O-Kiku; and the name "Kiku" signifies a chrysanthemum flower. Many precious things were intrusted to her charge, and among others ten costly dishes of gold. One of these was suddenly missed, and could not be found; and the girl, being responsible therefor, and knowing not how otherwise to prove her innocence, drowned herself in a well. But ever thereafter her ghost, returning nightly, could be heard counting the dishes slowly, with sobs:

Ichi-mai,	*Yo-mai,*	*Shichi-mai,*
Ni-mai,	*Go-mai,*	*Hachi-mai,*
San-mai,	*Roku-mai*	*Ku-mai*—

Then would be heard a despairing cry and a loudburst of weeping; and again the girl's voice counting the dishes plaintively: "One—two—three—four—five—six—seven—eight—*nine*"—

Her spirit passed into the body of a strange little insect, whose head faintly resembles that of a ghost with long disheveled hair; and it is called O-Kikumushi, or "the fly of O-Kiku," and it is found, they say, nowhere save in Himeji. A famous play was written about O-Kiku, which is still acted in all the popular theatres, entitled Banshu-O-Kiku-no-Sara-yashiki; or, The Manor of the Dish of O-Kiku of Banshu.

Some declare that Banshu is only the corruption of the name of an ancient quarter of Tōkyō (Yedo), where the story should have been laid. But the people of Himeji say that part of their city now called Go-Ken-Yashiki is identical with the site of the ancient manor. What is certainly true is that to cultivate chrysanthemum flowers in the part of Himeji called Go-Ken-Yashiki is deemed unlucky, because the name of O-Kiku signifies "Chrysanthemum." Therefore, nobody, I am told, ever cultivates chrysanthemums there.

IX.

Now of the ujō, or things having desire, which inhabit these gardens.

There are four species of frogs: three that dwell in the lotus pond, and one that lives in the trees. The tree frog is a very pretty little creature, exquisitely green; it has a shrill cry, almost like the note of a *semi;* and it is called amagaeru, or "the rain frog," because, like its kindred in other countries, its croaking is an omen of rain. The pond frogs are called babagaeru, shinagae-ru, and Tono-san-gaeru. Of these, the first named variety is the largest and the ugliest: its color is very disagreeable, and its full name ("babagaeru" being a decent abbreviation) is quite as offensive as its hue. The shinagaeru, or "striped frog," is not handsome, except by comparison with the previously mentioned creature. But the Tonosan-gaeru, so called after a famed daimyō who left behind him a memory of great splendor, is beautiful: its color is a fine bronze-red.

Besides these varieties of frogs there lives in the garden a huge uncouth goggle-eyed thing which, although called here hikigaeru, I take to be a toad. "Hikigaeru" is the term ordinarily used for a bullfrog. This creature enters the house almost daily to be fed, and seems to have no fear even of strangers. My people consider it a luck-bringing visitor; and it is credited with the power of drawing all the mosquitoes out of a room into its mouth by simply sucking its breath in. Much as it is cherished by gardeners and others, there is a legend about a goblin toad of old times, which, by thus sucking in its breath, drew into its mouth, not insects, but men.

The pond is inhabited also by many small fish; imori, or newts, with bright red bellies; and multitudes of little water-beetles, called maimaimushi, which pass their whole time in gyrating upon the surface of the water so rapidly that it is almost impossible to distinguish their shape clearly. A man who runs about aimlessly to and fro, under the influence of excitement, is compared to a maimaimushi. And there are some beautiful snails, with yellow stripes on their shells. Japanese children have a charm-song which is supposed to have power to make the snail put out its horns:

Daidaimushi,* daidaimushi, tsuno chitto dashare!
Ame kazefuku kara tsuno chitto dashare!†

The playground of the children of the better classes has always been the family garden, as that of the children of the poor is the temple court. It is in the garden that the little ones first learn something of the wonderful life of plants and the marvels of the insect world; and there, also, they are first taught those pretty legends and songs about birds and flowers which form so charming a part of Japanese folklore. As the home training of the child is left mostly to the mother, lessons of kindness to animals are early inculcated; and the results are strongly marked in after life. It is true, Japanese children are not entirely free from that unconscious tendency to cruelty characteristic of children in all countries, as a survival of primitive instincts. But in this regard the great moral difference between the sexes is strongly marked from the earliest years. The tenderness of the woman-soul appears even in the child. Little Japanese girls who play with insects or small animals rarely hurt them, and generally set them free after they have afforded a reasonable amount of amusement. Little boys are not nearly so good, when out of sight of parents or guardians. But if seen doing anything cruel, a child is made to feel ashamed of the act, and hears the Buddhist warning, "Thy future birth will be unhappy, if thou dost cruel things."

Somewhere among the rocks in the pond lives a small tortoise—left in the garden, probably, by the previous tenants of the house. It is very pretty, but manages to remain invisible for weeks at a time. In popular mythology, the tortoise is the servant of the divinity Kompira;‡ and if a pious fisherman finds a tortoise, he writes upon his back characters signifying "Servant

---

* *Daidaimushi* in Izumo. The dictionary word is *dedemushi*. The snail is supposed to he very fond of wet weather; and one who goes out much in the rain is compared to a snail—*dedemushi no yona.*

† "Snail, snail, put out your horns a little: it rains and the wind is blowing, so put out your horns, just for a little while."

‡ A Buddhist divinity, but within recent times identified by Shintō with the god Kotohira.

of the Deity Kompira," and then gives it a drink of saké and sets it free. It is supposed to be very fond of saké.

Some say that the land tortoise, or "stone tortoise," only, is the servant of Kompira, and the sea tortoise, or turtle, the servant of the Dragon Empire beneath the sea. The turtle is said to have the power to create, with its breath, a cloud, a fog, or a magnificent palace. It figures in the beautiful old folk-tale of Urashima.* All tortoises are supposed to live for a thousand years, wherefore one of the most frequent symbols of longevity in Japanese art is a tortoise. But the tortoise most commonly represented by native painters and metal-workers has a peculiar tail, or rather a multitude of small tails, extending behind it like the fringes of a straw rain-coat, mino, whence it is called minogamé. Now, some of the tortoises kept in the sacred tanks of Buddhist temples attain a prodigious age, and certain waterplants attach themselves to the creatures' shells and stream behind them when they walk. The myth of the minogamé is supposed to have had its origin in old artistic efforts to represent the appearance of such tortoises with confervae fastened upon their shells.

X.

Early in summer the frogs are surprisingly numerous, and, after dark, are noisy beyond description; but week by week their nightly clamor grows feebler, as their numbers diminish under the attacks of many enemies. A large family of snakes, some fully three feet long, make occasional inroads into the colony. The victims often utter piteous cries, which are promptly responded to, whenever possible, by some inmate of the house, and many a frog has been saved by my servant-girl, who, by a gentle tap with a bamboo rod, compels the snake to let its prey go. These snakes are beautiful swimmers. They make themselves quite free about the garden; but they come out only on hot days. None of my

---

* See Professor Chamberlain's version of it in The Japanese Fairy Tale Series, with charming illustrations by a native artist.

people would think of injuring or killing one of them. Indeed, in Izumo it is said that to kill a snake is unlucky. "If you kill a snake without provocation," a peasant assured me, "you will afterwards find its head in the komebitsu [the box in which cooked rice is kept] when you take off the lid."

But the snakes devour comparatively few frogs. Impudent kites and crows are their most implacable destroyers; and there is a very pretty weasel which lives under the kura (go-down), and which does not hesitate to take either fish or frogs out of the pond, even when the lord of the manor is watching. There is also a cat which poaches in my preserves, a gaunt outlaw, a master thief, which I have made sundry vain attempts to reclaim from vagabondage. Partly because of the immorality of this cat, and partly because it happens to have a long tail, it has the evil reputation of being a nekomata, or goblin cat.

It is true that in Izumo some kittens are born with long tails; but it is very seldom that they are suffered to grow up with long tails. For the natural tendency of cats is to become goblins; and this tendency to metamorphosis can be checked only by cutting off their tails in kittenhood. Cats are magicians, tails or no tails, and have the power of making corpses dance. Cats are ungrateful. "Feed a dog for three days," says a Japanese proverb, "and he will remember your kindness for three years; feed a cat for three years and she will forget your kindness in three days." Cats are mischievous: they tear the mattings, and make holes in the shōji, and sharpen their claws upon the pillars of tokonoma. Cats are under a curse: only the cat and the venomous serpent wept not at the death of Buddha; and these shall never enter into the bliss of the Gokuraku. For all these reasons, and others too numerous to relate, cats are not much loved in Izumo, and are compelled to pass the greater part of their lives out of doors.

XI.

Not less than eleven varieties of butterflies have visited the neighborhood of the lotus pond within the past few days. The most common variety is snowy white. It is supposed to be especially attracted by the *na*, or rapeseed plant; and when little girls see it, they sing:

> Chō-chō, chō-chō, na no ha ni tomare;
> Na no ha ga iyenara, te ni tomare.*

But the most interesting insects are certainly the semi (cicadae). These Japanese tree crickets are much more extraordinary singers than even the wonderful cicadae of the tropics; and they are much less tiresome, for there is a different species of semi, with a totally different song, for almost every month during the whole warm season. There are, I believe, seven kinds; but I have become familiar with only four. The first to be heard in my trees is the natsuzemi, or summer semi: it makes a sound like the Japanese monosyllable *ji,* beginning wheezily, slowly swelling into a crescendo shrill as the blowing of steam, and dying away in another wheeze. This *j-i-i-iiiiiiiii* is so deafening that when two or three natsuzemi come close to the window I am obliged to make them go away. Happily the natsuzemi is soon succeeded by the minminzemi, a much finer musician, whose name is derived from its wonderful note. It is said "to chant like a Buddhist priest reciting the kyō; and certainly, upon hearing it the first time, one can scarcely believe that one is listening to a mere cicada. The minminzemi is followed, early in autumn, by a beautiful green semi, the higurashi, which makes a singularly clear sound, like the rapid ringing of a small bell—*kanokana-kana-kana-kana.* But the most astonishing visitor of all comes still later, the tsuku-tsuku-bōshi.† I fancy this creature can have no rival in the whole world of cicadae: its music is exactly like the song of a bird. Its name, like that of the minminzemi, is onomatopoetic; but in Izumo the sounds of its chant are given thus:

---

* "Butterfly, little butterfly, light upon the *na* leaf. But if thou dost not like the *na* leaf, light, I pray thee, upon my hand."

† *Bōshi* means "a hat," *tsukeru,* "to put on." But this etymology is more than doubtful.

> *Tsuku-tsuku uisu,* *
> *Tsuku-tsuku uisu;*
> *Tsuku-tsuku uisu;*
>> Ui-ōsu,
>> Ui-ōsu,
>> Ui-ōsu,
>> Ui-ōs-s-s-s-s-s-s-su.

However, the semi are not the only musicians of the garden. Two remarkable creatures aid their orchestra. The first is a beautiful bright green grasshopper, known to the Japanese by the curious name of hotoke-no-uma, or "the horse of the dead." This insect's head really bears some resemblance in shape to the head of a horse—hence the fancy. It is a queerly familiar creature, allowing itself to be taken in the hand without struggling, and generally making itself quite at home in the house, which it often enters. It makes a very thin sound, which the Japanese write as a repetition of the syllables *jun-ta;* and the name junta is sometimes given to the grasshopper itself. The other insect is also a green grasshopper, somewhat larger, and much shyer: it is called gisu,† on account of its chant:

> *Chon,*
>> *Gisu;*
> *Chon,*
>> *Gisu;*
> *Chon,*
>> *Gisu;*
> *Chon*...(ad libitum).

Several lovely species of dragon-flies *(tombō)* hover about the pondlet on hot bright days. One variety—the most beautiful creature of the kind I ever saw, gleaming with metallic colors indescribable, and spectrally slender—is called Tenshi-tombō, "the Emperor's dragon-fly." There is another, the largest of Japanese

---

* Some say "*Chokko-chokko-uisu.*" "Uisu" would be pronounced in English very much like "weece," the final *u* being silent. "Uiōsu" would be something like "we-oce."

† Pronounced almost as "geece."

dragon-flies, but somewhat rare, which is much sought after by children as a plaything. Of this species it is said that there are many more males than females; and what I can vouch for as true is that, if you catch a female, the male can be almost immediately attracted by exposing the captive. Boys, accordingly, try to secure a female, and when one is captured they tie it with a thread to some branch, and sing a curious little song, of which these are the original words:

> *Konna* danshō Korai ō*
> *Adzuma no metō ni makete*
> *Nigeru wa haji dewa naikai?*

Which signifies, "Thou, the male, King of Korea, dost thou not feel shame to flee away from the Queen of the East?" (This taunt is an allusion to the story of the conquest of Korea by the Empress Jin-gō.) And the male comes invariably, and is also caught. In Izumo the first seven words of the original song have been corrupted into *"konna unjo Korai abura no mito;"* and the name of the male dragonfly, *unjo,* and that of the female, *mito,* are derived from two words of the corrupted version.

XII.

Of warm nights all sorts of unbidden guests invade the house in multitudes. Two varieties of mosquitoes do their utmost to make life unpleasant, and these have learned the wisdom of not approaching a lamp too closely; but hosts of curious and harmless things cannot be prevented from seeking their death in the flame. The most numerous victims of all, which come thick as a shower of rain, are called Sanemori. At least they are so called in Izumo, where they do much damage to growing rice.

Now the name Sanemori is an illustrious one, that of a famous warrior of old times belonging to the Genji clan. There is a legend that while he was fighting with an enemy on horseback

---

* Contraction of *kore naru.*

his own steed slipped and fell in a rice-field, and he was consequently overpowered and slain by his antagonist. He became a
rice-devouring insect, which is still respectfully called, by the
peasantry of Izumo, Sanemori-San. They light fires, on certain
summer nights, in the rice-fields, to attract the insect, and
beat gongs and sound bamboo flutes, chanting the while, "O
Sanemori, augustly deign to come hither!" A kannushi performs
a religious rite, and a straw figure representing a horse and rider
is then either burned or thrown into a neighboring river or
canal. By this ceremony it is believed that the fields are cleared
of the insect.

This tiny creature is almost exactly the size and color of a rice-
husk. The legend concerning it may have arisen from the fact
that its body, together with the wings, bears some resemblance
to the helmet of a Japanese Warrior.*

Next in number among the victims of fire are the moths, some
of which are very strange and beautiful. The most remarkable
is an enormous creature popularly called okori-chōchō, or the
"ague moth," because there is a superstitious belief that it brings
intermittent fever into any house it enters. It has a body quite
as heavy and almost as powerful as that of the largest humming-
bird, and its struggles, when caught in the hand, surprise by
their force. It makes a very loud whirring sound while flying.
The wings of one which I examined measured, outspread, five

---

* A kindred legend attaches to the shiwan, a little yellow insect which preys upon
cucumbers. The shiwan is said to have been once a physician, who, being detected in an
amorous intrigue, had to fly for his life; but as he went his foot caught in a cucumber
vine, so that he fell and was overtaken and killed, and his ghost became an insect, the
destroyer of cucumber vines.

In the zoological mythology and plant mythology of Japan there exist many legends
offering a curious resemblance to the old Greek tales of metamorphoses. Some of the
most remarkable bits of such folklore have originated, however, in comparatively modern time. The legend of the crab called heikegani, found at Nagato, is an example. The
souls of the Taira warriors who perished in the great naval battle of Dan-no-ura (now
Seto-Naikai), 1185, are supposed to have been transformed into heikegani. The shell of
the heikegani is certainly surprising. It is wrinkled into the likeness of a grim face, or
rather into exact semblance of one of those black iron visors, or masks, which feudal
warriors wore in battle, and which were shaped like frowning visages.

inches from tip to tip, yet seemed small in proportion to the heavy body. They were richly mottled with dusky browns and silver grays of various tones.

Many flying night-comers, however, avoid the lamp. Most fantastic of all visitors is the tōrō or kamakiri, called in Izumo kamakaké, a bright green praying mantis, extremely feared by children for its capacity to bite. It is very large. I have seen specimens over six inches long. The eyes of the kamakaké are a brilliant black at night, but by day they appear grass-colored, like the rest of the body. The mantis is very intelligent and surprisingly aggressive. I saw one attacked by a vigorous frog easily put its enemy to flight. It fell a prey subsequently to other inhabitants of the pond, but it required the combined efforts of several frogs to vanquish the monstrous insect, and even then the battle was decided only when the kamakaké had been dragged into the water.

Other visitors are beetles of divers colors, and a sort of small roach called goki-kaburi, signifying "one whose head is covered with a bowl." It is alleged that the goki-kaburi likes to eat human eyes, and is therefore the abhorred enemy of Ichibata-Sama—Yakushi-Nyorai of Ichibata—by whom diseases of the eye are healed. To kill the goki-kaburi is consequently thought to be a meritorious act in the sight of this Buddha. Always welcome are the beautiful fireflies *(hotaru)*, which enter quite noiselessly, and at once seek the darkest place in the house, slow-glimmering, like sparks moved by a gentle wind. They are supposed to be very fond of water; wherefore children sing to them this little song:

> *Hotaru kōe midzu nomashō;*
> *Achi no midzu wa nigaizo;*
> *Kochi no midzu wa amaizo.**

A pretty gray lizard, quite different from some which usually haunt the garden, also makes its appearance at night, and pur-

---

* "Come, firefly, I will give you water to drink. The water of that place is bitter; the water here is sweet."

sues its prey along the ceiling. Sometimes an extraordinarily large centipede attempts the same thing, but with less success, and has to be seized with a pair of fire-tongs and thrown into the exterior darkness. Very rarely, an enormous spider appears. This creature seems inoffensive. If captured, it will feign death until certain that it is not watched, when it will run away with surprising swiftness if it gets a chance. It is hairless, and very different from the tarantula, or fukurogumo. It is called miyamagumo, or mountain spider. There are four other kinds of spiders common in this neighborhood: tenagakumo, or "long-armed spider," hiratakumo, or "flat spider," jikumo, or "earth spider," and totatekumo, or "door-shutting spider." Most spiders are considered evil beings. A spider seen anywhere at night, the people say, should be killed; for all spiders that show themselves after dark are goblins. While people are awake and watchful, such creatures make themselves small; but when everybody is fast asleep, then they assume their true goblin shape, and become monstrous.

XIII.

The high wood of the hill behind the garden is full of bird life. There dwell wild uguisu, owls, wild doves, too many crows, and a queer bird that makes weird noises at night—long deep sounds of *hoo, hoo.* It is called awamakidori or the "millet-sowing bird," because when the farmers hear its cry, they know that it is time to plant the millet. It is quite small and brown, extremely shy, and, so far as I can learn, altogether nocturnal in its habits.

But rarely, very rarely, a far stranger cry is heard in those trees at night, a voice as of one crying in pain the syllables "*ho-to-to-gi-su.*" The cry and the name of that which utters it are one and the same, *hototogisu.*

It is a bird of which weird things are told; for they say it is not really a creature of this living world, but a night wanderer from the Land of Darkness. In the Meido its dwelling is among those sunless mountains of Shide over which all souls must pass to reach the place of judgment. Once in each year it comes; the time of its coming is the end of the fifth month, by the antique counting of moons; and the peasants, hearing its voice, say one to the other, "Now must we sow the rice; for the Shide-no-taosa is with us." The word taosa signifies the headman of a mura, or village, as villages were governed in the old days; but why the hototogisu is called the taosa of Shide I do not know. Perhaps it is deemed to be a soul from some shadowy hamlet of the Shide hills, whereat the ghosts are wont to rest on their weary way to the realm of Emma, the King of Death.

Its cry has been interpreted in various ways. Some declare that the hototogisu does not really repeat its own name, but asks, *"Honzon kaketaka?"* (Has the honzon* been suspended?) Others, resting their interpretation upon the wisdom of the Chinese, aver that the bird's speech signifies, "Surely it is better to return home." This, at least, is true: that all who journey far from their native place, and hear the voice of the hototogisu in other distant provinces, are seized with the sickness of longing for home.

Only at night, the people say, is its voice heard, and most often upon the nights of great moons; and it chants while hovering high out of sight, wherefore a poet has sung of it thus:

> *Hito koe wa.*
> *Tsuki ga naitaka*
> *Hototogisu!†*

And another has written:

> *Hototogisu*
> *Nakitsuru kata wo*

---

* By *honzon* is here meant the sacred kakemono, or picture, exposed to public view in the temples only upon the birthday of the Buddha, which is the eighth day of the old fourth month. *Honzon* also signifies the principal image in a Buddhist temple.

† "A solitary voice!
  Did the Moon cry?
  'Twas but the hototogisu."

Nagamureba—
Tada ariake no
*Tsuki zo nokoreru.**

The dweller in cities may pass a lifetime without hearing the hototogisu. Caged, the little creature will remain silent and die. Poets often wait vainly in the dew, from sunset till dawn, to bear the strange cry which has inspired so many exquisite verses. But those who have heard found it so mournful that they have likened it to the cry of one wounded suddenly to death.

Hototogisu
Chi ni naku koe wa
Ariake no
Tsuki yori hokani
Kiku hito mo nashi.†

Concerning Izumo owls, I shall content myself with citing a composition by one of my Japanese students:

"The Owl is a hateful bird that sees in the dark. Little children who cry are frightened by the threat that the Owl will come to take them away; for the Owl cries, '*Ho! ho! sorōtto kōka! sorōtto kōka!*' which means, 'Thou! must I enter slowly?' It also cries '*Noritsuke hose! ho! ho!*' which, means, 'Do thou make the starch to use in washing tomorrow!' And when the women hear that cry, they know that tomorrow will be a fine day. It also cries, '*Tototo,*' 'The man dies,' and '*Kōtokokko,*' 'The boy dies.' So people hate it. And crows hate it so much that it is used to catch crows. The Farmer puts an Owl in the rice-field; and all the crows come to kill it, and they get caught fast in the snares. This should teach us not to give way to our dislikes for other people."

The kites which hover over the city all day do not live in the neighborhood. Their nests are far away upon the blue peaks;

---

* "When I gaze towards the place where I heard the hototogisu cry, lo! there is naught save the wan morning moon."

† "Save only the morning moon, none heard the heart's-blood cry of the hototogisu."

but they pass much of their time in catching fish, and in stealing from back yards. They pay the wood and the garden swift and sudden piratical visits; and their sinister cry—*pi-yorōyorō, pi-yorōyorō*—sounds at intervals over the town from dawn till sundown. Most insolent of all feathered creatures they certainly are—more insolent than even their fellow-robbers, the crows. A kite will drop five miles to filch a tai out of a fish-seller's bucket, or a fried-cake out of a child's hand, and shoot back to the clouds before the victim of the theft has time to stoop for a stone. Hence the saying, "to look as surprised as if one's aburagé* had been snatched from one's hand by a kite." There is, moreover, no telling what a kite may think proper to steal. For example, my neighbor's servant-girl went to the river the other day, wearing in her hair a string of small scarlet beads made of rice-grains prepared and dyed in a certain ingenious way. A kite lighted upon her head, and tore away and swallowed the string of beads. But it is great fun to feed these birds with dead rats or mice which have been caught in traps over night and subsequently drowned. The instant a dead rat is exposed to view a kite pounces from the sky to bear it away. Sometimes a crow may get the start of the kite, but the crow must be able to get to the woods very swiftly indeed in order to keep his prize. The children sing this song:

> *Tobi, tobi, maute mise!*
> *Ashita no ba ni*
> *Karasu ni kakushite*
> *Nezumi yaru.*†

The mention of dancing refers to the beautiful balancing motion of the kite's wings in flight. By suggestion this motion is poetically compared to the graceful swaying of a maiko, or dancing-girl, extending her arms and waving the long wide sleeves of her silken robe.

---

* A sort of doughnut made of bean flour, or tofu.

† "Kite, kite, let me see you dance, and tomorrow evening, when the crows do not know, I will give you a rat."

Although there is a numerous sub-colony of crows in the wood behind my house, the headquarters of the corvine army are in the pine grove of the ancient castle grounds, visible from my front rooms. To see the crows all flying home at the same hour every evening is an interesting spectacle, and popular imagination has found an amusing comparison for it in the hurry-skurry of people running to a fire. This explains the meaning of a song which children sing to the crows returning to their nests:

> *Ato no karasu saki ine,*
> *Ware ga iye ga yakeru ken*
> *Hayō inde midzu kake,*
> *Midzu ga nakya yarozo,*
> *Amattara ko ni yare,*
> *Ko ga nakya modose.**

Confucianism seems to have discovered virtue in the crow. There is a Japanese proverb, "*Karasu ni hampo no ko ari,*" meaning that the crow performs the filial duty of hampo, or, more literally, "the filial duty of hampo exists in the crow." "Hampo" means, literally, "to return a feeding." The young crow is said to requite its parents' care by feeding them when it becomes strong. Another example of filial piety has been furnished by the dove. "*Hato ni sanshi no rei ari,*"—the dove sits three branches below its parent; or, more literally, "has the three-branch etiquette to perform."

The cry of the wild dove (*yamabato*), which I hear almost daily from the wood, is the most sweetly plaintive sound that ever reached my ears. The Izumo peasantry say that the bird utters these words, which it certainly seems to do if one listen to it after having learned the alleged syllables:

---

* "O tardy crow, hasten forward! Your house is all on fire. Hurry to throw water upon it. If there be no water, I will give you. If you have too much, give it to your child. If you have no child, then give it back to me."

Tété
  poppō,
Kaka
  poppō,
Tété
  poppō,
Kaka
  poppō,
Tété...(sudden pause).

"Tété" is the baby word for "father," and "kaka" for "mother;" and "poppō" signifies, in infantile speech, "the bosom."*

Wild uguisu also frequently sweeten my summer with their song, and sometimes come very near the house, being attracted, apparently, by the chant of my caged pet. The uguisu is very common in this province. It haunts all the woods and the sacred groves in the neighborhood of the city, and I never made a journey in Izumo during the warm season without hearing its note from some shadowy place. But there are uguisu and uguisu. There are uguisu to be had for one or two yen, but the finely trained, cage-bred singer may command not less than a hundred.

It was at a little village temple that I first heard one curious belief about this delicate creature. In Japan, the coffin in which a corpse is borne to burial is totally unlike an Occidental coffin. It is a surprisingly small square box, wherein the dead is placed in a sitting posture. How any adult corpse can he put into so small a space may well be an enigma to foreigners. In cases of pronounced _rigor mortis_ the work of getting the body into the coffin is difficult even for the professional dōshin-bozu. But the devout followers of Nichiren claim that after death their bodies will remain perfectly flexible; and the dead body of an uguisu, they affirm, likewise never stiffens, for this little bird is of their

---

* The words _papa_ and _mamma_ exist in Japanese baby language, but their meaning is not at all what might be supposed. _Mamma_, or, with the usual honorific, _O-mamma_, means "boiled rice." _Papa_ means "tobacco."

faith, and passes its life in singing praises unto the Sutra of the Lotus of the Good Law.

XIV.

I have already become a little too fond of my dwelling-place. Each day, after returning from my college duties, and exchanging my teacher's uniform for the infinitely more comfortable Japanese robe, I find more than compensation for the weariness of five class-hours in the simple pleasure of squatting on the shaded veranda overlooking the gardens. Those antique garden walls, high-mossed below their ruined coping of tiles, seem to shut out even the murmur of the city's life. There are no sounds but the voices of birds, the shrilling of semi, or, at long, lazy intervals, the solitary splash of a diving frog. Nay, those walls seclude me from much more than city streets. Outside them hums the changed Japan of telegraphs and newspapers and steamships; within dwell the all-reposing peace of nature and the dreams of the sixteenth century. There is a charm of quaintness in the very air, a faint sense of something viewless and sweet all about one; perhaps the gentle haunting of dead ladies who looked like the ladies of the old picture-books, and who lived here when all this was new. Even in the summer light— touching the gray strange shapes of stone, thrilling through the foliage of the long-loved trees—there is the tenderness of a phantom caress. These are the gardens of the past. The future will know them only as dreams, creations of a forgotten art, whose charm no genius may reproduce.

Of the human tenants here no creature seems to be afraid. The little frogs resting upon the lotus-leaves scarcely shrink from my touch; the lizards sun themselves within easy reach of my hand; the watersnakes glide across my shadow without fear; bands of semi establish their deafening orchestra on a plum branch just above my head, and a praying mantis insolently poses on my knee. Swallows and sparrows not only build their nests on my roof, but even enter my rooms without concern—one swallow has actually built its nest in the ceiling of the bath-room—and the weasel purloins fish under my very eyes without any scruples of conscience. A wild uguisu perches on a cedar by the window, and in a burst of savage sweetness challenges my caged pet to a contest in song; and always through the golden air, from the green twilight of the mountain pines, there purls to me the plaintive, caressing, delicious call of the yamabato:

> *Tété*
> > *poppō,*
> *Kaka*
> > *poppō,*
> *Tété*
> > *poppō,*
> *Kaka*
> > *poppō,*
> *Tété...*

No European dove has such a cry. He who can hear, for the first time, the voice of the yamabato without feeling a new sensation at his heart little deserves to dwell in this happy world.

Yet all this—the old katchiū-yashiki and its gardens—will doubless have vanished forever before many years. Already a multitude of gardens, more spacious and more beautiful than mine, have been converted into rice-fields or bamboo groves; and the quaint Izumo city, touched at last by some long-projected railway line—perhaps even within the present decade—will swell, and change, and grow commonplace, and demand these grounds for the building of factories and mills. Not from here alone, but from all the land the ancient peace and the ancient charm seem doomed to pass away. For impermanency is the nature of things, more particularly in Japan; and the changes and the changers shall also be changed until there is found no place for them—and regret is vanity. The dead art that made the beauty of this place was the art, also, of that faith to which belongs the all-consoling text, *"Verily, even plants and trees, rocks and stones, all shall enter into Nirvana."*

17

THE HOUSEHOLD SHRINE

I.

IN Japan there are two forms of the Religion of the Dead—that which belongs to Shintō, and that which belongs to Buddhism. The first is the primitive cult, commonly called ancestor-worship. But the term ancestor-worship seems to me much too confined for the religion which pays reverence not only to those ancient gods believed to be the fathers of the Japanese race, but likewise to a host of deified sovereigns, heroes, princes, and illustrious men. Within comparatively recent times, the great Daimyō of Izumo, for example, were apotheosized; and the peasants of Shimane still pray before the shrines of the Matsudaira. Moreover Shintō, like the faiths of Hellas and of Rome, has its deities of the elements and special deities who preside over all the various affairs of life. Therefore ancestor-worship, though still a striking feature of Shintō, does not alone constitute the State Religion: neither does the term fully describe the Shintō cult of the dead—a cult which in Izumo retains its primitive character more than in other parts of Japan.

And here I may presume, though no sinologue, to say something about that State Religion of Japan—that ancient faith of Izumo—which, although even more deeply rooted in national life than Buddhism, is far less known to the Western world. Except in special works by such men of erudition as Chamberlain and

Satow—works with which the Occidental reader, unless himself a specialist, is not likely to become familiar outside of Japan—little has been written in English about Shintō which gives the least idea of what Shintō is. Of its ancient traditions and rites much of rarest interest may be learned from the works of the philologists just mentioned; but, as Mr. Satow himself acknowledges, a definite answer to the question, "What is the nature of Shintō?" is still difficult to give. How define the common element in the six kinds of Shintō which are known to exist, and some of which no foreign scholar has yet been able to examine for lack of time or of authorities or of opportunity? Even in its modern external forms, Shintō is sufficiently complex to task the united powers of the historian, philologist, and anthropologist, merely to trace out the multitudinous lines of its evolution, and to determine the sources of its various elements: primeval polytheisms and fetichisms, traditions of dubious origin, philosophical concepts from China, Korea, and elsewhere—all mingled with Buddhism, Taoism, and Confucianism. The so-called "Revival of Pure Shintō"—an effort, aided by Government, to restore the cult to its archaic simplicity, by divesting it of foreign characteristics, and especially of every sign or token of Buddhist origin—resulted only, so far as the avowed purpose was concerned, in the destruction of priceless art, and in leaving the enigma of origins as complicated as before. Shintō had been too profoundly modified in the course of fifteen centuries of change to be thus remodeled by a fiat. For the like reason scholarly efforts to define its relation to national ethics by mere historical and philological analysis must fail: as well seek to define the ultimate secret of Life by the elements of the body which it animates. Yet when the result of such efforts shall have been closely combined with a deep knowledge of Japanese thought and feeling—the thought and sentiment, not of a special class, but of the people at large—then indeed all that Shintō was and is may be fully comprehended. And this may be accomplished, I fancy, through the united labor of European and Japanese scholars.

Yet something of what Shintō signifies—in the simple poetry of its beliefs—in the home-training of the child—in the worship of filial piety before the tablets of the ancestors—may be learned during a residence of some years among the people, by one who lives their life and adopts their manners and customs. With such experience he can at least claim the right to express his own conception of Shintō.

II.

Those far-seeing rulers of the Meiji era, who disestablished Buddhism to strengthen Shintō, doubtless knew they were giving new force not only to a faith in perfect harmony with their own state policy, but likewise to one possessing in itself a far more profound vitality than the alien creed, which although omnipotent as an art-influence, had never found deep root in the intellectual soil of Japan. Buddhism was already in decrepitude, though transplanted from China scarcely more than thirteen centuries before; while Shintō, though doubtless older by many a thousand years, seems rather to have gained than to have lost force through all the periods of change. Eclectic like the genius of the race, it had appropriated and assimilated all forms of foreign thought which could aid its material manifestation or fortify its ethics. Buddhism had attempted to absorb its gods, even as it had adopted previously the ancient deities of Brahmanism; but Shintō, while seeming to yield, was really only borrowing strength from its rival. And this marvelous vitality of Shintō is due to the fact that in the course of its long development out of unrecorded beginnings, it became at a very ancient epoch, and below the surface still remains, a religion of the heart. Whatever be the origin of its rites and traditions, its ethical spirit has become identified with all the deepest and best emotions of the race. Hence, in Izumo especially, the attempt to create a Buddhist-Shintōism resulted only in the formation of a Shintō-Buddhism.

And the secret living force of Shintō today—that force which repels missionary efforts at proselytizing—means something much more profound than tradition or worship or ceremonialism. Shintō may yet, without loss of real power, survive all these. Certainly the expansion of the popular mind through education, the influences of modern science, must compel modification or abandonment of many ancient Shintō conceptions; but the ethics of Shintō will surely endure. For Shintō signifies character in the higher sense—courage, courtesy, honor, and above all things, loyalty. The spirit of Shintō is the spirit of filial piety, the zest of duty, the readiness to surrender life for a principle without a thought of wherefore. It is the docility of the child; it is the sweetness of the Japanese woman. It is conservatism likewise; the wholesome check upon the national tendency to cast away the worth of the entire past in rash eagerness to assimilate too much of the foreign present. It is religion—but religion transformed into hereditary moral impulse—religion transmuted into ethical instinct. It is the whole emotional life of the race—the Soul of Japan.

The child is born Shintō. Home teaching and school training only give expression to what is innate: they do not plant new seed; they do but quicken the ethical sense transmitted as a trait ancestral. Even as a Japanese infant inherits such ability to handle a writing-brush as never can be acquired by Western fingers, so does it inherit ethical sympathies totally different from our own. Ask a class of Japanese students—young students of fourteen to sixteen—to tell their dearest wishes; and if they have confidence in the questioner, perhaps nine out of ten will answer: "To die for His Majesty Our Emperor." And the wish soars from the heart pure as any wish for martyrdom ever born. How much this sense of loyalty may or may not have been weakened in such great centers as Tōkyō by the new agnosticism and by the rapid growth of other nineteenth century ideas among the student class, I do not know; but in the country it remains as natural to boyhood as joy. Unreasoning it also is—unlike those loyal sentiments with us, the results of maturer knowledge and settled conviction. Never does the Japanese youth ask himself why; the beauty of self-sacrifice alone is the all-sufficing motive. Such ecstatic loyalty is a part of the national life; it is in the blood—inherent as the impulse of the ant to perish for its little republic—unconscious as the loyalty of bees to their queen. It is Shintō.

That readiness to sacrifice one's own life for loyalty's sake, for the sake of a superior, for the sake of honor, which has distinguished the race in modern times, would seem also to have been a national characteristic from the earliest period of its independent existence. Long before the epoch of established feudalism, when honorable suicide became a matter of rigid etiquette, not for warriors only, but even for women and little children, the giving one's life for one's prince, even when the sacrifice could avail nothing, was held a sacred duty. Among various instances which might be cited from the ancient Kojiki, the following is not the least impressive:

Prince Mayowa, at the age of only seven years, having killed his father's slayer, fled into the house of the Grandee *(Omi)* Tsubura. "Then Prince Oho-hatsuse raised an army, and besieged that house. And the arrows that were shot were for multitude like the ears of the reeds. And the Grandee Tsubura came forth himself, and having taken off the weapons with which he was girded, did obeisance eight times, and said: 'The maiden-princess Kara, my daughter whom thou deignedst anon to woo, is at thy service. Again I will present to thee five granaries. Though a vile slave of a Grandee exerting his utmost strength in the fight can scarcely hope to conquer, yet must he die rather than desert a prince who, trusting in him, has entered into his house.' Having thus spoken, he again took his weapons, and went in once more to fight. Then, their strength being exhausted, and their arrows finished, he said to the Prince: 'My hands are wounded, and our arrows are finished. We cannot now fight: what shall be done?' The Prince replied saying: 'There is nothing more to do. Do thou now slay me.' So the Grandee Tsubura thrust the Prince to death with his sword, and forthwith killed himself by cutting off his own head."

Thousands of equally strong examples could easily be quoted from later Japanese history, including many which occurred even within the memory of the living. Nor was it for persons alone that to die might become a sacred duty: in certain contingencies conscience held it scarcely less a duty to die for a purely personal conviction; and he who held any opinion which he believed of paramount importance would, when other means failed, write his views in a letter of farewell, and then take his own life, in order to call attention to his beliefs and to prove their sincerity. Such an instance occurred only last year in Tōkyō,* when the young lieutenant of militia, Ōhara Takeyoshi, killed kimself by *harakiri* in the cemetery of Saitokuji, leaving a letter stating as the reason for his act, his hope to force public recognition of the danger to Japanese independence from the growth of Russian power in the North Pacific. But a much more touching sacrifice, in May of the same year—a sacrifice conceived in the purest and most innocent spirit of loyalty—was that of the young girl Yoko Hatakeyama, who, after the attempt to assassinate the Czarevitch, traveled from Tōkyō to Kyōto and there killed herself before the gate of the Kenchō, merely as a vicarious atonement for the incident which had caused shame to Japan and grief to the Father of the people—His Sacred Majesty the Emperor.

III.

As to its exterior forms, modern Shintō is indeed difficult to analyze; but through all the intricate texture of extraneous beliefs so thickly interwoven about it, indications of its earliest character are still easily discerned. In certain of its primitive rites, in its archaic prayers and texts and symbols, in the history of its shrines, and even in many of the artless ideas of its poorest worshipers, it is plainly revealed as the most ancient of all forms of worship—that which Herbert Spencer terms "the root of all religions,"—devotion to the dead. Indeed, it has been frequently

---

* This was written early in 1892.

so expounded by its own greatest scholars and theologians. Its divinities are ghosts; *all* the dead become deities. In the Tama-no-mihashira the great commentator Hirata says "the spirits of the dead continue to exist in the unseen world which is everywhere about us, and they all become gods of varying character and degrees of influence. Some reside in temples built in their honor; others hover near their tombs; and they continue to render services to their prince, parents, wife, and children, as when in the body."* And they do more than this, for they control the lives and the doings of men. "Every human action," says Hirata, "is the work of a god."† And Motowori, scarcely less famous an exponent of pure Shintō doctrine, writes: "All the moral ideas which a man requires are implanted in his bosom by the gods, and are of the same nature with those instincts which impel him to eat when he is hungry or to drink when he is thirsty."‡ With this doctrine of Intuition no decalogue is required, no fixed code of ethics; and the human conscience is declared to be the only necessary guide. Though every action be "the work of a Kami," yet each man has within him the power to discern the righteous impulse from the unrighteous, the influence of the good deity from that of the evil. No moral teacher is so infallible as one's own heart. "To have learned that there is no way *(michi),*"§ says Motowori, "to be learned and practiced, is really to have learned the Way of the Gods."¶ And Hirata writes: "If you desire to practice true virtue, learn to stand in awe of the Unseen; and that will prevent you from doing wrong. Make a vow to the Gods who

---

* Quoted from Mr. Satow's masterly essay, "The Revival of Pure Shintō," published in the *Transactions* of the Asiatic Society of Japan. By "gods" are not necessarily meant beneficent *Kami*. Shintō has no devils; but it has its "bad gods" as well as good deities.

† Satow, "The Revival of Pure Shintō."

‡ *Ibid.*

§ In the sense of *Moral Path—i.e.* an ethical system.

¶ Satow, "The Revival of Pure Shintō." The whole force of Motowori's words will not be fully understood unless the reader knows that the term "Shintō" is of comparatively modern origin in Japan—having been borrowed from the Chinese to distinguish the ancient faith from Buddhism; and that the old name for the primitive religion is Kami-no-michi, "the Way of the Gods."

rule over the Unseen, and cultivate the conscience (*ma-gokoro*) implanted in you; and then you will never wander from the way." How this spiritual self-culture may best be obtained, the same great expounder has stated with almost equal brevity: "Devotion to the memory of ancestors is the mainspring of all virtues. No one who discharges his duty to them will ever be disrespectful to the Gods or to his living parents. Such a man will be faithful to his prince, loyal to his friends, and kind and gentle with his wife and children."*

How far are these antique beliefs removed from the ideas of the nineteenth century? Certainly not so far that we can afford to smile at them. The faith of the primitive man and the knowledge of the most profound psychologist may meet in strange harmony upon the threshold of the same ultimate truth, and the thought of a child may repeat the conclusions of a Spencer or a Schopenhauer. Are not our ancestors in very truth our *Kami*? Is not every action indeed the work of the Dead who dwell within us? Have not our impulses and tendencies, our capacities and weaknesses, our heroisms and timidities, been created by those vanished myriads from whom we received the all-mysterious bequest of Life? Do we still think of that infinitely complex Something which is each one of us, and which we call EGO, as "I" or as "They?" What is our pride or shame but the pride or shame of the Unseen in that which They have made?—and what our Conscience but the inherited sum of countless dead experiences with varying good and evil? Nor can we hastily reject the Shintō thought that all the dead become gods, while we respect the convictions of those strong souls of today who proclaim the divinity of man.

IV.

Shintō ancestor-worship, no doubt, like all ancestor-worship, was developed out of funeral rites, according to that general

---

* Satow, "The Revival of Pure Shintō."

law of religious evolution traced so fully by Herbert Spencer. And there is reason to believe that the early forms of Shintō public worship may have been evolved out of a yet older family worship—much after the manner in which M. Fustel de Coulanges, in his wonderful book, "La Cité Antique," has shown the religious public institutions among the Greeks and Romans to have been developed from the religion of the hearth. Indeed, the word ujigami, now used to signify a Shintō parish temple, and also its deity, means "*family* God," and in its present form is a corruption or contraction of uchi-no-Kami, meaning the "god of the interior" or "the god of the house." Shintō expounders have, it is true, attempted to interpret the term otherwise; and Hirata, as quoted by Mr. Ernest Satow, declared the name should be applied only to the *common ancestor,* or ancestors, or to one so entitled to the gratitude of a community as to merit equal honors. Such, undoubtedly, was the just use of the term in his time, and long before it; but the etymology of the word would certainly seem to indicate its origin in family worship, and to confirm modern scientific beliefs in regard to the evolution of religious institutions.

Now just as among the Greeks and Latins the family cult always continued to exist through all the development and expansion of the public religion, so the Shintō family worship has continued concomitantly with the communal worship at the countless ujigami, with popular worship at the famed Oho-yashiro of various provinces or districts, and with national worship at the great shrines of Ise and Kitzuki. Many objects connected with the family cult are certainly of alien or modern origin; but its simple rites and its unconscious poetry retain their archaic charm. And, to the student of Japanese life, by far the most interesting aspect of Shintō is offered in this home worship, which, like the home worship of the antique Occident, exists in a dual form.

V.

In nearly all Izumo dwellings there is a kamidana,* or "Shelf of the Gods." On this is usually placed a small Shintō shrine (*miya*) containing tablets bearing the names of gods (one at least of which tablets is furnished by the neighboring Shintō parish temple), and various ofuda, holy texts or charms, which most often are written promises in the name of some Kami to protect his worshiper. If there be no miya, the tablets or ofuda are simply placed upon the shelf in a certain order, the most sacred having the middle place. Very rarely are images to be seen upon a kamidana: for primitive Shintōism excluded images as rigidly as Jewish or Mohammedan law; and all Shintō iconography belongs to a comparatively modern era—especially to the period of Ryōbu-Shintō—and must be considered of Buddhist origin. If there be any images, they will probably be such as have been made only within recent years at Kitzuki: those small twin figures of Oho-kuni-nushi-no-Kami and of Koto-shiro-nushi-no-Kami, described in a former paper upon the Kitzuki-no-oho-yashiro. Shintō kakemono, which are also of latter-day origin, representing incidents from the Kojiki, are much more common than Shintō icons: these usually occupy the toko, or alcove, in the same room in which the kamidana is placed; but they will not be seen in the houses of the more cultivated classes. Ordinarily there will be found upon the kamidana nothing but the simple miya containing some ofuda: very, very seldom will a mirror† be seen, or gohei—except the gohei attached to the small shi-

---

* From *Kami*, "the [Powers] Above," or the Gods, and *tana*, "a shelf." The initial "t" of the latter word changes into "d" in the compound—just as that of *tokkuri*, "a jar" or "bottle," becomes *dokkuri* in the compound *o-mikidokkuri*.

† The mirror, as an emblem of female divinities, is kept in the secret innermost shrine of various Shintō temples. But the mirror of metal commonly placed before the public gaze in a Shintō shrine is not really of Shintō origin, but was introduced into Japan as a Buddhist symbol of the Shingon sect. As the mirror is the symbol in Shintō of female divinities, the sword is the emblem of male deities. The real symbols of the god or goddess are not, however, exposed to human gaze under any circumstances.

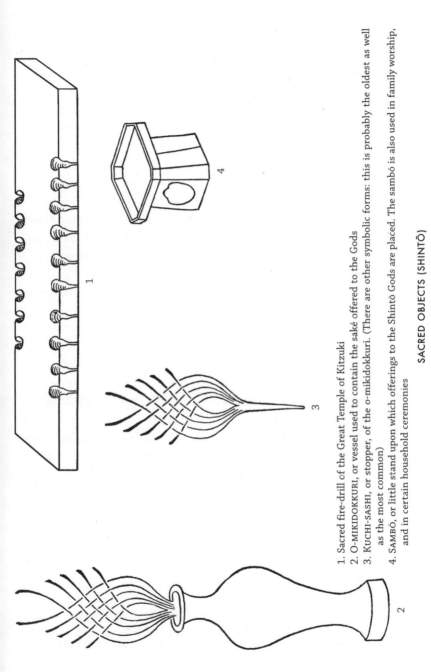

1. Sacred fire-drill of the Great Temple of Kitzuki
2. O-MIKIDOKKURI, or vessel used to contain the saké offered to the Gods
3. KUCHI-SASHI, or stopper, of the o-mikidokkuri. (There are other symbolic forms: this is probably the oldest as well as the most common)
4. SAMBŌ, or little stand upon which offerings to the Shintō Gods are placed. The sambō is also used in family worship, and in certain household ceremonies

SACRED OBJECTS (SHINTŌ)

menawa either hung just above the kamidana or suspended to the box-like frame in which the miya sometimes is placed. The shimenawa and the paper gohei are the true emblems of Shintō: even the ofuda and the mamori are quite modern. Not only before the household shrine, but also above the house-door of almost every home in Izumo, the shimenawa is suspended. It is ordinarily a thin rope of rice straw; but before the dwellings of high Shintō officials, such as the Taisha-Guji of Kitzuki, its size and weight are enormous. One of the first curious facts that the traveler in Izumo cannot fail to be impressed by is the universal presence of this symbolic rope of straw, which may sometimes even be seen round a rice-field. But the grand displays of the sacred symbol are upon the great festivals of the new year, the accession of Jimmu Tennō to the throne of Japan, and the Emperor's birthday. Then all the miles of streets are festooned with shimenawa thick as shipcables.

VI.

A particular feature of Matsue are the miya-shops—establishments not, indeed, peculiar to the old Izumo town, but much more interesting than those to be found in larger cities of other provinces. There are miya of a hundred varieties and sizes, from the child's toy miya which sells for less than one sen, to the large shrine destined for some rich home, and costing perhaps ten yen or more. Besides these, the household shrines of Shintō, may occasionally be seen massive shrines of precious wood, lacquered and gilded, worth from three hundred even to fifteen hundred yen. These are not household shrines; but festival shrines, and are made only for rich merchants. They are displayed on Shintō holidays, and twice a year are borne through the streets in procession, to shouts of *"Chosaya! chosaya!"** Each temple parish

---

* Anciently the two great Shintō festivals on which the miya were thus carried in procession were the Toshigami-no-matsuri, or festival of the God of the New Year, and the anniversary of Jimmu Tennō to the throne. The second of these is still observed. The celebration of the Emperor's birthday is the only other occasion when the miya are pa-

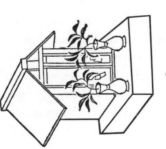

1
SUZU: Instrument used
by the Shintō priestess
in her sacred dance

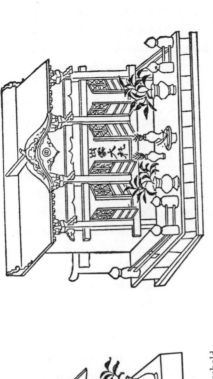

2
MIYA, or Shintō household
shrine of the cheapest
form

3
MIYA, or household shrine of
a wealthy family

SACRED OBJECTS (SHINTŌ)

also possesses a large portable miya which is paraded on these occasions with much chanting and beating of drums. The majority of household miya are cheap constructions. A very fine one can be purchased for about two yen; but those little shrines one sees in the houses of the common people cost, as a rule, considerably less than half a yen. And elaborate or costly household shrines are contrary to the spirit of pure Shintō. The true miya should be made of spotless white hinoki* wood, and be put together without nails. Most of those I have seen in the shops had their several parts joined only with rice-paste; but the skill of the maker rendered this sufficient. Pure Shintō requires that a miya should be without gilding or ornamentation. The beautiful miniature temples in some rich homes may justly excite admiration by their artistic structure and decoration; but the ten or thirteen cent miya, in the house of a laborer or a kurumaya, of plain white wood, truly represents that spirit of simplicity characterizing the primitive religion.

VII.

The kamidana or "God-shelf," upon which are placed the miya and other sacred objects of Shintō worship, is usually fastened at a height of about six or seven feet above the floor. As a rule it should not be placed higher than the hand can reach with ease; but in houses having lofty rooms the miya is sometimes put up at such a height that the sacred offerings cannot be made without the aid of a box or other object to stand upon. It is not commonly a part of the house structure, but a plain shelf attached with brackets either to the wall itself, at some angle of the apartment, or, as is much more usual, to the kamoi, or horizontal grooved

---

raded. On both days the streets are beautifully decorated with lanterns and shimenawa, the fringed ropes of rice straw which are the emblems of Shintō. Nobody now knows exactly what the words chanted on these days (*chosaya! chosaya!*) mean. One theory is that they are a corruption of Sagicho, the name of a great samurai military festival, which was celebrated nearly at the same time as the Yoshigami-no-matsuri—both holidays now being obsolete.

* *Thuya obtusa.*

beam, in which the screens of opaque paper *(fusuma),* which divide room from room, slide to and fro. Occasionally it is painted or lacquered. But the ordinary kamidana is of white wood, and is made larger or smaller in proportion to the size of the miya, or the number of the ofuda and other sacred objects to be placed upon it. In some houses, notably those of innkeepers and small merchants, the kamidana is made long enough to support a number of small shrines dedicated to different Shintō deities, particularly those believed to preside over wealth and commercial prosperity. In the houses of the poor it is nearly always placed in the room facing the street; and Matsue shopkeepers usually erect it in their shops—so that the passer-by or the customer can tell at a glance in what deities the occupant puts his trust. There are many regulations concerning it. It may be placed to face south or east, but should not face west, and under no possible circumstances should it be suffered to face north or northwest. One explanation of this is the influence upon Shintō of Chinese philosophy, according to which there is some fancied relation between South or East and the Male Principle, and between West or North and the Female Principle. But the popular notion on the subject is that because a dead person is buried with the head turned north, it would be very wrong to place a miya so as to face north—since everything relating to death is impure; and the regulation about the west is not strictly observed. Most kamidana in Izumo, however, face south or east. In the houses of the poorest—often consisting of but one apartment—there can be little choice as to rooms; but it is a rule, observed in the dwellings of the middle classes, that the kamidana must not be placed either in the guest room *(zashiki)* nor in the kitchen; and in shizoku houses its place is usually in one of the smaller family apartments. Respect must be shown it. One must not sleep, for example, or even lie down to rest, with his feet turned towards it. One must not pray before it, or even stand before it, while in a state of religious impurity—such as that entailed by having touched a corpse, or attended a Buddhist funeral, or even during the period of mourning for kindred buried according to the Buddhist rite. Should any member of the family be thus buried, then during fifty days* the kamidana must be entirely screened from view with pure white paper, and even the Shintō ofuda, or pious invocations fastened upon the house-door, must have white paper pasted over them. During the same mourning period the fire in the house is considered unclean; and at the close of the term all the ashes of the braziers and of the kitchen must be cast away, and new fire kindled with a flint and steel. Nor are funerals the only source of legal uncleanliness. Shintō, as the religion of purity and purification, has a Deuteronomy of quite an extensive kind. During certain periods women must not even pray before the miya, much less make offerings or touch the sacred vessels, or kindle the lights of the Kami.

VIII.

Before the miya, or whatever holy object of Shintō worship be placed upon the kamidana, are set two quaintly shaped jars for the offerings of saké; two small vases, to contain sprays of the sacred plant sakaki, or offerings of flowers; and a small lamp, shaped like a tiny saucer, where a wick of rush-pith floats in rapeseed oil. Strictly speaking, all these utensils except the flower-vases should be made of unglazed red earthenware, such as we find described in the early chapters of the Kojiki: and still at Shintō festivals in Izumo, when saké is drunk in honor of the gods, it is drunk out of cups of red baked unglazed clay shaped like shallow round dishes. But of late years it has become the fashion to make all the utensils of a fine kamidana of brass or bronze—even the hanaiké, or flower-vases. Among the poor, the most archaic utensils are still used to a great extent, especially in the remoter country districts; the lamp being a simple saucer or kawaraké of red clay; and the flower-vases most often bamboo

---

* Such at least is the mourning period under such circumstances in certain samurai families. Others say twenty days is sufficient. The Buddhist code of mourning is extremely varied and complicated, and would require much space to dilate upon.

cups, made by simply cutting a section of bamboo immediately below a joint and about five inches above it.

The brazen lamp is a much more complicated object than the kawaraké, which costs but one rin. The brass lamp costs about twenty-five sen, at least. It consists of two parts. The lower part, shaped like a very shallow, broad wineglass, with a very thick stem, has an interior as well as an exterior rim; and the bottom of a correspondingly broad and shallow brass cup, which is the upper part and contains the oil, fits exactly into this inner rim. This kind of lamp is always furnished with a small brass object in the shape of a flat ring, with a stem set at right angles to the surface of the ring. It is used for moving the floating wick and keeping it at any position required; and the little perpendicular stem is long enough to prevent the fingers from touching the oil.

The most curious objects to be seen on any ordinary kamidana are the stoppers of the saké-vessels or o-mikidokkuri ("honorable saké-jars"). These stoppers—o-mikidokkuri-no-kuchisashi—may be made of brass, or of fine thin slips of wood jointed and bent into the singular form required. Properly speaking, the thing is not a real stopper, in spite of its name; its lower part does not fill the mouth of the jar at all: it simply hangs in the orifice like a leaf put there stem downwards. I find it difficult to learn its history; but, though there are many designs of it—the finer ones being of brass—the shape of all seems to hint at a Buddhist origin. Possibly the shape was borrowed from a Buddhist symbol—the Hoshi-no-tama, that mystic gem whose lambent glow (iconographically suggested as a playing of flame) is the emblem of Pure Essence; and thus the object would be typical at once of the purity of the wine-offering and the purity of the heart of the giver.

The little lamp may not be lighted every evening in all homes, since there are families too poor to afford even this infinitesimal nightly expenditure of oil. But upon the first, fifteenth, and twenty-eighth of each month the light is always kindled; for these are Shintō holidays of obligation, when offerings must be made to the gods, and when all uji-ko, or parishioners of a Shintō temple, are supposed to visit their ujigami. In every home on these days saké is poured as an offering into the o-mikidokkuri, and in the vases of the kamidana are placed sprays of the holy sakaki, or sprigs of pine, or fresh flowers. On the first day of the new year the kamidana is always decked with sakaki, moromoki (ferns), and pinesprigs, and also with a shimenawa; and large double rice cakes are placed upon it as offerings to the gods.

IX.

But only the ancient gods of Shintō are worshiped before the kamidana. The family ancestors or family dead are worshiped either in a separate room (called the mitamaya, or "Spirit Chamber"), or, if worshiped according to the Buddhist rites, before the butsuma or butsudan.

The Buddhist family worship coexists in the vast majority of Izumo homes with the Shintō family worship; and whether the dead be honored in the mitamaya or before the butsudan altogether depends upon the religious traditions of the household. Moreover, there are families in Izumo—particularly in Kitzuki— whose members do not profess Buddhism in any form, and a very few, belonging to the Shinshū or Nichiren-shū,* whose members do not practice Shintō. But the domestic cult of the dead is maintained, whether the family be Shintō or Buddhist. The ihai or tablets of the Buddhist family dead (Hotoke) are never placed in a special room or shrine, but in the Buddhist household shrine† along with the images or pictures of Buddhist divinities

---

* In spite of the supposed rigidity of the Nichiren sect in such matters, most followers of its doctrine in Izumo are equally fervent Shintōists. I have not been able to observe whether the same is true of Izumo Shin-shū families as a rule; but I know that some Shin-shū believers in Matsue worship at Shintō shrines. Adoring only that form of Buddha called Amida, the Shin sect might be termed a Buddhist "Unitarianism." It seems never to have been able to secure a strong footing in Izumo on account of its doctrinal hostility to Shintō. Elsewhere throughout Japan it is the most vigorous and prosperous of all Buddhist sects.

† Mr. Morse, in his *Japanese Homes*, published on hearsay a very strange error when he stated: "The Buddhist household shrines *rest on the floor*—at least so I was informed." They never rest on the floor under any circumstances. In the better class of houses spe-

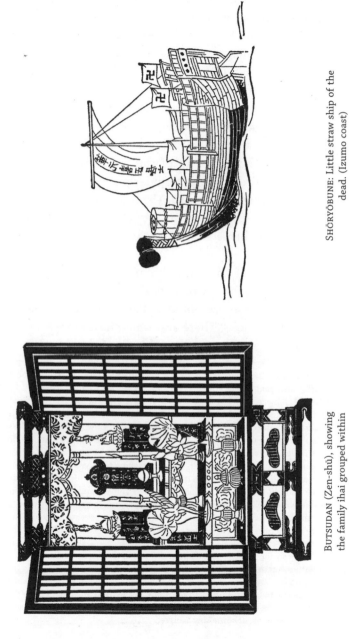

BUTSUDAN (Zen-shū), showing
the family ihai grouped within

SHŌRYŌBUNE: Little straw ship of the
dead. (Izumo coast)

SACRED OBJECTS (BUDDHIST)

usually there inclosed—or, at least, this is always the case when the honors paid them are given according to the Buddhist instead of the Shintō rite. The form of the butsudan or butsuma, the character of its holy images, its ofuda, or its pictures, and even the prayers said before it, differ according to the fifteen different shū, or sects; and a very large volume would have to be written in order to treat the subject of the butsuma exhaustively. Therefore I must content myself with stating that there are Buddhist household shrines of all dimensions, prices, and degrees of magnificence; and that the butsudan of the Shin-shū, although to me the least interesting of all, is popularly considered to be the most beautiful in design and finish. The butsudan of a very poor household may be worth a few cents, but the rich devotee might purchase in Kyōto a shrine worth as many thousands of yen as he could pay.

Though the forms of the butsuma and the character of its contents may greatly vary, the form of the ancestral or mortuary tablet is generally that represented in Fig. 4 of the illustrations of ihai given in this book.* There are some much more elaborate shapes, costly and rare, and simpler shapes of the cheapest and

---

cial architectural arrangements are made for the butsudan; an alcove, recess, or other contrivance, often so arranged as to be concealed from view by a sliding panel or a little door. In smaller dwellings it may be put on a shelf, for want of a better place, and in the homes of the poor, on the top of the tansu, or clothes-chest. It is never placed so high as the kamidana, but seldom at a less height than three feet above the floor. In Mr. Morse's own illustration of a Buddhist household shrine (p. 226) it does not rest on the floor at all, but on the upper shelf of a cupboard, which must not be confounded with the butsudan—a very small one. The sketch in question seems to have been made during the Festival of the Dead, for the offerings in the picture are those of the Bommatsuri. At that time the household butsudan is always exposed to view, and often moved from its usual place in order to obtain room for the offerings to be set before it. To place any holy object on the floor is considered by the Japanese very disrespectful. As for Shintō objects, to place even a mamori on the floor is deemed a sin.

* Two ihai are always made for each Buddhist dead. One usually larger than that placed in the family shrine, is kept in the temple of which the deceased was a parishioner, together with a cup in which tea or water is daily poured out as an offering. In almost any large temple, thousands of such ihai may be seen, arranged in rows, tier above tier—each with its cup before it—for even the souls of the dead are supposed to drink tea. Sometimes, I fear, the offering is forgotten, for I have seen rows of cups containing only dust, the fault, perhaps, of some lazy acolyte.

SHINTŌ IHAI. (IZUMO)

1

2
Ihai of a Samurai
lady

3
Ihai of a child —
a little boy

4
Ordinary form of
a man's ihai

5
Elaborately ornamented
ihai of a Samurai
official

BUDDHIST IHAI. (ZEN-SHŪ)

plainest description; but the form thus illustrated is the common one in Izumo and the whole San-indo country. There are differences, however, of size; and the ihai of a man is larger than that of a woman, and has a headpiece also, which the tablet of a female has not; while a child's ihai is always very small. The average height of the ihai made for a male adult is a little more than a foot, and its thickness about an inch. It has a top, or headpiece, surmounted by the symbol of the Hoshi-no-tama or Mystic Gem, and ordinarily decorated with a cloud-design of some kind, and the pedestal is a lotus-flower rising out of clouds. As a general rule all this is richly lacquered and gilded; the tablet itself being lacquered in black, and bearing the posthumous name, or kaimyō, in letters of gold—*ken-mu-ji-shō-shin-ji,* or other syllables indicating the supposed virtues of the departed. The poorest people, unable to afford such handsome tablets, have ihai made of plain wood; and the kaimyo is sometimes simply written on these in black characters; but more commonly it is written upon a strip of white paper, which is then pasted upon the ihai with ricepaste. The living name is perhaps inscribed upon the back of the tablet. Such tablets accumulate, of course, with the passing of generations; and in certain homes great numbers are preserved.

A beautiful and touching custom still exists in Izumo, and perhaps throughout Japan, although much less common than it used to be. So far as I can learn, however, it was always confined to the cultivated classes. When a husband dies, two ihai are made, in case the wife resolves never to marry again. On one of these the kaimyō of the dead man is painted in characters of gold, and on the other that of the living widow; but, in the latter case, the first character of the kaimyō ia painted in red, and the other characters in gold. These two tablets are then placed in the household butsuma. Two larger ones, similarly inscribed, are placed in the parish temple; but no cup is set before that of the wife. The solitary crimson ideograph signifies a solemn pledge to remain faithful to the memory of the dead. Furthermore, the wife loses her living name among all her friends and relatives, and is thereafter addressed only by a fragment of her kaimyō—as, for example, "Shin-toku-in-San," an abbreviation of the much longer and more sonorous posthumous name, *Shin-toku-in-den-jōyo-teisō-daishi.** Thus to be called by one's kaimyō is at once an honor to the memory of the husband and the constancy of the bereaved wife. A precisely similar pledge is taken by a man after the loss of a wife to whom he was passionately attached; and one crimson letter upon his ihai registers the vow not only in the home but also in the place of public worship. But the widower is never called by his kaimyō, as is the widow.

The first religious duty of the morning in a Buddhist household is to set before the tablets of the dead a little cup of tea, made with the first hot water prepared—*O-Hotoke-San-ni-o-cha-to-ageru.*† Daily offerings of boiled rice are also made; and fresh flowers are put in the shrine vases; and incense—although not allowed by Shintō—is burned before the tablets. At night, and also during the day upon certain festivals, both candles and a small oil-lamp are lighted in the butsuma—a lamp somewhat differently shaped from the lamp of the miya and called rintō. On the day of each month corresponding to the date of death a little repast is served before the tablets, consisting of shōjin-ryōri only, the vegetarian food of the Buddhists. But as Shintō family worship has its special annual festival, which endures from the first to the third day of the new year, so Buddhist ancestor-worship has its yearly Bonku, or Bommatsuri, lasting from the thirteenth to the sixteenth day of the seventh month. This is the Buddhist Feast of Souls. Then the butsuma is decorated to the utmost, special offerings of food and of flowers are made, and all the house is made beautiful to welcome the coming of the ghostly visitors.

---

* This is a fine example of a samurai kaimyō. The kaimyō of kwazoku or samurai are different from those of humbler dead; and a Japanese, by a single glance at an ihai, can tell at once to what class of society the deceased belonged, by the Buddhist words used.

† "Presenting the honorable tea to the august Buddhas,"—for by Buddhist faith it is hoped, if not believed, that the dead become Buddhas and escape the sorrows of farther transmigration. Thus the expression "is dead" is often rendered in Japanese by the phrase "is become a Buddha."

Now Shintō, like Buddhism, has its ihai; but these are of the simplest possible shape and material—mere slips of plain white wood. The average height is only about eight inches. These tablets are either placed in a special miya kept in a different room from that in which the shrine of the Kami is erected, or else simply arranged on a small shelf called by the people *Mitama-San-no-tana*—"the Shelf of the August *Spirits*." The shelf or the shrine of the ancestors and household dead is placed always at a considerable height in the mitamaya or soreisha (as the Spirit Chamber is sometimes called), just as is the miya of the Kami in the other apartment. Sometimes no tablets are used, the name being simply painted upon the woodwork of the Spirit Shrine. But Shintō has no kaimyō: the living name of the dead is written upon the ihai, with the sole addition of the word "*Mitama*" (Spirit). And monthly upon the day corresponding to the menstrual date of death, offerings of fish, wine, and other food are made to the spirits, accompanied by special prayer.* The Mitama-San have also their particular lamps and flower-vases, and, though in lesser degree, are honored with rites like those of the Kami.

The prayers uttered before the ihai of either faith begin with the respective religious formulas of Shintō or of Buddhism. The Shintōist, clapping his hands thrice or four times,† first utters the sacramental *Harai-tamai*. The Buddhist, according to his sect, murmurs *Namu-myō-hō-ren-ge-kyō,* or *Namu Amida Butsu*, or some other holy words of prayer or of praise to the Buddha,

---

* The idea underlying this offering of food and drink to the dead, or to the gods, is *not* so irrational as unthinking critics have declared it to be. The dead are not supposed to consume any of the visible substance of the food set before them, for they are thought to be in an ethereal state requiring only the most vapory kind of nutrition. The idea is that they absorb only the invisible essence of the food. And as fruits and other such offerings lose something of their flavor after having been exposed to the air for several hours, this slight change would have been taken in other days as evidence that the spirits had feasted upon them. Scientific education necessarily dissipates these consoling illusions, and with them a host of tender and beautiful fancies as to the relation between the living and the dead.

† I find that the number of clappings differs in different provinces somewhat. In Kyūshū the clapping is very long, especially before the prayer to the Rising Sun.

ere commencing his prayer to the ancestors. The words said to them are seldom spoken aloud, either by Shintōist or Buddhist: they are either whispered very low under the breath, or shaped only within the heart.

X.

At nightfall in Izumo homes the lamps of the gods and of the ancestors are kindled, either by a trusted servant or by some member of the family. Shintō orthodox regulations require that the lamps should be filled with pure vegetable oil only—tomo-shiabura—and oil of rapeseed is customarily used. However, there is an evident inclination among the poorer classes to sub-stitute a microscopic kerosene lamp for the ancient form of uten-sil. But by the strictly orthodox this is held to be very wrong, and even to light the lamps with a match is somewhat heretical. For it is not supposed that matches are always made with pure sub-stances, and the lights of the Kami should be kindled only with purest fire—that holy natural fire which lies hidden within all things. Therefore in some little closet in the home of any strictly orthodox Shintō family there is always a small box containing the ancient instruments used for the lighting of holy fire. These consist of the hi-uchi-ishi, or "fire-strike-stone," the hi-uchi-gane, or steel; the hokuchi, or tinder, made of dried moss; and the tsukegi, fine slivers of resinous pine. A little tinder is laid upon the flint and set smoldering with a few strokes of the steel, and blown upon until it flames. A slip of pine is then ignited at this flame, and with it the lamps of the ancestors and the gods are lighted. If several great deities are represented in the miya or upon the kamidana by several ofuda, then a separate lamp is sometimes lighted for each; and if there be a butsuma in the dwelling, its tapers or lamp are lighted at the same time.

Although the use of the flint and steel for lighting the lamps of the gods will probably have become obsolete within another generation, it still prevails largely in Izumo, especially in the

country districts. Even where the safety-match has entirely sup-
planted the orthodox utensils, the orthodox sentiment shows
itself in the matter of the choice of matches to be used. Foreign
matches are inadmissible: the native matchmaker quite successfully represented that foreign matches contained phosphorus
"made from the bones of dead animals," and that to kindle the
lights of the Kami with such unholy fire would be sacrilege. In
other parts of Japan the matchmakers stamped upon their boxes
the words: "*Saikyō go honzon yo*" (Fit for the use of the August
High Temple of Saikyō*). But Shintō sentiment in Izumo was
too strong to be affected much by any such declaration: indeed,
the recommendation of the matches as suitable for use in a
Shin-shū temple was of itself sufficient to prejudice Shintōists
against them. Accordingly special precautions had to be taken
before safety-matches could be satisfactorily introduced into the
Province of the Gods. Izumo match-boxes now bear the inscription: "*Pure, and fit to use for kindling the lamps of the Kami, or of
the Hotoke!*"

The inevitable danger to all things in Japan is fire. It is the
traditional rule that when a house takes fire, the first objects
to be saved, if possible, are the household gods and the tablets
of the ancestors. It is even said that if these are saved, most of
the family valuables are certain to be saved, and that if these are
lost, all is lost.

XI.

The terms soreisha and mitamaya, as used in Izumo, may, I
am told, signify either the small miya in which the Shintō ihai
(usually made of cherrywood) is kept, or that part of the dwelling
in which it is placed, and where the offerings are made. These,
by all who can afford it, are served upon tables of plain white
wood, and of the same high narrow form as the tables upon

---

* Another name for Kyōto, the Sacred City of Japanese Buddhism.

which offerings are made in the temples and at public funeral ceremonies.

The most ordinary form of prayer addressed to the ancient ancestors in the household cult of Shintō is not uttered aloud. After pronouncing the initial formula of all popular Shintō prayer, "*Harai-tamai*" etc., the worshiper says, with his heart only—

"Spirits august of our far-off ancestors, ye forefathers of the generations, and of our families and of our kindred, unto you, the founders of our homes, we this day utter the gladness of our thanks."

In the family cult of the Buddhists a distinction is made between the household Hotoke—the souls of those long dead—and the souls of those but recently deceased. These last are called Shin-botoke, "new Buddhas," or more strictly, "the newly dead." No direct request for any supernatural favor is made to a Shin-botoke; for, though respectfully called Hotoke, the freshly departed soul is not really deemed to have reached Buddhahood: it is only on the long road thither, and is in need itself, perhaps, of aid, rather than capable of giving aid. Indeed, among the deeply pious its condition is a matter of affectionate concern. And especially is this the case when a little child dies; for it is thought that the soul of an infant is feeble and exposed to many dangers. Wherefore a mother, speaking to the departed soul of her child, will advise it, admonish it, command it tenderly, as if addressing a living son or daughter. The ordinary words said in Izumo homes to any Shin-botoke take rather the form of adjuration or counsel than of prayer, such as these:

"*Jōbutsu seyō*," or "*Jōbutsu shimasare*." [Do thou become a Buddha.]

"*Mayō na yo*." [Go not astray; or, Be never deluded.]

"*Miren-wo nokorazu*." [Suffer no regret (for this world) to linger with thee.]

These prayers are never uttered aloud. Much more in accordance with the Occidental idea of prayer is the following, uttered by Shin-shū believers on behalf of a Shin-botoke:

"*O-mukai kudasare Amida-Sama.*" [Vouchsafe, O Lord Amida, augustly to welcome (this soul).]

Needless to say that ancestor-worship, although adopted in China and Japan into Buddhism, is not of Buddhist origin. Needless also to say that Buddhism discountenances suicide. Yet in Japan, anxiety about the condition of the soul of the departed often caused suicide—or at least justified it on the part of those who, though accepting Buddhist dogma, might adhere to primitive custom. Retainers killed themselves in the belief that by dying they might give to the soul of their lord or lady, counsel, aid, and service. Thus in the novel Hogen-no-monogatari, a retainer is made to say after the death of his young master:

"Over the mountain of Shide, over the ghostly River of Sanzu, who will conduct him? If he be afraid, will he not call my name, as he was wont to do? Surely better that, by slaying myself, I go to serve him as of old, than to linger here, and mourn for him in vain."

In Buddhist household worship, the prayers addressed to the family Hotoke proper, the souls of those long dead, are very different from the addresses made to the Shin-botoke. The following are a few examples: they are always said under the breath.

"*Kanai anzen.*" [(Vouchsafe) that our family may be preserved.]

"*Enmei sakusai.*" [That we may enjoy long life without sorrow.]

"*Shōbai hanjo.*" [That our business may prosper.] Said only by merchants and tradesmen.]

"*Shison chōkin.*" [That the perpetuity of our descent may be assured.]

"*Onteki taisan.*" [That our enemies be scattered.]

"*Yakubyō shōmetsu.*" [That pestilence may not come nigh us.]

Some of the above are used also by Shintō worshipers.

The old samurai still repeat the special prayers of their caste:

"*Tenka taihei.*" [That long peace may prevail throughout the world.]

"*Bu-un chōkyu.*" [That we may have eternal good-fortune in war.]

"*Ka-ei-manzoku.*" [That our house (*family*) may forever remain fortunate.]

But besides these silent formulae, any prayers prompted by the heart, whether of supplication or of gratitude, may, of course, be repeated. Such prayers are said, or rather thought, in the speech of daily life. The following little prayer uttered by an Izumo mother to the ancestral spirit, besought on behalf of a sick child, is an example:

"*O-kage ni kodomo no byōki mo zenkwai itashimashite, arigatō-gozarimasu!*" [By thine august influence the illness of my child has passed away; I thank thee.]

"*O-kage ni*" literally signifies "in the august shadow of." There is a ghostly beauty in the original phrase that neither a free nor yet a precise translation can preserve.

XII.

Thus, in this home-worship of the Far East, by love the dead are made divine; and the foreknowledge of this tender apotheosis must temper with consolation the natural melancholy of age. Never in Japan are the dead so quickly forgotten as with us: by simple faith they are deemed still to dwell among their beloved; and their place within the home remains ever holy. And the aged patriarch about to pass away knows that loving lips will nightly murmur to the memory of him before the household shrine; that faithful hearts will beseech him in their pain and bless him in their joy; that gentle hands will place before his ihai pure offerings of fruits and flowers, and dainty repasts of the things which he was wont to like; and will pour out for him, into the little cup of ghosts and gods, the fragrant tea of guests or the amber rice-wine. Strange changes are coming upon the land: old customs are vanishing; old beliefs are weakening; the thoughts of today will not be the thoughts of another age—but of all this he knows happily nothing in his own quaint, simple, beautiful Izumo. He dreams that for him, as for his fathers, the little lamp will burn on through the generations; he sees, in softest fancy, the yet unborn—the children of his children's children—clapping their tiny hands in Shintō prayer, and making filial obeisance before the little dusty tablet that bears his unforgotten name.

18

OF WOMEN'S HAIR

I.

THE hair of the younger daughter of the family is very long; and it is a spectacle of no small interest to see it dressed. It is dressed once in every three days; and the operation, which costs four sen, is acknowledged to require one hour. As a matter of fact it requires nearly two. The hairdresser *(kamiyui)* first sends her maiden apprentice, who cleans the hair, washes it, perfumes it, and combs it with extraordinary combs of at least five different kinds. So thoroughly is the hair cleansed that it remains for three days, or even four, immaculate beyond our Occidental conception of things. In the morning, during the dusting time, it is carefully covered with a handkerchief or a little blue towel; and the curious Japanese wooden pillow, which supports the neck, not the head, renders it possible to sleep at ease without disarranging the marvelous structure.*

After the apprentice has finished her part of the work, the hairdresser herself appears, and begins to build the coiffure. For this task she uses, besides the extraordinary variety of combs, fine loops of gilt thread or colored paper twine, dainty bits of deliciously tinted crape-silk, delicate steel springs, and curious

---

* Formerly both sexes used the same pillow for the same reason. The long hair of a samurai youth, tied up in an elaborate knot, required much time to arrange. Since it has become the almost universal custom to wear the hair short, the men have adopted a pillow shaped like a small bolster.

little basket-shaped things over which the hair is moulded into the required forms before being fixed in place.

The kamiyui also brings razors with her; for the Japanese girl is shaved—cheeks, ears, brows, chin, even nose! What is there to shave? Only that peachy floss which is the velvet of the finest human skin, but which Japanese taste removes. There is, however, another use for the razor. All maidens bear the signs of their maidenhood in the form of a little round spot, about an inch in diameter, shaven clean upon the very top of the head. This is only partially concealed by a band of hair brought back from the forehead across it, and fastened to the back hair. The girl-baby's head is totally shaved. When a few years old the little creature's hair is allowed to grow except at the top of the head, where a large tonsure is maintained. But the size of the tonsure diminishes year by year, until it shrinks after childhood to the small spot above described; and this, too, vanishes after marriage, when a still more complicated fashion of wearing the hair is adopted.

II.

Such absolutely straight dark hair as that of most Japanese women might seem, to Occidental ideas at least, ill-suited to the highest possibilities of the art of the *coiffeuse*.* But the skill of the kamiyui has made it tractable to every aesthetic whim. Ringlets, indeed, are unknown, and curling irons. But what wonderful and beautiful shapes the hair of the girl is made to assume: volutes, jets, whirls, eddyings, foliations, each passing into the other blandly as a linking of brush-strokes in the writing of a Chinese master! Far beyond the skill of the Parisian *coiffeuse*

---

* It is an error to suppose that all Japanese have blue-black hair. There are two distinct racial types. In one the hair is a deep brown instead of a pure black, and is also softer and finer. Rarely, but very rarely, one may see a Japanese *chevelure* having a natural tendency to ripple. For curious reasons, which cannot be stated here, an Izumo woman is very much ashamed of having wavy hair—more ashamed than she would be of a natural deformity.

is the art of the kamiyui. From the mythical era* of the race, Japanese ingenuity has exhausted itself in the invention and the improvement of pretty devices for the dressing of woman's hair; and probably there have never been so many beautiful fashions of wearing it in any other country as there have been in Japan. These have changed through the centuries; sometimes becoming wondrously intricate of design, sometimes exquisitely simple—as in that gracious custom, recorded for us in so many quaint drawings, of allowing the long black tresses to flow unconfined below the waist.† But every mode of which we have any pictorial record had its own striking charm. Indian, Chinese, Malayan, Kōrean ideas of beauty found their way to the Land of the Gods, and were appropriated and transfigured by the finer native conceptions of comeliness. Buddhism, too, which so profoundly influenced all Japanese art and thought, may possibly have influenced fashions of wearing the hair; for its female divinities appear with the most beautiful coiffures. Notice the hair of a Kwannon or a Benten, and the tresses of the Tennin—those angel-maidens who float in azure upon the ceilings of the great temples.

III.

The particular attractiveness of the modern styles is the way in which the hair is made to serve as an elaborate nimbus for the features, giving delightful relief to whatever of fairness or sweetness the young face may possess. Then behind this charming black aureole is a riddle of graceful loopings and weavings whereof neither the beginning nor the ending can possibly be discerned. Only the kamiyui knows the key to that riddle. And the whole is held in place with curious ornamental combs, and shot through with long fine pins of gold, silver, nacre, trans-

---

* Even in the time of the writing of the *Kojiki* the art of arranging the hair must have been somewhat developed. See Professor Chamberlain's introduction to translation, p. xxxi.; also vol. i. section ix.; vol. vii. section xii.; vol. ix. section xviii., *et passim*.

† An art expert can decide the age of an unsigned kakemono or other work of art in which human figures appear by the style of the coiffure of the female personages.

parent tortoise-shell, or lacquered wood, with cunningly carven heads.*

IV.

Not less than fourteen different ways of dressing the hair are practiced by the *coiffeuses* of Izumo; but doubtless in the capital, and in some of the larger cities of eastern Japan, the art is much more elaborately developed. The hairdressers *(kamiyui)* go from house to house to exercise their calling, visiting their clients upon fixed days at certain regular hours. The hair of little girls from seven to eight years old is in Matsue dressed usually after the style called O-tabako-bon, unless it be simply "banged." In the O-tabako-bon ("honorable smoking-box" style) the hair is cut to the length of about four inches all round except above the forehead, where it is clipped a little shorter; and on the summit of the bead it is allowed to grow longer and is gathered up into a peculiarly shaped knot, which justifies the curious name of the coiffure. As soon as the girl becomes old enough to go to a female public day-school, her hair is dressed in the pretty, simple style called katsurashita, or perhaps in the new, ugly, semi-foreign "bundle-style" called sokuhatsu, which has become the regulation fashion in boarding-schools. For the daughters of the poor, and even for most of those of the middle classes, the public-school period is rather brief; their studies usually cease a few years before they are marriageable, and girls marry very early in Japan. The maiden's first elaborate coiffure is arranged for her when she reaches the age of fourteen or fifteen, at earliest. From twelve to fourteen her hair is dressed in the fashion called Omoyedzuki; then the style is changed to the beautiful coiffure called jōrowage. There are various forms of this style, more or less complex. A couple of years later, the jorōwage yields place in

---

* The principal and indispensable hair-pin (*kanzashi*), usually about seven inches long, is split, and its well-tempered double shaft can be used like a small pair of chopsticks for picking up small things. The head is terminated by a tiny spoon-shaped projection, which has a special purpose in the Japanese toilette.

the turn to the shinjōchō* ("new-butterfly" style), or the shima-da, also called takawage. The shinjocho style is common, is worn by women of various ages, and is not considered very genteel. The shimada, exquisitely elaborate, is; but the more respectable the family, the smaller the form of this coiffure; geisha and jorō wear a larger and loftier variety of it, which properly answers to the name takawage, or "high coiffure." Between eighteen and twenty years of age the maiden again exchanges this style for another termed Tenjingaeshi; between twenty and twenty-four years of age she adopts the fashion called mitsuwage, or the "triple coiffure" of three loops; and a somewhat similar but still more complicated coiffure, called mitsuwakudzushi is worn by young women of from twenty-five to twenty-eight. Up to that age every change in the fashion of wearing the hair has been in the direction of elaborateness and complexity. But after twenty-eight a Japanese woman is no longer considered young, and there is only one more coiffure for her—the mochiriwage or bobai, the simple and rather ugly style adopted by old women.

But the girl who marries wears her hair in a fashion quite different from any of the preceding. The most beautiful, the most elaborate, and the most costly of all modes is the bride's coiffure, called hanayome, a word literally signifying "flower-wife." The structure is dainty as its name, and must be seen to be artistically appreciated. Afterwards the wife wears her hair in the styles called kumesa or maruwage, another name for which is katsuyama. The kumesa style is not genteel, and is the coiffure of the poor; the maruwage or katsuyama is refined. In former times the samurai women wore their hair in two particular styles: the maiden's coiffure was ichōgaeshi, and that of the married folk katahajishi. It is still possible to see in Matsue a few katahajishi coiffures.

---

* The shinjōchō is also called Ichōgaeshi by old people, although the original Ichōgaeshi was somewhat different. The samurai girls used to wear their hair in the true Ichogaeshi manner; the name is derived from the ichō-tree (*Salisburia andiantifolia*), whose leaves have a queer shape, almost like that of a duck's foot. Certain bands of the hair in this coiffure bore a resemblance in form to ichō-leaves.

V.

The family kamiyui, O-Koto-San, the most skillful of her craft in Izumo, is a little woman of about thirty, still quite attractive. About her neck there are three soft pretty lines, forming what connoisseurs of beauty term "the necklace of Venus." This is a rare charm; but it once nearly proved the ruin of Koto. The story is a curious one.

Koto had a rival at the beginning of her professional career— a woman of considerable skill as a *coiffeuse*, but of malignant disposition, named Jin. Jin gradually lost all her respectable custom, and little Koto became the fashionable hairdresser. But her old rival, filled with jealous hate, invented a wicked story about Koto, and the story found root in the rich soil of old Izumo superstition, and grew fantastically. The idea of it had been suggested to Jin's cunning mind by those three soft lines about Koto's neck. She declared that Koto had a "NUKE-KUBI."

What is a nuke-kubi? "Kubi" signifies either the neck or head. "Nukeru" means to creep, to skulk, to prowl, to slip away stealthily. To have a nuke-kubi is to have a head that detaches itself from the body, and prowls about at night—by itself.

Koto has been twice married, and her second match was a happy one. But her first husband caused her much trouble, and ran away from her at last, in company with some worthless woman. Nothing was ever heard of him afterward—so that Jin thought it quite safe to invent a nightmare-story to account for his disappearance. She said that he abandoned Koto because, on awaking one night, he saw his young wife's head rise from the pillow, and her neck lengthen like a great white serpent, while the rest of her body remained motionless. He saw the head, supported by the ever lengthening neck, enter the farther apartment and drink all the oil in the lamps, and then return to the pillow slowly—the neck simultaneously contracting. "Then he rose up and fled away from the house in great fear," said Jin.

As one story begets another, all sorts of queer rumors soon

began to circulate about poor Koto. There was a tale that some police-officer, late at night, saw a woman's head without a body, nibbling fruit from a tree overhanging some garden-wall; and that, knowing it to be a nuke-kubi, he struck it with the flat of his sword. It shrank away as swiftly as a bat flies, but not before he had been able to recognize the face of the kamiyui. "Oh! it is quite true!" declared Jin, the morning after the alleged occurrence; "and if you don't believe it, send word to Koto that you want to see her. She can't go out: her face is all swelled up." Now the last statement was fact—for Koto had a very severe toothache at that time—and the fact helped the falsehood. And the story found its way to the local newspaper, which published it—only as a strange example of popular credulity; and Jin said, "Am I a teller of the truth? See, the paper has printed it!"

Wherefore crowds of curious people gathered before Koto's little house, and made her life such a burden to her that her husband had to watch her constantly to keep her from killing herself. Fortunately she had good friends in the family of the Governor, where she had been employed for years as *coiffeuse;* and the Governor, hearing of the wickedness, wrote a public denunciation of it, and set his name to it, and printed it. Now the people of Matsue reverenced their old samurai Governor as if he were a god, and believed his least word; and seeing what he had written, they became ashamed, and also denounced the lie and the liar; and the little hairdresser soon became more prosperous than before through popular sympathy.

Some of the most extraordinary beliefs of old days are kept alive in Izumo and elsewhere by what are called in America "traveling side-shows," and the inexperienced foreigner could never imagine the possibilities of a Japanese side-show. On certain great holidays the showmen make their appearance, put up their ephemeral theatres of rush-matting and bamboos in some temple court, surfeit expectation by the most incredible surprises, and then vanish as suddenly as they came. The Skeleton of a Devil, the Claws of a Goblin, and "a Rat as large as a sheep," were some of the least extraordinary displays which I saw. The Goblin's Claws were remarkably fine shark's teeth; the Devil's Skeleton had belonged to an orangoutang—all except the horns ingeniously attached to the skull; and the wondrous Rat I discovered to be a tame kangaroo. What I could not fully understand was the exhibition of a nuke-kubi, in which a young woman stretched her neck, apparently, to a length of about two feet, making ghastly faces during the performance.

VI.

There are also some strange old superstitions about women's hair.

The myth of Medusa has many a counterpart in Japanese folk-lore: the subject of such tales being always some wondrously beautiful girl, whose hair turns to snakes only at night, and who is discovered at last to be either a dragon or a dragon's daughter. But in ancient times it was believed that the hair of any young woman might, under certain trying circumstances, change into serpents. For instance: under the influence of long-repressed jealousy.

There were many men of wealth who, in the days of Old Japan, kept their concubines *(mekaké* or *aishō)* under the same roof with their legitimate wives *(okusama)*. And it is told that, although the severest patriarchal discipline might compel the mekaké and the okusama to live together in perfect seeming harmony by day, their secret hate would reveal itself by night in the transformation of their hair. The long black tresses of each would uncoil and hiss and strive to devour those of the other; and even the mirrors of the sleepers would dash themselves together; for, saith an ancient proverb, *kagami onna-no tamashii*—"a Mirror is the Soul of a Woman."* And there is a famous tradition of one

---

* The old Japanese mirrors were made of metal, and were extremely beautiful. *Kagami ga kumoru to tamashii ga kumoru* ("When the Mirror is dim, the Soul is unclean") is another curious proverb relating to mirrors. Perhaps the most beautiful and teaching

Kato Sayemon Shigenji, who beheld in the night the hair of his wife and the hair of his concubine, changed into vipers, writhing together and hissing and biting. Then Kato Sayemon grieved much for that secret bitterness of hatred which thus existed through his fault; and he shaved his head and became a priest in the great Buddhist monastery of Koya-San, where he dwelt until the day of his death under the name of Karukaya.

VII.

The hair of dead women is arranged in the manner called tabanegami, somewhat resembling the shimada extremely simplified, and without ornaments of any kind. The name tabanegami signifies hair tied into a bunch, like a sheaf of rice. This style must also be worn by women during the period of mourning.

Ghosts, nevertheless, are represented with hair loose and long, falling weirdly over the face. And no doubt because of the melancholy suggestiveness of its drooping branches, the willow is believed to be the favorite tree of ghosts. Thereunder, 'tis said, they mourn in the night, mingling their shadowy hair with the long disheveled tresses of the tree.

Tradition says that Ōkyo Maruyama was the first Japanese artist who drew a ghost. The Shōgun, having invited him to his palace, said: "Make a picture of a ghost for me." Ōkyo promised to do so; but he was puzzled how to execute the order satisfactorily. A few days later, hearing that one of his aunts was very ill, he visited her. She was so emaciated that she looked like one already long dead. As he watched by her bedside, a ghastly inspiration came to him: he drew the fleshless face and long disheveled hair, and created from that hasty sketch a ghost that surpassed all the Shōgun's expectations. Afterwards Okyo became very famous as a painter of ghosts.

---

story of a mirror in any language is that called Matsuyama-nokagami, which has been translated by Mrs. James.

Japanese ghosts are always represented as diaphanous, and preternaturally tall—only the upper part of the figure being distinctly outlined, and the lower part fading utterly away. As the Japanese say, "a ghost has no feet"—its appearance is like an exhalation, which becomes visible only at a certain distance above the ground; and it wavers and lengthens and undulates in the conceptions of artists, like a vapor moved by wind. Occasionally phantom women figure in picture-books in the likeness of living women; but these are not true ghosts. They are fox-women or other goblins; and their supernatural character is suggested by a peculiar expression of the eyes and a certain impossible elfish grace.

Little children in Japan, like little children in all countries, keenly enjoy the pleasure of fear; and they have many games in which such pleasure forms the chief attraction. Among these is O-bake-goto, or Ghost-play. Some nurse-girl or elder sister loosens her hair in front, so as to let it fall over her face, and pursues the little folk with moans and weird gestures, miming all the attitudes of the ghosts of the picturebooks.

VIII.

As the hair of the Japanese woman is her richest ornament, it is of all her possessions that which she would most suffer to lose; and in other days the man too manly to kill an erring wife deemed it vengeance enough to turn her away with all her hair shorn off. Only the greatest faith or the deepest love can prompt a woman to the voluntary sacrifice of her entire *chevelure,* though partial sacrifices, offerings of one or two long thick cuttings, may be seen suspended before many an Izumo shrine.

What faith can do in the way of such sacrifice, he best knows who has seen the great cables, woven of women's hair, that hang in the vast Hongwanji temple at Kyōto. And love is stronger than faith, though much less demonstrative. According to ancient custom a wife bereaved sacrifices a portion of her hair to be placed in the coffin of her husband, and buried with him. The quantity is not fixed: in the majority of cases it is very small, so that the appearance of the coiffure is thereby nowise affected. But she who resolves to remain forever loyal to the memory of the lost yields up all. With her own hand she cuts off her hair, and lays the whole glossy sacrifice—emblem of her youth and beauty—upon the knees of the dead.

It is never suffered to grow again.

19

FROM THE DIARY OF
AN ENGLISH TEACHER

I.

MATSUE, September 2, 1890.

I AM under contract to serve as English teacher in the Jinjō Chūgakkō, or Ordinary Middle School, and also in the Shihan-Gakkō, or Normal School, of Matsue, Izumo, for the term of one year.

The Jinjō Chūgakkō is an immense two-story wooden building in European style, painted a dark gray-blue. It has accommodations for nearly three hundred day scholars. It is situated in one corner of a great square of ground, bounded on two sides by canals, and on the other two by very quiet streets. This site is very near the ancient castle.

The Normal School is a much larger building occupying the opposite angle of the square. It is also much handsomer, is painted snowy white, and has a little cupola upon its summit. There are only about one hundred and fifty students in the Shihan-Gakko, but they are boarders.

Between these two schools are other educational buildings, which I shall learn more about later.

It is my first day at the schools. Nishida Sentaro, the Japanese teacher of English, has taken me through the buildings, introduced me to the Directors, and to all my future colleagues, given me all necessary instructions about hours and about text-books, and furnished my desk with all things necessary. Before teaching begins, however, I must be introduced to the Governor of the Province, Koteda Yasusada, with whom my contract has been made, through the medium of his secretary. So Nishida leads the way to the Kenchō, or Prefectural office, situated in another foreign-looking edifice across the street.

We enter it, ascend a wide stairway, and enter a spacious room carpeted in European fashion—a room with bay windows and cushioned chairs. One person is seated at a small round table, and about him are standing half a dozen others: all are in full Japanese costume, ceremonial costume—splendid silken haka-ma, or Chinese trousers, silken robes, silken haori or overdress, marked with their mon or family crests: rich and dignified attire which makes me ashamed of my commonplace Western garb. These are officials of the Kenchō, and teachers: the person seated is the Governor. He rises to greet me, gives me the handgrasp of a giant: and as I look into his eyes, I feel I shall love that man to the day of my death. A face fresh and frank as a boy's, expressing much placid force and large-hearted kindness—all the calm of a Buddha. Beside him, the other officials look very small: indeed the first impression of him is that of a man of another race. While I am wondering whether the old Japanese heroes were cast in a similar mould, he signs to me to take a seat, and questions my guide in a mellow basso. There is a charm in the fluent depth of the voice pleasantly confirming the idea suggested by the face. An attendant brings tea.

"The Governor asks," interprets Nishida, "if you know the old history of Izumo."

I reply that I have read the Kojiki, translated by Professor Chamberlain, and have therefore some knowledge of the story of Japan's most ancient province. Some converse in Japanese follows. Nishida tells the Governor that I came to Japan to study the ancient religion and customs, and that I am particularly interested in Shintō and the traditions of Izumo. The Governor suggests that I make visits to the celebrated shrines of Kitzuki, Yaegaki, and Kumano, and then asks:

"Does he know the tradition of the origin of the clapping of hands before a Shintō shrine?"

I reply in the negative; and the Governor says the tradition is given in a commentary upon the Kojiki.

"It is in the thirty-second section of the fourteenth volume, where it is written that Ya-he-Koto-Shiro-nushi-no-Kami clapped his hands."

I thank the Governor for his kind suggestions and his citation. After a brief silence I am graciously dismissed with another genuine hand grasp; and we return to the school.

II.

I have been teaching for three hours in the Middle School, and teaching Japanese boys turns out to be a much more agreeable task than I had imagined. Each class has been so well prepared for me beforehand by Nishida that my utter ignorance of Japanese makes no difficulty in regard to teaching: moreover, although the lads cannot understand my words always when I speak, they can understand whatever I write upon the blackboard with chalk. Most of them have already been studying English from childhood, with Japanese teachers. All are wonderfully docile and patient. According to old custom, when the teacher enters, the whole class rises and bows to him. He returns the bow, and calls the roll.

Nishida is only too kind. He helps me in every way he possibly can, and is constantly regretting that he cannot help me more. There are, of course, some difficulties to overcome. For instance, it will take me a very, very long time to learn the names of the boys—most of which names I cannot even pronounce, with the class-roll before me. And although the names of the different classes have been painted upon the doors of their respective rooms in English letters, for the benefit of the foreign teacher, it will take me some weeks at least to become quite familiar with them. For the time being Nishida always guides me to the rooms.

He also shows me the way, through long corridors, to the Normal School, and introduces me to the teacher Nakayama who is to act there as my guide.

I have been engaged to teach only four times a week at the Normal School; but I am furnished there also with a handsome desk in the teachers' apartment, and am made to feel at home almost immediately. Nakayama shows me everything of interest in the building before introducing me to my future pupils. The introduction is pleasant and novel as a school experience. I am conducted along a corridor, and ushered into a large luminous whitewashed room full of young men in dark blue military uniform. Each sits at a very small desk, supported by a single leg, with three feet. At the end of the room is a platform with a high desk and a chair for the teacher. As I take my place at the desk, a voice rings out in English: "*Stand up!*" And all rise with a springy movement as if moved by machinery. "*Bow down!*" the same voice again commands—the voice of a young student wearing a captain's stripes upon his sleeve; and all salute me. I bow in return; we take our seats; and the lesson begins.

All teachers at the Normal School are saluted in the same military fashion before each class-hour—only the command is given in Japanese. For my sake only, it is given in English.

III.

September 22, 1890.

The Normal School is a State institution. Students are admitted upon examination and production of testimony as to good character; but the number is, of course, limited. The young men pay no fees, no boarding money, nothing even for books, college outfits, or wearing apparel. They are lodged, clothed, fed, and educated by the State; but they are required in return, after their graduation, to serve the State as teachers for the space of five years. Admission, however, by no means assures graduation. There are three or four examinations each year; and the students who fail to obtain a certain high average of examination marks must leave the school, however exemplary their conduct or earnest their study. No leniency can be shown where the educational needs of the State are concerned, and these call for natural ability and a high standard of its proof.

The discipline is military and severe. Indeed, it is so thorough that the graduate of a Normal School is exempted by military law from more than a year's service in the army: he leaves college a trained soldier. Deportment is also a requisite: special marks are given for it; and however gawky a freshman may prove at the time of his admission, he cannot remain go. A spirit of manliness is cultivated, which excludes roughness but develops self-reliance and self-control. The student is required, when speaking, to look his teacher in the face, and to utter his words not only distinctly, but sonorously. Demeanor in class is partly enforced by the classroom fittings themselves. The tiny tables are too narrow to allow of being used as supports for the elbows; the seats have no backs against which to lean, and the student must hold himself rigidly erect as he studies. He must also keep himself faultlessly neat and clean. Whenever and wherever he encounters one of his teachers he must halt, bring his feet together, draw himself erect, and give the military salute. And this is done with a swift grace difficult to describe.

The demeanor of a class during study hours is if anything too faultless. Never a whisper is heard; never is a head raised from the book without permission. But when the teacher addresses a student by name, the youth rises instantly, and replies in a tone of such vigor as would seem to unaccustomed ears almost startling by contrast with the stillness and self-repression of the others.

The female department of the Normal School, where about fifty young women are being trained as teachers, is a separate two-story quadrangle of buildings, large, airy, and so situated, together with its gardens, as to be totally isolated from all other buildings and invisible from the street. The girls are not only taught European science by the most advanced methods, but are trained as well in Japanese arts—the arts of embroidery, of decoration, of painting, and of arranging flowers. European drawing is also taught, and beautifully taught, not only here, but in all the schools. It is taught, however, in combination with Japanese methods; and the results of this blending may certainly be expected to have some charming influence upon future art-production. The average capacity of the Japanese student in drawing is, I think, at least fifty percent, higher than that of European students. The soul of the race is essentially artistic; and the extremely difficult art of learning to write the Chinese characters, in which all are trained from early childhood, has already disciplined the hand and the eye to a marvelous degree—a degree undreamed of in the Occident—long before the drawing-master begins his lessons of perspective.

Attached to the great Normal School, and connected by a corridor with the Jinjō Chūgakkō likewise, is a large elementary school for little boys and girls: its teachers are male and female students of the graduating classes, who are thus practically trained for their profession before entering the service of the State. Nothing could be more interesting as an educational spectacle to any sympathetic foreigner than some of this elementary teaching. In the first room which I visit a class of very little girls and boys—some as quaintly pretty as their own dolls—are bending at their desks over sheets of coal-black paper which you would think they were trying to make still blacker by energetic use of writing-brushes and what we call Indian-ink. They are really learning to write Chinese and Japanese characters, stroke by stroke. Until one stroke has been well learned, they are not suffered to attempt another—much less a combination. Long before the first lesson is thoroughly mastered, the white paper has become all evenly black under the multitude of tyro brush-strokes. But the same sheet is still used; for the wet ink makes a yet blacker mark upon the dry, so that it can easily be seen.

In a room adjoining, I see another child-class learning to use scissors—Japanese scissors, which, being formed in one piece, shaped something like the letter U, are much less easy to manage than ours. The little folk are being taught to cut out patterns, and shapes of special objects or symbols to be studied. Flower-forms are the most ordinary patterns; sometimes certain ideographs are given as subjects.

And in another room a third small class is learning to sing; the teacher writing the music notes *(do, re, mi)* with chalk upon a blackboard, and accompanying the song with an accordion. The little ones have learned the Japanese national anthem *(Kimi ga yo wa)* and two native songs set to Scotch airs—one of which calls back to me, even in this remote corner of the Orient, many a charming memory: *Auld Lang Syne.*

No uniform is worn in this elementary school: all are in Japanese dress—the boys in dark blue kimono, the little girls in robes of all tints, radiant as butterflies. But in addition to their robes, the girls wear hakama,* and these are of a vivid, warm skyblue.

Between the hours of teaching, ten minutes are allowed for play or rest. The little boys play at Demon-Shadows or at blind-man's-buff or at some other funny game: they laugh, leap, shout, race, and wrestle, but, unlike European children, never quarrel or fight.† As for the little girls, they get by themselves, and either play at hand-ball, or form into circles to play at some round game, accompanied by song. Indescribably soft and sweet the chorus of those little voices in the round.

> *Kango-kango shō-ya,*
> *Naka yoni shō-ya,*
> *Dan-don to kunde*
> *Jizō-San no midzu wo*
> *Alatsuba no midzu irete,*
> *Makkuri kaéso.*‡

---

* There is a legend that the Sun-Goddess invented the first hakama, by tying together the skirts of her robe.

† Since the above was written I have had two years' experience as a teacher in various large Japanese schools; and I have never had personal knowledge of any serious quarrel between students, and have never even heard of a fight among my pupils. And I have taught some eight hundred boys and young men.

‡ "Let us play the game called kango-kango. Plenteously the water of Jizō-San

I notice that the young men, as well as the young women, who teach these little folk, are extremely tender to their charges. A child whose kimono is out of order, or dirtied by play, is taken aside and brushed and arranged as carefully as by an elder brother.

Besides being trained for their future profession by teaching the children of the elementary school, the girl students of the Shihan-Gakkō are also trained to teach in the neighboring kindergarten. A delightful kindergarten it is, with big cheerful sunny rooms, where stocks of the most ingenious educational toys are piled upon shelves for daily use.

IV.

October 1, 1890.

Nevertheless I am destined to see little of the Normal School. Strictly speaking, I do not belong to its staff: my services being only lent by the Middle School, to which I give most of my time. I see the Normal School students in their classrooms only, for they are not allowed to go out to visit their teachers' homes in the town. So I can never hope to become as familiar with them as with the students of the Chūgakkō, who are beginning to call me "Teacher" instead of "Sir," and to treat me as a sort of elder brother. (I objected to the word "master," for in Japan the teacher has no need of being masterful.) And I feel less at home in the large, bright, comfortable apartments of the Normal School teachers than in our dingy, chilly teachers' room, at the Chūgakkō, where my desk is next to that of Nishida.

On the walls there are maps, crowded with Japanese ideographs; a few large charts representing zoological facts in the light of evolutional science; and an immense frame filled with little black lacquered wooden tablets, so neatly fitted together that the entire surface is uniform as that of a blackboard. On these are written, or rather painted, in white, names of teachers, sub-

---

quickly draw—and pour on the pine-leaves—and turn back again." Many of the games of Japanese children, like many of their toys, have a Buddhist origin, or at least a Buddhist significance.

jects, classes, and order of teaching hours; and by the ingenious tablet arrangement any change of hours can be represented by simply changing the places of the tablets. As all this is written in Chinese and Japanese characters, it remains to me a mystery, except in so far as the general plan and purpose are concerned. I have learned only to recognize the letters of my own name, and the simpler form of numerals.

On every teacher's desk there is a small hibachi of glazed blue-and-white ware, containing a few lumps of glowing charcoal in a bed of ashes. During the brief intervals between classes each teacher smokes his tiny Japanese pipe of brass, iron, or silver. The hibachi and a cup of hot tea are our consolations for the fatigues of the classroom.

Nishida and one or two other teachers know a good deal of English, and we chat together sometimes between classes. But more often no one speaks. All are tired after the teaching hour, and prefer to smoke in silence. At such times the only sounds within the room are the ticking of the clock, and the sharp clang of the little pipes being rapped upon the edges of the hibachi to empty out the ashes.

V.

October 15, 1890.

Today I witnessed the annual athletic contests (undō-kwai) of all the schools in Shimane Ken. These games were celebrated in the broad castle grounds of Ninomaru. Yesterday a circular race-track had been staked off, hurdles erected for leaping, thousands of wooden seats prepared for invited or privileged spectators, and a grand lodge built for the Governor, all before sunset. The place looked like a vast circus, with its tiers of plank seats rising one above the other, and the Governor's lodge magnificent with wreaths and flags. School children from all the villages and towns within twenty-five miles had arrived in surprising multitude. Nearly six thousand boys and girls were entered to take part in the contests. Their parents and relatives and teachers made an imposing assembly upon the benches and within the gates. And on the ramparts overlooking the huge inclosure a much larger crowd had gathered, representing perhaps one third of the population of the city.

The signal to begin or to end a contest was a pistolshot. Four different kinds of games were performed in different parts of the grounds at the same time, as there was room enough for an army; and prizes were awarded to the winners of each contest by the hand of the Governor himself.

There were races between the best runners in each class of the different schools; and the best runner of all proved to be Sakane, of our own fifth class, who came in first by nearly forty yards without seeming even to make an effort. He is our champion athlete, and as good as he is strong—so that it made me very happy to see him with his arms full of prize books. He won also a fencing contest decided by the breaking of a little earthenware saucer tied to the left arm of each combatant. And he also won a leaping match between our older boys.

But many hundreds of other winners there were too, and many hundreds of prizes were given away. There were races in which the runners were tied together in pairs, the left leg of one to the right leg of the other. There were equally funny races, the winning of which depended on the runner's ability not only to run, but to crawl, to climb, to vault, and to jump alternately. There were races also for the little girls—pretty as butterflies they seemed in their sky-blue hakama and many colored robes—races in which the contestants had each to pick up as they ran three balls of three different colors out of a number scattered over the turf. Besides this, the little girls had what is called a flag-race, and a contest with battledores and shuttlecocks.

Then came the tug-of-war. A magnificent tug-of-war, too—one hundred students at one end of a rope, and another hundred at the other. But the most wonderful spectacles of the day were the dumb-bell exercises. Six thousand boys and girls, massed in ranks about five hundred deep; six thousand pairs of arms rising and falling exactly together; six thousand pairs of san-daled feet advancing or retreating together, at the signal of the masters of gymnastics, directing all from the tops of various little wooden towers; six thousand voices chanting at once the "one, two, three," of the dumb-bell drill: *"Ichi, ni—san, shi—go, roku—shichi, hachi."*

Last came the curious game called "Taking the Castle." Two models of Japanese towers, about fifteen feet high, made with paper stretched over a framework of bamboo, were set up, one at each end of the field. Inside the castles an inflammable liquid had been placed in open vessels, so that if the vessels were over-turned the whole fabric would take fire. The boys, divided into two parties, bombarded the castles with wooden balls, which passed easily through the paper walls; and in a short time both models were making a glorious blaze. Of course the party whose castle was the first to blaze lost the game.

The games began at eight o'clock in the morning, and at five in the evening came to an end. Then at a signal fully ten thousand voices pealed out the superb national anthem, *"Kimi ga yo"* and concluded it with three cheers for their Imperial Majesties, the Emperor and Empress of Japan.

The Japanese do not shout or roar as we do when we cheer. They chant. Each long cry is like the opening tone of an immense musical chorus: *A-a-a-a-a-a-a-a!*

VI.

It is no small surprise to observe how botany, geology, and other sciences are daily taught even in this remotest part of old Japan. Plant physiology and the nature of vegetable tissues are studied under excellent microscopes, and in their relations to chemistry; and at regular intervals the instructor leads his classes into the country to illustrate the lessons of the term by examples taken from the flora of their native place. Agriculture, taught by a graduate of the famous Agricultural School at Sapporo, is practically illustrated upon farms purchased and maintained by the schools for purely educational ends. Each series of lessons in geology is supplemented by visits to the mountains about the lake, or to the tremendous cliffs of the coast, where the students are taught to familiarize themselves with forms of stratification and the visible history of rocks. The basin of the lake, and the country about Matsue, is physiographically studied, after the plans of instruction laid down in Huxley's excellent manual. Natural History, too, is taught according to the latest and best methods, and with the help of the microscope. The results of such teaching are sometimes surprising. I know of one student, a lad of only sixteen, who voluntarily collected and classified more than two hundred varieties of marine plants for a Tōkyō professor. Another, a youth of seventeen, wrote down for me in my notebook, without a work of reference at hand, and, as I afterward discovered, almost without an omission or error, a scientific list of all the butterflies to be found in the neighborhood of the city.

VII.

Through the Minister of Public Instruction, His Imperial Majesty has sent to all the great public schools of the Empire a letter bearing date of the thirteenth day of the tenth month of the twenty-third year of Meiji. And the students and teachers of the various schools assemble to hear the reading of the Imperial Words on Education.

At eight o'clock we of the Middle School are all waiting in our own assembly hall for the coming of the Governor, who will read the Emperor's letter in the various schools.

We wait but a little while. Then the Governor comes with all the officers of the Kenchō and the chief men of the city. We rise to salute him: then the national anthem is sung.

Then the Governor, ascending the platform, produces the Imperial Missive—a scroll of Chinese manuscript sheathed in silk. He withdraws it slowly from its woven envelope, lifts it reverentially to his forehead, unrolls it, lifts it again to his forehead, and after a moment's dignified pause begins in that clear deep voice of his to read the melodious syllables after the ancient way, which is like a chant:

"*CHO-KU-GU. Chin omommiru ni waga kōso kosō kuni wo....*

"We consider that the Founder of Our Empire and the ancestors of Our Imperial House placed the foundation of the country on a grand and permanent basis, and established their authority on the principles of profound humanity and benevolence.

"That Our subjects have throughout ages deserved well of the state by their loyalty and piety and by their harmonious cooperation is in accordance with the essential character of Our nation; and on these very same principles Our education has been founded.

"You, Our subjects, be therefore filial to your parents; be affectionate to your brothers; be harmonious as husbands and wives; and be faithful to your friends; conduct yourselves with propriety and carefulness; extend generosity and benevolence towards your neighbors; attend to your studies and follow your pursuits; cultivate your intellects and elevate your morals; advance public benefits and promote social interests; be always found in the good observance of the laws and constitution of the land; display your personal courage and public spirit for the sake of the country whenever required; and thus support the Imperial prerogative, which is coexistent with the Heavens and the Earth.

"Such conduct on your part will not only strengthen the character of Our good and loyal subjects, but conduce also to the maintenance of the fame of your worthy forefathers.

"This is the instruction bequeathed by Our ancestors and to be followed by Our subjects; for it is the truth which has guided and guides them in their own affairs and in their dealings towards aliens.

"We hope, therefore, We and Our subjects will regard these sacred precepts with one and the same heart in order to attain the same ends."*

Then the Governor and the Head-master speak a few words— dwelling upon the full significance of His Imperial Majesty's august commands, and exhorting all to remember and to obey them to the uttermost.

After which the students have a holiday, to enable them the better to recollect what they have heard.

VIII.

All teaching in the modern Japanese system of education is conducted with the utmost kindness and gentleness. The teacher is a teacher only: he is not, in the English sense of mastery, a master. He stands to his pupils in the relation of an elder brother. He never tries to impose his will upon them: he never scolds, he seldom criticises, he scarcely ever punishes. No Japanese teacher ever strikes a pupil: such an act would cost him his post at once. He never loses his temper: to do so would disgrace him in the eyes of his boys and in the judgment of his colleagues. Practically speaking, there is no punishment in Japanese schools. Sometimes very mischievous lads are kept in the schoolhouse during recreation time; yet even this light penalty is not inflicted directly by the teacher, but by the director of the school on complaint of the teacher. The purpose in such cases is not to inflict pain by deprivation of enjoyment, but to give public illustration of a fault; and in the great majority of instances, consciousness of the fault thus brought home to a lad before his comrades is quite enough to prevent its repetition.

---

* I take the above translation from a Tōkyō educational journal, entitled *The Museum*. The original document, however, was impressive to a degree that perhaps no translation could give. The Chinese words by which the Emperor refers to himself and his will are far more impressive than our Western "We" or "Our," and the words relating to duties, virtues, wisdom, and other matters are words that evoke in a Japanese mind ideas which only those who know Japanese life perfectly can appreciate, and which, though variant from our own, are neither less beautiful nor less sacred.

No such cruel punition as that of forcing a dull pupil to learn an additional task, or of sentencing him to strain his eyes copying four or five hundred lines, is ever dreamed of. Nor would such forms of punishment, in the present state of things, be long tolerated by the pupils themselves. The general policy of the educational authorities everywhere throughout the empire is to get rid of students who cannot be perfectly well managed without punishment; and expulsions, nevertheless, are rare.

I often see a pretty spectacle on my way home from the school, when I take the short cut through the castle grounds. A class of about thirty little boys, in kimono and sandals, bareheaded, being taught to march and to sing by a handsome young teacher, also in Japanese dress. While they sing, they are drawn up in line; and keep time with their little bare feet. The teacher has a pleasant high clear tenor: he stands at one end of the rank and sings a single line of the song. Then all the children sing it after him. Then he sings a second line, and they repeat it. If any mistakes are made, they have to sing the verse again.

It is the Song of Kusunoki Masashigé, noblest of Japanese heroes and patriots.

IX.

I have said that severity on the part of teachers would scarcely be tolerated by the students themselves—a fact which may sound strange to English or American ears. Tom Brown's school does not exist in Japan; the ordinary public school much more resembles the ideal Italian institution so charmingly painted for us in the "Cuoré" of De Amicis. Japanese students furthermore claim and enjoy an independence contrary to all Occidental ideas of disciplinary necessity. In the Occident the master expels the pupil. In Japan it happens quite as often that the pupil expels the master. Each public school is an earnest, spirited little republic, to which director and teachers stand only in the relation of president and cabinet. They are indeed appointed by the prefectural government upon recommendation by the Educational Bureau at the capital; but in actual practice they maintain their positions by virtue of their capacity and personal character as estimated by their students, and are likely to be deposed by a revolutionary movement whenever found wanting. It has been alleged that the students frequently abuse their power. But this allegation has been made by European residents, strongly prejudiced in favor of masterful English ways of discipline. (I recollect that an English Yokohama paper, in this connection, advocated the introduction of the birch.) My own observations have convinced me, as larger experience has convinced some others, that in most instances of pupils rebelling against a teacher, reason is upon their side. They will rarely insult a teacher whom they dislike, or cause any disturbance in his class: they will simply refuse to attend school until he be removed. Personal feeling may often be a secondary, but it is seldom, so far as I have been able to learn, the primary cause for such a demand. A teacher whose manners are unsympathetic, or even positively disagreeable, will be nevertheless obeyed and revered while his students remain persuaded of his capacity as a teacher, and his sense of justice; and they are as keen to discern ability as they are to detect partiality. And, on the other hand, an amiable disposition alone will never atone with them either for want of knowledge or for want of skill to impart it. I knew one case, in a neighboring public school, of a demand by the students for the removal of their professor of chemistry. In making their complaint, they frankly declared: "We like him. He is kind to all of us; he does the best he can. But he does not know enough to teach us as we wish to be taught. He cannot answer our questions. He cannot explain the experiments which he shows us. Our former teacher could do all these things. We must have another teacher." Investigation proved that the lads were quite right. The young teacher had graduated at the university; he had come well recommended: but he had no thorough knowledge of the science which he undertook to impart, and no experience as a teacher. The instructor's success in Japan is not guaranteed by a degree, but by his *practical* knowledge and his capacity to communicate it simply and thoroughly.

X.

November 3, 1890.

Today is the birthday of His Majesty the Emperor. It is a public holiday throughout Japan; and there will be no teaching this morning. But at eight o'clock all the students and instructors enter the great assembly hall of the Jinjō Chūgakkō to honor the anniversary of His Majesty's august birth.

On the platform of the assembly hall a table, covered with dark silk, has been placed; and upon this table the portraits of Their Imperial Majesties, the Emperor and the Empress of Japan, stand side by side upright, framed in gold. The alcove above the platform has been decorated with flags and wreaths. Presently the Governor enters, looking like a French general in his gold-embroidered uniform of office, and followed by the Mayor of the city, the Chief Military Officer, the Chief of Police, and all the officials of the provincial government. These take their places in silence to left and right of the platform. Then the school organ suddenly rolls out the slow, solemn, beautiful national anthem; and all present chant those ancient syllables, made sacred by the reverential love of a century of generations:

> Ki-mi ga-a yo-o wa
> Chi-yo ni-i-i yachi-yo ni sa-za-re
> I-shi no
> I-wa o to na-ri-te
> Ko-ke no
> Mu-u su-u ma-a-de.*

---

* *Kimi ga yo wa chiyo ni yachiyo ni sazare ishi no iwa o to narite oke no musu made.* Freely translated: "May Our Gracious Sovereign reign a thousand years—reign ten thousand thousand years—reign till the little stone grow into a mighty rock, thick-velveted with ancient moss!"

The anthem ceases. The Governor advances with a slow dignified step from the right side of the apartment to the center of
the open space before the platform and the portraits of Their
Majesties, turns his face to them, and bows profoundly. Then he
takes three steps forward toward the platform, and halts, and
bows again. Then he takes three more steps forward, and bows
still more profoundly. Then he retires, walking backward six
steps, and bows once more. Then he returns to his place.

After this the teachers, by parties of six, perform the same
beautiful ceremony. When all have saluted the portrait of His
Imperial Majesty, the Governor ascends the platform and makes
a few eloquent remarks to the students about their duty to
their Emperor, to their country, and to their teachers. Then the
anthem is sung again; and all disperse to amuse themselves for
the rest of the day.

XI.

March 1, 1891.

The majority of the students of the Jinjō Chūgakkō are day-scholars only *(externes,* as we would say in France): they go to school in the morning, take their noon meal at home, and return at one o'clock to attend the brief afternoon classes. All the city students live with their own families; but there are many boys from remote country districts who have no city relatives, and for such the school furnishes boarding-houses, where a wholesome moral discipline is maintained by special masters. They are free, however, if they have sufficient means, to choose another boarding-house (provided it be a respectable one), or to find quarters in some good family; but few adopt either course.

I doubt whether in any other country the cost of education—education of the most excellent and advanced kind—is so little as in Japan. The Izumo student is able to live at a figure so far below the Occidental idea of necessary expenditure that the mere statement of it can scarcely fail to surprise the reader. A sum equal in American money to about twenty dollars supplies him with board and lodging *for one year.* The whole of his expenses, including school fees, are about seven dollars a month. For his room and three ample meals a day he pays every four weeks only one yen eighty-five sen—not much more than a dollar and a half in American currency. If very, very poor, he will not be obliged to wear a uniform; but nearly all students of the higher classes do wear uniforms, as the cost of a complete uniform, including cap and shoes of leather, is only about three and a half yen for the cheaper quality. Those who do not wear leather shoes, however, are required, while in the school, to exchange their noisy wooden geta for zori or light straw sandals.

XII.

But the mental education so admirably imparted in an ordinary middle school is not, after all, so cheaply acquired by the student as might be imagined from the cost of living and the low rate of school fees. For Nature exacts a heavier school fee, and rigidly collects her debt—in human life.

To understand why, one should remember that the modern knowledge which the modern Izumo student must acquire upon a diet of boiled rice and bean-curd was discovered, developed, and synthetized by minds strengthened upon a costly diet of flesh. National underfeeding offers the most cruel problem which the educators of Japan must solve in order that she may become fully able to assimilate the civilization we have thrust upon her. As Herbert Spencer has pointed out, the degree of human energy, physical or intellectual, must depend upon the nutritiveness of food; and history shows that the well-fed races have been the energetic and the dominant. Perhaps mind will rule in the future of nations; but mind is a mode of force, and must be fed—through the stomach. The thoughts that have shaken the world were never framed upon bread and water: they were created by beefsteak and mutton-chops, by ham and eggs, by pork and puddings, and were stimulated by generous wines, strong ales, and strong coffee. And science also teaches us that the growing child or youth requires an even more nutritious diet than the adult; and that the student especially needs strong nourishment to repair the physical waste involved by brain-exertion.

And what is the waste entailed upon the Japanese schoolboy's system by study? It is certainly greater than that which the system of the European or American student must suffer at the same period of life. Seven years of study are required to give the Japanese youth merely the necessary knowledge of his own triple system of ideographs—or, in less accurate but plainer speech, the enormous alphabet of his native literature. That literature, also, he must study, and the art of two forms of his language—the written and the spoken: likewise, of course, he must learn native history and native morals. Besides these Oriental studies, his course includes foreign history, geography, arithmetic, astronomy, physics, geometry, natural history, agriculture, chemistry, drawing, and mathematics. Worst of all, he must learn English—a language of which the difficulty to the Japanese cannot be even faintly imagined by any one unfamiliar with the construction of the native tongue—a language so different from his own that the very simplest Japanese phrase cannot be intelligibly rendered into English by a literal translation of the words or even the form of the thought. And he must learn all this upon a diet no English boy could live on; and always thinly clad in his poor cotton dress without even a fire in his school-room during the terrible winter, only a hibachi containing a few lumps of glowing charcoal in a bed of ashes.* Is it to be wondered at that even those Japanese students who pass successfully through all the educational courses the Empire can open to them can only in rare instances show results of their long training as large as those manifested by students of the West? Better conditions are coming; but at present, under the new strain, young bodies and young minds too often give way. And those who break down are not the dullards, but the pride of schools, the captains of classes.

XII.

Yet, so far as the finances of the schools allow, everything possible is done to make the students both healthy and happy—to furnish them with ample opportunities both for physical exercise and for mental enjoyment. Though the course of study is severe, the hours are not long: and one of the daily five is devoted to military drill—made more interesting to the lads by the use of real rifles and bayonets, furnished by government. There is a fine gymnastic ground near the school, furnished with trapezes, parallel bars, vaulting horses, etc.; and there are two masters of gymnastics attached to the Middle School alone. There are row-boats, in which the boys can take their pleasure on the beautiful

---

* Stoves, however, are being introduced. In the higher government schools, and in the Normal Schools, the students who are boarders obtain a better diet than most poor boys can get at home. Their rooms are also well warmed.

lake whenever the weather permits. There is an excellent fenc-ing-school conducted by the Governor himself, who, although so heavy a man, is reckoned one of the best fencers of his own generation. The style taught is the old one, requiring the use of both hands to wield the sword; thrusting is little attempted, it is nearly all heavy slashing. The foils are made of long splinters of bamboo tied together so as to form something resembling elongated fasces: masks and wadded coats protect the head and body, for the blows given are heavy. This sort of fencing requires considerable agility, and gives more active exercise than our severer Western styles. Yet another form of healthy exercise consists of long journeys on foot to famous places. Special holi-days are allowed for these. The students march out of town in military order, accompanied by some of their favorite teachers, and perhaps a servant to cook for them. Thus they may travel for a hundred, or even a hundred and fifty miles and back; but if the journey is to be a very long one, only the strong lads are allowed to go. They walk in waraji, the true straw sandal, closely tied to the naked foot, which it leaves perfectly supple and free, without blistering or producing corns. They sleep at night in Buddhist temples; and their cooking is done in the open fields, like that of soldiers in camp.

For those little inclined to such sturdy exercise there is a school library which is growing every year. There is also a monthly school magazine, edited and published by the boys. And there is a Students' Society, at whose regular meetings debates are held upon all conceivable subjects of interest to students.

XIV.

April 4, 1891.

The students of the third, fourth, and fifth year classes write for me once a week brief English compositions upon easy themes which I select for them. As a rule the themes are Japanese. Considering the immense difficulty of the English language to Japanese students, the ability of some of my boys to express their thoughts in it is astonishing. Their compositions have also another interest for me as revelations, not of individual character, but of national sentiment, or of aggregate sentiment of some sort or other. What seems to me most surprising in the compositions of the average Japanese student is that they have no personal *cachet* at all. Even the handwriting of twenty English compositions will be found to have a curious family resemblance; and striking exceptions are too few to affect the rule. Here is one of the best compositions on my table, by a student at the head of his class. Only a few idiomatic errors have been corrected:

"THE MOON.

"The Moon appears melancholy to those who are sad, and joyous to those who are happy. The Moon makes memories of home come to those who travel, and creates homesickness. So when the Emperor Godaigo, having been banished to Oki by the traitor Hojō, beheld the moonlight upon the seashore, he cried out, *'The Moon is heartless!'* The sight of the Moon *makes an immeasurable feeling in our hearts* when we look up at it through the clear air of a beauteous night.

"Our hearts ought to be pure and calm like the light of the Moon.

"Poets often compare the Moon to a Japanese [metal] mirror *(kagami);* and indeed its shape is the same when it is full.

"The refined man amuses himself with the Moon. He seeks some house looking out upon water, to watch the Moon, and to make verses about it.

"The best places from which to see the Moon are Tsukigashi, and the mountain Obasute.

"The light of the Moon shines alike upon foul and pure, upon high and low. That beautiful Lamp is neither yours nor mine, but everybody's.

"When we look at the Moon we should remember that its waxing and its waning are the signs of the truth that the culmination of all things is likewise the beginning of their decline."

Any person totally unfamiliar with Japanese educational methods might presume that the foregoing composition shows some original power of thought and imagination. But this is not the case. I found the same thoughts and comparisons in thirty other compositions upon the same subject. Indeed, the compositions of any number of middle-school students upon the same subject are certain to be very much alike in idea and sentiment—though they are none the less charming for that. As a rule the Japanese student shows little originality in the line of imagination. His imagination was made for him long centuries ago—partly in China, partly in his native land. From his childhood he is trained to see and to feel Nature exactly in the manner of those wondrous artists who, with a few swift brush-strokes, fling down upon a sheet of paper the color-sensation of a chilly dawn, a fervid noon, an autumn evening. Through all his boyhood he is taught to commit to memory the most beautiful thoughts and comparisons to be found in his ancient native literature. Every boy has thus learned that the vision of Fuji against the blue resembles a white half-opened fan, hanging inverted in the sky. Every boy knows that cherry-trees in full blossom look as if the most delicate of flushed summer clouds were caught in their branches. Every boy knows the comparison between the falling of certain leaves on snow and the casting down of texts upon a sheet of white paper with a brush. Every boy and girl knows the verses comparing the print of cat's-feet on snow to plum-flowers,* and that comparing the impression of bokkuri on snow to the Japanese character for the number "two."† These were thoughts of old, old poets; and it would be very hard to invent prettier ones. Artistic power in composition is chiefly shown by the correct memorizing and clever combination of these old thoughts.

And the students have been equally well trained to discover a moral in almost everything, animate or inanimate. I have tried them with a hundred subjects—Japanese subjects—for composition; I have never found them to fail in discovering a moral when the theme was a native one. If I suggested "Fireflies," they at once

---

* *Hachi yuki ya*
 Neko no ashi ato
 Ume no hana.
† *Ni no ji fumi dasu*
 Bokkuri kana.

approved the topic, and wrote for me the story of that Chinese student who, being too poor to pay for a lamp, imprisoned many fireflies in a paper lantern, and thus was able to obtain light enough to study after dark, and to become eventually a great scholar. If I said "Frogs," they wrote for me the legend of Ono-no-Tofu, who was persuaded to become a learned celebrity by witnessing the tireless perseverance of a frog trying to leap up to a willow-branch. I subjoin a few specimens of the moral ideas which I thus evoked. I have corrected some common mistakes in the originals, but have suffered a few singularities to stand:

"THE BOTAN.

"The *botan* [Japanese peony] is large and beautiful to see; but it has a disagreeable smell. This should make us remember that what is only outwardly beautiful in human society should not attract us. *To be attracted by beauty only may lead us into fearful and fatal misfortune.* The best place to see the *botan* is the island of Daikonshima in the lake Nakaumi. There in the season of its flowering all the island is red with its blossoms."

"THE DRAGON.

"When the Dragon tries to ride the clouds and come into heaven there happens immediately a furious storm. When the Dragon dwells on the ground it is supposed to take the form of a stone or other object; but when it wants to rise it calls a cloud. Its body is composed of parts of many animals. It has the eyes of a tiger and the horns of a deer and the body of a crocodile and the claws of an eagle and two trunks like the trunk of an elephant. It has a moral. *We should try to be like the dragon, and find out and adopt all the good qualities of others.*"

At the close of this essay on the dragon is a note to the teacher, saying: "I believe not there is any Dragon. But there are many stories and curious pictures about Dragon."

"MOSQUITOES.

"On summer nights we hear the sound of faint voices; and little things come and sting our bodies very violently. We call them *ka*—in English 'mosquitoes.' I think the sting is useful for us, because if we begin to sleep, the *ka* shall come and sting us, uttering a small voice; *then we shall be bringed back to study by the sting.*"

The following, by a lad of sixteen, is submitted only as a characteristic expression of half-formed ideas about a less familiar subject.

"EUROPEAN AND JAPANESE CUSTOMS.

"Europeans wear very narrow clothes and they wear shoes always in the house. Japanese wear clothes which are very *lenient* and they do not *shoe* except when they walk *out-of-the-door.*

"What we think very strange is that in Europe every wife loves her husband more than her parents. In Nippon there is no wife who more loves not her parents than her husband.

"And Europeans walk out in the road with their wives, which we utterly refuse to, except on the festival of Hachiman.

"The Japanese woman is treated by man as a servant, while the European woman is respected as a master. I think these customs are both bad.

"We think it is very much trouble to treat European ladies; and we do not know why ladies are so much respected by Europeans."

Conversation in the classroom about foreign subjects is often equally amusing and suggestive:

"Teacher, I have been told that if a European and his father and his wife were all to fall into the sea together, and that he only could swim, he would try to save his wife first. Would he really?"

"Probably," I reply.

"But why?"

"One reason is that Europeans consider it a man's duty to help the weaker first—especially women and children."

"And does a European love his wife more than his father and mother?"

"Not always—but generally, perhaps, he does."

"Why, Teacher, according to our ideas that is very immoral."

"Teacher, how do European women carry their babies?"

"In their arms."

"Very tiring! And how far can a woman walk carrying a baby in her arms?"

"A strong woman can walk many miles with a child in her arms."

"But she cannot use her hands while she is carrying a baby that way, can she?"

"Not very well."

"Then it is a very bad way to carry babies," etc.

XV.

May 1, 1891.

My favorite students often visit me of afternoons. They first send me their cards, to announce their presence. On being told to come in they leave their footgear on the doorstep, enter my little study, prostrate themselves; and we all squat down together on the floor, which is in all Japanese houses like a soft mattress. The servant brings zabuton or small cushions to kneel upon, and cakes, and tea.

To sit as the Japanese do requires practice; and some Europeans can never acquire the habit. To acquire it, indeed, one must become accustomed to wearing Japanese costume. But once the habit of thus sitting has been formed, one finds it the most natural and easy of positions, and assumes it by preference for eating, reading, smoking, or chatting. It is not to be recommended, perhaps, for writing with a European pen—as the motion in our Occidental style of writing is from the supported wrist; but it is the best posture for writing with the Japanese fude, in using which the whole arm is unsupported, and the motion from the elbow. After having become habituated to Japanese habits for more than a year, I must confess that I find it now somewhat irksome to use a chair.

When we have all greeted each other, and taken our places upon the kneeling cushions, a little polite silence ensues, which I am the first to break. Some of the lads speak a good deal of English. They understand me well when I pronounce every word slowly and distinctly—using simple phrases, and avoiding idioms. When a word with which they are not familiar must be used, we refer to a good English-Japanese dictionary, which gives each vernacular meaning both in the kana and in the Chinese characters.

Usually my young visitors stay a long time, and their stay is rarely tiresome. Their conversation and their thoughts are of the simplest and frankest. They do not come to learn: they know that to ask their teacher to teach out of school would be unjust. They speak chiefly of things which they think have some particular interest for me. Sometimes they scarcely speak at all, but appear to sink into a sort of happy reverie. What they come really for is the quiet pleasure of sympathy. Not an intellectual sympathy, but the sympathy of pure good-will: the simple pleasure of being quite comfortable with a friend. They peep at my books and pictures; and sometimes they bring books and pictures to show me—delightfully queer things—family heirlooms which I regret much that I cannot buy. They also like to look at my garden, and enjoy all that is in it even more than I. Often they bring me gifts of flowers. Never by any possible chance are they troublesome, impolite, curious, or even talkative. Courtesy in its utmost possible exquisiteness—an exquisiteness of which even the French have no conception—seems natural to the Izumo boy as the color of his hair or the tint of his skin. Nor is he less kind than courteous. To contrive pleasurable surprises for me is one of the particular delights of my boys; and they either bring or cause to be brought to the house all sorts of strange things.

Of all the strange or beautiful things which I am thus privileged to examine, none gives me so much pleasure as a certain wonderful kakemono of Amida Nyorai. It is rather a large picture, and has been borrowed from a priest that I may see it. The Buddha stands in the attitude of exhortation, with one hand uplifted. Behind his head a huge moon makes an aureole; and across the face of that moon stream winding lines of thinnest cloud. Beneath his feet, like a rolling of smoke, curl heavier and darker clouds. Merely as a work of color and design, the thing is a marvel. But the real wonder of it is not in color or design at all. Minute examination reveals the astonishing fact that every shadow and clouding is formed by a fairy text of Chinese characters so minute that only a keen eye can discern them; and this text is the entire text of two famed sutras—the Kwammuryō-ju-kyō and the Amida-kyō—"text no larger than the limbs of fleas." And all the strong dark lines of the figure, such as the seams of the Buddha's robe, are formed by the characters of the holy invocation of the Shin-shū sect, repeated thousands of times: "*Namu Amida Butsu!*" Infinite patience, tireless silent labor of loving faith, in some dim temple, long ago.

Another day one of my boys persuades his father to let him bring to my house a wonderful statue of Kōshi (Confucius), made, I am told, in China, toward the close of the period of the Ming dynasty. I am also assured it is the first time the statue has ever been removed from the family residence to be shown to any one. Previously, whoever desired to pay it reverence had to visit the house. It is truly a beautiful bronze. The figure of a smiling, bearded old man, with fingers uplifted and lips apart as if discoursing. He wears quaint Chinese shoes, and his flowing robes are adorned with the figure of the mystic phoenix. The microscopic finish of detail seems indeed to reveal the wonderful cunning of a Chinese hand: each tooth, each hair, looks as though it had been made the subject of a special study.

Another student conducts me to the home of one of his relatives, that I may see a cat made of wood, said to have been chiseled by the famed Hidari Jingorō—a cat crouching and watching, and so lifelike that real cats "have been known to put up their backs and spit at it."

XVI.

Nevertheless I have a private conviction that some old artists even now living in Matsue could make a still more wonderful cat. Among these is the venerable Arakawa Junosuke, who wrought many rare things for the Daimyō of Izumo in the Tempō era, and whose acquaintance I have been enabled to make through my school-friends. One evening he brings to my house something very odd to show me, concealed in his sleeve. It is a doll: just a small carven and painted head without a body—the body being represented by a tiny robe only, attached to the neck. Yet as Arakawa Junosuke manipulates it, it seems to become alive. The back of its head is like the back of a very old man's head; but its face is the face of an amused child, and there is scarcely any forehead nor any evidence of a thinking disposition. And whatever way the head is turned, it looks so funny that one cannot help laughing at it. It represents a kirakubo—what we might call in English "a jolly old boy,"—one who is naturally too hearty and too innocent to feel trouble of any sort. It is not an original, but a model of a very famous original—whose history is recorded in a faded scroll which Arakawa takes out of his other sleeve, and which a friend translates for me. This little history throws a curious light upon the simplehearted ways of Japanese life and thought in other centuries:

"Two hundred and sixty years ago this doll was made by a famous maker of No-masks in the city of Kyōto, for the Emperor Go-midzu-no-O. The Emperor used to have it placed beside his pillow each night before he slept, and was very fond of it. And he composed the following poem concerning it:

> *Yo no naka wo*
> *Kiraku ni kurase*
> *Nani goto mo*
> *Omoeba omou*
> *Omowaneba koso.**

"On the death of the Emperor this doll became the property of Prince Konoye, in whose family it is said to be still preserved.

---

* This little poem signifies that whoever in this world thinks much, must have care, and that not to think about things is to pass one's life in untroubled felicity.

"About one hundred and seven years ago, the then Ex-Empress, whose posthumous name is Sei-Kwa-Mon-Yin, borrowed the doll from Prince Konoye, and ordered a copy of it to be made. This copy she kept always beside her, and was very fond of it.

"After the death of the good Empress this doll was given to a lady of the court, whose family name is not recorded. Afterwards this lady, for reasons which are not known, cut off her hair and became a Buddhist nun—taking the name of Shingyō-in.

"And one who knew the Nun Shingyō-in—a man whose name was Kondo-ju-haku-in-Hokyō—had the honor of receiving the doll as a gift.

"Now I, who write this document, at one time fell sick; and my sickness was caused by despondency. And my friend Kondo-ju-haku-in-Hokyō, coming to see me, said: 'I have in my house something which will make you well.' And he went home and, presently returning, brought to me this doll, and lent it to me—putting it by my pillow that I might see it and laugh at it.

"Afterward, I myself, having called upon the Nun Shingyō-in, whom I now also have the honor to know, wrote down the history of the doll, and made a poem thereupon."

(Dated about ninety years ago: no signature.)

XVII.

June 1, 1891.

I find among the students a healthy tone of skepticism in regard to certain forms of popular belief. Scientific education is rapidly destroying credulity in old superstitions yet current among the unlettered, and especially among the peasantry—as, for instance, faith in mamori and ofuda. The outward forms of Buddhism—its images, its relics, its commoner practices—affect the average student very little. He is not, as a foreigner may be, interested in iconography, or religious folk-lore, or the comparative study of religions; and in nine cases out of ten he is rather ashamed of the signs and tokens of popular faith all around him. But the deeper religious sense, which underlies all symbolism, remains with him; and the Monistic Idea in Buddhism is being strengthened and expanded, rather than weakened, by the new education. What is true of the effect of the public schools upon the lower Buddhism is equally true of its effect upon the lower Shintō. Shintō the students all sincerely are, or very nearly all; yet not as fervent worshipers of certain Kami, but as rigid observers of what the higher Shintō signifies—loyalty, filial piety, obedience to parents, teachers, and superiors, and respect to ancestors. For Shintō means more than faith.

When, for the first time, I stood before the shrine of the Great Deity of Kitzuki, as the first Occidental to whom that privilege had been accorded, not without a sense of awe there came to me the thought: "This is the Shrine of the Father of a Race; this is the symbolic center of a nation's reverence for its past." And I, too, paid reverence to the memory of the progenitor of this people.

As I then felt, so feels the intelligent student of the Meiji era whom education has lifted above the common plane of popular creeds. And Shintō also means for him—whether he reasons upon the question or not—all the ethics of the family, and all that spirit of loyalty which has become so innate that, at the call of duty, life itself ceases to have value save as an instrument for duty's accomplishment. As yet, this Orient little needs to reason about the origin of its loftier ethics. Imagine the musical sense in our own race so developed that a child could play a complicated instrument so soon as the little fingers gained sufficient force and flexibility to strike the notes. By some such comparison only can one obtain a just idea of what inherent religion and instinctive duty signify in Izumo.

Of the rude and aggressive form of skepticism so common in the Occident, which is the natural reaction after sudden emancipation from superstitious belief, I find no trace among my students. But such sentiment may be found elsewhere—especially in Tōkyō—among the university students, one of whom, upon hearing the tones of a magnificent temple bell, exclaimed to a friend of mine: "*Is it not a shame that in this nineteenth century we must still hear such a sound?*"

For the benefit of curious travelers, however, I may here take occasion to observe that to talk Buddhism to Japanese gentlemen of the new school is in just as bad taste as to talk Christianity at home to men of that class whom knowledge has placed above creeds and forms. There are, of course, Japanese scholars willing to aid researches of foreign scholars in religion or in folklore; but these specialists do not undertake to gratify idle curiosity of the "globetrotting" description. I may also say that the foreigner desirous to learn the religious ideas or superstitions of the common people must obtain them from the people themselves—not from the educated classes.

XVIII.

Among all my favorite students—two or three from each class—I cannot decide whom I like the best. Each has a particular merit of his own. But I think the names and faces of those of whom I am about to speak will longest remain vivid in my remembrance—Ishihara, Otani-Masanobu, Adzukizawa, Yokogi, Shida.

Ishihara is a samurai, a very influential lad in his class because of his uncommon force of character. Compared with others, he has a somewhat brusque, independent manner, pleasing, however, by its honest manliness. He says everything he thinks, and precisely in the tone that he thinks it, even to the degree of being a little embarrassing sometimes. He does not hesitate, for example, to find fault with a teacher's method of explanation, and to insist upon a more lucid one. He has criticised me more than once; but I never found that he was wrong. We like each other very much. He often brings me flowers.

One day that he had brought two beautiful sprays of plum-blossoms, he said to me:

"I saw you bow before our Emperor's picture at the ceremony on the birthday of His Majesty. You are not like a former English teacher we had."

"How?"

"He said we were savages."

"Why?"

"He said there is nothing respectable except God—*his* God—and that only vulgar and ignorant people respect anything else."

"Where did he come from?"

"He was a Christian clergyman, and said he was an English subject."

"But if he was an English subject, he was bound to respect Her Majesty the Queen. He could not even enter the office of a British consul without removing his hat."

"I don't know what he did in the country he came from. But that was what he said. Now we think we should love and honor our Emperor. We think it is a duty. We think it is a joy. We think it is happiness to be able to give our lives for our Emperor.* But he said we were only savages—ignorant savages. What do you think of that?"

"I think, my dear lad, that he himself was a savage—a vulgar, ignorant, savage bigot. I think it is your highest social duty to honor your Emperor, to obey his laws, and to be ready to give your blood whenever he may require it of you for the sake of Japan. I think it is your duty to respect the gods of your fathers, the religion of your country—even if you yourself cannot believe all that others believe. And I think, also, that it is your duty, for your Emperor's sake and for your country's sake, to resent any such wicked and vulgar language as that you have told me of, no matter by whom uttered."

Masanobu visits me seldom and always comes alone. A slender, handsome lad, with rather feminine features, reserved and per-

---

* Having asked in various classes for written answers to the question, "What is your dearest wish?" I found about twenty percent of the replies expressed, with little variation of words, the simple desire to die "for His Sacred Majesty, Our Beloved Emperor." But a considerable proportion of the remainder contained the same aspiration, less directly stated in the wish to emulate the glory of Nelson, or to make Japan first among nations by heroism and sacrifice. While this splendid spirit lives in the hearts of her youth, Japan should have little to fear for the future.

fectly self-possessed in manner, refined. He is somewhat serious, does not often smile; and I never heard him laugh. He has risen to the head of his class, and appears to remain there without any extraordinary effort. Much of his leisure time he devotes to botany—collecting and classifying plants. He is a musician, like all the male members of his family. He plays a variety of instruments never seen or heard of in the West, including flutes of marble, flutes of ivory, flutes of bamboo of wonderful shapes and tones, and that shrill Chinese instrument called shō—a sort of mouth-organ consisting of seventeen tubes of different lengths fixed in a silver frame. He first explained to me the uses in temple music of the taiko and shōko, which are drums; of the flutes called fei or teki; of the flageolet termed hichiriki; and of the kakko, which is a little drum shaped like a spool with very narrow waist. On great Buddhist festivals, Masanobu and his father and his brothers are the musicians in the temple services, and they play the strange music called Ōjō and Batto—music which at first no Western ear can feel pleasure in, but which, when often heard, becomes comprehensible, and is found to possess a weird charm of its own. When Masanobu comes to the house, it is usually in order to invite me to attend some Buddhist or Shintō festival *(matsuri)* which he knows will interest me.

Adzukizawa bears so little resemblance to Masanobu that one might suppose the two belonged to totally different races. Adzukizawa is large, raw-boned, heavy-looking, with a face singularly like that of a North American Indian. His people are not rich; he can afford few pleasures which cost money, except one—buying books. Even to be able to do this he works in his leisure hours to earn money. He is a perfect bookworm, a natural-born researcher, a collector of curious documents, a haunter of all the queer second-hand stores in Teramachi and other streets where old manuscripts or prints are on sale as waste paper. He is an omnivorous reader, and a perpetual borrower of volumes, which he always returns in perfect condition after having copied what he deemed of most value to him. But his special delight is philosophy and the history of philosophers in all countries. He has read various epitomes of the history of philosophy in the Occident, and everything of modern philosophy which has been translated into Japanese—including Spencer's "First Principles." I have been able to introduce him to Lewes and John Fiske—both of which he appreciates—although the strain of studying philosophy in English is no small one. Happily he is so strong that no amount of study is likely to injure his health, and his nerves are tough as wire. He is quite an ascetic withal. As it is the Japanese custom to set cakes and tea before visitors, I always have both in readiness, and an especially fine quality of kwashi, made at Kitzuki, of which the students are very fond. Adzukizawa alone refuses to taste cakes or confectionery of any kind, saying: "As I am the youngest brother, I must begin to earn my own living soon. I shall have to endure much hardship. And if I allow myself to like dainties now, I shall only suffer more later on." Adzukizawa has seen much of human life and character. He is naturally observant; and he has managed in some extraordinary way to learn the history of everybody in Matsue. He has brought me old tattered prints to prove that the opinions now held by our director are diametrically opposed to the opinions he advocated fourteen years ago in a public address. I asked the director about it. He laughed and said, "Of course that is Adzukizawa! But he is right: I was very young then." And I wonder if Adzukizawa was ever young.

Yokogi, Adzukizawa's dearest friend, is a very rare visitor; for he is always studying at home. He is always first in his class—the third year class—while Adzukizawa is fourth. Adzukizawa's account of the beginning of their acquaintance is this: "I watched him when he came and saw that he spoke very little, walked very quickly, and looked straight into everybody's eyes. So I knew he had a particular character. I like to know people with a particular character." Adzukizawa was perfectly right: under a very gentle exterior, Yokogi has an extremely strong character. He is the son of a carpenter and his parents could not afford to send him

to the Middle School. But he had shown such exceptional qualities while in the Elementary School that a wealthy man became
interested in him, and offered to pay for his education.* He is
now the pride of the school. He has a remarkably placid face,
with peculiarly long eyes, and a delicious smile. In class he is
always asking intelligent questions—questions so original that
I am sometimes extremely puzzled how to answer them; and he
never ceases to ask until the explanation is quite satisfactory to
himself. He never cares about the opinion of his comrades if he
thinks he is right. On one occasion when the whole class refused
to attend the lectures of a new teacher of physics, Yokogi alone
refused to act with them—arguing that although the teacher was
not all that could be desired, there was no immediate possibility
of his removal, and no just reason for making unhappy a man
who, though unskilled, was sincerely doing his best. Adzukizawa
finally stood by him. These two alone attended the lectures
until the remainder of the students, two weeks later, found that
Yokogi's views were rational. On another occasion when some
vulgar proselytism was attempted by a Christian missionary,
Yokogi went boldly to the proselytizer's house, argued with him
on the morality of his effort, and reduced him to silence. Some
of his comrades praised his cleverness in the argument.

"I am not clever," he made answer: "it does not require cleverness to argue against what is morally wrong; it requires only the
knowledge that one is morally right." At least such is about the
translation of what he said as told me by Adzukizawa.

Shida, another visitor, is a very delicate, sensitive boy, whose
soul is full of art. He is very skillful at drawing and painting; and
he has a wonderful set of picture-books by the old Japanese masters. The last time he came he brought some prints to show me—
rare ones—fairy maidens and ghosts. As I looked at his beautiful
pale face and weirdly frail fingers, I could not help fearing for
him—fearing that he might soon become a little ghost.

---

* Beautiful generosities of this kind are not uncommon in Japan.

I have not seen him now for more than two months. He has been very, very ill; and his lungs are so weak that the doctor has forbidden him to converse. But Adzukizawa has been to visit him, and brings me this translation of a Japanese letter which the sick boy wrote and pasted upon the wall above his bed:

"Thou, my Lord-Soul, dost govern me. Thou knowest that I cannot now govern myself. Deign, I pray thee, to let me be cured speedily. Do not suffer me to speak much. Make me to obey in all things the command of the physician.

"This ninth day of the eleventh month of the twenty-fourth year of Meiji.

"From the sick body of Shida to his Soul."

XIX.

September 4, 1891.

The long summer vacation is over; a new school year begins.

There have been many changes. Some of the boys I taught are dead. Others have graduated and gone away from Matsue forever. Some teachers, too, have left the school, and their places have been filled; and there is a new Director.

And the dear good Governor has gone—been transferred to cold Niigata in the northwest. It was a promotion. But he had ruled Izumo for seven years, and everybody loved him, especially, perhaps, the students, who looked upon him as a father. All the population of the city crowded to the river to bid him farewell. The streets through which he passed on his way to take the steamer, the bridge, the wharves, even the roofs were thronged with multitudes eager to see his face for the last time. Thousands were weeping. And as the steamer glided from the wharf such a cry arose—"A-*a-a-a-a-a-a-a-a-a*!" It was intended for a cheer, but it seemed to me the cry of a whole city sorrowing, and so plaintive that I hope never to hear such a cry again.

The names and faces of the younger classes are all strange to me. Doubtless this was why the sensation of my first day's teaching in the school came back to me with extraordinary vividness when I entered the class-room of First Division A this morning.

Strangely pleasant is the first sensation of a Japanese class, as you look over the ranges of young faces before you. There is nothing in them familiar to inexperienced Western eyes; yet there is an indescribable pleasant something common to all. Those traits have nothing incisive, nothing forcible: compared with Occidental faces they seem but "half-sketched," so soft their outlines are—indicating neither aggressiveness nor shyness, neither eccentricity nor sympathy, neither curiosity nor indifference. Some, although faces of youths well grown, have a childish freshness and frankness indescribable; some are as uninteresting as others are attractive; a few are beautifully feminine. But all are equally characterized by a singular placidity—expressing neither love nor hate nor anything save perfect repose and gentleness—like, the dreamy placidity of Buddhist images. At a later day you will no longer recognize this aspect of passionless composure: with growing acquaintance each face will become more and more individualized for you by characteristics before imperceptible. But the recollection of that first impression will remain with you; and the time will come when you will find, by many varied experiences, how strangely it foreshadowed something in Japanese character to be fully learned only after years of familiarity. You will recognize in the memory of that first impression one glimpse of the race-soul, with its impersonal lovableness and its impersonal weaknesses—one glimpse of the nature of a life in which the Occidental, dwelling alone, feels a psychic comfort comparable only to the nervous relief of suddenly emerging from some stifling atmospheric pressure into thin, clear, free living air.

XX.

Was it not the eccentric Fourier who wrote about the horrible faces of "the *civilizes?*" Whoever it was would have found seeming confirmation of his physiognomical theory could he have known the effect produced by the first sight of European faces in the most eastern East. What we are taught at home to consider handsome, interesting, or characteristic in physiognomy does not produce the same impression in China or Japan. Shades of facial expression familiar to us as letters of our own alphabet are not perceived at all in Western features by these Orientals at first acquaintance. What they discern at once is the race-characteristic, not the individuality. The evolutional meaning of the deep-set Western eye, protruding brow, accipitrine nose, ponderous jaw—symbols of aggressive force and habit—was revealed to the gentler race by the same sort of intuition through which a tame animal immediately comprehends the dangerous nature of the first predatory enemy which it sees. To Europeans the smooth-featured, slender, low-statured Japanese seemed like boys; and "boy" is the term by which the native attendant of a Yokohama merchant is still called. To Japanese the first red-haired, rowdy, drunken European sailors seemed fiends, shōjō, demons of the sea; and by the Chinese the Occidentals are still called "foreign devils." The great stature and massive strength and fierce gait of foreigners in Japan enhanced the strange impression created by their faces. Children cried for fear on seeing them pass through the streets. And in remoter districts, Japanese children are still apt to cry at the first sight of a European or American face.

A lady of Matsue related in my presence this curious souvenir of her childhood: "When I was a very little girl," she said, "our daimyō hired a foreigner to teach the military art. My father and a great many samurai went to receive the foreigner; and all the people lined the streets to see—for no foreigner had ever come to Izumo before; and we all went to look. The foreigner came by ship: there were no steamboats here then. He was very tall, and walked quickly with long steps; and the children began to cry at the sight of him, because his face was not like the faces of the people of Nihon. My little brother cried out loud, and hid his face in mother's robe; and mother reproved him and said:

'This foreigner is a very good man who has come here to serve our prince; and it is very disrespectful to cry at seeing him.' But he still cried. I was not afraid; and I looked up at the foreigner's face as he came and smiled. He had a great beard; and I thought his face was good though it seemed to me a very strange face and stern. Then he stopped and smiled too, and put something in my hand, and touched my head and face very softly with his great fingers, and said something I could not understand, and went away. After he had gone I looked at what he put into my hand and found that it was a pretty little glass to look through. If you put a fly under that glass it looks quite big. At that time I thought the glass was a very wonderful thing. I have it still." She took from a drawer in the room and placed before me a tiny, dainty pocket-microscope.

The hero of this little incident was a French military officer. His services were necessarily dispensed with on the abolition of the feudal system. Memories of him still linger in Matsue; and old people remember a popular snatch about him—a sort of rapidly-vociferated rigmarole, supposed to be an imitation of his foreign speech.

> Tōjin no negoto niwa kinkarakuri medagashō,
> Saiboji ga shimpeishite harishite keisan,
> Hanryō na *Sacr-r r r-r-é-na-nom-da-Jiu.*

XXI.

November 2, 1891

Shida will never come to school again. He sleeps under the shadow of the cedars, in the old cemetery of Tōkōji. Yokogi, at the memorial service, read a beautiful address *(saibun)* to the soul of his dead comrade.

But Yokogi himself is down. And I am very much afraid for him. He is suffering from some affection of the brain, brought on, the doctor says, by studying a great deal too hard. Even if he gets well, he will always have to be careful. Some of us hope much; for the boy is vigorously built and so young. Strong Sakane burst a blood vessel last month and is now well. So we trust that Yokogi may rally. Adzukizawa daily brings news of his friend.

But the rally never comes. Some mysterious spring in the mechanism of the young life has been broken. The mind lives only in brief intervals between long hours of unconsciousness. Parents watch, and friends, for these living moments to whisper caressing things, or to ask: "Is there anything thou dost wish?" And one night the answer comes:

"Yes: I want to go to the school; I want to see the school."

Then they wonder if the fine brain has not wholly given way, while they make answer:

"It is midnight past, and there is no moon. And the night is cold."

"No; I can see by the stars—I want to see the school again."

They make kindliest protests in vain: the dying boy only repeats, with the plaintive persistence of a last wish—

"I want to see the school again; I want to see it now."

So there is a murmured consultation in the neighboring room; and tansu-drawers are unlocked, warm garments prepared. Then Fusaichi, the strong servant, enters with lantern lighted, and cries out in his kind rough voice:

"Master Tomi will go to the school upon my back: 'tis but a little way; he shall see the school again."

Carefully they wrap up the lad in wadded robes; then he puts his arms about Fusaichi's shoulders like a child; and the strong servant bears him lightly through the wintry street; and the father hurries beside Fusaichi, bearing the lantern. And it is not far to the school, over the little bridge.

The huge dark gray building looks almost black in the night; but Yokogi can see. He looks at the windows of his own classroom; at the roofed sidedoor where each morning for four happy years he used to exchange his getas for soundless sandals of straw; at the lodge of the slumbering Kodzukai;* at the silhouette of the bell hanging black in its little turret against the stars.

Then he murmurs:

"I can remember all now. I had forgotten—so sick I was. I remember everything again. Oh, Fusaichi, you are very good. I am so glad to have seen the school again."

And they hasten back through the long void streets.

XXII.

November 26, 1891.

Yokogi will be buried tomorrow evening beside his comrade Shida.

When a poor person is about to die, friends and neighbors come to the house and do all they can to help the family. Some bear the tidings to distant relatives; others prepare all necessary things; others, when the death has been announced, summon the Buddhist priests.†

It is said that the priests know always of a parishioner's death at night, before any messenger is sent to them; for the soul of the dead knocks heavily, once, upon the door of the family temple. Then the priests arise and robe themselves, and when the messenger comes make answer: "We know: we are ready."

Meanwhile the body is carried out before the family butsudan, and laid upon the floor. No pillow is placed under the head. A naked sword is laid across the limbs to keep evil spirits away. The doors of the butsudan are opened; and tapers are lighted before the tablets of the ancestors; and incense is burned. All friends send gifts of incense. Wherefore a gift of incense, however rare and precious, given upon any other occasion, is held to be unlucky.

---

* The college porter.

† Except in those comparatively rare instances where the family is exclusively Shintō in its faith, or, although belonging to both faiths, prefers to bury its dead according to Shintō rites. In Matsue, as a rule, high officials only have Shintō funerals.

But the Shintō household shrine must be hidden from view with white paper; and the Shintō ofuda fastened upon the house door must be covered up during all the period of mourning.* And in all that time no member of the family may approach a Shintō temple, or pray to the Kami, or even pass beneath a torii.

A screen *(biōbu)* is extended between the body and the principal entrance of the death chamber; and the kaimyō, inscribed upon a strip of white paper, is fastened upon the screen. If the dead be young the screen must be turned upside-down; but this is not done in the case of old people.

Friends pray beside the corpse. There a little box is placed, containing one thousand peas, to be used for counting during the recital of those one thousand pious invocations, which, it is believed, will improve the condition of the soul on its unfamiliar journey.

The priests come and recite the sutras; and then the body is prepared for burial. It is washed in warm water, and robed all in white. But the kimono of the dead is lapped over to the left side. Wherefore it is considered unlucky at any other time to fasten one's kimono thus, even by accident.

When the body has been put into that strange square coffin which looks something like a wooden palanquin, each relative puts also into the coffin some of his or her hair or nail parings, symbolizing their blood. And six rin are also placed in the coffin, for the six Jizō who stand at the heads of the ways of the Six Shadowy Worlds.

---

* Unless the dead be buried according to the Shintō rite. In Matsue the mourning period is usually fifty days. On the fifty-first day after the decease, all members of the family go to Enjōji-nada (the lake-shore at the foot of the hill on which the great temple of Enjōji stands) to perform the ceremony of purification. At Enjōji-nada, on the beach, stands a lofty stone statue of Jizō. Before it the mourners pray; then wash their months and hands with the water of the lake. Afterwards they go to a friend's house for breakfast, the purification being always performed at daybreak, if possible. During the mourning period, no member of the family can eat at a friend's house. But if the burial has been according to the Shintō rite, all these ceremonial observances may be dispensed with.

The funeral procession forms at the family residence. A priest leads it, ringing a little bell; a boy bears the ihai of the newly dead. The van of the procession is wholly composed of men—relatives and friends. Some carry hata, white symbolic bannerets; some bear flowers; all carry paper lanterns—for in Izumo the adult dead are buried after dark: only children are buried by day. Next comes the kwan or coffin, borne palanquin-wise upon the shoulders of men of that pariah caste whose office it is to dig graves and assist at funerals. Lastly come the women mourners.

They are all white-hooded and white-robed from head to feet, like phantoms.* Nothing more ghostly than this sheeted train of an Izumo funeral procession, illuminated only by the glow of paper lanterns, can be imagined. It is a weirdness that, once seen, will often return in dreams.

At the temple the kwan is laid upon the pavement before the entrance; and another service is performed, with plaintive music and recitation of sutras. Then the procession forms again, winds once round the temple court, and takes its way to the cemetery. But the body is not buried until twenty-four hours later, lest the supposed dead should awake in the grave.

Corpses are seldom burned in Izumo. In this, as in other matters, the predominance of Shintō sentiment is manifest.

XXIII.

For the last time I see his face again, as he lies upon his bed of death—white-robed from neck to feet—white-girdled for his shadowy journey—but smiling with closed eyes in almost the same queer gentle way he was wont to smile at class on learning the explanation of some seeming riddle in our difficult English tongue. Only, methinks, the smile is sweeter now, as with sudden larger knowledge of more mysterious things. So smiles, through dusk of incense in the great temple of Tōkōji, the golden face of Buddha.

---

* But at samurai funerals in the olden time the women were robed in black.

XXIV.

December 23, 1891.

The great bell of Tōkōji is booming for the memorial service—for the tsuito-kwai of Yokogi—slowly and regularly as a minute-gun. Peal on peal of its rich bronze thunder shakes over the lake, surges over the roofs of the town, and breaks in deep sobs of sound against the green circle of the hills.

It is a touching service, this tsuito-kwai, with quaint ceremonies which, although long since adopted into Japanese Buddhism, are of Chinese origin and are beautiful. It is also a costly ceremony; and the parents of Yokogi are very poor. But all the expenses have been paid by voluntary subscription of students and teachers. Priests from every great temple of the Zen sect in Izumo have assembled at Tōkōji. All the teachers of the city and all the students have entered the hondo of the huge temple, and taken their places to the right and to the left of the high altar—kneeling on the matted floor, and leaving, on the long broad steps without, a thousand shoes and sandals.

Before the main entrance, and facing the high shrine, a new butsudan has been placed, within whose open doors the ihai of the dead boy glimmers in lacquer and gilding. And upon a small stand before the butsudan have been placed an incense-vessel with bundles of senko-rods and offerings of fruits, confections, rice, and flowers. Tall and beautiful flower vases on each side of the butsudan are filled with blossoming sprays, exquisitely arranged. Before the honzon tapers burn in massive candelabra whose stems of polished brass are writhing monsters—the Dragon Ascending and the Dragon Descending; and incense curls up from vessels shaped like the sacred deer, like the symbolic tortoise, like the meditative stork of Buddhist legend. And beyond these, in the twilight of the vast alcove, the Buddha smiles the smile of Perfect Rest.

Between the butsudan and the honzon a little table has been placed; and on either side of it the priests kneel in ranks, facing each other: rows of polished heads, and splendors of vermilion silks and vestments gold-embroidered.

The great bell ceases to peal; the Segaki prayer, which is the prayer uttered when offerings of food are made to the spirits of the dead, is recited; and a sudden sonorous measured tapping, accompanied by a plaintive chant, begins the musical service. The tapping is the tapping of the mokugyo—a huge wooden fish-head, lacquered and gilded, like the head of a dolphin grotesquely idealized—marking the time; and the chant is the chant of the Chapter of Kwannon in the Hokkekyō, with its magnificent invocation:

"O Thou whose eyes are clear, whose eyes are kind, whose eyes are full of pity and of sweetness—O Thou Lovely One, with thy beautiful face, with thy beautiful eyes—

"O Thou Pure One, whose luminosity is without spot, whose knowledge is without shadow—O Thou forever shining like that Sun whose glory no power may repel—Thou Sun-like in the course of Thy mercy, pourest Light upon the world!"

And while the voices of the leaders chant clear and high in vibrant unison, the multitude of the priestly choir recite in profoundest undertone the mighty verses; and the sound of their recitation is like the muttering of surf.

The mokugyo ceases its dull echoing, the impressive chant ends, and the leading officiants, one by one, high priests of famed temples, approach the ihai. Each bows low, ignites an incense-rod, and sets it upright in the little vase of bronze. Each at a time recites a holy verse of which the initial sound is the sound of a letter in the kaimyō of the dead boy; and these verses, uttered in the order of the characters upon the ihai, form the sacred Acrostic whose name is The Words of Perfume.

Then the priests retire to their places; and after a little silence begins the reading of the saibun—the reading of the addresses to the soul of the dead. The students speak first—one from each class, chosen by election. The elected rises, aproaches the little table before the high altar, bows to the honzon, draws from his bosom a paper and reads it in those melodious, chanting, and plaintive tones which belong to the reading of Chinese texts. So each one tells the affection of the living to the dead, in words of loving grief and loving hope. And last among the students a gentle girl rises—a pupil of the Normal School—to speak in tones soft as a bird's. As each saibun is finished, the reader lays the written paper upon the table before the honzon, and bows, and retires.

It is now the turn of the teachers; and an old man takes his place at the little table—old Katayama, the teacher of Chinese, famed as a poet, adored as an instructor. And because the students all love him as a father, there is a strange intensity of silence as he begins— *Kō-Shimane-Ken-Jinjō-Chūgakkō-yo-nensei.*

"Here upon the twenty-third day of the twelfth month of the twenty-fourth year of Meiji, I, Katayama Shōkei, teacher of the Jinjō Chūgakkō of Shimane Ken, attending in great sorrow the holy service of the dead *[tsui-fuku]*, do speak unto the soul of Yokogi Tomisaburo, my pupil.

"Having been, as thou knowest, for twice five years, at different periods, a teacher of the school, I have indeed met with not a few most excellent students. But very, very rarely in any school may the teacher find one such as thou—so patient and so earnest, so diligent and so careful in all things—so distinguished among thy comrades by thy blameless conduct, observing every precept, never breaking a rule.

"Of old in the land of Kihoku, famed for its horses, whenever a horse of rarest breed could not be obtained, men were wont to say: *'There is no horse.'* Still there are many fine lads among our students—many *ryume*, fine young steeds; but we have lost the best.

"To die at the age of seventeen—the best period of life for study—even when of the Ten Steps thou hadst already ascended six! Sad is the thought; but sadder still to know that thy last illness was caused only by thine own tireless zeal of study. Even yet more sad our conviction that with those rare gifts, and with that rare character of thine, thou wouldst surely, in that career to which thou wast destined, have achieved good and great things, honoring the names of thine ancestors, couldst thou have lived to manhood.

"I see thee lifting thy hand to ask some question; then, bending above thy little desk to make note of all thy poor old teacher was able to tell thee. Again I see thee in the ranks—thy rifle upon thy shoulder—so bravely erect during the military exercises. Even now thy face is before me, with its smile, as plainly as if thou wert present in the body; thy voice I think I hear distinctly as though thou hadst but this instant finished speaking; yet I know that, except in memory, these never will be seen and heard again. O Heaven, why didst thou take away that dawning life from the world, and leave such a one as I—old Shōkei, feeble, decrepit, and of no more use?

"To thee my relation was indeed only that of teacher to pupil. Yet what is my distress! I have a son of twenty-four years; he is now far from me, in Yokohama. I know he is only a worthless youth;* yet never for so much as the space of one hour does the thought of him leave his old father's heart. Then how must the father and mother, the brothers and the sisters of this gentle and gifted youth feel now that he is gone! Only to think of it forces the tears from my eyes: I cannot speak—so full my heart is.

"*Aa! aa!*—thou hast gone from us; thou hast gone from us! Yet though thou hast died, thy earnestness, thy goodness, will long be honored and told of as examples to the students of our school.

"Here, therefore, do we, thy teachers and thy schoolmates, hold this service in behalf of thy spirit—with prayer and offerings. Deign thou, O gentle Soul, to honor our love by the acceptance of our humble gifts."

---

* Said only in courteous self-depreciation. In the same way a son, writing to his parent, would never according to Japanese ideas of true courtesy and duty sign himself "*Your affectionate son,*" but "*Your ungrateful [or] unloving son.*"

Then a sound of sobbing is suddenly whelmed by the resonant booming of the great fish's-head, as the high-pitched voices of the leaders of the chant begin the grand Nehan-gyō, the Sutra of Nirvana, the song of passage triumphant over the Sea of Death and Birth; and deep below those high tones and the hollow echoing of the mokugyo, the surging bass of a century of voices reciting the sonorous words, sounds like the breaking of a sea:

"*Shō-gyō ma-jō, Je-sho meppō.—Transient are all. They, being born, must die. And being born, are dead. And being dead, are glad to be at rest.*"

20

TWO STRANGE FESTIVALS

I

THE outward signs of any Japanese matsuri are the most puzzling of enigmas to the stranger who sees them for the first time. They are many and varied; they are quite unlike anything in the way of holiday decoration ever seen in the Occident; they have each a meaning founded upon some belief or some tradition—a meaning known to every Japanese child; but that meaning is utterly impossible for any foreigner to guess. Yet whoever wishes to know something of Japanese popular life and feeling must learn the signification of at least the most common among festival symbols and tokens. Especially is such knowledge necessary to the student of Japanese art: without it, not only the delicate humor and charm of countless designs must escape him, but in many instances the designs themselves must remain incomprehensible to him. For hundreds of years the emblems of festivity have been utilized by the Japanese in graceful decorative ways: they figure in metalwork, on porcelain, on the red or black lacquer of the humblest household utensils, on little brass pipes, on the clasps of tobacco-pouches. It may even be said that the majority of common decorative design is emblematical. The very figures of which the meaning seems most obvious— those matchless studies* of animal or vegetable life with which

---

* As it has become, among a certain sect of Western Philistines and self-constituted

the Western curio-buyer is most familiar—have usually some ethical signification which is not perceived at all. Or take the commonest design dashed with a brush upon the fusuma of a cheap hotel—a lobster—sprigs of pine—tortoises waddling in a curl of water—a pair of storks—a spray of bamboo. It is rarely that a foreign tourist thinks of asking why such designs are used instead of others—even when he has seen them repeated, with slight variation, at twenty different places along his route. They have become conventional simply because they are emblems of which the sense is known to all Japanese, however ignorant, but is never even remotely suspected by the stranger.

The subject is one about which a whole encyclopedia might be written, but about which I know very little—much too little for a special essay. But I may venture, by way of illustration, to speak of the curious objects exhibited during two antique festivals still observed in all parts of Japan.

II.

The first is the Festival of the New Year, which lasts for three days. In Matsue its celebration is particularly interesting, as the old city still preserves many matsuri customs which have either become, or are rapidly becoming, obsolete elsewhere. The streets are then profusely decorated, and all shops are closed. Shimenawa or shimekazari—the straw ropes which have been sacred symbols of Shintō from the mythical age—are festooned along the façades

---

art critics, the fashion to sneer at any writer who becomes enthusiastic about the *truth to nature* of Japanese art, I may cite here the words of England's most celebrated living *naturalist* on this very subject. Mr. Wallace's authority will scarcely, I presume, be questioned, even by the Philistines referred to:

"Dr. Mohnike possesses a large collection of colored sketches of the plants of Japan made by a Japanese lady, *which are the most masterly things I have ever seen*. Every stem, twig, and leaf is produced by single touches of the brush, the character and perspective of very complicated plants being admirably given, and the articulations of stem and leaves shown *in a most scientific manner*." (*Malay Archipelago*, chap, xx.)

Now this was written in 1857, before European methods of drawing had been introduced. The same art of painting leaves, etc., with single strokes of the brush is still common in Japan—even among the poorest class of decorators.

of the dwellings, and so interjoined that you see to right or left what seems but a single mile-long shimenawa, with its straw pendents and white fluttering paper gohei, extending along either side of the street as far as the eye can reach. Japanese flags—bearing on a white ground the great crimson disk which is the emblem of the Land of the Rising Sun—flutter above the gateways; and the same national emblem glows upon countless paper lanterns strung in rows along the eaves or across the streets and temple avenues. And before every gate or doorway a kadomatsu ("gate pine-tree") has been erected. So that all the ways are lined with green, and full of bright color.

The kadomatsu is more than its name implies. It is a young pine, or part of a pine, conjoined with plum branches and bamboo cuttings.* Pine, plum, and bamboo are growths of emblematic significance. Anciently the pine alone was used; but from the era of O-ei, the bamboo was added; and within more recent times the plum-tree.

The pine has many meanings. But the fortunate one most generally accepted is that of endurance and successful energy in time of misfortune. As the pine keeps its green leaves, when other trees lose their foliage, so the true man keeps his courage and his strength in adversity. The pine is also, as I have said elsewhere, a symbol of vigorous old age.

No European could possibly guess the riddle of the bamboo. It represents a sort of pun in symbolism. There are two Chinese characters both pronounced *setsu*—one signifying the *node* or joint of the bamboo, and the other virtue, fidelity, constancy. Therefore is the bamboo used as a felicitous sign. The name "Setsu," be it observed, is often given to Japanese maidens—

---

* There is a Buddhist saying about the kadomatsu:

Kadomatsu
Meido no tabi no
Ichi-ri-zuka.

The meaning is that each kadomatsu is a milestone on the journey to the Meido; or, in other words, that each New Year's festival signals only the completion of another stage of the ceaseless journey to death.

just as the names "Faith," "Fidelia," and "Constance" are given to
English girls.

The plum-tree—of whose emblematic meaning I said something in a former paper about Japanese gardens—is not invariably used, however; sometimes sakaki, the sacred plant of Shintō,
is substituted for it; and sometimes only pine and bamboo form
the kadomatsu.

Every decoration used upon the New Year's festival has a
meaning of a curious and unfamiliar kind; and the very commonest of all—the straw rope—possesses the most complicated
symbolism. In the first place it is scarcely necessary to explain
that its origin belongs to that most ancient legend of the Sun-
Goddess being tempted to issue from the cavern into which she
had retired, and being prevented from returning thereunto by a
deity who stretched a rope of straw across the entrance—all of
which is written in the Kojiki. Next observe that, although the
shimenawa may be of any thickness, it must be twisted so that
the direction of the twist is to the left; for in ancient Japanese
philosophy the left is the "pure" or fortunate side: owing perhaps
to the old belief, common among the uneducated of Europe to
this day, that the heart lies to the left. Thirdly, note that the
pendent straws, which hang down from the rope at regular
intervals, in tufts, like fringing, must be of different numbers
according to the place of the tufts, beginning with the number
three: so that the first tuft has three straws, the second five, the
third seven, the fourth again three, the fifth five, and the sixth
seven—and so on, the whole length of the rope. The origin of the
pendent paper cuttings (*gohei*), which alternate with the straw
tufts, is likewise to be sought in the legend of the Sun-Goddess;
but the gohei also represent offerings of cloth anciently made to
the gods according to a custom long obsolete.

But besides the gohei, there are many other things attached to
the shimenawa of which you could not imagine the signification.
Among these are fern-leaves, bitter oranges, yuzuri-leaves, and
little bundles of charcoal.

Why fern-leaves *(moromoki* or *urajirō)?* Because the fern-leaf is the symbol of the hope of exuberant posterity: even as it branches and rebranches so may the happy family increase and multiply through the generations.

Why bitter oranges *(daidai)?* Because there is a Chinese word daidai signifying "from generation unto generation." Wherefore the fruit called daidai has become a fruit of good omen.

But why charcoal *(sumi)?* It signifies "prosperous *changelessness.*" Here the idea is decidedly curious. Even as the color of charcoal cannot be changed, so may the fortunes of those we love remain forever unchanged in all that gives happiness! The signification of the yuzuri-leaf I explained in a former paper.

Besides the great shimenawa in front of the house, shimenawa or shimekazari* are suspended above the toko, or alcoves, in each apartment; and over the back gate, or over the entrance to the gallery of the second story (if there be a second story), is hung a wajime, which is a very small shimekazari twisted into a sort of wreath, and decorated with fern-leaves, gohei, and yuzuri-leaves.

But the great domestic display of the festival is the decoration of the kamidana—the shelf of the Gods. Before the household miya are placed great double rice cakes; and the shrine is beautified with flowers, a tiny shimekazari, and sprays of sakaki. There also are placed a string of cash; kabu (turnips); daikon (radishes); a tai-fish, which is the "king of fishes," dried slices of salt cuttlefish; jinbaso, or "the Seaweed of the Horse of the God;"†—also the seaweed kombu, which is a symbol of pleasure and of joy, because its name is deemed to be a homonym for gladness; and mochibana, artificial blossoms formed of rice flour and straw.

The sambō is a curiously shaped little table on which offerings are made to the Shintō gods; and almost every well-to-do

---

* The difference between the shimenawa and shimekazari is that the latter is a strictly decorative straw rope, to which many curious emblems are attached.

† It belongs to the sargassum family, and is full of air sacs. Various kinds of edible seaweed form a considerable proportion of Japanese diet.

household in Izumo has its own sambō; such a family sambō being smaller, however, than sambō used in the temples. At the advent of the New Year's Festival, bitter oranges, rice, and rice-flour cakes, native sardines *(iwashi),* chikara-iwai ("strength-rice-bread"), black peas, dried chestnuts, and a fine lobster, are all tastefully arranged upon the family sambō. Before each visitor the sambō is set; and the visitor, by saluting it with a prostration, expresses not only his heartfelt wish that all the good-fortune symbolized by the objects upon the sambō may come to the family, but also his reverence for the household gods. The black peas *(mame)* signify bodily strength and health, because a word similarly pronounced, though written with a different ideograph, means "robust." But why a lobster? Here we have another curious conception. The lobster's body is bent double: the body of the man who lives to a very great old age is also bent. Thus the lobster stands for a symbol of extreme old age; and in artistic design signifies the wish that our friends may live so long that they will become bent like lobsters—under the weight of years. And the dried chestnuts *(kachiguri)* are emblems of success, because the first character of their name in Japanese is the homonym of kachi, which means "victory," "conquest."

There are at least a hundred other singular customs and emblems belonging to the New Year's Festival which would require a large volume to describe. I have mentioned only a few which immediately appeal to even casual observation.

III.

The other festival I wish to refer to is that of the Setsubun, which, according the ancient Japanese calendar, corresponded with the beginning of the natural year—the period when winter first softens into spring. It is what we might term, according to Professor Chamberlain, "a sort of movable feast," and it is chiefly famous for the curious ceremony of the casting out of devils—Oni-yarai. On the eve of the Setsubun, a little after dark, the Yaku-otoshi, or caster-out of devils, wanders through the streets from house to house, rattling his shakujō,* and uttering his strange professional cry: "*Oni wa soto!—fuku wa uchi!*" [Devils out! Good-fortune in!] For a trifling fee he performs his little exorcism in any house to which he is called. This simply consists in the recitation of certain parts of a Buddhist kyō, or sutra, and the rattling of the shakujō. Afterwards dried peas *(shiro-mame)* are thrown about the house in four directions. For some mysterious reason, devils do not like dried peas—and flee therefrom. The peas thus scattered are afterward swept up and carefully preserved until the first clap of spring thunder is heard, when it is the custom to cook and eat some of them. But just why, I cannot find out; neither can I discover the origin of the dislike of devils for dried peas. On the subject of this dislike, however, I confess my sympathy with devils.

After the devils have been properly cast out, a small charm is placed above all the entrances of the dwelling to keep them from coming back again. This consists of a little stick about the length and thickness of a skewer, a single holly-leaf, and the head of a dried iwashi—a fish resembling a sardine. The stick is stuck through the middle of the hollyleaf; and the fish's head is fastened into a split made in one end of the stick; the other end being slipped into some joint of the timber-work immediately above a door. But why the devils are afraid of the holly-leaf and the fish's head, nobody seems to know. Among the people the origin of all these curious customs appears to be quite forgotten; and the families of the upper classes who still maintain such customs believe in the superstitions relating to the festival just as little as Englishmen today believe in the magical virtues of mistletoe or ivy.

---

* This is a curiously shaped staff with which the divinity Jizō is commonly represented. It is still carried by Buddhist mendicants, and there are several sizes of it. That carried by the Yaku-otoshi is usually very short. There is a tradition that the shakujo was first invented as a means of giving warning to insects or other little creatures in the path of the Buddhist pilgrim, so that they might not be trodden upon unawares.

This ancient and merry annual custom of casting out devils has been for generations a source of inspiration to Japanese artists. It is only after a fair acquaintance with popular customs and ideas that the foreigner can learn to appreciate the delicious humor of many art-creations which he may wish, indeed, to buy just because they are so oddly attractive in themselves, but which must really remain enigmas to him, so far as their inner meaning is concerned, unless he knows Japanese life. The other day a friend gave me a little card-case of perfumed leather. On one side was stamped in relief the face of a devil, through the orifice of whose yawning mouth could be seen—painted upon the silk lining of the interior—the laughing, chubby face of Otafuku, joyful Goddess of Good Luck. In itself the thing was very curious and pretty; but the real merit of its design was this comical symbolism of good wishes for the New Year: *"Oni wa soto!—fuku wa uehi!"*

IV.

Since I have spoken of the custom of eating some of the Setsubun peas at the time of the first spring thunder, I may here take the opportunity to say a few words about superstitions in regard to thunder which have not yet ceased to prevail among the peasantry.

When a thunder storm comes, the big brown mosquito curtains are suspended, and the women and children—perhaps the whole family—squat down under the curtains till the storm is over. From ancient days it has been believed that lightning cannot kill anybody under a mosquito curtain. The Raijū, or Thunder-Animal, cannot pass through a mosquito curtain. Only the other day, an old peasant who came to the house with vegetables to sell told us that he and his whole family, while crouching under their mosquito-netting during a thunder-storm, actually saw the Lightning rushing up and down the pillar of the balcony opposite their apartment—furiously clawing the woodwork, but unable to enter because of the mosquito-netting. His house had been badly damaged by a flash; but he supposed the mischief to have been accomplished by the Claws of the Thunder-Animal. The Thunder-Animal springs from tree to tree during a storm, they say; wherefore to stand under trees in time of thunder and lightning is very dangerous: the Thunder-Animal might step on one's head or shoulders.

The Thunder-Animal is also alleged to be fond of eating the human navel; for which reason people should be careful to keep their navels well covered during storms, and to lie down upon their stomachs if possible. Incense is always burned during storms, because the Thunder-Animal hates the smell of incense. A tree stricken by lightning is thought to have been torn and scarred by the claws of the Thunder-Animal; and fragments of its bark and wood are carefully collected and preserved by dwellers in the vicinity; for the wood of a blasted tree is alleged to have the singular virtue of curing toothache.

There are many stories of the Raijū having been caught and caged. Once, it is said, the Thunder-Animal fell into a well, and got entangled in the ropes and buckets, and so was captured alive. And old Izumo folk say they remember that the Thunder-Animal was once exhibited in the court of the Temple of Tenjin in Matsue, inclosed in a cage of brass; and that people paid one sen each to look at it. It resembled a badger. When the weather was clear it would sleep contentedly in its cage. But when there was thunder in the air, it would become excited, and seem to obtain great strength, and its eyes would flash dazzlingly.

V.

There is one very evil spirit, however, who is not in the least afraid of dried peas, and who cannot be so easily got rid of as the common devils; and that is Bimbogami.

But in Izumo people know a certain household charm whereby Bimbogami may sometimes be cast out.

Before any cooking is done in a Japanese kitchen, the little charcoal fire is first blown to a bright red heat with that most useful and simple household utensil called a hifukidake. The hifukidake ("fireblow-bamboo") is a bamboo tube usually about three feet long and about two inches in diameter. At one end—the end which is to be turned toward the fire—only a very small orifice is left; the woman who prepares the meal places the other end to her lips, and blows through the tube upon the kindled charcoal. Thus a quick fire may be obtained in a few minutes.

In course of time the hifukidake becomes scorched and cracked and useless. A new "fire-blow-tube" is then made; and the old one is used as a charm against Bimbogami. One little copper coin *(rin)* is put into it, some magical formula is uttered, and then the old utensil, with the rin inside of it, is either simply thrown out through the front gate into the street, or else flung into some neighboring stream. This—I know not why—is deemed equivalent to pitching Bimbogami out of doors, and rendering it impossible for him to return during a considerable period.

It may be asked how is the invisible presence of Bimbogami to be detected.

The little insect which makes that weird ticking noise at night called in England the *Death-watch* has a Japanese relative named by the people Bimbomushi, or the "Poverty-Insect." It is said to be the servant of Bimbogami, the God of Poverty; and its ticking in a house is believed to signal the presence of that most unwelcome deity.

VI.

One more feature of the Setsubun festival is worthy of mention—the sale of the hitogata ("people-shapes"). These are little figures, made of white paper, representing men, women, and children. They are cut out with a few clever scissors strokes; and the difference of sex is indicated by variations in the shape of the sleeves and the little paper obi. They are sold in the Shintō temples. The purchaser buys one for every member of the family—the priest writing upon each the age and sex of the person for whom it is intended. These hitogata are then taken home and distributed; and each person slightly rubs his body or her body with the paper, and says a little Shintō prayer. Next day the hitogata are returned to the kannushi, who, after having recited certain formulae over them, burns them with holy fire.* By this ceremony it is hoped that all physical misfortunes will be averted from the family during a year.

---

* I may make mention here of another matter, in no way relating to the Setsubun.

There lingers in Izumo a wholesome—and I doubt not formerly a most valuable—superstition about the sacredness of writing. Paper upon which anything has been written, or even printed, must not be crumpled up, or trodden upon, or dirtied, or put to any base use. If it be necessary to destroy a document, the paper should be burned. I have been gently reproached in a little hotel at which I stopped for tearing up and crumpling some paper covered with my own writing.

21

BY THE JAPANESE SEA

I.

IT is the fifteenth day of the seventh month—and I am in Hōki.

The blanched road winds along a coast of low cliffs—the coast of the Japanese Sea. Always on the left, over a narrow strip of stony land, or a heaping of dunes, its vast expanse appears, blue-wrinkling to that pale horizon beyond which Korea lies, under the same white sun. Sometimes, through sudden gaps in the cliff's verge, there flashes to us the running of the surf. Always upon the right another sea—a silent sea of green, reaching to far misty ranges of wooded hills, with huge pale peaks behind them—a vast level of rice-fields, over whose surface soundless waves keep chasing each other under the same great breath that moves the blue today from Chōsen to Japan.

Though during a week the sky has remained unclouded, the sea has for several days been growing angrier; and now the muttering of its surf sounds far into the land. They say that it always roughens thus during the period of the Festival of the Dead—the three days of the Bon, which, are the thirteenth, fourteenth, and fifteenth of the seventh month by the ancient calendar. And on the sixteenth day, after the shōryōbune, which are the Ships of Souls, have been launched, no one dares to enter it: no boats can then be hired; all the fishermen remain at home. For on that day the sea is the highway of the dead, who must pass back over its waters to their mysterious home; and therefore upon that day is it called Hotoke-umi—the Buddha-Flood—the Tide of the Returning Ghosts. And ever upon the night of that sixteenth day—whether the sea be calm or tumultnous—all its surface shimmers with faint lights gliding out to the open—the dim fires of the dead; and there is heard a murmuring of voices, like the murmur of a city far-off—the indistinguishable speech of souls.

II.

But it may happen that some vessel, belated in spite of desperate effort to reach port, may find herself far out at sea upon the night of the sixteenth day. Then will the dead rise tall about the ship, and reach long hands and murmur: *"Tago, tago o-kure!—tago o-kure!"** Never may they be refused; but, before the bucket is given, the bottom of it must be knocked out. Woe to all on board should an entire tago be suffered to fall even by accident into the sea!—for the dead would at once use it to fill and sink the ship.

Nor are the dead the only powers invisible dreaded in the time of the Hotoke-umi. Then are the Ma most powerful, and the Kappa.†

---

* "A bucket honorably condescend [to give]."

† The Kappa is not properly a sea goblin, but a river goblin, and haunts the sea only in the neighborhood of river months.

About a mile and a half from Matsue, at the little village of Kawachi-mura, on the river called Kawachi, stands a little temple called Kawako-no-miya, or the Miya of the Kappa. (In Izumo, among the common people, the word "Kappa "is not used, but the term *Kawako,* or "The Child of the River.") In this little shrine is preserved a document said to have been signed by a Kappa. The story goes that in ancient times, the Kappa dwelling in the Kawachi used to seize and destroy many of the inhabitants of the village and many domestic animals. One day, however, while trying to seize a horse that had entered the river to drink, the Kappa got its head twisted in some way under the belly-band of the horse, and the terrified animal, rushing out of the water, dragged the Kappa into a field. There the owner of the horse and a number of peasants seized and bound the Kappa. All the villagers gathered to see the monster, which bowed its head to the ground, and audibly begged for mercy. The peasants desired to kill the goblin at once; but the owner of the horse, who happened to be the head man of the mura, said: "It is better to make it swear never again to touch any person or animal belonging to Kawachi-mura." A written form of oath was prepared and read to the Kappa. It said that it could not write, but that it would sign the paper by dipping its hand in ink, and pressing the imprint thereof at the bottom of the document. This having been agreed

But in all times the swimmer fears the Kappa, the Ape of Waters, hideous and obscene, who reaches up from the deeps to draw men down, and to devour their entrails.

Only their entrails.

The corpse of him who has been seized by the Kappa may be cast on shore after many days. Unless long battered against the rocks by heavy surf, or nibbled by fishes, it will show no outward wound, but it will be light and hollow—empty like a long-dried gourd.

III.

Betimes, as we journey on, the monotony of undulating blue on the left, or the monotony of billowing green upon the right, is broken by the gray apparition of a cemetery—a cemetery so long that our jinrikisha men, at full run, take a full quarter of an hour to pass the huge congregation of its perpendicular stones. Such visions always indicate the approach of villages; but the villages prove to be as surprisingly small as the cemeteries are surprisingly large. By hundreds of thousands do the silent populations of the hakaba outnumber the folk of the hamlets to which they belong—tiny thatched settlements sprinkled along the leagues of coast, and sheltered from the wind only by ranks of somber pines. Legions on legions of stones—a host of sinister witnesses of the cost of the present to the past—and old, old, old!—hundreds so long in place that they have been worn into shapelessness merely by the blowing of sand from the dunes, and their inscriptions utterly effaced. It is as if one were passing through the burial-ground of all who ever lived on this wind-blown shore since the being of the land.

And in all these hakaba—for it is the Bon—there are new lanterns before the newer tombs—the white lanterns which are the lanterns of graves. Tonight the cemeteries will be all aglow with lights like the fires of a city for multitude. But there are also

---

to and done, the Kappa was set free. From that time forward no inhabitant or animal of Kawachi-mura was ever assaulted by the goblin.

unnumbered tombs before which no lanterns are—elder myriads, each the token of a family extinct, or of which the absent descendants have forgotten even the name. Dim generations whose ghosts have none to call them back, no local memories to love—so long ago obliterated were all things related to their lives.

IV.

Now many of these villages are only fishing settlements, and in them stand old thatched homes of men who sailed away on some eve of tempest, and never came back. Yet each drowned sailor has his tomb in the neighboring hakaba, and beneath it something of him has been buried.

What?

Among these people of the west something is always preserved which in other lands is cast away without a thought—the hozono-o, the flower-stalk of a life, the navel-string of the newly born. It is enwrapped carefully in many wrappings; and upon its outermost covering are written the names of the father, the mother, and the infant, together with the date and hour of birth—and it is kept in the family o-mamori-bukuro. The daughter, becoming a bride, bears it with her to her new home: for the son it is preserved by his parents. It is buried with the dead; and should one die in a foreign land, or perish at sea, it is entombed in lieu of the body.

V.

Concerning them that go down into the sea in ships, and stay there, strange beliefs prevail on this far coast—beliefs more primitive, assuredly, than the gentle faith which hangs white lanterns before the tombs. Some hold that the drowned never journey to the Meido. They quiver forever in the currents; they billow in the swaying of tides; they toil in the wake of the junks; they shout in the plunging of breakers. 'Tis their white hands that toss in the leap of the surf; their clutch that clatters the shingle, or seizes the swimmer's feet in the pull of the undertow.

And the seamen speak euphemistically of the O-baké, the honorable ghosts, and fear them with a great fear.

Wherefore cats are kept on board!

A cat, they aver, has power to keep the O-baké away. How or why, I have not yet found any to tell me. I know only that cats are deemed to have power over the dead. If a cat be left alone with a corpse, will not the corpse arise and dance? And of all cats a mike-neko, or cat of three colors, is most prized on this account by sailors. But if they cannot obtain one—and cats of three colors are rare—they will take another kind of cat; and nearly every trading junk has a cat; and when the junk comes into port, its cat may generally be seen—peeping through some little window in the vessel's side, or squatting in the opening where the great rudder works—that is, if the weather be fair and the sea still.

VI.

But these primitive and ghastly beliefs do not affect the beautiful practices of Buddhist faith in the time of the Bon; and from all these little villages the shōryōbune are launched upon the sixteenth day. They are much more elaborately and expensively constructed on this coast than in some other parts of Japan; for though made of straw only, woven over a skeleton framework, they are charming models of junks, complete in every detail. Some are between three and four feet long. On the white paper sail is written the kaimyō or soul-name of the dead. There is a small water-vessel on board, filled with fresh water, and an incense-cup; and along the gunwales flutter little paper banners bearing the mystic manji, which is the Sanscrit svastika.*

The form of the shōryōbune and the customs in regard to the time and manner of launching them differ much in different provinces. In most places they are launched for the family dead in general, wherever buried; and they are in some places launched only at night, with small lanterns on board. And I am told also

* The Buddhist symbol 卍.

that it is the custom at certain sea-villages to launch the lanterns all by themselves, in lieu of the shōryōbune proper—lanterns of a particular kind being manufactured for that purpose only.

But on the Izumo coast, and elsewhere along this western shore, the soul-boats are launched only for those who have been drowned at sea, and the launching takes place in the morning instead of at night. Once every year, for ten years after death, a shōryōbune is launched; in the eleventh year the ceremony ceases. Several shōryōbune which I saw at Inasa were really beautiful, and must have cost a rather large sum for poor fisher-folk to pay. But the ship-carpenter who made them said that all the relatives of a drowned man contribute to purchase the little vessel, year after year.

VII.

Near a sleepy little village called Kami-ichi I make a brief halt in order to visit a famous sacred tree. It is in a grove close to the public highway, but upon a low hill. Entering the grove I find myself in a sort of miniature glen surrounded on three sides by very low cliffs, above which enormous pines are growing, incalculably old. Their vast coiling roots have forced their way through the face of the cliffs, splitting rocks; and their mingling crests make a green twilight in the hollow. One pushes out three huge roots of a very singular shape; and the ends of these have been wrapped about with long white papers bearing written prayers, and with offerings of seaweed. The shape of these roots, rather than any tradition, would seem to have made the tree sacred in popular belief: it is the object of a special cult; and a little torii has been erected before it, bearing a votive annunciation of the most artless and curious kind. I cannot venture to offer a translation of it—though for the anthropologist and folklorist it certainly possesses peculiar interest. The worship of the tree, or at least of the Kami supposed to dwell therein, is one rare survival of a phallic cult probably common to most primitive races, and formerly widespread in Japan. Indeed it was suppressed by the government scarcely more than a generation ago. On the opposite side of the little hollow, carefully posed upon a great loose rock, I see something equally artless and almost equally curious—a ki-tōja-no-mono, or ex-voto. Two straw figures joined together and reclining side by side: a straw man and a straw woman. The workmanship is childishly clumsy; but still the woman can be distinguished from the man by the ingenious attempt to imitate the female coiffure with a straw wisp. And as the man is represented with a queue—now worn only by aged survivors of the feudal era—I suspect that this kitōja-no-mono was made after some ancient and strictly conventional model.

Now this queer ex-voto tells its own story. Two who loved each other were separated by the fault of the man; the charm, of some jorō, perhaps, having been the temptation to faithlessness. Then the wronged one came here and prayed the Kami to dispel the delusion of passion and touch the erring heart. The prayer has been heard; the pair have been reunited; and she has therefore made these two quaint effigies with her own hands, and brought them to the Kami of the pine—tokens of her innocent faith and her grateful heart.

VIII.

Night falls as we reach the pretty hamlet of Hamamura, our last resting-place by the aea, for tomorrow our way lies inland. The inn at which we lodge is very small, but very clean and cosy; and there is a delightful bath of natural hot water; for the yadoya is situated close to a natural spring. This spring, so strangely close to the sea beach, also furnishes, I am told, the baths of all the houses in the village.

The best room is placed at our disposal; but I linger awhile to examine a very fine shōryōbune, waiting, upon a bench near the street entrance, to be launched tomorrow. It seems to have been finished but a short time ago; for fresh clippings of straw lie scattered around it, and the kaimyō has not yet been written upon its sail. I am surprised to hear that it belongs to a poor widow and her son, both of whom are employed by the hotel.

I was hoping to see the Bon-odori at Hamamura, but I am disappointed. At all the villages the police have prohibited the dance. Fear of cholera has resulted in stringent sanitary regulations. In Hamamura the people have been ordered to use no water for drinking, cooking, or washing except the hot water of their own volcanic springs.

A little middle-aged woman, with a remarkably sweet voice, comes to wait upon us at supper-time. Her teeth are blackened and her eyebrows shaved after the fashion of married women twenty years ago; nevertheless her face is still a pleasant one, and in her youth she must have been uncommonly pretty. Though acting as a servant, it appears that she is related to the family owning the inn, and that she is treated with the consideration due to kindred. She tells us that the shōryōbune is to be launched for her husband and brother—both fishermen of the village, who perished in sight of their own home eight years ago. The priest of the neighboring Zen temple is to come in the morning to write the kaimyo upon the sail, as none of the household are skilled in writing the Chinese characters.

I make her the customary little gift, and, through my attendant, ask her various questions about her history. She was married to a man much older than herself, with whom she lived very happily; and her brother, a youth of eighteen, dwelt with them. They had a good boat and a little piece of ground, and she was skillful at the loom; so they managed to live well. In summer the fishermen fish at night: when all the fleet is out, it is pretty to see the line of torch-fires in the offing, two or three miles away, like a string of stars. They do not go out when the weather is threatening; but in certain months the great storms (taifu) come so quickly that the boats are overtaken almost before they have time to hoist sail. Still as a temple pond the sea was on the night when her husband and brother last sailed away; the taifu rose before daybreak. What followed, she relates with a simple pathos that I cannot reproduce in our less artless tongue.

"All the boats had come back except my husband's; for my husband and my brother had gone out farther than the others, so they were not able to return as quickly. And all the people were looking and waiting. And every minute the waves seemed to be growing higher and the wind more terrible; and the other boats had to be dragged far up on the shore to save them. Then suddenly we saw my husband's boat coming very, very quickly. We were so glad! It came quite near, so that I could see the face of my husband and the face of my brother. But suddenly a great wave struck it upon one side, and it turned down into the water, and it did not come up again. And then we saw my husband and my brother swimming; but we could see them only when the waves lifted them up. Tall like hills the waves were, and the head of my husband, and the head of my brother would go up, up, up, and then down, and each time they rose to the top of a wave so that we could see them they would cry out, 'Tasukete! tamkete!'* But the strong men were afraid; the sea was too terrible; I was only a woman! Then my brother could not be seen any more. My husband was old, but very strong; and he swam a long time—so near that I could see his face was like the face of one in fear—and he called 'Tasukete!' But none could help him; and he also went down at last. And yet I could see his face before he went down.

"And for a long time after, every night, I used to see his face as I saw it then, so that I could not rest, but only weep. And I prayed and prayed to the Buddhas and to the Kami-Sama that I might not dream that dream. Now it never comes; but I can still see his face, even while I speak...In that time my son was only a little child."

Not without sobs can she conclude her simple recital. Then, suddenly bowing her head to the matting, and wiping away her

---

* "Help! help!"

tears with her sleeve, she humbly prays our pardon for this little exhibition of emotion, and laughs—the soft low laugh *de rigueur* of Japanese politeness. This, I must confess, touches me still more than the story itself. At a fitting moment my Japanese attendant delicately changes the theme, and begins a light chat about our journey, and the danna-sama's interest in the old customs and legends of the coast. And he succeeds in amusing her by some relation of our wanderings in Izumo.

She asks whither we are going. My attendant answers probably as far as Tottori.

"Aa! Tottori! So degozarimasu ka? Now, there is an old story—the Story of the Futon of Tottori. But the danna-sama knows that story?"

Indeed, the danna-sama does not, and begs earnestly to hear it. And the story is set down, somewhat as I learn it through the lips of my interpreter.

IX.

Many years ago, a very small yadoya in Tottori town received its first guest, an itinerant merchant. He was received with more than common kindness, for the landlord desired to make a good name for his little inn. It was a new inn, but as its owner was poor, most of its dōgu—furniture and utensils—had been purchased from the furuteya.* Nevertheless, everything was clean, comforting, and pretty. The guest ate heartily and drank plenty of good warm saké; after which his bed was prepared on the soft floor, and he laid himself down to sleep.

[But here I must interrupt the story for a few moments, to say a word about Japanese beds. Never unless some inmate happen to be sick, do you see a bed in any Japanese house by day, though you visit all the rooms and peep into all the corners. In fact, no bed exists, in the Occidental meaning of the word. That which the Japanese call bed has no bedstead, no spring,

---

* *Furuteya*, the establishment of a dealer in second-hand wares—*furute*.

no mattress, no sheets, no blankets. It consists of thick quilts only, stuffed, or, rather, padded with cotton, which are called futon. A certain number of futon are laid down upon the tatami (the floor mats), and a certain number of others are used for coverings. The wealthy can lie upon five or six quilts, and cover themselves with as many as they please, while poor folk must content themselves with two or three. And of course there are many kinds, from the servant's cotton futon which is no larger than a Western hearth rug, and not much thicker, to the heavy and superb futon silk, eight feet long by seven broad, which only the kanemochi can afford. Besides these there is the yogi, a massive quilt made with wide sleeves like a kimono, in which you can find much comfort when the weather is extremely cold. All such things are neatly folded up and stowed out of sight by day in alcoves contrived in the wall and closed with fusuma-pretty sliding screen doors covered with opaque paper usually decorated with dainty designs. There also are kept those curious wooden pillows, invented to preserve the Japanese coiffure from becoming disarranged during sleep.

The pillow has a certain sacredness; but the origin and the precise nature of the beliefs concerning it I have not been able to learn. Only this I know, that to touch it with the foot is considered very wrong; and that if it be kicked or moved thus, even by accident, the clumsiness must be atoned for by lifting the pillow to the forehead with the hands, and replacing it in its original position respectfully, with the word "go-men," signifying, I pray to be excused.]

Now, as a rule, one sleeps soundly after having drunk plenty of warm saké, especially if the night be cool and the bed very snug. But the guest, having slept but a very little while, was aroused by the sound of voices in his room—voices of children, always asking each other the same questions:

"Ani-San samukarō?"

"Omae samukarō?"

The presence of children in his room might annoy the guest, but could not surprise him, for in these Japanese hotels there are no doors, but only papered sliding screens between room and room. So it seemed to him that some children must have wandered into his apartment, by mistake, in the dark. He uttered some gentle rebuke. For a moment only there was silence; then a sweet, thin, plaintive voice queried, close to his ear, "Ani-San samukarō?" [Elder Brother probably is cold?], and another sweet voice made answer caressingly, "Omae samukarō?" [Nay, thou probably art cold?]

He arose and rekindled the candle in the andon,* and looked about the room. There was no one. The shōji were all closed. He examined the cupboards; they were empty. Wondering, he lay down again, leaving the light still burning; and immediately the voices spoke again, complainingly, close to his pillow;

"Ani-San samukarō?"

"Omae samukarō?"

Then, for the first time, he felt a chill creep over him, which was not the chill of the night. Again and again he heard, and each time he became more afraid. For he knew that the voices were *in the futon!* It was the covering of the bed that cried out thus.

He gathered hurriedly together the few articles belonging to him, and, descending the stairs, aroused the landlord and told what had passed. Then the host, much angered, made reply: "That to make pleased the honorable guest everything has been done, the truth is; but the honorable guest too much august saké having drank, bad dreams has seen." Nevertheless the guest insisted upon paying at once that which he owed, and seeking lodging elsewhere.

Next evening there came another guest who asked for a room for the night. At a late hour the landlord was aroused by his lodger with the same story. And this lodger, strange to say, had not taken

---

* *Andon*, a paper lantern of peculiar construction, used as a night light. Some forms of the andon are remarkably beautiful.

any saké. Suspecting some envious plot to ruin his business, the landlord answered passionately: "Thee to please all things honorably have been done: nevertheless, ill-omened and vexatious words thou utterest, And that my inn my means-of-livelihood is—that also thou knowest. Wherefore that such things be spoken, right-there-is-none!" Then the guest, getting into a passion, loudly said things much more evil; and the two parted in hot anger.

But after the guest was gone, the landlord, thinking all this very strange, ascended to the empty room to examine the futon. And while there, he heard the voices, and he discovered that the guests had said only the truth. It was one covering—only one—which cried out. The rest were silent. He took the covering into his own room, and for the remainder of the night lay down beneath it. And the voices continued until the hour of dawn: "Ani-San samukarō?" "Omae samukarō?" So that he could not sleep.

But at break of day he rose up and went out to find the owner of the furuteya at which the futon had been purchased. The dealer knew nothing. He had bought the futon from a smaller shop, and the keeper of that shop had purchased it from a still poorer dealer dwelling in the farthest suburb of the city. And the innkeeper went from one to the other, asking questions.

Then at last it was found that the futon had belonged to a poor family, and had been bought from the landlord of a little house in which the family had lived, in the neighborhood of the town. And the story of the futon was this:

The rent of the little house was only sixty sen a month, but even this was a great deal for the poor folks to pay. The father could earn only two or three yen a month, and the mother was ill and could not work; and there were two children—a boy of six years and a boy of eight. And they were strangers in Tottori.

One winter's day the father sickened; and after a week of suffering he died, and was buried. Then the long-sick mother followed him, and the children were left alone. They knew no one whom they could ask for aid; and in order to live they began to sell what there was to sell.

That was not much: the clothes of the dead father and mother, and most of their own; some quilts of cotton, and a few poor houshold utensils—hibachi, bowls, cups, and other trifles. Every day they sold something, until there was nothing left but one futon. And a day came when they had nothing to eat; and the rent was not paid.

The terrible Dai-kan had arrived, the season of greatest cold; and the snow had drifted too high that day for them to wander far from the little house. So they could only lie down under their one futon, and shiver together, and compassionate each other in their own childish way—

"Ani-San, samukarō?"

"Omae samukarō?"

They had no fire, nor anything with which to make fire; and the darkness came; and the icy wind screamed into the little house.

They were afraid of the wind, but they were more afraid of the house-owner, who roused them roughly to demand his rent. He was a hard man, with an evil face. And finding there was none to pay him, he turned the children into the snow, and took their one futon away from them, and locked up the house.

They had but one thin blue kimono each, for all their other clothes had been sold to buy food; and they had nowhere to go. There was a temple of Kwannon not far away, but the snow was too high for them to reach it. So when the landlord was gone, they crept back behind the house. There the drowsiness of cold fell upon them, and they slept, embracing each other to keep warm. And while they slept, the gods covered them with a new futon—ghostly-white and very beautiful. And they did not feel cold any more. For many days they slept there; then somebody found them, and a bed was made for them in the hakaba of the Temple of Kwannon-of-the-Thousand-Arms.

And the innkeeper, having heard these things, gave the futon to the priests of the temple, and caused the kyō to be recited for the little souls. And the futon ceased thereafter to speak.

X.

One legend recalls another; and I hear tonight many strange ones. The most remarkable is a tale which my attendant suddenly remembers—a legend of Izumo.

Once there lived in the Izumo village called Mochida-no-ura a peasant who was so poor that he was afraid to have children. And each time that his wife bore him a child he cast it into the river, and pretended that it had been born dead. Sometimes it was a son, sometimes a daughter; but always the infant was thrown into the river at night. Six were murdered thus.

But, as the years passed, the peasant found himself more prosperous. He had been able to purchase land and to lay by money. And at last his wife bore him a seventh child—a boy.

Then the man said: "Now we can support a child, and we shall need a son to aid us when we are old. And this boy is beautiful. So we will bring him up."

And the infant thrived; and each day the hard peasant wondered more at his own heart—for each day he knew that he loved his son more.

One summer's night he walked out into his garden, carrying his child in his arms. The little one was five months old.

And the night was so beautiful, with its great moon, that the peasant cried out—

"*Aa! kon ya medzurashii e yo da!*" [Ah! tonight truly a wondrously beautiful night is!]

Then the infant, looking up into his face and speaking the speech of a man, said—

"Why, father! *the* LAST *time you threw me away* the night was just like this, and the moon looked just the same, did it not?"*

And thereafter the child remained as other children of the same age, and spoke no word.

---

* "*Ototsan! washi wo shimai ni shitesashita toki mo, chōdo kon ya no yona tsuki yo data-ne?*"—Izumo dialect.

The peasant became a monk.

XI.

After the supper and the bath, feeling too warm to sleep, I wander out alone to visit the village hakaba, a long cemetery upon a sandhill, or rather a prodigious dune, thinly covered at its summit with soil, but revealing through its crumbling flanks the story of its creation by ancient tides, mightier than tides of today.

I wade to my knees in sand to reach the cemetery. It is a warm moonlight night, with a great breeze. There are many bon-lanterns (*bondōrō*), but the seawind has blown out most of them; only a few here and there still shed a soft white glow—pretty shrine-shaped cases of wood, with apertures of symbolic outline, covered with white paper. Visitors beside myself there are none, for it is late. But much gentle work has been done here today, for all the bamboo vases have been furnished with fresh flowers or sprays, and the water basins filled with fresh water, and the monuments cleansed and beautified. And in the farthest nook of the cemetery I find, before one very humble tomb, a pretty zen or lacquered dining tray, covered with dishes and bowls containing a perfect dainty little Japanese repast. There is also a pair of new chopsticks, and a little cup of tea, and some of the dishes are still warm. A loving woman's work; the prints of her little sandals are fresh upon the path.

XII.

There is an Irish folk-saying that any dream may be remembered if the dreamer, after awakening, forbear to scratch his head in the effort to recall it. But should he forget this precaution, never can the dream be brought back to memory: as well try to reform the curlings of a smoke-wreath blown away.

Nine hundred and ninety-nine of a thousand dreams are indeed hopelessly evaporative. But certain rare dreams, which come when fancy has been strangely impressed by unfamiliar experiences—dreams particularly apt to occur in time of travel—remain in recollection, imaged with all the vividness of real events.

Of such was the dream I dreamed at Hamamura, after having seen and heard those things previously written down.

Some pale broad paved place—perhaps the thought of a temple court—tinted by a faint sun; and before me a woman, neither young nor old, seated at the base of a great gray pedestal that supported I know not what, for I could look only at the woman's face. Awhile I thought that I remembered her—a woman of Izumo; then she seemed a weirdness. Her lips were moving, but her eyes remained closed, and I could not choose but look at her.

And in a voice that seemed to come thin through distance of years she began a soft wailing chant; and, as I listened, vague memories came to me of a Celtic lullaby. And as she sang, she loosed with one hand her long black hair, till it fell coiling upon the stones. And, having fallen, it was no longer black, but blue—pale day-blue—and was moving sinuously, crawling with swift blue ripplings to and fro. And then, suddenly, I became aware that the ripplings were far, very far away, and that the woman was gone. There was only the sea, blue, billowing to the verge of heaven, with long slow flashings of soundless surf.

And wakening, I heard in the night the muttering of the real sea—the vast husky speech of the Hotoke-Umi—*the Tide of the Returning Ghosts.*

22

OF A DANCING-GIRL

NOTHING is more silent than the beginning of a Japanese banquet; and no one, except a native, who observes the opening scene could possibly imagine the tumultuous ending.

The robed guests take their places, quite noiselessly and without speech, upon the kneeling-cushions. The lacquered services are laid upon the matting before them by maidens whose bare feet make no sound. For a while there is only smiling and flitting, as in dreams. You are not likely to hear any voices from without, as a banqueting-house is usually secluded from the street by spacious gardens. At last the master of ceremonies, host or provider, breaks the hush with the consecrated formula: "*O-somatsu degozarimasu ga!—dōzo o-hashi!*" whereat all present bow silently, take up their hashi (chopsticks), and fall to. But hashi, deftly used, cannot be heard at all. The maidens pour warm saké into the cup of each guest without making the least sound; and it is not until several dishes have been emptied, and several cups of saké absorbed, that tongues are loosened.

Then, all at once, with a little burst of laughter, a number of young girls enter, make the customary prostration of greeting, glide into the open space between the ranks of the guests, and begin to serve the wine with a grace and dexterity of which no common maid is capable. They are pretty; they are clad in very costly robes of silk; they are girdled like queens; and the beautifully dressed hair of each is decked with mock flowers, with wonderful combs and pins, and with curious ornaments of gold. They greet the stranger as if they had always known him; they jest, laugh, and utter funny little cries. These are the geisha,* or dancing-girls, hired for the banquet.

Samisen† tinkle. The dancers withdraw to a clear space at the farther end of the banqueting-hall, always vast enough to admit of many more guests than ever assemble upon common occasions. Some form the orchestra, under the direction of a woman of uncertain age; there are several samisen, and a tiny drum played by a child. Others, singly or in pairs, perform the dance. It may be swift and merry, consisting wholly of graceful posturing—two girls dancing together with such coincidence of step and gesture as only years of training could render possible. But more frequently it is rather like acting than like what we Occidentals call dancing—acting accompanied with extraordinary waving of sleeves and fans, and with a play of eyes and features, sweet, subtle, subdued, wholly Oriental. There are more voluptuous dances known to geisha, but upon ordinary occasions and before refined audiences they portray beautiful old Japanese traditions, like the legend of the fisher Urashima, beloved by the Sea God's daughter; and at intervals they sing ancient Chinese poems, expressing a natural emotion with delicious vividness by a few exquisite words. And always they pour the wine—that warm, pale yellow, drowsy wine which fills the veins with soft contentment, making a faint sense of ecstasy, through which, as through some poppied sleep, the commonplace becomes wondrous and blissful, and the geisha Maids of Paradise, and the world much sweeter than, in the natural order of things, it could ever possibly be.

The banquet, at first so silent, slowly changes to a merry tumult. The company break ranks, form groups; and from group to group the girls pass, laughing, prattling—still pouring saké

* The Kyōto word is *maiko*.
† Guitars of three strings.

into the cups which are being exchanged and emptied with low bows.* Men begin to sing old samurai songs, old Chinese poems. One or two even dance. A geisha tucks her robe well up to her knees; and the samisen strike up the quick melody, "*Kompira funé-funé.*" As the music plays, she begins to run lightly and swiftly in a figure of 8, and a young man, carrying a saké bottle and cup, also runs in the same figure of 8. If the two meet on a line, the one through whose error the meeting happens must drink a cup of saké. The music becomes quicker and quicker and the runners run faster and faster, for they must keep time to the melody; and the geisha wins. In another part of the room, guests and geisha are playing ken. They sing as they play, facing each other, and clap their hands, and fling out their fingers at intervals with little cries; and the samisen keep time.

> *Choito—don-don!*
> *Otagaidané;*
> *Choito—don-don!*
> *Oidemashitané;*
> *Choito—don-don!*
> *Shimaimashitané.*

Now, to play ken with a geisha requires a perfectly cool head, a quick eye, and much practice. Having been trained from childhood to play all kinds of ken—and there are many—she generally loses only for politeness, when she loses at all. The signs of the most common ken are a Man, a Fox, and a Gun. If the geisha make the sign of the Gun, you must instantly, and in exact time to the music, make the sign of the Fox, who cannot use the Gun. For if you make the sign of the Man, then she will answer with the sign of the Fox, who can deceive the Man, and you lose. And if she make the sign of the Fox first; then you should make the sign of the Gun, by which the Fox can be killed. But all the while you must watch her bright eyes and supple hands. These are pretty;

---

* It is sometimes customary for guests to exchange cups, after duly rinsing them. It is always a compliment to ask for your friend's cup.

and if you suffer yourself, just for one fraction of a second, to think how pretty they are, you are bewitched and vanquished.

Notwithstanding all this apparent comradeship, a certain rigid decorum between guest and geisha is invariably preserved at a Japanese banquet. However flushed with wine a guest may have become; you will never see him attempt to caress a girl; he never forgets that she appears at the festivities only as a human flower, to be looked at, not to be touched. The familiarity which foreign tourists in Japan freqnently permit themselves with geisha or with waitergirls, though endured with smiling patience, is really much disliked, and considered by native observers an evidence of extreme vulgarity.

For a time the merriment grows; but as midnight draws near, the guests begin to slip away, one by one, unnoticed. Then the din gradually dies down, the music stops; and at last the geisha, having escorted the latest of the feasters to the door, with laughing cries of *Sayōnara,* can sit down alone to break their long fast in the deserted hall.

Such is the geisha's role. But what is the mystery of her? What are her thoughts, her emotions, her secret self? What is her veritable existence beyond the night circle of the banquet lights, far from the illusion formed around her by the mist of wine? Is she always as mischievous as she seems while her voice ripples out with mocking sweetness the words of the ancient song?

> *Kimi to neyaru ka, go sengoku toruka?*
> *Nanno gosengoku kimi to neyo?**

Or might we think her capable of keeping that passionate promise she utters so deliciously?

---

* "Once more to rest beside her, or keep five thousand koku?
What care I for koku? Let me be with her!"

There lived in ancient times a hatamoto called Fuji-eda Geki, a vassal of the Shōgun. He had an income of five thousand koku of rice, a great income in those days. But he fell in love with an inmate of the Yoshiwara, named Ayaginu, and wished to marry her. When his master bade the vassal choose between his fortune and his passion, the lovers fled secretly to a farmer's house, and there committed suicide together. And the above song was made about them. It is still sung.

Omae shindara tera ewa yaranu!
*Yaete konishite sake de nomu.**

"Why, as for that," a friend tells me, "there was O-Kama of Ōsaka who realized the song only last year. For she, having collected from the funeral pile the ashes of her lover, mingled them with saké, and at a banquet drank them, in the presence of many guests." In the presence of many guests! Alas for romance!

Always in the dwelling which a band of geisha occupy there is a strange image placed in the alcove; sometimes it is of clay, rarely of gold, most commonly of porcelain. It is reverenced: offerings are made to it, sweetmeats and rice bread and wine; incense smolders in front of it, and a lamp is burned before it. It is the image of a kitten erect, one paw outstretched as if inviting—whence its name, "the Beckoning Kitten."† It is the *genius loci:* it brings good-fortune, the patronage of the rich, the favor of banquet-givers. Now, they who know the soul of the geisha aver that the semblance of the image is the semblance of herself—playful and pretty, soft and young, lithe and caressing, and cruel as a devouring fire.

Worse, also, than this they have said of her: that in her shadow treads the God of Poverty, and that the Fox-women are her sisters; that she is the rain of youth, the waster of fortunes, the destroyer of families; that she knows love only as the source of the follies which are her gain, and grows rich upon the substance of men whose graves she has made; that she is the most consummate of pretty hypocrites, the most dangerous of schemers, the most insatiable of mercenaries, the most pitiless of mistresses. This cannot all be true. Yet thus much is true—that, like the kitten, the geisha is by profession a creature of prey. There are many really lovable kittens. Even so there must be really delightful dancing-girls.

---

　　　* "Dear, shouldst thou die, grave shall hold thee never!
　　　　I thy body's ashes, mixed with wine, will drink."
† Maneki-Neko.

The geisha is only what she has been made in answer to foolish human desire for the illusion of love mixed with youth and grace, but without regrets or responsibilities: wherefore she has been taught, besides ken, to play at hearts. Now, the eternal law is that people may play with impunity at any game in this unhappy world except three, which are called Life, Love, and Death. Those the gods have reserved to themselves, because nobody else can learn to play them without doing mischief. Therefore, to play with a geisha any game much more serious than ken, or at least *go,* is displeasing to the gods.

The girl begins her career as a slave, a pretty child bought from miserably poor parents under a contract, according to which her services may be claimed by the purchasers for eighteen, twenty, or even twenty-five years. She is fed, clothed, and trained in a house occupied only by geisha; and she passes the rest of her childhood under severe discipline. She is taught etiquette, grace, polite speech; she has daily lessons in dancing; and she is obliged to learn by heart a multitude of songs with their airs. Also she must learn games, the service of banquets and weddings, the art of dressing and looking beautiful. Whatever physical gifts she may have are carefully cultivated. Afterwards she is taught to handle musical instruments: first, the little drum (*tsudzumi),* which cannot be sounded at all without considerable practice; then she learns to play the samisen a little, with a plectrum of tortoise-shell or ivory. At eight or nine years of age she attends banquets, chiefly as a drum-player. She is then the most charming little creature imaginable, and already knows how to fill your wine-cup exactly full, with a single toss of the bottle and without spilling a drop, between two taps of her drum.

Thereafter her discipline becomes more cruel. Her voice may be flexible enough, but lacks the requisite strength. In the iciest hours of winter nights, she must ascend to the roof of her dwelling-house, and there sing and play till the blood oozes from her fingers and the voice dies in her throat. The desired result is an atrocious cold. After a period of hoarse whispering, her voice changes its tone and strengthens. She is ready to become a public singer and dancer.

In this capacity she usually makes her first appearance at the age of twelve or thirteen. If pretty and skillful, her services will be much in demand, and her time paid for at the rate of twenty to twenty-five sen per hour. Then only do her purchasers begin to reimburse themselves for the time, expense, and trouble of her training; and they are not apt to be generous. For many years more all that she earns must pass into their hands. She can own nothing, not even her clothes.

At seventeen or eighteen she has made her artistic reputation. She has been at many hundreds of entertainments, and knows by sight all the important personages of her city, the character of each, the history of all. Her life has been chiefly a night life; rarely has she seen the sun rise since she became a dancer. She has learned to drink wine without ever losing her head, and to fast for seven or eight hours without ever feeling the worse. She has had many lovers. To a certain extent she is free to smile upon whom she pleases; but she has been well taught, above all else, to use her power of charm for her own advantage. She hopes to find somebody able and willing to buy her freedom—which somebody would almost certainly thereafter discover many new and excellent meanings in those Buddhist texts that tell about the foolishness of love and the impermanency of all human relationships.

At this point of her career we may leave the geisha: thereafter her story is apt to prove unpleasant, unless she die young. Should that happen, she will have the obsequies of her class, and her memory will be preserved by divers curious rites.

Some time, perhaps, while wandering through Japanese streets at night, you hear sounds of music, a tinkling of samisen floating through the great gateway of a Buddhist temple, together with shrill voices of singing-girls; which may seem to you a strange happening. And the deep court is thronged with people looking and listening. Then, making your way through the press to the temple steps, you see two geisha seated upon the matting within, playing and singing, and a third dancing before a little table. Upon the table is an ihai, or mortuary tablet; in front of the tablet burns a little lamp, and incense in a cup of bronze; a small repast has been placed there, fruits and dainties—such a repast as, upon festival occasions, it is the custom to offer to the dead. You learn that the kaimyō upon the tablet is that of a geisha; and that the comrades of the dead girl assemble in the temple on certain days to gladden her spirit with songs and dances. Then whosoever pleases may attend the ceremony free of charge.

But the dancing-girls of ancient times were not as the geisha of today. Some of them were called shirabyōshi; and their hearts were not extremely hard. They were beautiful; they wore queerly shaped caps bedecked with gold; they were clad in splendid attire, and danced with swords in the dwellings of princes. And there is an old story about one of them which I think it worth while to tell.

I.

It was formerly, and indeed still is, a custom with young Japanese artists to travel on foot through various parts of the empire, in order to see and sketch the most celebrated scenery as well as to study famous art objects preserved in Buddhist temples, many of which occupy sites of extraordinary picturesqueness. It is to such wanderings, chiefly, that we owe the existence of those beautiful books of landscape views and life studies which are now so curious and rare, and which teach better than aught else that only the Japanese can paint Japanese scenery. After you have become acquainted with their methods of interpreting their own nature, foreign attempts in the same line will seem to you strangely flat and soulless. The foreign artist will give you realistic reflections of what he sees; but he will give you nothing more. The Japanese artist gives you that which he feels—the mood of a season, the precise sensation of an hour and place; his work is qualified by a power of suggestiveness rarely found in the art of the West. The Occidental painter renders minute detail; he satisfies the imagination he evokes. But his Oriental brother either suppresses or idealizes detail—steeps his distances in mist, bands his landscapes with cloud, makes of his experience a memory in which only the strange and the beautiful survive, with their sensations. He surpasses imagination, excites it, leaves it hungry with the hunger of charm perceived in glimpses only. Nevertheless, in such glimpses he is able to convey the feeling of a time, the character of a place, after a fashion that seems magical. He is a painter of recollections and of sensations rather than of clear-cut realities; and in this lies the secret of his amazing power—a power not to be appreciated by those who have never witnessed the scenes of his inspiration. He is above all things impersonal. His human figures are devoid of all individuality; yet they have inimitable merit as types embodying the characteristics of a class: the childish curiosity of the peasant, the shyness of the maiden, the fascination of the joro, the self-consciousness of the samurai, the funny, placid prettiness of the child, the resigned gentleness of age. Travel and observation were the influences which developed this art; it was never a growth of studios.

A great many years ago, a young art student was traveling on foot from Kyoto to Yedo, over the mountains. The roads then were few and bad, and travel was so difficult compared to what it is now that a proverb was current, *Kawai ko wa tabi wo sasé* (A pet child should be made to travel). But the land was what it is today. There were the same forests of cedar and of pine, the same groves of bamboo, the same peaked villages with roofs of thatch, the same terraced rice-fields dotted with the great yellow straw hats of peasants bending in the slime. From the wayside, the same statues of Jizō smiled upon the same pilgrim figures passing to the same temples; and then, as now, of summer days, one might see naked brown children laughing in all the shallow rivers, and all the rivers laughing to the sun. The young art student, however, was no *kawai ko:* he had already traveled a great deal, was inured to hard fare and rough lodging, and accustomed to make the best of every situation. But upon this journey he found himself, one evening after sunset, in a region where it seemed possible to obtain neither fare nor lodging of any sort— out of sight of cultivated land. While attempting a short cut over a range to reach some village, he had lost his way.

There was no moon, and pine shadows made blackness all around him. The district into which he had wandered seemed utterly wild; there were no sounds but the humming of the wind in the pine-needles; and an infinite tinkling of bell-insects. He stumbled on, hoping to gain some river bank, which he could follow to a settlement. At last a stream abruptly crossed his way; but it proved to be a swift torrent pouring into a gorge between precipices. Obliged to retrace his steps, he resolved to climb to the nearest summit, whence he might be able to discern some sign of human life; but on reaching it he could see about him only a heaping of hills.

He had almost resigned himself to passing the night under the stars, when he perceived, at some distance down the farther slope of the hill he had ascended, a single thin yellow ray of light, evidently issuing from some dwelling. He made his way towards it, and soon discerned a small cottage, apparently a peasant's home. The light he had seen still streamed from it, through a chink in the closed storm-doors. He hastened forward, and knocked at the entrance.

II.

Not until he had knocked and called several times did he hear any stir within; then a woman's voice asked what was wanted. The voice was remarkably sweet, and the speech of the unseen questioner surprised him, for she spoke in the cultivated idiom of the capital. He responded that he was a student, who had lost his way in the mountains; that he wished, if possible, to obtain food and lodging for the night; and that if this could not be given, he would feel very grateful for information how to reach the nearest village—adding that he had means enough to pay for the services of a guide. The voice, in return, asked several other questions, indicating extreme surprise that any one could have reached the dwelling from the direction he had taken. But his answers evidently allayed suspicion, for the inmate exclaimed: "I will come in a moment. It would be difficult for you to reach any village tonight; and the path is dangerous."

After a brief delay the storm-doors were pushed open, and a woman appeared with a paper lantern, which she so held as to illuminate the stranger's face, while her own remained in shadow. She scrutinized him in silence, then said briefly, "Wait; I will bring water." She fetched a wash basin, set it upon the doorstep, and offered the guest a towel. He removed his sandals, washed from his feet the dust of travel, and was shown into a neat room which appeared to occupy the whole interior, except a small boarded space at the rear, used as a kitchen. A cotton zabuton was laid for him to kneel upon, and a brazier set before him.

It was only then that he had a good opportunity of observing his hostess, and he was startled by the delicacy and beauty of her features. She might have been three or four years older than he, but was still in the bloom of youth. Certainly she was not a peasant girl. In the same singularly sweet voice she said to him: "I am now alone, and I never receive guests here. But I am sure it would be dangerous for you to travel farther tonight. There are some peasants in the neighborhood, but you cannot find your way to them in the dark without a guide. So I can let you stay here until morning. You will not be comfortable, but I can give you a bed. And I suppose you are hungry. There is only some shōjin-ryōri*—not at all good, but you are welcome to it."

---

* Buddhist food, containing no animal substance. Some kinds of shōjin-ryōri are quite appetizing.

The traveler was quite hungry, and only too glad of the offer. The young woman kindled a little fire, prepared a few dishes in silence—stewed leaves of na, some aburagé, some kampyō, and a bowl of coarse rice—and quickly set the meal before him, apologizing for its quality. But during his repast she spoke scarcely at all, and her reserved manner embarrassed him. As she answered the few questions he ventured upon merely by a bow or by a solitary word, he soon refrained from attempting to press the conversation.

Meanwhile, he had observed that the small house was spotlessly clean, and the utensils in which his food was served were immaculate. The few cheap objects in the apartment were pretty. The fusuina of the oshiire and zendana* were of white paper only, but had been decorated with large Chinese characters exquisitely written, characters suggesting, according to the law of such decoration, the favorite themes of the poet and artist: Spring Flowers, Mountain and Sea, Summer Rain, Sky and Stars, Autumn Moon, River Water, Autumn Breeze. At one side of the apartment stood a kind of low altar, supporting a butsudan, whose tiny lacquered doors, left open, showed a mortuary tablet within, before which a lamp was burning between offerings of wild flowers. And above this household shrine hung a picture of more than common merit, representing the Goddess of Mercy, wearing the moon for her aureole.

As the student ended his little meal the young woman observed: "I cannot offer you a good bed, and there is only a paper mosquito-curtain. The bed and the curtain are mine, but tonight I have many things to do, and shall have no time to sleep; therefore I beg you will try to rest, though I am not able to make you comfortable."

He then understood that she was, for some strange reason, entirely alone, and was voluntarily giving up her only bed to

* The terms *oshiire* and *zendana* might be partly rendered by "wardrobe" and "cupboard." The *fusuma* are sliding screens serving as doors.

him upon a kindly pretext. He protested honestly against such an excess of hospitality, and assured her that he could sleep quite soundly anywhere on the floor, and did not care about the mosquitoes. But she replied, in the tone of an elder sister, that he must obey her wishes. She really had something to do, and she desired to be left by herself as soon as possible; therefore, understanding him to be a gentleman, she expected he would suffer her to arrange matters in her own way. To this he could offer no objection, as there was but one room. She spread the mattress on the floor, fetched a wooden pillow, suspended her paper mosquito-curtain, unfolded a large screen on the side of the bed toward the butsudan, and then bade him good-night in a manner that assured him she wished him to retire at once; which he did, not without some reluctance at the thought of all the trouble he had unintentionally caused her.

III.

Unwilling as the young traveler felt to accept a kindness involving the sacrifice of another's repose, he found the bed more than comfortable. He was very tired, and had scarcely laid his head upon the wooden pillow before he forgot everything in sleep.

Yet only a little while seemed to have passed when he was awakened by a singular sound. It was certainly the sound of feet, but not of feet walking softly. It seemed rather the sound of feet in rapid motion, as of excitement. Then it occurred to him that robbers might have entered the house. As for himself, he had little to fear because he had little to lose. His anxiety was chiefly for the kind person who had granted him hospitality. Into each side of the paper mosquito-curtain a small square of brown netting had been fitted, like a little window, and through one of these he tried to look; but the high screen stood between him and whatever was going on. He thought of calling, but this impulse was checked by the reflection that in case of real danger it would be both useless and imprudent to announce his presence before understanding the situation. The sounds which had made him uneasy continued, and were more and more mysterious. He resolved to prepare for the worst, and to risk his life, if necessary, in order to defend his young hostess. Hastily girding up his robes, he slipped noiselessly from under the paper curtain, crept to the edge of the screen, and peeped. What he saw astonished him extremely.

Before her illuminated butsudan the young woman, magnificently attired, was dancing all alone. Her costume he recognized as that of a shirabyōshi, though much richer than any he had ever seen worn by a professional dancer. Marvelously enhanced by it, her beauty, in that lonely time and place, appeared almost supernatural; but what seemed to him even more wonderful was her dancing. For an instant he felt the tingling of a weird doubt. The superstitions of peasants, the legends of Fox-women, flashed before his imagination; but the sight of the Buddhist shrine, of the sacred picture, dissipated the fancy, and shamed him for the folly of it. At the same time he became conscious that he was watching something she had not wished him to see, and that it was his duty, as her guest, to return at once behind the screen; but the spectacle fascinated him. He felt, with not less pleasure than amazement, that he was looking upon the most accomplished dancer he had ever seen; and the more he watched, the more the witchery of her grace grew upon him. Suddenly she paused, panting, unfastened her girdle, turned in the act of doffing her upper robe, and started violently as her eyes encountered his own.

He tried at once to excuse himself to her. He said he had been suddenly awakened by the sound of quick feet, which sound had caused him some uneasiness, chiefly for her sake, because of the lateness of the hour and the lonesomeness of the place. Then he confessed his surprise at what he had seen, and spoke of the manner in which it had attracted him. "I beg you," he continued, "to forgive my curiosity, for I cannot help wondering who you are, and how you could have become so marvelous a dancer. All the dancers of Saikyō I have seen, yet I have never seen among the most celebrated of them a girl who could dance like you; and once I had begun to watch you, I could not take away my eyes."

At first she had seemed angry, but before he had ceased to speak her expression changed. She smiled, and seated herself before him. "No, I am not angry with you," she said. "I am only sorry that you should have watched me, for I am sure you must have thought me mad when you saw me dancing that way, all by myself; and now I must tell you the meaning of what you have seen."

So she related her story. Her name he remembered to have heard as a boy—her professional name, the name of the most famous of shirabyōshi, the darling of the capital, who, in the zenith of her fame and beauty, had suddenly vanished from public life, none knew whither or why. She had fled from wealth and fortune with a youth who loved her. He was poor, but between them they possessed enough means to live simply and happily in the country. They built a little house in the mountains, and there for a number of years they existed only for each other. He adored her. One of his greatest pleasures was to see her dance. Each evening he would play some favorite melody, and she would dance for him. But one long cold winter he fell sick, and, in spite of her tender nursing, died. Since then she had lived alone with the memory of him, performing all those small rites of love and homage with which the dead are honored. Daily before his tablet she placed the customary offerings, and nightly danced to please him, as of old. And this was the explanation of what the young traveler had seen. It was indeed rude, she continued, to have awakened her tired guest; but she had waited until she thought him soundly sleeping, and then she had tried to dance very, very lightly. So she hoped he would pardon her for having unintentionally disturbed him.

When she had told him all, she made ready a little tea, which they drank together; then she entreated him so plaintively to please her by trying to sleep again that he found himself obliged to go back, with many sincere apologies, under the paper mosquito-curtain.

He slept well and long; the sun was high before he woke. On rising, he found prepared for him a meal as simple as that of the evening before, and he felt hungry. Nevertheless he ate sparingly, fearing the young woman might have stinted herself in thus providing for him; and then he made ready to depart. But when he wanted to pay her for what he had received, and for all the trouble he had given her, she refused to take anything from him, saying: "What I had to give was not worth money, and what I did was done for kindness alone. So I pray that you will try to forget the discomfort you suffered here, and will remember only the good-will of one who had nothing to offer."

He still endeavored to induce her to accept something; but at last, finding that his insistence only gave her pain, he took leave of her with such words as he could find to express his gratitude, and not without a secret regret, for her beauty and her gentleness had charmed him more than he would have liked to acknowledge to any but herself. She indicated to him the path to follow, and watched him descend the mountain until he had passed from sight. An hour later he found himself upon a highway with which he was familiar. Then a sudden remorse touched him: he had forgotten to tell her his name. For an instant he hesitated; then said to himself, "What matters it? I shall be always poor." And he went on.

IV.

Many years passed by, and many fashions with them; and the painter became old. But ere becoming old he had become famous. Princes, charmed by the wonder of his work, had vied with one another in giving him patronage; so that he grew rich, and possessed a beautiful dwelling of his own in the City of the Emperors. Young artists from many provinces were his pupils, and lived with him, serving him in all things while receiving his instruction; and his name was known throughout the land.

Now, there came one day to his house an old woman, who asked to speak with him. The servants, seeing that she was meanly dressed and of miserable appearance, took her to be some common beggar, and questioned her roughly. But when she answer-

ed: "I can tell to no one except your master why I have come,"
they believed her mad, and deceived her, saying: "He is not now
in Saikyo, nor do we know how soon he will return."

But the old woman came again and again—day after day, and
week after week—each time being told something that was not
true: "Today he is ill," or, "Today he is very busy," or, "Today he
has much company, and therefore cannot see you." Nevertheless
she continued to come, always at the same hour each day, and
always carrying a bundle wrapped in a ragged covering; and the
servants at last thought it were best to speak to their master
about her. So they said to him: "There is a very old woman,
whom we take to be a beggar, at our lord's gate. More than fifty
times she has come, asking to see our lord, and refusing to tell
us why—saying that she can tell her wishes only to our lord.
And we have tried to discourage her, as she seemed to be mad;
but she always comes. Therefore we have presumed to mention
the matter to our lord, in order that we may learn what is to be
done hereafter."

Then the Master answered sharply: "Why did none of you tell
me of this before?" and went out himself to the gate, and spoke
very kindly to the woman, remembering how he also had been
poor. And he asked her if she desired alms of him.

But she answered that she had no need of money or of food,
and only desired that he would paint for her a picture. He wondered at her wish, and bade her enter his house. So she entered
into the vestibule, and, kneeling there, began to untie the knots
of the bundle she had brought with her. When she had un-
wrapped it, the painter perceived curious rich quaint garments
of silk broidered with designs in gold, yet much frayed and dis-
colored by wear and time—the wreck of a wonderful costume of
other days, the attire of a shirabyoshi.

While the old woman unfolded the garments one by one, and
tried to smooth them with her trembling fingers, a memory
stirred in the Master's brain, thrilled dimly there a little space,
then suddenly lighted up. In that soft shock of recollection, he

saw again the lonely mountain dwelling in which he had received unremunerated hospitality—the tiny room prepared for his rest, the paper mosquito-curtain, the faintly burning lamp before the Buddhist shrine, the strange beauty of one dancing there alone in the dead of the night. Then, to the astonishment of the aged visitor, he, the favored of princes, bowed low before her, and said: "Pardon my rudeness in having forgotten your face for a moment; but it is more than forty years since we last saw each other. Now I remember you well. You received me once at your house. You gave up to me the only bed you had. I saw you dance, and you told me all your story. You had been a shirabyōshi, and I have not forgotten your name."

He uttered it. She, astonished and confused, could not at first reply to him, for she was old and had suffered much, and her memory had begun to fail. But he spoke more and more kindly to her, and reminded her of many things which she had told him, and described to her the house in which she had lived alone, so that at last she also remembered; and she answered, with tears of pleasure: "Surely the Divine One who looketh down above the sound of prayer has guided me. But when my unworthy home was honored by the visit of the august Master, I was not as I now am. And it seems to me like a miracle of our Lord Buddha that the Master should remember me."

Then she related the rest of her simple story. In the course of years, she had become, through poverty, obliged to part with her little house; and in her old age she had returned alone to the great city, in which her name had long been forgotten. It had caused her much pain to lose her home; but it grieved her still more that, in becoming weak and old, she could no longer dance each evening before the butsudan, to please the spirit of the dead whom she had loved. Therefore she wanted to have a picture of herself painted, in the costume and the attitude of the dance, that she might suspend it before the butsudan. For this she had prayed earnestly to Kwannon. And she had sought out the Master because of his fame as a painter, since she desired, for the sake of the dead, no common work, but a picture painted with great skill; and she had brought her dancing attire, hoping that the Master might be willing to paint her therein.

He listened to all with a kindly smile, and answered her: "It will be only a pleasure for me to paint the picture which you want. This day I have something to finish which cannot be delayed. But if you will come here tomorrow, I will paint you exactly as you wish, and as well as I am able."

But she said: "I have not yet told to the Master the thing which most troubles me. And it is this—that I can offer in return for so great a favor nothing except these dancer's clothes; and they are of no value in themselves, though they were costly once. Still, I hoped the Master might be willing to take them, seeing they have become curious; for there are no more shirabyōshi, and the maiko of these times wear no such robes."

"Of that matter," the good painter exclaimed, "you must not think at all! No; I am glad to have this present chance of paying a small part of my old debt to you. So tomorrow I will paint you just as you wish."

She prostrated herself thrice before him, uttering thanks, and then said, "Let my lord pardon, though I have yet something more to say. For I do not wish that he should paint me as I now am, but only as I used to be when I was young, as my lord knew me."

He said: "I remember well. You were very beautiful."

Her wrinkled features lighted up with pleasure, as she bowed her thanks to him for those words. And she exclaimed: "Then indeed all that I hoped and prayed for may be done! Since he thus remembers my poor youth, I beseech my lord to paint me, not as I now am, but as he saw me when I was not old and, as it has pleased him generously to say, not uncomely. O Master, make me young again! Make me seem beautiful that I may seem beautiful to the soul of him for whose sake I, the unworthy, beseech this! He will see the Master's work: he will forgive me that I can no longer dance."

Once more the Master bade her have no anxiety, and said: "Come tomorrow, and I will paint you.

"I will make a picture of you just as you were when I saw you, a young and beautiful shirabyōshi, and I will paint it as carefully and as skillfully as if I were painting the picture of the richest person in the land. Never doubt, but come."

V.

So the aged dancer came at the appointed hour; and upon soft white silk the artist painted a picture of her. Yet not a picture of her as she seemed to the Master's pupils, but the memory of her as she had been in the days of her youth, bright-eyed as a bird, lithe as a bamboo, dazzling as a tennin* in her raiment of silk and gold. Under the magic of the Master's brush, the vanished grace returned, the faded beauty bloomed again. When the kakemono had been finished, and stamped with his seal, he mounted it richly upon silken cloth, and fixed to it rollers of cedar with ivory weights, and a silken cord by which to hang it; and he placed it in a little box of white wood, and so gave it to the shirabyōshi. And he would also have presented her with a gift of money. But though he pressed her earnestly, he could not persuade her to accept his help. "Nay," she made answer, with tears, "indeed I need nothing. The picture only I desired. For that I prayed; and now my prayer has been answered, and I know that I never can wish for anything more in this life, and that if I come to die thus desiring nothing, to enter upon the way of Buddha will not be difficult. One thought alone causes me sorrow—that I have nothing to offer to the Master but this dancer's apparel, which is indeed of little worth, though I beseech him to accept it; and I will pray each day that his future life may be a life of happiness, because of the wondrous kindness which he has done me."

"Nay," protested the painter, smiling, "what is it that I have done? Truly nothing. As for the dancer's garments, I will accept

---

* *Tennin*, a "Sky-Maiden," a Buddhist angel.

them, if that can make you more happy. They will bring back pleasant memories of the night I passed in your home, when you gave up all your comforts for my unworthy sake, and yet would not suffer me to pay for that which I used; and for that kindness I hold myself to be still in your debt. But now tell me where you live, so that I may see the picture in its place." For he had resolved within himself to place her beyond the reach of want.

But she excused herself with humble words, and would not tell him, saying that her dwelling-place was too mean to be looked upon by such as he; and then, with many prostrations, she thanked him again and again, and went away with her treasure, weeping, for joy.

Then the Master called to one of his pupils: "Go quickly after that woman, but so that she does not know herself followed, and bring me word where she lives." So the young man followed her, unperceived.

He remained long away, and when he returned he laughed in the manner of one obliged to say something which it is not pleasant to hear, and he said: "That woman, O Master, I followed out of the city to the dry bed of the river, near to the place where criminals are executed. There I saw a hut such as an Eta might dwell in, and that is where she lives. A forsaken and filthy place, O Master!"

"Nevertheless," the painter replied, "tomorrow you will take me to that forsaken and filthy place. What time I live she shall not suffer for food or clothing or comfort."

And as all wondered, he told them the story of the shirabyōshi, after which it did not seem to them that his words were strange.

VI.

On the morning of the day following, an hour after sunrise, the Master and his pupil took their way to the dry bed of the river, beyond the verge of the city, to the place of outcasts.

The entrance of the little dwelling they found closed by a single shutter, upon which the Master tapped many times without evoking a response. Then, finding the shutter unfastened from within, he pushed it slightly aside, and called through the aperture. None replied, and he decided to enter. Simultaneously, with extraordinary vividness, there thrilled back to him the sensation of the very instant when, as a tired lad, he stood pleading for admission to the lonesome little cottage among the hills.

Entering alone softly, he perceived that the woman was lying there, wrapped in a single thin and tattered futon, seemingly asleep. On a rude shelf he recognized the butsudan of forty years before, with its tablet, and now, as then, a tiny lamp was burning in front of the kaimyō. The kakemono of the Goddess of Mercy with her lunar aureole was gone, but on the wall facing the shrine he beheld his own dainty gift suspended, and an ofuda beneath it—an ofuda of Hito-koto-Kwannon*—that Kwannon unto whom it is unlawful to pray more than once, as she answers but a single prayer. There was little else in the desolate dwelling; only the garments of a female pilgrim, and a mendicant's staff and bowl.

But the Master did not pause to look at these things, for he desired to awaken and to gladden the sleeper, and he called her name cheerily twice and thrice.

Then suddenly he saw that she was dead, and he wondered while he gazed upon her face, for it seemed less old. A vague sweetness, like a ghost of youth, had returned to it; the lines of sorrow had been softened, the wrinkles strangely smoothed, by the touch of a phantom Master mightier than he.

---

* Her shrine is at Nara—not far from the temple of the giant Buddha.

23

FROM HŌKI TO OKI

I.

I RESOLVED to go to Oki.

Not even a missionary had ever been to Oki, and its shores had never been seen by European eyes, except on those rare occasions when men-of-war steamed by them, cruising about the Japanese Sea. This alone would have been a sufficient reason for going there; but a stronger one was furnished for me by the ignorance of the Japanese themselves about Oki. Excepting the far-away Riu-Kiu, or Loo-Choo Islands, inhabited by a somewhat different race with a different language, the least-known portion of the Japanese Empire is perhaps Oki. Since it belongs to the same prefectural district as Izumo, each new governor of Shimane-Ken is supposed to pay one visit to Oki after his inauguration; and the chief of police of the province sometimes goes there upon a tour of inspection. There are also some mercantile houses in Matsue and in other cities which send a commercial traveler to Oki once a year. Furthermore, there is quite a large trade with Oki—almost all carried on by small sailing-vessels. But such official and commercial communications have not been of a nature to make Oki much better known today than in the mediaeval period of Japanese history. There are still current among the common people of the west coast extraordinary stories of Oki much like those about that fabulous Isle of Women, which figures so largely in the imaginative literature of various

Oriental races. According to these old legends, the moral notions of the people of Oki were extremely fantastic: the most rigid ascetic could not dwell there and maintain his indifference to earthly pleasures; and, however wealthy at his arrival, the visiting stranger must soon return to his native land naked and poor, because of the seductions of women. I had quite sufficient experiences of travel in queer countries to feel certain that all these marvelous stories signified nothing beyond the bare fact that Oki was a *terra incognita;* and I even felt inclined to believe that the average morals of the people of Oki—judging by those of the common folk of the western provinces—must be very much better than the morals of our ignorant classes at home.

Which I subsequently ascertained to be the case.

For some time I could find no one among my Japanese acquaintances to give me any information about Oki, beyond the fact that in ancient times it had been a place of banishment for the Emperors Go-Daigo and Go-Toba, dethroned by military usurpers and this I already knew. But at last, quite unexpectedly, I found a friend—a former fellow-teacher—who had not only been to Oki, but was going there again within a few days about some business matter. We agreed to go together. His accounts of Oki differed very materially from those of the people who had never been there. The Oki folks, he said, were almost as much civilized as the Izumo folks: they had nice towns and good public schools. They were very simple, and honest beyond belief, and extremely kind to strangers. Their only boast was that of having kept their race unchanged since the time that the Japanese had first come to Japan; or, in more romantic phrase, since the Age of the Gods. They were all Shintōists, members of the Izumo Taisha faith, but Buddhism was also maintained among them, chiefly through the generous subscription of private individuals. And there were very comfortable hotels, so that I would feel quite at home.

He also gave me a little book about Oki, printed for the use of the Oki schools, from which I obtained the following brief summary of facts:

II.

Oki-no-Kuni, or the Land of Oki, consists of two groups of small islands in the Sea of Japan, about one hundred miles from the coast of Izumo. Dōzen, as the nearer group is termed, comprises, besides various islets, three islands lying close together: Chiburishima, or the Island of Chiburi (sometimes called Higashinoshima, or Eastern Island); Nishinoshima, or the Western Island, and Nakanoshima, or the Middle Island. Much larger than any of these is the principal island, Dōgo, which together with various islets, mostly uninhabited, form the remaining group. It is sometimes called Oki—though the name Oki is more generally used for the whole archipelago.*

Officially, Oki is divided into four kōri or counties. Chiburi and Nishinoshima together form Chiburigōri; Nakanoshima, with an islet, makes Amgōri, and Dōgo is divided into Ochigōri and Sukigōri.

All these islands are very mountainous, and only a small portion of their area has ever been cultivated. Their chief sources of revenue are their fisheries, in which nearly the whole population has always been engaged from the most ancient times.

During the winter months the sea between Oki and the west coast is highly dangerous for small vessels, and in that season the islands hold little communication with the mainland. Only one passenger steamer runs to Oki from Sakai in Hōki. In a direct line, the distance from Sakai in Hōki to Saigo, the chief port of Oki, is said to be thirty-nine ri; but the steamer touches at the other islands upon her way thither.

There are quite a number of little towns, or rather villages, in Oki, of which forty-five belong to Dōgo. The villages are nearly all

* The names Dōzen or Tōzen, and Dōgo or Tōgo, signify "the Before-Islands" and "the Behind-Islands."

situated upon the coast. There are large schools in the principal towns. The population of the islands is stated to be 80,196, but the respective populations of towns and villages are not given.

III.

From Matsue in Izumo to Sakai in Hōki is a trip of barely two hours by steamer. Sakai is the chief seaport of Shimane-Ken. It is an ugly little town, full of unpleasant smells; it exists only as a port; it has no industries, scarcely any shops, and only one Shintō temple of small dimensions and smaller interest. Its principal buildings are warehouses, pleasure resorts for sailors, and a few large dingy hotels, which are always overcrowded with guests waiting for steamers to Ōsaka, to Bakkan, to Hamada, to Niigata, and various other ports. On this coast no steamers run regularly anywhere; their owners attach no business value whatever to punctuality, and guests have usually to wait for a much longer time than they could possibly have expected, and the hotels are glad.

But the harbor is beautiful—along frith between the high land of Izumo and the low coast of Hōki. It is perfectly sheltered from storms, and deep enough to admit all but the largest steamers. The ships can lie close to the houses, and the harbor is nearly always thronged with all sorts of craft, from junks to steam packets of the latest construction.

My friend and I were lucky enough to secure back rooms at the best hotel. Back rooms are the best in nearly all Japanese buildings; at Sakai they have the additional advantage of overlooking the busy wharves and the whole luminous bay, beyond which the Izumo hills undulate in huge green billows against the sky. There was much to see and to be amused at. Steamers and sailing craft of all sorts were lying two and three deep before the hotel, and the naked dock laborers were loading and unloading in their own peculiar way. These men are recruited from among the strongest peasantry of Hōki and of Izumo, and some were really fine men, over whose brown backs the muscles rippled at every movement. They were assisted by boys of fifteen or sixteen apparently— apprentices learning the work, but not yet strong enough to bear heavy burdens. I noticed that nearly all had bands of blue cloth bound about their calves to keep the veins from bursting. And all sang as they worked. There was one curious alternate chorus, in which the men in the hold gave the signal by chanting "*dokoe, dokoe!*" (haul away!) and those at the hatch responded by improvisations on the appearance of each package as it ascended:

> *Dokoe, dokoe!*
> *Onnago no ko da.*
> *Dokoe, dokoe!*
> *Oya da yo, oya da yo.*
> *Dokoe, dokoe!*
> *Choi-choi da, choi-choi da.*
> *Dokoe, dokoe!*
> *Matsue da, Matsue da.*
> *Dokoe, dokoe!*
> *Koetsumo Yonago da,* * etc.

But this chant was for light quick work. A very different chant accompanied the more painful and slower labor of loading heavy sacks and barrels upon the shoulders of the stronger men:

> *Yan-yui!*
> *Yan-yui!*
> *Yan-yui!*
> *Yan-yui!*
> *Yoi-ya-sa-a-a-no-do-koe-shi!*†

Three men always lifted the weight. At the first *yan-yui* all stooped; at the second all took hold; the third signified ready; at

---

* "*Dokoe, dokoe!*" "This is only a woman's baby" (a very small package.) "*Dokoe, dokoe!*" "This is the daddy, this is the daddy" (a big package)." "*Dokoe, dokoe!*" "'Tis very small, very small!" "*Dokoe, dokoe!*" "This is for Matsue, this is for Matsue!" "*Dokoe, dokoe!*" "This is for Koetsumo of Yonago," etc.

† These words seem to have no more meaning than our "yo-heave-ho." *Yan-yui* is a cry used by all Izumo and Hōki sailors.

the fourth the weight rose from the ground; and with the long cry of *yoiyasa no dokoeshi* it was dropped on the brawny shoulder waiting to receive it.

Among the workers was a naked laughing boy, with a fine contralto that rang out so merrily through all the din as to create something of a sensation in the hotel. A young woman, one of the guests, came out upon the balcony to look, and exclaimed: "That boy's voice is RED,"—whereat everybody smiled. Under the circumstances I thought the observation very expressive, although it recalled a certain famous story about scarlet and the sound of a trumpet, which does not seem nearly so funny now as it did at a time when we knew less about the nature of light and sound.

The Oki steamer arrived the same afternoon, but she could not approach the wharf, and I could only obtain a momentary glimpse of her stern through a telescope, with which I read the name, in English letters of gold—OKI-SAIGO. Before I could obtain any idea of her dimensions, a huge black steamer from Nagasaki glided between, and moored right in the way.

I watched the loading and unloading, and listened to the song of the boy with the red voice, until sunset, when all quit work; and after that I watched the Nagasaki steamer. She had made her way to our wharf as the other vessels moved out, and lay directly under the balcony. The captain and crew did not appear to be in a hurry about anything. They all squatted down together on the foredeck, where a feast was spread for them by lantern-light. Dancing-girls climbed on board and feasted with them, and sang to the sound of the samisen, and played with them the game of ken. Late into the night the feasting and the fun continued; and although an alarming quantity of saké was consumed, there was no roughness or boisterousness. But saké is the most soporific of wines; and by midnight only three of the men remained on deck. One of these had not taken any saké at all, but still desired to eat. Happily for him there climbed on board a night walking mochiya with a box of mochi, which are cakes of rice-flour sweetened with native sugar. The hungry one bought all, and reproached the mochiya because there were no more, and offered, nevertheless, to share the mochi with his comrades. Whereupon the first to whom the offer was made answered somewhat after this manner:

"I-your-servant mochi-for this-world-in no-use-have. Saké-alone this-life-in if-there-be, nothing-beside-desirable-is."

"For me-your-servant," spake the other, "Woman this-fleeting-life-in the-supreme-thing is; mochi-or-saké-for earthly-use have-I-none."

But, having made all the mochi to disappear, he that had been hungry turned himself to the mochiya, and said:

"O Mochiya San, I-your-servant Woman-or-saké-for earthly-requirement have-none. Mochi-than things better this-life-of-sorrow-in existence-have-not!"

IV.

Early in the morning we were notified that the Oki-Saigo would start at precisely eight o'clock, and that we had better secure our tickets at once. The hotel-servant, according to Japanese custom, relieved us of all anxiety about baggage, etc., and bought our tickets: first-class fare, eighty sen. And after a hasty breakfast the hotel boat came under the window to take us away.

Warned by experience of the discomforts of European dress on Shimane steamers, I adopted Japanese costume and exchanged my shoes for sandals. Our boatmen sculled swiftly through the confusion of shipping and junkery; and as we cleared it I saw, far out in midstream, the joki waiting for us. Joki is a Japanese name for steam-vessel. The word had not yet impressed me as being capable of a sinister interpretation.

She seemed nearly as long as a harbor tug, though much more squabby; and she otherwise so much resembled the Lilliputian steamers of Lake Shinji, that I felt somewhat afraid of her, even

for a trip of one hundred miles. But exterior inspection afforded
no clue to the mystery of her inside. We reached her and climbed
into her starboard through a small square hole. At once I found
myself cramped in a heavily-roofed gangway, four feet high and
two feet wide, and in the thick of a frightful squeeze—passengers stifling in the effort to pull baggage three feet in diameter
through the two-foot orifice. It was impossible to advance or
retreat; and behind me the engine-room gratings were pouring
wonderful heat into this infernal corridor. I had to wait with
the back of my head pressed against the roof until, in some
unimaginable way, all baggage and passengers had squashed and
squeezed through. Then, reaching a doorway, I fell over a heap of
sandals and geta, into the first-class cabin. It was pretty, with its
polished woodwork and mirrors; it was surrounded by divans five
inches wide; and in the center it was nearly six feet high. Such
altitude would have been a cause for comparative happiness, but
that from various polished bars of brass extended across the
ceiling all kinds of small baggage, including two cages of singing-
crickets *(chon-gisu)*, had been carefully suspended. Furthermore
the cabin was already extremely occupied: everybody, of course,
on the floor, and nearly everybody lying at extreme length; and
the heat struck me as being supernatural. Now they that go down
to the sea in ships, out of Izumo and such places, for the purpose
of doing business in great waters, are never supposed to stand
up, but to squat in the ancient patient manner; and coast or lake
steamers are constructed with a view to render this attitude only
possible. Observing an open door in the port side of the cabin, I
picked my way over a tangle of bodies and limbs—among them a
pair of fairy legs belonging to a dancing-girl—and found myself
presently in another gangway, also roofed, and choked up to the
roof with baskets of squirming eels. Exit there was none: so I
climbed back over all the legs and tried the starboard gangway
a second time. Even during that short interval, it had been half
filled with baskets of unhappy chickens. But I made a reckless
dash over them, in spite of frantic cacklings which hurt my soul,

and succeeded in finding a way to the cabin-roof. It was entirely occupied by watermelons, except one corner, where there was a big coil of rope. I put melons inside of the rope, and sat upon them in the sun. It was not comfortable; but I thought that there I might have some chance for my life in case of a catastrophe, and I was sure that even the gods could give no help to those below. During the squeeze I had got separated from my companion, but I was afraid to make any attempt to find him. Forward I saw the roof of the second cabin crowded with third-class passengers squatting round a hibachi. To pass through them did not seem possible, and to retire would have involved the murder of either eels or chickens. Wherefore I sat upon the melons.

And the boat started, with a stunning scream. In another moment her funnel began to rain soot upon me—for the so-called first-class cabin was well astern—and then came small cinders mixed with the soot, and the cinders were occasionally red-hot. But I sat burning upon the watermelons for some time longer, trying to imagine a way of changing my position without committing another assault upon the chickens. Finally, I made a desperate endeavor to get to leeward of the volcano, and it was then for the first time that I began to learn the peculiarities of the joki. What I tried to sit on turned upside down, and what I tried to hold by instantly gave way, and always in the direction of overboard. Things clamped or rigidly braced to outward seeming proved, upon cautious examination, to be dangerously mobile; and things that, according to Occidental ideas, ought to have been movable, were fixed like the roots of the perpetual hills. In whatever direction a rope or stay could possibly have been stretched so as to make somebody unhappy, it was there. In the midst of these trials the frightful little craft began to swing, and the watermelons began to rush heavily to and fro, and I came to the conclusion that this joki had been planned and constructed by demons.

Which I stated to my friend. He had not only rejoined me quite unexpectedly, but had brought along with him one of the ship's boys to spread an awning above ourselves and the water-melons, so as to exclude cinders and sun.

"Oh, no!" he answered reproachfully. "She was designed and built at Hyōgo, and really she might have been made much worse..."

"I beg your pardon," I interrupted; "I don't agree with you at all."

"Well, you will see for yourself," he persisted, "Her hull is good steel, and her little engine is wonderful; she can make her hundred miles in five hours. She is not very comfortable, but she is very swift and strong."

"I would rather be in a sampan," I protested, "if there were rough weather."

"But she never goes to sea in rough weather. If it only looks as if there might possibly be some rough weather, she stays in port. Sometimes she waits a whole month. She never runs any risks."

I could not feel sure of it. But I soon forgot all discomforts, even the discomfort of sitting upon watermelons, in the delight of the divine day and the magnificent view that opened wider and wider before us, as we rushed from the long frith into the Sea of Japan, following the Izumo coast. There was no fleck in the soft blue vastness above, not one flutter on the metallic smoothness of the all-reflecting sea; if our little steamer rocked, it was doubtless because she had been overloaded. To port, the Izumo hills were flying by, a long, wild procession of broken shapes, somber green, separating at intervals to form mysterious little bays, with fishing hamlets hiding in them. Leagues away to starboard, the Hōki shore receded into the naked white horizon, an ever-diminishing streak of warm blue edged with a thread-line of white, the gleam of a sand beach; and beyond it, in the center, a vast shadowy pyramid loomed up into heaven—the ghostly peak of Daisen.

My companion touched my arm to call my attention to a group of pine-trees on the summit of a peak to port, and laughed and sang a Japanese song. How swiftly we had been traveling I then for the first time understood, for I recognized the four famous pines of Mionoseki, on the windy heights above the shrine of Koto-shiro-nushi-no-Kami. There used to be five trees: one was uprooted by a storm, and some Izumo poet wrote about the remaining four the words which my friend had sung:

> *Seki no gohon matsu*
> *Ippun kirya, shihon;*
> *Ato wa kirarenu*
> *Miyōto matsu.*

Which means: "Of the five pines of Seki one has been cut, and four remain; and of these no one must now be cut—they are wedded pairs." And in Mionoseki there are sold beautiful little saké cups and saké bottles, upon which are pictures of the four pines, and above the pictures, in spidery text of gold, the verses, "*Seki no gohon matsu.*" These are for keepsakes, and there are many other curious and pretty souvenirs to buy in those pretty shops: porcelains bearing the picture of the Mionoseki temple, and metal clasps for tobacco pouches representing Koto-shiro-nushi-no-Kami trying to put a big tai-fish into a basket too small for it, and funny masks of glazed earthenware representing the laughing face of the god. For a jovial god is this Ebisu, or Koto-shiro-nushi-no-Kami, patron of honest labor and especially of fishers, though less of a laughter-lover than his father, the Great Deity of Kitzuki, about whom 'tis said: "Whenever the happy laugh, the God rejoices."

We passed the Cape—the *Miho* of the Kojiki—and the harbor of Mionoseki opened before us, showing its islanded shrine of Benten in the midst, and the crescent of quaint houses with their feet in the water, and the great torii and granite lions of the far-famed temple. Immediately a number of passengers rose to their feet, and, turning their faces toward the torii, began to clap their hands in Shintō prayer.

I said to my friend:

"There are fifty baskets full of chickens in the gangway; and yet these people are praying to Kotoshiro-nushi-no-Kami that nothing horrible may happen to this boat."

"More likely," he answered, "they are praying for good fortune; though there is a saying: 'The gods only laugh when men pray to them for wealth. But of the Great Deity of Mionoseki there is a good story told. Once there was a very lazy man who went to Mionoseki and prayed to become rich. And the same night he saw the god in a dream; and the god laughed, and took off one of his own divine sandals, and told him to examine it. And the man saw that it was made of solid brass, but had a big hole worn through the sole of it. Then said the god: 'You want to have money without working for it. I am a god; but I am never lazy. See! my sandals are of brass: yet I have worked and walked so much that they are quite worn out.'"

V.

The beautiful bay of Mionoseki opens between two headlands: Cape Mio (or Miho, according to the archaic spelling) and the Cape of Jizō (Jizōzaki), now most inappropriately called by the people "The Nose of Jizō" (Jizō-no-hana). This Nose of Jizō is one of the most dangerous points of the coast in time of surf, and the great terror of small ships returning from Oki. There is nearly always a heavy swell there, even in fair weather. Yet as we passed the ragged promontory I was surprised to see the water still as glass. I felt suspicious of that noiseless sea: its Boundlessness recalled the beautiful treacherous sleep of waves and winds which precedes a tropical hurricane. But my friend said:

"It may remain like this for weeks. In the sixth month and in the beginning of the seventh, it is usually very quiet; it is not likely to become dangerous before the Bon. But there was a little squall last week at Mionoseki; and the people said that it was caused by the anger of the god."

"Eggs?" I queried.

"No, a Kudan." "What is a Kudan?"

"Is it possible you never heard of the Kudan? The Kudan has

the face of a man, and the body of a bull. Sometimes it is born of a cow, and that is a Sign-of-things-going-to-happen. And the Kudan always tells the truth. Therefore in Japanese letters and documents it is customary to use the phrase, *Kudan-no-gotoshi*—'like the Kudan'—or 'on the truth of the Kudan.'"*

"But why was the God of Mionoseki angry about the Kudan?"

"People said it was a stuffed Kudan. I did not see it, so I cannot tell you how it was made. There were some traveling showmen from Ōsaka at Sakai. They had a tiger and many curious animals and the stuffed Kudan; and they took the Izumo Maru for Mionoseki. As the steamer entered the port, a sudden squall came; and the priests of the temple said the god was angry because things impure—bones and parts of dead animals—had been brought to the town. And the show people were not even allowed to land: they had to go back to Sakai on the same steamer. And as soon as they had gone away, the sky became clear again, and the wind stopped blowing: so that some people thought what the priests had said was true."

VI.

Evidently there was much more moisture in the atmosphere than I had supposed. On really clear days, Daisen can be distinctly seen even from Oki; but we had scarcely passed the Nose of Jizō when the huge peak began to wrap itself in vapor of the same color as the horizon; and in a few minutes it vanished, as a spectre might vanish. The effect of this sudden disappearance was very extraordinary; for only the peak passed from sight, and that which had veiled it could not be in any way distinguished from horizon and sky.

Meanwhile the Oki-Saigo, having reached the farthest outlying point of the coast upon her route, began to race in a straight line across the Japanese Sea. The green hills of Izumo fled away

---

* This curious meaning is not given in Japanese-English dictionaries, where the idiom is translated merely by the phrase "as aforesaid."

and turned blue, and the spectral shores of Hōki began to melt
into the horizon, like bands of cloud. Then I was obliged to confess my surprise at the speed of the horrid little steamer. She
moved, too, with scarcely any sound, so smooth was the working
of her wonderful little engine. But she began to swing heavily,
with deep, slow swingings. To the eye, the sea looked level as
oil; but there "were long invisible swells—ocean-pulses—that
made themselves felt beneath the surface. Hōki evaporated;
the Izumo hills turned gray, and their gray steadily paled as I
watched them. They grew more and more colorless—seemed to
become transparent. And then they were not. Only blue sky and
blue sea, welded together in the white horizon.

It was just as lonesome as if we had been a thousand leagues
from land. And in that weirdness we were told some very lonesome things by an ancient mariner who found leisure to join us
among the watermelons. He talked of the Hotoke-umi, and the ill
luck of being at sea on the sixteenth day of the seventh month.
He told us that even the great steamers never went to sea during
the Bon: no crew would venture to take a ship out then. And he
related the following stories with such simple earnestness that I
think he must have believed what he said:

"The first time I was very young. From Hokkaido we had sailed,
and the voyage was long, and the winds turned against us. And
the night of the sixteenth day fell as we were working on over
this very sea.

"And all at once in the darkness we saw behind us a great
junk—all white—that we had not noticed till she was quite close
to us. It made us feel queer, because she seemed to have come
from nowhere. She was so near us that we could hear voices; and
her hull towered up high above us. She seemed to be sailing very
fast; but she came no closer. We shouted to her; but we got no
answer. And while we were watching her, all of us became afraid,
because she did not move like a real ship. The sea was terrible,
and we were lurching and plunging; but that great junk never

rolled. Just at the same moment that we began to feel afraid she vanished so quickly that we could scarcely believe we had really seen her at all.

"That was the first time. But four years ago I saw something still more strange. We were bound for Oki, in a junk, and the wind again delayed us, so that we were at sea on the sixteenth day. It was in the morning, a little before midday; the sky was dark, and the sea very ugly. All at once we saw a steamer running in our track, very quickly. She got so close to us that we could hear her engines, *katakata, katakata!*—but we saw nobody on deck. Then she began to follow us, keeping exactly at the same distance, and whenever we tried to get out of her way she would turn after us and keep exactly in our wake. And then we suspected what she was. But we were not sure until she vanished. She vanished like a bubble, without making the least sound. None of us could say exactly when she disappeared. None of us saw her vanish. The strangest thing was that after she was gone we could still hear her engines working behind us—*katakata, katakata, katakata!*

"That is all I saw. But I know others, sailors like myself, who have seen more. Sometimes many ships will follow you—though never at the same time. One will come close and vanish, then another, and then another. As long as they come behind you, you need never be afraid. But if you see a ship of that sort running *before* you, against the wind, that is very bad! It means that all on board will be drowned."

VII.

The luminous blankness circling us continued to remain unflecked for less than an hour. Then out of the horizon toward which we steamed, a small gray vagueness began to grow. It lengthened fast, and seemed a cloud. And a cloud it proved; but slowly, beneath it, blue filmy shapes began to define against the whiteness, and sharpened into a chain of mountains. They grew taller and bluer—a little sierra, with one paler shape towering in the middle to thrice the height of the rest, and filleted with cloud—Takuhizan, the sacred mountain of Oki, in the island Nishinoshima.

Takuhizan has legends, which I learned from my friend. Upon its summit stands an ancient shrine of the deity Gongen-Sama. And it is said that upon the thirty-first night of the twelfth month three ghostly fires arise from the sea and ascend to the place of the shrine, and enter the stone lanterns which stand before it, and there remain, burning like lamps. These lights do not arise at once, but separately, from the sea, and rise to the top of the peak one by one. The people go out in boats to see the lights mount from the water. But only those whose hearts are pure can see them; those who have evil thoughts or desires look for the holy fires in vain.

Before us, as we steamed on, the sea-surface appeared to become suddenly speckled with queer craft previously invisible— light, long fishing-boats, with immense square sails of a beautiful yellow color. I could not help remarking to my comrade how pretty those sails were; he laughed, and told me they were made of old tatami.* I examined them through a telescope, and found that they were exactly what he had said—woven straw coverings of old floor-mats. Nevertheless, that first tender yellow sprinkling of Oki sails over the soft blue water was a charming sight.

They fleeted by, like a passing of yellow butterflies, and the sea was void again. Gradually, a little to port, a point in the approaching line of blue cliffs shaped itself and changed color— dull green above, reddish gray below; it defined into a huge rock,

---

* The floor of a Japanese dwelling might be compared to an immense but very shallow wooden tray, divided into compartments corresponding to the various rooms. These divisions are formed by grooved and polished woodwork, several inches above the level, and made for the accommodation of the fusuma, or sliding screens, separating room from room. The compartments are filled up level with the partitions with tatami, or mats about the thickness of light mattresses, covered with beautifully woven rice-straw. The squared edges of the mats fit exactly together, and as the mats are not made for the house, but the house for the mats, all tatami are exactly the same size. The fully finished floor of each room is thus like a great soft bed. No shoes, of course, can be worn in a Japanese house. As soon as the mats become in the least soiled they are replaced by new ones.

with a dark patch on its face, but the rest of the land remained blue. The dark patch blackened as we came nearer—a great gap full of shadow. Then the blue cliffs beyond also turned green, and their bases reddish gray. We passed to the right of the huge rock, which proved to be a detached and uninhabited islet, Hakashima; and in another moment we were steaming into the archipelago of Oki, between the lofty islands Chiburishima and Nakashima.

VIII.

The first impression was almost uncanny. Rising sheer from the flood on either hand, the tall green silent hills stretched away before us, changing tint through the summer vapor, to form a fantastic vista of blue cliffs and peaks and promontories. There was not one sign of human life. Above their pale bases of naked rock the mountains sloped up beneath a somber wildness of dwarf vegetation. There was absolutely no sound, except the sound of the steamer's tiny engine—*poum-poum, poum! poum-poum, poum!* like the faint tapping of a geisha's drum. And this savage silence continued for miles: only the absence of lofty timber gave evidence that those peaked hills had ever been trodden by human foot. But all at once, to the left, in a mountain wrinkle, a little gray hamlet appeared; and the steamer screamed and stopped, while the hills repeated the scream seven times.

This settlement was Chiburimura, of Chiburishima (Nakashima being the island to starboard)—evidently nothing more than a fishing station. First a wharf of uncemented stone rising from the cove like a wall; then great trees through which one caught sight of a torii before some Shintō shrine, and of a dozen houses climbing the hollow hill one behind another, roof beyond roof; and above these some terraced patches of tilled ground in the midst of desolation: that was all. The packet halted to deliver mail, and passed on.

But then, contrary to expectation, the scenery became more beautiful. The shores on either side at once receded and heightened: we were traversing an inland sea bounded by three lofty islands. At first the way before us had seemed barred by vapory hills; but as these, drawing nearer, turned green, there suddenly opened magnificent chasms between them on both sides— mountain-gates revealing league-long wondrous vistas of peaks and cliffs and capes of a hundred blues, ranging away from velvety indigo into far tones of exquisite and spectral delicacy. A tinted haze made dreamy all remotenesses, and veiled with illusions of color the rugged nudities of rock.

The beauty of the scenery of Western and Central Japan is not as the beauty of scenery in other lands; it has a peculiar character of its own. Occasionally the foreigner may find memo-ries of former travel suddenly stirred to life by some view on a mountain road, or some stretch of beetling coast seen through a fog of spray. But this illusion of resemblance vanishes as swiftly as it comes; details immediately define into strangeness, and you become aware that the remembrance was evoked by form only, never by color. Colors indeed there are which delight the eye, but not colors of mountain verdure, not colors of the land. Cultivated plains, expanses of growing rice, may offer some ap-proach to warmth of green; but the whole general tone of this nature is dusky; the vast forests are somber; the tints of grasses are harsh or dull. Fiery greens, such as burn in tropical scenery, do not exist; and blossom-bursts take a more exquisite radi-ance by contrast with the heavy tones of the vegetation out of which they flame. Outside of parks and gardens and cultivated fields, there is a singular absence of warmth and tenderness in the tints of verdure; and nowhere need you hope to find any such richness of green as that which makes the loveliness of an English lawn.

Yet these Oriental landscapes possess charms of color extraor-dinary—phantom-color, delicate, elfish, indescribable—created by the wonderful atmosphere. Vapors enchant the distances, bathing peaks in bewitchments of blue and gray of a hundred tones, transforming naked cliffs to amethyst, stretching spectral gauzes across the topazine morning, magnifying the splendor of noon by effacing the horizon, filling the evening with smoke of gold, bronzing the waters, banding the sundown with ghostly purple and green of nacre. Now, the old Japanese artists who made those marvelous *ehon*—those picture-books which have now become so rare—tried to fix the sensation of these enchantments in color, and they were successful in their backgrounds to a degree almost miraculous. For which very reason some of their foregrounds have been a puzzle to foreigners unacquainted with certain features of Japanese agriculture. You will see blazing saffron-yellow fields, faint purple plains, crimson and snow-white trees, in those old picture-books; and perhaps you will exclaim: "How absurd!" But if you knew Japan you would cry out: "How deliciously real." For you would know those fields of burning yellow are fields of flowering rape, and the purple expanses are fields of blossoming miyako, and the snow-white or crimson trees are not fanciful, but represent faithfully certain phenomena of efflorescence peculiar to the plum-trees and the cherry-trees of the country. But these chromatic extravaganzas can be witnessed only during very brief periods of particular seasons: throughout the greater part of the year, the foreground of an inland landscape is apt to be dull enough in the matter of color.

It is the mists that make the magic of the backgrounds; yet even without them there is a strange, wild, dark beauty in Japanese landscapes, a beauty not easily defined in words. The secret of it must be sought in the extraordinary lines of the mountains, in the strangely abrupt crumpling and jagging of the ranges: no two masses closely resembling each other, every one having a fantasticality of its own. Where the chains reach to any considerable height, softly swelling lines are rare: the general characteristic is abruptness, and the charm is the charm of Irregularity.

Doubtless this weird Nature first inspired the Japanese with their unique sense of the value of irregularity in decoration—taught them that single secret of composition which distinguishes their art from all other art, and which Professor Chamberlain

has said it is their special mission to teach to the Occident.*
Certainly, whoever has once learned to feel the beauty and significance of the old Japanese decorative art can find thereafter
little pleasure in the corresponding art of the West. What he has
really learned is that Nature's greatest charm is irregularity. And
perhaps something of no small value might be written upon the
question whether the highest charm of human life and work is
not also irregularity.

IX.

From Chiburimura we made steam west for the port of Urago,
which is in the island of Nishinoshima. As we approached it
Takuhizan came into imposing view. Far away it had seemed a
soft and beautiful shape; but as its blue tones evaporated its
aspect became rough, and even grim: an enormous jagged bulk
all robed in somber verdure, through which, as through tatters,
there protruded here and there naked rock of the wildest shapes.
One fragment, I remember, as it caught the slanting sun upon
the irregularities of its summit, seemed an immense gray skull.
At the base of this mountain, and facing the shore of Nakashima,
rises a pyramidal mass of rock, covered with scraggy under-
growth, and several hundred feet in height—Mongakuzan. On
its desolate summit stands a little shrine.

"Takuhizan" signifies The Fire-burning Mountain—a name due
perhaps either to the legend of its ghostly fires, or to some ancient memory of its volcanic period. "Mongakuzan" means The
Mountain of Mongaku—Mongaku Shōnin, the great monk. It is
said that Mongaku Shōnin fled to Oki, and that he dwelt alone
upon the top of that mountain many years, doing penance for
his deadly sin. Whether he really ever visited Oki, I am not able
to say; there are traditions which declare the contrary. But the
peaklet has borne his name for hundreds of years.

Now this is the story of Mongaku Shōnin:

---

* See article on Art in his *Things Japanese*.

Many centuries ago, in the city of Kyōto, there was a captain of the garrison whose name was Endō Moritō. He saw and loved the wife of a noble samurai; and when she refused to listen to his desires, he vowed that he would destroy her family unless she consented to the plan which he submitted to her. The plan was that upon a certain night she should suffer him to enter her house and to kill her husband; after which she was to become his wife.

But she, pretending to consent, devised a noble stratagem to save her honor. For, after having persuaded her husband to absent himself from the city, she wrote to Endo a letter, bidding him come upon a certain night to the house. And on that night she clad herself in her husband's robes, and made her hair like the hair of a man, and laid herself down in her husband's place, and pretended to sleep.

And Endo came in the dead of the night with his sword drawn, and smote off the head of the sleeper at a blow, and seized it by the hair and lifted it up and saw it was the head of the woman he had loved and wronged.

Then a great remorse came upon him, and hastening to a neighboring temple, he confessed his sin, and did penance, and cut off his hair, and became a monk, taking the name of Mongaku. And in after years he attained to great holiness, so that folk still pray to him, and his memory is venerated throughout the land.

Now at Asakusa in Tokyō, in one of the curious little streets which lead to the great temple of Kwannon the Merciful, there are always wonderful images to be seen—figures that seem alive, though made of wood only—figures illustrating the ancient legends of Japan. And there you may see Endō standing: in his right hand the reeking sword; in his left the head of a beautiful woman. The face of the woman you may forget soon, because it is only beautiful.

But the face of Endō you will not forget, because it is naked hell.

X.

Urago is a queer little town, perhaps quite as large as Mionoseki, and built, like Mionoseki, on a narrow ledge at the base of a steep semicircle of hills. But it is much more primitive and colorless than Mionoseki; and its houses are still more closely cramped between cliffs and water, so that its streets, or rather alleys, are no wider than gangways. As we cast anchor, my attention was suddenly riveted by a strange spectacle—a white wilderness of long fluttering vague shapes, in a cemetery on the steep hillside, rising by terraces high above the roofs of the town. The cemetery was full of gray haka and images of divinities; and over every haka there was a curious white paper banner fastened to a thin bamboo pole. Through a glass one could see that these banners were inscribed with Buddhist texts—*"Namu-myō-hō-renge-kyō," "Namu Amida Butsu," "Namu Daij Dai-hi Kwanze-on Bosatsu,"*—and other holy words. Upon inquiry I learned that it was an Urago custom to place these banners every year above the graves during one whole month preceding the Festival of the Dead, together with various other ornamental or symbolic things.

The water was full of naked swimmers, who shouted laughing welcomes; and a host of light, swift boats, sculled by naked fishermen, darted out to look for passengers and freight. It was my first chance to observe the physique of Oki islanders; and I was much impressed by the vigorous appearance of both men and boys. The adults seemed to me of a taller and more powerful type than the men of the Izumo coast; and not a few of those brown backs, and shoulders displayed, in the motion of sculling, what is comparatively rare in Japan, even among men picked for heavy labor—a magnificent development of muscles.

As the steamer stopped an hour at Urago, we had time to dine ashore in the chief hotel. It was a very clean and pretty hotel, and the fare infinitely superior to that of the hotel at Sakai. Yet the price charged was only seven sen; and the old landlord refused to accept the whole of the chadai-gift offered him, retaining less than half, and putting back the rest, with gentle force, into the sleeve of my yukata.

XI.

From Urago we proceeded to Hishi-ura, which is in Nakanoshima, and the scenery grew always more wonderful as we steamed between the islands. The channel was just wide enough to create the illusion of a grand river flowing with the stillness of vast depth between mountains of a hundred forms. The long lovely vision was everywhere walled in by peaks, bluing through sea-haze, and on either hand the ruddy gray cliffs, sheering up from profundity, sharply mirrored their least asperities in the flood with never a distortion, as in a sheet of steel. Not until we reached Hishi-ura did the horizon reappear; and even then it was visible only between two lofty headlands, as if seen through a river's mouth.

Hishi-ura is far prettier than Urago, but it is much less populous, and has the aspect of a prosperous agricultural town, rather than of a fishing station. It bends round a bay formed by low hills which slope back gradually toward the mountainous interior, and which display a considerable extent of cultivated surface. The buildings are somewhat scattered, and in many cases isolated by gardens; and those facing the water are quite handsome modern constructions. Urago boasts the best hotel in all Oki; and it has two new temples—one a Buddhist temple of the Zen sect, one a Shintō temple of the Izumo Taisha faith, each the gift of a single person. A rich widow, the owner of the hotel, built the Buddhist temple; and the wealthiest of the merchants contributed the other—one of the handsomest miya for its size that I ever saw.

XII.

Dōgo, the main island of the Oki archipelago, sometimes itself called "Oki," lies at a distance of eight miles, northeast of the

Dōzen group, beyond a stretch of very dangerous sea. We made for it immediately after leaving Urago; passing to the open through a narrow and fantastic strait between Nakanoshima and Nishinoshima, where the cliffs take the form of enormous fortifications—bastions and ramparts, rising by tiers. Three colossal rocks, anciently forming but a single mass, which would seem to have been divided by some tremendous shock, rise from deep water near the mouth of the channel, like shattered towers. And the last promontory of Nishinoshima, which we pass to port, a huge red naked rock, turns to the horizon a point so strangely shaped that it has been called by a name signifying "The Hat of the Shintō priest."

As we glide out into the swell of the sea other extraordinary shapes appear, rising from great depths. Komori, "The Bat," a ragged silhouette against the horizon, has a great hole worn through it, which glares like an eye. Farther out two bulks, curved and pointed, and almost joined at the top, bear a grotesque resemblance to the uplifted pincers of a crab; and there is also visible a small dark mass which, until closely approached, seems the figure of a man sculling a boat. Beyond these are two islands: Matsushima, uninhabited and inaccessible, where there is always a swell to beware of; Omorishima, even loftier, which rises from the ocean in enormous ruddy precipices. There seemed to be some grim force in those sinister bulks; some occult power which made our steamer reel and shiver as she passed them. But I saw a marvelous effect of color under those formidable cliffs of Omorishima. They were lighted by a slanting sun; and where the glow of the bright rock fell upon the water, each black-blue ripple flashed bronze: I thought of a sea of metallic violet ink.

From Dōzen the cliffs of Dōgo can be clearly seen when the weather is not foul: they are streaked here and there with chalky white, which breaks through their blue, even in time of haze. Above them a vast bulk is visible—a *point-de-repère* for the mariners of Hōki—the mountain of Daimanji. Dōgo, indeed, is one great cluster of mountains.

Its cliffs rapidly turned green for us, and we followed them eastwardly for perhaps half an hour. Then they opened unexpectedly and widely, revealing a superb bay, widening far into the land, surrounded by hills, and full of shipping. Beyond a confusion of masts there crept into view a long gray line of house-fronts, at the base of a crescent of cliffs—the city of Saigo; and in a little while we touched a wharf of stone. There I bade farewell for a month to the Oki-Saigo.

XIII.

Saigo was a great surprise. Instead of the big fishing village I had expected to see, I found a city much larger and handsomer and in all respects more modernized than Sakai; a city of long streets full of good shops; a city with excellent public buildings; a city of which the whole appearance indicated commercial prosperity. Most of the edifices were roomy two-story dwellings of merchants, and everything had a bright, new look. The unpainted woodwork of the houses had not yet darkened into gray; the blue tints of the tiling were still fresh. I learned that this was because the town had been recently rebuilt, after a conflagration, and rebuilt upon a larger and handsomer plan.

Saigo seems still larger than it really is. There are about one thousand houses, which number in any part of Western Japan means a population of at least five thousand, but must mean considerably more in Saigo. These form three long streets—Nishimachi, Nakamachi, and Higashimachi (names respectively signifying the Western, Middle, and Eastern Streets), bisected by numerous cross-streets and alleys. What makes the place seem disproportionately large is the queer way the streets twist about, following the irregularities of the shore, and even doubling upon themselves, so as to create from certain points of view an impression of depth which has no existence. For Saigo is peculiarly, although admirably situated. It fringes both banks of a river, the Yabigawa, near its mouth, and likewise extends round a large point within the splendid bay, besides stretching itself out upon various tongues of land. But though smaller than it looks, to walk through all its serpentine streets is a good afternoon's work.

Besides being divided by the Yabigawa, the town is intersected by various water-ways, crossed by a number of bridges. On the hills behind it stand several large buildings, including a public school, with accommodation for three hundred students; a pretty Buddhist temple (quite new), the gift of a rich citizen; a prison; and a hospital, which deserves its reputation of being for its size the handsomest Japanese edifice not only in Oki, but in all Shimane-Ken; and there are several small but very pretty gardens.

As for the harbor, you can count more than three hundred ships riding there of a summer's day. Grumblers, especially of the kind who still use wooden anchors, complain of the depth; but the men-of-war do not.

XIV.

Never, in any part of Western Japan, have I been made more comfortable than at Saigo. My friend and myself were the only guests at the hotel to which we had been recommended. The broad and lofty rooms of the upper floor which we occupied overlooked the main street on one side, and on the other commanded a beautiful mountain landscape beyond the mouth of the Yabigawa, which flowed by our garden. The sea breeze never failed by day or by night, and rendered needless those pretty fans which it is the Japanese custom to present to guests during the hot season. The fare was astonishingly good, and curiously varied; and I was told that I might order Seyō-ryōri (Occidental cooking) if I wished—beefsteak with fried potatoes, roast chicken, and so forth. I did not avail myself of the offer, as I make it a rule while traveling to escape trouble by keeping to a purely Japanese diet; but it was no small surprise to be offered in Saigo what is almost impossible to obtain in any other Japanese town of five thousand inhabitants. From a romantic point of view, however, this discovery was a disappointment. Having made my way into the most primitive region of all Japan, I had imagined myself far beyond the range of all modernizing influences; and the suggestion of beefsteak with fried potatoes was a disillusion. Nor was I entirely consoled by the subsequent discovery that there were no newspapers or telegraphs. But there was one serious hindrance to the enjoyment of these comforts: an omnipresent, frightful, heavy, all-penetrating smell, the smell of decomposing fish, used as a fertilizer. Tons and tons of cuttlefish entrails are used upon the fields beyond the Yabigawa, and the never-sleeping sea wind blows the stench into every dwelling. Vainly do they keep incense burning in most of the houses during the heated term. After having remained three or four days constantly in the city you become better able to endure this odor; but if you should leave town even for a few hours only, you will be astonished on returning to discover how much your nose had been numbed by habit and refreshed by absence.

XV.

On the morning of the day after my arrival at Saigo, a young physician called to see me, and requested me to dine with him at his house. He explained very frankly that as I was the first foreigner who had ever stopped in Saigo, it would afford much pleasure both to his family and to himself to have a good chance to see me; but the natural courtesy of the man overcame any scruple I might have felt to gratify the curiosity of strangers. I was not only treated charmingly at his beautiful home, but actually sent away loaded with presents, most of which I attempted to decline in vain. In one matter, however, I remained obstinate, even at the risk of offending—the gift of a wonderful specimen of bateiseki (a substance which I shall speak of hereafter). This I persisted in refusing to take, knowing it to be not only very costly, but very rare. My host at last yielded, but afterwards secretly sent to the hotel two smaller specimens, which Japanese etiquette rendered it impossible to return. Before leaving Saigo, I experienced many other unexpected kindnesses from the same gentleman.

Not long after, one of the teachers of the Saigo public school paid me a visit. He had heard of my interest in Oki, and brought with him two fine maps of the islands made by himself, a little book about Saigo, and, as a gift, a collection of Oki butterflies and insects which he had made. It is only in Japan that one is likely to meet with these wonderful exhibitions of pure goodness on the part of perfect strangers.

A third visitor, who had called to see my friend, performed an action equally characteristic, but which caused me not a little pain. We squatted down to smoke together. He drew from his girdle a remarkably beautiful tobacco-pouch and pipe-case, containing a little silver pipe, which he began to smoke. The pipe-case was made of a sort of black coral, curiously carved, and attached to the tabako-iré, or pouch, by a heavy cord of plaited silk of three colors, passed through a ball of transparent agate. Seeing me admire it, he suddenly drew a knife from his sleeve, and before I could prevent him, severed the pipe-case from the pouch, and presented it to me. I felt almost as if he had cut one of his own nerves asunder when he cut that wonderful cord; and, nevertheless, once this had been done, to refuse the gift would have been rude in the extreme. I made him accept a present in return; but after that experience I was careful never again while in Oki to admire anything in the presence of its owner.

XVI.

Every province of Japan has its own peculiar dialect; and that of Oki, as might be expected in a country so isolated, is particularly distinct. In Saigo, however, the Izumo dialect is largely used. The townsfolk in their manners and customs much resemble Izumo country-folk; indeed, there are many Izumo people among them, most of the large businesses being in the hands of strangers. The women did not impress me as being so attractive as those of Izumo: I saw several very pretty girls, but these proved to be strangers.

However, it is only in the country that one can properly study the physical characteristics of a population. Those of the Oki islanders may best be noted at the fishing villages, many of which I visited. Everywhere I saw fine strong men and vigorous women; and it struck me that the extraordinary plenty and cheapness of nutritive food had quite as much to do with this robustness as climate and constant execise. So easy, indeed, is it to live in Oki, that men of other coasts, who find existence difficult, emigrate to Oki if they can get a chance to work there, even at less remuneration. An interesting spectacle to me were the vast processions of fishing-vessels which always, weather permitting, began to shoot out to sea a couple of hours before sundown. The surprising swiftness with which those light craft were impelled by their sinewy scullers—many of whom were women—told of a skill acquired only through the patient experience of generations. Another matter that amazed me was the number of boats. One night in the offing I was able to count three hundred and five torch-fires in sight, each one signifying a crew; and I knew that from almost any of the forty-five coast villages I might see the same spectacle at the same time. The main part of the population, infact, spends its summer nights at sea. It is also a revelation to travel from Izumo to Hamada by night upon a swift steamer during the fishing season. The horizon for a hundred miles is alight with torch-fire; the toil of a whole coast is revealed in that vast illumination.

Although the human population appears to have gained rather than lost vigor upon this barren soil the horses and cattle of the country seem to have degenerated. They are remarkably diminutive. I saw cows not much bigger than Izumo calves, with calves about the size of goats. The horses, or rather ponies, belong to a special breed of which Oki is rather proud—very small, but hardy. I was told that there were larger horses, but I saw none, and could not learn whether they were imported. It seemed to me a curious thing, when I saw Oki ponies for the first time, that

Sasaki Takatsuna's battle-steed—not less famous in Japanese story than the horse Kyrat in the ballads of Kurroglou—is declared by the islanders to have been a native of Oki. And they have a tradition that it once swam from Oki to Mionoseki.

XVII.

Almost every district and town in Japan has its meibutsu or its kembutsu. The meibutsu of any place are its special productions, whether natural or artificial. The kembutsu of a town or district are its sights—its places worth visiting for any reason—religious, traditional, historical, or pleasurable. Temples and gardens, remarkable trees and curious rocks, are kembutsu. So, likewise, are any situations from which beautiful scenery may be looked at, or any localities where one can enjoy such charming spectacles as the blossoming of cherry-trees in spring, the flickering of fireflies in summer nights, the flushing of maple-leaves in autumn, or even that long snaky motion of moonlight upon water to which Chinese poets have given the delightful name of Kinryō, "the Golden Dragon."

The great meibutsu of Oki is the same as that of Hinomisaki—dried cuttlefish; an article of food much in demand both in China and Japan. The cuttlefish of Oki and Hinomisaki and Mionoseki are all termed ika (a kind of sepia); but those caught at Mionoseki are white and average fifteen inches in length, while those of Oki and Hinomisaki rarely exceed twelve inches and have a reddish tinge. The fisheries of Mionoseki and Hinomisaki are scarcely known; but the fisheries of Oki are famed not only throughout Japan, but also in Korea and China. It is only through the tilling of the sea that the islands have become prosperous and capable of supporting thirty thousand souls upon a coast of which but a very small portion can be cultivated at all. Enormous quantities of cuttlefish are shipped to the mainland; but I have been told that the Chinese are the best customers of Oki for this product. Should the supply ever fail, the result would be disastrous beyond conception; but at present it seems inexhaustible, though the fishing has been going on for thousands of years. Hundreds of tons of cuttlefish are caught, cured, and prepared for exportation month after month; and many hundreds of acres are fertilized with the entrails and other refuse. An officer of police told me several strange facts about this fishery. On the northeastern coast of Saigo it is no uncommon thing for one fisherman to capture upwards of two thousand cuttlefish in a single night. Boats have been burst asunder by the weight of a few hauls, and caution has to be observed in loading. Besides the sepia, however, this coast swarms with another variety of cuttlefish which also furnishes a food-staple—the formidable tako, or true octopus. Tako weighing fifteen kwan each, or nearly one hundred and twenty-five pounds, are sometimes caught near the fishing settlement of Nakamura. I was surprised to learn that there was no record of any person having been injured by these monstrous creatures.

Another meibutsu of Oki is much less known than it deserves to be—the beautiful jet-black stone called bateiseki, or "horse-hoof stone."* It is found only in Dōgo, and never in large masses. It is about as heavy as flint, and chips like flint; but the polish which it takes is like that of agate. There are no veins or specks in it; the intense black color never varies. Artistic objects are made of bateiseki: inkstones, wine-cups, little boxes, small dai, or stands for vases or statuettes; even jewelry, the material being worked in the same manner as the beautiful agates of Yumachi in Izumo. These articles are comparatively costly, even in the place of their manufacture.

There is an odd legend about the origin of the bateiseki. It owes its name to some fancied resemblance to a horse's hoof, either in color, or in the semicircular marks often seen upon the stone in its natural state, and caused by its tendency to split in curved lines. But the story goes that the bateiseki was formed by the

---

* It seems to be a black obsidian.

touch of the hoofs of a sacred steed, the wonderful mare of the great Minamoto warrior, Sasaki Takatsuna. She had a foal, which fell into a deep lake in Dōgo, and was drowned. She plunged into the lake herself, but could not find her foal, being deceived by the reflection of her own head in the water. For a long time she sought and mourned in vain; but even the hard rocks felt for her, and where her hoofs touched them beneath the water they became changed into bateiseki.*

Scarcely less beautiful than bateiseki, and equally black, is another Oki-meibutsu, a sort of coralline marine product called umi-matsu, or "sea-pine." Pipe-cases, brush-stands, and other small articles are manufactured from it; and these when polished seem to be covered with black lacquer. Objects of umi-matsu are rare and dear.

Nacre wares, however, are very cheap in Oki; and these form another variety of meibutsu. The shells of the awabi, or "sea-ear," which reaches a surprising size in these western waters, are converted by skillful polishing and cutting into wonderful dishes bowls, cups, and other articles, over whose surfaces the play of iridescence is like a flickering of fire of hundred colors.

XVIII.

According to a little book published at Matsue, the kembutsu of Oki-no-Kuni are divided among "three of the four principal islands; Chiburishima only possessing nothing of special interest. For many generations the attractions of Dōgo have been the shrine of Agonashi Jizō, at Tsubamezato; the waterfall (Dangyo-taki) at Yuenimura; the mighty cedar-tree *(sugi)* before the shrine of Tama-Wakusa-jinja at Shimomura, and the lakelet called Sai-no-ike where the bateiseki is said to be found. Naka-noshima possesses the tomb of the exiled Emperor Go-Toba, at Amamura, and the residence of the ancient Chōja, Shikekurō,

---

* There are several other versions of this legend. In one, it is the mare, and not the foal, which was drowned.

where he dwelt betimes, and where relics of him are kept even to this day. Nishinoshima possesses at Beppu a shrine in memory of the exiled Emperor Go-Daigo, and on the summit of Takuhizan that shrine of Gongen-Sama, from the place of which a wonderful view of the whole archipelago is said to be obtainable on cloudless days.

Though Chiburishima has no kembutsu, her poor little village of Chiburi—the same Chiburimura at which the Oki steamer always touches on her way to Saigo—is the scene of perhaps the most interesting of all the traditions of the archipelago.

Five hundred and sixty years ago, the exiled Emperor Go-Daigo managed to escape from the observation of his guards, and to flee from Nishinoshima to Chiburi. And the brown sailors of that little hamlet offered to serve him, even with their lives if need be. They were loading their boats with "dried fish," doubtless the same dried cuttlefish which their descendants still carry to Izumo and to Hōki. The emperor promised to remember them, should they succeed in landing him either in Hōki or in Izumo; and they put him in a boat.

But when they had sailed only a little way they saw the pursuing vessels. Then they told the emperor to lie down, and they piled the dried fish high above him. The pursuers came on board and searched the boat, but they did not even think of touching the strong-smelling cuttlefish. And when the men of Chiburi were questioned they invented a story, and gave to the enemies of the emperor a false clue to follow. And so, by means of the cuttlefish, the good emperor was enabled to escape from banishment.

XIX.

I found there were various difficulties in the way of becoming acquainted with some of the kembutsu. There are no roads, properly speaking, in all Oki, only mountain paths; and consequently there are no jinrikisha, with the exception of one especially imported by the leading physician of Saigo, and available for use only in the streets. There are not even any kago, or palanquins, except one for the use of the same physician. The paths are terribly rough, according to the testimony of the strong peasants themselves; and the distances, particularly in the, hottest period of the year, are disheartening. Ponies can be hired; but my experiences of a similar wild country in western Izumo persuaded me that neither pleasure nor profit was to be gained by a long and painful ride over pine-covered hills, through slippery gullies and along torrent-beds, merely to look at a waterfall. I abandoned the idea of visiting Dangyotaki, but resolved, if possible, to see Agonashi-Jizō.

I had first heard in Matsue of Agonashi-Jizō while suffering from one of those toothaches in which the pain appears to be several hundred miles in depth—one of those toothaches which disturb your ideas of space and time. And a friend who, sympathized said:

"People who have toothache pray to Agonashi-Jizō. Agonashi-Jizō is in Oki, but Izumo people pray to him. When cured they go to Lake Shinji, to the river, to the sea, or to any running stream, and drop into the water twelve pears *(nashi)*, one for each of the twelve months. And they believe the currents will carry all these to Oki across the sea.

"Now, Agonashi-Jizō means 'Jizō-who-has-no-Jaw.' For it is said that in one of his former lives Jizō had such a toothache in his lower jaw that he tore off his jaw, and threw it away, and died. And he became a Bosatsu. And the people of Oki made a statue of him without a jaw; and all who suffer toothache pray to that Jizō of Oki."

This story interested me; for more than once I had felt a strong desire to do like Agonashi-Jizō, though lacking the necessary courage and indifference to earthly consequences. Moreover, the tradition suggested so humane and profound a comprehension of toothache, and so large a sympathy with its victims, that I felt myself somewhat consoled.

Nevertheless, I did not go to see Agonashi-Jizō, because I found out there was no longer any Agonashi-Jizō to see. The news was brought one evening by some friends, shizoku of Matsue, who had settled in Oki, a young police officer and his wife. They had walked right across the island to see us, starting before daylight, and crossing no less than thirty-two torrents on their way. The wife, only nineteen, was quite slender and pretty, and did not appear tired by that long rough journey.

What we learned about the famous Jizō was this: The name Agonashi-Jizō was only a popular corruption of the true name, Agonaoshi-Jizō, or "Jizō-the-Healer-of-Jaws." The little temple in which the statue stood had been burned, and the statue along with it, except a fragment of the lower part of the figure, now piously preserved by some old peasant woman. It was impossible to rebuild the temple, as the disestablishment of Buddhism had entirely destroyed the resources of that faith in Oki. But the peasantry of Tsubamezato had built a little Shintō miya on the site of the temple, with a torii before it, and people still prayed there to Agonaoshi-Jizō.

This last curious fact reminded me of the little torii I had seen erected before the images of Jizō in the Cave of the Children's Ghosts. Shintō, in these remote districts of the west, now appropriates the popular divinities of Buddhism, just as of old Buddhism used to absorb the divinities of Shintō in other parts of Japan.

XX.

I went to the Sai-no-ike, and to Tama-Wakasu-jinja, as these two kembutsu can be reached by boat. The Sai-no-ike, however, much disappointed me. It can only be visited in very calm weather, as the way to it lies along a frightfully dangerous coast, nearly all sheer precipice. But the sea is beautifully clear, and the eye can distinguish forms at an immense depth below the surface. After following the cliffs for about an hour, the boat reaches a sort of cove, where the beach is entirely composed of small round boulders. They form a long ridge, the outer verge of which is always in motion, rolling to and fro with a crash like a volley of musketry at the rush and ebb of every wave. To climb over this ridge of moving stone balls is quite disagreeable; but after that one has only about twenty yards to walk, and the Sai-no-ike appears, surrounded on three sides by wooded hills. It is little more than a large freshwater pool, perhaps fifty yards wide, not in any way wonderful. You can see no rocks under the surface—only mud and pebbles. That any part of it was ever deep enough to drown a foal is hard to believe. I wanted to swim across to the farther side to try the depth, but the mere proposal scandalized the boatmen. The pool was sacred to the gods, and was guarded by invisible monsters; to enter it was impious and dangerous. I felt obliged to respect the local ideas on the subject, and contented myself with inquiring where the bateiseki was found. They pointed to the hill on the western side of the water. This indication did not tally with the legend. I could discover no trace of any human labor on that savage hillside; there was certainly no habitation within miles of the place; it was the very abomination of desolation.*

It is never wise for the traveler in Japan to expect much on the strength of the reputation of kembutsu. The interest attaching to the vast majority of kembutsu depends altogether upon the exercise of imagination; and the ability to exercise such imagination again depends upon one's acquaintance with the history and mythology of the country. Knolls, rocks, stumps of trees, have been for hundreds of years objects of reverence for the peasantry, solely because of local traditions relating to them. Broken iron kettles, bronze mirrors covered with verdigris, rusty pieces of sword blades, fragments of red earthenware, have drawn generations of pilgrims to the shrines in which they are preserved.

---

* There are two ponds not far from each other. The one I visited was called O-ike, or "The Male Pond," and the other, Me-ike, or "The Female Pond."

At various small temples which I visited, the temple treasures consisted of trays full of small stones. The first time I saw those little stones I thought that the priests had been studying geology or mineralogy, each stone being labeled in Japanese characters. On examination, the stones proved to be absolutely worthless in themselves, even as specimens of neighboring rocks. But the stories which the priests or acolytes could tell about each and every stone were more than interesting. The stones served as rude beads, in fact, for the recital of a litany of Buddhist legends.

After the experience of the Sai-no-ike, I had little reason to expect to see anything extraordinary at Shimonishimura. But this time I was agreeably mistaken. Shimonishimura is a pretty fishing village within an hour's row from Saigo. The boat follows a wild but beautiful coast, passing one singular truncated hill, Oshiroyama, upon which a strong castle stood in ancient times. There is now only a small Shintō shrine there, surrounded by pines. From the hamlet of Shimonishimura to the Temple of Tama-Wakasu-jinja is a walk of twenty minutes over very rough paths between rice-fields and vegetable gardens. But the situation of the temple, surrounded by its sacred grove, in the heart of a landscape framed in by mountain ranges of many colors, is charmingly impressive. The edifice seems to have once been a Buddhist temple; it is now the largest Shintō structure in Oki. Before its gate stands the famous cedar, not remarkable for height, but wonderful for girth. Two yards above the soil its circumference is forty-five feet. It has given its name to the holy place; the Oki peasantry scarcely ever speak of Tama-Wakasu-jinja, but only of "Ō-Sugi," the Great Cedar.

Tradition avers that this tree was planted by a Buddhist nun more than eight hundred years ago. And it is alleged that whoever eats with chopsticks made from the wood of that tree will never have the toothache, and will live to become exceedingly old.*

---

* Speaking of the supposed power of certain trees to cure toothache. I may men-

XXI.

The shrine dedicated to the spirit of the Emperor Go-Daigo is in Nishinoshima, at Beppu, a picturesque fishing village composed of one long street of thatched cottages fringing a bay, at the foot of a demilune of hills. The simplicity of manners and the honest healthy poverty of the place are quite wonderful, even for Oki. There is a kind of inn for strangers at which hot water is served instead of tea, and dried beans instead of kwashi, and millet instead of rice. The absence of tea, however, is much more significant than that of rice. But the people of Beppu do not suffer for lack of proper nourishment, as their robust appearance bears witness: there are plenty of vegetables, all raised in tiny gardens which the women and children till during the absence of the boats; and there is abundance of fish. There is no Buddhist temple, but there is an ujigami.

The shrine of the emperor is at the top of a hill called Kuro-kizan, at one end of the bay. The hill is covered with tall pines, and the path is very steep, so that I thought it prudent to put on straw sandals, in which one never slips. I found the shrine to be a small wooden miya, scarcely three feet high, and black with age. There were remains of other miya, much older, lying in some bushes near by. Two large stones, unhewn and without inscriptions of any sort, have been placed before the shrine. I looked into it, and saw a crumbling metal-mirror, dingy paper gohei attached to splints of bamboo, two little o-mikidokkuri, or Shintō saké-vessels of red earthenware, and one rin. There was nothing else to see, except, indeed, certain delightful glimpses of coast and peak, visible in the bursts of warm blue light which penetrated the consecrated shadow, between the trunks of the great pines.

---

tion a curious superstition about the yanagi, or willow-tree. Sufferers from toothache sometimes stick needles into the tree, believing that the pain caused to the tree-spirit will force it to exercise its power to cure. I could not, however, find any record of this practice in Oki.

Only this humble shrine commemorates the good emperor's sojourn among the peasantry of Oki but there is now being erected by voluntary subscription, at the little village of Go-sen-goku-mura, near Yonago in Tottori, quite a handsome monument of stone to the memory of his daughter, the princess Hinako-Nai-Shinnō, who died there while attempting to follow her august parent into exile. Near the place of her rest stands a famous chestnut-tree, of which this story is told: While the emperor's daughter was ill, she asked for chestnuts; and some were given to her. But she took only one, and bit it a little, and threw it away. It found root and became a grand tree. But all the chestnuts of that tree bear marks like the marks of little teeth; for in Japanese legend even the trees are loyal, and strive to show their loyalty in all sorts of tender dumb ways. And that tree is called Hagata-guri-no-ki, which signifies; "The Tree-of-the-Tooth-marked-Chestnuts."

XXII.

Long before visiting Oki I had heard that such a crime as theft was unknown in the little archipelago; that it had never been found necessary there to lock things up; and that, whenever weather permitted, the people slept with their houses all open to the four winds of heaven.

And after careful investigation, I found these surprising statements were, to a great extent, true. In the Dōzen group, at least, there are no thieves, and practically no crime. Ten policemen are sufficient to control the whole of both Dōzen and Dōgo, with their population of thirty thousand one hundred and ninety-six souls. Each policeman has under his inspection a number of villages, which he visits on regular days; and his absence for any length of time from one of these seems never to be taken advantage of. His work is mostly confined to the enforcement of hygienic regulations, and to the writing of reports. It is very seldom that he finds it necessary to make an arrest, for the people scarcely ever quarrel.

In the island of Dōgo alone are there ever any petty thefts, and only in that part of Oki do the people take any precautions against thieves. Formerly there was no prison, and thefts were never heard of; and the people of Dōgo still claim that the few persons arrested in their island for such offenses are not natives of Oki, but strangers from the mainland. What appears to be quite true is that theft was unknown in Oki before the port of Saigo obtained its present importance. The whole trade of Western Japan has been increased by the rapid growth of steam communications with other parts of the empire; and the port of Saigo appears to have gained commercially, but to have lost morally, by the new conditions.

Yet offenses against the law are still surprisingly few, even in Saigo. Saigo has a prison; and there were people in it during my stay in the city; but the inmates had been convicted only of such misdemeanors as gambling (which is strictly prohibited in every form by Japanese law), or the violation of lesser ordinances. When a serious offense is committed, the offender is not punished in Oki, but is sent to the great prison at Matsue, in Izumo.

The Dōzen islands, however, perfectly maintain their ancient reputation for irreproachable honesty. There have been no thieves in those three islands within the memory of man; and there are no serious quarrels, no fighting, nothing to make life miserable for anybody. Wild and bleak as the land is, all can manage to live comfortably enough; food is cheap and plenty, and manners and customs have retained their primitive simplicity.

XXIII.

To foreign eyes the defenses of even an Izumo dwelling against thieves seem ludicrous. *Chevaux-de-frise* of bamboo stakes are used extensively in eastern cities of the empire, but in Izumo these are not often to be seen, and do not protect the really weak points of the buildings upon which they are placed. As for outside walls and fences, they serve only for screens, or for ornamental boundaries; any one can climb over them. Any one can also cut his way into an ordinary Japanese house with a pocket knife. The amadō are thin sliding screens of soft wood, easy to break with a single blow; and in most Izumo homes there is not a lock which could resist one vigorous pull. Indeed, the Japanese themselves are so far aware of the futility of their wooden panels against burglars that all who can afford it build kura—small heavy fire-proof and (for Japan) almost burglar-proof structures, with very thick earthen walls, a narrow ponderous door fastened with a gigantic padlock, and one very small iron-barred window, high up, near the roof. The kura are whitewashed, and look very neat. They cannot be used for dwellings, however, as they are mouldy and dark; and they serve only as storehouses for valuables. It is not easy to rob a kura.

But there is no trouble in "burglariously" entering an Izumo dwelling unless there happen to be good watchdogs on the premises. The robber knows the only difficulties in the way of his enterprise are such as he is likely to encounter after having effected an entrance. In view of these difficulties, he usually carries a sword.

Nevertheless, he does not wish to find himself in any predicament requiring the use of a sword; and to avoid such an unpleasant possibility he has recourse to magic.

He looks about the premises for a tarai—a kind of tub. If he finds one, he performs a nameless operation in a certain part of the yard, and covers the spot with the tub, turned upside down. He believes if he can do this that a magical sleep will fall upon all the inmates of the house, and that he will thus be able to carry away whatever he pleases, without being heard or seen.

But every Izumo household knows the countercharm. Each evening, before retiring, the careful wife sees that a hocho, or kitchen knife, is laid upon the kitchen floor, and covered with a kanadarai, or brazen wash-basin, on the upturned bottom of which is placed a single straw sandal, of the noiseless sort called zōri, also turned upside down. She believes this little bit of witchcraft will not only nullify the robber's spell, but also render it impossible for him—even should he succeed in entering the house without being seen or heard—to carry anything whatever away. But, unless very tired indeed, she will also see that the tarai is brought into the house before the amadō are closed for the night.

If through omission of these (precautions as the good wife might aver), or in despite of them, the dwelling be robbed while the family are asleep, search is made early in the morning for the footprint of the burglar; and a moxa* is set burning upon each footprint. By this operation it is hoped or believed that the burglar's feet will be made so sore that he cannot run far, and that the police may easily overtake him.

XXIV.

It was in Oki that I first heard of an extraordinary superstition about the cause of okori (ague, or intertermittent fever), mild forms of which prevail in certain districts at certain seasons; but I have since learned that this quaint belief is an old one in Izume and in many parts of the San-indo. It is a curious example of the manner in which Buddhism has been used to explain all mysteries.

Okori is said to be caused by the Gaki-botoke, or hungry ghosts. Strictly speaking, the Gaki-botoke are the Pretas of Indian Buddhism, spirits condemned to sojourn in the Gakidō, the sphere of the penance of perpetual hunger and thirst. But in Japanese Buddhism, the name Gaki is given also to those souls who have none among the living to remember them, and to prepare for them the customary offerings of food and tea.

---

* *Moxa*, a corruption of the native name of the mugwort plant *more-kusa*, or *mogusa*, "the burning weed." Small cones of its fiber are used for cauterizing, according to the old Chinese system of medicine—the little cones being placed upon the patient's skin, lighted, and left to smolder until wholly consumed. The result is a profound scar. The moxa is not only used therapeutically, but also as a punishment for very naughty children. See the interesting note on this subject in Professor Chamberlain's *Things Japanese*.

These suffer, and seek to obtain warmth and nutriment by entering into the bodies of the living. The person into whom a gaki enters at first feels intensely cold and shivers, because the gaki is cold. But the chill is followed by a feeling of intense heat, as the gaki becomes warm. Having warmed itself and absorbed some nourishment at the expense of its unwilling host, the gaki goes away, and the fever ceases for a time. But at exactly the same hour upon another day the gaki will return, and the victim must shiver and burn until the haunter has become warm and has satisfied its hunger. Some gaki visit their patients every day; others every alternate day, or even less often. In brief, the paroxysms of any form of intermittent fever are explained by the presence of the gaki, and the intervals between the paroxysms by its absence.

XXV.

Of the word hotoke (which becomes botoke in such compounds as nure-botoke,* gaki-botoke), there is something curious to say.

Hotoke signifies a Buddha.

Hotoke signifies also the Souls of the Dead—since faith holds that these, after worthy life, either enter upon the way to Buddhahood, or become Buddhas.

Hotoke, by euphemism, has likewise come to mean a corpse: hence the verb hotoke-zukuri, "to look ghastly," to have the semblance of one long dead.

And Hotoke-San is the name of the Image of a Face seen in the pupil of the eye—Hotoke-San, "the Lord Buddha." Not the Supreme of the Hokkekyo, but that lesser Buddha who dwelleth in each one of us—the Spirit.†

---

* *Nure-botoke,* "a wet god." This term is applied to the statue of a deity left exposed to the open air.

† According to popular legend, in each eye of the child of a god or a dragon *two Buddhas* are visible. The statement in some of the Japanese ballads, that the hero sung of had *four Buddhas* in his eyes, is equivalent to the declaration that each of his eyes had a double-pupil.

Sang Rossetti: "*I looked and saw your heart in the shadow of your eyes.*" Exactly converse is the Oriental thought. A Japanese lover would have said: "I looked and saw *my own Buddha* in the shadow of your eyes."

What is the psychical theory connected with so singular a belief?* I think it might be this: the Soul, within its own body, always remains viewless; yet may reflect itself in the eyes of another, as in the mirror of a necromancer. Vainly you gaze into the eyes of the beloved to discern her soul: you see there only your own soul's shadow, diaphanous; and beyond is mystery alone—reaching to the Infinite.

But is not this true? The Ego, as Schopenhauer wonderfully said, is the dark spot in consciousness, even as the point whereat the nerve of sight enters the eye is blind. We see ourselves in others only: only through others do we dimly guess that which we are. And in the deepest love of another being do we not indeed love ourselves? What are the personalities, the individualities of us but countless vibrations in the Universal Being? Are we not all One in the unknowable Ultimate? One with the inconceivable past? One with the everlasting future?

XXVI.

In Oki, as in Izumo, the public school is slowly but surely destroying many of the old superstitions. Even the fishermen of the new generation laugh at things in which their fathers believed. I was rather surprised to receive from an intelligent young sailor, whom I had questioned through an interpreter about the ghostly fire of Takuhizan, this scornful answer: "Oh, we used to believe those things when we were savages; but we are civilized now!"

Nevertheless, he was somewhat in advance of his time. In the village to which he belonged I discovered that the Fox-superstition prevails to a degree scarcely paralleled in any part of Izumo.

---

* The idea of the *Atman* will perhaps occur to many readers.

The history of the village was quite curious. From time immemorial it had been reputed a settlement of kitsune-mochi: in other words, all its inhabitants were commonly believed, and perhaps believed themselves, to be the owners of goblin-foxes. And being all alike kitsune-mochi, they could eat and drink together, and marry and give in marriage among themselves without affliction. They were feared with a ghostly fear by the neighboring peasantry, who obeyed their demands both in matters reasonable and unreasonable. They prospered exceedingly. But some twenty years ago an Izumo stranger settled among them. He was energetic, intelligent, and possessed of some capital. He bought land, made various shrewd investments, and in a surprisingly short time became the wealthiest citizen in the place. He built a very pretty Shintō temple and presented it to the community. There was only one obstacle in the way of his becoming a really popular person: he was not a kitsune-mochi and he had even said that he hated foxes. This singularity threatened to beget discords in the mura, especially as he married his children to strangers, and thus began in the midst of the kitsune-mochi to establish a sort of anti-Fox-holding colony.

Wherefore, for a long time past, the Fox-holders have been trying to force their superfluous goblins upon him. Shadows glide about the gate of his dwelling on moonless nights, muttering: "*Kaere! kyō kara kokoye: kuruda!*" [Be off now! from now hereafter it is here that ye must dwell: go!] Then are the upper shōji violently pushed apart; and the voice of the enraged house owner is heard: "*Koko wa kiraida! modori!*" [Detestable is that which ye do! get ye gone!] And the Shadows flee away.*

---

* In 1892 a Japanese newspaper, published in Tōkyō, stated upon the authority of a physician who had visited Shimane, that the people of Oki believe in ghostly dogs instead of ghostly foxes. This is a mistake caused by the literal rendering of a term often used in Shimane, especially in Iwami, namely, inu-gami-mochi. It is only a euphemism for kitsune-mochi; the inu-gami is only the hito-kitsune, which is supposed to make itself visible in various animal forms.

XXVII.

Because there were no cuttlefish at Hishi-ura, and no horrid smells, I enjoyed myself there more than I did anywhere else in Oki. But, in any event; Hishi-ura would have interested me more than Saigo. The life of the pretty little town is peculiarly old-fashioned; and the ancient domestic industries, which the introduction of machinery has almost destroyed in Izumo and elsewhere, still exist in Hiahi-ura. It was pleasant to watch the rosy girls weaving robes of cotton and robes of silk, relieving each other whenever the work became fatiguing. All this quaint gentle life is open to inspection, and I loved to watch it. I had other pleasures also: the bay is a delightful place for swimming, and there were always boats ready to take me to any place of interest along the coast. At night the sea breeze made the rooms which I occupied deliciously cool; and from the balcony I could watch the bay-swell breaking in slow, cold fire on the steps of the wharves—a beautiful phosphorescence; and I could hear Oki mothers singing their babes to sleep with one of the oldest lullabys in the world:

> *Nenneko,*
> *O-yama no*
> *Usagi no ho,*
> *Naze mata*
> *O-mimi ga*
> *Nagai e yara?*
> *Ohkasan no*
> *O-naka ni*
> *Oru toku ni,*
> *Biwa no ha,*
> *Sasa no ha,*
> *Tabeta sona;*
> *Sore de*
> *O-mimi ga*
> *Nagai e sona.**

---

* Which words signify something like this:
"*Sleep, baby, sleep! Why are the honorable ears of the Child of the Hare of the honorable*

The air was singularly sweet and plaintive, quite different from that to which the same words are sung in Izumo, and in other parts of Japan.

One morning I had hired a boat to take me to Beppu, and was on the point of leaving the hotel for the day, when the old landlady, touching my arm, exclaimed: "Wait a little while; it is not good to cross a funeral." I looked round the corner, and saw the procession coming along the shore. It was a Shintō funeral—a child's funeral. Young lads came first, carrying Shintō emblems—little white flags, and branches of the sacred sakaki; and after the coffin the mother walked, a young peasant, crying very loud, and wiping her eyes with the long sleeves of her coarse blue dress. Then the old woman at my side murmured: "She sorrows; but she is very young: perhaps it will come back to her." For she was a pious Buddhist, my good old landlady, and doubtless supposed the mother's belief like her own, although the funeral was conducted according to the Shintō rite.

XXVIII.

There are in Buddhism certain weirdly beautiful consolations unknown to Western faith.

The young mother who loses her first child may at least pray that it will come back to her out of the night of death—not in dreams only, but through reincarnation. And so praying, she writes within the hand of the little corpse the first ideograph of her lost darling's name.

Months pass; she again becomes a mother. Eagerly she examines the flower-soft hand of the infant. And lo! the self-same ideograph is there—a rosy birth-mark on the tender palm; and the Soul returned looks out upon her through the eyes of the newly born with the gaze of other days.

---

mountain so long? 'Tis because when he dwelt within her honored womb, his mamma ate the leaves of the loquat, the leaves of the bamboo-grass. That is why his honorable ears are so long."

XXIX.

While on the subject of death I may speak of a primitive but touching custom which exists both in Oki and Izumo—that of calling the name of the dead immediately after death. For it is thought that the call may be heard by the fleeting soul, which might sometimes be thus induced to return. Therefore, when a mother dies, the children should first call her, and of all the children first the youngest (for she loved that one most); and then the husband and all those who loved the dead cry to her in turn.

And it is also the custom to call loudly the name of one who faints, or becomes insensible from any cause; and there are curious beliefs underlying this custom.

It is said that of those who swoon from pain or grief especially, many approach very nearly to death, and these always have the same experience. "You feel," said one to me in answer to my question about the belief, "as if you were suddenly somewhere else, and quite happy—only tired. And you know that you want to go to a Buddhist temple which is quite far away. At last you reach the gate of the temple court, and you see the temple inside, and it is wonderfully large and beautiful. And you pass the gate and enter the court to go to the temple. But suddenly you hear voices of friends far behind you calling your name—very, very earnestly. So you turn back, and all at once you come to yourself again. At least it is so if your heart cares to live. But one who is really tired of living will not listen to the voices, and walks on to the temple. And what there happens no man knows, for they who enter that temple never return to their friends.

"That is why people call loudly into the ear of one who swoons.

"Now, it is said that all who die, before going to the Meido, make one pilgrimage to the great temple of Zenkōji, which is in the country of Shinano, in Nagano-Ken. And they say that whenever the priest of that temple preaches, he sees the Souls gather there in the hondō to hear him, all with white wrappings about their heads. So Zenkōji might be the temple which is seen by those who swoon. But I do not know."

XXX.

I went by boat from Hishi-ura to Amamura, in Nakanoshima, to visit the tomb of the exiled Emperor Go-Toba. The scenery along the way was beautiful, and of softer outline than I had seen on my first passage through the archipelago. Small rocks rising from the water were covered with sea gulls and cormorants, which scarcely took any notice of the boat, even when we came almost within an oar's length. This fearlessness of wild creatures is one of the most charming impressions of travel in these remoter parts of Japan, yet unvisited by tourists with shotguns. The early European and American hunters in Japan seem to have found no difficulty and felt no compunction in exterminating what they considered "game" over whole districts, destroying life merely for the wanton pleasure of destruction. Their example is being imitated now by "Young Japan," and the destruction of bird life is only imperfectly checked by game laws. Happily, the government does interfere sometimes to check particular forms of the hunting vice. Some brutes who had observed the habits of swallows to make their nests in Japanese houses, last year offered to purchase some thousands of swallow-skins at a tempting price. The effect of the advertisement was cruel enough, but the police were promptly notified to stop the murdering, which they did. About the same time, in one of the Yokohama papers, there appeared a letter from some holy person announcing, as a triumph of Christian sentiment, that a "converted" fisherman had been persuaded by foreign proselytizers to kill a turtle, which his Buddhist comrades had vainly begged him to spare.

Amamura, a very small village, lies in a narrow plain of rice-fields extending from the sea to a range of low hills. From the landing-place to the village is about a quarter of a mile. The narrow path leading to it passes round the base of a small hill, covered with pines, on the outskirts of the village. There is quite a handsome Shintō temple on the hill, small, but admirably constructed, approached by stone steps and a paved walk. There are the usual lions and lamps of stone, and the ordinary simple offerings of paper and women's hair before the shrine. But I saw among the ex-voto a number of curious things which I had never seen in Izunmo—tiny miniature buckets, well-buckets, with rope and pole complete, neatly fashioned out of bamboo. The boatman said that farmers bring these to the shrine when praying for rain. The deity was called Suwa-Dai-Myōjin.

It was at the neighboring village, of which Suwa-Dai-Myōjin seems to be the ujigami, that the Emperor Go-Toba is said to have dwelt, in the house of the Chōja Shikekurō. The Shikekurō homestead remains, and still belongs to the Chōja's descendants, but they have become very poor. I asked permission to see the cups from which the exiled emperor drank, and other relics of his stay said to be preserved by the family; but in consequence of illness in the house I could not be received. So I had only a glimpse of the garden, where there is a celebrated pond—a kembutsu.

The pond is called Shikekurō's Pond—Shike-kurō-no-ike. And for seven hundred years, 'tis said, the frogs of that pond have never been heard to croak.

For the Emperor Go-Toba, having one night been kept awake by the croaking of the frogs in that pond, arose and went out and commanded them, saying: "Be silent!" Wherefore they have remained silent through all the centuries even unto this day.

Near the pond there was in that time a great pine-tree, of which the rustling upon windy nights disturbed the emperor's rest. And he spoke to the pine-tree, and said to it: "Be still!" And never thereafter was that tree heard to rustle, even in time of storms.

But that tree has ceased to be. Nothing remains of it but a few fragments of its wood and bark, which are carefully preserved as relics by the ancients of Oki. Such a fragment was shown to me in the toko of the guest chamber of the dwelling of a physician of Saigo—the same gentleman whose kindness I have related elsewhere.

The tomb of the emperor lies on the slope of a low hill, at a distance of about ten minutes' walk from the village. It is far less imposing than the least of the tombs of the Matsudaira at Matsue, in the grand old courts of Gesshōji; but it was perhaps the best which the poor little country of Oki could furnish. This is not, however, the original place of the tomb, which was moved by imperial order in the sixth year of Meiji to its present site. A lofty fence, or rather stockade of heavy wooden posts, painted black, incloses a piece of ground perhaps one hundred and fifty feet long, by about fifty broad, and graded into three levels, or low terraces. All the space within is shaded by pines. In the center of the last and highest of the little terraces the tomb is placed: a single large slab of gray rock laid horizontally. A narrow paved walk leads from the gate to the tomb, ascending each terrace by three or four stone steps. A little within this gateway, which is opened to visitors only once a year, there is a torii facing the sepulchre; and before the highest terrace there are a pair of stone lamps. All this is severely simple, but effective in a certain touching way. The country stillness is broken only by the shrilling of the semi and the tintinnabulation of that strange little insect, the suzumushi, whose calling sounds just like the tinkling of the tiny bells which are shaken by the miko in her sacred dance.

XXXI.

I remained nearly eight days at Hishi-ura on the occasion of my second visit there, but only three at Urago. Urago proved a less pleasant place to stay in—not because its smells were any stronger than those of Saigo, but for other reasons which shall presently appear.

More than one foreign man-of-war has touched at Saigo, and English and Russian officers of the navy have been seen in the streets. They were tall, fairhaired, stalwart men; and the people of Oki still imagine that all foreigners from the West have the same stature and complexion. I was the first foreigner who ever remained even a night in the town, and I stayed there two weeks; but being small and dark, and dressed like a Japanese, I excited little attention among the common people: it seemed to them that I was only a curious-looking Japanese from some remote part of the empire. At Hishi-ura the same impression prevailed for a time; and even after the fact of my being a foreigner had become generally known; the population caused me no annoyance whatever: they had already become accustomed to see me walking about the streets or swimming across the bay. But it was quite otherwise at Urago. The first time I landed there I had managed to escape notice, being in Japanese costume, and wearing a very large Izumo hat, which partly concealed my face. After I left for Saigo, the people must have found out that a foreigner—the very first ever seen in Dōzen—had actually been in Urago without their knowledge; for my second visit made a sensation such as I had never been the cause of anywhere else, except at Kaka-ura.

I had barely time to enter the hotel, before the street became entirely blockaded by an amazing crowd desirous to see. The hotel was unfortunately situated on a corner, so that it was soon besieged on two sides. I was shown to a large back room on the second floor; and I had no sooner squatted down on my mat, than the people began to come upstairs quite noiselessly, all leaving their sandals at the foot of the steps. They were too polite to enter the room; but four or five would put their heads through the doorway at once, and bow, and smile, and look, and retire to make way for those who filled the stairway behind them. It was no easy matter for the servant to bring me my dinner. Meanwhile, not only had the upper rooms of the houses across the way become packed with gazers, but all the roofs—north, east, and south—which commanded a view of my apartment had been occupied by men and boys in multitude.

Numbers of lads had also climbed (I never could imagine how) upon the narrow eaves over the galleries below my windows; and all the openings of my room, on three sides, were full of faces. Then tiles gave way, and boys fell, but nobody appeared to be hurt. And the queerest fact was that during the performance of these extraordinary gymnastics there was a silence of death: had I not seen the throng, I might have supposed there was not a soul in the street.

The landlord began to scold; but, finding scolding of no avail, he summoned a policeman. The policeman begged me to excuse the people, who had never seen a foreigner before; and asked me if I wished him to clear the street. He could have done that by merely lifting his little finger; but as the scene amused me, I begged him not to order the people away, but only to tell the boys not to climb upon the awnings, some of which they had already damaged. He told them most effectually, speaking in a very low voice. During all the rest of the time I was in Urago, no one dared to go near the awnings. A Japanese policeman never speaks more than once about anything new, and always speaks to the purpose.

The public curiosity, however, lasted without abate for three days, and would have lasted longer if I had not fled from Urago. Whenever I went out I drew the population after me with a pattering of geta like the sound of surf moving shingle. Yet, except for that particular sound, there was silence. No word was spoken. Whether this was because the whole mental faculty was so strained by the intensity of the desire to see that speech became impassible, I am not able to decide. But there was no roughness in all that curiosity; there was never anything approaching rudeness, except in the matter of ascending to my room without leave; and that was done so gently that I could not wish the intruders rebuked. Nevertheless, three days of such experience proved trying. Despite the heat, I had to close the doors and windows at night to prevent myself being watched while asleep. About my effects I had no anxiety at all: thefts are never committed in the island. But that perpetual silent crowding about me became at last more than embarrassing. It was innocent, but it was weird. It made me feel like a ghost—a new arrival in the Meido, surrounded by shapes without voice.

XXXII.

There is very little privacy of any sort in Japanese life. Among the people, indeed, what we term privacy, in the Occident, does not exist. There are only walls of paper dividing the lives of men; there are only sliding screens instead of doors; there are neither locks nor bolts to be used by day; and whenever weather permits, the fronts, and perhaps even the sides of the house are literally removed, and its interior widely opened to the air, the light, and the public gaze. Not even the rich man closes his front gate by day. Within a hotel or even a common dwelling-house, nobody knocks before entering your room: there is nothing to knock at except a shōji or fusuma, which cannot be knocked upon without being broken. And in this world of paper walls and sunshine, nobody is afraid or ashamed of fellow-men or fellow-women. Whatever is done, is done, after a fashion, in public. Your personal habits, your idiosyncrasies (if you have any), your foibles, your likes and dislikes, your loves or your hates, must be known to everybody. Neither vices nor virtues can be hidden: there is absolutely nowhere to hide them. And this condition has lasted from the most ancient time. There has never been, for the common millions at least, even the idea of living unobserved. Life can be comfortably and happily lived in Japan only upon the condition that all matters relating to it are open to the inspection of the community. Which implies exceptional moral conditions, such as have no being in the West. It is perfectly comprehensible only to those who know by experience the extraordinary charm of Japanese character, the infinite goodness of the common people, their instinctive politeness, and the absence among them of any tendencies to indulge in criticism, ridicule, irony, or sarcasm. No one endeavors to expand his own individuality by belittling his fellow; no one tries to make himself appear a superior being:

any such attempt would be vain in a community where the weaknesses of each are known to all, where nothing can be concealed or disguised, and where affectation could only be regarded as a mild form of insanity.

XXXIII

Some of the old samurai of Matsue are living in the Oki Islands. When the great military caste was disestablished, a few shrewd men decided to try their fortunes in the little archipelago, where customs remained old-fashioned and lands were cheap. Several succeeded—probably because of the whole-souled honesty and simplicity of manners in the islands; for samurai have seldom elsewhere been able to succeed in business of any sort when obliged to compete with experienced traders. Others failed, but were able to adopt various humble occupations which gave them the means to live.

Besides these aged survivors of the feudal period, I learned there were in Oki several children of once noble families—youths and maidens of illustrious extraction—bravely facing the new conditions of life in this remotest and poorest region of the empire. Daughters of men to whom the population of a town once bowed down were learning the bitter toil of the rice-fields. Youths, who might in another era have aspired to offices of state, had become the trusted servants of Oki heimin. Others, again, had entered the police,* and rightly deemed themselves fortunate.

No doubt that change of civilization forced upon Japan by Christian bayonets, for the holy motive of gain, may yet save the empire from perils greater than those of the late social disintegration; but it was cruelly sudden. To imagine the consequence of depriving the English landed gentry of their revenues would not enable one to realize exactly what a similar privation signified to

---

* The Japanese police are nearly all of the samurai class, now called shizoku. I think this force may be considered the most perfect police in the world; but whether it will retain those magnificent qualities which at present distinguish it, after the lapse of another generation, is doubtful. It is now the samurai blood that tells.

the Japanese samurai. For the old warrior caste knew only the arts of courtesy and the arts of war.

And hearing of these things, I could not help thinking about a strange pageant at the last great Izumo festival of Rakusan-jinja.

XXXIV.

The hamlet of Rakuzan, known only for its bright yellow pottery and its little Shintō temple, drowses at the foot of a wooded hill about one ri from Matsue, beyond a wilderness of rice-fields. And the deity of Rakuzan-jinja is Naomasa, grandson of Iyeyasu, and father of the Daimyō of Matsue.

Some of the Matsudaira slumber in Buddhist ground, guarded by tortoises and lions of stone, in the marvelous old courts of Gesshōōji. But Naomasa, the founder of their long line, is enshrined at Rakuzan; and the Izumo peasants still clap their hands in prayer before his miya, and implore his love and protection.

Now formerly upon each annual matsuri, or festival, of Rakuzan-jinja, it was customary to carry the miya of Naomasa-San from the village temple to the castle of Matsue. In solemn procession it was borne to those strange old family temples in the heart of the fortress-grounds—Go-jō-nai-Inari-Daimyōjin, and Kusunoki-Matsuhira-Inari-Daimyōjin—whose moldering courts, peopled with lions and foxes of stone, are shadowed by enormous trees. After certain Shintō rites had been performed at both temples, the miya was carried back in procession to Rakuzan.

And this annual ceremony was called the miyuki or togyo—"the August Going," or Visit, of the ancestor to the ancestral home.

But the revolution changed all things. The daimyō passed away; the castles fell to ruin; the samurai caste was abolished and dispossessed. And the miya of Lord Naomasa made no August Visit to the home of the Matsudaira for more than thirty years.

But it came to pass a little time ago, that certain old men of Matsue bethought them to revive once more the ancient customs of the Rakuzan matsuri. And there was a miyuki.

The miya of Lord Naomasa was placed within a barge, draped

and decorated, and so conveyed by river and canal to the eastern end of the old Matubara road, along whose pine-shaded way the daimyō formerly departed to Yedo on their annual visit, or returned therefrom. All those who rowed the barge were aged samurai who had been wont in their youth to row the barge of Matsudaira-Dewa-no-Kami, the last Lord of Izumo. They wore their ancient feudal costume; and they tried to sing their ancient boatsong—*o-funa-uta*. But more than a generation had passed since the last time they had sung it; and some of them had lost their teeth, so that they could not pronounce the words well; and all, being aged, lost breath easily in the exertion of wielding the oars. Nevertheless they rowed the barge to the place appointed.

Thence the shrine was borne to a spot by the side of the Matsubara road, where anciently stood an August Tea-House, O-Chaya, at which the daimyō, returning from the Shogun's capital, were accustomed to rest and to receive their faithful retainers, who always came in procession to meet them. No teahouse stands there now; but, in accord with old custom, the shrine and its escort waited at the place, among the wild flowers and the pines. And then was seen a strange sight.

For there came to meet the ghost of the great lord a long procession of shapes that seemed ghosts also—shapes risen out of the dust of cemeteries: warriors in crested helmets and masks of iron and breastplates of steel, girded with two swords; and spearmen wearing queues; and retainers in kamishimo; and bearers of hasami-bako. Yet ghosts these were not, but aged samurai of Matsue, who had borne arms in the service of the last of the daimyō. And among them appeared his surviving ministers, the venerable karō; and these, as the procession turned city-ward, took their old places of honor, and marched before the shrine valiantly, though bent with years.

How that pageant might have impressed other strangers I do not know. For me, knowing something of the history of each of those aged men, the scene had a significance apart from its story of forgotten customs, apart from its interest as a feudal procession. Today each and all of those old samurai are unspeakably poor. Their beautiful homes vanished long ago; their gardens have been turned into rice-fields; their household treasures were cruelly bargained for, and bought for almost nothing by curio-dealers to be resold at high prices to foreigners at the open ports. And yet what they could have obtained considerable money for, and what had ceased to be of any service to them, they clung to fondly through all their poverty and humiliation. Never could they be induced to part with their armor and their swords, even when pressed by direst want, under the new and harder conditions of existence.

The riverbanks, the streets, the balconies, and blue-tiled roofs were thronged. There was a great quiet as the procession passed. Young people gazed in hushed wonder, feeling the rare worth of that chance to look upon what will belong in the future to picture-books only and to the quaint Japanese stage. And old men wept silently, remembering their youth.

Well spake the ancient thinker: *"Everything is only for a day, both that which remembers, and that which is remembered."*

XXXV.

Once more, homeward bound, I sat upon the cabin-roof of the Oki-Saigo—this time happily unencumbered by watermelons—and tried to explain to myself the feeling of melancholy with which I watched those wild island-coasts vanishing over the pale sea into the white horizon. No doubt it was inspired partly by the recollection of kindnesses received from many whom I shall never meet again; partly, also, by my familiarity with the ancient soil itself, and remembrance of shapes and places: the long blue visions down channels between islands—the faint gray fishing hamlets hiding in stony bays—the elfish oddity of narrow streets in little primitive towns—the forms and tints of peak and vale made lovable by daily intimacy—the crooked broken paths to shadowed shrines of gods with long mysterious names—the butterfly-drifting of yellow sails out of the glow of an unknown horizon. Yet I think it was due much more to a particular sensation in which every memory was steeped and toned, as a landscape is steeped in the light and toned in the colors of the morning: the sensation of conditions closer to Nature's heart, and farther from the monstrous machine-world of Western life than any into which I had ever entered north of the torrid zone. And then it seemed to me that I loved Oki—in spite of the cuttlefish—chiefly because of having felt there, as nowhere else in Japan, the full joy of escape from the far-reaching influences of high-pressure civilization—the delight of knowing one's self, in Dōzen at least, well beyond the range of everything artificial in human existence.

24

OF SOULS

KINJURŌ, the ancient gardener, whose head shines like an ivory ball, sat him down a moment on the edge of the ita-no-ma outside my study to smoke his pipe at the hibachi always left there for him. And as he smoked he found occasion to reprove the boy who assists him. What the boy had been doing I did not exactly know; but I heard Kinjurō bid him try to comport himself like a creature having more than one Soul. And because those words interested me I went out and sat down by Kinjurō.

"O Kinjurō," I said, "whether I myself have one or more Souls I am not sure. But it would much please me to learn how many Souls have you."

"I-the-Selfish-One have only four Souls," made answer Kinjurō, with conviction imperturbable.

"Four?" reechoed I, feeling doubtful of having understood.

"Four," he repeated. "But that boy I think can have only one Soul, so much is he wanting in patience."

"And in what manner," I asked, "came you to learn that you have four Souls?"

"There are wise men," made he answer, while knocking the ashes out of his little silver pipe, "there are wise men who know these things. And there is an ancient book which discourses of them. According to the age of a man, and the time of his birth, and the stars of heaven, may the number of his Souls be divined. But this is the knowledge of old men: the young folk of these times who learn the things of the West do not believe."

"And tell me, O Kinjurō, do there now exist people having more Souls than you?"

"Assuredly. Some have five, some six, some seven, some eight Souls. But no one is by the gods permitted to have more Souls than nine."

[Now this, as a universal statement, I could not believe, remembering a woman upon the other side of the world who possessed many generations of Souls, and knew how to use them all. She wore her Souls just as other women wear their dresses, and changed them several times a day; and the multitude of dresses in the wardrobe of Queen Elizabeth was as nothing to the multitude of this wonderful person's Souls. For which reason she never appeared the same upon two different occasions; and she changed her thought and her voice with her Souls. Sometimes she was of the South, and her eyes were brown; and again she was of the North, and her eyes were gray. Sometimes she was of the thirteenth, and sometimes of the eighteenth century; and people doubted their own senses when they saw these things; and they tried to find out the truth by begging photographs of her, and then comparing them. Now the photographers rejoiced to photograph her because she was more than fair; but presently they also were confounded by the discovery that she was never the same subject twice. So the men who most admired her could not presume to fall in love with her because that would have been absurd. She had altogether too many Souls. And some of you who read this I have written will bear witness to the verity thereof.]

"Concerning this Country of the Gods, O Kinjurō, that which you say may be true. But there are other countries having only gods made of gold; and in those countries matters are not so well arranged; and the inhabitants thereof are plagued with a plague of Souls. For while some have but half a Soul, or no Soul at all, others have Souls in multitude thrust upon them for which neither nutriment nor employ can be found. And Souls thus situated torment exceedingly their owners....That is to say, Western Souls....But tell me, I pray you, what is the use of having more than one or two Souls?"

"Master, if all had the same number and quality of Souls, all would surely be of one mind. But that people are different from each other is apparent; and the differences among them are because of the differences in the quality and the number of their Souls."

"And it is better to have many Souls than a few?"

"It is better."

"And the man having but one Soul is a being imperfect?"

"Very imperfect."

"Yet a man very imperfect might have had an ancestor perfect?"

"That is true."

"So that a man of today possessing but one Soul may have had an ancestor with nine Souls?"

"Yes."

"Then what has become of those other eight Souls which the ancestor possessed, but which the descendant is without?"

"Ah! that is the work of the gods. The gods alone fix the number of Souls for each of us. To the worthy are many given; to the unworthy few."

"Not from the parents, then, do the Souls descend?"

"Nay! Most ancient the Souls are: innumerable the years of them."

"And this I desire to know: Can a man separate his Souls? Can he, for instance, have one Soul in Kyōto and one in Tōkyō and one in Matsue, all at the same time?"

"He cannot; they remain always together."

"How? One within the other—like the little lacquered boxes of an inrō?"

"Nay: that none but the gods know."

"And the Souls are never separated?"

"Sometimes they may be separated. But if the Souls of a man

be separated, that man becomes mad. Mad people are those who have lost one of their Souls."

"But after death what becomes of the Souls?"

"They remain still together....When a man dies his Souls ascend to the roof of the house. And they stay upon the roof for the space of nine and forty days."

"On what part of the roof?"

"On the yane-no-mune—upon the Ridge of the Roof they stay."

"Can they be seen?"

"Nay: they are like the air is. To and fro upon the Ridge of the Roof they move, like a little wind."

"Why do they not stay upon the roof for fifty days instead of forty-nine?"

"Seven weeks is the time allotted them before they must depart: seven weeks make the measure of forty-nine days. But why this should be, I cannot tell."

I was not unaware of the ancient belief that the spirit of a dead man haunts for a time the roof of his dwelling, because it is referred to quite impressively in many Japanese dramas, among others in the play called Kagami-yama, which makes the people weep. But I had not before heard of triplex and quadruplex and other yet more highly complex Souls; and I questioned Kinjurō vainly in the hope of learning the authority for his beliefs. They were the beliefs of his fathers: that was all he knew.*

Like most Izumo folk, Kinjurō was a Buddhist as well as a Shintōist. As the former he belonged to the Zen-shū, as the

---

* Afterwards I found that the old man had expressed to me only one popular form of a belief which would require a large book to fully explain—a belief founded upon Chinese astrology, but possibly modified by Buddhist and by Shintō ideas. This notion of compound Souls cannot be explained at all without a prior knowledge of the astrological relation between the Chinese Zodiacal Signs and the Ten Celestial Stems. Some understanding of these may be obtained from the curious article "Time," in Professor Chamberlain's admirable little book, *Things Japanese*. The relation having been perceived, it is further necessary to know that under the Chinese astrological system each year is under the influence of one or other of the "Five Elements"—Wood, Fire, Earth, Metal, Water; and according to the day and year of one's birth, one's temperament is celestially decided.

latter to the Izumo-Taisha. Yet his ontology seemed to me not of either. Buddhism does not teach the doctrine of compound-multiple Souls. There are old Shintō books inaccessible to the multitude which speak of a doctrine very remotely akin to Kinjurō's; but Kinjurō had never seen them. Those books say that each of us has two souls—the Ara-tama, or Rough Soul, which is vindictive; and the Nigi-tama, or Gentle Soul, which is all-forgiving. Furthermore, we are all possessed by the spirit of Oho-maga-tsu-hi-no-Kami, the "Wondrous Deity of Exceeding Great Evils," also by the spirit of Oho-naho-bi-no-Kami, the "Wondrous Great Rectifying Deity," a counteracting influence. These were not exactly the ideas of Kinjurō. But I remembered something Hirata wrote which reminded me of Kinjurō's words about a possible separation of souls. Hirata's teaching was that the ara-tama of a man may leave his body, assume his shape, and without his knowledge destroy a hated enemy. So I asked Kinjurō about it.

A Japanese mnemonic verse tells us the number of souls or natures corresponding to each of the Five Elemental Influences—namely, nine souls for Wood, three for Fire, one for Earth, seven for Metal, five for Water:

> *Kiku karani*
> *Himitsu no yama ni*
> *Tsuchi hitotsu*
> *Nanatsu kane to zo*
> *Go suiryō are.*

Multiplied into ten by being each one divided into "Elder" and "Younger," the Five Elements become the Ten Celestial Stems; and their influences are commingled with those of the Rat, Bull, Tiger, Hare, Dragon, Serpent, Horse, Goat, Ape, Cock, Dog, and Boar (the twelve Zodiacal Signs)—all of which have relations to time, place, life, luck, misfortune, etc. But even these hints give no idea whatever how enormously complicated the subject really is.

The book the old gardener referred to—once as widely known in Japan as ever fortune-telling book in any European country—was the *San-ze-sō*, copies of which may still be picked up. Contrary to Kinjurō's opinion, however, it is held, by those learned in such Chinese matters, just as bad to have too many souls as to have too few. To have nine souls is to be too "many-minded"—without fixed purpose; to have only one soul is to lack quick intelligence. According to the Chinese astrological ideas, the word "natures" or "characters" would perhaps be more accurate than the word "souls" in this case. There is a world of curious fancies, born out of these beliefs. For one example of hundreds, a person having a Fire-nature must not marry one having a Water-nature. Hence the proverbial saying about two who cannot agree—"They are like Fire and Water."

He said he had never heard of a nigi-tama or an ara-tama; but be told me this:

"Master, when a man has been discovered by his wife to be secretly enamored of another, it sometimes happens that the guilty woman is seized with a sickness that no physician can cure. For one of the Souls of the wife, moved exceedingly by anger, passes into the body of that woman to destroy her. But the wife also sickens, or loses her mind awhile, because of the absence of her Soul.

"And there is another and more wonderful thing known to us of Nippon, which you, being of the West, may never have heard. By the power of the gods, for a righteous purpose, sometimes a Soul may be withdrawn a little while from its body, and be made to utter its most secret thought. But no suffering to the body is then caused. And the wonder is wrought in this wise:

"A man loves a beautiful girl whom he is at liberty to marry; but he doubts whether he can hope to make her love him in return. He seeks the kannushi of a certain Shintō temple,* and tells of his doubt, and asks the aid of the gods to solve it. Then the priests demand, not his name, but his age and the year and day and hour of his birth, which they write down for the gods to know; and they bid the man return to the temple after the space of seven days.

"And during those seven days the priests offer prayer to the gods that the doubt may be solved; and one of them each morning bathes all his body in cold, pure water, and at each repast eats only food prepared with holy fire. And on the eighth day the man returns to the temple, and enters an inner chamber where the priests receive him.

"A ceremony is performed, and certain prayers are said, after which all wait in silence. And then, the priest who has performed the rites of purification suddenly begins to tremble violently in all his body, like one trembling with a great fever. And this is

---

* Usually an Inari temple. Such things are never done at the great Shintō shrines.

because, by the power of the gods, the Soul of the girl whose love is doubted has entered, all fearfully, into the body of that priest. She does not know; for at that time, wherever she may be, she is in a deep sleep from which nothing can arouse her. But her Soul, having been summoned into the body of the priest, can speak nothing save the truth; and it is made to tell all its thought. And the priest speaks not with his own voice, but with the voice of the Soul; and he speaks in the person of the Soul, saying: 'I love,' or 'I hate,' according as the truth may be, and in the language of women. If there be hate, then the reason of the hate is spoken; but if the answer be of love, there is little to say. And then the trembling of the priest stops, for the Soul passes from him; and he falls forward upon his face like one dead, and long so remains."

"Tell me, Kinjurō," I asked, after all these queer things had been related to me, "have you yourself ever known of a Soul being removed by the power of the gods, and placed in the heart of a priest?"

"Yes, I myself have known it."

I remained silent and waited. The old man emptied his little pipe, threw it down beside the hibachi, folded his hands, and looked at the lotus-flowers for some time before he spoke again. Then he smiled and said:

"Master, I married when I was very young. For many years we had no children: then my wife at last gave me a son, and became a Buddha. But my son lived and grew up handsome and strong; and when the Revolution came, he joined the armies of the Son of Heaven; and he died the death of a man in the great war of the South, in Kyūshū. I loved him; and I wept with joy when I heard that he had been able to die for our Sacred Emperor: since there is no more noble death for the son of a samurai. So they buried my boy far away from me in Kyūshū, upon a hill near Kumamoto, which is a famous city with a strong garrison; and I went there to make his tomb beautiful. But his name is here also, is Ninomaru, graven on the monument to the men of Izumo who fell in the good fight for loyalty and honor in our emperor's holy cause; and when I see his name there, my heart laughs, and I speak to him, and then it seems as if he were walking beside me again, under the great pines...But all that is another matter.

"I sorrowed for my wife. All the years we had dwelt together, no unkind word had ever been uttered between us. And when she died, I thought never to marry again. But after two more years had passed, my father and mother desired a daughter in the house, and they told me of their wish, and of a girl who was beautiful and of good family, though poor. The family were of our kindred, and the girl was their only support: she wove garments of silk and garments of cotton, and for this she received but little money. And because she was filial and comely, and our kindred not fortunate, my parents desired that I should marry her and help her people; for in those days we had a small income of rice. Then, being accustomed to obey my parents, I suffered them to do what they thought best. So the nakōdo was summoned, and the arrangements for the wedding began.

"Twice I was able to see the girl in the house of her parents. And I thought myself fortunate the first time I looked upon her; for she was very comely and young. But the second time, I perceived she had been weeping, and that her eyes avoided mine. Then my heart sank, for I thought: She dislikes me, and they are forcing her to this thing. Then I resolved to question the gods, and I caused the marriage to be delayed, and I went to the temple of Yanagi-no-Inari-Sama, which is in the Street Zaimokuchō.

"And when the trembling came upon him, the priest, speaking with the Soul of that maid, declared to me: 'My heart hates you, and the sight of your face gives me sickness, because I love another, and because this marriage is forced upon me. Yet though my heart hates you, I must marry you because my parents are poor and old, and I alone cannot long continue to support them, for my work is killing me. But though I may strive to be a dutiful wife, there never will be gladness in your house because of me, for my heart hates you with a great and lasting hate, and the sound of your voice makes a sickness in my breast *(koe kiite mo mune ga waruku naru),* and only to see your face makes me wish that I were dead *(kao miru to shinitaku naru).*"

"Thus knowing the truth, I told it to my parents, and I wrote a letter of kind words to the maid, praying pardon for the pain I had unknowingly caused her, and I feigned long illness, that the marriage might be broken off without gossip, and we made a gift to that family, and the maid was glad. For she was enabled at a later time to marry the young man she loved. My parents never pressed me again to take a wife, and since their death I have lived alone....O Master, look upon the extreme wickedness of that boy!"

Taking advantage of our conversation, Kinjurō's young assistant had improvised a rod and line with a bamboo stick and a bit of string; and had fastened to the end of the string a pellet of tobacco stolen from the old man's pouch. With this bait he had been fishing in the lotus pond; and a frog had swallowed it, and was now suspended high above the pebbles, sprawling in rotary motion, kicking in frantic spasms of disgust and despair. "Kaji!" shouted the gardener.

The boy dropped his rod with a laugh, and ran to us unabashed; while the frog, having disgorged the tobacco, plopped back into the lotus pond. Evidently Kaji was not afraid of scoldings.

"Gooshō ga warui!" declared the old man, shaking his ivory head. "O Kaji, much I fear that your next birth will be bad! Do I buy tobacco for frogs? Master, said I not rightly this boy has but one Soul?"

25

OF GHOSTS AND GOBLINS

I.

THERE was a Buddha, according to the Hokkekyō, who "even assumed the shape of a goblin to preach to such as were to be converted by a goblin." And in the same Sutra may be found this promise of the Teacher: "*While he is dwelling lonely in the wilderness, I will send thither goblins in great number to keep him company.*" The appalling character of this promise is indeed somewhat modified by the assurance that gods also are to be sent. But if ever I become a holy man, I shall take heed not to dwell in the wilderness, because I have seen Japanese goblins, and I do not like them.

Kinjurō showed them to me last night. They had come to town for the matsuri of our own ujigami, or parish-temple; and, as there were many curious things to be seen at the night festival, we started for the temple after dark, Kinjurō carrying a paper lantern painted with my crest.

It had snowed heavily in the morning; but now the sky and the sharp still air were clear as diamond; and the crisp snow made a pleasant crunching sound under our feet as we walked; and it occurred to me to say: "O Kinjurō, is there a God of Snow?"

"I cannot tell," replied Kinjurō. "There be many gods I do not know; and there is not any man who knows the names of all the gods. But there is the Yuki-Onna, the Woman of the Snow."

"And what is the Yuki-Onna?"

"She is the White One that makes the Faces in the snow. She does not any harm, only makes afraid. By day she lifts only her head, and frightens those who journey alone. But at night she rises up sometimes, taller than the trees, and looks about a little while, and then falls back in a shower of snow."*

"What is her face like?"

"It is all white, white. It is an enormous face. And it is a *lonesome* face."

[The word Kinjurō used was *samushii*. Its common meaning is "lonesome"; but he used it, I think, in the sense of "weird."]

"Did you ever see her, Kinjurō?"

"Master, I never saw her. But my father told me that once when he was a child, he wanted to go to a neighbor's house through the snow to play with another little boy; and that on the way he saw a great white Face rise up from the snow and look lonesomely about, so that he cried for fear and ran back. Then his people all went out and looked; but there was only snow; and then they knew that he had seen the Yuki-Onna."

"And in these days, Kinjurō, do people ever see her?"

"Yes. Those who make the pilgrimage to Yabumura, in the period called Dai-Kan, which is the Time of the Greatest Cold,† they sometimes see her."

"What is there at Yabumura, Kinjurō?"

"There is the Yabu-jinja, which is an ancient and famous temple of Yabu-no-Tenno-San—the God of Colds, Kaze-no-Kami. It is high upon a hill, nearly nine ri from Matsue. And the great matsuri of that temple is held upon the tenth and eleventh days of the Second Month. And on those days strange things may be seen. For one who gets a very bad cold prays to the deity of Yabu-jinja to cure it, and takes a vow to make a pilgrimage naked to the temple at the time of the matsuri."

---

* In other parts of Japan I have heard the Yuki-Onna described as a very beautiful phantom who lures young men to lonesome places for the purpose of sucking their blood.

† In Izumo the Dai-Kan, or Period of Greatest Cold, falls in February.

"Naked?"

"Yes: the pilgrims wear only waraji, and a little cloth round their loins. And a great many men and women go naked through the snow to the temple, though the snow is deep at that time. And each man carries a bunch of gohei and a naked sword as gifts to the temple; and each woman carries a metal mirror. And at the temple, the priests receive them, performing curious rites. For the priests then, according to ancient custom, attire themselves like sick men, and lie down and groan, and drink potions made of herbs, prepared after the Chinese manner."

"But do not some of the pilgrims die of cold, Kinjurō?"

"No: our Izumo peasants are hardy. Besides, they run swiftly, so that they reach the temple all warm. And before returning they put on thick warm robes. But sometimes, upon the way, they see the Yuki-Onna."

II.

Each side of the street leading to the miya was illuminated with a line of paper lanterns bearing holy symbols; and the immense court of the temple had been transformed into a town of booths, and shops, and temporary theatres. In spite of the cold, the crowd was prodigious. There seemed to be all the usual attractions of a matsuri, and a number of unusual ones. Among the familiar lures, I missed at this festival only the maiden wearing an obi of living snakes; probably it had become too cold for the snakes. There were several fortune-tellers and jugglers; there were acrobats and dancers; there was a man making pictures out of sand; and there was a menagerie containing an emu from Australia, and a couple of enormous bats from the Loo Choo Islands—bats trained to do several things. I did reverence to the gods, and bought some extraordinary toys; and then we went to look for the goblins. They were domiciled in a large permanent structure, rented to showmen on special occasions.

Gigantic characters signifying "IKI-NINGYŌ," painted upon the sign-board at the entrance, partly hinted the nature of the exhibition. Iki-ningyō ("living images") somewhat correspond to our Occidental "wax figures," but the equally realistic Japanese creations are made of much cheaper material. Having bought two wooden tickets for one sen each, we entered, and passed behind a curtain to find ourselves in a long corridor lined with booths, or rather matted compartments, about the size of small rooms. Each space, decorated with scenery appropriate to the subject, was occupied by a group of life-size figures. The group nearest the entrance, representing two men playing samisen and two geisha dancing, seemed to me without excuse for being, until Kinjurō had translated a little placard before it, announcing that one of the figures was a living person. We watched in vain for a wink or palpitation. Suddenly one of the musicians laughed aloud, shook his head, and began to play and sing. The deception was perfect.

The remaining groups, twenty-four in number, were powerfully impressive in their peculiar way, representing mostly famous popular traditions or sacred myths. Feudal heroisms, the memory of which stirs every Japanese heart; legends of filial piety; Buddhist miracles, and stories of emperors were among the subjects. Sometimes, however, the realism was brutal, as in one scene representing the body of a woman lying in a pool of blood, with brains scattered by a sword stroke. Nor was this unpleasantness altogether atoned for by her miraculous resuscitation in the adjoining compartment, where she reappeared returning thanks in a Nichiren temple, and converting her slaughterer, who happened, by some extraordinary accident, to go there at the same time.

At the termination of the corridor there hung a black curtain, behind which screams could be heard. And above the black curtain was a placard inscribed with the promise of a gift to anybody able to traverse the mysteries beyond without being frightened.

"Master," said Kinjurō, "the goblins are inside."

We lifted the veil, and found ourselves in a sort of lane between hedges, and behind the hedges we saw tombs; we were in a graveyard. There were real weeds and trees, and sotoba and haka, and the effect was quite natural. Moreover, as the roof was very lofty, and kept invisible by a clever arrangement of lights, all seemed darkness only; and this gave one a sense of being out under the night, a feeling accentuated by the chill of the air. And here and there we could discern sinister shapes, mostly of super-human stature, some seeming to wait in dim places, others floating above the graves. Quite near us, towering above the hedge on our right, was a Buddhist priest, with his back turned to us.

"A yamabushi, an exorciser?" I queried of Kinjurō.

"No," said Kinjurō; "see how tall he is. I think that must be a Tanuki-Bōzu."

The Tanuki-Bōzu is the priestly form assumed by the goblin-badger *(tanuki)* for the purpose of decoying belated travelers to destruction. We went on, and looked up into his face. It was a nightmare—his face.

"In truth a Tanuki-Bozu," said Kinjurō. "What does the Master honorably think concerning it?"

Instead of replying, I jumped back; for the monstrous thing had suddenly reached over the hedge and clutched at me, with a moan. Then it fell back, swaying and creaking. It was moved by invisible strings.

"I think, Kinjurō, that it is a nasty, horrid thing. But I shall not claim the present."

We laughed, and proceeded to consider a Three-Eyed Friar *(Mitsu-me-Nyūdō)*. The Three-Eyed Friar also watches for the unwary at night. His face is soft and smiling as the face of a Buddha, but he has a hideous eye in the summit of his shaven pate, which can only be seen when seeing it does no good. The Mitsu-me-Nyūdō made a grab at Kinjurō, and startled him almost as much as the Tanuki-Bōzu had startled me.

Then we looked at the Yama-Uba—the "Mountain Nurse." She catches little children and nurses them for a while, and then devours them. In her face she has no mouth; but she has a mouth in the top of her head, under her hair. The Yama-Uba did not clutch at us, because her hands were occupied with a nice little boy, whom she was just going to eat. The child had been made wonderfully pretty to heighten the effect.

Then I saw the spectre of a woman hovering in the air above a tomb at some distance, so that I felt safer in observing it. It had no eyes; its long hair hung loose; its white robe floated light as smoke. I thought of a statement in a composition by one of my pupils about ghosts: "Their greatest Peculiarity is that They have no feet." Then I jumped again, for the thing, quite soundlessly but very swiftly, made through the air at me.

And the rest of our journey among the graves was little more than a succession of like experiences; but it was made amusing by the screams of women, and bursts of laughter from people who lingered only to watch the effect upon others of what had scared themselves.

III.

Forsaking the goblins, we visited a little open-air theatre to see two girls dance. After they had danced awhile, one girl produced a sword and cut off the other girl's head, and put it upon a table, where it opened its mouth and began to sing. All this was very prettily done; but my mind was still haunted by the goblins. So I questioned Kinjurō:

"Kinjurō, those goblins of which we the ningyō have seen—do folk believe in the reality thereof?"

"Not any more," answered Kinjurō—"not at least among the people of the city. Perhaps in the country it may not be so. We believe in the Lord Buddha; we believe in the ancient gods; and there be many who believe the dead sometimes return to avenge a cruelty or to compel an act of justice. But we do not now believe all that was believed in ancient time...Master," he added, as we reached another queer exhibition, "it is only one sen to go to hell, if the Master would like to go."

"Very good, Kinjurō," I made reply. "Pay two sen that we may both go to hell."

IV.

And we passed behind a curtain into a big room full of curious clicking and squeaking noises. These noises were made by unseen wheels and pulleys moving a multitude of ningyō upon a broad shelf about breast-high, which surrounded the apartment upon three sides. These ningyō were not iki-ningyō, but very small images—puppets. They represented all things in the Under-World.

The first I saw was Sozu-Baba, the Old Woman of the River of Ghosts, who takes away the garments of Souls. The garments were hanging upon a tree behind her. She was tall; she rolled her green eyes and gnashed her long teeth, while the shivering of the little white souls before her was as a trembling of butterflies. Farther on appeared Emma Dai-O great King of Hell, nodding grimly. At his right hand, upon their tripod, the heads of Kaguhana and Mirume, the Witnesses, whirled as upon a wheel. At his left, a devil was busy sawing a Soul in two; and I noticed that he used his saw like a Japanese carpenter—pulling it towards him instead of pushing it. And then various exhibitions of the tortures of the damned. A liar bound to a post was having his tongue pulled out by a devil—slowly, with artistic jerks; it was already longer than the owner's body. Another devil was pounding another Soul in a mortar so vigorously that the sound of the braying could be heard above all the din of the machinery. A little farther on was a man being eaten alive by two serpents having women's faces; one serpent was white, the other blue. The white had been his wife, the blue his concubine. All the tortures known to mediaeval Japan were being elsewhere deftly practiced by swarms of devils. After reviewing them, we visited the Sai-no-Kawara, and saw Jizō with a child in his arms, and a circle of other children running swiftly around him, to escape from demons who brandished their clubs and ground their teeth.

Hell proved, however, to be extremely cold; and while meditating on the partial inappropriateness of the atmosphere, it occurred to me that in the common Buddhist picture-books of the Jigoku I had never noticed any illustrations of torment by cold. Indian Buddhism, indeed, teaches the existence of cold hells. There is one, for instance, where people's lips are frozen so that they can say only "Ah-ta-ta!"—wherefore that hell is called Atata. And there is the hell where tongues are frozen, and where people say only "Ah-baba!" for which reason it is called Ababa. And there is the Pundarika, or Great White-Lotus hell, where the spectacle of the bones laid bare by the cold is "like a blossoming of white lotus-flowers." Kinjuro thinks there are cold hells according to Japanese Buddhism; but he is not sure. And I am not sure that the idea of cold could be made very terrible to the Japanese. They confess a general liking for cold, and compose Chinese poems about the loveliness of ice and snow.

V.

Out of hell, we found our way to a magic-lantern show being given in a larger and even much colder structure. A Japanese magic-lantern show is nearly always interesting in more particulars than one, but perhaps especially as evidencing the native genius for adapting Western inventions to Eastern tastes. A Japanese magic-lantern show is essentially dramatic.

It is a play of which the dialogue is uttered by invisible personages, the actors and the scenery being only luminous shadows. Wherefore it is peculiarly well suited to goblinries and weirdnesses of all kinds; and plays in which ghosts figure are the favorite subjects. As the hall was bitterly cold, I waited only long enough to see one performance—of which the following is an epitome:

SCENE I. A beautiful peasant girl and her aged mother, squatting together at home. Mother weeps violently, gesticulates agonizingly. From her frantic speech, broken by wild sobs, we learn that the girl must be sent as a victim to the Kami-Sama of some lonesome temple in the mountains. That god is a bad god. Once a year he shoots an arrow into the thatch of some farmer's house as a sign that he wants a girl—to eat! Unless the girl be sent to him at once, he destroys the crops and the cows. Exit mother, weeping and shrieking, and pulling out her gray hair. Exit girl, with downcast head, and air of sweet resignation.

SCENE II. Before a wayside inn; cherry-trees in blossom. Enter coolies carrying, like a palanquin, a large box, in which the girl is supposed to be. Deposit box; enter to eat; tell story to loquacious landlord. Enter noble samurai, with two swords. Asks about box. Hears the story of the coolies repeated by loquacious landlord. Exhibits fierce indignation; vows that the Kami-Sama are good— do not eat girls. Declares that so-called Kami-Sama to be a devil. Observes that devils must be killed. Orders box opened. Sends girl home. Gets into box himself, and commands coolies under pain of death to bear him right quickly to that temple.

SCENE III. Enter coolies, approaching temple through forest at night. Coolies afraid. Drop box and run. Exeunt coolies. Box alone in the dark. Enter veiled figure, all white. Figure moans unpleasantly; utters horrid cries. Box remains impassive. Figure removes veil, showing Its face—a skull with phosphoric eyes. [*Audience unanimously utter the sound "Aaaaaa!"*] Figure displays its hands—monstrous and apish, with claws. [*Audience utter a second "Aaaaaa!"*] Figure approaches the box, touches the box, opens the box! Up leaps noble samurai. A wrestle; drums sound the roll of battle. Noble samurai practices successfully noble art of jiujutsu. Casts demon down, tramples upon him triumphantly, cuts off his head. Head suddenly enlarges, grows to the size of a house, tries to bite off head of samurai. Samurai slashes it with his sword. Head rolls backward, spitting fire, and vanishes. Finis. *Exeunt omnes.*

VI.

The vision of the samurai and the goblin reminded Kinjurō of a queer tale, which he began to tell me as soon as the shadow-play was over. Ghastly stories are apt to fall flat after such an exhibition; but Kinjurō's stories are always peculiar enough to justify the telling under almost any circumstances. Wherefore I listened eagerly, in spite of the cold:

"A long time ago, in the days when Fox-women and goblins haunted this land, there came to the capital with her parents a samurai girl, so beautiful that all men who saw her fell enamored of her. And hundreds of young samurai desired and hoped to marry her, and made their desire known to her parents. For it has ever been the custom in Japan that marriages should be arranged by parents. But there are exceptions to all customs, and the case of this maiden was such an exception. Her parents declared that they intended to allow their daughter to choose her own husband, and that all who wished to win her would be free to woo her.

"Many men of high rank and of great wealth were admitted to the house as suitors; and each one courted her as he best knew how—with gifts, and with fair words, and with poems written in her honor, and with promises of eternal love. And to each one she spoke sweetly and hopefully; but she made strange conditions. For every suitor she obliged to bind himself by his word of honor as a samurai to submit to a test of his love for her, and never to divulge to living person what that test might be. And to this all agreed.

"But even the most confident suitors suddenly ceased their importunities after having been put to the test; and all of them appeared to have been greatly terrified by something. Indeed, not a few even fled away from the city, and could not be persuaded by their friends to return. But no one ever so much as hinted why. Therefore it was whispered by those who knew nothing of the mystery, that the beautiful girl must be either a Fox-woman or a goblin.

"Now, when all the wooers of high rank had abandoned their suit, there came a samurai who had no wealth but his sword.

He was a good man and true, and of pleasing presence; and the girl seemed to like him. But she made him take the same pledge which the others had taken; and after he had taken it, she told him to return upon a certain evening.

"When that evening came, he was received at the house by none but the girl herself. With her own hands she set before him the repast of hospitality, and waited upon him, after which she told him that she wished him to go out with her at a late hour. To this he consented gladly, and inquired to what place she desired to go. But she replied nothing to his question, and all at once became very silent, and strange in her manner. And after a while she retired from the apartment, leaving him alone.

"Only long after midnight she returned, robed all in white—like a Soul—and, without uttering a word, signed to him to follow her. Out of the house they hastened while all the city slept. It was what is called an oborozuki-yo—'moon-clouded night.' Always upon such a night, 'tis said, do ghosts wander. She swiftly led the way; and the dogs howled as she flitted by; and she passed beyond the confines of the city to a place of knolls shadowed by enormous trees, where an ancient cemetery was. Into it she glided, a white shadow into blackness. He followed, wondering, his hand upon his sword. Then his eyes became accustomed to the gloom; and he saw.

"By a new-made grave she paused and signed to him to wait. The tools of the grave-maker were still lying there. Seizing one, she began to dig furiously, with strange haste and strength. At last her spade smote a coffin-lid and made it boom: another moment and the fresh white wood of the kwan was bare. She tore off the lid, revealing a corpse within—the corpse of a child. With goblin gestures she wrung an arm from the body, wrenched it in twain, and, squatting down, began to devour the upper half. Then, flinging to her lover the other half, she cried to him, '*Eat, if thou lovest me! this is what I eat!*'

"Not even for a single instant did he hesitate. He squatted down upon the other side of the grave, and ate the half of the arm, and said, '*Kekkō degozarimasu! mo sukoshi chōdai?** For that arm was made of the best kwashi† that Saikyō could produce. Then the girl sprang to her feet with a burst of laughter, and cried: 'You only, of all my brave suitors, did not run away! And I wanted a husband who could not fear. I will marry you; I can love you: you are a *man!*'"

VII.

"O Kinjurō," I said, as we took our way home, "I have heard and I have read many Japanese stories of the returning of the dead. Likewise you yourself have told me it is still believed the dead return, and why. But according both to that which I have read and that which you have told me, the coming back of the dead is never a thing to be desired. They return because of hate, or because of envy, or because they cannot rest for sorrow. But of any who return for that which is not evil—where is it written? Surely the common history of them is like that which we have this night seen: much that is horrible and much that is wicked and nothing of that which is beautiful or true."

Now this I said that I might tempt him. And he made even the answer I desired, by uttering the story which is hereafter set down:

"Long ago, in the days of a daimyō whose name has been forgotten, there lived in this old city a young man and a maid who loved each other very much. Their names are not remembered, but their story remains. From infancy they had been betrothed; and as children they played together, for their parents were neighbors. And as they grew up, they became always fonder of each other.

"Before the youth had become a man, his parents died. But he was able to enter the service of a rich samurai, an officer of

---

* "It is excellent: I pray you give me a little more."

† *Kwashi:* Japanese confectionery.

high rank, who had been a friend of his people. And his protector soon took him into great favor, seeing him to be courteous, intelligent, and apt at arms. So the young man hoped to find himself shortly in a position that would make it possible for him to marry his betrothed. But war broke out in the north and east; and he was summoned suddenly to follow his master to the field.

Before departing, however, he was able to see the girl; and they exchanged pledges in the presence of her parents; and he promised, should he remain alive, to return within a year from that day to marry his betrothed.

"After his going much time passed without news of him, for there was no post in that time as now; and the girl grieved so much for thinking of the chances of war that she became all white and thin and weak. Then at last she heard of him through a messenger sent from the army to bear news to the daimyō, and once again a letter was brought to her by another messenger. And thereafter there came no word. Long is a year to one who waits. And the year passed, and he did not return.

"Other seasons passed, and still he did not come; and she thought him dead; and she sickened and lay down, and died, and was buried. Then her old parents, who had no other child, grieved unspeakably, and came to hate their home for the lonesomeness of it. After a time they resolved to sell all they had, and to set out upon a sengaji—the great pilgrimage to the Thousand Temples of the Nichiren-Shū, which requires many years to perform. So they sold their small house with all that it contained, excepting the ancestral tablets, and the holy things which must never be sold, and the ihai of their buried daughter, which were placed, according to the custom of those about to leave their native place, in the family temple. Now the family was of the Nichiren-Shū; and their temple was Myōkōji.

"They had been gone only four days when the young man who had been betrothed to their daughter returned to the city. He had attempted, with the permission of his master, to fulfill his promise. But the provinces upon his way were full of war, and the roads and passes were guarded by troops, and he had been long delayed by many difficulties. And when he heard of his misfortune he sickened for grief, and many days remained without knowledge of anything, like one about to die.

"But when he began to recover his strength, all the pain of memory came back again; and he regretted that he had not died. Then he resolved to kill himself upon the grave of his betrothed; and, as soon as be was able to go out unobserved, he took his sword and went to the cemetery where the girl was buried: it is a lonesome place—the cemetery of Myōkōji. There he found her tomb, and knelt before it, and prayed and wept, and whispered to her that which he was about to do. And suddenly he heard her voice cry to him: '*Anata!*' and felt her hand upon his hand; and he turned, and saw her kneeling beside him, smiling, and beautiful as he remembered her, only a little pale. Then his heart leaped so that he could not speak for the wonder and the doubt and the joy of that moment. But she said: 'Do not doubt: it is really I. I am not dead. It was all a mistake. I was buried, because my people thought me dead—buried too soon. And my own parents thought me dead, and went upon a pilgrimage.

"'Yet you see I am not dead—not a ghost. It is I: do not doubt it! And I have seen your heart, and that was worth all the waiting and the pain....But now let us go away at once to another city, so that people may not know this thing and trouble us; for all still believe me dead.'

"And they went away, no one observing them. And they went even to the village of Minobu, which is in the province of Kai. For there is a famous temple of the Nichiren-Shū in that place; and the girl had said: 'I know that in the course of their pilgrimage my parents will surely visit Minobu: so that if we dwell there, they will find us, and we shall be all again together.' And when they came to Minobu, she said: 'Let us open a little shop.' And they opened a little food-shop, on the wide way leading to the holy place; and there they sold cakes for children, and toys, and food for pilgrims. For two years they so lived and prospered; and there was a son born to them.

"Now when the child was a year and two months old, the parents of the wife came in the course of their pilgrimage to Minobu; and they stopped at the little shop to buy food. And seeing their daughter's betrothed, they cried out and wept and asked questions.

"Then he made them enter, and bowed down before them, and astonished them, saying: 'Truly as I speak it, your daughter is not dead; and she is my wife; and we have a son. And she is even now within the farther room, lying down with the child, I pray you go in at once and gladden her, for her heart longs for the moment of seeing you again.'

"So while he busied himself in making all things ready for their comfort, they entered the inner room very softly—the mother first.

"They found the child asleep; but the mother they did not find. She seemed to have gone out for a little while only: her pillow was still warm. They waited long for her: then they began to seek her. But never was she seen again.

"And they understood only when they found, beneath the coverings which had covered the mother and child, something which they remembered having left years before in the temple of Myōkōji—a little mortuary tablet— the ihai of their buried daughter."

I suppose I must have looked thoughtful after this tale; for the old man said:

"Perhaps the Master honorably thinks concerning the story that it is foolish?"

"Nay, Kinjurō, the story is in my heart."

26

THE JAPANESE SMILE

I.

THOSE whose ideas of the world and its wonders have been formed chiefly by novels and romance still indulge a vague belief that the East is more serious than the West. Those who judge things from a higher standpoint argue, on the contrary, that, under present conditions, the West must be more serious than the East; and also that gravity, or even something resembling its converse, may exist only as a fashion. But the fact is that in this, as in all other questions, no rule susceptible of application to either half of humanity can be accurately framed. Scientifically, we can do no more just now than study certain contrasts in a general way, without hoping to explain satisfactorily the highly complex causes which produced them. One such contrast, of particular interest, is that afforded by the English and the Japanese.

It is a commonplace to say that the English are a serious people—not superficially serious, but serious all the way down to the bedrock of the race character. It is almost equally safe to say that the Japanese are not very serious, either above or below the surface, even as compared with races much less serious than our own. And in the same proportion, at least, that they are less serious, they are more happy: they still, perhaps, remain the happiest people in the civilized world. We serious folk of the West cannot call ourselves very happy. Indeed, we do not yet fully know how serious we are; and it would probably frighten us to learn how much more serious we are likely to become under the ever-swelling pressure of industrial life. It is, possibly, by long sojourn among a people less gravely disposed that we can best learn our own temperament. This conviction came to me very strongly when, after having lived for nearly three years in the interior of Japan, I returned to English life for a few days at the open port of Kobe. To hear English once more spoken by Englishmen touched me more than I could have believed possible; but this feeling lasted only for a moment. My object was to make some necessary purchases. Accompanying me was a Japanese friend, to whom all that foreign life was utterly new and wonderful, and who asked me this curious question: "Why is it that the foreigners never smile? You smile and bow when you speak to them; but they never smile. Why?"

The fact was, I had fallen altogether into Japanese habits and ways, and had got out of touch with Western life; and my companion's question first made me aware that I had been acting somewhat curiously. It also seemed to me a fair illustration of the difficulty of mutual comprehension between the two races— each quite naturally, though quite erroneously, estimating the manners and motives of the other by its own. If the Japanese are puzzled by English gravity, the English are, to say the least, equally puzzled by Japanese levity. The Japanese speak of the "angry faces" of the foreigners. The foreigners speak with strong contempt of the Japanese smile: they suspect it to signify insincerity; indeed, some declare it cannot possibly signify anything else. Only a few of the more observant have recognized it as an enigma worth studying. One of my Yokohama friends—a thoroughly lovable man, who had passed more than half his life in the open ports of the East—said to me, just before my departure for the interior: "Since you are going to study Japanese life, perhaps you will be able to find out something for me. I can't understand the Japanese smile. Let me tell you one experience out of many. One day, as I was driving down from the Bluff, I saw an empty kuruma coming up on the wrong side of the curve.

I could not have pulled up in time if I had tried; but I didn't try, because I didn't think there was any particular danger. I only yelled to the man in Japanese to get to the other side of the road; instead of which he simply backed his kuruma against a wall on the lower side of the curve, with the shafts outwards. At the rate I was going, there wasn't room even to swerve; and the next minute one of the shafts of that kuruma was in my horse's shoulder. The man wasn't hurt at all. When I saw the way my horse was bleeding, I quite lost my temper, and struck the man over the head with the butt of my whip. He looked right into my face and smiled, and then bowed. I can see that smile now. I felt as if I had been knocked down. The smile utterly non-plused me—killed all my anger instantly. Mind you, it was a polite smile. But what did it mean? Why the devil did the man smile? I can't understand it."

Neither, at that time, could I; but the meaning of much more mysterious smiles has since been revealed to me. A Japanese can smile in the teeth of death, and usually does. But he then smiles for the same reason that he smiles at other times. There is neither defiance nor hypocrisy in the smile; nor is it to be confounded with that smile of sickly resignation which we are apt to associate with weakness of character. It is an elaborate and long-cultivated etiquette.

It is also a silent language. But any effort to interpret it according to Western notions of physiognomical expression would be just about as successful as an attempt to interpret Chinese ideographs by their real or fancied resemblance to shapes of familiar things.

First impressions, being largely instinctive, are scientifically recognized as partly trustworthy; and the very first impression produced by the Japanese smile is not far from the truth. The stranger cannot fail to notice the generally happy and smiling character of the native faces; and this first impression is, in most cases, wonderfully pleasant. The Japanese smile at first charms. It is only at a later day, when one has observed the same smile under extraordinary circumstances—in moments of pain, shame, disappointment—that one becomes suspicious of it. Its apparent inopportuneness may even, on certain occasions, cause violent anger. Indeed, many of the difficulties between foreign residents and their native servants have been due to the smile. Any man who believes in the British tradition that a good servant must be solemn is not likely to endure with patience the smile of his "boy." At present, however, this particular phase of Western eccentricity is becoming more fully recognized by the Japanese; they are beginning to learn that the average English-speaking foreigner hates smiling, and is apt to consider it insulting; wherefore Japanese employees at the open ports have generally ceased to smile, and have assumed an air of sullenness.

At this moment there comes to me the recollection of a queer story told by a lady of Yokohama about one of her Japanese servants. "My Japanese nurse came to me the other day, smiling as if something very pleasant had happened, and said that her husband was dead, and that she wanted permission to attend his funeral. I told her she could go. It seems they burned the man's body. Well, in the evening she returned, and showed me a vase containing some ashes of bones (I saw a tooth among them); and she said: 'That is my husband.' And she actually *laughed* as she said it! Did you ever hear of such disgusting creatures?"

It would have been quite impossible to convince the narrator of this incident that the demeanor of her servant, instead of being heartless, might have been heroic, and capable of a very touching interpretation. Even one not a Philistine might be deceived in such a case by appearances. But quite a number of the foreign residents of the open ports are pure Philistines, and never try to look below the surface of the life around them, except as hostile critics. My Yokohama friend who told me the story about the kurumaya was quite differently disposed: he recognized the error of judging by appearances.

II.

Miscomprehension of the Japanese smile has more than once led to extremely unpleasant results, as happened in the case of T——, a Yokohama merchant of former days. T—— had employed in some capacity (I think partly as a teacher of Japanese) a nice old samurai, who wore, according to the fashion of the era, a queue and two swords. The English and the Japanese do not understand each other very well now; but at the period in question they understood each other much less. The Japanese servants at first acted in foreign employ precisely as they would have acted in the service of distinguished Japanese;* and this innocent mistake provoked a good deal of abuse and cruelty. Finally the discovery was made that to treat Japanese like West Indian negroes might be very dangerous. A certain number of foreigners were killed, with good moral consequences.

But I am digressing. T—— was rather pleased with his old samurai, though quite unable to understand his Oriental politeness, his prostrations, or the meaning of the small gifts which he presented occasionally, with an exquisite courtesy entirely wasted upon T——. One day he came to ask a favor. (I think it was the eve of the Japanese New Year, when everybody needs money, for reasons not here to be dwelt upon.) The favor was that T——

---

* The reader will find it well worth his while to consult the chapter entitled "Domestic Service," in Miss Bacon's *Japanese Girls and Women,* for an interesting and just presentation of the practical side of the subject, as relating to servants of both sexes. The poetical side, however, is not treated of—perhaps because intimately connected with religions beliefs which one writing from the Christian standpoint could not be expected to consider sympathetically. Domestic service in ancient Japan was both transfigured and regulated by religion; and the force of the religious sentiment concerning it may be divined from the Buddhist saying, still current:

> *Oya-ko wa is-se,*
> *Fufu wa ni-se,*
> *Shujū wa san-se.*

The relation of parent and child endures for the space of one life only; that of husband and wife for the space of two lives; but the relation between master and servant continues for the period of three existences.

would lend him a little money upon one of his swords, the long one. It was a very beautiful weapon, and the merchant saw that it was also very valuable, and lent the money without hesitation. Some weeks later the old man was able to redeem his sword.

What caused the beginning of the subsequent unpleasantness nobody now remembers. Perhaps T——'s nerves got out of order. At all events, one day he became very angry with the old man, who submitted to the expression of his wrath with bows and smiles. This made him still more angry, and he used some extremely bad language; but the old man still bowed and smiled; wherefore he was ordered to leave the house. But the old man continued to smile, at which T—— losing all self-control, struck him.

And then T——suddenly became afraid, for the long sword instantly leaped from its sheath, and swirled above him; and the old man ceased to seem old. Now, in the grasp of any one who knows how to use it, the razor-edged blade of a Japanese sword wielded with both hands can take a head off with extreme facility. But, to T——'s astonishment, the old samurai, almost in the same moment, returned the blade to its sheath with the skill of a practiced swordsman, turned upon his heel, and withdrew.

Then T—— wondered, and sat down to think. He began to remember some nice things about the old man—the many kindnesses unasked and unpaid, the curious little gifts, the impeccable honesty. T—— began to feel ashamed. He tried to console himself with the thought: "Well, it was his own fault; he had no right to laugh at me when he knew I was angry." Indeed, T—— even resolved to make amends when an opportunity should offer.

But no opportunity ever came, because on the same evening the old man performed hara-kiri, after the manner of a samurai. He left a very beautifully written letter explaining his reasons. For a samurai to receive an unjust blow without avenging it was a shame not to be borne. He had received such a blow. Under any other circumstances he might have avenged it. But the circumstances were, in this instance, of a very peculiar kind. His code of honor forbade him to use his sword upon the man to whom he had pledged it once for money, in an hour of need. And being thus unable to use his sword, there remained for him only the alternative of an honorable suicide.

In order to render this story less disagreeable, the reader may suppose that T—— was really very sorry, and behaved generously to the family of the old man. What he must not suppose is that T—— was ever able to imagine why the old man had smiled the smile which led to the outrage and the tragedy.

III.

To comprehend the Japanese smile, one must be able to enter a little into the ancient, natural, and popular life of Japan. From the modernized upper classes nothing is to be learned. The deeper signification of race differences is being daily more and more illustrated in the effects of the higher education. Instead of creating any community of feeling, it appears only to widen the distance between the Occidental and the Oriental. Some foreign observers have declared that it does this by enormously developing certain latent peculiarities—among others an inherent materialism little perceptible among the common people. This explanation is one I cannot quite agree with; but it is at least undeniable that, the more highly he is cultivated, according to Western methods, the farther is the Japanese psychologically removed from us. Under the new education, his character seems to crystallize into something of singular hardness, and to Western observation, at least, of singular opacity. Emotionally, the Japanese child appears incomparably closer to us than the Japanese mathematician, the peasant than the statesman. Between the most elevated class of thoroughly modernized Japanese and the Western thinker anything akin to intellectual sympathy is non-existent: it is replaced on the native side by a cold and faultless politeness. Those influences which in other lands appear most potent to develop the higher emotions seem here to have the extraordinary effect of suppressing them. We are accustomed abroad to associate emotional sensibility with intellectual expansion: it would be a grievous error to apply this rule in Japan. Even the foreign teacher in an ordinary school can feel, year by year, his pupils drifting farther away from him, as they pass from class to class; in various higher educational institutions, the separation widens yet more rapidly, so that, prior to graduation, students may become to their professor little more than casual acquaintances. The enigma is perhaps, to some extent, a physiological one, requiring scientific explanation; but its solution must first be sought in ancestral habits of life and of imagination. It can be fully discussed only when its natural causes are understood; and these, we may be sure, are not simple. By some observers it is asserted that because the higher education in Japan has not yet had the effect of stimulating the higher emotions to the Occidental pitch, its developing power cannot have been exerted uniformly and wisely, but in special directions only, at the cost of character. Yet this theory involves the unwarrantable assumption that character can be created by education; and it ignores the fact that the best results are obtained by affording opportunity for the exercise of preexisting inclination rather than by any system of teaching.

The causes of the phenomenon must be looked for in the race character; and whatever the higher education may accomplish in the remote future, it can scarcely be expected to transform nature. But does it at present atrophy certain finer tendencies? I think that it unavoidably does, for the simple reason that, under existing conditions, the moral and mental powers are overtasked by its requirements. All that wonderful national spirit of duty, of patience, of self-sacrifice, anciently directed to social, moral, or religious idealism, must, under the discipline of the higher training, be concentrated upon an end which not only demands, but exhausts its fullest exercise. For that end, to be accomplished at all, must be accomplished in the face of difficulties that the Western student rarely encounters, and could scarcely be made even to understand. All those moral qualities which made the old Japanese character admirable are certainly the same which make the modern Japanese student the most indefatigable, the most docile, the most ambitious in the world. But they are also qualities which urge him to efforts in excess of his natural powers, with the frequent result of mental and moral enervation. The nation has entered upon a period of intellectual overstrain. Consciously or unconsciously, in obedience to sudden necessity, Japan has undertaken nothing less than the tremendous task of forcing mental expansion up to the highest existing standard; and this means forcing the development of the nervous system. For the desired intellectual change, to be accomplished within a few generations, must involve a physiological change never to be effected without terrible cost. In other words, Japan has attempted too much; yet under the circumstances she could not have attempted less. Happily, even among the poorest of her poor the educational policy of the government is seconded with an astonishing zeal; the entire nation has plunged into study with a fervor of which it is utterly impossible to convey any adequate conception in this little essay. Yet I may cite a touching example. Immediately after the frightful earthquake of 1891, the children of the ruined cities of Gifu and Aichi, crouching among the ashes of their homes, cold and hungry and shelterless, surrounded by horror and misery unspeakable, still continued their small studies, using tiles of their own burnt dwellings in lieu of slates, and bits of lime for chalk, even while the earth still trembled beneath them.* What future miracles may justly be expected from the amazing power of purpose such a fact reveals!

But it is true that as yet the results of the higher training have not been altogether happy. Among the Japanese of the old regime one encounters a courtesy, an unselfishness, a grace of pure goodness, impossible to overpraise. Among the modernized of the new generation these have almost disappeared. One meets

---

* The shocks continued, though with lessening frequency and violence, for more than six months after the cataclysm.

a class of young men who ridicule the old times and the old ways without having been able to elevate themselves above the vulgarism of imitation and the commonplaces of shallow skepticism.

What has become of the noble and charming qualities they must have inherited from their fathers? Is it not possible that the best of those qualities have been transmuted into mere effort—an effort so excessive as to have exhausted character, leaving it without weight or balance?

It is to the still fluid, mobile, natural existence of the common people that one must look for the meaning of some apparent differences in the race feeling and emotional expression of the West and the Far East. With those gentle, kindly, sweet-hearted folk, who smile at life, love, and death alike, it is possible to enjoy community of feeling in simple, natural things; and by familiarity and sympathy we can learn why they smile.

The Japanese child is born with this happy tendency, which is fostered through all the period of home education. But it is cultivated with the same exquisiteness that is shown in the cultivation of the natural tendencies of a garden plant. The smile is taught like the bow; like the prostration; like that little sibilant sucking-in of the breath which follows, as a token of pleasure, the salutation to a superior; like all the elaborate and beautiful etiquette of the old courtesy. Laughter is not encouraged, for obvious reasons. But the smile is to be used upon all pleasant occasions, when speaking to a superior or to an equal, and even upon occasions which are not pleasant; it is a part of deportment. The most agreeable face is the smiling face; and to present always the most agreeable face possible to parents, relatives, teachers, friends, well-wishers, is a rule of life. And furthermore, it is a rule of life to turn constantly to the outer world a mien of happiness, to convey to others as far as possible a pleasant impression. Even though the heart is breaking, it is a social duty to smile bravely. On the other hand, to look serious or unhappy is rude, because this may cause anxiety or pain to those who love us; it is likewise foolish, since it may excite unkindly curiosity on the part of those who love us not. Cultivated from childhood as a duty, the smile soon becomes instinctive. In the mind of the poorest peasant lives the conviction that to exhibit the expression of one's personal sorrow or pain or anger is rarely useful, and always unkind. Hence, although natural grief must have, in Japan as elsewhere, its natural issue, an uncontrollable burst of tears in the presence of superiors or guests is an impoliteness; and the first words of even the most unlettered country woman, after the nerves give way in such a circumstance, are invariably: "Pardon my selfishness in that I have been so rude!" The reasons for the smile, be it also observed, are not only moral; they are to some extent aesthetic; they partly represent the same idea which regulated the expression of suffering in Greek art. But they are much more moral than aesthetic, as we shall presently observe.

From this primary etiquette of the smile there has been developed a secondary etiquette, the observance of which has frequently impelled foreigners to form the most cruel misjudgments as to Japanese sensibility. It is the native custom that whenever a painful or shocking fact *must* be told, the announcement should be made, by the sufferer, with a smile.* The grayer the subject, the more accentuated the smile; and when the matter is very unpleasant to the person speaking of it, the smile often changes to a low, soft laugh. However bitterly the mother who has lost her first-born may have wept at the funeral, it is probable that, if in your service, she will tell of her bereavement with a smile: like the Preacher, she holds that there is a time to weep and a time to laugh. It was long before I myself could understand how it was possible for those whom I believed to have loved a person recently dead to announce to me that death with a laugh. Yet the laugh was politeness carried to the utmost point of self-abnegation.

---

* Of course the converse is the rule in condoling with the sufferer.

It signified: "This you might honorably think to be an unhappy event; pray do not suffer your superiority to feel concern about so inferior a matter, and pardon the necessity which causes us to outrage politeness by speaking about such an affair at all."

The key to the mystery of the most unaccountable smiles is Japanese politeness. The servant sentenced to dismissal for a fault prostrates himself, and asks for pardon with a smile. That smile indicates the very reverse of callousness or insolences "Be assured that I am satisfied with the great justice of your honorable sentence, and that I am now aware of the gravity of my fault. Yet my sorrow and my necessity have caused me to indulge the unreasonable hope that I may be forgiven for my great rudeness in asking pardon." The youth or girl beyond the age of childish tears, when punished for some error, receives the punishment with a smile which means: "No evil feeling arises in my heart; much worse than this my fault has deserved." And the kurumaya cut by the whip of my Yokohama friend smiled for a similar reason, as my friend must have intuitively felt, since the smile at once disarmed him: "I was very wrong, and you are right to be angry: I deserve to be struck, and therefore feel no resentment."

But it should be understood that the poorest and humblest Japanese is rarely submissive under injustice.

His apparent docility is due chiefly to his moral sense. The foreigner who strikes a native for sport may have reason to find that he has made a serious mistake. The Japanese are not to be trifled with; and brutal attempts to trifle with them have cost several worthless lives.

Even after the foregoing explanations, the incident of the Japanese nurse may still seem incomprehensible; but this, I feel quite sure, is because the narrator either suppressed or overlooked certain facts in the case. In the first half of the story, all is perfectly clear. When announcing her husband's death, the young servant smiled, in accordance with the native formality already referred to. What is quite incredible is that, of her own accord, she should have invited the attention of her mistress to the contents of the vase, or funeral urn. If she knew enough of Japanese politeness to smile in announcing her husband's death, she must certainly have known enough to prevent her from perpetrating such an error. She could have shown the vase and its contents only in obedience to some real or fancied command; and when so doing, it is more than possible she may have uttered the low, soft laugh which accompanies either the unavoidable performance of a painful duty, or the enforced utterance of a painful statement. My own opinion is that she was obliged to gratify a wanton curiosity. Her smile or laugh would then have signified: "Do not suffer your honorable feelings to be shocked upon my unworthy account; it is indeed very rude of me, even at your honorable request, to mention so contemptible a thing as my sorrow."

IV.

But the Japanese smile must not be imagined as a kind of *sourire figé,* worn perpetually as a soulmask. Like other matters of deportment, it is regulated by an etiquette which varies in different classes of society. As a rule, the old samurai were not given to smiling upon all occasions; they reserved their amiability for superiors and intimates, and would seem to have maintained toward inferiors an austere reserve. The dignity of the Shintō priesthood has become proverbial; and for centuries the gravity of the Confucian code was mirrored in the decorum of magistrates and officials. From ancient times the nobility affected a still loftier reserve; and the solemnity of rank deepened through all the hierarchies up to that awful state surrounding the Tenshi-Sama, upon whose face no living man might look. But in private life the demeanor of the highest had its amiable relaxation; and even today, with some hopelessly modernized exceptions, the noble, the judge, the high priest, the august minister, the military officer, will resume at home, in the intervals of duty, the charming habits of the antique courtesy.

The smile which illuminates conversation is in itself but a small detail of that courtesy; but the sentiment which it symbolizes certainly comprises the larger part. If you happen to have a cultivated Japanese friend who has remained in all things truly Japanese, whose character has remained untouched by the new egotism and by foreign influences, you will probably be able to study in him the particular social traits of the whole people— traits in his case exquisitely accentuated and polished. You will observe that, as a rule, he never speaks of himself, and that, in reply to searching personal questions, he will answer as vaguely and briefly as possible, with a polite bow of thanks. But, on the other hand, he will ask many questions about yourself: your opinions, your ideas, even trifling details of your daily life, appear to have deep interest for him; and you will probably have occasion to note that he never forgets anything which he has learned concerning you. Yet there are certain rigid limits to his kindly curiosity, and perhaps even to his observation: he will never refer to any disagreeable or painful matter, and he will seem to remain blind to eccentricities or small weaknesses, if you have any. To your face he will never praise you; but he will never laugh at you nor criticise you. Indeed, you will find that he never criticises persons, but only actions in their results. As a private adviser, he will not even directly criticise a plan of which he disapproves, but is apt to suggest a new one in some such guarded language as: "Perhaps it might be more to your immediate interest to do thus and so." When obliged to speak of others, he will refer to them in a curious indirect fashion, by citing and combining a number of incidents sufficiently characteristic to form a picture. But in that event the incidents narrated will almost certainly be of a nature to awaken interest, and to create a favorable impression. This indirect way of conveying information is essentially Confucian. "Even when you have no doubts," says the Li-Ki, "do not let what you say appear as your own view." And it is quite probable that you will notice many other traits in your friend requiring some knowledge of the Chinese classics to understand. But no such knowledge is necessary to convince you of his exquisite consideration for others, and his studied suppression of self. Among no other civilized people is the secret of happy living so thoroughly comprehended as among the Japanese; by no other race is the truth so widely understood that our pleasure in life must depend upon the happiness of those about us, and consequently upon the cultivation in ourselves of unselfishness and of patience. For which reason, in Japanese society, sarcasm, irony, cruel wit, are not indulged. I might almost say that they have no existence in refined life. A personal failing is not made the subject of ridicule or reproach; an eccentricity is not commented upon; an involuntary mistake excites no laughter.

Stiffened somewhat by the Chinese conservatism of the old conditions, it is true that this ethical system was maintained to the extreme of giving fixity to ideas, and at the cost of individuality. And yet, if regulated by a broader comprehension of social requirements, if expanded by scientific understanding of the freedom essential to intellectual evolution, the very same moral policy is that through which the highest and happiest results may be obtained. But as actually practiced it was not favorable to originality; it rather tended to enforce that amiable mediocrity of opinion and imagination which still prevails.

Wherefore a foreign dweller in the interior cannot but long sometimes for the sharp, erratic inequalities of Western life, with its larger joys and pains and its more comprehensive sympathies. But sometimes only, for the intellectual loss is really more than compensated by the social charm; and there can remain no doubt in the mind of one who even partly understands the Japanese, that they are still the best people in the world to live among.

V.

As I pen these lines, there returns to me the vision of a Kyōto night. While passing through, some wonderfully thronged and illuminated street, of which I cannot remember the name, I had turned aside to look at a statue of Jizō, before the entrance of a very small temple. The figure was that of a kozo, an acolyte— a beautiful boy; and its smile was a bit of divine realism. As I stood gazing, a young lad, perhaps ten years old, ran up beside me, joined his little hands before the image, bowed his head, and prayed for a moment in silence. He had but just left some comrades, and the joy and glow of play were still upon his face; and his unconscious smile was so strangely like the smile of the child of stone that the boy seemed the twin brother of the god. And then I thought: "The smile of bronze or stone is not a copy only; but that which the Buddhist sculptor symbolizes thereby must be the explanation of the smile of the race."

That was long ago; but the idea which then suggested itself still seems to me true. However foreign to Japanese soil the origin of Buddhist art, yet the smile of the people signifies the same conception as the smile of the Bosatsu—the happiness that is born of self-control and self-suppression. "If a man conquer in battle a thousand times a thousand, and another conquer himself, he who conquers himself is the greatest of conquerors." "Not even a god can change into defeat the victory of the man who has vanquished himself."* Such Buddhist texts as these—and they are many—assuredly express, though they cannot be assumed to have created, those moral tendencies which form the highest charm of the Japanese character. And the whole moral idealism of the race seems to me to have been imaged in that marvelous Buddha of Kamakura, whose countenance, "calm like a deep, still water,"† expresses, as perhaps no other work of human hands can have expressed, the eternal truth: "There is no higher happiness than rest."‡ It is toward that infinite calm that the aspirations of the Orient have been turned; and the ideal of the Supreme Self-Conquest it has made its own. Even now, though agitated at its surface by those new influences which must soon-

---

* Dhammapada.
† Dammikkasutta.
‡ Dhaamapada.

er or later move it even to its uttermost depths, the Japanese mind retains, as compared with the thought of the West, a wonderful placidity. It dwells but little, if at all, upon those ultimate abstract questions about which we most concern ourselves. Neither does it comprehend our interest in them as we desire to be comprehended. "That you should not be indifferent to religious speculations," a Japanese scholar once observed to me, "is quite natural; but it is equally natural that we should never trouble ourselves about them. The philosophy of Buddhism has a profundity far exceeding that of your Western theology, and we have studied it. We have sounded the depths of speculation only to find that there are depths unfathomable below those depths; we have voyaged to the farthest limit that thought may sail, only to find that the horizon forever recedes. And you, you have remained for many thousand years as children playing in a stream, but ignorant of the sea. Only now you have reached its shore by another path than ours, and the vastness is for you a new wonder; and you would sail to Nowhere because you have seen the infinite over the sands of life."

Will Japan be able to assimilate Western civilization, as she did Chinese more than ten centuries ago, and nevertheless preserve her own peculiar modes of thought and feeling? One striking fact is hopeful: that the Japanese admiration for Western material superiority is by no means extended to Western morals. Oriental thinkers do not commit the serious blunder of confounding mechanical with ethical progress, nor have they failed to perceive the moral weaknesses of our boasted civilization. One Japanese writer has expressed his judgment of things Occidental after a fashion that deserves to be noticed by a larger circle of readers than that for which it was originally written:

"Order or disorder in a nation does not depend upon something that falls from the sky or rises from the earth. It is determined by the disposition of the people. The pivot on which the public disposition turns towards order or disorder is the point where public and private motives separate. If the people be influenced chiefly by public considerations, order is assured; if by private, disorder is inevitable. Public considerations are those that prompt the proper observance of duties; their prevalence signifies peace and prosperity in the case alike of families, communities, and nations. Private considerations are those suggested by selfish motives: when they prevail, disturbance and disorder are unavoidable. As members of a family, our duty is to look after the welfare of that family; as units of a nation, our duty is to work for the good of the nation. To regard our family affairs with all the interest due to our family, and our national affairs with all the interest due to our nation—this is to fitly discharge our duty, and to be guided by public considerations. On the other hand, to regard the affairs of the nation as if they were our own family affairs—this is to be influenced by private motives and to stray from the path of duty....

"Selfishness is born in every man; to indulge it freely is to become a beast. Therefore it is that sages preach the principles of duty and propriety, justice and morality, providing restraints for private aims and encouragements for public spirit....What we know of Western civilization is that it struggled on through long centuries in a confused condition, and finally attained a state of some order; but that even this order, not being based upon such principles as those of the natural and immutable distinctions between sovereign and subject, parent and child, with all their corresponding rights and duties, is liable to constant change, according to the growth of human ambitions and human aims. Admirably suited to persons whose actions are controlled by selfish ambition, the adoption of this system in Japan is naturally sought by a certain class of politicians. From a superficial point of view, the Occidental form of society is very attractive, inasmuch as, being the outcome of a free development of human desires from ancient times, it represents the very extreme of luxury and extravagance. Briefly speaking, the state of things obtaining in the West; is based upon the free play of human selfishness, and can only be reached by giving full sway to that quality. Social disturbances are little heeded in the Occident; yet they are at once the evidences and the factors of the present evil state of affairs. Do Japanese enamored of Western ways propose to have their nation's history written in similar terms? Do they seriously contemplate turning their country into a new field for experiments in Western civilization?

"In the Orient, from ancient times, national government has been based on benevolence, and directed to securing the welfare and happiness of the people. No political creed has ever held that intellectual strength should be cultivated for the purpose of exploiting inferiority and ignorance....The inhabitants of this empire live, for the most part, by manual labor. Let them be never so industrious, they hardly earn enough to supply their daily wants. They earn on the average about twenty sen daily. There is no question with them of aspiring to wear fine clothes or to inhabit handsome houses. Neither can they hope to reach positions of fame and honor. What offense have these poor people committed that they, too, should not share the benefits of Western civilization?...By some, indeed, their condition is explained off the hypothesis that their desires do not prompt them to better themselves. There is no truth in such a supposition. They have desires, but nature has limited their capacity to satisfy them; their duty as men limits it, and the amount of labor physically possible to a human being limits it. They achieve as much as their opportunities permit. The best and finest products of their labor they reserve for the wealthy; the worst and roughest they keep for their own use. Yet there is nothing in human society that does not owe its existence to labor. Now, to satisfy the desires of one luxurious man, the toil of a thousand is needed. Surely it is monstrous that those who owe to labor the pleasures suggested by their civilization should forget what they owe to the laborer, and treat him as if he were not a fellow-being. But civilization, according to the interpretation of the Occident, serves only to satisfy men of large desires. It is of no benefit to the masses, but is simply a system under which ambitions compete to accomplish their aims....That the Occidental system is gravely disturbing to the order and peace of a country is seen by men who have eyes, and heard by men who have ears. The future of Japan under such a system fills us with anxiety. A system based on the principle that ethics and religion are made to serve human ambition naturally accords with the wishes of selfish individuals; and such theories as those embodied in the modern formula of liberty and equality annihilate the established relations of society, and outrage decorum and propriety.... Absolute equality and absolute liberty being unattainable, the limits prescribed by right and duty are supposed to be set. But as each person seeks to have as much right and to be burdened with as little duty as possible, the results are endless disputes and legal contentions. The principles of liberty and equality may succeed in changing the organization of nations, in overthrowing the lawful distinctions of social rank, in reducing all men to one nominal level; but they can never accomplish the equal distribution of wealth and property. Consider America....It is plain that if the mutual rights of men and their status are made to depend on degrees of wealth, the majority of the people, being without wealth, must fail to establish their rights; whereas the minority who are wealthy will assert their rights, and, under society's sanction, will exact oppressive duties from the poor, neglecting the dictates of humanity and benevolence. The adoption of these principles of liberty and equality in Japan would vitiate the good and peaceful customs of our country, render the general disposition of the people harsh and unfeeling, and prove finally a source of calamity to the masses....

"Though at first sight Occidental civilization presents an attractive appearance, adapted as it is to the gratification of selfish desires, yet, since its basis is the hypothesis that men's wishes constitute natural laws, it must ultimately end in disappointment and demoralization....Occidental nations have become what they are after passing through conflicts and vicissitudes of the most serious kind; and it is their fate to continue the struggle. Just now their motive elements are in partial equilibrium, and their social condition is more or less ordered. But if this slight equilibrium happens to be disturbed, they will be thrown once more into confusion and change, until, after a period of renewed struggle and suffering, temporary stability is once more attained. The poor and powerless of the present may become the wealthy and strong of the future, and *vice versa.* Perpetual disturbance is their doom. Peaceful equality can never be attained until built up among the ruins of annihilated Western states and the ashes of extinct Western peoples."*

Surely, with perceptions like these, Japan may hope to avert some of the social perils which menace her. Yet it appears inevitable that her approaching transformation must be coincident with a moral decline. Forced into the vast industrial competition of nations whose civilizations were never based on altruism, she must eventually develop those qualities of which the comparative absence made all the wonderful charm of her life. The national character must continue to harden, as it has begun to harden already. But it should never be forgotten that old Japan was quite as much in advance of the nineteenth century morally as she was behind it materially. She had made morality instinctive, after having made it rational. She had realized, though within restricted limits, several among those social conditions which our ablest thinkers regard as the happiest and the high-

---

* These extracts from a translation in the *Japan Daily Mail,* November 19 and 20, 1890, of Viscount Tōrio's famous conservative essay do not give a fair idea of the force and logic of the whole. The essay is too long to quote entire; and any extracts from the *Mail's* admirable translation suffer by their isolation from the singular chains of ethical, religions, and philosophical reasoning which bind the various parts of the composition together. The essay was further more remarkable as the production of a native scholar, totally uninfluenced by Western thought. He correctly predicted those social and political disturbances which have occurred in Japan since the opening of the new parliament. Viscount Tōrio is also well known as a master of Buddhist philosophy. He holds a high rank in the Japanese army.

est. Throughout all the grades of her complex society she had cultivated both the comprehension and the practice of public and private duties after a manner for which it were vain to seek any Western parallel. Even her moral weakness was the result of an excess of that which all civilized religions have united in proclaiming virtue—the self-sacrifice of the individual for the sake of the family, of the community, and of the nation. It was the weakness indicated by Percival Lowell in his "Soul of the Far East," a book of which the consummate genius cannot be justly estimated without some personal knowledge of the Far East.* The progress made by Japan in social morality, although greater than our own, was chiefly in the direction of mutual dependence. And it will be her coming duty to keep in view the teaching of that mighty thinker whose philosophy she has wisely accepted†—the teaching that "the highest individuation must be

---

* In expressing my earnest admiration of this wonderful book, I must, however, declare that several of its conclusions, and especially the final ones, represent the extreme reverse of my own beliefs on the subject. I do not think the Japanese without individuality; but their individuality is less superficially apparent, and reveals itself much less quickly, than that of Western people. I am also convinced that much of what we call "personality" and "force of character" in the West represents only the survival and recognition of primitive aggressive tendencies, more or less disguised by culture. What Mr. Spencer calls the *highest* individuation surely does not include extraordinary development of powers adapted to merely aggressive ends; and yet it is rather through these than through any others that Western individuality most commonly and readily manifests itself. Now there is, as yet, a remarkable scarcity in Japan, of domineering, brutal, aggressive, or morbid individuality. What does impress one as an apparent weakness in Japanese intellectual circles is the comparative absence of spontaneity, creative thought, original perceptivity of the highest order. Perhaps this seeming deficiency is racial: the peoples of the Far East seem to have been throughout their history receptive lather than creative. At all events I cannot believe Buddhism—originally the faith of an Aryan race—can be proven responsible. The total exclusion of Buddhist influence from public education would not seem to have been stimulating; for the masters of the old Buddhist philosophy still show a far higher capacity for thinking in relations than that of the average graduate of the Imperial University. Indeed, I am inclined to believe that an intellectual revival of Buddhism—a harmonizing of its loftier truths with the best and broadest teachings of modern science—would have the most important results for Japan. A native scholar, Mr. Iuouye Enryō, has actually founded at Tōkyō with this noble object in view, a college of philosophy which seems likely, at the present writing, to become an influential institution.

† Herbert Spencer.

joined with the greatest mutual dependence," and that, however seemingly paradoxical the statement, "the law of progress is at once toward complete separateness and complete union."

Yet to that past which her younger generation now affect to despise Japan will certainly one day look back, even as we ourselves look back to the old Greek civilization. She will learn to regret the forgotten capacity for simple pleasures, the lost sense of the pure joy of life, the old loving divine intimacy with nature, the marvelous dead art which reflected it. She will remember how much more luminous and beautiful the world then seemed. She will mourn for many things—the old-fashioned patience and self-sacrifice, the ancient courtesy, the deep human poetry of the ancient faith. She will wonder at many things; but she will regret. Perhaps she will wonder most of all at the faces of the ancient gods, because their smile was once the likeness of her own.

27

SAYŌNARA!

I.

I AM going away—very far away. I have already resigned my post as teacher, and am waiting only for my passport.

So many familiar faces have vanished that I feel now less regret at leaving than I should have felt six months ago. And nevertheless, the quaint old city has become so endeared to me by habit and association that the thought of never seeing it again is one I do not venture to dwell upon. I have been trying to persuade myself that some day I may return to this charming old house, in shadowy Kitaborimachi, though all the while painfully aware that in past experience such imaginations invariably preceded perpetual separation.

The facts are that all things are impermanent in the Province of the Gods; that the winters are very severe; and that I have received a call from the great Government college in Kyūshū, far south, where snow rarely falls. Also I have been very sick; and the prospect of a milder climate had much influence in shaping my decision.

But these few days of farewells have been full of charming surprises. To have the revelation of gratitude where you had no right to expect more than plain satisfaction with your performance of duty; to find affection where you supposed only goodwill to exist: these are assuredly delicious experiences.

The teachers of both schools have sent me a farewell gift—a superb pair of vases nearly three feet high, covered with designs representing birds, and flowering-trees overhanging a slope of beach where funny pink crabs are running about—vases made in the old feudal days at Rakusan—rare souvenirs of Izumo. With the wonderful vases came a scroll bearing in Chinese text the names of the thirty-two donors; and three of these are names of ladies—the three lady-teachers of the Normal School.

The students of the Jinjō-Chūgakkō have also sent me a present—the last contribution of two hundred and fifty-one pupils to my happiest memories of Matsue: a Japanese sword of the time of the daimyō.

Silver karashishi with eyes of gold—in Izumo, the Lions of Shintō—swarm over the crimson lacquer of the sheath, and sprawl about the exquisite hilt. And the committee who brought the beautiful thing to my house requested me to accompany them forthwith to the college assembly-room, where the students were all waiting to bid me good-by, after the oldtime custom.

So I went there. And the things which we said to each other are hereafter set down.

II.

DEAR TEACHER: You have been one of the best and most benevolent teachers we ever had. We thank you with all our heart for the knowledge we obtained through your kindest instruction. Every student in our school hoped you would stay with us at least three years. When we learned you had resolved to go to Kyūshū, we all felt our hearts sink with sorrow. We entreated our Director to find some way to keep you, but we discovered that could not be done. We have no words to express our feeling at this moment of farewell. We sent you a Japanese sword as a memory of us. It was only a poor ugly thing; we merely thought you would care for it as a mark of our gratitude. We will never forget your kindest instruction; and we all wish that you may ever be healthy and happy.

MASANABU ŌTANI,
Representing all the Students of the Middle School of Shimane-Ken.

MY DEAR BOYS: I cannot tell you with what feelings I received your present; that beautiful sword with the silver karashishi ramping upon its sheath, or crawling through the silken cording of its wonderful hilt. At least I cannot tell you all. But there flashed to me, as I looked at your gift, the remembrance of your ancient proverb: "*The Sword is the Soul of the Samurai*" and then it seemed to me that in the very choice of that exquisite souvenir you had symbolized something of your own souls. For we English also have some famous sayings and proverbs about swords. Our poets call a good blade "trusty" and "true," and of our best friend we say, "He is true as *steel*"—signifying in the ancient sense the steel of a perfect sword—the steel to whose temper a warrior could trust his honor and his life. And so in your rare gift, which I shall keep and prize while I live, I find an emblem of your true-heartedness and affection. May you always keep fresh within your hearts those impulses of generosity and kindliness and loyalty which I have learned to know so well, and of which your gift will ever remain for me the graceful symbol!

And a symbol not only of your affection and loyalty as students to teachers, but of that other beautiful sense of duty you expressed, when so many of you wrote down for me, as your dearest wish, the desire to die for His Imperial Majesty, your Emperor. That wish is holy: it means perhaps even more than you know, or can know, until you shall have become much older and wiser. This is an era of great and rapid change; and it is probable that many of you, as you grow up, will not be able to believe everything that your fathers believed before you—though I sincerely trust you will at least continue always to respect the faith, even as you still respect the memory, of your ancestors. But however much the life of New Japan may change about you, however much your own thoughts may change with the times, never suffer that noble wish you expressed to me to pass away from your souls. Keep it burning there, clear and pure as the flame of the little lamp that glows before your household shrine.

Perhaps some of you may have that wish. Many of you must become soldiers. Some will become officers. Some will enter the Naval Academy to prepare for the grand service of protecting the empire by sea; and your Emperor and your country may even require your blood. But the greater number among you are destined to other careers, and may have no such chances of bodily self-sacrifice—except perhaps in the hour of some great national danger, which I trust Japan will never know. And there is another desire, not less noble, which may be your compass in civil life: to live for your country though you cannot die for it. Like the kindest and wisest of fathers, your Government has provided for you these splendid schools, with all opportunities for the best instruction this scientific century can give, at a far less cost than any other civilized country can offer the same advantages. And all this in order that each of you may help to make your country wiser and richer and stronger than it has ever been in the past. And whoever does his best, in any calling or profession, to ennoble and develop that calling or profession, gives his life to his Emperor and to his country no less truly than the soldier or the seaman who dies for duty.

I am not less sorry to leave you, I think, than you are to see me go. The more I have learned to know the hearts of Japanese students, the more I have learned to love their country. I think, however, that I shall see many of you again, though I never return to Matsue: some I am almost sure I shall meet elsewhere in future summers; some I may even hope to teach once more, in the Government college to which I am going. But whether we meet again or not, be sure that my life has been made happier by knowing you, and that I shall always love you. And, now, with renewed thanks for your beautiful gift, good-by!

III.

The students of the Normal School gave me a farewell banquet in their hall. I had been with them so little during the year—less even than the stipulated six hours a week—that I could not have supposed they would feel much attachment for their foreign teacher. But I have still much to learn about my Japanese students. The banquet was delightful. The captain of each class in turn read in English a brief farewell address which he had prepared; and more than one of those charming compositions, made beautiful with similes and sentiments drawn from the old Chinese and Japanese poets, will always remain in my memory. Then the students sang their college songs for me, and chanted the Japanese version of "Auld Lang Syne" at the close of the banquet. And then all, in military procession, escorted me home, and cheered me farewell at my gate, with shouts of

"*Manzai!*" "Good-by!" "We will march with you to the steamer when you go."

IV.

But I shall not have the pleasure of seeing them again. They are all gone far away—some to another world. Yet it is only four days since I attended that farewell banquet at the Normal School! A cruel visitation has closed its gates and scattered its students through the province.

Two nights ago, the Asiatic cholera, supposed to have been brought to Japan by Chinese vessels, broke out in different parts of the city, and, among other places, in the Normal School. Several students and teachers expired within a short while after having been attacked; others are even now lingering between life and death. The rest marched to the little healthy village of Tamatsukuri, famed for its hot springs. But there the cholera again broke out among them, and it was decided to dismiss the survivors at once to their several homes. There was no panic. The military discipline remained unbroken. Students and teachers fell at their posts. The great college building was taken charge of by the medical authorities, and the work of disinfection and sanitation is still going on. Only the convalescents and the fearless samurai president, Saitō Kumatarō, remain in it. Like the captain who scorns to leave his sinking ship till all souls are safe, the president stays in the center of danger, nursing the sick boys, overlooking the work of sanitation, transacting all the business usually intrusted to several subordinates, whom he promptly sent away in the first hour of peril. He has had the joy of seeing two of his boys saved.

Of another, who was buried last night, I hear this: Only a little while before his death, and in spite of kindliest protest, he found strength, on seeing his president approaching his bedside, to rise on his elbow and give the military salute. And with that brave greeting to a brave man, he passed into the Great Silence.

V.

At last my passport has come. I must go.

The Middle School and the adjacent elementary schools have been closed on account of the appearance of cholera, and I protested against any gathering of the pupils to bid me good-by, fearing for them the risk of exposure to the chilly morning air by the shore of the infected river. But my protest was received only with a merry laugh. Last night the Director sent word to all the captains of classes. Wherefore, an hour after sunrise, some two hundred students, with their teachers, assemble before my gate to escort me to the wharf, near the long white bridge, where the little steamer is waiting. And we go.

Other students are already assembled at the wharf. And with them wait a multitude of people known to me: friends or friendly acquaintances, parents and relatives of students, every one to whom I can remember having ever done the slightest favor, and many more from whom I have received favors which I never had the chance to return—persons who worked for me, merchants from whom I purchased little things, a host of kind faces, smiling salutation. The Governor sends his secretary with a courteous message; the President of the Normal School hurries down for a moment to shake hands. The Normal students have been sent to their homes, but not a few of their teachers are present. I most miss friend Nishida. He has been very sick for two long months, bleeding at the lungs, but his father brings me the gentlest of farewell letters from him, penned in bed, and some pretty souvenirs.

And now, as I look at all these pleasant faces about me, I cannot but ask myself the question: "Could I have lived in the exercise of the same profession for the same length of time in any other country, and have enjoyed a similar unbroken experience of human goodness?" From each and all of these I have received only kindness and courtesy. Not one has ever, even through inadvertence, addressed to me a single ungenerous word. As a teacher of more than five hundred boys and men, I have never even had my patience tried. I wonder if such an experience is possible only in Japan.

But the little steamer shrieks for her passengers. I shake many hands—most heartily, perhaps, that of the brave, kind President of the Normal School—and climb on board. The Director of the Jinjō Chūgakkō, a few teachers of both schools, and one of my favorite pupils, follow; they are going to accompany me as far as the next port, whence my way will be over the mountains to Hiroshima.

It is a lovely vapory morning, sharp with the first chill of winter. From the tiny deck I take my last look at the quaint vista of the Ōhashigawa, with its long white bridge—at the peaked host of queer dear old houses, crowding close to dip their feet in its glassy flood—at the sails of the junks, gold-colored by the early sun—at the beautiful fantastic shapes of the ancient hills.

Magical indeed the charm of this land, as of a land veritably haunted by gods: so lovely the spectral delicacy of its colors—so lovely the forms of its hills blending with the forms of its clouds—so lovely, above all, those long trailings and bandings of mists which make its altitudes appear to hang in air. A land where sky and earth so strangely intermingle that what is reality may not be distinguished from what is illusion—that all seems a mirage, about to vanish. For me, alas! it is about to vanish, forever.

The little steamer shrieks again, puffs, backs into midstream, turns from the long white bridge. And as the gray wharves recede, a long *Aaaaaaaaaa* rises from the uniformed ranks, and all the caps wave, flashing their Chinese ideographs of brass. I clamber to the roof of the tiny deck cabin, wave my hat, and shout in English: "Good-by, good-by!" And there floats back to me the cry: "*Manzai, manzai!*" [Ten thousand years to you! ten thousand years!] But already it comes faintly from far away. The packet glides out of the river-mouth, shoots into the blue lake, turns a pine-shadowed point; and the faces, and the voices, and the wharves, and the long white bridge have become memories.

Still for a little while looking back, as we pass into the silence of the great water, I can see, receding on the left, the crest of the ancient castle, over grand shaggy altitudes of pine—and the place of my home, with its delicious garden—and the long blue roofs of the schools. These, too, swiftly pass out of vision. Then only faint blue water, faint blue mists, faint blues and greens and grays of peaks looming through varying distance, and beyond all, towering ghost white into the east, the glorious spectre of Daisen.

And my heart sinks a moment under the rush of those vivid memories which always crowd upon one the instant after parting—memories of all that make attachment to places and to things. Remembered smiles; the morning gathering at the threshold of the old yashiki to wish the departing teacher a happy day; the evening gathering to welcome his return; the dog waiting by the gate at the accustomed hour; the garden with its lotus-flowers and its cooing of doves; the musical boom of the temple bell from the cedar groves; songs of children at play; afternoon shadows upon many-tinted streets; the long lines of lantern-fires upon festal nights; the dancing of the moon upon the lake; the clapping of hands by the river shore in salutation to the Izumo sun; the endless merry pattering of geta over the windy bridge: all these and a hundred other happy memories revive for me with almost painful vividness—while the far peaks, whose names are holy, slowly turn away their blue shoulders, and the little steamer bears me, more and more swiftly, ever farther and farther from the Province of the Gods.

INDEX

TUTTLE CLASSICS

LITERATURE   (* = for sale in Japan only)

ABE, Kobo   安部公房
  The Woman in the Dunes   砂の女   ISBN 978-4-8053-0900-1*

AKUTAGAWA, Ryunosuke   芥川龍之介
  Kappa   河童   ISBN 978-4-8053-0901-8*
  Rashomon and Other Stories   羅生門   ISBN 978-4-8053-0882-0

DAZAI, Osamu   太宰治
  No Longer Human   人間失格   ISBN 978-4-8053-1017-5*

ENDO, Shusaku   遠藤周作
  The Final Martyrs   最後の殉教者   ISBN 978-4-8053-0625-3*
  The Golden Country 黄金の国   ISBN 978-0-8048-3337-0*

HEARN, Lafcadio   ラフカディオ・ハーン
  Glimpses of Unfamiliar Japan   知られざる日本の面影
    ISBN 978-4-8053-1025-0
  In Ghostly Japan   霊の日本   ISBN 978-0-8048-3661-6;
    978-4-8053-0749-6*
  Kokoro 心   ISBN 978-0-8048-3660-9; 978-4-8053-0748-9*
  Kwaidan 怪談   ISBN 978-0-8048-3662-3; 978-4-8053-0750-2*
  Lafcadio Hearn's Japan   ラフカディオ・ハーンの日本
    ISBN 978-4-8053-0873-8

INOUE, Yasushi   井上靖
  The Samurai Banner of Furin Kazan   風林火山
    ISBN 978-0-8048-3701-9; 978-4-8053-0910-0*

KAWABATA, Yasunari   川端康成
  The Izu Dancer and Other Stories   伊豆の踊り子
    ISBN 978-4-8053-0744-1*
  The Master of Go   名人   ISBN 978-4-8053-0673-4*
  The Old Capital   古都   ISBN 978-4-8053-0972-8*
  Snow Country   雪国   ISBN 978-4-8053-0635-2*

SUMII, Sue   The River With No Bridge   橋のない川
ISBN 978-4-8053-0650-5*

TAKEYAMA, Michio   Harp of Burma   ビルマの竪琴
ISBN 978-0-8048-0232-1

TSUBOI, Sakae   Twenty-Four Eyes   二十四の瞳
ISBN 978-4-8053-0772-4*

YOSHIKAWA, Eiji

The Heike Story   新平家物語   ISBN 978-0-8048-3318-9;
978-4-8053-1044-1*

ANTHOLOGY   選集

A.L. Sadler   Japanese Plays   ISBN 978-4-8053-1073-1

Arthur Waley   The Noh Plays of Japan   ISBN 978-4-8053-1033-5

Donald Keene *(compiled & edited)*

Anthology of Japanese Literature   日本文学選集
ISBN 978-4-8053-1014-4*

Modern Japanese Literature   現代日本文学
ISBN 978-4-8053-0752-6*

Ellery Queen *(compiled & edited)*

Ellery Queen's Japanese Detective Stories   日本傑作推理12選
ISBN 978-4-8053-0851-6*

Ivan Moris   Modern Japanese Stories   近代日本文学
ISBN 978-0-8048-3336-3; 978-4-8053-0751-9*

Lane Dunlop *(compiled & trans.)*

Autumn Wind and Other Stories   秋風ほか
ISBN 978-4-8053-0850-9

Yei Theodora Ozaki   Japanese Fairy Tales   日本のお伽話
ISBN 978-4-8053-0881-3

CLASSICS

C. H. Brewitt-Taylor *(trans.)*
Romance of the Three Kingdom　三国志演義
Volume 1: ISBN 978-0-8048-3467-4
Volume 2: ISBN 978-0-8048-3468-1

IHARA, Saikaku　井原西鶴　Five Women Who Loved Love
好色五人女　ISBN 978-0-8048-0184-3; 978-4-8053-1020-0

This Scheming World　世間胸算用　ISBN 978-0-8048-3339-4;
978-4-8053-0643-7*

MURASAKI Shikibu　紫式部

Arthur Waley *(trans.)*　The Tale of Genji　源氏物語
ISBN 978-4-8053-1081-6

Edward G. Seidensticker *(trans.)*　The Tale of Genji (2 Volumes)
源氏物語（2巻組）　ISBN 978-4-8053-0921-6*

William J. Puette
The Tale of Genji A Reader's Guide　源氏物語読本
ISBN 978-0-8048-3832-8; 978-4-8053-1084-7*

William N. Porter *(trans.)*　A Hundred Verses from Old Japan
百人一首　ISBN 978-4-8053-0853-0*

YOSHIDA, Kenko　Essays in Idleness　徒然草
ISBN 978-4-8053-0631-4*

HISTORY

A.L. Sadler　Shogun: The Life of Tokugawa Ieyasu　将軍徳川家
康の生涯　ISBN 978-4-8053-1042-7

B. H. Chamberlain Kojiki　古事記　ISBN 978-0-8048-3675-3;
978-4-8053-1076-2*

Charles J. Dunn

Everyday Life in Traditional Japan　江戸の暮らし
ISBN 978-4-8053-1005-2

Edwin O. Reischauer　Japan : The Story of a Nation *(4th ed.)*
日本：その歴史と文化（第四版）　ISBN 978-4-8053-0666-6*

George Karr

Okinawa; The History of an Island People *(rev.)*
ISBN 978-4-8053-1356-5

Hans Brinckmann   Showa Japan   ISBN 978-4-8053-1002-1

R.H.P Mason, J.G. Caiger   A History of Japan   日本の歴史
ISBN 978-0-8048-2097-4; 978-4-8053-0792-2*

Stephen Mansfield   Tokyo: A Biography
ISBN 978-4-8053-1329-9

JAPANESE SOCIETY & NON-FICTION

Boyé De Mente

Japan's Cultural Code Words   ISBN 978-0-8048-3574-9;
978-4-8053-1104-2*

Kata   ISBN 978-0-8048-3386-8; 978-4-8053-1105-9*

Edwin O. Reischauer

The Meaning of Internationalization   ISBN 978-4-8053-1034-2

NAKANO, Chie   Japanese Society   タテ社会の人間関係
ISBN 978-4-8053-1026-7*

Rebecca Otowa   At Home in Japan   ISBN 978-4-8053-1078-6

Roger Davis, Osamu Ikeno   The Japanese Mind
ISBN 978-0-8048-3295-3; 978-4-8053-1021-2*

Roger J. Davies   Japanese Culture   ISBN 978-4-8053-1163-9

Stephen Longstree, Ethel Longstreett   Yoshiwara
ISBN 978-4-8053-1027-4

JAPANESE CULTURE

A. L. Sadler

Japanese Architecture   ISBN 978-4-8053-1043-4

The Japanese Tea Ceremony   ISBN 978-4-8053-0914-8

David Benjamin   Sumo   ISBN 978-4-8053-1087-8

TAKEI, Jiro, Marc P. Keane   Sakuteiki
ISBN 978-0-8048-3968-6, 978-4-8053-1051-9* (paperback);
978-0-8048-3294-6 (hardcover)

TSUDA, Noritake   A History of Japanese Art
ISBN 978-4-8053-1031-1

Vincent T. Covello, Yuji Yoshida

The Japanese Art of Stone Appreciation   ISBN 978-4-8053-1013-7

SAMURAI, BUSHIDO

NITOBE, Inazo   Bushido   武士道   ISBN 978-0-8048-3628-9;
978-4-8053-1112-7*

O. Ratti, A. Westbook   Secret of the Samurai
ISBN 978-0-8048-1684-7* (paperback); 978-4-8053-0960-5 (hardcover)

R. Hillsborough   Shinsengumi   新選組   ISBN 978-0-8048-3627-2

Ruth Benedict

The Chrysanthemum and the Sword   菊と刀
ISBN 978-4-8053-0671-0*

Stephen F. Kaufman *(trans.)*

Musashi's Book of Five Rings   五輪の書
ISBN 978-0-8048-3520-6

Sun Tzu's the Art of War   孫子「兵法」   ISBN 978-0-8048-3080-5

TABATA, Kazumi   Secret Tactics   葉隠
ISBN 978-0-8048-3488-9

Thomas Cleary

Code of the Samurai   ISBN 978-0-8048-3190-1

Soul of the Samurai   ISBN 978-0-8048-3690-6

Samurai Wisdom   ISBN 978-0-8048-4008-8

ZEN & SHINTO

Nyogen Senzaki, Paul Reps *(trans. & compiled)*

Zen Fresh, Zen Bones   ISBN 978-0-8048-3186-4 (paperback);
978-0-8048-3706-4 (hardcover)

SUZUKI, Daisetsu   Zen and Japanese Culture
ISBN 978-4-8053-0623-9*

ONO, Sokyo   Shinto   ISBN 978-0-8048-3557-2; 978-4-8053-1106-6*